S0-BYY-458

The Key To Understanding U.S. History and Government

Fifth Edition

James Killoran
Social Studies Supervisor, New York City

Mark Jarrett
Former Social Studies Teacher, New York City

Stuart Zimmer
Social Studies Teacher, New York City

JP

JARRETT PUBLISHING COMPANY

East Coast Office:
19 Cross Street
Lake Ronkonkoma, NY 11779

West Coast Office:
10 Folin Lane
Lafayette, CA 94549

(516) 981-4248 ☎ 1-800-859-7679

Fax (516) 588-4722

www.rwmg.com/jarrettpub

ABOUT THE AUTHORS

James Killoran is a retired Assistant Principal from Jamaica High School in New York. He has written *Mastering Global Studies*, *Mastering U.S. History and Government*, *Government and You*, *Economics and You*, *The Key To Understanding Global Studies*, *Nuestro Mundo: Su Historia, Sus Culturas*; *Los Estados Unidos: Su Historia, Su Gobierno*; *Ohio: Its Land and Its People; Mastering Ohio's 9th Grade Citizenship Test,* and *Mastering Ohio's 12th Grade Citizenship Test.* Mr. Killoran has extensive experience in test writing for the New York State Board of Regents in Social Studies and has served on the Committee for Testing of the National Council of Social Studies. His article on social studies testing was recently published in *Social Education*, the country's leading social studies journal. In addition, he has won a number of awards for outstanding teaching and curriculum development, including "Outstanding Social Studies Teacher" and "Outstanding Social Studies Supervisor" in New York City. In 1993, he was awarded an Advanced Certification for Teachers of Social Studies by the National Council of Social Studies.

Mark Jarrett is a former Social Studies teacher and a practicing attorney at the San Francisco office of Baker & McKenzie. He has written *Mastering Global Studies*, *Mastering U.S. History and Government*, *The Key To Understanding Global Studies*, *Nuestro Mundo: Su Historia, Sus Culturas*; *Los Estados Unidos: Su Historia, Su Gobierno*; *Ohio: Its Land and Its People; Mastering Ohio's 9th Grade Citizenship Test,* and *Mastering Ohio's 12th Grade Citizenship Test.* He has served as a test writer for the New York State Board of Regents, and has taught at Hofstra University. Mr. Jarrett was educated at Columbia University, the London School of Economics, the Law School of the University of California at Berkeley, and Stanford University, where he is a doctoral candidate in history.

Stuart Zimmer is a retired Social Studies teacher from Jamaica High School in New York. He has written *Mastering Global Studies*, *Mastering U.S. History and Government*, *Government and You*, *Economics and You*, *The Key To Understanding Global Studies*, *Nuestro Mundo: Su Historia, Sus Culturas*; *Los Estados Unidos: Su Historia, Su Gobierno*; *Ohio: Its Land and Its People; Mastering Ohio's 9th Grade Citizenship Test,* and *Mastering Ohio's 12th Grade Citizenship Test.* Mr. Zimmer has served as a test writer for the New York State Board of Regents in Social Studies, and has written for the National Merit Scholarship Examination. He has presented many demonstrations and educational workshops at state and national teachers' conferences. Mr. Zimmer's achievements have been recognized by the New York State Legislature with a Special Resolution.

Acknowledgements

Cover design by Peter R. Fleck. Illustrations by Ronald Scott Zimmer. Maps by Morris Kantor. Layout and typesetting by Maple Hill Press, Huntington, New York.

ISBN 1-882422-28-7
Printed in the United States
Fifth Edition

HOW TO USE THIS BOOK

The Regents and RCT Competency Tests in U.S. History and Government are tests given to students in New York State. This book helps students to pass these tests. If you are not from New York State, however, this book will be just as useful to you in developing your understanding and knowledge of U.S. History and Government. Completing the exercises and practice tests in this book will reinforce your learning and help you to master U.S. History and Government.

It is no secret that the New York State 11th and 12th grade U.S. History and Government Regents and RCT examinations are quite demanding tests. How can you be expected to learn and remember so much about the nation's history and its system of government? With this book as your guide, you should find the subject less difficult and maybe even fun to learn about.

The philosophy of this book is best expressed by an old Chinese adage, "Give a man a fish and you feed him for a day, but teach him how to fish and you feed him for a lifetime." *The Key To Understanding U.S. History and Government* will teach you how to answer Regents and RCT questions—not just provide you with past tests and their answers. The following section-by-section examination will give you an overview of the approach used in this book.

A PRE-TEST

How much do you already know about U.S. History and Government? The Pre-test section, containing an RCT-type examination and a recent Regents, evaluates your knowledge. There are two tests: select the one most appropriate for you. How well you do on this Pre-test will give you an idea of how much preparation you need in order to get ready for the examination.

TEST-TAKING STRATEGIES

This section highlights test-taking strategies to help you become "test-wise" in answering questions.

HOW TO ANSWER MULTIPLE CHOICE QUESTIONS

This section explores the many types of questions in the short-answer section of the Regents and RCT examinations. You will learn how to differentiate and handle assumptions, concepts, comparisons, cause and effect, and other types of multiple choice questions.

HOW TO ANSWER DATA-BASED QUESTIONS

On the New York State examinations, you will confront many kinds of data-based materials. This unit examines the different kinds of data that are found on the Regents and RCTs: political cartoons, maps, tables, bar graphs, line graphs, pie charts, timelines, and reading comprehension.

HOW TO ANSWER ESSAY QUESTIONS

This section deals with answering Regents and RCT essay questions. You will learn how to outline, organize and then answer essay questions.

CONTENT REVIEWS

This section contains brief reviews of the most important facts you need to know about each of the ten historical periods covered by the U.S. History and Government curriculum: Constitutional Foundations, The Constitution Tested, Industrialization, Changing American Life, Protest and Reform, Early Foreign Policy, Prosperity and Depression, the Age of Global Crisis, America in Uncertain Times, and The Limits of Power. In addition, there is an important concluding chapter that examines major concerns, issues and trends facing the United States today and in the future. Each content area, except for the last, is divided into identical sections:

OVERVIEW AND TIMELINE

This section introduces you to the main highlights of the period.

KEY HISTORICAL DEVELOPMENTS

This section contains concise descriptions of the major historical events and developments that you are expected to know about and understand. Each period is broken down into smaller separate units focusing on key historical trends. Emphasis is placed on the causes of key developments, what took place, and what were the effects. This section will help you to narrow down the factual content of U.S. History and Government so that you can better understand and remember the developments that are really important.

PERSONALITIES OF THE PERIOD

This section looks at the experiences and accomplishments of a small number of individuals from all walks of life who contributed significantly to their times.

THE CONSTITUTION AT WORK

This section looks at the continuing role which the Constitution has played in American life by focusing on key legislation, key Supreme Court cases and key amendments.

SUMMARIZING YOUR UNDERSTANDING

Most high school students make the mistake of studying for a test only by reading. To do your best on a test, you must practice applying the knowledge you have learned. This section enables you to apply your knowledge by requiring you to summarize the key terms, concepts and other important information discussed in the chapter you have just reviewed.

TESTING YOUR UNDERSTANDING

Each unit ends by testing your understanding of the chapter. The test consists of short answer questions and concludes with essay questions in both an RCT and Regents format.

"LOOKING AT" SECTIONS

In front of each chapter you will find a special "Looking At" section. The aim of these sections is ***not*** to give you more material to memorize, but to give you new ways to think about the material contained in the historical chapters. Each "Looking At" section explores a major theme that runs through several chapters, such as the structure of the American legal system, the nature of history, decision-making in foreign policy, the role of American leaders in shaping this country, and the effects of cultural diversity. After analyzing the theme, each "Looking At" section then applies what you have learned by helping you to answer Regents and RCT essay questions on the same theme.

PERFORMANCE-BASED ASSESSMENT SECTIONS

Each chapter concludes with a performance-based assessment task. These activities may be used to enrich your understanding of the region under review. They may also be used by your teacher as a means of evaluating your performance, with an emphasis on research skills, analytical skills, proficiency in written and oral expression, and the ability to cooperate with others.

GLOSSARY AND ADDITIONAL TESTS

In the closing sections of this book, you will have the opportunity to further sharpen your test-taking skills.

LOOKING AT THE MOST IMPORTANT CONCEPTS AND TERMS

This section —a glossary— provides an explanatory list of the most important terms and concepts that you must know in order to pass the RCT or Regents Examination. An analysis of past Regents and RCTs has shown these terms and concepts to be the ones most frequently tested.

POST-TEST

You are provided with a post-test consisting of a recent U.S. History and Government Regents Examination and an RCT. If you have carefully read through this book and completed all the exercises and chapter tests, your post-test score should show a marked improvement over your pre-test score.

A TEST FOR FURTHER REVIEW

An additional recent Regents Examination is provided for further practice.

By paying careful attention to your teachers, by completing your homework assignments, and by preparing for the Regents and RCT examinations with this review book, you can be confident that you will do your best when the day of the real test arrives.

TABLE OF CONTENTS

PART ONE: HOW MUCH DO YOU KNOW?

PART TWO: HOW TO TAKE A TEST

PART THREE: A REVIEW OF UNITED STATES HISTORY

1607-1820

1820-1877

1865-1920

Photo Credits

Chapter 5:	U. S. Capitol Building in Washington D. C., where Congress makes the laws. (Library of Congress)
Chapter 6:	Bodies of Union soldiers after the first battle of Gettysburg. (Library of Congress)
Chapter 7:	The Carnegie Steel Company plant in Pennsylvania. (Library of Congress)
Chapter 8:	Immigrants coming to America aboard the Atlantic liner SS Patricia. (Library of Congress)
Chapter 9:	Suffragettes demonstrating for the right to vote, New York City, 1912. (Library of Congress)
Chapter 10:	U. S. Marines in China, part of an international force to put down the Boxer Rebellion. (National Archives)
Chapter 11:	Poverty-stricken farm family during the Great Depression. (National Archives)
Chapter 12:	The USS Shaw exploding during Japan's attack on Pearl Harbor in 1941. (Library of Congress)
Chapter 13:	Dr. Martin Luther King, Jr. leading the March on Washington for civil rights, 1963. (National Archives)
Chapter 14:	Oil wells in Kuwait set ablaze by Iraqi forces during the Gulf War in 1991. (United Nations Photo)
Chapter 15:	The New York City skyline at dusk, obscured by air pollution. (National Archives)

CHAPTER 1
PRETEST

How much do you know about the history of the United States and its government? This chapter is comprised of two tests: an RCT examination (constructed to be like the actual RCT you may be taking) and an actual Regents Examination. You should take whichever of these two tests is appropriate for you as a pretest **before** you begin to review the content areas in this book.

This pretest will help you to evaluate your strengths and weaknesses in United States History and Government. Once you know your weak points, you can tailor a study program that will permit you to concentrate on those areas where you need the most help. Good luck on this pretest!

RCT-TYPE EXAMINATION

Directions: This practice RCT has two parts: Part I contains 50 multiple choice questions. You must answer all 50 questions; *circle* the number of the word or expression that best completes the statement or answers the question. Part II contains 4 essay questions, from which you must answer 2.

PART I (50 Credits)

Base your answers to questions 1 through 3 on the following political cartoon and your knowledge of social studies.

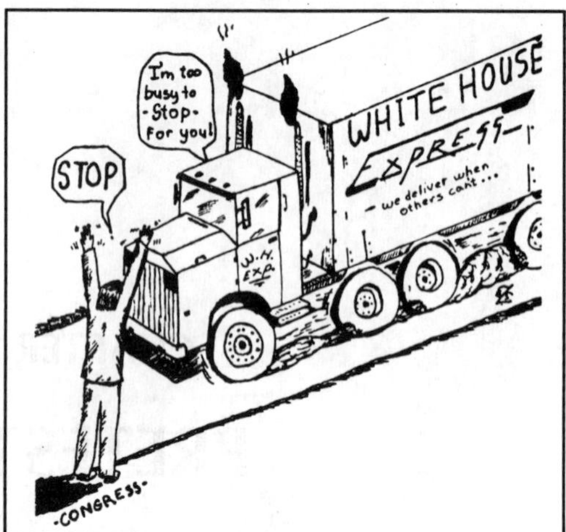
I'm too busy to -Stop- For you!
STOP
WHITE HOUSE
EXPRESS
we deliver when others can't...
W.H. EXP.
-CONGRESS-

1 Which branch of government is represented by the truck?

1 legislative	3 judicial
2 executive	4 bureaucratic

2 Which principle of government is illustrated in the cartoon?
1 checks and balances
2 limited government
3 Bill of Rights
4 judicial review

3 Which power could the person use to stop the truck?
1 appointment of ambassadors
2 impeachment proces
3 judicial review
4 negotiating treaties

---

4 The ultimate power of the United States government comes from the

1 people	3 Congress
2 president	4 Supreme Court

5 The "Bill of Rights" refers to the
1 Declaration of Independence
2 first ten amendments to the Constitution
3 separation of powers in the federal government
4 emancipation of the slaves

6 The main function of Congress is to
1 pass laws for particular states
2 judge whether laws are constitutional
3 appoint and receive ambassadors
4 make federal laws

7 The term " judicial review" means that
1 states and the federal government share power
2 the Supreme Court can determine if laws are unconstitutional
3 Congress can review presidential appointments to the Supreme Court
4 the president can appoint Supreme Court judges

8 Which document was written first?
1 the Truman Doctrine
2 the Declaration of Independence
3 the Articles of Confederation
4 the Monroe Doctrine

9 The right to have a lawyer represent you at a criminal trial best illustrates the right to
1 freedom of speech
2 equal opportunity
3 checks and balances
4 due process

10 In *Marbury v. Madison*, the Supreme Court ruled that
1 racial segregation is constitutional
2 it can declare federal laws unconstitutional
3 in certain cases, defendants are entitled to a lawyer
4 defendants must be informed of their rights

11 Presidents, governors, and mayors are similar in that they all
1 make laws
2 enforce laws
3 judge laws
4 make treaties

12 The topics "freedom of speech" and "due process" would most likely be discussed in an essay on
1 federalism
2 checks and balances
3 the Bill of Rights
4 judicial review

13 Which was a major cause of the Civil War?
1 disputes between England and the colonies concerning taxation
2 Japan's bombing of Pearl Harbor
3 sectional differences turning parts of the country against each other
4 Germany's sinking of United States ships

14 Which event took place during the administration of Abraham Lincoln?
1 issuing of the Emancipation Proclamation
2 signing of the Declaration of Independence
3 outbreak of the Spanish-American War
4 arranging of the Missouri Compromise

15 Which group was most affected by the passage of the Civil War amendments?
1 women
2 former slaves
3 northern manufacturers
4 immigrants

16 A person speaking about "black codes," "carpetbaggers," and Thaddeus Stevens would most likely be referring to which period in American history?
1 the American Revolution
2 Reconstruction
3 the Harlem Renaissance
4 the Cold War

17 John D. Rockefeller, Andrew Carnegie, and Cornelius Vanderbilt were all famous
1 labor leaders
2 civil right leaders
3 military leaders
4 industrialists

18 The Granger Movement consisted of
1 southern whites who terrorized blacks
2 industrial workers who cooperated to obtain higher wages
3 farmers who united to overcome the power of the railroads
4 societies formed by immigrants to learn the American way of life.

Base your answer to questions 19 and 20 on the following bar graph and your knowledge of social studies.

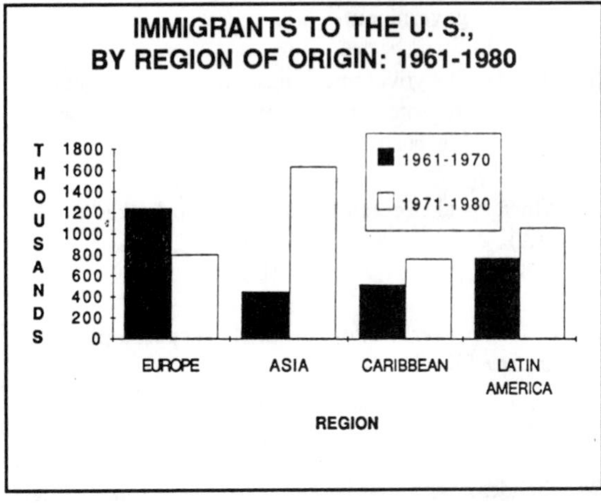
IMMIGRANTS TO THE U. S.,
BY REGION OF ORIGIN: 1961-1980
THOUSANDS
1800
1600
1400
1200
1000
800
600
400
200
0
1961-1970
1971-1980
EUROPE
ASIA
CARIBBEAN
LATIN AMERICA
REGION

19 From which region of the world did immigration to the United States decrease in the period 1961-1980?
1 Europe
2 Asia
3 the Caribbean
4 Latin America

20 Which area, in the time period indicated, contributed the most immigrants to the United States?
1 Europe in the period 1961-1970
2 Asia in the period 1971-1980
3 Caribbean in the period 1961-1970
4 Latin America in the period 1971-1980

---

21 Who is correctly paired with a field in which he/she achieved distinction?
1 Samuel Gompers—women's movement
2 Jane Addams—social reform
3 John Muir—prison reform
4 Dorothea Dix—environmental conservation

Base your answers to questions 22 to 24 on the following statements and on your knowledge of social studies.

Speaker A: Government should not interfere in the affairs of business.

Speaker B: Journalists must continue to expose the wrongs of big business in order to bring about needed reforms.

Speaker C: People must be given the power to control their government. I strongly believe in giving people a greater voice in the affairs of government.

Speaker D: Our government must take a more active role in protecting workers against the abuses of big business.

22 Which speaker could be called a "muckraker"?
1 (A)
2 (B)
3 (C)
4 (D)

23 Which speaker would most likely support a policy of "laissez-faire"?
1 (A)
2 (B)
3 (C)
4 (D)

24 The ideas expressed by the speakers most likely refer to which time period in American history?
1 the Reconstruction Era
2 the Progressive Movement
3 the Great Depression
4 the Civil Rights Movement

---

25 Which was a major cause of the Progressive Movement in the United States?
1 the influence of muckrakers, Populists, and social reformers
2 the stock market crash of 1929
3 racial conflict in the west
4 the migration of people from the cities to the country

26 Which event took place during the administration of Theodore Roosevelt?
1 construction of the Panama Canal
2 passage of the 14th Amendment
3 the Spanish-American War
4 the creation of NATO

27 The term "Manifest Destiny" referred to the belief that America should devote its energies towards
1 greater industrial growth
2 further westward expansion
3 equality and justice for all
4 freedom of thought and religion

28 The Monroe Doctrine has basically been used to
1 justify U. S. intervention in Latin America
2 allow European powers to establish colonies in the New World
3 keep the United States out of European conflicts
4 open up Japan and China to American commerce

29 Which newspaper headline bests reflects the concept of "imperialism"?
1 "The Supreme Court Bans Segregation in Public Schools"
2 "The United Nations is Founded in San Francisco"
3 "President McKinley Announces U.S. Annexation of the Philippines"
4 "President Bush Meets Gorbachev at Summit Conference"

30 If a student's notes contain information about the sinking of the Lusitania, trench warfare, and the Central Powers, the student is most likely studying
1 the Korean War
2 World War I
3 World War II
4 the Vietnam War

31 Which was a major result of World War I?
1 American troops occupied Japan.
2 The Soviet Union gained control of Eastern Europe.
3 Britain and France lost control of their colonies.
4 Germany lost territories and colonies.

32 A primary result of the U. S. participation in the Vietnam War was that the
1 king was restored to power in South Vietnam
2 threat of a Communist takeover in Vietnam was eliminated
3 war created discontent and divisions within the United States
4 United States eliminated future immigration from Vietnam

33 Lockouts, blacklisting and yellow-dog contracts were "tools" once used by
1 management against workers
2 unions against management
3 the government against immigrants
4 political parties against voters

34 Which source would be most helpful to a person seeking information about the Jazz Age and the Harlem Renaissance?
1 the *Congressional Record*
2 an atlas
3 the *Economic Report of the President*
4 an encyclopedia

35 The "Crash of '29" refers to
1 a major railroad accident in 1829
2 the New York stock market crash of 1929
3 the sinking of the battleship *Maine* that started the Spanish-American War
4 the explosion of the *Challenger* space shuttle

36 Which was a major result of the Depression of the 1930's?
1 a rise in oil prices
2 shortages of consumer goods
3 the start of World War I
4 widespread unemployment

37 The terms "bank holiday," W.P.A., and C.C.C. would most likely be discussed in an essay dealing with the
1 Progressive Movement
2 New Deal
3 causes of World War II
4 Women's Movement

38 Which event took place during the administration of Franklin D. Roosevelt?
1 formation of the Freedmen's Bureau
2 passage of the 14th amendment
3 construction of the Panama Canal
4 start of World War II

39 Which was a basic cause of World War II?
1 European competition for colonies in Africa
2 the aggressiveness of Nazi Germany
3 tensions between the United States and the U.S.S.R.
4 human rights abuses in South Africa

40 The bombing of Hiroshima and Nagasaki resulted in
1 establishing the "Open Door" policy in Japan
2 the outbreak of World War II
3 the United States entering the war against Japan
4 the Japanese surrender to the United States

41 The term "Cold War" refers to
1 United States neutrality before World War I
2 Prime Minister Chamberlain's attempts to appease Hitler.
3 the long period of distrust between the U.S.S.R. and the U.S.
4 the westward movement across the United States.

Base your answer to questions 42 and 43 on the table and your knowledge of social studies.

POPULATION DATA BY REGION

Region	1987 Population (mil.)	% Change (1980-1987)
United States	243.4	+7.4%
Northeast	50.3	+2.3%
Midwest	59.5	+1.1%
South	83.9	+11.3%
West	49.7	+15.1%

42 Which region had the largest population in 1987?
1 Northwest
2 Midwest
3 South
4 West

43 Which statement is most accurate?
1 All regions of the United States experienced population gains.
2 The majority of Americans live in the South.
3 The Midwest has the smallest population.
4 The West has the largest population.

---

44 The terms "detente," "glasnost," and "perestroika" are words associated with relations between the United States and
1 Cuba
2 the U.S.S.R.
3 China
4 Japan

45 Susan B. Anthony, Betty Friedan, and Gloria Steinem are associated with the movement
1 to increase women's rights
2 for racial equality
3 for protection of the environment
4 to help the disabled

46 In *Roe v. Wade*, the Supreme Court ruled that
1 the Court can declare federal laws unconstitutional
2 racial segregation is unconstitutional
3 defendants must be informed of their rights
4 states cannot ban abortion for women in the early months of pregnancy

47 Which was a basic cause of the Vietnam War?
1 religious differences between Muslims and Jews
2 American fear of Communist expansion in Southeast Asia
3 the North Korean invasion of South Korea
4 the Soviet Union's placement of missiles in Cuba

48 During the administration of President Jimmy Carter, Iran
1 lowered world oil prices
2 declared war on Israel
3 invaded the Soviet Union
4 seized American hostages

49 The Reagan Administration faced its greatest foreign policy difficulties in
1 Nicaragua
2 Nigeria
3 Greece
4 Mexico

50 Which statement is an opinion rather than a fact?
1 President Theodore Roosevelt won the Nobel Peace prize.
2 The U.S. Senate voted not to join the League of Nations.
3 Japan bombed Pearl Harbor in 1941.
4 The United Nations has helped us to achieve world peace.

PART II

ANSWER TWO ESSAYS FROM THIS PART: 20 Credits

1 The principles contained in the U.S. Constitution serve to protect our liberties.

Principles

Separation of Powers
Federalism
Popular Sovereignty
Limited Government

Part A

Choose *one* of the principles listed. ______________________________

Define its meaning. ______________________________

State *one* way in which that principle protects our liberties. ______________________________

Choose *another* principle: ______________________________

Define its meaning. ______________________________

State *one* way in which that principle protects our liberties. ______________________________

Part B

In your Part B answer, you should use information you gave in Part A. However, you may also include different or additional information in your Part B answer.

On a separate sheet of paper, write an essay discussing how the principles contained in the United States Constitution help to protect our liberties.

2 A country's foreign policy is often determined by events in other countries.

Events

The battleship *Maine* explodes in Cuba—1898
Germany invades Poland—1939
Soviet missiles are found in Cuba—1962
Khomeini removes the Shah from power in Iran—1979

Part A

Select *two* events from the list. For *each* event:

- Describe the event.
- State how the United States responded to the event.

Event: ______________________	**U.S. Response:** ______________________
Event: ______________________	**U.S. Response:** ______________________

Part B

In your Part B answer, you should use information you gave in Part A. However, you may also include different or additional information in your Part B answer.

On a separate sheet of paper, write an essay discussing how a country's foreign policy has often been determined by events in other countries.

3 The ideas and actions of some individuals have brought about important changes in the United States.

Individuals

Thomas Jefferson
Abraham Lincoln
Susan B. Anthony
Thomas Edison
Henry Ford
Franklin Delano Roosevelt
Martin Luther King, Jr.

Part A

Choose *one* individual from the list above. ______________________________

State an idea or action of that individual that brought about at least one important change in the United States.

____

Choose *another* individual from the list: ______________________________

State an idea or action of that individual that brought about at least one important change in the United States.

____

Part B

In your Part B answer, you should use information you gave in Part A. However, you may also include different or additional information in your Part B answer.

On a separate sheet of paper, write an essay discussing how the ideas or actions of some individuals have brought about important changes in the United States.

4 Base your answer to this essay question on the following cartoon and on your knowledge of social studies.

ILLITERACY
DRUGS
AIDS EPIDEMIC
TOXIC WASTE
CRIME
HOMELESSNESS
$

Part A

1. What is the main idea of the cartoon? ______________________________

2. Select a problem shown in the cartoon. ______________________________

   Describe the problem. ______________________________

3. Select *another* problem shown in the cartoon ______________________________

   Describe the problem. ______________________________

Part B

In your Part B answer, you should use information you gave in Part A. However, you may also include different or additional information in your Part B answer.

On a separate sheet of paper, write an essay discussing one possible solution that might be taken to help resolve one of the problems you have selected.

JUNE 1996 REGENTS

Part I (55 credits)

ANSWER ALL 48 QUESTIONS IN THIS PART.

Directions (1-48): For each statement or question, write on the separate answer sheet the number of the word or expression that, of those given, best completes the statement or answers the question.

1 "The only representatives of the people of these colonies are persons chosen therein by themselves; and that no taxes ever have been, or can be constitutionally imposed on them but by their respective legislatures."

— *Statement by the Stamp Act Congress, 1765*

What is a valid conclusion that can be drawn from this quotation?
1 The colonial legislatures should be appointed by the English King with the consent of Parliament.
2 Only the colonists' elected representatives should have the power to levy taxes.
3 The English King should have the right to tax the colonists.
4 The colonists should be opposed to all taxation.

2 The authors of the Articles of Confederation established a decentralized political system mainly to
1 cancel state debts incurred during the Revolutionary War
2 assist the southern states in their efforts to gain a manufacturing base
3 promote the common goal of national sovereignty
4 prevent the abuses of power that had existed under British rule

3 Senate ratification of treaties negotiated by the President is required by the United States Constitution as a way of
1 maintaining United States prestige in international affairs
2 preventing Federal abuse of State power
3 implementing the principle of checks and balances
4 expanding the authority of the executive branch

4 The United States Constitution requires that a census be taken every ten years to reapportion
1 membership in the House of Representatives
2 the number of delegates to national conventions
3 Federal aid to localities
4 agricultural subsidies

5 In the United States Congress, differences between Senate and House of Representatives versions of a bill are usually resolved by accepting the version that is
1 preferred by a majority of the State legislatures
2 supported by the Supreme Court
3 preferred by the House in which the bill originated
4 agreed to by a joint conference committee of both Houses

6 "The privilege of the writ of habeas corpus shall not be suspended, unless when in cases of rebellion or invasion the public safety may require it."

This provision is evidence that the writers of the United States Constitution
1 wanted the President to have unlimited power during wartime
2 wanted to balance individual liberty with the needs of the nation
3 did not trust the common people to obey the laws
4 expected the American people to oppose most government policies

7 In the United States, activities such as Cabinet meetings and political party conventions are best described as
1 examples of direct democracy
2 responsibilities of the executive branch
3 features of the unwritten constitution
4 requirements of the system of checks and balances

Base your answer to question 8 on the cartoon below and on your knowledge of social studies.

CAMPAIGN COSTS
DEMOCRACY

8 The most commonly proposed solution to the problem shown in the cartoon is to
1 establish poll taxes
2 have candidates finance their own campaigns
3 eliminate primaries from the election system
4 use public funds to pay for political campaigns

9 Actions and policies of the Government under President George Washington generally resulted in the
1 establishment of strong political ties with other nations
2 liberation of many enslaved persons
3 failure to create a sound financial program for the country
4 strengthening of the Federal Government

10 "By the 1850s, the Constitution originally framed as an instrument of national unity, had become a source of sectional discord."

This quotation suggests that
1 vast differences of opinion existed over the issue of states rights
2 the Federal Government had become more interested in foreign affairs than in domestic problems
3 the Constitution had no provisions for governing new territories
4 the Southern States continued to import slaves

11 Early in his Presidency, Abraham Lincoln declared that his primary goal as President was to
1 enforce the Emancipation Proclamation
2 preserve the Union
3 end slavery throughout the entire country
4 encourage sectionalism

12 In their plans for Reconstruction, both President Abraham Lincoln and President Andrew Johnson sought to
1 punish the South for starting the Civil War
2 force the Southern States to pay reparations to the Federal Government
3 allow the Southern States to reenter the nation as quickly as possible
4 establish the Republican Party as the only political party in the South

13 The poll tax, the literacy test, and the actions of the Ku Klux Klan were all attempts to limit the effectiveness of
1 the 14th and 15th amendments
2 the Supreme Court's decision in *Brown v. Board of Education*
3 civil rights legislation passed in all states after the Civil War
4 immigration laws such as the Gentleman's Agreement and the Chinese Exclusion Act

14 According to the theory of laissez faire, the economy functions best when the government
1 subsidizes business so that it can compete worldwide
2 regulates businesses for the good of the majority
3 owns major industries
4 does not interfere in business

15 Businesses formed trusts, pools, and holding companies mainly to
1 increase profits by eliminating competition
2 offer a wide range of goods and services to consumers
3 provide employment opportunities for minorities
4 protect the interests of workers

16 The Rockefeller Foundation, Carnegie Hall, and the Morgan Library illustrate various ways that entrepreneurs and their descendants have
1 suppressed the growth of labor unions
2 supported philanthropic activities to benefit society
3 applied scientific discoveries to industry
4 attempted to undermine the United States economic system

17 The major reason the United States placed few restrictions on immigration during the 1800s was that
1 few Europeans wished to give up their economic security
2 little opposition to immigration existed
3 the growing economy needed a steady supply of cheap labor
4 most immigrants spoke English and thus needed little or no education

18 The American Federation of Labor became the first long-lasting, successful labor union in the United States mainly because it
1 refused to participate in strikes against employers
2 concentrated on organizing workers in industries in the South
3 formed its own political party and elected many pro-labor public officials
4 fought for the rights of skilled workers

19 In the late 1800s, the goal of the Federal Government's policy toward Native American Indians was to
1 destroy tribal bonds and thus weaken their traditional cultural values
2 grant them full citizenship and due process
3 give their tribal groups authority over their own affairs
4 increase the land holdings of western tribes

20 W.E.B. Du Bois believed that African Americans should attempt to gain equality in the United States by
1 setting up a separate nation within the United States
2 entering vocational training programs in separate schools
3 demanding full and immediate participation in American society
4 taking over the leadership of the two major political parties

21 In the United States during the late 19th century, much of the prejudice expressed toward immigrants was based on the belief that they would
1 cause overcrowding in farm areas
2 refuse to become citizens
3 support the enemies of the United States in wartime
4 fail to assimilate into American society

22 During the late 19th and early 20th centuries, United States policy toward Latin America was most strongly characterized by
1 friendship and trust
2 intervention and paternalism
3 tolerance and humanitarianism
4 indifference and neglect

23 A major purpose of the Federal Reserve System was to
1 deal with the trade deficit through tariffs and quotas
2 control the minimum wage
3 establish the Federal budget
4 regulate interest rates and the money supply

24 A major goal of reformers during the Progressive Era was to
1 end segregation in the South
2 correct the abuses of big business
3 limit immigration from Latin America
4 enact high tariffs to help domestic industry grow

25 "We are to be an instrument in the hands of God to see that liberty is made secure for mankind."
— *President Woodrow Wilson*

President Wilson tried to carry out the idea expressed in this quotation by
1 protesting the sinking of the *Lusitania*
2 proposing a program of civil rights for minorities in American society
3 urging the Allies to adopt the Fourteen Points
4 taking control of territories conquered in World War I

26 In stating the principle of a "clear and present danger" in *Schenck v. United States*, the Supreme Court established that
1 constitutional rights are not absolute
2 the Constitution guarantees the right to privacy
3 Congress can pass a law to eliminate any part of the Bill of Rights
4 all individual rights are eliminated during wartime

27 In the 1920s, the Immigration Act of 1924 and the Sacco-Vanzetti trial were typical of the
1 rejection of traditional customs and beliefs
2 acceptance of cultural differences
3 increase in nativism and intolerance
4 support of humanitarian causes

28 The economic boom and the financial speculation of the 1920s were caused in part by
1 installment buying and an unregulated stock market
2 the expansion of civil rights to women and minorities
3 the mobilization of the economy for war
4 increased government restrictions on big business

29 The popularity of escapist novels and movies during the Great Depression is evidence that
1 the Great Depression was not really a time of economic distress
2 popular culture is shaped by economic and social conditions
3 American society did not try to solve the problems of the Great Depression
4 the greatest employment opportunities for the average person in the 1930s were in the field of entertainment

30 The power of labor unions increased during the New Deal mainly because
1 a new spirit of cooperation existed between employers and government
2 a shortage of skilled and unskilled laborers developed
3 management changed its attitude toward organized labor
4 Federal legislation guaranteed labor's right to organize and bargain collectively

31 An immediate result of the Supreme Court decision in *Schecter Poultry Corporation v. United States* (1935) and *United States v. Butler* (1936) was that
1 some aspects of the New Deal were declared unconstitutional
2 State governments took over relief agencies
3 Congress was forced to abandon efforts to improve the economy
4 the constitutional authority of the President was greatly expanded

32 The United States became involved in World War II primarily because
1 Germany refused to pay its debts from World War I
2 European democracies supported United States policies toward Germany and Japan
3 President Franklin D. Roosevelt did not enforce the Neutrality Acts
4 Germany and Japan achieved important military successes in Europe and Asia

Base your answer to question 33 on the cartoon below and on your knowledge of social studies.

I WANT SIX SUBSTITUTES AT ONCE. THOSE FELLOWS DONT KNOW IT, BUT THEY'RE THROUGH, BUT I DONT WANT TO TAKE 'EM OFF THE FIELD!
CONGRESS
REFEREE
FDR
COURT
THE INGENIOUS QUARTERBACK!

33 This cartoon portrays Franklin D. Roosevelt's attempt to
1 continue life terms for Supreme Court Justices
2 increase Presidential influence on the Supreme Court
3 prevent Congress from interfering with the Federal Court system
4 strengthen the independence of the Supreme Court

34 In the United States during World War II, the role of women changed as they
1 were drafted and assigned military roles equal to those held by men
2 continued to work outside the home only in jobs traditionally performed by women
3 made major contributions to the war effort by taking jobs in factories
4 achieved positions of leadership in most major industries

35 After World War II, the United States occupied Japan, joined the North Atlantic Treaty Organization (NATO), and helped organize the United Nations. These actions show that the United States was
1 concerned solely with rebuilding Europe
2 taking on greater global responsibility
3 expanding its imperialistic empire
4 returning to its policy of neutrality

Base your answer to question 36 on the graph below and on your knowledge of social studies.

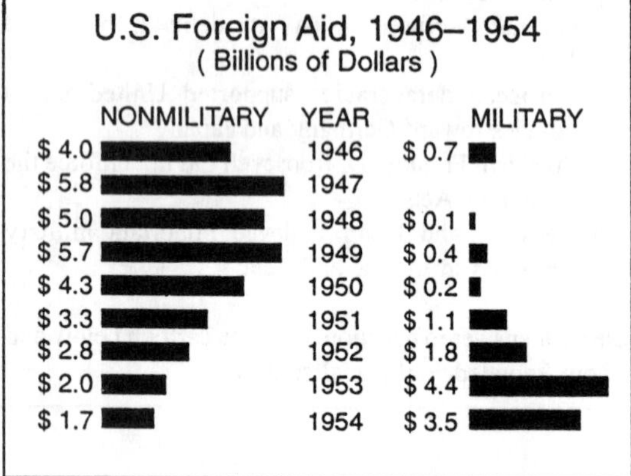
U.S. Foreign Aid, 1946–1954
(Billions of Dollars)
NONMILITARY
YEAR
MILITARY
$ 4.0 1946 $ 0.7
$ 5.8 1947
$ 5.0 1948 $ 0.1
$ 5.7 1949 $ 0.4
$ 4.3 1950 $ 0.2
$ 3.3 1951 $ 1.1
$ 2.8 1952 $ 1.8
$ 2.0 1953 $ 4.4
$ 1.7 1954 $ 3.5

36 Which United States program is most likely reflected in the amounts of non-military foreign aid given from 1947 to 1950?
1 Peace Corps
2 Marshall Plan
3 Alliance for Progress
4 Lend Lease

37 Which is a valid conclusion based on United States involvement in the Korean War?
1 The policy of containment was applied in Asia as well as in Europe.
2 United Nations economic sanctions are more effective than military action.
3 The American people will support United States participation in any war, whether declared or undeclared.
4 United States cooperation with a wartime ally ends when the war ends.

38 Which statement about public education in the United States is most accurate?
1 The Federal Government controls but does not fund education.
2 The problems that affect other segments of American society seldom affect education.
3 Education is largely controlled and financed by state governments and local communities.
4 High school enrollments have decreased over the last 100 years.

39 "Those of us who shout the loudest about Americanism in making character assassinations are all too frequently those who, by our own words and acts, ignore some of the basic principles of Americanism."

—*Senator Margaret Chase Smith, 1950*

This criticism of Senator Joseph McCarthy and his supporters suggest that
1 Senator McCarthy did not do enough to protect the nation from a Communist conspiracy
2 the tactics of Senator McCarthy were necessary to protect the basic principles of democracy
3 free speech must be limited in times of national crisis
4 Senator McCarthy was a greater threat to the nation than Communist sympathizers were

40 The Great Society programs of the 1960s used the power of the Federal Government to bring about
1 an all-volunteer military
2 anti-poverty reforms
3 deregulation of business
4 reduced defense spending

41 A major long-term effect of the Vietnam War has been
1 an end to communist governments in Asia
2 a change in United States foreign policy from containment to imperialism
3 a reluctance to commit United States troops for extended military action abroad
4 a continued boycott of trade with Asia

42 The Camp David accords negotiated during President Jimmy Carter's administration were an attempt to
1 decrease United States control of the Panama Canal
2 encourage the use of solar and other nonpolluting energy sources
3 end inflationary oil prices
4 establish peace in the Middle East

43 According to the supply-side economics principles promoted by President Ronald Reagan, economic growth would occur when
1 corporate business taxes were reduced
2 business was regulated by antitrust legislation
3 unemployment benefits were increased
4 investment in capital goods was decreased

44 The rulings of the Supreme Court in *Dred Scott v. Sanford* (1857), *Plessy v. Ferguson* (1896), and *Korematsu v. United States* (1944) all demonstrate that the Supreme Court has
1 continued to extend voting rights to minorities
2 protected itself from internal dissent
3 sometimes failed to protect the rights of minorities
4 often imposed restrictions on free speech during wartime

45 Which characteristic of the American frontier continues to be an important part of life in the United States today?
1 widespread support for the Populist Party
2 necessity for families to have many children
3 a predominately agricultural and mining economy
4 significant opportunities for social and economic mobility

46 The main purpose of a progressive income tax is to
1 base tax rates on person's ability to pay
2 increase government spending on welfare programs
3 tax everyone at the same percentage rate
4 ensure a balanced budget

Base your answers to questions 47 and 48 on the statements below and on your knowledge of social studies.

Speaker A: We must take action even if we are not sure it will work. To do nothing to stop them would be a repeat of the Munich mistake.

Speaker B: We must recognize the increasing interdependence of nations and join the United Nations.

Speaker C: Stopping the spread of communism can and must take several forms. We must be willing to do whatever is necessary.

Speaker D: Involvement in European affairs would be a mistake. We should not jeopardize our peace and prosperity over issues that Europe's ambitions and rivalries control.

47 Which speaker best describes the basic foreign policy of the United States until the late 1800s.?
(1) A
(2) B
(3) C
(4) D

48 The "Munich mistake" mentioned by speaker A refers to a policy of
1 interdependence
2 appeasement
3 balance of power
4 collective security

PART II

ANSWER ONE QUESTION FROM THIS PART.

1 The United States democratic system includes certain features that are intended to protect against the abuse of power by government and public officials.

Protective Features

Judicial review
Impeachment process
Freedom of expression
Protection against unreasonable searches
Equal protection under the law
Rights of the accused

Choose *three* of the features listed and for *each* one chosen:

- Explain how the feature is intended to protect against abuse of governmental power
- Discuss a specific situation in United States history in which the feature was used to protect against an abuse of governmental power [Use a different historical situation for each feature discussed.]
- Discuss the extent to which the feature was successful in protecting against abuse of governmental power in that situation [5,5,5]

2 Different groups have played a role in influencing policies and shaping legislation in the United States.

Influential Groups

Representatives of foreign nations
Lobbyists
Media
Political action committees
Political parties
Unions

Choose *three* of the groups listed and for *each* one chosen:

- Identify a specific group and show how that group attempted to influence a specific governmental policy or to shape legislation
- Discuss the extent to which the attempt was successful [5,5,5]

PART III

ANSWER TWO QUESTIONS FROM THIS PART.

3 At different times in the history of the United States, Presidents have taken various foreign policy actions.

Presidential Foreign Policy Actions

George Washington warns against "entangling alliances" in his Farewell Address. (1796)
James Monroe announces the Monroe Doctrine. (1823)
Theodore Roosevelt supports the independence of Panama from Colombia. (1903)
Franklin D. Roosevelt asks Congress for a declaration of war. (1941)
John F. Kennedy orders a blockade of Cuba. (1962)
Ronald Reagan begins a major military buildup. (early 1980s)
Bill Clinton sends United States forces to Bosnia. (1995)

Choose *three* of the foreign policy actions listed and for *each* one chosen:

- Describe a circumstance that motivated the Presidential foreign policy action
- Explain a goal of the United States in taking that action
- Discuss an impact of that action. [5,5,5]

4 Since colonial times, various methods of protest have been used to bring about change.

Methods of Protests

Boycott
Civil disobedience
Demonstration / protest march
Petition
Rebellion
Sit-in
Strike

a Choose *three* of the methods listed and for *each* one chosen, describe a specific historical situation in which that method of protest was used to bring about change and explain why that method was used. [Use a different historical situation for each method.] [4,4,4]

b For *one* of the methods of protest chosen in answer to part a, discuss the extent to which that method was successful in bringing about change. [3]

5 Certain actions have aroused controversy in American society. Some of these controversial actions are listed below

Controversial Actions

Proposal of the Virginia Plan (one-house federal legislature) at the Constitutional Convention (1787)
Election of Abraham Lincoln to the Presidency (1860)
Annexation of the Philippines by the United States (1898)
Proposal of United States membership in the League of Nations by President Woodrow Wilson (1919)
Ratification of the Prohibition amendment (1919)
Proposal of New Deal legislation by President Franklin D. Roosevelt (1933)
Decision concerning abortion in *Roe v. Wade* by the Supreme Court (1973)

Select *three* of the controversial actions listed and for *each* one chosen:

- Discuss one argument given by supporters and one argument given by opponents of the action.
- Discuss one result of the action [5,5,5]

6 Certain issues concern American society today. Some of these issues are listed below.

Issues of Concern to Americans
Changing family patterns
Crime
Health care reform
Homelessness
Immigration
Technological change

Choose *three* of the issues listed and for *each* one chosen:

- Discuss *two* reasons the issue concerns Americans today
- Describe a specific proposal that has been suggested to deal with the issue [5,5,5]

7 Songs sometimes describe the experiences and problems of various groups. Excerpts from some songs are given below. Choose *three* of the excerpts and for each *one* chosen:

- Identify the group described in the song and describe a problem suggested by the song
- Show how a specific political or economic policy of government attempted to deal with the problem [5,5,5]

"HARD TIMES" SONGS

Excerpt 1—
The farmer is the man, the farmer is the man
Lives on credit 'til the fall
With the interest rate so high, its a wonder he don't die
For the mortgage man's the one who gets it all

—Anonymous

Excerpt 2—
O it's all in the past you can say
But it's still going on here today
The Government now wants the Iroquois land
That of the Seneca and the Cheyenne
It's here and it's now you must help us, dear man
Now that the Buffalo's gone

—Buffy Sainte-Marie

Excerpt 3—
It is we who dug the ditches, built the cities where they trade
Blasted mines and built the workshops, endless miles of railroad laid
Now we stand outcast and starving 'mid the wonders we have made,
But the union makes us strong ...

—Ralph Chaplin

Excerpt 4—
Bumpy wagons moving through the days and nights
They've been travelin' far in search of women's rights
Not much comfort or supporters but within this country's borders
They won't quit 'til they've won all of the fights.

—Eileen Abrams

Excerpt 5—
Too old to work, too old to work
When you're too old to work and you're too young to die
Who will take care of you, how'll you get by
When your too old to work and you're too young to die?

—Joe Glazer

LOOKING AT HISTORY

WHAT IS HISTORY?

The word "history" refers to an inquiry into what happened in the past. In its focus on human behavior, history is similar to social science—yet it is also different. Social scientists are interested in uncovering common patterns of behavior and analyzing these patterns scientifically. Historians are more concerned with understanding and explaining particular events and occurrences. They especially want to know about people's ideas, plans, and actions and their effects.

THE IMPORTANCE OF HISTORY

People have been studying history for thousands of years because they are curious about the past. The study of history helps a society remember what it is and where it is going. Just as your own life would be quite meaningless if you had no memory of who you were or what you had done, each society looks to its history for a sense of identity. This is why dictators who want to control a society often rewrite the history books to suit their own needs. Although we cannot predict the future from studying the past, knowledge of history can give us insights into what may happen in some instances. Knowledge of Soviet history, for example, might have led one to foresee the collapse of Soviet Communism.

THE VARIETIES OF HISTORY

The past is so vast an area for study that there are many types of historians. Each type focuses on a different aspect of the past. Some study politics, diplomacy and wars; others study past economies, social structures and family life; and still others study the history of the arts, culture and ideas. Some historians recount a series of events, others attempt to establish a series of hypotheses about a period in history; some study one country, others a civilization or the entire world.

THE EMERGENCE OF MULTICULTURAL HISTORY

Throughout history most records have been kept by a relatively small group of powerful people—rulers, government officials, religious leaders, philosophers and landowners. Until quite recently, most historical writing was devoted to their concerns. In the United States, much of this historical writing also centered on European history, since European immigrants and their descendants had established most of the dominant institutions of the American republic.

Today, because many historians recognize that focusing on the most powerful segment of society provides only one historical perspective, they also investigate what it was like to be a poor farmer, a factory worker, or a slave. Historians have also become concerned with studying the experiences of women as well as men, and children as well as adults. In addition, historians today try to understand events from different perspectives. This attempt to understand events from multiple perspectives is sometimes referred to as **multicultural history**.

HOW HISTORIANS WORK: THE HISTORICAL METHOD

The study of history is especially difficult because it is neither literature nor science but combines the qualities of both. Like literature, history must be well-written to communicate its ideas effectively. Like science, history should be accurate.

FRAMING A HISTORICAL PROBLEM

We have seen that the job of the historian is to study the past and write about it. Usually a historian begins by framing a problem that needs to be solved. For example:

- When did the first Native American civilizations develop?
- How were women treated during Colonial times?
- What were the lives of slaves like before the Civil War?
- Why did the U. S. Senate refuse to ratify the Treaty of Versailles?

HISTORICAL SOURCES AND THEIR INTERPRETATION

Once the historian has framed a historical problem, he or she next gathers source materials that might help to solve the problem. These sources are of two kinds:

■ **Primary Sources** are original records of the event or matter under investigation. Primary sources include: documents left by eyewitnesses, records compiled at the time of the event, the texts of speeches and reports, letters sent or received by people involved in the event, photographs, and so forth. All historical knowledge about an event is ultimately derived from primary sources.

■ **Secondary sources** are the writings and interpretations of historians and other writers. Often secondary sources, like textbooks and articles, provide convenient summaries of the information contained in primary sources. Historians read these to find out about other historians' ideas as well as to find out where primary sources are located.

Using historical sources presents many problems. Primary sources are always incomplete, and the historian can never know with complete accuracy what happened before. History, therefore, relies on the interpretation of surviving sources. This can be a very tricky matter. Being an historian is like being a detective. When a historian discovers a particular record, he or she must interpret it. The historian asks:

- Is the document authentic or a forgery? Is the document really what it seems to be?
- What were the probable conditions that produced this record? In what ways is the record biased?

The historian must consider the ways in which the information in the document may be biased. For example, a Southern plantation owner writing about the election of Abraham Lincoln would have a different view from that of a New England abolitionist.

THE SELECTION AND INTERPRETATION OF SIGNIFICANT FACTS

There are thousands of facts that we can be reasonably certain took place. But which of these facts is important in telling the story of a past event? In selecting some facts to include in a historical account and in discarding others, each historian must make value judgments about what he or she thinks was really important. Other historians might not agree with these value judgments. History thus not only poses problems in interpreting specific documents and records, but also in deciding which facts had important effects and which did not. Therefore, in analyzing facts in any record or document the historian must also ask: What do the facts tell us about the society we are studying, the historical quesion we are trying to answer, or the problem we are trying to solve?

HISTORICAL CONTROVERSIES

Because historians often disagree about the interpretation of sources, there are many disagreements about what actually happened. What you find in your school text is often only a summary of key points about an issue on which some historians have agreed. For example, older textbooks often stated that Christopher Columbus "discovered" America. But in more recent history texts, Columbus has become the center of a historical controversy.

THE COLUMBUS CONTROVERSY

THE CHARACTER OF THE MAN

Many historians feel that he treated his crews and colonists harshly—although it can be argued that his conduct was justified by the rough frontier conditions. Other historians argue that in his eagerness to turn a profit for his royal masters, Columbus shipped Indians back to Spain as slaves. His defenders point out that these actions must be judged by 15th century standards; for example, the Carib Indians—one of the groups enslaved by the Spaniards—had practiced cannibalism on other tribes.

THE NATURE OF HIS IMPACT

Admirers of Columbus point to his unique contribution to world history. It took great courage to sail into the unknown. He is the only person in history to have brought together two hemispheres. Columbus' voyages brought important benefits to Europe—new foods, knowledge about other peoples of the world, and immense riches. These changes fueled social, intellectual, and economic changes, leading to the scientific and industrial revolutions. Critics of Columbus see some of the flaws of his personality as those of European society of his day. The demand for labor led to the Atlantic slave trade. His exploitation of other peoples and of the environment led to technological progress and increased riches, but at the cost of greater suffering and destruction. The encounter with Europeans led to the conquest of Native American civilizations, and the deaths of millions of Native Americans from European diseases.

Can one ever know the "real" Columbus? Was he a remarkable explorer or a cruel tyrant? Perhaps he was both. However, all historians agree that his voyages had a major impact on world history.

In trying to judge any historical controversy, or trying to evaluate any piece of historical writing, you should consider all the aspects of the historical method discussed in this "Looking At" section. The final question you should ask yourself is: Taking all surviving records into account, what would be the most likely explanation of that event?

ANSWERING AN ESSAY QUESTION ABOUT HISTORY

A large part of what you study about the United States concerns its history. Many Regents and RCT questions therefore focus on historical issues. The topics of these questions are quite varied. You may be asked what problems different groups faced, what foreign policies the U.S. followed, or what branches of the federal government were most powerful at various periods in our history. Or you might be asked about the problems and characteristics of a particular time period, such as the 1890s, 1920s, 1930s or 1960s.

Preceding each chapter of this book, you will find special "*Looking At*" sections. These sections are designed to help you understand and answer essay questions. They focus on such topics as foreign policy, economic policy, social policy, culture, and the problems, issues and trends facing the nation in the future. Each "*Looking At*" explores a different topic from an analytical perspective, and then applies what you have learned to answering RCT and Regents essay questions.

CHAPTER 2

HOW TO ANSWER MULTIPLE CHOICE QUESTIONS

Everyone wants to get a high score when taking an examination. But just wanting that high score is not enough; you really have to work for it. Although knowledge of the subject matter is the most important thing in achieving a high grade, being aware of certain test-taking strategies can also help increase your test score. This chapter will focus on these strategies.

COMPONENTS OF THE REGENTS AND RCT EXAMINATIONS

Each examination has certain mechanical aspects of which you should be aware.

U. S. History and Government Regents Examination

Part I. Consists of 47 to 50 short answer multiple choice questions. Each question has four choices. This section is worth 55 points.

Part II. Contains two essay choices about American government, of which you must answer one. This essay is worth 15 points.

Part III. Contains five essays on topics in American history and current problems. You are required to answer two essays. Each essay is worth 15 points.

To pass the Regents Examination, you must score at least 65 points out of a possible 100.

U.S. History and Government Regents Competency Test

Part I. Consists of 50 short answer multiple choice questions. Each question will have four choices. The point value for each question is 1 point.

Part II. Contains four essays. You must select two out of the four essays. Each essay is worth 10 points.

In order to pass the RCT examination, you must score at least 46 points out of a possible total of 70 points on the test.

GENERAL HINTS TO KEEP IN MIND

WHEN YOU START THE EXAMINATION

Take some time to find out what is expected of you by carefully reading all of the directions. There is no substitute for taking a few moments to make sure that the directions are fully understood.

BE AWARE OF THE TIME

Bring a watch when taking a timed test. You should have a general idea of how much time each section or part of the test will take you. If you are stumped on a particular question move on to other questions, but **mark** any omitted questions. If time allows, return to work on those questions you omitted.

WHAT TO LOOK FOR WHEN ANSWERING A QUESTION

Read the question carefully. As you read, underline the key word or expression that you think may be central to that question. If a word is used in the question that is unfamiliar, try breaking down the word into other words that are more familiar to you. See if looking at the prefix (start of the word), root or suffix (ending) in the word helps you find the meaning of the word.

MAKING A SELECTION

Consider all of the choices *before* you make a selection. Don't select an answer that may generally be true, but may be a wrong answer for that particular question. Always select an answer that provides the best response to the question posed. Don't panic if you do not know the answer. If a question is confusing, try putting the question into simpler language that makes it easier to understand.

GUESSING

Since there is no penalty for guessing, you should ***never*** omit any short answer question. Blank answers will *always* be counted as wrong. Make an educated guess, since there is a chance you may get the correct answer.

ANALYZING THE MULTIPLE CHOICE SECTION OF PAST REGENTS AND RCT'S

Over the past several years, students in New York State have been required to take either the U.S. History and Government Regents or RCT examinations. A careful study of the content tested on all past examinations indicates that a large number of questions focus on the government of the United States. We *strongly* recommend that you pay particular attention to this topic (covered in Chapter 5: Constitutional Foundations) in your studies. In addition, by looking at the multiple choice section of both the Regents and RCT's, it is possible to chart other important patterns that have emerged in the types of questions asked.

ANALYSIS OF PAST REGENTS (Numbers=Total Questions Asked)

	June 1990	Aug. 1990	Jan. 1991	June 1991	Aug. 1991	Jan. 1992	June 1992	Jan. 1993	June 1993
Total # Questions	48	49	48	48	48	48	48	47	48
Terms, Concepts and Events	23	24	15	18	21	23	26	24	18
Compare and Contrast	5	1	10	9	7	8	6	9	8
Generalizations	6	3	5	2	3	1	3	2	7
Cause and Effect	9	13	5	5	10	4	8	5	12
Special Types	-	-	-	-	-	-	1	-	-
Data Based:	4	8	13	16	7	12	4	7	3
a. Cartoons	-	-	4	1	1	4	2	2	2
b. Maps	-	-	-	-	-	-	-	-	-
c. Tables/Charts	-	2	-	2	1	-	2	-	-
d. Bar Graphs	-	-	2	-	-	-	-	-	-
e. Line Graphs	-	-	-	-	-	2	-	1	-
f. Pie Charts	-	-	-	-	-	-	-	2	-
g. Timelines	-	-	-	-	-	-	-	-	-
h. Speakers	-	3	2	2	-	3	-	-	-
i. Outlines	1	1	-	1	-	-	-	-	1
j. Readings	3	2	5	10	5	3	1	2	-

ANALYSIS OF PAST RCT'S (Numbers = Total Questions Asked)							
	June 1990	Jan. 1991	June 1991	Jan. 1992	June 1992	Jan. 1993	June 1993
Total # Questions	50	50	50	50	50	50	50
Terms, Concepts and Events	33	22	25	24	28	15	20
Compare and Contrast	7	9	3	6	6	3	7
Generalizations	-	2	2	1	2	6	4
Cause and Effect	5	6	6	8	10	8	4
Special Types	-	-	-	-	1	-	-
Data Based:	5	11	14	11	3	18	15
a. Cartoons	-	3	5	4	-	7	5
b. Maps	-	-	-	-	-	2	-
c. Tables/Charts	2	-	3	-	1	-	1
d. Bar Graphs	1	2	2	1	1	-	-
e. Line Graphs	-	1	3	-	1	4	1
f. Pie Graphs	-	-	-	-	-	2	1
g. Timelines	2	-	-	-	-	-	-
h. Speakers	-	-	-	2	-	2	2
i. Outline	-	-	-	-	-	-	-
j. Reading Selections	-	5	1	4	-	1	5

After looking at these charts it should now be possible for you to reach some conclusions about what the RCT's and Regents examinations focus on:

- The most frequently asked questions on both the RCT's and Regents examinations test the student's understanding of important terms, concepts, and people.

- The next type of question most frequently asked on both tests are compare/contrast and cause/effect questions.

- Although both tests contain data-based questions, there is a tendency to see a larger number of data-based questions on the RCT than on the Regents examination. Cartoons and Reading Selections material are the most frequently used type of data-based questions.

- On the Regents Examination, there is usually a series of Speaker-Type questions.
- The Regents Examination contains more generalization-type questions than the RCT.

Can understanding these items help you to achieve a better grade on the RCT or Regents Examination? The answer is a most definite **YES!** In the following sections, you will learn more about each type of question found on the RCT and Regents Examinations. Moreover, you will learn how to recognize these questions, how to identify which format they may be presented in, and what to concentrate on when answering them.

ANSWERING MULTIPLE CHOICE QUESTIONS

Although the multiple choice questions found on the RCT's and Regents examinations are quite varied, they can be grouped into basic types according to certain common characteristics. The aim of this section is to familiarize you with these basic types so that you will be able to grasp quickly what is being asked for in each question.

IMPORTANT TERMS, CONCEPTS AND EVENTS

The New York State curriculum has identified a specific body of information—terms, concepts and events—that students *must* know and understand. Certain questions will ask for recognition of these important terms, concepts and events. The following examples illustrate the variety with which these questions may be phrased. Keep in mind that although the [bracketed] term will change, depending on what is being tested, the form of the question will remain the same. Questions testing important terms, concepts, and events might appear as follows:

- The purpose of the [*Open Door Policy*] was to ....
- Which statement was true of [*nativism*]?
- The concept of [*manifest destiny*] is best illustrated by ......
- The decision of the Supreme Court in the [*Marbury v. Madison*] case was important because......
- Which statement about the [*Spanish-American War*] is most accurate?

Notice that it matters very little what form the question takes. The crucial factor is that each question asks you to recognize a term, a concept or an event. Thus it is important to know the major **terms, concepts** and **events** of each unit. To help you focus on these, each unit presents the major terms, concepts and events in **bold** print. Key terms and concepts are listed at the close of each section in the unit.

COMPARE AND CONTRAST

We often compare and contrast two things in order to better understand each of them. This act of comparing and contrasting highlights and separates each event, idea or concept from other data, placing it in sharper relief. Compare-and-contrast questions might appear as follows:

- [*Harriet Tubman, Booker T. Washington, Martin Luther King, Jr.*] were similar in that they all were active in......

- A study of [*World War I*] and [*World War II*] shows that both .....

- The most significant difference between the foreign policies of [*George Washington*] and [*Franklin D. Roosevelt*] was that .....

- Which belief is common to both [*imperialism*] and [*nationalism*]?

- A major difference between [*life in the city*] and [*frontier life*] in the late 19th century was ......

Notice that it matters very little what form the question takes. The crucial factor is that the question asks you to **compare or contrast** important people, places, or events. As you read through each unit, test yourself by comparing and contrasting **new** names and terms with those you already know. You must understand what these things have in common and how they differ.

GENERALIZATIONS

Generalizations are a basic tool of social studies. To form a generalization, we examine a group of facts, statistics, or trends. From this specific information we draw out a general principle, rule, opinion, or conclusion. For example, we may have several friends who study hard to get good grades. We might draw out, or infer, the generalization that hard study helps someone get good grades. Generalization questions may be phrased as follows:

- Which is the most accurate statement about [*social mobility*] in the United States?

- In an outline, one of these is a main topic, and the others are sub-topics. Which is the main topic?

- The idea that [*a nation's domestic policy can determine its foreign policy*] is best illustrated by ......

Notice that it matters very little what form the question takes. The crucial factor is that the question asks you to associate specific events or facts with a general idea. To help you focus on this type of question, important generalizations are highlighted at the end of each unit. In addition, you will find questions challenging your understanding of generalizations included in the tests at the end of each unit.

CAUSE AND EFFECT

History is a series of events that lead to other events. Causal explanations give history much of its meaning. The New York State curriculum has identified certain events, ideas, and people that have acted as forces causing other things to happen. Cause and effect questions test your understanding of the relationship between an action or event and its corresponding effect. In answering these questions, be sure to keep in mind which thing is the effect. Also, be careful to understand which question is being asked—the cause or the effect. These types of questions might appear as follows:

- Which was a significant cause of the United States entry into [*World War I*] ? (asks for a cause)
- Which best explains why U.S. [*labor unions*] were first organized in the late 1800's? (asks for a cause)
- Which situation led to the [*blockade of Cuba*] in 1962? (asks for a cause)
- Which is a direct result of the Supreme Court decision in [*Roe v. Wade*]? (asks for an effect)
- Which is a long term result of the [*Monroe Doctrine*]? (asks for an effect)

Notice that it matters very little what form the question takes. The crucial factor is that the question asks you to recognize a **cause and effect relationship**. To help you focus on these types of questions, important cause and effect relationships are identified in each unit. In addition, to help you further focus on this type of question, a cause and effect question is included in the test at the end of each unit.

SPECIAL TYPES

CHRONOLOGY

Chronology refers to the timing of events, that is to the order in which these events occurred. A list of events in chronological order starts from the earliest event and progresses to the latest event. This arrangement of time periods allows us to see patterns, order, or sequences in the events taking place. Chronological questions might appear as follows:

- Which historical time period occurred [*first/last*]?
- Which sequence of events best describes the historical development of the [*Women's Movement*] in the United States?
- Which group of events is in the correct chronological order?
- Which event took place in the administration of [*Woodrow Wilson*]?

FACT, OPINION, AND THEORY

Sometimes the RCT or Regent examination will ask you to distinguish between a fact, an opinion or a theory.

■ A **fact** is a statement that can be proven to be true. For example, a factual statement would be: "The Spanish-American War began in 1898."

■ An **opinion** is someone's belief and cannot be verified. An example of an opinion would be: "The United States was wrong when it declared war against Spain in 1898."

■ A **theory** is a plausible and careful explanation of something based on a body of facts. It is a type of opinion offered as true, but open for debate. An example of a theory would be: "If one nation in an area becomes Communist, others will soon follow."

Questions asking you to distinguish fact from opinion could be phrased as follows:

■ Which statement about the [*Reconstruction Period*] would be the most difficult to prove?

■ Which statement about [*World War II*] is an opinion rather than a fact?

■ Which statement about the [*Civil Rights Movement*] expresses an opinion rather than a fact?

USE OF SOURCES

Historians and social scientists often have to consult a variety of sources to discover what has happened in the past or what is happening in different parts of the world.

■ A **primary source** is one in which a participant or observer records the event as it happens. Examples of primary sources might be the diary of a person, an autobiography, a photograph or an artifact.

■ Any account or description of an event that is not a primary source is a **secondary source**. Examples of secondary sources are textbooks, encyclopedias, history books, biographies, or scholarly journals.

Questions asking you to distinguish primary from secondary sources could be phrased as follows:

■ Which would be an example of a primary source of information about the [*Progressive Era*]?

■ Which is a secondary source about the [*Civil War*] period?

USE OF REFERENCE BOOKS

Sometimes questions may ask you to identify a specific type of reference book in which particular information can be found. Thus it might be very helpful for you to be familiar with some common types of reference books:

General Reference Books:

■ An **atlas** is a book containing a collection of different maps on a given subject. It may also contain information about topography, resources, population, cities, etc.

■ An **encyclopedia** is a book or a series of books made up of articles covering a broad range of knowledge.

■ An **almanac** is a yearly publication of useful and interesting facts relating to countries of the world, sporting events, etc.

Specialized Reference Books:

■ The **Congressional Record** contains the speeches and the voting record of members of Congress.

■ The **Statistical Abstract of the United States** contains many statistical tables about the government, economy, and people of the United States.

■ The **Economic Report of the President** contains the president's annual report to Congress about the current condition of the nation's economy.

Questions testing your familiarity with reference books could be phrased as follows:

- To find information about a region's [*topography*], which source would you most likely consult?

- If you wanted to find information about the early years of [*President Nixon*] you would consult a ....

- Which would be the best source to consult to obtain accurate information about a recent [*speech of a U.S. Senator*]?

FRAMES OF REFERENCE

Sometimes Regents or RCT Examination questions ask you to identify a particular **social scientist** — people who study society from different viewpoints or "frames of reference". The most important types of social scientists are listed below.

■ **Anthropologists** study the origins, customs, beliefs, and cultures of mankind.

■ **Archaeologists** study past civilizations by examining their material artifacts. Archaeologists often specialize in the study of prehistoric and ancient civilizations.

■ **Sociologists** study social relationships and structures, such as social class and social mobility (the movement between classes).

■ **Economists** study the ways in which people make goods and perform services, and distribute and consume these goods and services. An economist might study unemployment levels, the growth of national production, inflation, and methods of production.

■ **Political Scientists** study political relationships and structures. These concern how people govern themselves. Political scientists study how people choose their leaders, what kind of government they have, and the relationships between governments.

■ **Historians** study the past. They are interested in the relationships of past events, as well as in all aspects of past societies. One historian might study the causes of World War I, while another might study the social structures of feudal Japan.

Questions testing your familiarity with the various types of social scientists could be phrased as follows:

- Which social scientist would be the most interested in studying a [*nation's system of government*]?
- Which social scientist uses [*artifacts, fossils, and ruins*] to study prehistoric cultures?
- With which statement would an [*historian*] be most in agreement?

To help you practice answering these types of questions, examples are included in the tests found at the end of each chapter.

HINTS ON REMEMBERING IMPORTANT INFORMATION

A large number of questions on the RCT's and Regents Examinations require knowledge of important terms, concepts, and people. This section will show you a technique to help you remember and make it easier for you to prepare for your tests.

KEY TERMS

In U.S. History and Government there are many key historical terms for you to learn about and remember. These terms are of several different types:

- document — U.S. Constitution
- time period — Industrial Revolution
- movement — Progressive Movement
- group — carpetbaggers
- event — bombing of Pearl Harbor
- policy — containment
- organization — United Nations
- court cases — *Roe v. Wade*

What all these terms have in common is that each refers to a specific thing that actually happened or existed, whether it be a document that was signed, a group that was formed, or a war that was fought. Questions about any of these terms will generally ask you to know its main features:

- what it is
- its purpose
- its causes/its effects
- its significance

NOTE: Terms differ; in some cases you will need to know its causes and effects (e.g., the Progressive Movement), while in others, you need to know its purpose or significance (e.g., the U.S. Constitution). The term itself will "tell" you what you need to know.

Your memory will be helped if you translate this information into a picture. We suggest that every time you read about an important term, concept, event, court case, or person, you fill in a 3x5 index card similar to this:

DECLARATION OF INDEPENDENCE

WHAT IS IT/PURPOSE: Document written mainly by Thomas Jefferson in 1776. It declared America's independence from England.

MAJOR CAUSE: The colonists wanted to announce to the world their reasons for declaring independence.

MAJOR EFFECT: The document established the basic principle upon which the U.S. government is based—that government is created to protect people's rights.

Declaration
of
Independence

(Your drawing may appear on the front as shown or on the back of the card.)

KEY CONCEPTS

In U.S. history there are also many key concepts for you to learn about and remember. Concepts are the building blocks of knowledge—they are words or phrases that denote categories of information. Concepts allow us to organize vast amounts of knowledge. Most questions about concepts will ask you about the meaning or definition of a concept, or to give an example of one. Thus, when you study, it will be most helpful if for each key concept you learn:

- its definition
- an example

Again, each time you read about an important concept, fill out a 3x5 index card similar to this:

DEMOCRACY

DEFINITION: When people govern themselves, usually through elected representatives.

EXAMPLE: The system of representative government found in the United States.

Ballot Box

(Your drawing may appear on the front as shown or on the back of the card.)

KEY PEOPLE

In U.S. history there are many famous individuals for you to learn about and remember. Most questions will ask you why they are famous. It would be most helpful when you study if for each key person you know:

- when the person lived
- what the person did
- the impact of the person's accomplishments

Again, for each individual you should fill out a 3x5 index card similar to the following:

FRANKLIN D. ROOSEVELT

TIME PERIOD: Early to mid-20th century.

WHAT F. D. R. DID: He passed New Deal legislation that helped bring the U. S. out of the Great Depression.

IMPACT: 1. Many of the laws proposed by F. D. R., such as the Social Security Act, are still in effect today.
2. He advanced the idea that the government should help protect individuals from risks they cannot deal with on their own.

NEW DEAL
WAGNER ACT
C.C.C.
SOCIAL SECURITY ACT

(Your drawing may appear on the front as shown or on the back of the card.)

Throughout each chapter, the names of the most important people appear in **bold** print. In addition, at the end of each chapter, there is a ***Summarizing Your Understanding*** section. In this section you will find a list of the most important terms and concepts. We strongly suggest that you use this index card approach as you read each chapter. At the end of the term you will then have a collection of cards that can be extremely helpful in preparing for class tests, the RCT or the Regents Examination.

CHAPTER 3

HOW TO ANSWER DATA-BASED QUESTIONS

Quite often on RCT's and Regents Examinations, you will face data-based questions. In general, a data-based question is one which is based on some form of information that is presented to you as part of the question. The data upon which questions are based can be quite varied—including such items as maps, tables of information, political cartoons, line graphs, pie charts, bar graphs, and timelines.

Although the data may be different, almost all of the questions asked about the data can be grouped into four general types of questions. It will be helpful if you can recognize **when** each of these types of questions is being asked.

GENERAL TYPES OF QUESTIONS

COMPREHENSION QUESTIONS

These questions ask you to locate or find a specific item, figure or number presented in the data. A comprehension question may take any of the following forms:

- The [*eagle*] in the cartoon is a symbol representing ....
- According to the table, in which time period was [*union membership*] the greatest?
- According to the graph, which section of the country had the [*largest decrease in manufacturing jobs*]?

CONCLUSION OR GENERALIZATION QUESTIONS

These questions ask you to make a generalization by tying together several elements found in the presented piece of data. This type of question may take any of the following forms:

- The main idea of the cartoon is that .....
- Which statement is best supported by the data in the table?
- Which generalization is best supported by an examination of the data in the bar graph?

EXPLANATORY QUESTIONS

These questions ask you to provide an explanation for the situation illustrated by the data. You must ***first*** analyze the data to get its overall meaning. ***Then*** you must use your knowledge of social studies to find an explanation for what the data indicates. This type of question may take any of the following forms:

- The situation illustrated in the cartoon was caused by ......
- Which factor best explains the events shown on the timeline?
- The trend shown in the graph is most probably related to ....

PREDICTION QUESTIONS

These questions ask you to make a prediction based on the situation shown in the data. Again, you must first analyze the data to get its overall meaning. Then you must use your knowledge of social studies to make an educated guess as to what will probably happen in the future. These questions take any of the following forms:

- The writer of the statement would most likely condemn ......
- Recent Supreme Court decisions about [*due process*] will most probably result in ....
- Based on the information in the line graph, which is most likely to occur?

TYPES OF DATA-BASES

On New York State Regents Examinations or RCT's, you will be faced with different kinds of data-based questions. *Knowing* the different types of data and understanding how to interpret them will be the focus of this section.

POLITICAL CARTOONS

What Is a Political Cartoon?

A political cartoon is a drawing or illustration that expresses an opinion about a topic or issue. Although most political cartoons are humorous, the point they make is serious.

Keys to Understanding a Cartoon

To understand a political cartoon you should look at its major components:

Medium. Cartoons are visual representations. Cartoonists will use the size and type of objects, facial expressions, exaggeration, highlights, or words spoken by one or more characters to persuade you to their point of view.

Symbols. Cartoonists often use symbols (objects that stand for, or represent, something else) to get across their point of view. There are certain common symbols that frequently appear in political cartoons. The following are some of the most common symbols with which you should be familiar:

Former Soviet Union ***United States*** ***Republican Party***

Democratic Party ***Liberty*** ***Congress***

What other symbols can you think of? ____________________

People. Cartoonists often depict certain important individuals who are closely identified with a particular issue or country. For example, President Bush is often shown in political cartoons dealing with current problems facing the U. S. Therefore, it would be helpful to recognize his picture, as well as those of some other key people who might be illustrated in a political cartoon.

Theodore Roosevelt
Franklin D. Roosevelt
Richard Nixon
Ronald Reagan
George Bush
Mikhail Gorbachev

Interpreting a Cartoon

Whenever you are asked to interpret a cartoon, start by answering the following questions about the cartoon:

- What objects, people, or symbols are being used by the artist?
- Which elements are exaggerated or highlighted?
- What is the situation presented in the cartoon?
- What do you think is the major idea of the cartoon?

A Final Thought

There are no hidden messages in cartoons. In their drawings cartoonists are usually taking a stand—giving a visual opinion—on a current issue or situation. Can you name two issues or situations that might serve as the basis of a political cartoon?

1. ______________________________

2. ______________________________

NOTE: Since cartoon questions often appear on state examinations, you will find questions challenging your understanding of cartoons in tests at the end of each unit.

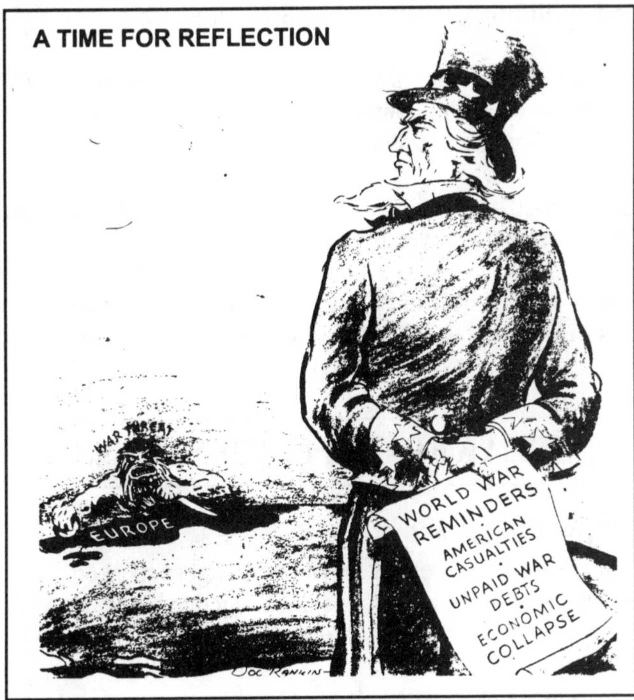
A TIME FOR REFLECTION
WAR THREATS
EUROPE
WORLD WAR REMINDERS
AMERICAN CASUALTIES
UNPAID WAR DEBTS
ECONOMIC COLLAPSE

Now that you have learned what to look for in a political cartoon, test your understanding by answering the following questions:

1 The man holding the list behind his back symbolizes
   1 European nations
   2 the United States
   3 the Soviet Union
   4 third world nations

2 The main idea of the cartoon is that the United States
   1 must collect unpaid war debts
   2 would like to increase its trade with Europe
   3 should stay out of European problems
   4 wants to help European nations solve their problems

3 Which would be the most accurate political label for someone who supports the foreign policy suggested by the cartoon?
   1 interventionist
   2 imperialist
   3 isolationist
   4 expansionist

4 Which might be a likely result of the situation shown in the cartoon?
  1 European countries will become more dependent on the Soviet Union.
  2 European countries will seize power in Asia.
  3 The United States will refuse to join any European alliances.
  4 A united Europe will emerge under United States leadership.

There are three other types of visuals that may occasionally appear on an RCT or Regents Examination: pictures, illustrations, and diagrams. Unlike cartoons, they do not express an opinion about something, but merely depict a scene, person, situation, or process.

■ **Pictures and illustrations.** Closely examine and identify all the parts of the picture or illustration. They will help you to understand its overall meaning.

■ **Diagrams.** A diagram most often will be used to show how something is organized or how a particular process works. Looking at the "flow" or direction of the arrows will help reveal the meaning of the diagram.

SPEAKER-TYPE QUESTIONS

What Is a Speaker-Type Question?

A speaker-type question presents a series of statements by different speakers. Usually there will be four speakers identified by the letters A, B, C, and D. The main function of this type of question is to present a discussion in which different viewpoints are expressed.

The Key to Understanding a Speaker-Type Question

To better understand speaker-type questions, you should recognize that each speaker's statement is usually an opinion about a social studies term, concept or situation.

Interpreting a Speaker-Type Question

Start by asking yourself the following questions about each speaker:

- What term, concept or situation is being described or discussed by the speaker?
- What is the speaker saying about the term, concept or situation?

Notice that the speakers usually are in disagreement.

- Why do they disagree?
- Do the opinions of the speakers remind you of the views of any groups or individuals with which you are already familiar?

NOTE: Since speaker-type questions appear on almost every state examination, you will find questions challenging your understanding of this type of question in the tests at the end of each unit.

Now that you have learned what to look for in a speaker-type question, test your understanding by reading the following passage and answering the questions that follow:

Speakers A, B, C, and D are discussing United States foreign policy. Base your answers to the following questions on their statements and on your knowledge of social studies.

Speaker A: Throughout its history, United States foreign policy has generally shown an idealistic concern and respect for all humanity.

Speaker B: An examination of United States foreign policy shows clearly that the dominant theme has been a desire to expand American power and influence.

Speaker C: The most successful American foreign policy was when the United States followed a policy of non-involvement in the affairs of Europe.

Speaker D: The United States has often shown a desire for international cooperation by playing the role of world leader.

1 Which speaker expresses the viewpoint that is closest to the advice that George Washington gave to the new nation in 1796?

1 (A) 3 (C)
2 (B) 4 (D)

2 Which two speakers disagree most sharply about U. S. foreign policy?

1 (A) and (B) 3 (A) and (C)
2 (C) and (D) 4 (A) and (D)

3 The history of United States relations with Latin America in the early 20th century could best be used to support the views of Speaker

1 (A) 3 (C)
2 (B) 4 (D)

4 If the speakers were on a television news program, the moderator would probably introduce the topic of their discussion as

1 New Paths to Isolationism
2 The Future of U.S. Foreign Policy
3 Capitalism vs. Communism in Today's World
4 Different Approaches to Foreign Policy

MAPS

What Is A Map?

A map is a diagram or representation of a land mass that is much larger. Although most maps show the political divisions, there is almost no limit to the different kinds of information that can be shown on a map.

Keys to Understanding a Map

An understanding of almost any map can be achieved by looking at some of its major components:

Title. Most maps depict the political boundaries or features of an area. The title of the map will indicate what information is being presented. For example, in the following map the title is: MIGRATION OF THE U.S. POPULATION, 1980-1990, AS A PERCENT OF THE 1980 POPULATION, BY SECTIONS. Thus, this map visually shows us a sectional map of the United States, indicating how the population has shifted in each section from 1980 to 1990.

Legend or Key. The legend, often called the "key," unlocks the information found on a map. It is a short way of listing the symbols used and what each symbol represents. For example, in our map the white represents areas where the population has increased by less than 10%. The shaded area represents where the population has increased by more than 20%.

Other Map Features. There are two other items that also help us to understand a map:

A. **Direction**. To find direction on a map you should look at the direction indicator often shown as a small compass. The indicator shows the four basic directions: north, south, east, and west. Unless otherwise indicated, most maps will show north at the top and south at the bottom of the map.

B. **Scale**. A scale is used to show distances. They are usually shown as a graduated line marked: Scale of Miles. We use the information in the scale to estimate the distance between any two points.

Interpreting a Map

Start by looking at the title. It will give you an indication of the type of information being illustrated.

- If it is a political map, note that the lines determine the political boundaries between areas.

- If it is another type of map, the legend will provide the major key to unlock the meaning of the map.

MIGRATION OF U.S. POPULATION, 1980-1990, AS A PERCENT OF 1980 POPULATION, BY SECTIONS

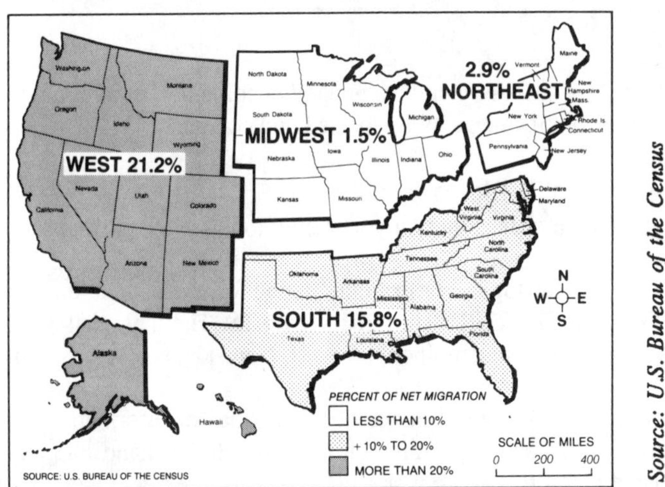
WEST 21.2%
MIDWEST 1.5%
2.9%
NORTHEAST
SOUTH 15.8%
Washington
Montana
Oregon
Idaho
Wyoming
Nevada
Utah
Colorado
California
Arizona
New Mexico
Alaska
Hawaii
North Dakota
Minnesota
South Dakota
Wisconsin
Michigan
Nebraska
Iowa
Illinois
Indiana
Ohio
Kansas
Missouri
Maine
Vermont
New Hampshire
Mass.
New York
Rhode Is
Connecticut
Pennsylvania
New Jersey
Delaware
Maryland
West Virginia
Virginia
Kentucky
North Carolina
Tennessee
South Carolina
Oklahoma
Arkansas
Mississippi
Alabama
Georgia
Texas
Louisiana
Florida
N
W
E
S
PERCENT OF NET MIGRATION
LESS THAN 10%
+10% TO 20%
MORE THAN 20%
SCALE OF MILES
0 200 400
SOURCE: U.S. BUREAU OF THE CENSUS

Source: U.S. Bureau of the Census

Now that you have studied the various parts of a map, test your understanding by answering the following questions, based on the preceding map:

1 Which section of the United States gained the largest percentage of population from 1980 to 1990?

1 the West
2 the South
3 the Northeast
4 the Midwest

2 Which statement is best supported by the information on the map?

1 The Midwest has the largest population.
2 The West was the only section of the nation to show a gain.
3 The Midwest showed the smallest increase in population.
4 Most of the nation's population is located in the South.

3 Concerning representation in Congress, what can be inferred from the information on the map?

1 The West will gain members in the House of Representatives.
2 The Midwest will lose one senator.
3 The Northeast will gain one senator.
4 The South will lose members in the House of Representatives.

4 Which factor probably contributed most to the pattern of population migration shown in the map?

1 the availability of low cost housing in the Northeast
2 the desire of people to enjoy Midwestern sports
3 the growth in the job market in the West
4 the increase in Asian immigrants in the South

TABLES

What Is A Table?

A table is an arrangement of words and numbers in parallel columns. Its main function is to organize large amounts of information so that it can easily be located and compared.

Keys to Understanding a Table

To help you understand a table of information you should look at its major components:

Title. The title will state the topic. For example, in the following table the title is: SELECTED STATISTICS FOR 20th CENTURY U.S. PRESIDENTS. The table lists various statistics (i.e. political party, sex, and age at inauguration) for all U.S. presidents who served in the 20th century.

Categories. Each table is composed of various categories of information. The categories are named in the headings across the top of the table and down the left-hand margin. In our illustration, the categories listed along the top row are: political party, sex, and age on taking office. The categories listed down the left-hand column are the names of the 20th century presidents.

Interpreting a Table

Start by looking at the title, to understand the overall meaning. For specific information, find where the columns and rows of categories intersect. For example, if you want to find the political party of President Taft, start from the top of the "Political Party" column and move your finger down the column to the name *William Taft*. The point at which they *intersect* shows that he was a member of the *Republican* political party.

SELECTED STATISTICS FOR 20th CENTURY U.S. PRESIDENTS

President	Political Party	Sex	Age On Taking Office
William McKinley	Republican	Male	54
Theodore Roosevelt	Republican	Male	42
William Taft	Republican	Male	51
Woodrow Wilson	Democrat	Male	56
Warren Harding	Republican	Male	55
Calvin Coolidge	Republican	Male	51
Herbert Hoover	Republican	Male	54
Franklin Roosevelt	Democrat	Male	51
Harry Truman	Democrat	Male	60
Dwight Eisenhower	Republican	Male	62
John Kennedy	Democrat	Male	43
Lyndon Johnson	Democrat	Male	55
Richard Nixon	Republican	Male	56
Gerald Ford	Republican	Male	61
Jimmy Carter	Democrat	Male	52
Ronald Reagan	Republican	Male	69
George Bush	Republican	Male	65

Now that you have learned how to read a table, test your understanding by answering the following questions:

1 Which president was the oldest at the time of his inauguration?
 1 Calvin Coolidge
 2 John Kennedy
 3 Gerald Ford
 4 Ronald Reagan

2 Which statement is best supported by the data in the table?
 1 All twentieth-century presidents were at least 45 years old when taking office.
 2 All twentieth-century presidents were Protestants.
 3 All twentieth-century presidents belonged to either the Democratic or Republican Party.
 4 All twentieth-century presidents were married.

3 Which statement best explains *why* all presidents in the 20th century were at least 40 years of age when becoming president of the United States?
 1 People live longer in the twentieth century.
 2 Candidates seek the presidency at a later age.
 3 The Constitution requires a person be at least 35 years of age.
 4 Most voters will only vote for an older person.

4 Based on the information in the table, the next U. S. president will *probably* be a
 1 female under 40 years old
 2 male between the ages of 50 and 70
 3 male under 40 years old
 4 female between the ages 50 and 70

BAR GRAPHS

What Is A Bar Graph?

A bar graph is a chart composed of parallel bars of varying lengths. Its main function is to show a comparison of two or more things.

Keys to Understanding a Bar Graph

To help you better understand a bar graph you should look at its main components:

Title. The title states the overall topic of the bar graph. For example, the title of the bar graph that follows is: IMMIGRANTS BY REGION: SELECTED YEARS. It indicates where immigrants came from to the U. S., for three selected years.

Legend. The legend lists what each bar represents. For example, in the graph that follows the black bars represent Asia, the shaded bars represent Europe, and the white bars represent the Americas.

Vertical and Horizontal Axis. Bar graphs are composed of a vertical and a horizontal axis which indicate the items that are being compared. In the following graph, the vertical axis, which runs from top to bottom, lists the number of immigrants. The horizontal axis, which runs from left to right, indicates the years being compared.

Interpreting a Bar Graph

The title, IMMIGRANTS, BY REGION: SELECTED YEARS, provides the overall meaning. To find specific information, examine particular axes and bars in the graph. For example, how many immigrants came to the U.S. from Europe in 1900? To find out, go to the horizontal axis and find the year 1900. Select the bar that represents Europe. Run your finger up the "Europe" bar, to the top of the bar. Now, reading across to the left, you will find the number is between 400,000 and 450,000—or about 425,000. Thus, the answer to the question—How many immigrants came to the U. S. from Europe in 1900?— is about 425,000.

IMMIGRANTS, BY REGION: SELECTED YEARS

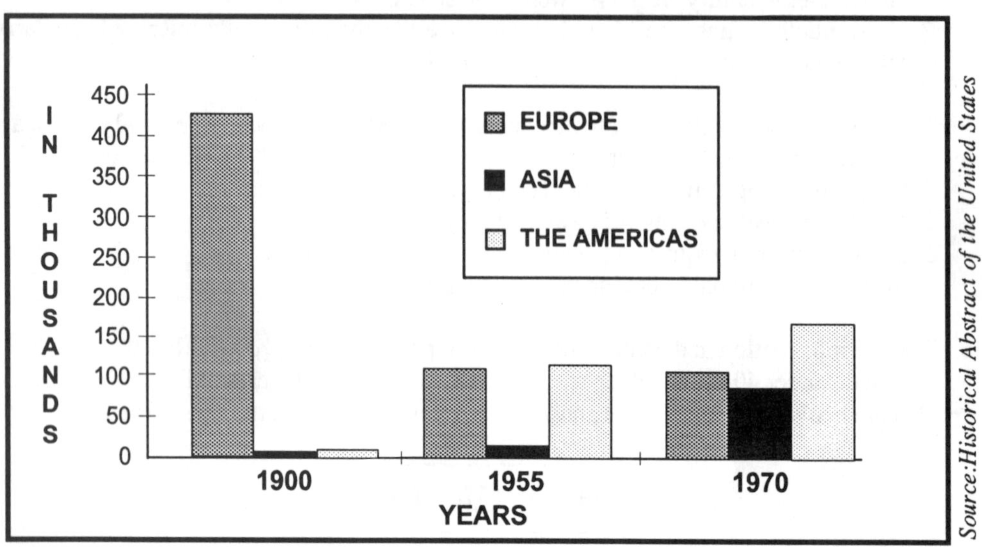
IN THOUSANDS
450
400
350
300
250
200
150
100
50
0
EUROPE
ASIA
THE AMERICAS
1900
1955
1970
YEARS
Source: Historical Abstract of the United States

Now that you have learned what to look for on a bar graph, test your understanding by answering the following questions:

1 How many immigrants came to the United States in 1970 from the Americas?

1 about 10,000
2 about 90,000
3 about 105,000
4 about 160,000

2 Which statement is best supported by the information in the bar graph?

1 The United States has become overcrowded.
2 U.S. immigration has basically remained the same over the years.
3 Immigration from the Americas has increased since 1900.
4 Asian immigration has declined since 1900.

3 Which is the best explanation for the absence of Asian immigration into the U. S. in 1900?

1 The Asian birth rate was quite low in 1900.
2 Asian workers were needed to work in eastern factories.
3 Asian immigrants were prohibited from coming to the United States.
4 U.S. immigration laws welcomed Asian immigrants.

4 Based on the trend shown on the bar graph, which is most likely to occur?
   1 Asian immigration to the United States will decline sharply.
   2 Labor unions will support increased Asian immigration to the U.S.
   3 The number of Asian immigrants to the United States will increase.
   4 European immigration will soon surpass Asian immigration.

LINE GRAPHS

What Is a Line Graph?

A line graph is a chart composed of a series of points that are connected in a line. Its main function is to show how something has increased, decreased, or otherwise changed over a period of time.

Keys to Understanding a Line Graph

To better understand a line graph you should look at its major components:

Title. The title states the overall topic of the line graph. For example, in the following graph the title is: U.S. IMPORTS/EXPORTS: 1983-1989. The title indicates that imports and exports to the United States are being compared over seven years.

Vertical and Horizontal Axis. Line graphs include a vertical and a horizontal axis indicating information about what items are being compared. In the following line graph, the vertical axis, which runs from bottom to top, lists amounts in billions of dollars. Notice that as you move up from the bottom, the amounts get larger. The horizontal axis, which runs from left to right, shows the years in ascending (lower to higher) order.

Legend. The legend indicates what each line represents. If the graph has only one line, there is no legend. However, if the graph has two or more lines a legend is needed. In our graph, the continuous line with black boxes shows imports, while the continuous line with white boxes shows exports.

Interpreting a Line Graph

Start by looking at the title. It will provide the overall meaning of the information presented. To find specific information you must examine the legends, the axes, and the lines on the graph. For example, what was the dollar amount of U.S. exports in 1983? To find out, run your finger across "Years" until you reach 1983. Now, move your finger up until you reach the line representing exports (line with white boxes). To find the actual number, slide your finger to the left to the numbers on the vertical axis. This point intersects at approximately 200 billion dollars. Thus, the answer to the question—What was the dollar amount of U.S. exports in 1983?—is about 200 billion dollars.

A Final Thought

Some questions may ask you to identify the **trend** in a line graph. A trend means a general direction or tendency. It is something we can generalize from the points on the line. For example, one trend indicated by the graph is that imports have been rising since 1983.

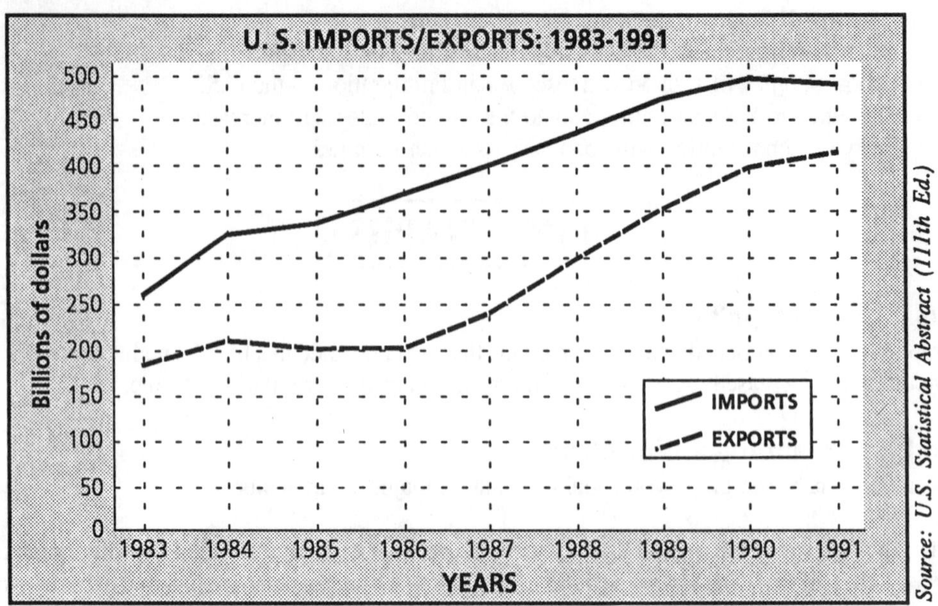
U. S. IMPORTS/EXPORTS: 1983-1991
Billions of dollars
500
450
400
350
300
250
200
150
100
50
0
1983
1984
1985
1986
1987
1988
1989
1990
1991
YEARS
IMPORTS
EXPORTS
Source: U.S. Statistical Abstract (111th Ed.)

Now that you have studied what to look for in a line graph, test your understanding by answering the following questions:

1 What was the dollar amount of goods imported to the United States in 1987?
- 1 about 350 billion
- 2 about 245 billion
- 3 about 400 billion
- 4 about 500 billion

2 Which statement is best supported by the information found in the graph?
- 1 U.S. exports have been decreasing each year.
- 2 U.S. imports have been decreasing each year.
- 3 U.S. imports have remained fairly constant from 1983 to 1989.
- 4 U.S. exports have generally increased from 1986 to 1989.

3 The trend dealing with U. S. imports was probably caused by
- 1 the declining cost of manufactured goods in the United States
- 2 the increasing demand by U.S. consumers for foreign goods
- 3 a falling birth rate in the United States
- 4 electing a new prime minister in Japan

4 Which would be one method of reducing the balance of payments deficit shown in the graph?
- 1 consumer boycotts of U.S.-made goods
- 2 exporting fewer U.S. manufactured items
- 3 government restrictions on buying foreign products
- 4 limiting the availability of U.S. natural resources

PIE CHARTS

What Is a Pie Chart?

A circle or pie chart is a diagram of a circle divided into slices of different sizes. Its main function is to show the relationship between a whole and its parts. Think of the pie as representing 100% of something. If you were to add each of the various parts of the pie together, they would total 100%.

Keys to Understanding a Pie Chart

To understand a pie chart you should look at its major components:

> ***Title.*** The title states the overall topic. For example, the following pie chart is entitled: ***Where The Federal Government Dollar Goes: 1990.*** It shows in which categories the federal government spent its money in 1990.
>
> ***Slices Of The Pie.*** Each slice or piece of the pie tells us what information is being examined and its size or relationship to the whole pie. For example, the following pie chart shows that 26 cents out of each dollar the Federal Government received was spent on national defense.
>
> ***Legend.*** Sometimes a pie chart will contain a legend, which shows what the different slices of the pie represent. Sometimes the information is contained within the pie chart instead.

Interpreting a Pie Chart

Look at the title, to learn the overall meaning. To find specific information, examine the size of each piece of the pie and its relationship to the other pieces or to the whole pie. For example, on what did the federal government spend the least amount of money? If we look at the chart, we see that the piece representing ***Other Federal Operations (5%)*** is the smallest slice of the pie. Thus, the answer to the question—On what did the federal government spend the least amount of money?—is "Other Federal Operations."

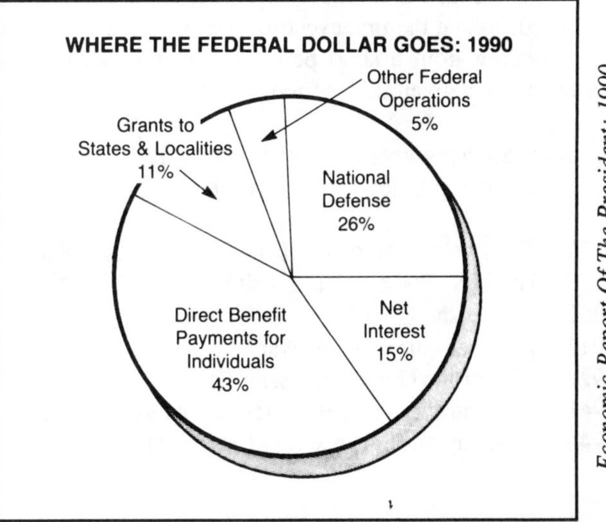
WHERE THE FEDERAL DOLLAR GOES: 1990
Other Federal Operations 5%
Grants to States & Localities 11%
National Defense 26%
Net Interest 15%
Direct Benefit Payments for Individuals 43%

Economic Report Of The President: 1990

Now that you have learned what to look for in a pie chart, test your understanding by answering the following questions:

1 On what item does the federal government spend the most money?
  1 national defense
  2 grants to states and localities
  3 net interest
  4 direct benefit payments for individuals

2 Which statement is best supported by the information in the pie chart?
  1 Local governments spend more on health care than the national government does.
  2 More federal money is devoted to non-military spending than to military spending.
  3 State and local governments have higher tax rates than the national government.
  4 National defense is a low priority for the federal government.

3 The data in the pie chart reflects the concern in the United States with
  1 being prepared in case of a military conflict
  2 taxing all its citizens at the same rate
  3 developing new computer technology for the future
  4 molding public opinion on economic issues of the day

4 Which would most likely be a major effect on federal spending if there were peace in the world?
  1 an increase in federal taxes being collected
  2 a decrease in state and local spending on education
  3 an increase in federal spending on regulating business
  4 a decrease in spending on military security

TIMELINES

What Is a Timeline?

A timeline shows a group of events arranged in *chronological order* along a line. Chronological order is the order in which the events occurred, so that the first event to have occurred is the first one on the line. The span of the timeline can be anything from a short period to several thousand years. Timelines show relationships between major events in a given time period.

Special Dates To Remember. Students are generally not required to memorize the dates of events in American history. However, there are a few significant dates with which you should be familiar, including:

- 1776—The Declaration of Independence is proclaimed
- 1787—The U.S. Constitution is written
- 1861—Start of the Civil War
- 1917—The U.S. enters World War I
- 1929—Start of the Great Depression
- 1941—Japan attacks Pearl Harbor; U.S. enters World War II
- 1945—Germany and Japan surrender; first atomic bomb used

Keys to Understanding a Timeline

To understand a timeline you should look at its major components:

Title. The title states the overall topic. For example, in the following timeline the title is: KEY EVENTS IN THE CIVIL RIGHTS MOVEMENT. The line lists important events in the history of the civil rights movement in the U.S.

Events. Each event listed is related to the topic of the timeline. For example, if the topic of a timeline were ***Wars in the 20th Century***, each event would be a war that occurred in the 20th century.

Special Terms. To understand some chronological questions you must be familiar with the following special terms:

■ **Decade** refers to a ten-year period.

■ **Century** refers to a hundred-year period.

■ **20th century** refers to the 100 years from 1900 to 1999. The actual dates of the years are less than the number of the century. For example, the 19th century refers to 1800-1899.

Interpreting a Timeline

Start by reading the title, which provides the overall meaning of the timeline. The events are arranged from the earliest to the most recent event. Which happened first: the issuance of the Emancipation Proclamation or the March on Washington? The timeline shows that the issuance of the Emancipation Proclamation was first.

KEY EVENTS IN THE CIVIL RIGHTS MOVEMENT

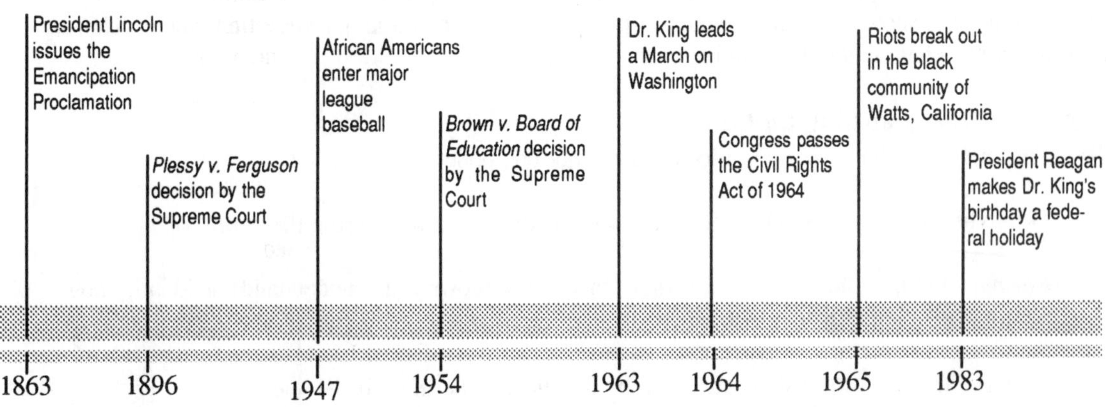
President Lincoln issues the Emancipation Proclamation
Plessy v. Ferguson decision by the Supreme Court
African Americans enter major league baseball
Brown v. Board of Education decision by the Supreme Court
Dr. King leads a March on Washington
Congress passes the Civil Rights Act of 1964
Riots break out in the black community of Watts, California
President Reagan makes Dr. King's birthday a federal holiday
1863
1896
1947
1954
1963
1964
1965
1983

Now that you have learned what to look for on a timeline, test your understanding by answering the following questions:

1 Which event occurred during the period of the Civil War?
  1 President Lincoln issued the Emancipation Proclamation
  2 *Plessy v. Ferguson* decision handed down by the Supreme Court
  3 First African American played in a major league baseball game
  4 *Brown v. Board of Education* decision handed down by the Supreme Court

2 Which decade saw the greatest changes in the Civil Rights Movement?
  1 1930-1939
  2 1940-1949
  3 1960-1969
  4 1980-1989

3 Which statement is best supported by the data in the timeline?
  1 The Supreme Court has played a major role in civil rights issues.
  2 Congress has declined to pass any civil rights legislation.
  3 Most Presidents have supported the civil rights movement.
  4 Prejudice against African Americans no longer exists.

4 Which statement is best supported by the events indicated on the timeline?
  1 African Americans wanted to achieve religious freedom.
  2 Basic changes in a society sometimes take a long time.
  3 The judicial system in the United States is weak.
  4 Enforcing civil rights legislation is everyone's job.

OUTLINES

What Is an Outline?

An outline is a brief plan in which a topic or major idea is divided up into smaller units. The main purpose of an outline is to show the logical relationships between a topic or a major idea and its parts. This serves as a blueprint to help guide the thinking of the writer.

Keys to Understanding an Outline

To understand an outline you should look at its major components:

Title. The title may be thought of as an umbrella or overview covering the entire topic.

Format. Outlines follow a specific format that quickly allows you to understand and identify how the topic is being broken down:

- The first major divisions are given by a *Roman numeral* (I, II, III, etc.).

- If the Roman numerals need to be further divided, the divisions/sub-divisions are identified by *capital letters* (A, B, C, etc.).
- If these sub-divisions are further divided, they are given *Arabic numbers* (1, 2, 3).

To illustrate this process, assume you want to write about your own life. It might be outlined as follows:

Title: My Autobiography

I. Early Childhood
- A. Parents
- B. Family
- C. Playmates

II. Pre-teen Years
- A. Grade School
  - 1. Teachers
  - 2. Friends
- B. Neighborhood

III. Teenage Years
- A. Junior High School
- B. Senior High School

Interpreting an Outline

Remember that outlines go from the general to the specific. In other words, you break down a larger idea into smaller and smaller units. Notice that in our example, each smaller unit helps to develop the larger concept. For example, the "Teachers" and "Friends" help to develop the larger concept "Grade School," while "Grade School" and "Neighborhood" help to develop the larger concept "Pre-teen Years." This larger unit is one of three main units that make up the topic: "My Autobiography."

Outlining not only helps you to answer data-based questions on the Regents and RCT, but also provides a useful tool for you to use in organizing your thoughts when writing an essay.

Now that you have seen what to look for in an outline, test your understanding by answering the following three questions:

Directions: *Three* items have been omitted from the following outline. For each blank space in the outline, select the number of the item from the following list that best completes the blank.

Items

1 The Cabinet
2 The Supreme Court
3 The Executive Branch
4 The Senate

THE ORGANIZATION OF THE U.S. GOVERNMENT

1 I The Legislative Branch
A ____________________
B The House of Representatives

2 II ____________________
A The President
B The Vice-President

3 III The Judicial Branch
A ____________
B Courts of Appeal
C District Courts

Note: Outline-type questions may also appear in another format. For example:

In an outline, one of these is a main topic, and the others are sub-topics. Which is the main topic?
1 The Executive Branch
2 Organization of the U.S. Government
3 The Legislative Branch
4 The Judicial Branch

> Remember that the major topic is the broadest one covering all of the smaller units. In the case of this outline, the main topic is "The Organization of the U.S. Government."

READING SELECTION

What Is a Reading Selection?

A reading selection consists of a statement or a group of statements about a particular topic or subject. It may be a short quotation or a short paragraph. The main function of the selection is to present someone's ideas about a topic.

The Key to Understanding a Reading Selection

To better understand a reading selection you should note that the writer presents a series of facts and/or arguments, to make a point.

Interpreting a Reading Selection

Start by asking yourself the following questions about each reading selection:

1. What do you know about the writer?
2. What term, concept or situation is being discussed by the writer?
3. What is the writer saying about the term, concept or situation?
4. What facts does the writer present to support his/her views?
5. What is the main idea of the passage?
6. What is the tone of the passage? Is the author angry, sad, hopeful, etc.?
7. Why might the author have written the passage?

Multiple choice questions about reading selections often ask about the main idea of the passage, the opinions of the author, or the tone of the passage.

Now that you are familiar with what to look for in a reading selection, test your understanding by reading the following selection and answering the questions that follow:

Reading Selection

> We hold these truths to be self-evident, that all men are created equal, that they are endowed by their Creator with certain unalienable Rights, that among these are Life, Liberty and the pursuit of Happiness. That to secure these rights, Governments are instituted among Men, deriving their just powers from the consent of the governed, That whenever any Form of Government becomes destructive of these ends, it is the right of the People to alter or abolish it, and to institute new Government...
>
> —*Thomas Jefferson*

1 The phrase "it is the right of the People to alter or abolish it, and to institute new Government" refers to the concept of

1 revolution
2 federalism
3 checks and balances
4 balance of power

2 The main idea of the reading selection is that

1 there are three separate powers of government
2 governments are established to promote racial equality
3 men and women are born with the same chance in life
4 the power of government comes from the people it governs

3 Which argument could be justified by the statements in the reading selection?

1 People have a right to overthrow their government if it fails to protect their rights.
2 People are born free but everywhere they are in chains; therefore, revolution is necessary to return their freedom.
3 Government authority prevents human progress; revolution will end all government control.
4 Economic conditions determine the course of history; thus, revolutionary struggle between classes is inevitable.

4 The argument used in the reading could be used to justify the idea that

1 people have natural rights as human beings
2 all governments are evil by their very nature
3 governments are best that rule least
4 there must be a separation of church and state

CHAPTER 4

HOW TO ANSWER ESSAY QUESTIONS

In addition to asking you to answer multiple choice questions, both the RCT's and the Regents Examinations require that you write several essays. These essays are short compositions of several paragraphs each, in which you must make comparisons, describe situations, discuss events, draw conclusions, or recommend courses of action. Unlike multiple choice questions, essay questions measure your ability by asking you to select information from your general reservoir of knowledge and present it in written form. You must back up your general statements by providing specific facts and examples. Most students know more than they think they know, but do not understand how to use this information to answer the question. The key is to understand the question well.

KEYS TO UNDERSTANDING THE QUESTION

GENERAL DIRECTIONS

In writing your essay, you must learn to pay particular attention to the directions provided by the test-makers. Familiarize yourself with these directions now, rather than during the test. On the examination booklet, you will find the following directions:

In developing your answers to the essays, be sure to:

(1) include specific factual information and evidence whenever possible.
(2) keep to the questions asked; don't go off on tangents.
(3) avoid over-generalizations or sweeping statements without sufficient proof; do not overstate your case.

What the directions mean in simple words is that you must answer just the question asked, and not write everything you know about the topic. This also means that when you answer the question you should include specific *examples* and *facts* to support your general statements and conclusions.

KEY VOCABULARY FOR REGENTS ESSAY QUESTIONS

Regents essay questions usually contain certain key words such as *describe*, *discuss*, *explain*, and *show*. Let us look at a sample essay question in which these four key words are used.

Throughout history minority groups in the United States have suffered from various forms of discrimination.

Forms of Discrimination

- Denied political and legal rights
- Denied an equal education
- Denied equality of job opportunity
- Forced to live in certain areas

Choose *one* of the forms of discrimination listed above. For the form of discrimination chosen:

A. *describe* a specific example of its use during a specific time in U.S. history
B. *discuss* an effect of this form of discrimination on a minority group
C. *explain* why a minority group may experience discrimination
D. *show* how a minority group has tried to overcome that discrimination

Although briefly defined for you on Regents Examinations, it will help you to gain maximum credit if you understand these key terms more fully.

DESCRIBE

Describe means "to illustrate something in words or tell about it." To *describe* a friend is to tell about his or her characteristics—his or her looks, personality, and attitudes. In Social Studies to *describe* is usually to tell about the "who," "what," "when," and "where" of an item. Of course, **not** every item requires *all four* of these descriptions. For example, if you wished to answer the sample "describe" question—*describe* a specific example of the use of a form of discrimination during a specific time in U.S. history—you might write as follows:

Answer: One form of discrimination against minority groups was the denial of political and legal rights to African Americans. All Americans were supposedly granted political and legal equality under the 13th, 14th, and 15th Amendments. However, after Reconstruction was over, many

Southern state governments found ways to deny giving African Americans their political and legal rights. Literacy tests, poll taxes, and other methods were used to prevent African Americans from voting. The Democratic Party in the South denied African Americans membership in the party. Law enforcement officials and juries were composed entirely of whites.

> Notice how the answer *describes* a specific kind of discrimination during a period in U.S. history. The description sets forth a verbal picture of **who** (African Americans), **what** (being denied membership in a political party, the use of literacy tests, poll taxes, and other methods to prevent African Americans from using their political and legal rights), **when** (Post-Reconstruction), and **where** (in the South). (*A helpful hint might be to go through a mental checklist — who, what, where, when — when asked to "describe" something.*)

DISCUSS

Discuss means "to make observations about something using facts, reasoning, and arguments; to present in some detail." To *discuss* something you must go beyond the "describing" stage of merely reciting the facts. You will usually include one of the following:

- the *reasons* (or causes) behind something, or
- a look at the possible *results* (or effects) of something, or
- different points of view about something

For example, to answer a sample "discuss" question—*discuss* an effect of this form of discrimination on a minority group—you might focus on the *effects* by writing as follows:

Answer: Discrimination against women had many important effects. Denying women their political and legal rights had a negative effect. Traditionally in America, women were legally under the control of their fathers or husbands. Women were not allowed to vote, participate in government, or attend most universities. This denial of rights handicapped women both socially and economically. Laws looked at problems from a man's point of view. Women felt like "second class" citizen. They were unable to enter many highly-paid professional jobs. They had limited control over their own life styles.

> Notice how the answer discusses the **effects** of discrimination on women: feelings of inferiority and low self-esteem. This was **caused** by women being denied political and legal rights (being denied the right to vote and participate in government). (*A helpful hint might be to go through a mental checklist—first describe it, then give its causes and/or its effects—when asked to "discuss" something.*)

EXPLAIN

Explain means "to make plain or understandable; to give reasons for or causes of; to show the logical development or relationship of." To *explain* is to present points that justify a position. Most of the time test writers use this word—*explain*—when they want you to answer the "why" of something. For example, if you were asked to *explain* why you should be given a passing grade for a course, you might *explain* that you regularly attended the class, did all the homeworks, and passed all the tests. Notice how your **reasons** add up to your **conclusion**.

+ attended the class (reason)
+ did the homework (reason)
+ passed all the tests (reason)

= why you deserve a passing grade (conclusion)

Thus, you have *explained* why you deserve to pass the class. To answer a sample "explain" question—*explain* why a minority group might have experienced discrimination—you might write as follows:

> **Answer**: Minority groups often experience discrimination. Asian Americans are no exception. By the early 1900's, Asian immigrants were no longer welcomed here; various groups tried to prevent the further immigration of Chinese and Japanese people into the United States. There were several reasons for this. Because new immigrants were often willing to work for low wages, labor unions viewed Asian immigrants as competing for their jobs. Asian immigrants also spoke different languages, wore different clothes and practiced unfamiliar customs. This led to many Americans to feel that Asian immigrants were "alien." They feared that Asians could not be assimilated into American life. As a result, immigrants from Asia experienced discrimination from many groups.

Notice how the answer **explains** the various reasons supporting the statement "why a minority group may have experienced discrimination." The answer lists the **reasons** for the discrimination:

+ job competition (reason)
+ working for low wages (reason)
+ different language and customs (reason)

= Why Asian Americans experienced discrimination (conclusion)

Thus, the answer adds up to an *explanation* of why a minority group (Asians) experienced discrimination. (*A helpful hint might be to go through a mental checklist—listing the various reasons or causes to be sure they add up to an explanation of the policy or practice—when asked to "explain" something.*)

SHOW

Show means "to point out; to set forth clearly a position or idea by stating it and giving data which supports it." Test writers usually use the word *show* when they want you to illustrate *how* something works or *how* something came about. "How" is the key word that usually follows "show." It is different from "explain" in that you are not asked to present an argument—a series of reasons to prove a point—but rather you are asked to present the parts that make up the whole. You are asked to provide *facts* and *examples* that demonstrate that a general statement is true. For example, if you wished to answer a sample "show" question—*show* how a minority group has tried to overcome discrimination—you might write as follows:

Answer: Hispanic Americans have made great strides in overcoming much of the political and legal discrimination once directed against them. Hispanic Americans make up an important voting bloc in elections. They have used their political strength to elect Hispanic-American candidates to legislative, judicial, and executive positions. Hispanic Americans have campaigned to have bilingual courses taught in public schools and they have won the right to have election materials printed in both English and Spanish.

> Notice that the answer **shows how** the minority group (Hispanic Americans) has overcome discrimination. The answer brings in specific facts that *show how* Hispanic Americans have overcome discrimination. The facts used in the answer include the use of political power to achieve the election of Hispanic-American officials in government, and the use of the Spanish language in schools and election ballots. (*A helpful hint might be to think of a "show how" answer as a picture. One must make sure that all the parts in your answer—the facts and examples—complete this picture.*)

REGENTS ESSAY CONTENT

On Regents Examinations, there are two essay sections. **Part II** focuses on the American system of government. **Part III** focuses on all other aspects of United States history and culture. In **Part II** of the Regents Examination, you must answer one of the two essays. An examination of the following chart reveals some important information that can help you prepare to do well on this part of the examination:

REGENTS EXAMINATIONS: PART II ESSAY CONTENT

	1/90	6/90	8/90	1/91	6/91	8/91	1/92	6/92	1/93	6/93
Goals, Principles, Flexibility of the U.S. System of Government	•	•	•	•	•	•		•		•
Branches of the Government		•			•	•	•			•
Civil Liberties, Court Cases, Constitution	•	•	••	••	•	•	•	•	•	
Articles of Confederation, Declaration of Independence, Constitutional Convention									•	

An analysis of **Part II** shows that both essays in this section always deal with some aspect of American government. One of the two essays will almost certainly deal with either: the principles of the Constitution, the institutions of American government, or the civil liberties of individuals. Therefore you should carefully read both *Looking At Government* and Chapter 5: Constitutional Foundations, which deal with the content material covered on this question.

In **Part III** of the examination, you must answer two out of five essays. An examination of the following chart reveals important information that can help you to prepare for this part of the examination:

REGENTS EXAMINATIONS: PART III ESSAY CONTENT

	1/90	6/90	8/90	1/91	6/91	8/91	1/92	6/92	1/93	6/93
Foreign Policy	•	•	•	•	•	•	•	•	•	•
Problems, Issues, Trends	•	•	•	••	••	•	•	•	•	•
Minorities, Reform Movements	•	••		•	•		•	••	•	
Immigration			•			•				•
Individuals/ Presidents					•	•	••		•	
Domestic/Economic Policies	•		••			•		•	•	
Regions/Historical Periods				•						••

This chart indicates the following about **Part III** Regents essay questions:

■ There has always been an essay question dealing with some aspect of foreign policy. The essay deals with either general types of foreign policy or a specific foreign policy event or action. To prepare for this type question, you should read the *Looking At Foreign Policy* section preceding Chapter 10. In addition, Chapters 10, 12 and 14 are especially helpful in preparing you for these types of essay questions.

■ There is almost always an essay question dealing with minorities (e.g. African Americans, Asians, Jews, Hispanics, disabled Americans) or reform movements (e.g. Civil Rights, the Women's Movement, the Labor Movement, the Progressives). In either case the question usually asks you to identify the problems some groups faced and the steps or reforms that were taken to overcome them. Chapters 8, 9 and 13 will help you prepare for these types of essay questions.

■ There is almost always some essay question dealing with the problems, issues or trends affecting the United States today. To help you answer this type of essay question, you should read Chapter 15: Prospects For The Future, which deals with the most important current concerns, issues, and trends.

■ At times essay questions deal with a particular immigrant group, or immigration legislation or government policies. To help you answer this type of essay question, you should read Chapter 8: Changing America, which has a section focusing on immigration and the problems they faced.

■ There has been a recent trend on Regents Examinations to ask about individuals and U.S. presidents. Questions on various presidential administrations may also be found on one of the **Part II** questions on government. To help you deal with such questions, you will find the names of many important people in the content portion of each chapter. To help you identify these individuals, their names appear in **bold** print. Additionally, at the end of each chapter a *Personalities of the Period* section features important persons who have had an important impact on U.S. history.

■ Often, questions touching on economic problems and policy are asked. To help you answer such questions, you should read *Looking At Economic Policy.* In addition, read Chapter 11: Prosperity and Depression, which deals with the Great Depression—a favored topic of the Regents test-makers.

■ Lastly, on occasion there has been a question focusing on specific historical time periods. This is probably the most difficult type of question to prepare for. These questions test your understanding and memory of the most important problems and events of a time period. Because this type of question usually focuses on domestic events, it is most likely to be about the Reconstruction Era, the Progressive Era (1890-1914), the 1920s, the 1930s, the Civil Rights Movement (1954-1960s), the 1960s, or more recent times. You should examine the timeline found at the beginning of each chapter, to become familiar with the main events and themes of each period.

RCT ESSAY CONTENT

In **Part II** of the RCT, you must answer two out of four essays. Part II has two sections. **Part A** asks you to list some points about a particular topic. Often these concern problems faced by groups or the nation as a whole. For example, "list two problems facing unions," or "two problems facing immigrants." **Part B** then asks you to elaborate in more detail on your **Part A** answer. For example, it may ask you to "state how the group solved the problem" or "how the group brought about a change" or "had some impact on the nation." Therefore, as you read each chapter and come across a major time period (e.g. Civil War, Reconstruction, World War I) or social group (e.g. women, African Americans, labor) you should make a mental checklist of: (a) the problems faced in that period or by that group and (b) attempts to overcome these problems. An examination of the following chart reveals some important information that can help you to prepare for this part of the test.

RCT: PART II ESSAY CONTENT

	1/90	6/90	6/91	1/92	6/92	1/93	6/93
Government	•	•	•	•	•	•	•
Foreign Policy	•			•			•
Problems, Issues, Trends	•	•	•	•	•	•	•
Minorities/Reform Movements	•			•	•	•	
Immigration		•					
Time Periods/Wars			•		•		
Economic Development						•	•

■ Each past RCT has contained an essay question about the American system of government. These questions have dealt with such areas as: civil rights (e.g., the Bill of Rights, 14th Amendment), the principles of government (federalism, checks and balances, separation of powers), or the branches of the federal government (Congress, the Presidency, the Supreme Court). *Looking At Government* and Chapter 5: Constitutional Foundations will prepare you for questions on the U. S. government.

■ Each past RCT has had an essay question on current problems, issues or trends affecting the U.S. To prepare for this type of question, read Chapter 15: Prospects For The Future.

■ Chapters 8, 9 and 13 will help you prepare for questions on minorities (e.g., African Americans, Asians, Jews, Hispanics) and reform movements (e.g., Civil Rights, the Women's Movement, the Progressives). In both cases the question usually asks you to identify the problems faced by certain groups and the steps taken to overcome them.

■ At times there is an essay question dealing with some aspect of foreign policy. The question asks about either general types of foreign policy or a specific foreign-policy event or action. As preparation for such questions, you should read *Looking At Foreign Policy,* and Chapters 10, 12 and 14.

■ Sometimes essay questions deal with immigrant groups, or legislation or government policies affecting immigrants. To help you answer this type of essay question, you should read Chapter 8: Changing America, which has a section focusing on immigration.

■ On occasion there has been a question focusing on a particular historical time period (e.g. the Reconstruction Era or the 1920s). These questions test your understanding and memory of the main problems and events of the time period. Usually they focus on domestic developments and domestic policy. To prepare for this type of question, you should examine the timeline found in the front of each chapter and become familiar with the main theme and events of each period.

HOW TO ANSWER A REGENTS ESSAY QUESTION

COMMON ELEMENTS OF REGENTS ESSAY QUESTIONS

The majority of essays on Regents examinations follow a pattern. The question begins with a general statement, followed by a list of items associated with it. You must select a given number of items from the list.

After making your selections, you are asked to use specific information from your knowledge of social studies to show how the items you selected illustrate or support the general statement. The general statement is phrased in many ways, but will most often follow one of the following formats:

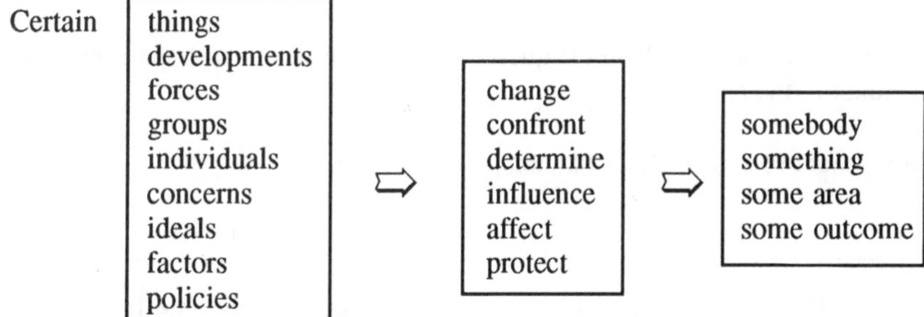
Certain
things
developments
forces
groups
individuals
concerns
ideals
factors
policies
change
confront
determine
influence
affect
protect
somebody
something
some area
some outcome

In each instance, you are being asked to prove your understanding of a generalization by giving specific instances that support it. Many students who know the information needed to support the general statement do poorly on this type of question, because they find the directions confusing.

To help you organize your answer to a typical Regents essay question, let's begin with an example:

The United States has followed various foreign policies to deal with international problems throughout its history.

Foreign Policies

Monroe Doctrine — Marshall Plan
Good Neighbor Policy — Membership in the United Nations
Truman Doctrine

Choose *two* of the policies listed:

- For *each* of the policies selected, describe the international problem that led to its formulation.
- For *one* of the policies chosen, discuss how effective the policy was in solving the problem.

PRE-WRITING THE ESSAY

Before beginning to write your answer, you should ***pre-write*** the essay. This pre-writing can be accomplished by using an answer box.

Setting Up An Answer Box

An answer box or grid can be useful in guiding you. The answer box will help by outlining the question and focusing your answer. This can be achieved by:

(A) Listing the issues, events, or in the case of our sample question, the programs or proposals involved in the first column.

(B) Looking at what the question asks you to do. This is shown by the words: "discuss," "explain," "describe," or "show."

(C) Circling the key vocabulary words in the question. List these words with their instructions at top of each column in the answer box.

Thus, your answer box should look something like this:

	[ ]	[ ]
Programs	**Describe the problem**	**Discuss the policy's effectiveness**
Monroe Doctrine	________ ________	________ ________
Good Neighbor Policy	________ ________	________ ________
Marshall Plan	________ ________	________ ________
U.N. Membership	________ ________	________ ________
Truman Doctrine	________ ________	________ ________

Filling in The Answer Box

Briefly jot down a word or two for each item that you are able to fill in.

(A) Remember, *do not* write full, detailed, complete sentences. This is only an outline. A word or two will help you to recall other details when writing out the answer.

(B) In answering the first part of the question, the directions call for selecting *two* of the policies listed. Above the column headed "**Describe**" are a pair of parentheses or brackets. Indicate a "2" between the parentheses to help remind you that you must describe two of the policies. Similarly, you should put a "1" in the parentheses above the "**Discuss**" column to help remind you to discuss one of the policies.

(C) It is quite unlikely that you will be able to jot something for every box in the grid. This should help guide you in selecting which parts of the question to answer. Place a check mark (✓) or star (✳) next to the two programs you think you know the most about.

Writing The Essay

After you have completed filling in the information that you know, your answer box might look something like this:

	[2]	[1]
Programs	**Describe the problem**	**Discuss the policy's effectiveness**
Monroe Doctrine	*France and Spain threatened newly-independent Latin American republics*	*prevented European powers from acquiring new colonies in Western Hemisphere*
Good Neighbor Policy	*[You are not sure of answer]*	*gave friendship/trade/defense to Latin American nations*
Marshall Plan	*Europe faced Communist threat threat after W.W. II*	*helped European economies to recover after W.W. II*
U.N. Membership	*World suffered two devastating wars in 20th century*	*provided a place to talk about world problems*
Truman Doctrine	*Communists groups threatened governments in Southern Europe*	*aided Greece and Turkey to combat and defeat Communist rebels*

(A) Based on your notes in the answer box, you think you know enough information to write about two of the five items. You should select the *two* about which you know the most.

(B) You are now ready to write your detailed answer. Convert your short word reminders into an essay by drawing on the knowledge you can recall. Place each example in a separate paragraph with a topic sentence. Use whatever facts, dates, names, and definitions apply to your example.

Here is one possible way part of this question could be answered. (The topic sentence has been underlined.)

> The United States has followed various foreign policies to deal with international problems throughout its history. One such foreign policy program was U. S. membership in the United Nations. This policy was designed to deal with problems caused by constant warfare between countries. The U.S. and the Allied Powers agreed to form a United Nations in 1945, just as World War II was ending. By providing an international organization in which all nations could participate, they hoped to prevent future acts of aggression and wars. A Security Council, composed of countries like the U.S. and the Soviet Union, was added to make the U.N. more effective than the League of Nations. However, because of disagreements between the U.S. and the Soviet Union, most of the U.N.'s peacekeeping functions have not been effective. Many nations continue to make war.

HOW TO ANSWER AN RCT ESSAY QUESTION

Even if you are not required to take the Regents examination, it would be helpful to read the preceding section: *How To Answer A Regents Essay Question.* The section on *Key Vocabulary* will be helpful in answering the RCT essays found in Part B. Let's begin by looking at a sample RCT-type essay question:

The U.S. Constitution set up a federal system of government.

Part A

Define "federalism:" ______________________________

List *two* powers of the national (federal) government.

1. ______________________ 2. ______________________

List *two* powers of the state governments.

1. ______________________ 2. ______________________

Part B

In your Part B answer, you should use information you gave in Part A. However, you may also include different or additional information in your part B answer.

Write an essay explaining how the writers of the U.S. Constitution created a federal system of government.

ORGANIZING THE ANSWER TO AN RCT ESSAY QUESTION

Unlike the Regents examination, essay questions on the RCT's are *already* partially organized for you. The essay question will consist of two parts: **Part A** and **Part B**. Let's examine each part separately.

ANSWERING PART A

In Part A you will usually be asked to **define, state, identify**, or **list** certain key factual information. Although these terms are similar—in that they ask for specific facts, events, factors, or ways—they have slightly different meanings.

- **define** means to set forth or to explain the meaning of a term or concept
- **state** or **identify** is usually used when *one* item is asked for in the answer
- **list** is usually used when *more than one* item is asked for in the answer

Notice how in Part A of our sample, you must outline the main facts. For example, you must *define* the term federalism. Then you must *list* two powers of the national and state governments. Your answers might be as follows:

Part A

Define "federalism:" *Federalism is a system of government in which the powers of government are divided between a central government and local governments. For example, in the United States power is divided between the central government located in Washington, D.C. and 50 local state governments.*

List *two* powers of the national (federal) government.

1. *declaring war* 2. *maintaining an army and navy*

List *two* powers of the state governments.

1. *issuing marriage licenses* 2. *controlling education*

ANSWERING PART B

You are now ready to write your detailed essay answer for **Part B**, based on the information you have already provided in **Part A. Part B** requires that you write an essay explaining how the writers of the U.S. Constitution created a federal system of government. To help you organize your **Part B** answer, try to imagine your answer as a hamburger consisting of a **top bun**, **patties of meat**, and a **bottom bun**:

- The "top bun" is the **topic sentence**. It is merely a restatement of the generalization that introduced the question. In this question, the topic sentence would be: *The writers of the United States Constitution created a federal system of government.*

- Next come the "patties of meat;" this is the **information** found in **Part A**. The "meat"starts with a **bridge sentence** linking the topic sentence to the main body of the essay. In this section you must expand on—*"describe," "explain," "discuss,"* or *"show"*—the information from **Part A**.

■ The "bottom bun" comes last. It is a **final restatement** of the first generalization. The one difference is that it is introduced with such words as "therefore" or "in conclusion one can see that." In the sample question, the concluding sentence could be: *In conclusion one can see that the writers of the United States Constitution created a federal system of government.*

Here is one possible way your answer to the **Part B** question could be written:

Topic Sentence	The writers of the United States Constitution created a federal system of government.
Bridge Sentence	Under federalism, powers are divided between a central government and many different local governments.
Patties of Meat	The national government was given the responsibility of handling the concerns of the entire nation. For example, the national government was given the power to declare war and maintain an army and navy. The state governments were given the responsibility of handling concerns that affected their particular state. For example, the state governments were given the power to issue marriage licenses and to control education.
Concluding Sentence	In conclusion one can see that the writers of the United States Constitution created a federal system of government.

Notice that your **Part B** answer used the information called for in answering **Part A**. As a final check you could "verify" your essay answer by asking yourself: Have I written an essay that would answer the topic sentence:

The writers of the United States Constitution created a federal system of government.

if the topic sentence were turned into a question:

How did the writers of the United States Constitution create a federal system of government?

LOOKING AT GOVERNMENT

In Part II of the Regents Examination, students are always asked to answer one essay question about the American system of government. The RCT frequently provides at least one essay question about American government. To prepare you for these questions, this section presents a general look at what government is, what the goals of our own system of government have been, and how our system of government has attempted to meet its goals in the course of its 200-year history.

WHAT IS GOVERNMENT?

It seems to be a fact of nature that human beings are communal. We live in groups or communities. This fact has important consequences. All communities need to make rules, to decide disputes between members, and to protect the community from aggressors. The ability to make these types of decisions, which are binding on others, is called **political power**. The body given the authority to carry out this political power is called **government**. Governments, by their very nature, posses three powers to implement their authority:

- Legislative power (to make laws)
- Executive power (to carry out the laws)
- Judicial power (to apply the laws to specific situations)

In fact, the word "govern" comes from the ancient Greek word for steering a ship. Just as a pilot guides a ship, a government guides the conduct of the members of a community in their dealings with each other and with outsiders.

CREATION OF A GOVERNMENT

The creation of governmental authority is a matter of great concern to each of us. Why do we give people whom we hardly know such tremendous power over our lives? And how much power can we give to government officials without threatening our personal liberties? To help answer these questions, look at some of the important issues that must be faced in framing any government.

- What are the purposes of a government?
- What institutions of government will be created to carry out the powers of the government?
- How will these institutions of government be organized?

Thinking about these issues helps you to appreciate the complexity of the problems that faced the authors of the American system of government.

THE FORMS OF GOVERNMENT

The members of the Constitutional Convention in 1787 had many different types of government from which to choose. They could have selected rule by:

- One person: **Monarchy** (rule by a king or queen)
- A select few: **Constitutional Monarchy** (rule by a king or queen, and parliament), or **Oligarchy** (rule by a privileged elite of wealthy and powerful citizens)
- All citizens: **Representative Democracy** (rule by representatives chosen by the people)

The delegates to the Constitutional Convention remained committed to the basic system of representative democracy, established a decade earlier when the U.S. had declared its independence from England. Ultimate power would remain in the hands of the people, who would choose their own representatives. After making this basic choice, the authors of the Constitution still had to decide what the specific aims of the new national government would be, how the representatives would be chosen, and what their particular powers would be.

THE GOALS OF THE UNITED STATES GOVERNMENT

The decision to adopt a democratic form of government was based on the framers' beliefs about the role of government in society. The aims of our national government are made clear in two important documents: the Declaration of Independence and the Constitution. The Declaration stated what its authors believed to be true of all governments generally — that they should aim to protect the rights of the individual members of the community, especially the rights to "life, liberty and the pursuit of happiness." The Preamble of the Constitution went on to spell out the specific goals of our own national government in particular:

DECLARATION OF INDEPENDENCE	THE U.S. CONSTITUTION
Right to Life	To Insure Domestic Tranquillity To Provide for the Common Defense
Right to Liberty	To Secure the Blessings of Liberty To Establish Justice
Right to Pursue Happiness	To Promote the General Welfare To Form a More Perfect Union

You should notice two important things about these statements of aims:

■ First, most of these aims are quite broad. For example, one of the goals of our national government is to "establish justice." What people believe to be justice may change over time. In the late 19th century, people did not consider it "unjust" to separate children of different races into different schools. Attitudes gradually changed as people came to see racial discrimination as "unjust," and racial segregation became unconstitutional. It is therefore important to see how the broad aims in both documents have been interpreted at different moments in our history.

■ Second, it is possible for some of these goals to come into conflict. For example, in taking measures for the "common defense," the government may be forced to deny some citizens the "blessings of liberty." Therefore, in evaluating the goals of our government, some goals are given priority over others. These priorities have also changed over time.

THE STRUCTURE OF THE UNITED STATES GOVERNMENT

Once they had arrived at the aims of the governmental system, the framers had to decide on how to create a system of government that could fulfill those aims. They wanted to strike a balance between the powers of the government and the rights of the individual. The central problem was seen as:

> How much power should be given to government officials—so that they can carry out their duties effectively—without taking away too many of the liberties of individual citizens?

The framers created structures that they thought would make the new government strong enough to meet national goals, but not so powerful that it would endanger individual liberties. They adopted several principles that you will review in greater detail in the next chapter. Consider how each of these principles contributed to the balancing of governmental power and the preservation of individual liberties:

Federalism	Power was divided between the federal and state governments.
Separation of powers	National governmental power was further divided among the legislative, executive and judicial branches of the federal government.
Checks and Balances	Each branch of the federal government had special powers to check the other branches.
Limited Government	The federal government could only exercise those powers given to it in the Constitution.
Judicial Review	The Supreme Court could rule that a law was unconstitutional.
Bill of Rights	Added to the Constitution in 1791, they guaranteed citizens certain rights against the actions of the federal government.

THE EVOLUTION OF OUR CONSTITUTIONAL SYSTEM

Our national system of government has changed over time. Constitutional amendments, the decisions of the Supreme Court, and informal political practices have played key roles in the adaptation of our system of government to the needs of our changing society. Some scholars go as far as to say that Americans have re-defined their Constitution at critical "Constitutional Moments" — such as Reconstruction and the New Deal. These moments have resulted in important changes in the goals and general structure of our system of government as well as in new laws.

Whether or not this view of our Constitution is correct, it is clear that there have been several key episodes in the growth and development of our national governmental power. Each of these is described in greater detail in later chapters of this book, as well as in special sections at the end of each chapter under the heading "The Constitution at Work." Three over-arching themes are readily apparent:

(1) the increasing power of the federal government over the states
(2) the increasing power of the federal government over our national economic life
(3) the increasing role of the federal government as the protector of individual rights and as the chief guarantor of the "equal protection" of the laws

PIVOTAL MOMENTS IN THE EVOLUTION OF THE AMERICAN POLITICAL SYSTEM

1776-1791	**Declaration of Independence**, **Constitution**, and **Bill of Rights**: These documents established the basic structures of the American political system.
1790s	**Rise of Parties**: The development of political parties brought new ideas and information to the public, made politics more organized, and made elections more competitive.
1830s	**Jacksonian Democracy**: Most states abolished property and income qualifications for voting; by 1840, almost all white males could vote. New campaign methods and the introduction of nominating conventions involved many more people in politics, making government more democratic.
1860s	**Civil War and Reconstruction**: Slavery was abolished and the supremacy of the federal government over the states was secured. The 14th Amendment greatly expanded the power of the federal government by giving it powers to protect individual citizens against the acts of state governments. Congress took a leading role over both the states and the presidency during the Reconstruction Era. Congress was unable, however, to impeach the president for differences in political views.

1890-1920	**The Progressive Era**: The federal government obtained limited powers to check some of the worst abuses of big business, such as monopolies. Other reforms, like the direct election of senators and the introduction of primaries made politics more democratic. The introduction of income tax changed the way government services were paid for. By 1920, the 19th Amendment had passed, giving women the vote.
1930s	**The New Deal**: The federal government took on a much more important role in regulating the national economy. After initial resistance, the Supreme Court authorized greater federal government interference in private economic activity on the basis of Congress' powers to regulate interstate commerce. New regulatory agencies were established to supervise many aspects of American economic life.
1950s-1960s	**The Civil Rights Era**: Starting with *Brown v. Board of Education*, the Supreme Court became much more assertive in defending both individual rights and the guarantee of "equal protection of the laws" found in the earlier 14th amendment. The Court also strengthened the rights of criminal defendants, guaranteed women the right to abortions, and ordered state legislatures to be reorganized on the basis of one person, one vote. The president and Congress also took a more active role in curbing discrimination and in protecting the rights of minority groups and women. New federal regulatory agencies were created to fight pollution and other abuses. The federal government assumed new responsibilities, like the "War on Poverty" and Medicare, to resolve major social problems.
1950s-1970s	**The Imperial Presidency**: The New Deal, the Cold War, the invention of nuclear weapons, and the development of radio and television resulted in the enormous growth of presidential power. Americans looked to the President for rapid decision-making on all issues of economic, social, defense and foreign policy. Presidents, in turn, sought to evade legislative and judicial controls—until Watergate ended the Nixon Presidency.
1980s	**The New Federalism**: President Reagan reduced the role of the federal government in dealing with social problems and in regulating the national economy. A more conservative Supreme Court began to limit the rights of criminal defendants, women seeking abortion, and minorities seeking "affirmative action" programs.

ANSWERING AN ESSAY QUESTION ON GOVERNMENT

RCT and Regents essay questions about government generally focus on the following issues and themes:

- What are the goals of our system of government?
- What are the main principles of our Constitution?

- What have been our enduring constitutional issues—especially:concerning federalism, individual rights, equality, representation, and the role of the judiciary?
- How has our Constitution managed to be flexible enough to adapt to the needs of our changing society? — requires knowledge of some chief amendments and Supreme Court cases.
- What has been the role of the Supreme Court in interpreting individual rights and the powers of our national government?
- How has the role of the presidency expanded in recent times?
- How do the different branches of our federal government act to check each other, and which branches have been dominant in particular periods of our history?

Very often the test-writers will try to test your knowledge of both government and history in the same question. For example, let's look at a question from a past Regents Examination:

The United States Supreme Court has interpreted the constitutional guarantees contained in amendments to the United States Constitution. Some of these guarantees are listed below:

Constitutional Guarantees

First Amendment guarantee of freedom of religion
First Amendment guarantee of freedom of speech
First Amendment guarantee of freedom of the press
Fourth Amendment guarantee concerning search and seizure
Sixth Amendment guarantee of the right to counsel
Fourteenth Amendment guarantee of equal protection of the law

Choose *three* of the constitutional guarantees listed and for *each* one chosen:

- Identify a United States Supreme Court case in which the decision was an interpretation of the guarantee
- Discuss the issue involved in the case
- Show how the ruling of the Court in that case has had a significant impact on United States society.

Note how each of these guarantees concerns striking a balance between governmental power and individual liberty. Note also that the question asks you to provide historical examples of Court decisions. You will find the "Constitution at Work" sections in each chapter particularly helpful in reviewing Supreme Court decisions and constitutional amendments. After you read about the principles and structures of American government in the following chapter, you should think about how those principles have been tested at various times in our national history, and how those structures have evolved to meet the needs of our changing society. Later chapters of this book will help you to focus on these themes.

CHAPTER 5

CONSTITUTIONAL FOUNDATIONS

What began as an attempt by loyal British colonial subjects to stand up for their rights as Englishmen, soon became a war for independence against British rule. The nation that emerged from the American Revolution became the first modern democratic republic. Facing many difficulties in its early existence, the United States managed to struggle through this critical period. The crisis the nation faced helped to create a new constitution that has become the model and inspiration for many other nations.

— TIMELINE OF KEY EVENTS —

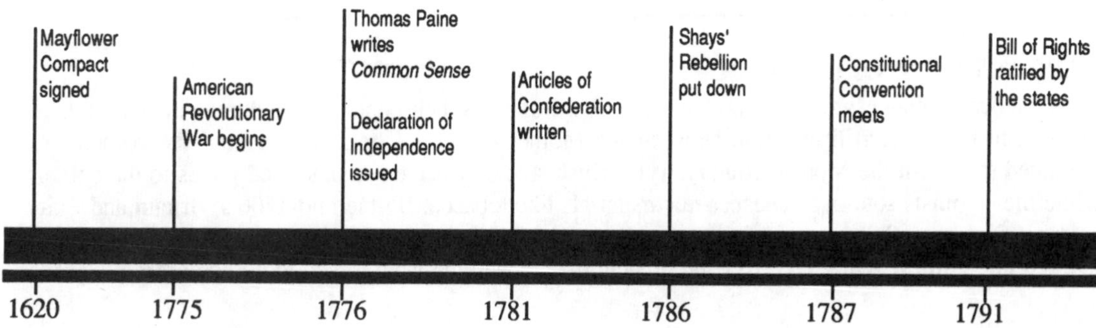
Mayflower Compact signed
1620
American Revolutionary War begins
1775
Thomas Paine writes *Common Sense*
Declaration of Independence issued
1776
Articles of Confederation written
1781
Shays' Rebellion put down
1786
Constitutional Convention meets
1787
Bill of Rights ratified by the states
1791

FROM COLONIES TO INDEPENDENT STATES

THE COLONIAL BACKGROUND

The first permanent British settlement in North America was established at the beginning of the 17th century. Most of the early British colonists came in search of wealth, property or religious freedom. One exception were the African slaves, forcibly brought to the colonies as captive laborers from 1619 onwards. British colonization gradually spread up and down the Atlantic coast, forming thirteen separate colonies. Many of the democratic institutions found in the colonies could trace their roots back to British political traditions.

- **Magna Carta (1215).** The English King promised not to take away the property or to imprison any subject except according to the laws of the land.

- **The British Parliament.** Parliament (the British lawmaking body) was composed of two houses, the House of Lords representing nobles, and the House of Commons representing the common people. In the 17th century, Parliament successfully established its supremacy over the king.

In addition, some important democratic principles were developed by the colonists themselves.

- **The Mayflower Compact.** In 1620, Pilgrims crossing the Atlantic on board the ship *Mayflower* signed a document establishing a government ruled by laws, deriving its powers from the consent of the governed.

- **The Virginia House of Burgesses.** This legislative body established the principle that the people in the colonies would have the right to elect their own representatives to the legislature. The colonial assemblies in Virginia and elsewhere acted as miniature law-making bodies in charge of local problems.

THE AMERICAN REVOLUTION: 1775-1783

ORIGINS OF THE CONFLICT

The American colonies grew in importance to Great Britain as their population and trade increased. Under the system of **mercantilism**, trade between the Mother Country (Great Britain) and the colonies was regulated to benefit the Mother Country. The British sold expensive manufactured goods to the colonists while the colonists sold back cheaper raw materials like tobacco. By the mid-1700's, Britain and France became rivals in a global contest for overseas colonies. In North America, this struggle was known as the **French and Indian Wars**. By 1763, the French lost the war and were forced to withdraw from Canada.

"NO TAXATION WITHOUT REPRESENTATION"

The war left the British facing the burden of a very large debt.The British government, wanting the colonists to help pay off the debt, imposed new taxes on them. The colonists objected, primarily because they were denied the right to be represented in Parliament. The problem was that the colonists could not be represented effectively there because of the great distance of the colonies from London.

■ **The Stamp Act.** In 1765, the British government passed a Stamp Act requiring all newspapers, books and documents in the colonies to carry an official government stamp. This led to a wave of protests by the colonists. The British repealed the tax, but passed an act declaring that Parliament had the right to tax the colonists if it wanted to.

■ **The Tea Tax**. Parliament next passed new taxes on paper, glass and tea. The colonists again protested that taxes were being imposed on them without their consent. Rioting broke out in several colonial cities, and the British repealed all the taxes except the duty on tea. In 1773, a group of protesters in Boston, disguised as Indians, threw tea off British ships in the harbor. The British closed Boston harbor and banned public meetings until the tea was paid for.

THE IDEA OF INDEPENDENCE GROWS

Representatives from the colonies met in Philadelphia for a Continental Congress in 1774 to deal with the crisis. The Congress sent a letter of protest to Great Britain and called for a boycott of British goods. In 1775, British soldiers searching for colonial supplies and arms exchanged gunfire with colonial volunteers in the colony of Massachusetts. This marked the start of the American Revolution.

A Second Continental Congress was held in Philadelphia. The Congress offered to negotiate with the British government, but the British refused. As the fighting continued, many of the delegates began to think about the possibility of becoming independent from Great Britain. The colonists were greatly influenced in 1776 by the publication of the pamphlet *Common Sense* by **Thomas Paine**. Paine wrote that it was ridiculous for the American colonies, occupying a great continent, to be ruled by a tiny island such as Great Britain.

A DECLARATION OF INDEPENDENCE IS ISSUED

By mid-1776, a committee headed by **Thomas Jefferson** was set up to draft a Declaration of Independence. The Declaration was approved and adopted on July 4, 1776.

■ **The Purpose of the Declaration**. Its main purpose was to explain and justify to the world the reasons for the American decision to declare independence from British colonial rule.

■ **The Key Paragraph**. The key paragraph of the Declaration contained a statement of principles upon which the colonists believed all governments should be based:

> *"We hold these truths to be self-evident, that all men are created equal, that they are endowed by their Creator with certain unalienable Rights, that among these are Life, Liberty and the pursuit of Happiness. That to secure these rights, Governments are instituted among Men, deriving their just powers from the consent of the governed, That whenever any Form of Government becomes destructive of these ends, it is the right of the People to alter or abolish it, and to institute new Government..."*

This paragraph was based on the following ideas:

- **Natural Rights and the Equality of Mankind.** The Declaration stated that all people have natural rights (unalienable rights) that cannot be taken away. Among these basic human rights are "life, liberty and the pursuit of happiness." In this sense, "all men are created equal." Although it would take 200 years before equality was extended to all Americans, the Declaration was a powerful force in laying the foundation for equality.

- **The Social Contract.** The Declaration was based on the Social Contract Theory of the English philosopher **John Locke**. According to this theory, people have a right to form a government to protect their inalienable rights. If the government fails to carry out its function and instead oppresses those it is meant to protect, the people have the right to overthrow the government and create a new one.

■ **Grievances Against the King.** The Declaration continued with a list of grievances against **King George III.** Because the king had repeatedly violated the colonists' liberties, the Declaration stated that the colonists were justified in breaking their connection with Great Britain.

■ **Significance of the Declaration.** The Declaration allowed foreign governments to recognize and support the colonists in their struggle for independence. The simplicity and logic of the Declaration laid the foundation for future revolutions—including the French Revolution (1789) and later revolutions in Asia, Africa, Latin America and the Middle East. Most importantly, the ideals contained within the Declaration influenced many provisions of the U.S. Constitution—especially the concept of democracy and the idea of achieving full equality for all citizens.

THE FIRST NATIONAL GOVERNMENT

The revolutionary army, led by **George Washington**, eventually triumphed over the British. In 1783, the British recognized the independence of the colonies. As a result, each of the thirteen original colonies now became an independent state. Although each colony created its own state constitution, establishing a new state government, Americans realized the need for some type of central government.

THE ARTICLES OF CONFEDERATION

Soon after independence was declared, the Second Continental Congress began to work out a plan for a more permanent national government. The agreement they arrived at was known as the Articles of Confederation, and it went into effect in 1781.

■ **The Nature of the Confederation.** The new confederation was a loose, weak association of states. Each state sent one representative to a new Confederation Congress, where each state had one vote. There was no national executive and no national courts. Under the Articles, the individual state governments remained more powerful than the limited national government. Although the new Confederation government had many powers — to declare war, make peace, send and receive ambassadors, enter treaties, borrow money, build a navy, set up a currency, ask states for troops in an emergency — they were difficult to put into effect.

■ **Laws and Amendments.** The agreement of nine out of the thirteen states was needed to make any new law, and this was difficult to obtain. Congress could not levy its own taxes, raise its own army, or enforce its own decisions. It was up to individual states to enforce and apply the acts of Congress. And all thirteen had to agree before any changes could be made to the Articles of Confederation.

THE CRITICAL PERIOD (1781-1786)

The Articles of Confederation successfully kept the nation together during the final years of the American Revolution. In addition, with the passage of the **Northwest Ordinance** in 1787, it provided a system for governing the western territories. Despite these successes, the period under the Articles is often called the "Critical Period" because of the serious problems which arose between 1781 and 1786.

■ **Weaknesses.** The major weakness of the government under the Articles was that it gave too little power to the national government. States taxed goods from other states, printed their own money, and refused to give the national Congress most of the tax money it requested. During all of this, the national government was powerless to do anything.

■ **Shays Rebellion (1786).** Another serious shortcoming of the national government was that it had no standing army. This weakness became apparent when a group of debtors and small farmers led by Daniel Shays rebelled in Massachusetts, demanding cheap money to pay off their debts. The rebellion was put down by state troops but instilled fear in many property-holders. If the rebellion had spread, the Confederation government would have been powerless to stop it.

KEY ITEMS TO REMEMBER

Mayflower Compact, House of Burgesses, mercantilism, *Common Sense*, Declaration of Independence, natural rights, Social Contract Theory, Articles of Confederation, Northwest Ordinance, Critical Period

THE ORIGINS OF THE U.S. CONSTITUTION

By the mid-1780s, many merchants were unhappy that some states were obstructing trade. Property owners no longer felt safe. Many people feared that if a foreign country attacked, the government would simply collapse. Several states called a meeting to be held in Philadelphia to revise the Articles of Confederation.

THE CONSTITUTIONAL CONVENTION

THE CONVENTION MEETS (1787)

The Convention was called primarily to give more power to the national government under the Articles of Confederation. However, almost immediately the delegates decided to abandon the Articles completely and to write a new national constitution (a document outlining the basic form and rules of government).

Did the Framers have the right to abandon the Articles of Confederation?	
POINT	**COUNTERPOINT**
Some historians have looked at the delegates to the Convention as members of a small elite, desperate to preserve their power and riches by creating a strong national government which they hoped to control.	Other historians have seen the delegates as representatives of the American people, taking steps to safeguard the liberties won during the American Revolution, and ensuring that the young country would not fall apart.

CONSTITUTIONAL COMPROMISES

The delegates at the Constitutional Convention agreed on the need for a strong central government with the power to tax, to create a national army, and to regulate commerce among the states. They also agreed on the need for a chief executive, a national court system and a national legislature. However, there were important disagreements among the delegates which were eventually settled through compromises. For this reason the Constitution is sometimes called a "**bundle of compromises.**" Some of the most important were:

■ **The Great Compromise**. Large states differed with small states on the method of representation in the legislature. To resolve the conflict, a **bicameral** (two-house) legislature was created.

- In the **House of Representatives**, states were represented according to the size of their population; the larger states had a greater number of representatives. This satisfied the larger states. The House of Representatives became the most democratic body in the new government, since the election of its members was directly in the hands of the people.

- In the **Senate**, each state—no matter how large or small—was represented by two senators. This satisfied the smaller states.

■ **The Three-Fifths Compromise.** Delegates from the South wanted to count their slaves as part of a state's population in order to increase their number of representatives in the House of Representatives. It was agreed that they would be allowed representation for three-fifths of their slave populations. In effect, every 5 slaves would be counted as 3 whites.

■ **The Slave Trade and Commerce Compromises.** Differences of opinion existed between the North and South over the slave trade and the taxing of exports. Two compromises were reached: the new Constitution provided that Congress could not pass any laws restricting the slave trade for at least another 20 years (until 1808), and the new government would have no power to impose taxes on exports.

THE DEBATE OVER RATIFICATION

The members of the Constitutional Convention decided to hold a special convention in each state to **ratify** (approve) the Constitution. Once nine states ratified the new Constitution, it would be put into effect. Those who supported ratification were known as **Federalists**, while those opposed were called **Anti-Federalists.**

THE FEDERALISTS SUPPORT RATIFICATION

The most persuasive Federalist arguments were presented by Alexander Hamilton, James Madison and John Jay during the debate over ratification in New York. Their 85 essays were published as **The Federalist Papers**. Some of the reasons the Federalists gave for adopting the Constitution were the following:

■ The Articles of Confederation were a failure and needed to be replaced. A stronger central government was needed to create a national army to protect Americans from internal rebellions or foreign enemies, and to regulate trade among the states. A President or chief executive was necessary to carry out or enforce the decisions of the national government. A national court system was similarly needed.

■ Citizens did not have to fear that the new government would become too strong, because its powers were divided among three separate branches. Federalism, the separation of powers, and the system of checks and balances created in the Constitution would prevent the rise of tyranny.

THE ANTI-FEDERALISTS OPPOSE RATIFICATION

Anti-Federalists argued against ratifying the Constitution because:

■ The Constitution would create a government so powerful it might take away the powers of state governments and the liberties of ordinary citizens.

■ The new government would create new and costly taxes. The wealthy members of Congress could use the army to collect unpopular taxes, and then use the taxes to build a stronger army.

■ There was no protection of the life, liberty and property of citizens, nor a guarantee of a fair trial and free speech. The debate over ratification thus led to adoption of the **Bill of Rights** (the first 10 amendments) in 1791.

Eleven state conventions ratified the Constitution by the end of 1788. In 1789, the first Congress assembled in New York City. The following month George Washington was inaugurated as the first president.

KEY ITEMS TO REMEMBER

Constitutional Convention, Constitution, Great Compromise, bicameralism, Three-fifths Compromise, the *Federalist Papers*, Bill of Rights

FUNDAMENTAL PRINCIPLES OF THE U.S. CONSTITUTION

The system of government established by the Constitution rests on a series of fundamental principles.

POPULAR SOVEREIGNTY

In the U. S., the final power of government rests with the people. This is reflected in the first words of the **Preamble**, "We, the people..." The people exercise their right to rule by choosing representatives in elections.

FEDERALISM

Federalism is a system for sharing power and authority between a national government and local governments. The U.S. Constitution divides the exercise of government power between two levels: the national (or **federal**) level of government and the local (or **state**) level of government. The federal government deals with national concerns and relations between the states, while the state governments deal with their own local affairs. To achieve this division, powers are shared as follows:

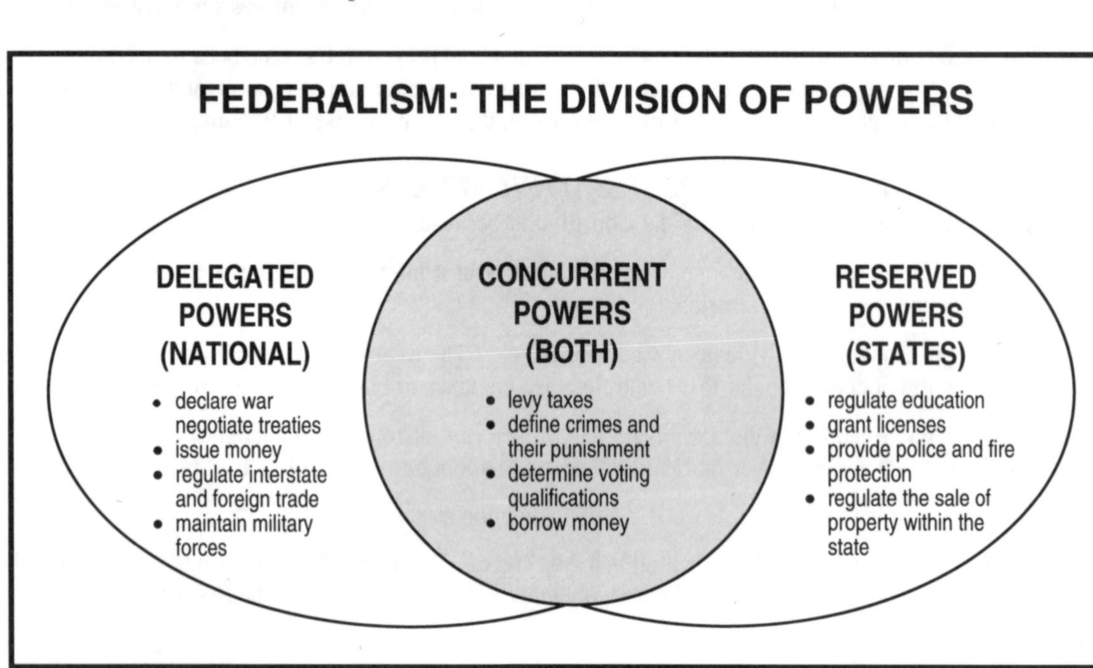
FEDERALISM: THE DIVISION OF POWERS
DELEGATED POWERS (NATIONAL)
• declare war negotiate treaties
• issue money
• regulate interstate and foreign trade
• maintain military forces
CONCURRENT POWERS (BOTH)
• levy taxes
• define crimes and their punishment
• determine voting qualifications
• borrow money
RESERVED POWERS (STATES)
• regulate education
• grant licenses
• provide police and fire protection
• regulate the sale of property within the state

■ **Delegated Powers.** The powers given to the national government are called delegated powers, and include: the regulation of interstate commerce, conducting a war, negotiating treaties with foreign countries, raising taxes, issuing money, running the national postal service, and maintaining the armed forces.

■ **Reserved Powers.** The exclusive powers of the state governments are called reserved powers and include: setting up public school systems, establishing rules for motor vehicles, making regulations for the sale of property within a state, and granting licenses.

■ **Concurrent Powers.** Some powers, commonly called concurrent powers, such as the power to tax and to borrow money, are exercised by both the national and state governments.

SEPARATION OF POWERS

At the national level, as well as within the various state governments, power is separated into three branches. This separation of powers makes it difficult for any one individual or group to gain control of the entire government, since power is obtained in each branch in different ways.

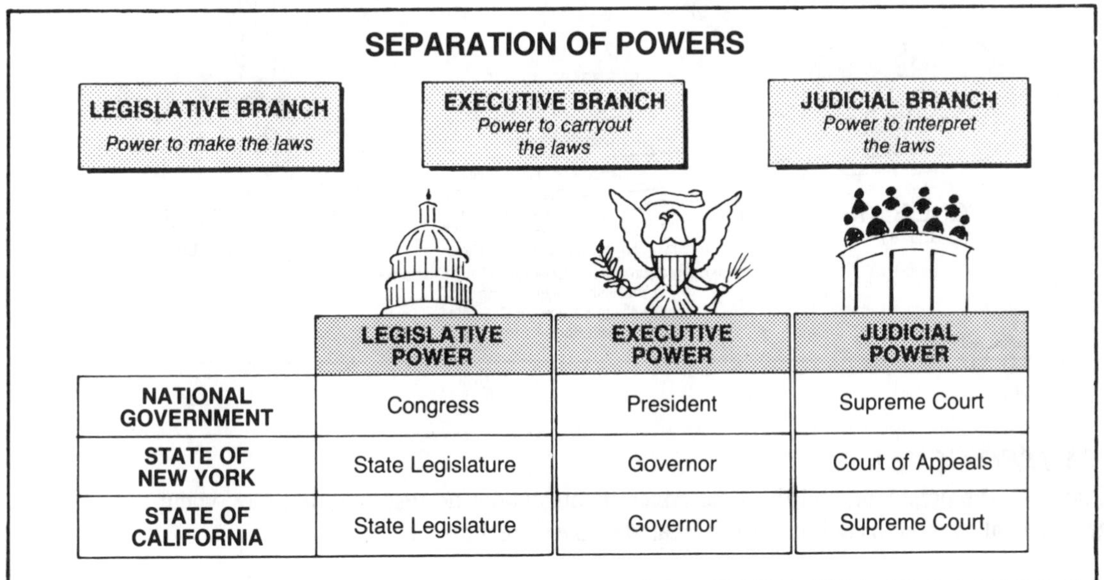
SEPARATION OF POWERS
LEGISLATIVE BRANCH
Power to make the laws
EXECUTIVE BRANCH
Power to carryout the laws
JUDICIAL BRANCH
Power to interpret the laws

	LEGISLATIVE POWER	EXECUTIVE POWER	JUDICIAL POWER
NATIONAL GOVERNMENT	Congress	President	Supreme Court
STATE OF NEW YORK	State Legislature	Governor	Court of Appeals
STATE OF CALIFORNIA	State Legislature	Governor	Supreme Court

CHECKS AND BALANCES

To make sure that the national government did not become too strong or oppress those it was supposed to govern, the Constitution also gave each branch of the federal government ways to stop or "**check**" the other branches. This system of checks and balances creates obstacles to government action, so that certain measures cannot be taken unless there is general agreement that they are needed.

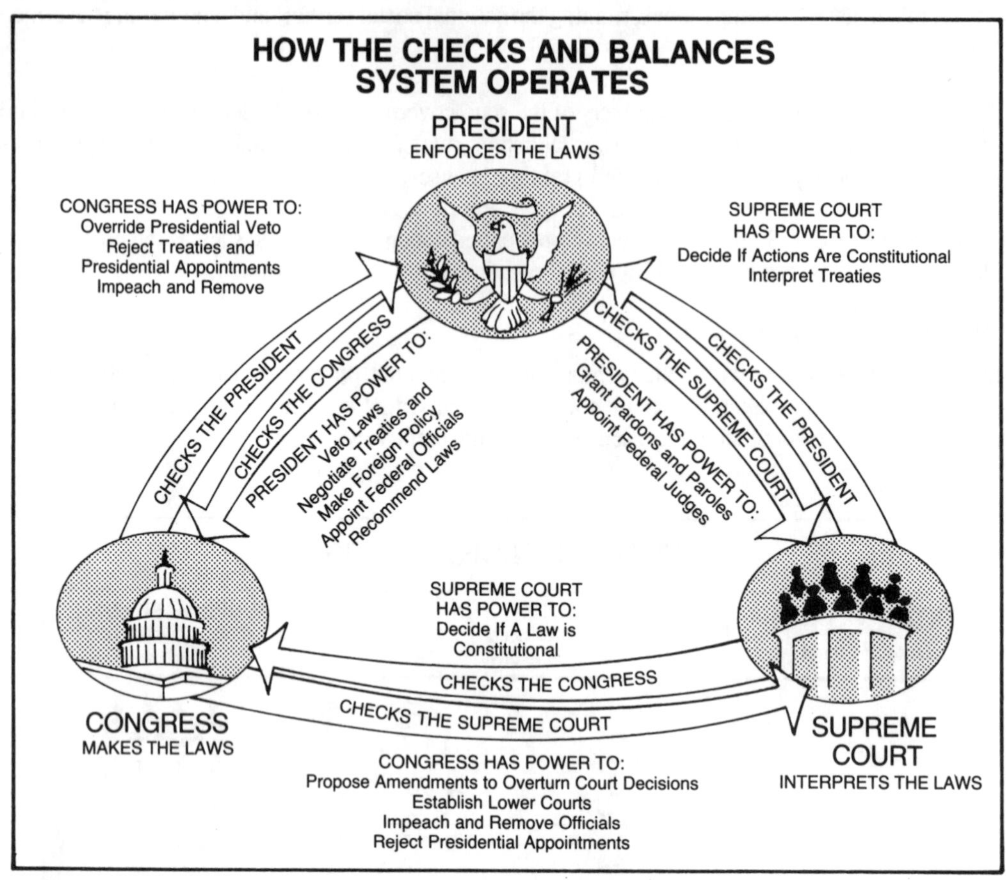
HOW THE CHECKS AND BALANCES SYSTEM OPERATES
PRESIDENT
ENFORCES THE LAWS
CONGRESS HAS POWER TO:
Override Presidential Veto
Reject Treaties and Presidential Appointments
Impeach and Remove
SUPREME COURT HAS POWER TO:
Decide If Actions Are Constitutional
Interpret Treaties
CHECKS THE PRESIDENT
CHECKS THE CONGRESS
PRESIDENT HAS POWER TO:
Veto Laws
Negotiate Treaties and Make Foreign Policy
Appoint Federal Officials
Recommend Laws
CHECKS THE SUPREME COURT
CHECKS THE PRESIDENT
PRESIDENT HAS POWER TO:
Grant Pardons and Paroles
Appoint Federal Judges
SUPREME COURT HAS POWER TO:
Decide If A Law is Constitutional
CHECKS THE CONGRESS
CHECKS THE SUPREME COURT
CONGRESS
MAKES THE LAWS
CONGRESS HAS POWER TO:
Propose Amendments to Overturn Court Decisions
Establish Lower Courts
Impeach and Remove Officials
Reject Presidential Appointments
SUPREME COURT
INTERPRETS THE LAWS

LIMITED GOVERNMENT

Congress, the president, and the state governments cannot do just anything they want; the power of government over our lives is strictly regulated by the Constitution.

■ **The Preamble.** The Preamble to the Constitution lists the purposes of the federal government. They are to establish justice, insure domestic peace, provide for the defense of the nation, promote the general welfare, and secure the blessings of liberty. All actions of the federal government are supposed to be directed towards these goals.

■ **Denied Powers.** Article I, Sections 9 and 10 of the U.S. Constitution list powers that are denied to both the federal and state governments:

Powers Denied to the Federal Government	Powers Denied To Both The Federal & State Governments	Powers Denied to the State Governments
· To suspend the writ of habeas corpus except in times of war. · To spend money without Congressional approval	· To pass ex post facto laws · To pass bills of attainder · To grant titles of nobility · To tax exports · To deny persons due process of law	· To coin money · To enter into treaties · To tax imports · To tax the federal government

■ **Delegated Powers.** The federal government has only those powers given to it by the Constitution. They are listed in Article I, Section 8. Some of the major powers include the power to collect taxes, to regulate interstate commerce, to borrow money, to provide a national currency (money), to declare war, and to maintain an army and navy.

■ **Implied Powers.** The **Elastic Clause** (Article I, Section 8, Clause 18) expands the powers of the federal government by giving it whatever additional powers are "necessary and proper" for carrying out those powers specifically listed in the Constitution. These additional powers are called the implied powers.

■ **The Bill of Rights.** The Bill of Rights and other later amendments also placed important limits on the powers of the federal and state governments.

FLEXIBILITY: THE CONSTITUTION AS A "LIVING DOCUMENT"

The Constitution is still in use today because it is a flexible document. It has been adapted to changing situations through the amending process and new interpretations.

■ **The Amending Process.** To prevent changes for unimportant reasons, the amending process was made far more difficult than the passing of an ordinary law. Although there are several ways to amend the Constitution, the two-thirds vote of approval in Congress combined with approval by three-fourths of the state legislatures is the one that has historically been used.

■ **New Interpretations.** Much of the language in the Constitution is vague. For example, Congress can regulate "interstate commerce," but what does "interstate commerce" mean? "Cruel and unusual punishments" are unconstitutional, but is capital punishment "cruel and unusual?" The Supreme Court is given the main job of interpreting the Constitution. Supreme Court decisions often apply the Constitution to new circumstances and find new meanings, helping to adapt the text to the needs of the times.

KEY ITEMS TO REMEMBER

Popular sovereignty, Preamble, federalism, delegated powers, reserved powers, separation of powers, checks and balances, implied powers, elastic clause

THE FEDERAL GOVERNMENT: ITS STRUCTURE AND FUNCTIONS

Although there have been some important changes, our federal government still operates today with the same basic structure that the Constitution established two hundred years ago. Federal power continues to be divided among the three separate branches—the Congress, the President, and the Supreme Court.

CONGRESS: THE LEGISLATIVE BRANCH

STRUCTURE AND FUNCTIONS OF CONGRESS

The main task of Congress is to make the nation's laws. It is composed of two houses:

- **Senate.** Today, the Senate has 100 members, two from each state. Each senator is elected for a six-year term by voters throughout his or her state. In addition to its law-making function, two-thirds of the Senate is needed to ratify (approve) all treaties negotiated by the President. The Senate must also confirm all presidential appointments of federal justices, cabinet officers and ambassadors.

- **House of Representatives.** Today, the House has 435 members. Each representative is elected for a two-year term by the voters of a single Congressional district. The number of representatives of each state is determined by that state's population. Every ten years a national **census** is taken and the seats in the House of Representatives are redistributed.

HOW A BILL BECOMES A LAW

A bill is a proposed law. It can start in either the Senate or the House of Representatives. However, all money bills must start in the House of Representatives. Once a representative or senator proposes a bill, it is sent to a Standing Committee.

- **The Committee Stage.** Standing Committees are permanent committees that deal with particular subject matters, like foreign affairs or the national budget. Committee members investigate and consider the bill. Then the committee either recommends, amends, or "kills" the bill.

- **Consideration By The Whole House.** If the committee recommends the bill, it must then go back to the whole house—either the Senate or the House of Representatives—for consideration. After the bill is debated, the house votes to approve or reject it. If the bill is approved, it goes to the other house of Congress and passes through a similar procedure.

- **Conference Committee.** If the bill is passed in one house but in a slightly different form in the other house, it is submitted to a Conference Committee composed of members of both houses, to iron out the differences.

■ **The President.** The bill is then submitted to the president. If the president signs the bill, it becomes law. If the president **vetoes** it, Congress can **override** the veto if two-thirds of each house votes again for the bill.

THE PRESIDENCY: THE EXECUTIVE BRANCH

QUALIFICATIONS AND TERM OF OFFICE

The president must be a natural-born citizen and at least 35 years old. The president is elected for a four-year term of office. Traditionally, presidents served only two terms, until Franklin D. Roosevelt was elected four times. The 22nd Amendment (1944) then limited the president to two elected terms.

CHOOSING THE PRESIDENTIAL CANDIDATES

Usually, to become president, a candidate must first win the nomination of a major political party. To do this, candidates participate in state **primaries**—elections among rivals from the same party seeking the support of delegates to the party's National Convention. At the **National Convention** held by each party, the delegates choose their party's nominee. The delegates also draw up a **party platform**, stating their party's position on important issues in the campaign. Then the nominees of the two parties travel around the country, campaigning against each other. Occasionally, a person may run for president without any party affiliation, as Ross Perot almost did in 1992. Thousands of citizens must sign petitions to get such a candidate on the presidential ballot in each state.

ELECTING A PRESIDENT: THE ELECTORAL COLLEGE PROCESS

The members of the Constitutional Convention did not trust the common people to elect the president directly. Instead, they turned over the selection of the president to special electors who form the **electoral college**. This system remains in effect, although the electors now follow the wishes of their state's voters.

■ To become president, a candidate needs to win a majority of the votes in the electoral college. The number of electors each state has is equal to the number of its representatives in the House combined with the number of its senators. The candidate with the majority wins *all* of the electors in that state.

■ If no candidate receives a majority of the electoral votes (270), the election is then decided in the House of Representatives, where each state gets one vote. The winner must receive a majority (26) of state votes.

THE MANY ROLES OF THE PRESIDENT

The Constitution defines and limits the powers of the presidency. However, in spite of this, the powers of the president have expanded and new powers have been added. Today, the president fills many roles:

■ As **Chief Executive**, the president is in charge of enforcing laws made by Congress. For example, if Congress passes laws restricting immigration, the president and his/her assistants set up the agencies to carry out this law. The president is also in charge of a vast federal government bureaucracy and submits an annual federal budget to Congress. The president can also pardon, parole or reprieve persons convicted of a federal crime.

■ As **Chief of State**, the president is the ceremonial head of the United States government and represents the country.

■ As **Commander-in-Chief**, the president commands our armed forces and controls the use of our nuclear weapons.

■ As **Foreign-Policy Chief**, the president conducts the nation's foreign relations, negotiates treaties with foreign countries, receives foreign ambassadors and diplomats, and appoints our ambassadors to other countries.

■ As **Chief Legislator**, the president can make recommendations to Congress which often become laws. In addition, the president can sign or veto bills passed by Congress.

■ As **Chief of a Political Party**, the president controls one of the two major national political parties: this gives the president influence over members of Congress from the same party.

Although this list is impressive, the president must cooperate with Congress to perform many of these tasks. For example, although the president is the Commander-in-Chief of the armed forces, Congress determines just how much money is spent on them.

FEDERAL COURTS: THE JUDICIAL BRANCH

The Supreme Court has nine members, each chosen by the president and confirmed by the Senate. Federal judges hold office for a life term to protect their decisions from political interference. Despite this fact, the Supreme Court is often influenced by public opinion and may reverse its previous decisions. Below the Supreme Court are other federal courts which try cases involving federal laws or disputes between citizens from different states. When a disagreement arises in the lower courts, it is the Supreme Court's job to review those cases that come to it on appeal. The Supreme Court can also review state court decisions.

In reviewing cases, the Supreme Court not only decides whether the law has been applied correctly by the lower court, but also whether the law itself is within the power of the government according to the Constitution. The power of the Supreme Court to decide whether or not laws are constitutional is known as **judicial review**. The Supreme Court's use of judicial review has created much controversy over the proper role of the Court. Some persons believe that the Court has overstepped its authority in taking on this added responsibility. Others feel that the Court's use of judicial review is necessary to protect citizens against possible constitutional violations by other branches of the government.

KEY ITEMS TO REMEMBER

Congress, Senate, House of Representatives, bill, law, veto, override, Chief Executive, Commander-in-Chief, Electoral College, primaries, National Convention, judicial review

CONSTITUTIONAL PROTECTION OF INDIVIDUAL LIBERTIES

One of the most important aspects of the Constitution is that it protects individuals against possible abuse by government. In fact, several states were so fearful of the potential for abuse that they refused to approve the Constitution until a Bill of Rights, guaranteeing individual freedoms, was added. However, the rights and liberties guaranteed to individuals are not limited to the Bill of Rights. Other parts of the Constitution as well as many Supreme Court decisions have helped to expand and ensure these protections.

PROTECTIONS FOUND IN THE ORIGINAL CONSTITUTION

The Constitution lists certain powers that are specifically denied to both federal and state governments. Both the Congress and the state governments are prohibited from passing laws—called **ex post facto laws**—that would punish someone for doing something that was not a crime when the act was committed. Neither Congress nor the state governments can pass an act—called a **Bill of Attainder**—that would punish an individual without a trial, nor can the federal government keep someone in prison without a trial, except during times of rebellion or riot. States are prohibited from impairing, altering or undoing the terms and obligations established by a proper business contract.

PROTECTIONS FOUND IN THE BILL OF RIGHTS

Some of the most important protections of individual rights were added to the Constitution in the Bill of Rights.

THE BILL OF RIGHTS	
1st Amendment	Guarantees freedoms of religion, speech, and the press, and rights of assembly and petition
2nd Amendment	Guarantees the right to keep and bear arms
3rd Amendment	Prohibits the quartering of soldiers in one's home
4th Amendment	Prohibits unreasonable searches and seizures
5th Amendment	Provides guarantees and prohibitions: • no citizen may be deprived of life, liberty or property without **due process of law** (legal procedures carried out according to established rules, such as a fair trial) • requires **grand jury** indictments (formal charge for comitting a serious crime) • prohibits **double jeopardy** (being tried twice for the same crime) • prohibits **self-incrimination** (no persons can be forced to give evidence against themselves).
6th Amendment	Guarantees that those accused of a crime have the: • right to a speedy trial by jury • right to confront accusers • right to be represented by a lawyer
7th Amendment	Guarantees a jury trial in most civil cases
8th Amendment	Prohibits excessive bail and cruel and unusual punishment
9th Amendment	The listing of some rights in the Constitution does not mean that the people do not enjoy other rights
10th Amendment	Reserves to the states and the people those rights not delegated to the federal government

CIVIL RIGHTS	
13th Amendment	Outlawed slavery
14th Amendment	Gave former slaves the right of citizenship
VOTING RIGHTS	
15th Amendment	Gave freed slaves the right to vote
17th Amendment	Changed election of Senators from selection by state legislatures to direct election by the people
19th Amendment	Gave women the right to vote
23rd Amendment	Gave residents of Washington, D.C. the right to vote for President
24th Amendment	Prohibited poll taxes in federal elections
26th Amendment	Gave persons the right to vote upon reaching the age of 18

KEY ITEMS TO REMEMBER

Ex post facto law, grand jury indictment, "due process" of law, double jeopardy

THE UNWRITTEN CONSTITUTION

The American government today relies on many practices that developed after the Constitution was put into effect. These practices became traditional and customary even though they were never formally incorporated into the Constitution. For this reason they are often referred to as the "unwritten Constitution."

THE CABINET

The Cabinet system began during George Washington's presidency. The Constitution provided the president with the power to appoint heads of executive departments, but did not specify what they should be. Washington selected several people to assist him in areas where he needed help. Every president has continued the tradition of appointing Cabinet members; these appointments must be approved by the Senate.

POLITICAL PARTIES

A political party is a group of people who work together to win elections and to place candidates into public office. Usually the members of a political party share common general goals. When the Constitution was first written, political parties did not exist in America.

■ **The First Political Parties Develop.** During George Washington's administration the first political parties developed out of disagreements between two members of Washington's cabinet, Alexander Hamilton and Thomas Jefferson. Those who supported Hamilton organized themselves into a political party known as the **Federalists**. Those who opposed his ideas rallied around Thomas Jefferson.

Jefferson's followers became known as the **Democratic-Republicans**. The two parties had opposing viewpoints on several key issues:

HAMILTON AND THE FEDERALISTS	JEFFERSON AND THE DEMOCRATIC-REPUBLICANS
1. Favored a broad construction of the Constitution, with a strong central government.	1. Favored a strict construction of the Constitution, with limitations preventing the central government from becoming too powerful.
2. Favored the wealthy, and business interests.	2. Favored independent small farmers and the common man.
3. Believed the chief aim of government was to protect property.	3. Believed the chief aim of government was to protect the people's liberties.

■ **Political Parties Today**. These first political parties were later replaced by the Democratic and Republican Parties. Americans have tended to organize themselves into two major political parties, known as a **two-party system**. American political parties perform many important functions:

- They unite Americans from distant regions and different backgrounds. They also provide a method for elected leaders in state and federal government to organize themselves into effective groups.
- They raise funds and provide support for candidates seeking election. They encourage eligible voters to participate in elections. They also help stimulate interest in elections by identifying issues and bringing them before the public.

JUDICIAL REVIEW

Since Chief Justice John Marshall first established judicial review in the case of *Marbury v. Madison*, this power has grown tremendously. Although not mentioned in the Constitution, judicial review gives the Supreme Court the right to review acts of the president and laws passed by Congress or the states, to determine if they are in keeping with the Constitution.

THE COMMITTEE SYSTEM

Congress does much of its important work in committees—holding hearings, discussing and evaluating proposed bills. Congressional committees help Congress to select the most worthwhile bills from among the thousands that are proposed during each session of Congress.

OUTSIDE INFLUENCES ON GOVERNMENT

Other groups in American society also help to make up a part of the unwritten Constitution.

■ **Pressure Groups and Lobbyists.** Pressure groups are organizations based on common economic interests or beliefs that attempt to "pressure" legislators to pass favorable laws. Often they hire agents, known as lobbyists, to pressure members of Congress and other public officials. Lobbyists try to develop friendships with members of Congress, forward information, testify at Congressional hearings, and campaign on behalf of their clients in the press and on television. Some critics charge that lobbyists hold too much influence over what gets passed in Congress by exposing members of Congress to the temptations of bribery and corruption.

■ **The News Media.** Although the news media are not considered a part of the government, they play a vital role in our political system. Freedom of the press is protected by the First Amendment. The news media provide information to the public and act as a watchdog over government. Investigative reporters are often the first to uncover misdeeds or to expose problems in official policies. Of all the forms of news media, television has become the most influential.

KEY ITEMS TO REMEMBER

Political parties, two-party system, Cabinet, pressure groups, lobbyists

PERSONALITIES OF THE PERIOD

JOHN PETER ZENGER (NEWSPAPER EDITOR)

John Peter Zenger helped establish freedom of the press in America during colonial times. He ran a series of articles in his newspaper accusing the colonial Governor of New York of corruption. For this he was arrested and put on trial in 1735. His lawyer, Andrew Hamilton, successfully defended him, encouraging others to write the truth as they saw it.

BENJAMIN FRANKLIN (STATESMAN)

In addition to helping to write the Declaration of Independence and the United States Constitution, Benjamin Franklin had a distinguished career. As a scientist he conducted experiments with lightning and electricity. He invented a heat-producing stove, bifocal glasses and a lightning rod. As an author he wrote *Poor Richard's Almanack*. He served the nation as an ambassador to France and as its first Postmaster General.

CRISPUS ATTUCKS (PATRIOT)

Crispus Attucks, a former slave, became the first American to sacrifice his life in the struggle for independence. He is regarded as a symbol of opposition to the harsh rule imposed by the British on the colonists. He was killed in 1770 by British soldiers while participating in a demonstration against British tyranny.

ALEXANDER HAMILTON (SECRETARY OF THE TREASURY)

Alexander Hamilton was a leader in the move for independence from England. His arguments in the *Federalist Papers* helped convince many Americans to approve the new Constitution. His financial plan as Secretary of the Treasury was to create a good credit rating for the new government by accepting responsibilities for revolutionary debts, to raise revenue, and to establish the nation's currency on a sound basis.

PHILLIS WHEATLEY (POET)

Phillis Wheatley came to the United States as a slave. She distinguished herself as the first African-American poetess in the United States. Her poems chronicled the American Revolutionary War. Her best known poems were "His Excellency George Washington" and "On The Death of Reverend George Whitefield."

For other personalities of this period, see Thomas Paine and Gilbert Stuart in the "Looking At The Arts" section.

THE CONSTITUTION AT WORK

John Marshall served as Chief Justice of the Supreme Court from 1801 to 1835. During that period, his interpretations of the Constitution and frequent use of judicial review laid the groundwork for establishing the importance of the federal judiciary and the supremacy of the national government over the states. His decisions helped create a sense of unity in the nation by enormously expanding the power of the federal government. Three of his most significant decisions were:

MARBURY v. MADISON (1803)

Background: President Adams, just before leaving office, appointed William Marbury as a justice of the peace. The new Secretary of State, James Madison, refused to deliver Marbury's commission (official papers) making him a justice of the peace. Marbury sued Madison, asking the Supreme Court to require Madison to deliver his commission. Marbury argued that the Judiciary Act of 1789 gave the Supreme Court the power to force Madison to deliver the commission.

Decision/Significance: The Court ruled that part of the Judiciary Act of 1789 was unconstitutional. Since the Constitution is the supreme law of the land, and part of the Act went against what Chief Justice John Marshall stated was in the Constitution, Marshall declared that part of the Act was null and void. He therefore refused to force Madison to deliver the commission. This case established **judicial review** (the right of the Court to declare a law unconstitutional if it goes against the Constitution). The decision greatly strengthened the power of the Supreme Court by making it the final authority in interpreting the Constitution.

McCULLOCH v. MARYLAND (1819)

Background: Congress established the Bank of the United States. One of the bank's branches was located in Maryland. Maryland said Congress had no constitutional right to create a bank, and its legislature passed a law requiring the U.S. bank to pay a tax. McCulloch, an official of the bank, refused to pay this state tax.

Decision/Significance: John Marshall, speaking for the Court, ruled that a state could not tax an agency (the bank) of the national government. Whenever a state law conflicts with a federal law, the federal law must be supreme. Marshall also said the national bank was constitutional. The decision supported the ability of Congress to interpret the Constitution in a loose (broad) manner, so long as it was doing whatever was "necessary and proper" to carry out one of its delegated powers.

GIBBONS v. OGDEN (1824)

Background: Ogden was granted a monopoly by New York State to operate a ferry boat that ran from New York to New Jersey. Gibbons was granted a similar license by the federal government. Ogden sued to stop Gibbons, and Gibbons appealed to the Supreme Court.

Decision/Significance: Marshall, speaking for the Court, ruled that New York State had no right to grant a monopoly to Ogden. Only the federal government, according to the U.S. Constitution, could regulate **interstate commerce** (trade between states). This decision established the right of the federal government to regulate businesses that were engaged in interstate commerce. Eventually, this power has come to include the regulation of railroads, buses, airlines, television broadcasting and most businesses.

SUMMARIZING YOUR UNDERSTANDING

Directions: How well do you understand what you have just read? Test yourself by answering the following questions.

MAJOR TERMS AND CONCEPTS

On separate 3x5 index cards, briefly define each of the following terms and concepts:

Note: Before answering this question, you should review the procedures for recalling key terms and concepts discussed in Chapter 2. To help you get started, one term and one concept have already been done for you.

Declaration of Independence	Bill of Rights	Judicial Review
Articles of Confederation	Due Process of Law	Unwritten Constitution
Constitutional Convention	Separation of Powers	Political Parties
Federalism	Checks and Balances	Cabinet

Articles of Confederation

What is it? A plan of government created by the Second Continental Congress in 1781 to bring all the states into one nation.

Purpose: The major purpose of the Articles of Confederation was to create some form of central government that would unite the newly independent states.

Significance: The Articles of Confederation successfully kept the nation together during the early stages of out nation's history. The Articles proved to be unsuccessful in large part because they gave too much power to the separate, independent states.

Checks and Balances

Definition: A system in which the three branches of government (legislative, executive and judicial) are given powers to check (stop) the other branches so that no one branch can become too powerful.

Example: In the national government of the United States, the president (executive) can veto bills passed by Congress (legislature).

THE STRUGGLE FOR INDEPENDENCE

Differences over certain issues led to the struggle for independence from British rule. Summarize your understanding of this struggle by answering the following questions:

- What factors contributed to the colonists' attempts to become independent of British control?
- How did the Declaration of Independence justify the move of the colonists to become free of British control? Why is the Declaration of Independence of such significance?

THE ARTICLES OF CONFEDERATION

The first government of the United States was created under the Articles of Confederation. Summarize your understanding of the Articles of Confederation by answering the following questions:

- Describe the government that was created under the Articles of Confederation and some of the problems it faced.
- Why are the years from 1781 to 1787 referred to as the "Critical Period"?

THE CONSTITUTIONAL CONVENTION

In 1787, several states met in Philadelphia to revise the Articles of Confederation. This meeting changed the fate of the United States forever. Summarize your understanding of this meeting by answering the following questions:

- Describe each of the major compromises reached at the Constitutional Convention.
- What arguments did opposing groups use in either supporting or opposing the ratification of the Constitution?
- How did the addition of the Bill of Rights aid in the ratification process?

FUNDAMENTAL PRINCIPLES OF THE CONSTITUTION

The Constitution set in motion a government founded on certain basic or fundamental principles. Describe each of the fundamental principles upon which the U.S. Constitution is founded, and explain how each of these principles helps to ensure a fair and decent government for the people of the United States.

STRUCTURE OF THE U. S. GOVERNMENT

Federal power is specifically divided between three separate branches of government—Congress, the President, and the Courts. Summarize your understanding of this separation by answering the following questions:

- Trace the process which a bill has to go through in order to become a law.
- Describe the various roles played by the president.
- How does a person go from being a candidate to becoming president of the United States?
- How does the use of judicial review increase the power of the Supreme Court?

PROTECTION OF INDIVIDUAL LIBERTIES

The Constitution provides many safeguards protecting the rights and liberties of individual citizens. Which protections in the Constitution of 1787, the Bill of Rights and later amendments do you think are the most important? Explain.

THE UNWRITTEN CONSTITUTION

Much of the U.S. Constitution relies on practices and traditions that developed after the Constitution went into effect. What are some of the practices of that have become a part of the "unwritten Constitution"?

PERSONALITIES OF THE PERIOD

People often have an important influence on the political, economic or social life of their times. Summarize your understanding of this statement by completing a separate 3 x 5 index card for each of the following individuals:

JOHN MARSHALL

Where/When: ______

What Marshall did: ______

Impact: ______

THOMAS JEFFERSON

Where/When: ______

What Jefferson did: ______

Impact: ______

PHILLIS WHEATLEY

Where/When: ______

What Wheatley did: ______

Impact: ______

THOMAS PAINE

Where/When: ______

What Paine did: ______

Impact: ______

TESTING YOUR UNDERSTANDING

Directions: Test your understanding of this unit by answering the following questions. Circle the number preceding the word or expression that correctly answers the statement or question. Following the short answer questions, answer either the RCT-type or Regents essay questions.

SKILL BUILDER: INTERPRETING A CARTOON

Base your answer to questions 1 through 3 on the following cartoon and on your knowledge of social studies.

SUPREME COURT DECISIONS
SUPREME COURT DECISIONS

1 Which constitutional concept is probably being referred to in the cartoon?
1 revenue sharing
2 due process rights
3 separation of powers
4 affirmative action

2 Which statement best expresses the main idea of the cartoon?
1 Police work is a physically dangerous occupation.
2 Police officers abuse the rights of the accused.
3 Criminals have too many constitutional protections.
4 The powers of the police are often limited by court decisions.

3 Which decision of the U.S. Supreme Court best accounts for the situation depicted in the cartoon?
1 *Brown v. Board of Education*
2 *McCulloch v. Maryland*
3 *Miranda v. Arizona*
4 *Marbury v. Madison*

SKILL BUILDER: INTERPRETING SPEAKERS

Base your answers to questions 4-6 on the speakers' statements and on your knowledge of social studies.

Speaker A: I was found guilty of a serious crime by a federal court. My conviction was based totally on the testimony of anonymous witnesses whose identities were concealed by the prosecution to "insure their safety."

Speaker B: I was indicted in a state court for the crime of murder. At the conclusion of my trial, the jury found me innocent. The following week, the police found new evidence that could be used against me. As a result, the prosecution wants me to be tried again.

Speaker C: I was arrested on suspicion of arson and was questioned by police for several days and nights. During that time I confessed in order to get some rest. The police never told me I had the right to call a lawyer, but I wasn't able to afford one anyway.

Speaker D: I was arrested for giving a peaceful speech on a street corner. A judge convicted and fined me on the grounds that I was creating a "clear and present danger." I believe that my freedom of speech was violated.

4 The constitutional provision that one shall not be compelled to be a witness against oneself has been violated in the case of Speaker
1 (A)
2 (B)
3 (C)
4 (D)

5 According to the U.S. legal system, Speaker B will most likely be
1 tried a second time in a state court
2 transferred to a higher court because of the nature of the crime
3 tried again by a judge without a jury
4 not be tried, in order to avoid double jeopardy

6 In cases similar to that of Speaker C, the United States Supreme Court has ruled that the accused
1 is guilty if he/she confesses before two witnesses
2 has a right to counsel at the start of questioning by police
3 should not have been arrested solely on suspicion of a crime
4 should have been furnished with a public defender after confessing

SKILL BUILDER: INTERPRETING A PIE CHART

Base your answers to questions 7-9 on the following pie charts and on your knowledge of social studies.

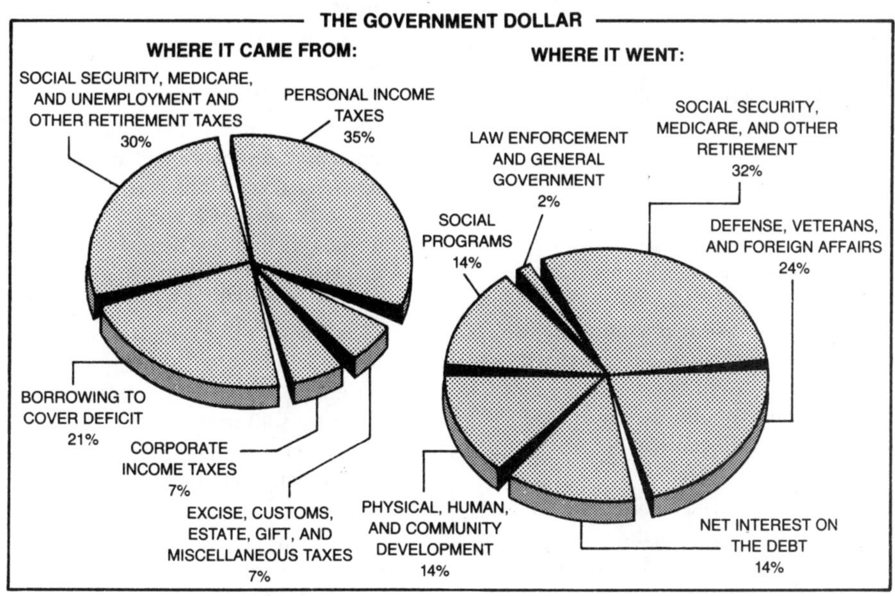
FISCAL YEAR 1992
THE GOVERNMENT DOLLAR
WHERE IT CAME FROM:
WHERE IT WENT:
SOCIAL SECURITY, MEDICARE, AND UNEMPLOYMENT AND OTHER RETIREMENT TAXES 30%
PERSONAL INCOME TAXES 35%
BORROWING TO COVER DEFICIT 21%
CORPORATE INCOME TAXES 7%
EXCISE, CUSTOMS, ESTATE, GIFT, AND MISCELLANEOUS TAXES 7%
LAW ENFORCEMENT AND GENERAL GOVERNMENT 2%
SOCIAL SECURITY, MEDICARE, AND OTHER RETIREMENT 32%
SOCIAL PROGRAMS 14%
DEFENSE, VETERANS, AND FOREIGN AFFAIRS 24%
PHYSICAL, HUMAN, AND COMMUNITY DEVELOPMENT 14%
NET INTEREST ON THE DEBT 14%

7 On which single item does the federal government spend the largest portion of its budget?
1 Medicare
2 national defense
3 social security
4 transportation

8 Which is the largest source of income for the federal government?
1 personal income taxes
2 corporation income taxes
3 excise taxes
4 borrowing

9 Which conclusion about federal government spending is most accurate?
1 education is primarily funded at the national level
2 parks and recreation are a major expense of the federal government
3 programs that take care of people make up the largest federal government expense
4 federal and state spending is the same amount for veterans benefits

10 Which is an essential feature of democratic government?
1 a bicameral legislature
2 free and open elections
3 a written constitution
4 separate branches of government

11 The basic purpose of constitutional checks and balances is to
1 protect states' rights
2 prevent one branch of the federal government from becoming too powerful
3 enable the federal government to run as efficiently as possible
4 provide a written guarantee of the rights of each citizen

12 The Bill of Rights refers to the
1 Declaration of Independence
2 first ten amendments to the Constitution
3 separation of powers in the federal government
4 emancipation of the slaves

13 An advantage of a federal system of government is that it
1 ensures speedy decisions
2 permits a republican form of government
3 permits both national and local approaches to problems
4 is the least costly form of government

14 Which document was written first?
1 the U.S. Constitution
2 the Articles of Confederation
3 the Declaration of Independence
4 the Bill of Rights

15 The purpose of most of the amendments to the United States Constitution has been to
1 guarantee individual civil and political rights
2 ensure the proper functioning of the checks and balances system
3 strengthen the authority of state governments
4 expand the power of the presidency

16 Which is part of the "unwritten constitution"?
1 political parties
2 electoral college
3 delegated powers
4 amending process

17 The primary purpose of the Declaration of Independence was to
1 establish the basic law of the land in the United States
2 justify the revolt of the American colonists against Great Britain
3 provide a clear plan for a meaningful and effective political system
4 guarantee human rights for all Americans

18 A major criticism directed against the Articles of Confederation was that too little power was given to
1 military leaders
2 the electoral college
3 the national government
4 the state governments

19 The major reason for a nation having a written constitution is to
1 fulfill the requirements of international law
2 prevent changes in the structure of government
3 define the government's powers and processes
4 encourage recognition of a government by other nations

20 The decision of the Supreme Court in *Marbury v. Madison* is important because it
1 defined the meaning of the Bill of Rights
2 established the power of the Court to declare laws unconstitutional
3 freed the slaves in the South
4 overturned the commerce clause of the U.S. Constitution

21 At the Constitutional Convention of 1787, the Great Compromise was concerned mainly with the issue of
1 representation in Congress
2 the legalization of slavery
3 the powers of the executive
4 the control of interstate commerce

22 Which feature of government was developed most fully during the colonial era?
1 separation of church and state
2 universal suffrage
3 an independent court system
4 representative assemblies

23 The idea that the U.S. Constitution establishes a central government of limited powers is best supported by the Constitutional provision that
1 powers not delegated to the U.S. shall be reserved to the states
2 Congress shall make all laws that are "necessary and proper" to its functions
3 the president shall act as commander in chief
4 the Supreme Court shall have both original and appellate jurisdiction

24 The statement in the U.S. Constitution that the president "shall nominate, by and with the advice and consent of the Senate, judges of the Supreme Court" illustrates which governmental principle?
1 judicial review
2 executive privilege
3 checks and balances
4 minority rights

25 Which group usually exercises the most control in the federal law-making process?
1 the National Security Council
2 congressional committees
3 the president's Cabinet
4 federal boards and commissions

26 The section of the U.S. Constitution that grants Congress the power to "make all laws which shall be necessary and proper for carrying into execution the foregoing powers" has come to be known as the
1 Great Compromise
2 supremacy clause
3 due process provision
4 elastic clause

27 Which is generally considered the major shortcoming of the electoral college system for selecting a president of the United States?
1 Electoral votes are evenly distributed among the states.
2 A candidate can win the popular vote but lose the presidency.
3 Too much time passes between the November election and the counting of electoral votes.
4 Candidates tend to ignore the states with young voters.

28 In the United States, the electoral college system influences presidential candidates to
1 make personal appearances in every state
2 spend more time campaigning in states with large populations
3 state their platforms in very specific terms
4 seek endorsements from state governors

29 Which action could legally override the ruling of the U.S. Supreme Court that a woman has a constitutional right to an abortion in the first three months of pregnancy?
1 passage of a law restricting abortion in a particular state
2 presidential veto
3 passage of congressional legislation
4 addition of an amendment to the United States Constitution

30 Which concept from the U.S. Constitution provides the basis for the variety of laws that govern teenage driving in different parts of the U.S.?
1 checks and balances
2 judicial review
3 reserved power
4 executive privilege

31 "*In framing a government which is to be administered by men over men, the great difficulty lies in this: you must first enable the government to control the governed; and next; oblige it to control itself.*"

—James Madison

Which concept of government was designed to help deal with the difficulty referred to in the last part of the quotation?
1 a unicameral legislature
2 a centralized executive branch
3 a cabinet system
4 a system of checks and balances

32 Which situation most clearly illustrates the constitutional principle of checks and balances?
1 Congress listens to the president's State of the Union Address.
2 A congressional committee kills a bill by majority vote.
3 The House of Representatives votes to impeach a federal judge.
4 A congressional committee revises the language of a bill.

Base your answers to questions 33 through 35 on the following quotation from a hypothetical Supreme Court decision and on your knowledge of social studies.

"The privilege to conduct business in any manner that one pleases is not guaranteed by the Constitution. The right to engage in certain businesses may be subject to various conditions. Laws regulating businesses have been found to be valid. We find no justification to reject the New York State law under question."

33 Which concept is best illustrated by the above passage?
1 residual powers
2 legislative consent
3 judicial review
4 executive order

34 Which concept would probably be rejected by the author of this passage?
1 laissez-faire
2 welfare
3 competition
4 profit motive

35 Which group would most likely have opposed this decision?
1 manufacturers
2 farmers
3 labor leaders
4 consumers

RCT-TYPE ESSAYS

Note: Before answering either the RCT or Regents essays found on this and the following pages, it would be helpful for you to review the procedures discussed in Chapter 4 on how to answer essay questions.

1 The principles of the U.S. Constitution protect our freedom.

Part A

Principles

Federalism	Flexibility
Checks and Balances	Popular Sovereignty
Separation of Powers	Limited Government

Select *one* principle: ______________________

Define the principle: ______________________

State *one* way in which the principle helps protect our freedom. ______________________

Select *another* principle: ______________________

Define the principle: ______________________

State *one* way in which the principle helps protect our freedom. ______________________

Part B

In your Part B answer, you should use information you gave in Part A. However, you may also include different or additional information in your Part B answer.

Write an essay describing how the principles of the U.S. Constitution help to protect our freedom.

2 The writers of the U.S. Constitution separated the major functions of government among three branches— the legislative, executive and judicial branches.

Part A

State the function (job) of each branch of government and name one power which that branch of government has over another branch.

Legislative function: ______________________

One power it has over another branch: ______________________

Executive function: ______________________________

One power it has over another branch: ______________________________

Judicial function: ______________________________

One power it has over another branch: ______________________________

Part B

In your Part B answer, you should use information you gave in Part A. However, you may also include different or additional information in your Part B answer.

Write an essay discussing how the writers of the U.S. Constitution separated the major function of government among three branches.

3 **Different individuals and groups have a role in how laws are made in the United States government.**

Individuals/Groups

The President
Congressional Committees
Political Parties
Special Interest Groups
Individual Citizens

Part A

Select *one* individual or group: ______________________________

State *one* way in which that individual or group helps make the laws. ______________________________

Select *another* individual or group: ______________________________

State *one* way in which that individual or group helps make the laws. ______________________________

Part B

In your Part B answer, you should use information you gave in Part A. However, you may also include different or additional information in your Part B answer.

Write an essay explaining how different individuals and groups have a role in making laws in the United States government.

REGENTS-TYPE ESSAYS

1 Government under the Articles of Confederation could not deal effectively with many problems that arose during the 1780s. Some of these problems involved:

Problem Areas

Currency	Commerce
National security	Domestic order
National leadership	Flexibility

Choose *three* of these problem areas. For *each* one chosen:

- Discuss why government under the Articles was ineffective in dealing with a problem in that area
- Show how the United States Constitution attempted to solve the problem

2 Since the U. S. Constitution was adopted, it has been described in many ways. Some of these descriptions include:

- The Constitution is essentially an economic document.
- The Constitution is a "bundle of compromises."
- The Constitution has both divided and limited governmental powers.
- The strength of the Constitution rests in its flexibility
- The Constitution combines European tradition with American colonial experiences.

Choose *three* of the generalizations. For *each* one chosen, discuss the extent to which the generalization is accurate. (Use *two* examples to support your position.)

3 The Constitution provides both basic principles of government and the means for adapting these principles to changing times.

Principles

Federalism	Popular Sovereignty
Checks and Balances	Separation of Powers
Limited Government	

a Choose *two* of the governmental principles listed, and for *each* one selected:

- define the principle
- discuss how it operates in the United States

b The Constitution provides for meeting the needs of changing times through such means as:

- The amending process
- The elastic clause (implied powers)
- Supreme Court decisions

Choose *two* of these means. For *each* one chosen, discuss a specific example of how this means was used to help the United States respond to social needs during a particular period in American history.

PERFORMANCE-BASED TASKS

In this activity, you will act as a delegate to a future Constitutional Convention held to revise the U.S. Constitution.

Setting: Some people have suggested that the original constitution, with its system of a President, a Congress and a Supreme Court, is no longer appropriate for the United States as it approaches the 21st century. Some have even suggested that during the year 2000, a convention ought to be held to revise the U.S. Constitution.

General Directions: Three excerpts from Articles I, II, and III of the Constitution appear below. In *italics* you will find **one** possible revision for each article:

Article I

Section 1. All legislative Powers herein granted shall be vested in a Congress of the United States, which shall consist of a Senate and House of Representatives.

Section 2. The House of Representatives shall be chosen every second year by the people of the several States ...

No person shall be a Representative who shall not have attained to the age of twenty-five years, and been seven years a citizen of the United States, and who shall not, when elected, be an inhabitant of that state in which he shall be chosen.

Any Person elected as a Representative shall serve no more than six terms, or a maximum of twelve years of service.

Article II

Section 1. The executive power shall be vested in a President of the United States of America. He shall hold office during the term of four years, and, together with the Vice-President, chosen for the same term, be elected, as follows:

The person having the greatest number of popular votes among all the eligible candidates shall be declared the President.

Article III

Section 1. The judicial power of the United States, shall be vested in one Supreme Court ...
Justices of the Supreme Court shall be appointed for a term of no more than fourteen years.

Your Task: In preparation for the Constitutional Convention, you are to select and consider one of the proposed changes in the U.S. Constitution:

- Consult a copy of the present U.S. Constitution. Determine how the italicized suggested revisions would change the original U.S. Constitution.
- Write a 300-word position paper in which you argue for or against one of the revisions.
- Prepare to make your arguments orally in a two minute speech before your fellow delegates attending the Constitutional Convention (your class).

NOTES FOR THE CONSTITUTIONAL CONVENTION

[1] How revision would change the original U.S. Constitution:

____

____

____

[2] Arguments to be used to support or oppose the proposed change:

____

____

____

____

____

____

____

____

____

A KEY TO UNDERSTANDING THE CONSTITUTION: LOOKING AT THE ENDURING ISSUES

Many questions on the Regents and RCT examination test your understanding of specific Constitutional issues. In this section we take a general look at these issues.

ENDURING CONSTITUTIONAL ISSUES

Constitutional issues are created when different groups disagree about the proper use of government power. In attempting to resolve these problems, the parties that disagree often turn to the Constitution to find an answer. Such disagreements almost always concern the:

- power of particular groups in government
- amount of power that government should have over society
- relations among the various levels and branches of government

There have been a number of Constitutional issues that have continually re-emerged in different forms throughout our history. **Thirteen Enduring Issues** were identified by a group of historians and political scientists in 1987 in honor of the 200th anniversary of the U.S. Constitution. You should become familiar with these issues and keep them in mind as you review other parts of this book. What follows is a list of the **Thirteen Enduring Issues**.

ENDURING ISSUE	QUESTIONS RAISED
1. NATIONAL POWER—LIMITS AND POTENTIALS	How much power should our government have over our society?
2. FEDERALISM—THE BALANCE BETWEEN NATION AND STATE	What powers should be given to the national government and what powers should be given to the state governments?

ENDURING ISSUE	QUESTIONS RAISED
3. THE JUDICIARY—INTERPRETER OF THE CONSTITUTION OR SHAPER OF PUBLIC POLICY	How much power should the Supreme Court have in defining and protecting the rights of citizens?
4. CIVIL LIBERTIES—THE BALANCE BETWEEN GOVERNMENT AND THE INDIVIDUAL	What are our civil liberties and what limits can be placed upon them?
5. RIGHTS OF THE ACCUSED AND PROTECTION OF THE COMMUNITY	How can we have rights protecting accused persons, who may be innocent, and still safeguard society by discouraging crime?
6. EQUALITY—ITS DEFINITION AS A CONSTITUTIONAL VALUE	How far should government go in treating all citizens equally, and in making them equal?
7. THE RIGHTS OF WOMEN UNDER THE CONSTITUTION	Should women enjoy equal rights with men?
8. THE RIGHTS OF ETHNIC AND RACIAL GROUPS	Should all ethnic and racial groups enjoy the same rights?
9. PRESIDENTIAL POWER IN WARTIME AND FOREIGN AFFAIRS	How much power over foreign affairs should the president be given in wartime?
10. SEPARATION OF POWERS AND THE CAPACITY TO GOVERN	How much power should each branch of our federal government have?
11. AVENUES OF REPRESENTATION	How representative is our national government?
12. PROPERTY RIGHTS AND ECONOMIC POLICY	How far can government go in infringing on individual property rights in order to promote the general prosperity?
13. CONSTITUTIONAL CHANGE AND FLEXIBILITY	Has the Constitution, in adapting to new situations and changing times, been stretched out of shape?

As you read through the chapters of this book, you will find these **Thirteen Enduring Issues** constantly reappearing. You will also discover that certain of these issues were especially dominant in specific time periods. For example, **Federalism—The Balance Between Nation and State** was particularly tested in the **Civil War**.

CHAPTER 6

THE CONSTITUTION TESTED

The Civil War (1861-1865) preserved the Union, but at a terrible cost: hundreds of thousands were killed or injured, and the South lay in ruins. The war changed the nation forever. The power of the national government was enormously increased. Slavery was abolished, but the former slaves had a long road to travel before achieving equality. During the Reconstruction period following the war, the nation devoted its energies to rebuilding the South and resolving major political, economic and social problems.

— TIMELINE OF KEY EVENTS —

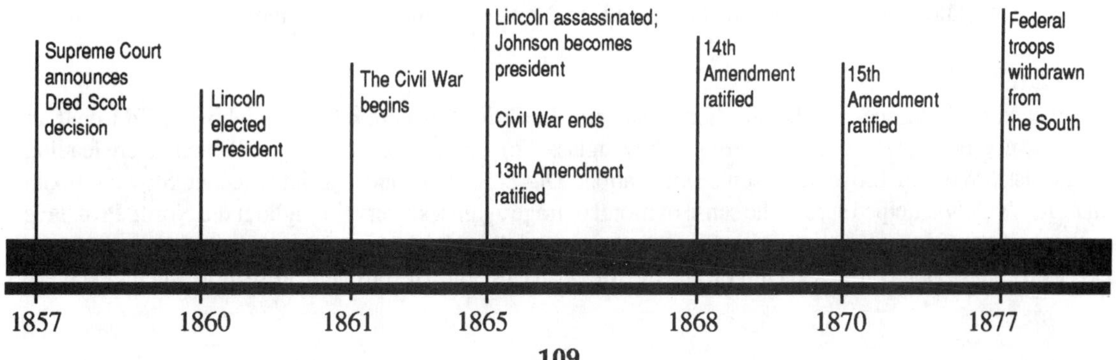

Supreme Court announces Dred Scott decision
Lincoln elected President
The Civil War begins
Lincoln assassinated; Johnson becomes president
Civil War ends
13th Amendment ratified
14th Amendment ratified
15th Amendment ratified
Federal troops withdrawn from the South
1857
1860
1861
1865
1868
1870
1877

THE CIVIL WAR: 1861-1865

The Civil War was the most divisive conflict in U. S. history. More Americans died in this war than in any other. The wounds created by the war took the nation more than a century to heal.

CAUSES OF THE CIVIL WAR

A complex event like the outbreak of the Civil War had many causes:

SECTIONALISM

In the early 19th century, as the United States grew in size and became more economically advanced, each region of the country developed its own special characteristics.

THE NORTHEAST	THE SOUTH	THE NORTHWEST
This section became a center of manufacturing, shipping, fishing and small farms. The Northeast witnessed the first growth of the new class of factory workers. Factories and cities were beginning to dramatically change lifestyles.	The dominant institution was slavery. Although most Southerners did not own slaves, much of the South's economy was based on profits obtained through the use of slave labor on large plantations, growing export crops such as cotton.	This section—now Wisconsin, Illinois, Indiana, Michigan, and Ohio—became the breadbasket of the nation. Its grain was shipped by river and canal to the Northeast and South. Small farmers predominated in this area.

These economic and social differences led to the rise of **sectionalism** as early as the 1820s. Sectionalism refers to the greater loyalty that many Americans felt towards their section or region than they did to the country as a whole. Each sectional group wanted the federal government to follow those policies that were most favorable to their own region. The economic and social differences between the three main regions of the United States (the Northeast, the South and the Northwest) made a clash inevitable.

SLAVERY

The most explosive issue was the question of slavery. **Abolitionists** were reformers who wanted to put an end to slavery. Former slaves such as Frederick Douglass, Sojourner Truth and Harriet Tubman were leading abolitionists. William Lloyd Garrison's publication, *The Liberator*, and Harriet Beecher Stowe's book, *Uncle Tom's Cabin*, helped spread the sense of moral outrage against slavery throughout the North. Pro-slave Southerners argued that Southern slaves were better treated than Northern factory workers. In the 1840s the U. S. won control of territories in Oregon and the Mexican Cession. The problem arose as to whether slavery should be established in the new territories. Southerners felt that only by extending slavery could they preserve the balance between slave states and free states in the United States Senate. Northerners were shocked at the possibility of the further expansion of slavery.

THE BREAKDOWN OF COMPROMISE

Despite sectional differences, the nation managed to preserve its fragile unity from the 1820s through the 1850s by a series of skillful compromises.

- **Missouri Compromise of 1820**. In the Missouri Compromise, Missouri was admitted as a slave state and Maine was admitted as a free state. Congress also decided that slavery would not be allowed in the lands of the Louisiana Purchase north of a certain line.

- **Compromise of 1850**. In the Compromise of 1850, California was admitted as a free state, but a new and harsher **Fugitive Slave Law** was imposed, requiring states in the North to cooperate in returning runaway slaves. The system of **popular sovereignty** was applied to the other territories taken from Mexico. Under popular sovereignty, settlers in the new territories could decide for themselves whether they wanted to have slavery or not.

In the 1850s, certain events tore apart these earlier compromises. This breakdown of compromise made a conflict between the North and South almost inevitable.

- **Kansas-Nebraska Act (1854)**. In this act Congress repealed the Missouri Compromise by introducing the principle of popular sovereignty in the Kansas and Nebraska Territories, where slavery had been previously prohibited. In Kansas, pro-slavery and anti-slavery forces clashed when each tried to determine the outcome of popular sovereignty by bringing in their own supporters. Killing and bloodshed took place on both sides. Federal troops were needed to restore order.

- **Dred Scott Decision (1857)**. In the Dred Scott decision, the Supreme Court ruled that slaves were not citizens and could not sue in the federal courts. The Court further stated that the prohibition of slavery in the Missouri Compromise had been unconstitutional, since slaves were property and Congress did not have the right to take away property. Northerners were angered by this decision, reached by a majority of Southern justices.

- **John Brown's Raid (1859)**. Brown, a Northern abolitionist, drew up secret plans for launching a slave revolt. He took over a federal arsenal in Virginia, but his tiny force was soon captured. Brown was hanged, but his attempt to stir the slaves to revolt created a sense of alarm among Southerners.

DIFFERENCES IN CONSTITUTIONAL INTERPRETATION

An important difference in interpreting the Constitution led to the secession of the Southern states. Southerners believed in **states' rights**, pointing out that the states were the ones that had created the federal government, and that each state possessed the power to leave the Union if it desired. Northerners, on the other hand, argued that the Constitution was the work of the American people as a whole, and states did not have the right to leave the Union whenever they pleased.

THE ELECTION OF LINCOLN

The election of the Republican candidate **Abraham Lincoln** in 1860 led most of the Southern slave-holding states to **secede** (break away) from the U.S. Lincoln was the candidate of the new Republican Party, which opposed the spread of slavery to new territories. Although Lincoln said he would not challenge the continuation of slavery in the South, distrust between Southerners and Northerners was so great that the Southern states seceded immediately after his election. The Southern states organized themselves into the **Confederate States of America**, and drew up their own Constitution. Lincoln was willing to take all steps necessary to preserve the unity of the United States.

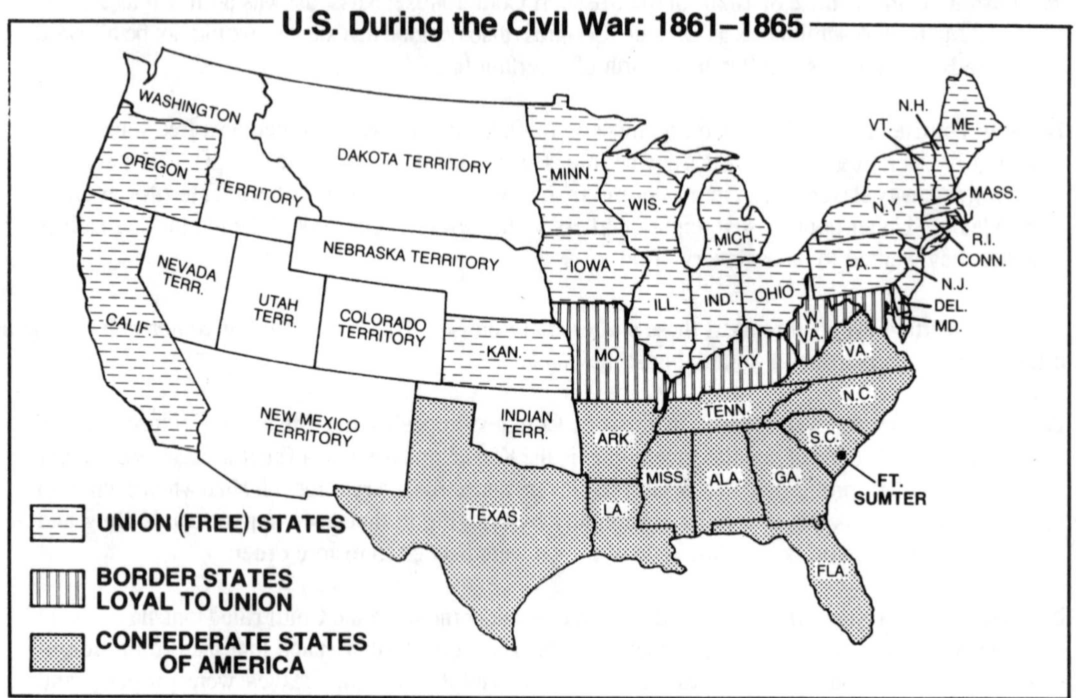
U.S. During the Civil War: 1861–1865
WASHINGTON
OREGON
TERRITORY
DAKOTA TERRITORY
MINN.
WIS.
MICH.
N.H.
VT.
ME.
MASS.
N.Y.
R.I.
CONN.
PA.
N.J.
DEL.
MD.
NEBRASKA TERRITORY
IOWA
NEVADA TERR.
UTAH TERR.
COLORADO TERRITORY
CALIF.
KAN.
MO.
ILL.
IND.
OHIO
W. VA.
VA.
KY.
N.C.
TENN.
NEW MEXICO TERRITORY
INDIAN TERR.
ARK.
S.C.
MISS.
ALA.
GA.
FT. SUMTER
TEXAS
LA.
FLA.
UNION (FREE) STATES
BORDER STATES LOYAL TO UNION
CONFEDERATE STATES OF AMERICA

THE FIGHTING

Actual combat began in 1861, when Fort Sumter, a federal fort in South Carolina, was attacked by Confederate forces. From the beginning, the North had immense advantages: a larger population, more money, more railroads, more manufacturing facilities, and greater naval power. The South was almost completely dependent on imports for manufactured goods, and the North quickly imposed a naval blockade on the South. In spite of all these advantages, it still took the Northern forces four years to defeat the Confederacy.

STEPS TOWARD FREEDOM

One of the most important events of the Civil War was the issuing of the **Emancipation Proclamation** in 1862. Lincoln announced that all slaves in states still in rebellion on January 1, 1863 would be freed. Lincoln had several motives for issuing this Proclamation:

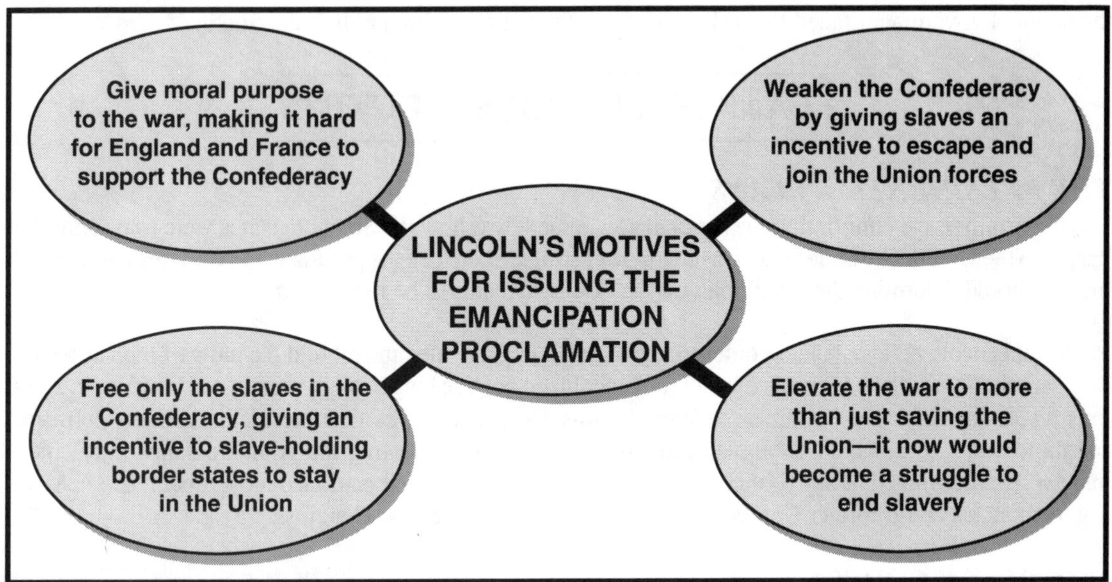
Give moral purpose to the war, making it hard for England and France to support the Confederacy
Weaken the Confederacy by giving slaves an incentive to escape and join the Union forces
LINCOLN'S MOTIVES FOR ISSUING THE EMANCIPATION PROCLAMATION
Free only the slaves in the Confederacy, giving an incentive to slave-holding border states to stay in the Union
Elevate the war to more than just saving the Union—it now would become a struggle to end slavery

Since it was unclear whether Lincoln had the Constitutional power to emancipate the slaves, Congress proposed the **Thirteenth Amendment**; when it was ratified in early 1865, it abolished slavery throughout the United States.

KEY ITEMS TO REMEMBER

Sectionalism, Civil War, abolitionists, *Uncle Tom's Cabin*, Missouri Compromise, Kansas-Nebraska Act, Dred Scott decision, states' rights, Emancipation Proclamation, Thirteenth Amendment

THE RECONSTRUCTION ERA: 1865-1877

The period immediately following the Civil War is known as the **Reconstruction Era**. It was a time in which the national government faced the task of unifying the nation and rebuilding the South.

PLANS FOR RECONSTRUCTION

THE PRESIDENTIAL PLANS

The first major issue confronting the national government was how the Southern states were to be admitted back into the Union. The issue created a bitter power struggle between the president and Congress over which branch should determine the conditions for the Southern states to be readmitted.

President Lincoln believed that in order to regain the South's loyalty and rebuild the unity of the nation, the Southern States needed to be treated leniently. Lincoln did not live long enough to carry out his plan; in 1865, only a few days after the South surrendered, he was assassinated. The new president, **Andrew Johnson**, sought to continue essentially the plan proposed by Lincoln for treating the Southern states in a lenient manner. He recognized newly formed Southern state governments and pardoned most rebel leaders. Many Southern states chose former Confederate leaders for seats in the new Congress.

THE BLACK CODES

Southern states were slow to extend the right to vote to the freedmen (former slaves). At the same time they passed "**Black Codes**," state laws enacted to regulate the lives of the former slaves in the South. The aim of the Black Codes was to preserve the structure of Southern society despite the abolition of slavery. For example:

- The Black Codes forbade freedmen to hold public office, to travel freely or to serve on juries.
- Freedmen were required to show that they had work for the current year, in effect forcing the former slaves to stay on plantations as workers.
- Any freedman found to be without a job could be fined and jailed.

THE CONGRESSIONAL PLAN

Public opinion in the North was outraged at the Black Codes and the election to Congress of southern rebel leaders. Although Johnson was willing to recognize the new Southern governments, Congress refused. Congress suspected Johnson, a Tennesseean, of being too sympathetic to the South. The **Radical Republicans**, a group of Congressmen, wanted blacks to be granted full political equality. They also sought to enlarge the **Freedmen's Bureau**, which had been established by Congress to help the former slaves adjust to freedom. Their plan called for passing a **Civil Rights Bill** and restoring military rule to the South.

To ensure that the Civil Rights Act would not be held unconstitutional by the Supreme Court, the Radical Republicans rewrote the act as the **Fourteenth Amendment.** This amendment has become especially important: besides granting U.S. citizenship to the former slaves, it prohibited state governments from denying any American the "rights and privileges" of citizens, including a fair trial and equal protection of the laws. Before being re-admitted into the Union, the Southern states were forced to ratify the amendment.

THE POLITICS OF RECONSTRUCTION

The Reconstruction Era provided a classic example of the "enduring issue" of how much power each branch of the federal government should have. President Johnson opposed Congressional Reconstruction, believing that the president should determine the conditions for the return of the Southern states. The members of Congress believed that Congress alone had the constitutional power to admit states back into the Union.

THE ATTEMPTED IMPEACHMENT OF PRESIDENT JOHNSON

To enforce its program, Congress also passed the **Tenure of Office Act**, limiting the president's power to dismiss his own Cabinet members. Johnson refused to obey this law, believing it was unconstitutional. When Johnson dismissed his Secretary of War, Congressional leaders attempted to remove Johnson from office through the process of **impeachment**. Johnson was impeached by the House of Representatives, but in the Senate the Radical Republicans fell one vote short of removing Johnson from the presidency.

THE GRANT PRESIDENCY

Shortly after the unsuccessful attempt to remove President Johnson from office, **Ulysses S. Grant** (1869-1877), the Radical Republican candidate, was elected president. His administration was characterized by weak presidential leadership and widespread political corruption on the national and local levels.

THE RECONSTRUCTION GOVERNMENTS

The Fourteenth Amendment had made freedmen citizens and excluded Confederate leaders from government. The **Fifteenth Amendment** gave the freedmen the right to vote. As a result of these two amendments, a new political leadership temporarily emerged in the South. It consisted of:

- **Carpetbaggers**—people from the North who went South either to help the freedmen with new business opportunities or for a chance to exploit the South.
- **Scalawags**—Southern whites who had opposed the Confederacy.
- **Freedmen**—who actively participated in running the Southern governments. During Reconstruction, over 600 African Americans served as state legislators and 16 were in Congress.

ACCOMPLISHMENTS

Among the greatest accomplishments of the Reconstruction governments were the creation of new public schools, laws banning racial discrimination, and the rebuilding of public roads, buildings and railroads. On the other hand, many of the Reconstruction governments were guilty of corruption and extravagance. White Southerners resented northern interference and did not recognize their former slaves as social equals. Without changing white Southern attitudes, Reconstruction policies were ultimately doomed to failure.

THE END OF RECONSTRUCTION

By the time Grant finished his second term in office, Reconstruction had come to an end. In 1877, the last remaining Northern troops were withdrawn from the South and home rule was restored to local state governments. Former Confederate leaders could now vote, and state legislatures quickly moved to bar African Americans from voting or participating in the political process. Most white Southerners hated the treatment they had received at the hands of the Radical Republicans in Congress. As a result, the South gave its political support almost entirely to the Democratic Party for many decades to come. In nearly every election, until recently, the South voted for Democratic candidates, becoming known as the "**Solid South**."

KEY ITEMS TO REMEMBER

Reconstruction, Black Codes, Freedmen's Bureau, carpetbaggers, "Solid South"

THE AFTERMATH OF RECONSTRUCTION

With the end of slavery and the widespread destruction of the Civil War, the economy of the South was changed permanently. Without slave labor, the old plantation system could not be restored.

THE ECONOMIC EFFECTS: THE NEW SOUTH

SHARE-CROPPING AND TENANT FARMING

For the most part, plantation owners entered into share-cropping arrangements with their former slaves. The landowner provided a cabin, a mule, tools, and a plot of land to the sharecropper. The sharecropper, in turn, gave a large share of his crop to the landowner. Some freedmen became tenant farmers; they rented land from the landowner but provided their own tools and provisions. Very few freedmen ever became landowners themselves.

AGRICULTURAL PROGRESS AND INDUSTRIAL GROWTH

After the war, new farming methods increased the yield per acre. New crops like fruits and vegetables were added to old staples like cotton, tobacco, rice and sugar. With heavy financial backing from the North, railroads, cotton mills, and steel furnaces were built. With the expansion of industry, people began moving from farms into Southern cities looking for jobs, which led to the development of several large cities.

THE SOCIAL EFFECTS: THE SEGREGATED SOUTH

The social system that followed the period of Reconstruction in the South was one of racial segregation and white supremacy, depriving African Americans of their basic political and civil rights.

FAILURE TO ACHIEVE EQUALITY

There were several reasons why Reconstruction failed to achieve complete equality for African Americans:

- **Economic Dependence of African Americans.** The failure to give freedmen their own land after the war meant that they remained dependent on their former masters. Most of the freedmen were uneducated, and this weakened their ability to compete with whites on equal terms. As a result, to protect their economic livelihoods, African Americans were often afraid to assert their political rights.

- **White Terrorism.** Secret societies like the **Ku Klux Klan** terrorized Southern blacks with threats and acts of violence against those who attempted to assert their full political and social rights. This frightened many African Americans into submission.

- **Loss of Northern Interest.** After the Civil War, Northerners were anxious to assert their supremacy over the South, but eventually they began to lose interest. Reformers in the North turned their attention away from the South and towards correcting the abuses of "big business" instead.

AFRICAN AMERICANS LOSE THE RIGHT TO VOTE

In the ten years following Reconstruction, Southern state governments systematically stripped African Americans of their rights. Southern legislators passed a series of laws in the 1890s designed to prevent them from voting.

- **Literacy Tests** were political devices used to determine if a person could read and write. Many freedmen, lacking a formal education, were unable to pass this test.

- **Poll Taxes** were special registration fees for voting. They were economically burdensome to poor African Americans, who could not afford to pay them.

- **"Grandfather Clauses"** were laws that allowed people who had been qualified to vote in 1867 to vote without passing a literacy test or paying a poll tax. This exempted "poor whites" from these new requirements but not poor African Americans, since few of them had been qualified to vote in 1867.

THE SYSTEM OF RACIAL SEGREGATION: JIM CROW LAWS

Southern legislatures in the 1880s and onwards passed laws segregating (or separating) blacks from whites. These laws were known as "Jim Crow" laws. In 1896, the Supreme Court upheld racial segregation in ***Plessy v. Ferguson***, resulting in whites and African Americans attending different schools, riding in separate railway cars, eating in different restaurants, using different public toilets and water fountains, and bathing on different public beaches. The Jim Crow laws can be compared to recent practices of apartheid in South Africa, where the government officially sponsored segregation.

AFRICAN AMERICAN LEADERS SPEAK OUT

African Americans responded to these unfair conditions in a variety of ways. They developed strong community and church ties and evolved their own unique, robust culture. In addition, a small trickle of African Americans began to move north. After 1910, this trickle became a flood: almost 2 million African Americans migrated to northern cities from 1910 to 1930. Finally, some African American leaders spoke out against the new forms of oppression. Two early African-American leaders who offered alternative responses to the dilemmas facing black Americans were Booker T. Washington and W.E.B. DuBois.

BOOKER T. WASHINGTON

Washington, who wrote *Up From Slavery*, came from a family of slaves. In 1881 he founded the Tuskegee Institute in Alabama. He believed that for the moment blacks should concentrate on achieving economic independence before seeking full social equality. Washington believed that economic prosperity could best be achieved by vocational training (practical, job-related education).

W. E. B. du BOIS

Unlike Washington, Du Bois believed that African Americans should work for full social equality immediately and not be content with an inferior social and economic status. In 1909, Du Bois helped form the **N.A.A.C.P.** (National Association for the Advancement of Colored People). This organization believed in working through the courts to win rights for African Americans and to bring an end to racial injustice. Du Bois was the director of the N.A.A.C.P. for twenty years and edited its official publication, *The Crisis*.

KEY ITEMS TO REMEMBER

Share-cropping, Ku Klux Klan, literacy tests, "Grandfather Clauses," "Jim Crow" laws, segregation, N.A.A.C.P.

PERSONALITIES OF THE PERIOD

HENRY DAVID THOREAU (ESSAYIST)

Thoreau believed it was his duty to disobey unjust laws. In protest against the nation's war with Mexico, he refused to pay his taxes, and was sent to jail. Thoreau felt people should follow their conscience when it conflicted with government policies. His ideas on civil disobedience later influenced Martin Luther King, Jr. and the Civil Rights Movement in the struggle to achieve equal rights for African Americans.

HARRIET TUBMAN (ABOLITIONIST)

Harriet Tubman, a former slave, was a leading "conductor" of the **Underground Rail-road.** This was a network of citizens who hid fugitive slaves on their dangerous trip north to freedom. Tubman is personally credited with helping over 300 slaves escape.

FREDERICK DOUGLASS (ABOLITIONIST)

Frederick Douglass was a well-known abolitionist; he published books and articles describing the horrors of slavery. Like Tubman, Douglass was born a slave. A self-educated man, he was a gifted speaker who traveled throughout the United States and England, inspiring crowds with anti-slavery speeches.

THADDEUS STEVENS AND CHARLES SUMNER (CONGRESSMEN)

Thaddeus Stevens and Charles Sumner were the chief leaders of the Radical Republicans in Congress. It was largely through their efforts that the Congressional Reconstruction Plan was adopted. Stevens and Sumner led the movement for treating the ex-Confederate states as "conquered provinces." They also wanted to promote complete equality for Southern blacks. Stevens proposed that each freedman be given his own land.

GEORGE WASHINGTON CARVER (BOTANIST)

Carver was an African-American scientist who trained at the Tuskegee Institute. His discoveries helped revolutionize Southern agriculture through scientific farming. Farmers learned to rotate their crops to prevent soil erosion. Carver taught them to plant peanuts, sweet potatoes, clover and other crops to replenish nitrates in the soil. He is credited with developing hundreds of new products and helping to end the South's dependence on cotton.

For other personalities of this period, see Harriet Beecher Stowe, Matthew Brady and Walt Whitman in the "Looking at the Arts" section.

THE CONSTITUTION AT WORK

KEY AMENDMENTS

During this period three amendments, often referred to as the **Civil War Amendments**, were added to the Constitution.

THIRTEENTH AMENDMENT (1865)
Slavery was prohibited.

FOURTEENTH AMENDMENT (1868)
This amendment gave the former slaves U.S. citizenship. It also prevented state governments from taking away a person's life, liberty or property without "due process" of law. In effect, states were required to follow a set of procedures established by the Constitution before any action could be taken to punish a person accused of violating the law. States were also required to give all their citizens the "equal protection of the laws."

FIFTEENTH AMENDMENT (1870)
This amendment guaranteed that the right to vote could not be denied because of race, color or having previously been a slave.

KEY LEGISLATION

"JIM CROW" LAWS (1881-1890s)
Tennessee passed the first "Jim Crow" law in 1881, which required that blacks and whites ride in separate railroad cars. Other states soon passed similar laws extending racial segregation to streetcars, railroad stations, restaurants, parks, playgrounds and beaches. The Supreme Court, in *Plessy v. Ferguson*, upheld the constitutionality of "separate but equal" facilities. These laws were only overturned in the 1950s and 1960s by the later Civil Rights Movement.

KEY COURT CASES

DRED SCOTT v. SANFORD (1857)
Background: Dred Scott, a slave, was taken by his owner Sanford to live in a territory which excluded slavery. Scott believed that this made him a free man. When he was taken back to a slave state to live, he sued his owner for his freedom.

Decision/Significance: The Supreme Court ruled that a slave was property and had no rights. Since Scott was not a citizen, he was prohibited from bringing his case before the Court. The Court further stated that Congress could not prohibit slavery in the territories. The case contributed to the tensions leading to the Civil War by opening the whole issue of Congressional control of slavery in newly annexed territories.

PLESSY v. FERGUSON (1896)
Background: Plessy was of racially mixed descent (part black/part white). He sat in a railroad car where only whites were permitted. When he refused to move, he was arrested and sent to jail for violating a state law that provided for "separate but equal" facilities for blacks. Plessy said this law was unconstitutional because it violated his "equal protection" rights under the Fourteenth Amendment.

Decision/Significance: The 14th Amendment requires state governments to give all citizens "equal protection of the laws." The Supreme Court held that as long as a state provided facilities that were "equal," it could separate African Americans from whites. This gave the South a green light to continue passing laws for "separate but equal" facilities that segregated black citizens. The decision was overturned many years later in *Brown v. Board of Education* (1954).

SUMMARIZING YOUR UNDERSTANDING

Directions: How well do you understand what you have just read? Test yourself by answering the following questions.

MAJOR ITEMS TO REMEMBER

On 3x5 index cards (as shown on pages 33-34), briefly define the following terms and concepts:

Civil War	Freedmen's Bureau	Emancipation Proclamation
Abolitionists	Jim Crow laws	Reconstruction
Dred Scott decision	*Plessy v. Ferguson*	14th Amendment

THE CIVIL WAR

The Civil War was the most divisive war in U. S. history, in which more Americans died than in any other war. Summarize your understanding of this conflict by answering the following questions:

- What factors led to the outbreak of the Civil War?
- What factors contributed to the Northern victory in the Civil War?
- Why did President Lincoln issue the Emancipation Proclamation?

THE RECONSTRUCTION ERA

The Reconstruction Era was a time in which the national government faced the task of unifying the nation and rebuilding the South. Describe the major plans for reconstructing the South. Describe some of the positive and negative effects of the Reconstruction period.

THE RISE OF SEGREGATION IN THE SOUTH

Following Reconstruction, the social and political system in the South deprived African Americans of many of their basic rights. Summarize your understanding of this by answering the following questions: What methods were used by Southerners to prevent African Americans from enjoying their newly won freedom? What were some suggestions offered by African-American leaders to overcome such treatment?

PERSONALITIES OF THE PERIOD

People often have an important influence on the political, economic or social life of their times. Summarize your understanding of this statement by completing a 3x5 index card (use the procedure on page 34) for each of the following people: ***Abraham Lincoln***, ***Dred Scott***, ***Booker T. Washington***, and ***Thaddeus Stevens***.

TESTING YOUR UNDERSTANDING

Directions: Test your understanding of this unit by answering the following questions. *Circle* the number preceding the word or expression that correctly answers the statement or question. Following the short answer questions, answer either the RCT-type or Regents essay questions.

SKILL BUILDER: INTERPRETING A CARTOON

Base your answers to questions 1 through 3 on the following cartoon and on your knowledge of social studies.

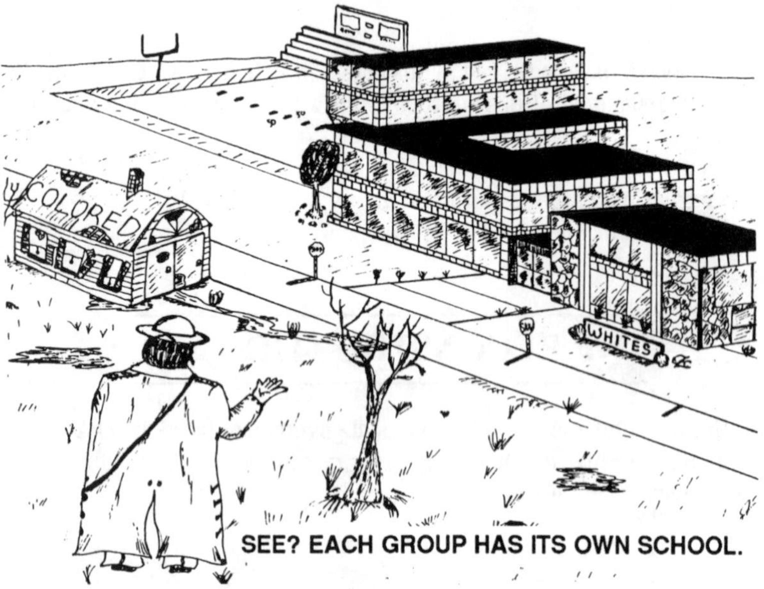
COLORED
WHITES
SEE? EACH GROUP HAS ITS OWN SCHOOL.

1 Which time period is being depicted in the cartoon?
  1 1600-1800 3 1900-1954
  2 1800-1860 4 1955-1990

2 What is the main idea of the cartoon?
  1 Everybody has a right to a good education.
  2 Separate and unequal facilities existed for African Americans.
  3 Education is the main road to success in the United States.
  4 All schools teach essentially the same thing.

3 Which Supreme Court decision permitted a continuation of the situation depicted in the cartoon?
  1 *Marbury v. Madison* 3 *Dred Scott v. Sanford*
  2 *Plessy v. Ferguson* 4 *Gibbons v. Ogden*

SKILL BUILDER: SPEAKER-TYPE QUESTION

Base your answers to questions 4 through 6 on the statements of the following speakers and on your knowledge of social studies.

Speaker A: Since the states were the ones that created the Union, they have a right to leave it.

Speaker B: The Constitution is the work of the American people as a group.

Speaker C: Let the people be the judge as to whether slavery should be introduced in the new territories. If not, I fear we will surely lose our political power in Congress.

Speaker D: Although there are differences between various sections of the nation, they must try to resolve these differences.

4 Which two speakers would support the position taken by the South during the Civil War?
  1 Speakers A and B 3 Speakers B and C
  2 Speakers A and C 4 Speakers C and D

5 Which speaker would most likely have supported the passage of the Kansas-Nebraska Act (1854)?
  1 Speaker A 3 Speaker C
  2 Speaker B 4 Speaker D

6 Speaker C would be most worried about
  1 abolitionists being elected to Congress
  2 carpetbaggers becoming judges
  3 anti-Federalists forming a political party
  4 an alliance with England

SKILL BUILDER: COMPLETING AN OUTLINE

Base your answers to questions 7, 8 and 9 on your understanding of an outline. Four items have been omitted from the following outline. In each blank space in the outline, write the number of the item from the list which best completes the blank.

ITEMS

(1) Emancipation Proclamation
(2) Causes
(3) Louisiana Purchase
(4) Slavery

THE CIVIL WAR

7 I Causes
  A. Sectionalism
8 B. Slavery
  C. The Failure of Compromise
  D. Different Constitutional Interpretations

  II Highlights
  A. Outbreak of the Civil War
  B. Why the North Won
9 C. Luisiana purchase

10 The term "abolitionist" is used to describe a person who
  1 believes in free trade
  2 opposes foreign alliances
  3 desires to end slavery
  4 supports colonial rule

11 Which was a major result of the Civil War?
  1 slavery was ended
  2 the U.S. won its independence
  3 states secured the right to secede
  4 women gained the right to vote

12 The purpose of the Black Codes in the South was to
1 give civil rights to blacks
2 return blacks to Africa
3 keep blacks in an inferior position
4 provide blacks with better jobs

13 Which group was most affected by the passage of the Civil War Amendments?
1 women
2 immigrants
3 former slaves
4 northern manufacturers

14 Booker T. Washington believed that African Americans should
1 return to Africa
2 concentrate on vocational education to improve their lives
3 use force to secure their full civil rights
4 establish a separate state within the United States

15 The significance of the passage of the 14th Amendment was that it
1 prevented Congress from making laws on religion
2 banned the sale and consumption of alcoholic beverages
3 prohibited states from depriving citizens of the equal protection of the laws
4 gave women the right to vote in national elections

16 Booker T. Washington and W.E.B. du Bois were similar in that they both believed that African-American success depended upon
1 progress through education
2 a total restructuring of American society
3 being given the land they worked as slaves
4 improved benefits from Southern state governments

17 Which pair of people actively opposed slavery in the United States?
1 Jefferson Davis / George Washington
2 Thomas Jefferson / Robert E. Lee
3 Frederick Douglass / Harriet Tubman
4 John Brown / John Marshall

18 During the Reconstruction era, a major Congressional objective was to
1 destroy the economy of the South
2 restore pre-Civil War conditions in the South
3 help the freedmen in the South
4 develop two equal political parties in the South

19 The practice of racial segregation in the South was based on the belief that
1 each culture has contributed to American society
2 some racial groups are superior to others
3 people should be treated equally regardless of race
4 mixing racial groups creates a nice blend in society

20 Which documents are presented in the correct chronological order in which they were written?
1 U.S. Constitution, Declaration of Independence, Emancipation Proclamation
2 Emancipation Proclamation, Declaration of Independence, Articles of Confederation
3 Articles of Confederation, Declaration of Independence, Mayflower Compact
4 Mayflower Compact, Articles of Confederation, U.S. Constitution

RCT-TYPE ESSAYS

1 How opposing groups handle their differences often affects future generations in society.

Groups

North / South before the Civil War
Large States / Small States at the Constitutional Convention
Radical Republicans / Southern Governments during Reconstruction

Part A

Choose *one* pair of groups from the list: __________

State *one* way in which the beliefs of the two groups were different: __________

Choose *another* pair of groups listed: __________

State *one* way in which the beliefs of the two groups were different: __________

Part B

In your Part B answer, you should use information you gave in Part A. However, you may also include different or additional information in your Part B answer.

Write an essay discussing how the handling of differences by certain groups often affects future generations.

2 People sometimes disagree in dealing with the same issue.

People/Issue

Thomas Jefferson / Alexander Hamilton:
interpreting the United States Constitution

Andrew Johnson / Thaddeus Stevens:
dealing with the South after the Civil War

Booker T. Washington / W.E.B. du Bois:
the plight of African Americans after the Civil War

Part A

Choose *one* pair of persons from the list: __________

State *one* way in which their positions differed: __________

Choose *another* pair of persons from the list: __________

State *one* way in which their positions differed: __________

Part B

In your Part B answer, you should use information you gave in Part A. However, you may also include different or additional information in your Part B answer.

Write an essay discussing how different people sometimes disagree in dealing with the same issue.

REGENTS-TYPE ESSAYS

1 How competing groups handle their differences affects future generations.

Groups

North / South before the Civil War
Large States / Small States at the Constitutional Convention
Radical Republicans / Southern Governments during Reconstruction

Select *two* groups from the list above. For *each* one selected:

- Describe their major differences.
- Show how the outcome of the conflict affected future generations.

2 People sometimes differ in dealing with issues.

People/Issues

Thomas Jefferson / Alexander Hamilton:
interpreting the United States Constitution

Andrew Johnson / Thaddeus Stevens:
dealing with the South after the Civil War

Booker T. Washington / W.E.B. du Bois:
the plight of African Americans after the Civil War

For *each* pair of people:

- Describe their differences in trying to solve the problem.
- Explain which approach you are most in agreement with.

PERFORMANCE-BASED TASKS

Setting: During the Civil War, brothers fought brothers and the American nation was torn apart. During the early years of the war, many Northerners questioned the conduct of the war and Lincoln's leadership. Despite the North's larger size, industrial wealth, and control of the seas, the Union army seemed incapable of achieving a decisive victory. The South seemed more prepared for war. In 1861, Southerners defeated Union forces at Bull Run. Confederate General Robert E. Lee inflicted a second defeat on the Union army on the same battlefield in 1862. Lincoln replaced his chief commander for his lack of aggressiveness. Despite this change, Lee again defeated Union forces the following year at Chancellorsville. Lee's advance into Pennsylvania was finally stopped at the Battle of Gettysburg — a battle that proved to be the turning point of the war.

General Directions: Your class will be divided into groups of 5 students. Each group will constitute a Board of Editors issuing an imaginary newspaper published either in the pre-war period, during the Civil War, or during the Reconstruction Era. Your group must select from among the following possible headlines for your newspaper:

POSSIBLE HEADLINES FOR YOUR NEWSPAPER

- John Brown Executed
- Lincoln Elected and South Carolina Secedes from Union
- Southern Rebels Fire on Fort Sumter
- President Lincoln Calls for 75,000 Volunteers
- Monitor defeats Merrimac in Sea Battle
- Blood Bath at Battle of Antietam
- President Lincoln Issues Emancipation Proclamation
- General Grant Captures Vicksburg
- Confederate General Lee Surrenders
- President Lincoln Assassinated
- Senate Seeks To Impeach President Andrew Johnson
- Fourteenth Amendment Ratified

Your Task: Each newspaper should be based on a single event and must include the following:

- **News Stories**: one or two news features about the lead story
- **Opinion Pieces**: one editorial or opinion piece
- **Interviews**: an interview with the President, a general, or a leading historical figure of the time about the news event
- **Speeches**: an imaginary speech given in Congress or a state legislature about the event.
- **Advertisement**: a local advertisement from that time period

To Find Information: To find information about your event, you should visit your school or local library. Consult history books, biographies, and encyclopedia articles that provide information on the events you have chosen. Primary sources, such as collections of documents, old newspapers, or personal narratives will give you the flavor of the period. Remember to write your newspaper from the standpoint of someone living at that time, not living today.

LOOKING AT ECONOMIC CHANGE

The Industrial Revolution, discussed in the following chapter, began a period of growth and change unprecedented in human history. The changes begun by the Industrial Revolution help point out the cause-and-effect relationship between many historical events and economic change. In order for you to better understand the Industrial Revolution and the influence of economic change on American life, this section takes a look at what an economy is, how a market economy works, and the main causes and effects of economic change.

HOW SOCIETIES MEET THEIR ECONOMIC NEEDS

We all have wants and needs. Unfortunately, our wants are unlimited and can never be fully satisfied because we have limited resources at our disposal. As a result, every society must make some choices in answering the three most basic economic questions:

***What* should be produced?**

***How* should it be produced?**

***Who* gets what is produced?**

Economics is the study of how societies use their limited resources to satisfy these unlimited wants.

TYPES OF ECONOMIC SYSTEMS

Societies usually answer these economic basic questions in one of three ways, each of which is called an **economic system**. In a **Traditional Economy**, the basic economic questions are answered by doing what was traditionally done in the past. In a **Command Economy**, all important economic decisions are made by government leaders. In a **Market Economy**, people are free to produce whatever they wish, and to consume whatever they can afford. These decisions, taken together, determine the answers to the basic economic questions.

HOW THE FREE MARKET WORKS

In a free market economy like the United States, the **profit motive** provides an incentive for people to produce goods and provide services, while competition and the laws of supply and demand determine how much will be produced and what will be charged. Even in a free market system, there is some government influence on the economy. The government provides stable conditions and a system of laws under which people can conduct business. The government also acts as a policeman of the marketplace, making sure that persons and businesses do not treat each other unfairly.

WHAT CAUSES AN ECONOMY TO DEVELOP AND CHANGE?

Economists have identified a number of important causes of economic change. Think about these reasons of economic change as you read about the causes for the Industrial Revolution in the next chapter.

TECHNOLOGICAL INNOVATION

One of the most important factors influencing an economy is technology—the use of knowledge, skills and tools for making things. Each generation builds on past technological achievements. The Industrial Revolution was one of the great turning points in the development of technology. People learned to use new sources of energy to replace human and animal power. Factories and machines replaced hand-produced goods. When a society fails to keep pace with technological changes, it usually falls behind economically.

CAPITAL INVESTMENTS AND PRODUCTIVITY

When a society invests labor and resources to build homes, roads, schools, factories and equipment, its workers and businesses become more productive. As technology improves and investment in the equipment used by each worker increases, each worker can produce more in the same amount of time. If a society fails to maintain its facilities, it becomes less productive. Thus, capital investment is the key to laying the foundation for future productivity.

NEW FORMS OF BUSINESS ORGANIZATION

The development of new forms of business organization and finance make it possible to bring together labor and resources in large amounts to mass-produce goods. For example, the rise of corporations in 19th century America allowed a greater pooling of private resources.

POPULATION CHANGES

Although populations usually expand, they sometimes decline because of disease, famine or war. Populations can also change in terms of age or location. For example, populations can move from the countryside to the city, or from the east to the west. Such changes affect the demand for goods and services.

NATURAL RESOURCES

Natural resources provide sources of energy and raw materials for agriculture, manufacturing and other purposes. The discovery of new resources or the development of new ways to process or use existing resources can stimulate economic change. For example, during the early stages of the Industrial Revolution, the availability of cheaper energy sources (coal and oil) helped speed industrialization.

CONTACTS WITH OTHER SOCIETIES

Contacts with others can help introduce new products, markets, or ways of producing things. However, such contact often leads to disputes and wars, which can have significant economic consequences.

GOVERNMENT POLICY

Government policy can greatly affect a nation's economy. To learn more about how the government can influence the economy, read the section *Looking at Economic Policy.*

THE IMPACT OF ECONOMIC CHANGE

The political, social and cultural life of a people is always closely tied to its economic life. As technology develops and the national economy is transformed, aspects of national life also change. Here are some of the ways in which economic changes can affect the rest of society:

CHANGES IN STANDARDS OF LIVING

Economic improvements generally raise standards of living—how well people live, and how much they have and can do. Economic catastrophes like wars or depressions often lead to a decline in living standards.

NEW OPPORTUNITIES, EXPECTATIONS AND LIFE STYLES

The opportunities available to people are also affected by the economic system in which they live. For example, in a traditional economy people are expected to follow in the footsteps of their parents. In more advanced economies, individuals can choose from among many career paths; education and special talents or abilities play a greater role in determining career choices and life styles; and people generally have more leisure time to pursue non-work-related activities.

BELIEFS, ARTS AND CULTURE

Economic changes can affect art styles, fashions, and even people's beliefs. For example, the plight of workers during early industrialization led to the rise of socialism and communism. The increasing use of machines influenced such art styles as futurism and cubism.

FAMILY LIFE

Even family life has been affected by economic change. Before industrialization, most people lived in extended families, with grandparents, parents and children all living under the same roof. After the industrial revolution, people moved to crowded cities and began living in smaller families composed of parents and their children. Men and women were also affected, as new forms of work required less physical strength, placing women on almost equal terms with men.

RELATIONS WITH OTHER SOCIETIES

New forms of production may require raw materials found in other countries. The need of industries for raw materials often leads to competition with other developed societies for global resources and markets. The result is a greater interdependence among nations.

KEY EVENTS IN THE DEVELOPMENT OF THE U.S. ECONOMY

Now that you have examined some of the main causes and effects of economic change in general, it might be useful to focus more specifically on the development of the American economy. The following chart represents the major events in American economic history in summary form. All of these events are described more fully in subsequent chapters:

MAJOR DEVELOPMENT	MILESTONES IN AMERICAN ECONOMIC HISTORY
Creation of the National Economy	The decision in *Gibbons v. Ogden* (1824) helped create a national economy in which citizens could do business in other states on equal terms—encouraging the free movement of goods, money and people—and greatly speeding up the growth of the American economy.
Spread of the Factory System	Factories, by greatly increasing the scale of production, marked the beginnings of the Industrial Revolution—changing where people lived, and what they produced and consumed.
Abolition of Slavery	The plantation system of the South was replaced by sharecropping and light industry; the South fell behind the North in economic power and influence.
Building the Transcontinental Railroad	The construction of railroads opened the interior of the U.S. for settlement, speeded up the pace of industrialization, and linked production centers to large city markets. In addition, railroads helped settle the prairies, eventually leading to less expensive food being available to feed the city dwellers.
Urbanization and Immigration	Cities became crowded and faced new problems in providing housing, sanitation and other services to their increasing populations. A new urban culture developed as the U. S. was transformed into a nation of city dwellers. As America's need for labor expanded, immigrants filled jobs in factories and sweatshops. They often faced discrimination and hardship, but they contributed to the establishment of a prosperous economy.
Business Consolidation in the Gilded Age	The rise of corporations allowed private individuals to undertake vast enterprises like the construction of steel plants. However, the trend toward unfair business practices had to be limited by federal anti-trust laws.
Rise of Labor Unions	Workers gained the right to bargain collectively with their employers over pay and working conditions. Labor unions helped obtain better working conditions for all American workers. Some economists argue that unionization contributed to making American products more expensive than comparable foreign goods.
Establishment of the Federal Reserve and the Income Tax	President Wilson introduced a Federal Reserve System to provide stability and flexibility to our national monetary system, and a progressive income tax which became the main source of federal revenue.

MAJOR DEVELOPMENT	MILESTONES IN AMERICAN ECONOMIC HISTORY
Mass Production of the Automobile	The rise of automobiles created a new industry employing large numbers of Americans. Cars, buses and trucks increased the mobility of people, brought different parts of the country closer together, and transformed the American way of life.
The Great Depression and the New Deal	After the stock market crash of 1929, people were thrown out of work, families lost their homes, banks failed, and national production shrank by 50%. The Great Depression was the greatest economic disaster in American history. It led to increased federal involvement in the economy, as President Roosevelt made the federal government responsible for supervising the performance of the national economy.
World War II and the Post-War Recovery	The U.S. came out of the war as the chief economic producer for the allied powers. Wartime research improved our uses of atomic energy, aircraft and computers. Following the war, the U.S. became the world's leading producer of manufactured goods.
The Great Society and the Vietnam War	President Johnson introduced new social programs that helped some groups but failed to help others. These new programs and the costs of the war in Asia led to increased federal spending and inflation.
Reaganomics	President Reagan's deficit spending and easing of government regulations led to economic prosperity for middle-class and upper-income Americans. However, minority and low income groups suffered from reduced spending on social programs; deregulation led to stockbroker scandals and the Savings and Loan Crisis, and military spending led to a vast national debt.
The Computer Revolution	Almost every facet of modern life has been affected by the computer revolution—from manufacturing techniques, to banking, to children's toys. Writers are now more productive because of word-processing; lawyers and doctors have immediate access to large computerized databases. However, computerization and automation have also led to the loss of many jobs, especially in manufacturing.

ANSWERING AN ESSAY QUESTION ON ECONOMIC CHANGE

Essay questions about economics generally focus on economic change or on government economic policy. Those questions about economic change ask you to explain the causes of a particular change, to describe the change, and to discuss one or more effects of the change. For example, the following question appeared on the June 1991 Regents.

> During the period from 1865 to 1920, the industrialization of the United States led to many changes. Some areas of change included:
>
> | | |
> |---|---|
> | Production Techniques | Labor |
> | Immigration Patterns | Energy Sources |
> | Urbanization | Business Organization |
>
> Choose *three* of the areas of change listed and for *each one* chosen:
>
> - Show how that area was changed as a result of industrialization during the period from 1865 to 1920.
> - Discuss one positive and one negative effect of the change on American society.

Another question, also exploring economic change, appeared on the August 1991 Regents:

> Some of the major economic events that have shaped United States history are included in the list below.
>
> **Economic Events**
>
> *Gibbons v. Ogden* decision (1824)
> Passage of the Sherman Anti-Trust Act (1890)
> Creation of the Federal Reserve System (1913)
> Ratification of the 16th Amendment establishing a personal income tax (1913)
> Stock Market crash (1929)
> Oil Embargo (1973)
> Increase in the United States national debt (1980s)
>
> Choose *three* of the economic events listed and for *each one* chosen:
>
> - Discuss one reason the event occurred.
> - Show how the event had a listing impact on the United States economy.

CHAPTER 7

AMERICA INDUSTRIALIZES

In the 1850s, most Americans lived in the countryside and were employed in farming. The next half-century saw the transformation of the nation into the world's leading industrial power. By then, half of all Americans lived in cities. Large corporations produced goods for the entire nation. Railroads and telephone lines spanned the country. Factories were powered by electricity. The use of automobiles was spreading. Many workers were organized into labor unions.

— TIMELINE OF KEY EVENTS —

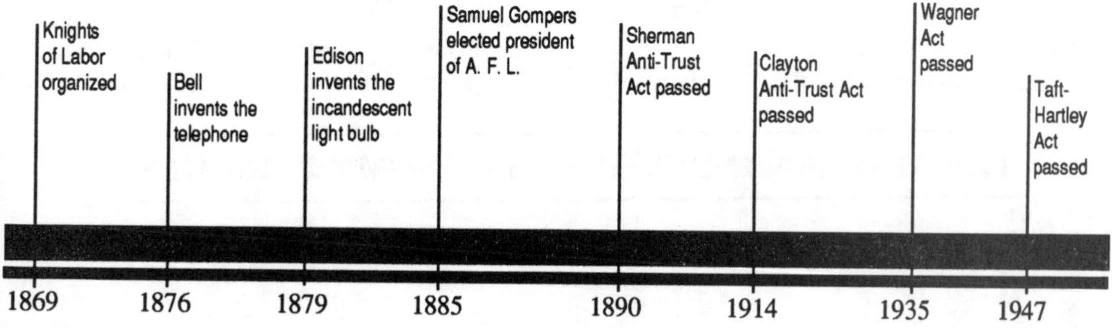

Knights of Labor organized
Bell invents the telephone
Edison invents the incandescent light bulb
Samuel Gompers elected president of A. F. L.
Sherman Anti-Trust Act passed
Clayton Anti-Trust Act passed
Wagner Act passed
Taft-Hartley Act passed
1869
1876
1879
1885
1890
1914
1935
1947

THE RISE OF AMERICAN INDUSTRY

In the 1750s the **Industrial Revolution** began in Great Britain and soon spread to the United States. New inventions and ideas brought about new ways of making goods and meeting people's needs. Instead of hand-producing goods at home, factories were built which produced goods in large amounts at lower prices. The newly invented steam engine ran the factories' machines. As goods became cheaper, demand for goods increased, leading to more jobs. Cities grew up around factories, as workers sought to live closer to where they worked.

THE FOUNDATIONS OF ECONOMIC GROWTH

The foundations for America's extraordinary economic growth were already in place by the end of the Civil War. In addition to its abundance of natural resources (plentiful land, fertile soil, swift-flowing streams, vast quantities of timber, and rich deposits of coal, iron, oil and copper), the economic development of the U. S. was supported by other factors:

THE FREE ENTERPRISE SYSTEM

The United States enjoyed the benefits of the "free enterprise," or **capitalist** system of economic organization. Under this system "capital" (wealth) is privately owned and invested. People are free to buy and sell goods. The producers who stay in business are those most able to compete effectively.

AMERICA'S WORK ETHIC

American culture stressed individualism, thrift and hard work. It taught that an individual's efforts would be rewarded with material success. By the late 19th century, the philosophy of **Social Darwinism** was used to justify America's work ethic. It stressed "survival of the fittest" and the necessity of free competition: those who were the most successful were considered to be the best.

THE CONTRIBUTION OF GOVERNMENT

The 19th century American government officially followed a "hands-off" or **laissez-faire** policy towards the economy. However, government policies still promoted industrialization in some ways. Laws protected property and contracts. Congress often passed protective tariffs, which helped guard U.S. manufacturerers from competing with foreign-made goods. The tariff was a tax which made foreign imports more costly for American consumers, encouraging them instead to buy goods made in the United States. Finally, a system of patent protection encouraged new inventions by protecting an inventor's ideas from being copied.

THE MODERN INDUSTRIAL ECONOMY EMERGES

There were several reasons for the emergence of the modern industrial economy in the United States:

THE EXPANSION OF RAILROADS

The key to the development of the modern industrial economy in the United States was the expansion of the railroads. The first transcontinental railroad, linking the east and west coasts, was completed in 1869. The construction of railroad trackage increased fivefold in the next 25 years. The railroads affected just about every aspect of American life:

■ **Stimulated Industry.** Construction of the railroads provided a tremendous stimulus to the steel, iron and coal industries. Railroads brought raw materials to factories and finished goods to consumers.

■ **Helped Settle the Frontier.** The railroads promoted the settlement of the frontier. They brought settlers to the Great Plains with the promise of cheap farmland, linking farmers on the plains to urban markets.

■ **Promoted Immigration.** Railroad companies promoted immigration by advertising in Europe for settlers. Irish and Chinese immigrants provided an inexpensive labor force for the construction of the great transcontinental lines.

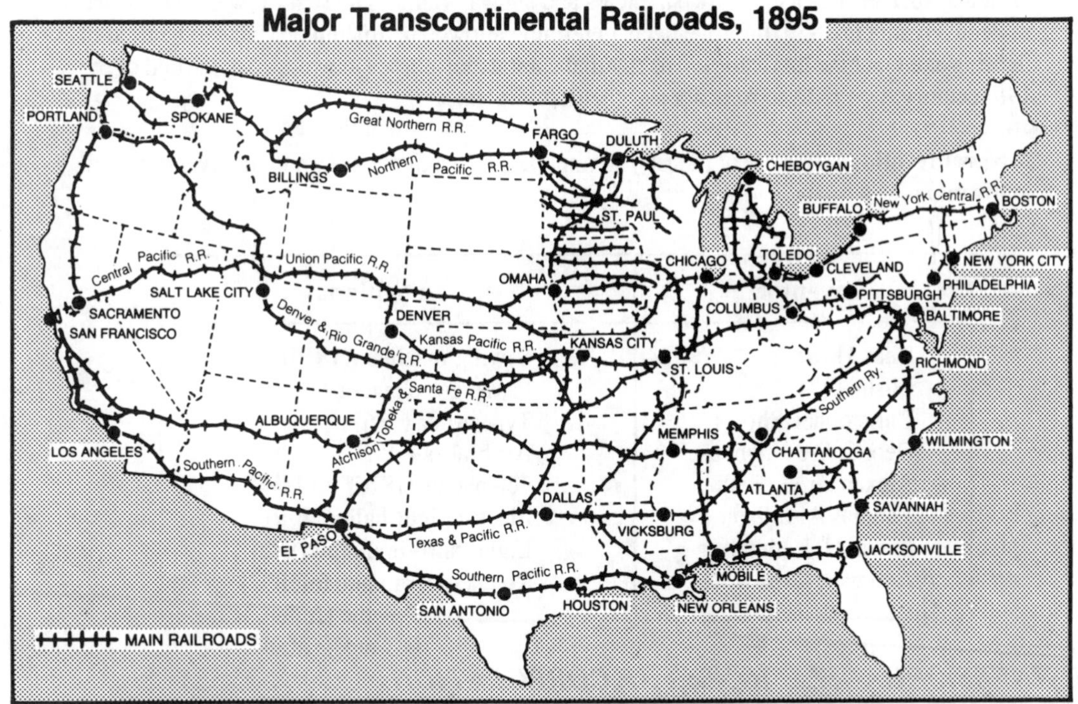
SEATTLE
PORTLAND
SPOKANE
Great Northern R.R.
FARGO
DULUTH
BILLINGS
Northern Pacific R.R.
CHEBOYGAN
ST. PAUL
BUFFALO
New York Central R.R.
BOSTON
Central Pacific R.R.
Union Pacific R.R.
CHICAGO
TOLEDO
CLEVELAND
NEW YORK CITY
OMAHA
PHILADELPHIA
SALT LAKE CITY
PITTSBURGH
SACRAMENTO
SAN FRANCISCO
DENVER
COLUMBUS
BALTIMORE
Denver & Rio Grande R.R.
Kansas Pacific R.R.
KANSAS CITY
ST. LOUIS
RICHMOND
Southern Ry.
Santa Fe R.R.
Atchison Topeka &
ALBUQUERQUE
MEMPHIS
WILMINGTON
LOS ANGELES
CHATTANOOGA
Southern Pacific R.R.
ATLANTA
DALLAS
SAVANNAH
EL PASO
VICKSBURG
Texas & Pacific R.R.
JACKSONVILLE
MOBILE
Southern Pacific R.R.
SAN ANTONIO
HOUSTON
NEW ORLEANS
MAIN RAILROADS

Major Transcontinental Railroads, 1895

THE GROWTH OF POPULATION

Between 1860 and 1900, the population of the United States more than doubled. The population increase was partly fueled by a constant stream of European immigrants. Population growth created favorable conditions for business expansion: a steadily rising demand for goods and a source of cheap labor.

DEVELOPMENT OF A NATIONAL MARKET

The high investment costs of mass production required a large market to remain profitable. In the late 19th century, a national market developed as a result of a number of factors:

- Railroads, telegraphs and telephones linked together different parts of the country.
- National producers could make and ship goods more cheaply than local producers, by taking advantage of more machinery and economies of scale.
- New methods of selling were developed, such as department stores, chain stores (Woolworths), and mail order houses (Sears, Roebuck and Co.).

TECHNOLOGICAL PROGRESS

New technologies, innovations and inventions helped fuel the economic expansion of the late 19th century.

- **New Technologies.** The Bessemer Process, developed in the 1850s, made the production of steel more economical. By 1900, electricity was being used to power an increasing number of items, such as motors, electric streetcars and subway trains. The first oil well was drilled in Pennsylvania in 1859. Improvements in refining allowed petroleum products to be used in lighting and machine lubrication. The internal combustion engine, developed at the end of the 19th century, was used to run cars and the first airplanes.
- **New Inventions.** The rise of industry was sparked by a number of important inventions and innovations.

Inventor	Invention
Elias Howe	Sewing machine (1846)
Elisha Otis	Passenger elevator (1852)
Christopher Sholes	Typewriter (1867)
George Westinghouse	Air brakes (1868)
Alexander G. Bell	Telephone (1876)
Thomas A. Edison	Electric light bulb (1879)
Lewis H. Latimer	Light bulb filament (1882)
Andrew J. Beard	Rotary steam engine (1892)

BUSINESS ORGANIZATIONS: THE CORPORATION

Before the Civil War, most businesses were owned by individuals or partners. In the years following the Civil War, the corporate form of business became much more popular. A **corporation** is a company that is chartered by a state and recognized in law as a separate "person." The corporation issues stocks, or shares in ownership, to investors. Each **stockholder** is a partial owner of the corporation and receives a share of its profits in the form of dividends. Corporations enjoyed many advantages because of the large amounts of money they could raise.

THE GREAT ENTREPRENEURS: ROBBER BARONS OR CAPTAINS OF INDUSTRY?

During the period from 1865 through 1900, many Americans became involved in the pursuit of material wealth and luxuries. Because of the lavish lifestyle of those who became rich from industry, this period was called the **Gilded Age**. Entrepreneurs who invested their money in business began to exercise a dominant influence on American life. Some observers thought of these entrepreneurs as "**captains of industry**" because they helped create the modern industrial economy. They had the vision to see the possibilities. Others called them "**robber barons**" because of the ruthless tactics they used to destroy competition and keep down the wages of their workers.

CORNELIUS VANDERBILT (1794-1877)	ANDREW CARNEGIE (1835-1919)	JOHN D. ROCKEFELLER (1839-1937)
Vanderbilt made his fortune in the steamship business before turning to railroads. He built the New York Central Railroad, replaced iron rails with steel, and consolidated under his own control the railroads running from New York to Chicago. A few years before he died, he gave one million dollars to build and endow a university in Nashville, Tennessee, which bears his name.	Andrew Carnegie worked his way up from a penniless immigrant to one of America's richest men. His steel mills undercut all competition. His workers put in 12-hour shifts at very low wages, and he crushed their attempts to unionize. Carnegie spent his later life giving away his fortune in support of education, medical research and world peace.	In 1870 Rockefeller formed the Standard Oil Company. He forced the railroad companies to give him special secret rates for shipping his oil, while they charged his competitors higher prices. By 1900, Rockefeller had a virtual monopoly over the oil business, controlling over 90% of all oil refining in the United States. Like Carnegie, he gave millions to education and science.

BIG BUSINESS CONSOLIDATION

Beginning with the Depression of 1873, larger producers like Carnegie and Rockefeller began driving smaller companies out of business and acquiring their companies. In other cases, rival companies reached agreements to consolidate (join together).

TYPES OF CONSOLIDATION

The aim of most consolidations was to eliminate competition and raise prices by establishing a monopoly —complete control of the manufacture of a product. This would allow producers to dictate their own prices to consumers. There were three major methods by which businesses tried to achieve monopolistic control:

METHODS TO ACHIEVE CONTROL	DEFINITION
Pooling Agreements	Informal agreements to fix prices or divide markets.
Trusts	Stockholders of existing companies give their stocks to the board of directors of the trust in exchange for "trust certificates" entitling them to dividends based on the profits of the entire trust.
Mergers	Two or more companies join together into a single company.

THE DEMAND FOR REFORM

Since the dominant economic belief during the late 19th century was laissez-faire capitalism, the response of the government to the abuses of "big business" was to do very little. Government leaders believed that the operations of the free market eliminated inefficient businesses, leading to the best and cheapest goods. They also doubted that the Constitution gave them powers to regulate business. However, the abuses of big business became so glaring that lawmakers gradually recognized that monopolies posed a greater threat to the free market than the evils of government intervention. Although the first laws passed by Congress tended to be weak, they did establish the right of Congress to regulate business. Congress passed two major laws: the Interstate Commerce Act and the Sherman Anti-Trust Act (see The Constitution At Work section at the end of this chapter for more details about these acts).

THE IMPACT OF BIG BUSINESS ON AMERICA

The growth of big business had profound effects on the United States.

CONTRIBUTIONS	ABUSES
1. Big business, through efficiency, lowered the cost of many items, making them more affordable.	1. Big business exploited workers by paying low wages and creating unsafe working conditions.
2. Big business helped raise the standard of living and improved the quality of life by creating new inventions and technology.	2. Big business polluted the environment and wasted many of the nation's natural resources.
3. Big business developed new and innovative practices that created jobs and helped America prosper.	3. Big business abused the free enterprise system by using cutthroat competition to bankrupt small businesses.

KEY ITEMS TO REMEMBER

Free enterprise system, laissez-faire capitalism, entrepreneurs, Gilded Age

THE RISE OF ORGANIZED LABOR

INDUSTRIAL WORKERS FACE NEW PROBLEMS

One of the main reasons for America's rapid economic growth in the late 1800s was the increasing exploitation of the industrial worker. Gains in productivity and higher profits were made at terrible costs to workers.

POOR WORKING CONDITIONS

Conditions at work were often extremely hazardous. There were insufficient safeguards around machinery. Overworked employees were prone to accidents; thousands were injured or killed in accidents each year.

■ **Long Hours and Low Wages.** Hours were incredibly long by today's standards. Workers faced a six-day work week of between 10 and 14 hours of work each day. Employers hired the cheapest possible laborers. Pay averaged between $3 and $12 weekly, but immigrants were willing to work for low wages. Women and children, frequently used as workers, were especially low-paid.

■ **Impersonal Conditions and Boring, Repetitive Tasks.** As factories and work places grew larger, the worker lost all personal contact with his actual employers. The job was offered on a take-it-or-leave-it basis. Usually the worker had no choice but to accept. As industrialists sought to achieve greater speed and efficiency, the worker became nothing more than a human cog in a vast machine. Work became less skilled, more repetitive, monotonous and boring.

CHILD LABOR

Textile mills and coal mines made use of child labor to perform special tasks, because it was cheaper. It is estimated that one out of five children under 15 was working in 1910. These children missed sunshine, fresh air, play, and the chance to better their lives through schooling.

LACK OF SECURITY

The industrial worker could be fired at any time for any reason. In bad economic times, manufacturers simply halted production and fired their employees. Workers did not have many of the benefits of today's workers. There was no unemployment insurance, worker's compensation to pay them for injuries on the job, health insurance, old-age pensions, paid holidays or paid sickdays. In some company towns, the company even controlled housing, town officials and police, making it impossible for workers to complain or organize.

RISE OF LABOR UNIONS

With the rise of big business in the later half of the 19th century, the individual worker lost all bargaining power with his employer. Since most work was unskilled, workers could easily be replaced. The workers realized that some form of labor organization was needed, and they turned to **unions**, since acting as a group gave them more power than they had as individuals. By organizing, workers could demand better pay, shorter hours and better working conditions. If an employer refused their demands, all the union workers threatened to **strike** (walk off the job at the same time). In addition, unions acted as pressure groups on government. Union leaders could coordinate the worker's vote to create pressure for their demands. Unions could contribute to campaign funds and lobby for bills in legislatures.

TACTICS USED BY LABOR AND MANAGEMENT

Attempts to achieve their own special economic ends often pitted labor and management against each other. Each used a host of different tactics to try to achieve its goal.

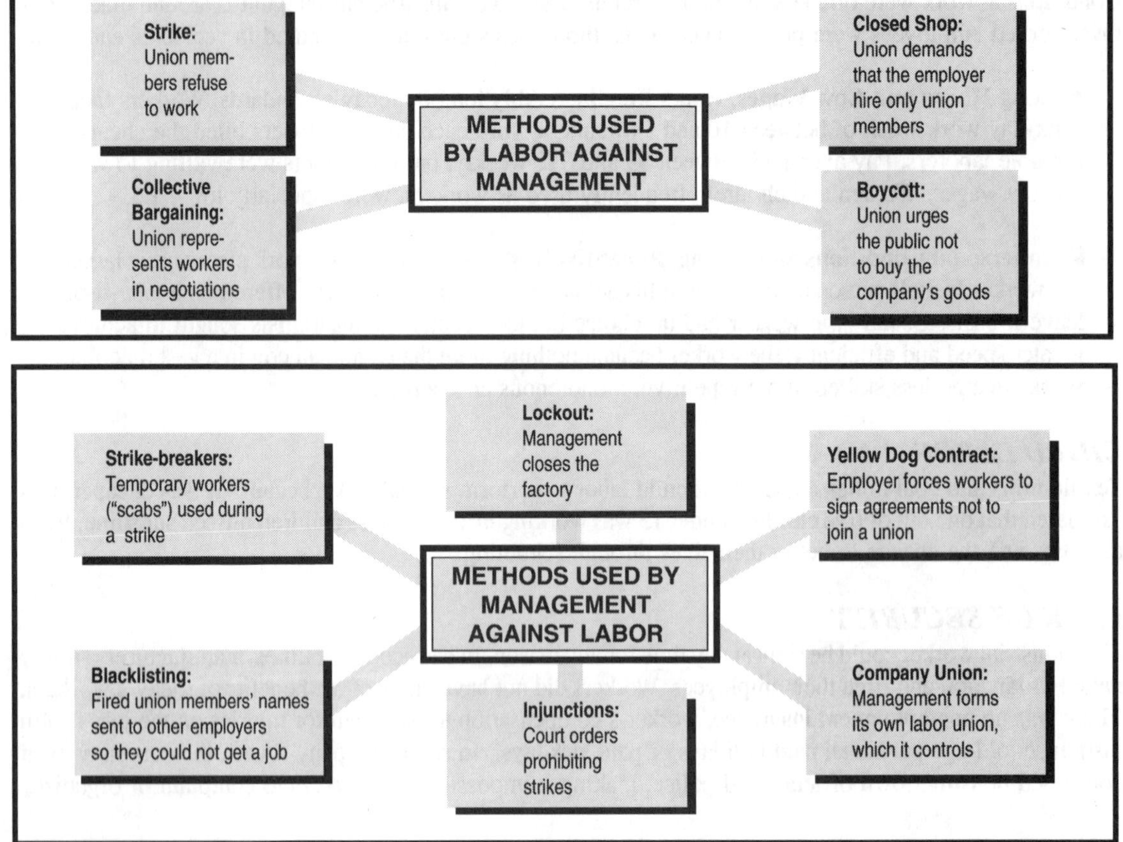
METHODS USED BY LABOR AGAINST MANAGEMENT
Strike: Union members refuse to work
Collective Bargaining: Union represents workers in negotiations
Closed Shop: Union demands that the employer hire only union members
Boycott: Union urges the public not to buy the company's goods
METHODS USED BY MANAGEMENT AGAINST LABOR
Strike-breakers: Temporary workers ("scabs") used during a strike
Lockout: Management closes the factory
Yellow Dog Contract: Employer forces workers to sign agreements not to join a union
Blacklisting: Fired union members' names sent to other employers so they could not get a job
Injunctions: Court orders prohibiting strikes
Company Union: Management forms its own labor union, which it controls

WORKERS SEEK A NATIONAL VOICE

By the end of the 19th century, workers realized that the only way to overcome the obstacles presented by big business was to band together to form national worker organizations.

THE KNIGHTS OF LABOR

The Knights of Labor was begun in 1869. It hoped to form one large union that would take in skilled and unskilled workers. The Knights grew rapidly in the prosperous times of the 1880s. Under the leadership of **Terrence Powderly**, the Knights reached their peak of 700,000 members by 1886.

■ **Aims.** The Knights demanded an 8-hour work day, higher wages and safety codes in factories. They opposed child and convict labor and supported equal pay for women. They supported restrictions on immigration, which they saw as competition for their jobs.

■ **Weaknesses.** The Knights were too loosely organized. Skilled workers resented being grouped in the same union with the unskilled, who had little bargaining power. After losing several important strikes, the Knights of Labor fell apart.

THE AMERICAN FEDERATION OF LABOR

The American Federation of Labor was founded in 1881 by **Samuel Gompers.** Gompers hoped to create a powerful union by uniting workers with the same economic interests. Unlike the Knights of Labor, the A.F.L. brought together unions of skilled workers into a single federation of national craft unions. These craft unions limited their membership to skilled workers such as carpenters, cigarmakers and shoemakers.

■ **Aims.** Gompers' approach was known as "bread and butter" unionism, in which he limited his goals to winning economic improvements for workers. Gompers' goals included higher pay, an 8-hour work day and better working conditions.

■ **Tactics.** Gompers sought to balance the concentration of industry in the hands of a few owners by having skilled workers band together in a singe national union. He fought hard to win job security for his members by seeking a **closed shop** (where only union members were hired).

■ **The A.F.L. and Minorities.** The A.F.L. did not admit women. At first, Gompers insisted that the affiliated craft unions admit African Americans, but when several refused to do so, Gompers backed down. As a result, only a few A.F.L. unions, the United Mine Workers among them, admitted African Americans in those years. Gompers also failed to counteract ethnic prejudice against some nationalities in particular craft unions.

■ **Growth and Limits.** The American Federation of Labor quickly emerged as the voice of organized labor. By 1900, it had half a million members. But the A.F.L. was severely weakened by the fact that in its early years it excluded unskilled workers, who continued to make up the bulk of the labor force. By 1910, less than 5% of American workers were unionized.

GOVERNMENT'S ATTITUDE TOWARD UNIONS AND BUSINESSES

The attitude of the government was crucial to the fortunes of the early labor movement. In the late 19th century, government leaders were partial towards business and took hostile views of unions. There were several reasons for the government's hostility.

THE GREATER POLITICAL INFLUENCE OF BUSINESS

In general, unions lacked the political strength to influence or pressure government, while businesses contributed heavily to political campaigns. Furthermore, business leaders and politicians often shared the same outlook. They believed that successful businessmen were chiefly responsible for America's greatness.

PROTECTOR OF THE ECONOMY

Government leaders feared the disruptive effect of strikes on the economy. There were more than 20,000 strikes involving over 6 million workers between 1880 and 1900. In 1895, the Supreme Court supported the use of the **Sherman Anti-Trust Act** against unions, ruling that many strikes were illegal interference with interstate commerce. Frequently a state governor or the president sent in troops to put down a strike.

PUBLIC OPINION

The public supported a laissez-faire attitude; they believed in the power of businessmen to hire and fire as they pleased. People were often hostile to unions because union wage demands led to higher prices. In addition, union activities were often associated with violence, anarchy and radical ideas.

- **Haymarket Affair**. In 1886, labor leaders were blamed when a bomb exploded as police were breaking up a demonstration of striking workers at Haymarket Square in Chicago. Seven policemen were killed and 67 others were wounded.

- **Homestead Strike**. In 1892, managers closed one of Carnegie's steel plants when workers protested wage cuts. Violence broke out and Pennsylvania sent in state troops to allow the use of strike-breakers to run the mill.

- **Pullman Strike**. In 1894, Pullman workers went on strike. In sympathy, railroad workers refused to handle Pullman cars, bringing railroads to a virtual standstill. The president sent in federal troops to end the strike, contending that the strike prevented mail deliveries. The government also used an injunction to stop the strike, claiming it interfered with interstate commerce.

A SHIFT IN GOVERNMENT ATTITUDE

Starting in the early 20th century, the attitude of the government and the public towards unions began to change. One of the events that stimulated this change was the fire at the **Triangle Shirtwaist Factory** in 1911. The fire killed 146 garment workers, mainly women, because the doors were bolted shut from the outside, and there was only one inadequate fire escape. The fire led to widespread public sympathy for workers, and the passage of local fire codes to improve safety in the factories. The disaster also encouraged demands for women's rights.

Later, additional legislation favorable to unions was passed by Congress.

- **The Department of Labor (1913).** Congress created a separate cabinet post, charged with studying the problems of labor, collecting statistics and enforcing federal labor laws.

- **Clayton Anti-Trust Act (1914).** This act prevented the application of anti-trust laws to unions. It helped unions by banning the issuance of federal injunctions in labor disputes.

IMPACT OF THE NEW DEAL ON ORGANIZED LABOR

The greatest growth in union membership took place in the 1930s because of President Franklin D. Roosevelt's New Deal.

NEW DEAL LABOR LEGISLATION

Roosevelt wanted to raise wages to help fight the Great Depression. The federal government switched from an anti-union to a pro-union position by enacting a series of laws favorable to unions. The **Norris-LaGuardia Act** (1932) prohibited the use of injunctions against peaceful strikes. The **National Industrial Recovery Act** (1933) guaranteed workers the right to form unions. Employers could not refuse to hire union members. The act was declared unconstitutional in 1935, but was replaced by the Wagner Act. The **Wagner Act** (1935) was a landmark act that greatly stimulated the unionization of American workers. (See the Constitution at Work section for more details about the Wagner Act).

THE A.F.L. AND C.I.O. MERGE

The A.F.L. was still predominantly made up of skilled craft unions. **John L. Lewis**, head of the United Mine Workers, formed the **C.I.O.** (Congress of Industrial Organizations) to organize unskilled as well as skilled workers. Its membership grew to 4 million by 1938. At first, the C.I.O. was part of the A.F.L., but differences between the leaders of the two organizations led the C.I.O. to leave the A.F.L. in 1937. The two organizations merged again in 1955, becoming the A.F.L.-C.I.O.

POST-NEW DEAL LEGISLATION: THE TAFT-HARTLEY ACT

Concern over the growth of union power led Congress to pass the **Taft-Hartley Act** in 1947, outlawing the closed shop and secondary boycotts. Under the Taft-Hartley Act, union officials were required to file financial reports with the government, and were forbidden from membership in the Communist Party. Unions also had to notify employers of their intention to strike and sometimes had to agree to series of cooling-off periods. During the cooling-off period, the government often encouraged the union and employer to submit their arguments to an impartial third party for mediation.

EFFECTS OF ORGANIZED LABOR ON AMERICAN SOCIETY

The union movement continued to grow in the 20th century. Currently, about 20% of the United States work force is unionized. This growth in union membership has had a significant impact on American society.

POSITION OF THE WORKER

Organized labor has improved the position of the worker, who is now far better than a century ago. Even workers who are not organized into unions have benefitted, since unions have acted to establish wage levels and safety standards that have become the norm in many industries.

POLITICAL INVOLVEMENT

Today, unions are very sensitive to state and national politics. They try to exert political force in order to counterbalance the influence of big business on government. Unions frequently lobby for pro-labor legislation. Many unions seek funds from their members to contribute to political candidates who are sympathetic to their cause.

INTERNATIONAL COMPETITION

Improved wage settlements have at times made American industry less competitive. Foreign companies, which pay their workers far less, can usually make goods more cheaply. This has led some companies to open manufacturing plants in foreign lands. To make American industry more competitive with foreign-made goods, unions have opposed immigration, supported higher tariffs, and accepted lower wages and increased automation in return for contracts that provide increased job security.

KEY ITEMS TO REMEMBER

Unions, American Federation of Labor (A.F.L.), closed shops, collective bargaining, strikes, boycotts, injunctions, Haymarket Affair, Wagner Act, Taft-Hartley Act

PERSONALITIES OF THE PERIOD

THOMAS EDISON (INVENTOR)

Thomas Edison, considered by many to be the greatest inventor in American history, patented more than one thousand devices. After his first invention at age 22, he set up a laboratory in Menlo Park, New Jersey, where he and his staff invented the phonograph, incandescent light bulb and the motion picture projector. His inventions created industries that affected the development of the United States and the world.

THOMAS NAST (CARTOONIST)

Thomas Nast, an artist, reached national prominence for his political cartoons. He is credited with raising political cartoons to a serious art form. Nast's illustrations focused on the political situation as it existed in America after the Civil War. His cartoons highlighted the corruption and graft that existed under "political machines," especially in New York politics. His symbols of the Democratic Party as a donkey and the Republican Party as an elephant have come to represent both to the public today.

PAULINE FELDMAN (UNION ORGANIZER)

In 1909, when she was only 16 years old, she was a leader in the movement to organize the International Ladies Garment Workers Union (I.L.G.W.U.). She led a general strike in New York City against the horrible conditions that existed in the garment industry. Her efforts were successful in getting the standard garment industry work week reduced from 59 hours to 52 hours.

A. PHILIP RANDOLPH (LABOR LEADER)

A. Philip Randolph was both a union organizer and a civil rights leader. In 1925, he founded the Brotherhood of Sleeping Car Porters to raise the weekly pay of $15 that a porter received for working 100 hours. Most porters were African Americans. Randolph's union won higher wages and a shorter work week. Later in life he worked to bring about equality in federal employment and the armed forces.

For other personalities of this period, see Horatio Alger, John Audubon and Thomas Eakins in the "Looking at the Arts" section.

THE CONSTITUTION AT WORK

KEY LEGISLATION

INTERSTATE COMMERCE ACT (1887)

Congress established regulations to outlaw unfair practices by railroads. A special regulatory commission (the I.C.C.) was established to enforce the act.

SHERMAN ANTI-TRUST ACT (1890)

The major purpose of the Sherman Act was to limit combinations and the growth of monopolies. It outlawed some of the practices of big business that diminished competition, such as trusts, combinations, and conspiracies in restraint of trade. Although the act lacked substantial penalties and provided little enforcement, it did mark a significant change in the attitude of Congress toward limiting the abuses of big business.

NATIONAL LABOR RELATIONS ACT (1935)

This act, often called the **Wagner Act**, was largely responsible for helping legitimatize unions and spurring on union membership in America. A special **National Labor Relations Board** was created to protect the right of labor to organize, and to guarantee the right of unions to bargain collectively with their employers. Unions grew rapidly with this new law to protect them.

A KEY COURT CASE

IN RE DEBS (1895)

Background: Eugene Debs, a union official, refused to honor a federal **injunction** (a court order requiring some action) ordering him to halt a strike of railroad workers. Debs argued that the federal government had no right to prevent workers from striking.

Decision/Significance: The Court upheld the right of the federal government to issue injunctions halting a strike. This decision permitted employers to use the federal courts as a tool to prevent strikes. The Clayton Anti-Trust Act (1914) later restricted the power of federal courts to issue injunctions for this purpose.

SUMMARIZING YOUR UNDERSTANDING

Directions: How well do you understand what you have just read? Test yourself by answering the following questions.

MAJOR ITEMS TO REMEMBER

On 3x5 index cards (as shown on pp. 33-34), briefly define the following terms and concepts:

Free Enterprise System	Corporations	Laissez-faire
Strikes	Boycotts	Injunctions
Sherman Anti-Trust Act	Unions	Wagner Act

THE RISE OF BIG BUSINESS

During the latter half of the 19th century the development of big business brought about enormous changes in America. Summarize your understanding of these changes by answering the following questions:

- What factors contributed to America's economic development in the second half of the 19th century?

- Do you think the entrepreneurs of this period were "captains of industry" or "robber barons"? Explain.

- In what ways did government respond to the demand for limiting the abuses of big business?
- What has been the impact of big business on America?

THE DEVELOPMENT OF LABOR UNIONS

Increases in industrial productivity and higher corporate profits were made at terrible costs to workers. Summarize your understanding of this statement by answering the following questions:

- What problems did the worker face in America during the second half of the 19th century?
- Describe the tactics used by both workers and management to achieve their particular goals.
- Trace the changing attitude of government towards labor unions.
- What has been the impact of labor unions on America?

PERSONALITIES OF THE PERIOD

People often have an important influence on the political, economic or social life of their times. Summarize your understanding of this statement by completing a separate 3x5 index card (follow the procedures outlined on page 34) for each of the following individuals: ***Andrew Carnegie***, ***John D. Rockefeller***, ***Samuel Gompers***, and ***A. Philip Randolph***.

TESTING YOUR UNDERSTANDING

Directions: Test your understanding of this unit by answering the following questions. Circle the number preceding the word or expression that correctly answers the statement or question. Following the short answer questions, answer either the RCT-type or Regents essay questions.

SKILL BUILDER: INTERPRETING A CARTOON

Base your answer to questions 1 through 3 on the following cartoon and on your knowledge of social studies.

FACTORY
THE NERVE OF THESE WORKERS, THE NEXT THING THEY WILL BE ASKING FOR IS A 10 HOUR WORK DAY!!!

1 The men with the cigars symbolize
 1 19th-century industrialists
 2 turn-of-the-century muckrakers
 3 union organizers
 4 trustbusters

2 What is the main idea of the cartoon?
 1 There should be a ten-hour work day.
 2 Unions should demand greater pay increases.
 3 Workers were treated unfairly by industrialists.
 4 Union leaders are concerned about government.

3 The cartoonist would most likely support the use of
 1 boycotts 3 lockouts
 2 yellow dog contracts 4 company unions

SKILL-BUILDER: ANALYZING SPEAKERS

Base your answers to questions 4 and 5 on the speakers' statements and on your knowledge of social studies.

Speaker A: America is the land of opportunity. All one needs to do to achieve success is work hard and save money.

Speaker B: Many large corporations exploit workers by paying them low wages and creating unsafe working conditions.

Speaker C: The job of government is to act as an umpire and not as a participant in the marketplace.

Speaker D: The growth of a large business is merely the process of weeding out the weak. This is not an evil tendency in business. It is merely the interaction of forces in the free market.

4 Speaker A would most likely agree with the ideas expressed by
 1 Thaddeus Stevens 3 Andrew Carnegie
 2 Samuel Gompers 4 Pauline Feldman

5 Which speaker would be most likely to oppose the idea of laissez-faire capitalism?
 1 A 3 C
 2 B 4 D

SKILL-BUILDER: ANALYZING A BAR GRAPH

Base your answer to questions 6 and 7 on the following bar graph and on your knowledge of social studies.

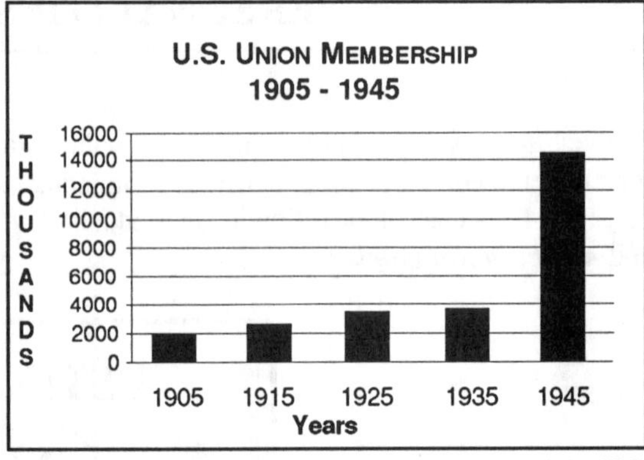
U.S. UNION MEMBERSHIP
1905 - 1945
THOUSANDS
16000
14000
12000
10000
8000
6000
4000
2000
0
1905 1915 1925 1935 1945
Years

Source: Historical Statistics of the U.S.

6 Union membership in the United States during 1905 was about
 1 two thousand 3 twenty million
 2 two million 4 two hundred million

7 Which is the best explanation for the increase in union membership from 1935 to 1945?
 1 end of World War II
 2 election of Calvin Coolidge
 3 passage of the Wagner Act
 4 creation of the assembly line

8 Which of the following people is most closely identified with the growth of industry in the United States?
1 George Washington Carver
2 Cornelius Vanderbilt
3 Thomas Nast
4 Paul Dunbar

9 Which term most accurately describes the economic system found in the United States?
1 mercantilism
2 free enterprise
3 Communism
4 balance of trade

10 The right to bargain collectively means that
1 workers are forbidden to strike
2 businesses must accept the demands of its workers
3 workers have a right to negotiate with their employers through unions
4 employers are prohibited from asking for injunctions

11 If you are a stockholder, then you would be considered
1 a carpetbagger from the north
2 a part owner of a corporation
3 a member of a labor union
4 a member of the president's Cabinet

12 A major cause of industrialization in the United States was the
1 issuing of the Emancipation Proclamation
2 expansion of railroads
3 passage of the Sherman Anti-Trust Act
4 development of labor unions

13 The use of the term "Gilded Age" to describe American society during the latter part of the 19th century suggests that, at that time, the nation was concerned primarily with
1 materialistic goals
2 social equality
3 overseas expansion
4 artistic achievement

14 The primary reason for workers to join a union is to
1 improve their working conditions
2 eliminate corporate injustices
3 achieve equal opportunities for minorities
4 improve the quality of goods they produce

15 What was the major problem facing industrial workers in the late 19th century in the United States?
1 shortage of farm crops
2 failure to vote in elections
3 decreased rates charged by railroads
4 unfair practices used by big business

16 Injunctions, lockouts and blacklisting were weapons used by
1 unions against workers
2 government against unions
3 business against workers
4 corporations against government

17 Which was a major reason for the failure of early 19th century labor unions in the United States?
1 the public disapproved of unions
2 congressional measures outlawed collective bargaining
3 there was an abundance of technical workers
4 workers were generally satisfied with their working conditions

18 Which belief was held by the leaders of big business in the U. S. during the early part of the 20th century?
1 Labor unions should be prohibited or closely controlled.
2 The United States should return to an agrarian society.
3 Government must closely regulate the economy.
4 Legislation must be enacted to limit business investment.

19 Which practice characterized big business in the United States during the period 1850-1900?
1 the demand for government action to end immigration
2 the use of business combinations to control prices
3 pressure on the government to prevent inflation
4 opposition to the introduction of automation

20 Decisions in the collective bargaining process primarily involve
1 labor leaders and Congress
2 unions and management
3 producers and consumers
4 government and unions

21 Which statement about the Sherman Anti-Trust Act of 1890 is most accurate?
1 It gave states the power to regulate interstate railways.
2 It outlawed monopolies that restrict interstate commerce.
3 It established the Federal Trade Commission.
4 The Supreme Court ruled that it was unconstitutional.

22 Which statement is an opinion rather than a fact?
1 The Knights of Labor were organized in 1869.
2 Thomas Edison invented the incandescent light bulb.
3 The primary reason for business mergers is to limit competition.
4 Early craft unions limited their membership to skilled workers.

23 Which belief was common to both Knights of Labor and the American Federation of Labor?
1 Unions must limit membership to become strong.
2 Unskilled workers should be excluded from union membership.
3 Yellow dog contracts can help union membership.
4 Unions should represent the voice of workers.

24 In an outline, one of these is the main topic, and the other three are sub-topics. Which one is the main topic?
1 Weapons of Labor
2 Strikes
3 Collective Bargaining
4 Boycotts

25 "All human life revolves around the struggle for survival."
This quotation best expresses the philosophy of
1 mercantilism
2 Social Darwinism
3 civil disobedience
4 collective bargaining

RCT-TYPE ESSAYS

1 Workers in the latter part of the 19th century faced many problems. They took various steps to overcome these problems.

Part A

List *two* problems that workers faced in the latter part of the 19th century.

1. ____________________

2. ____________________

List *two* steps that workers took to overcome their problems.

1. ____________________

2. ____________________

Part B

In your Part B answer, you should use information you gave in Part A. However, you may also include different or additional information in your Part B answer.

Write an essay discussing the problems that workers faced in the latter part of the 19th century and explain how they overcame some of these problems.

2 Many individuals have played an important role in changing the course of U. S. history.

Individuals

Samuel Gompers	Thaddeus Stevens
Booker T. Washington	W. E. B. du Bois
Andrew Carnegie	John D. Rockefeller

Part A

Choose *one* individual listed above: ____________________

Identify *one* way in which that person's ideas or actions affected the course of U. S. history.

____

Choose *another* individual: ____________________

Identify *one* way in which that person's ideas or actions affected the course of U. S. history.

____

Part B

In your Part B answer, you should use information you gave in Part A. However, you may also include different or additional information in your Part B answer.

Write an essay discussing how individuals have played an important role in changing the course of U. S. history.

3 Labor and management have different tools when they conflict with each other.

Tools of Labor	Tools of Management
Strikes	Injunctions
Boycotts	Lockouts
Closed shop	Company unions
Collective bargaining	Blacklisting

Part A

Select *two* tools of labor and *two* tools of management, and define *each* tool.

Tools of Labor	Definition
1. ____________	____________________
2. ____________	____________________

Tools of Management	Definition
1. ________________	________________________________
2. ________________	________________________________

Part B

In your Part B answer, you should use information you gave in Part A. However, you may also include different or additional information in your Part B answer.

Write an essay explaining how labor and management use different tools when they compete against each other.

REGENTS-TYPE ESSAYS

1 Certain groups have had a significant impact on developments in American history.

Group / Development

Industrialists / Rise of American Business
Radical Republicans / Reconstruction
Labor Unions / Rise of Organized Labor

Choose *two* groups from the list. For *each* one selected, show how that group had an impact on developments in American history.

2 State your view concerning each of *three* of the statements listed below. Using specific evidence, give reasons to support your position in each case.

- The post-Civil War amendments played a key role in bringing about equality in the United States.
- Congressional Reconstruction was too harsh on the South.
- Government should follow a policy of laissez-faire in dealing with big business in America.
- America's "captains of industry" contributed greatly to the growth of industry.
- Railroads helped stimulate industrial growth and tied the nation together.
- The weapons used by management are far more powerful than the weapons used by labor.

PERFORMANCE-BASED TASKS

Setting: America was transformed by the Industrial Revolution. In 1860, just over a million Americans worked in factories. However, by the 1890s, that number had grown to over 5 million. As factories grew, abuses against workers also increased. For example, in one New York carriage factory, workers were not even permitted to get a drink of water unless they had their foreman's permission.

General Directions: Class members will assume various roles during a Congressional hearing about working conditions at the turn of the 20th century. The members of the committee and those testifying consist of the following roles:

- Committee Chairperson
- Congressperson #1
- Congressperson #2
- Hat Factory Worker
- Union Leader
- Painter
- Chinese Miner
- Mother Jones

Committee Chairperson: Today we have several witnesses who will provide testimony to this committee regarding conditions faced by working people and their attempts to improve their lives through the labor union movement.

Congressperson #1: Please state your name and explain why you are here.

Hat Factory Worker: My name is Sarah Smith, and I have worked in a factory as a hat maker for three years. Instead of conditions at the factory getting better, they were getting worse. The bosses kept reducing our pay. They cut our wages by half a cent for each dozen hats we make.

Congressperson #2: What action did you take, if any, to improve your situation?

Hat Factory Worker: We joined the Hatmakers Union and then went on strike. The result was a victory, which resulted in a $2.00 average increase in our weekly wages. However, the bosses tried to fight the union by bringing in child workers and immigrants who were not union members, and were willing to work for almost nothing. As a result, we went on strike for 13 weeks. We won again, not only getting the employers to agree to hire only union workers, but also gaining the support of many non-union workers as well.

Committee Chairperson: Can you tell us about the experiences of black workers?

Union Leader: I am here to tell black workers that they are welcomed in the Knights of Labor. I myself belong to a local that is made up of whites, with two exceptions, and I hold a very high position of trust in that local. I would say to all men of color, organize. I also appeal to members of Congress to support the Knights of Labor. Let us put our shoulders to the wheel and victory is ours.

continued...

Congressperson #1: Sir, I understand that you, as a black painter, had a much different experience with organized labor than the previous speaker.

Painter: I certainly did. Not only weren't the white painters friendly toward us, but they didn't allow us to join their union under any circumstances. The plumbers were under somewhat the same ban.

Congressperson #2: Can you tell us something about the experiences of Chinese miners and organized labor?

Chinese Miner: Several times we were requested by the white miners to join them in asking the companies for an increase in wages for both Chinese and whites. We asked what we should do if the companies refused, and they said we should strike, so the companies would be forced to raise our pay. Afraid we would lose our jobs, we disagreed. During the past two years, an organization of white miners was created. Its goal is to force all Chinese workers out of the territory of Wyoming. In fact, this month notices were posted demanding that all Chinese be thrown out of the country.

Committee Chairperson: I understand that our last speaker is here to discuss with us the conditions of child workers.

Mother Jones: In Pennsylvania in 1903, I saw the conditions under which children worked in textile mills. I observed children with missing fingers, stooped little things, round shouldered and skinny. Many of them were not over ten years old, although state laws prohibit their working before age twelve. The mothers of these children lied about their ages because their families were starving and they needed the work.

Your Task: You are to write a newspaper article under the headline provided below. Use the "testimony" provided in the Congressional hearing and any other material you may wish to add from your research on American factory labor conditions at the turn of the 20th century.

1¢	DAILY GAZETTE	1¢

CONGRESS FINDS HELP IS NEEDED TO IMPROVE WORKERS' CONDITIONS

By ______________________________

____

____

____

____

LOOKING AT DIVERSITY

The United States is composed of many different kinds of people. Each of us is unique, yet each of us also bears some similarities to others. It is these similarities that Americans tend to use when classifying themselves.

HOW DO AMERICANS CATEGORIZE THEMSELVES?

Throughout American history, the most persistent classifications have been along the lines of race, gender, nationality, ethnic group, religion and social class. Before we begin to examine these terms, please indicate how you might classify yourself.

HOW WOULD YOU DEFINE YOURSELF?

My race is: ____________	My ethnic group is: ____________
My gender is: ____________	My religion is: ____________
My nationality is: ____________	My social class is: ____________

These various categories are not necessarily the most useful in determining what a person is like, but they have had a great impact on American history and culture. People have often lived in separate communities based on these characteristics, where they have developed their own cultures and life-styles. In addition, individuals have often been discriminated against by others on the basis of these same characteristics. Let's take a closer look at each of these classifications:

RACE

Over the course of time, human beings living in different regions of the world developed some physical and genetic differences, such as lighter and darker skin colors. These differences have served as the basis for classifying people into separate groups called races. The main racial groups in the U. S. are Caucasians (white European Americans), African Americans (blacks), Asian Americans and Native Americans.

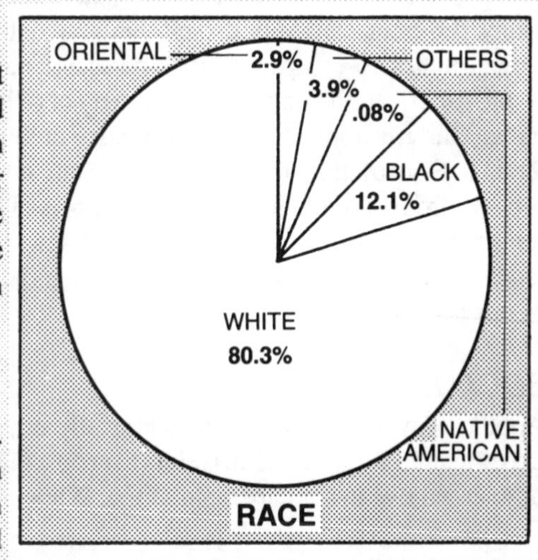
ORIENTAL
2.9%
OTHERS
3.9%
.08%
BLACK
12.1%
WHITE
80.3%
NATIVE
AMERICAN
RACE

GENDER

People can also be classified by gender (male/female). Gender divisions have played an important role in American history. Until the 20th century, American women could not vote in most states, could not attend universities or enter the professions, and had limited rights in their own families. With the passage of various civil rights laws, gender classification has taken on greater importance.

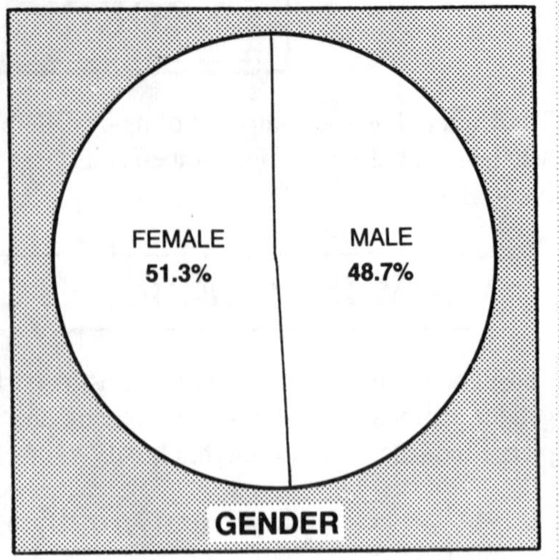
FEMALE
51.3%
MALE
48.7%
GENDER

ETHNICITY

An ethnic group is a group of people of common origin *or* common culture. How a particular ethnic group is defined can vary: its members may share a common race (African Americans, Asian Americans), a common religion (Jewish Americans, Mormons), a common language (Hispanic Americans) or a common national origin (Italian Americans, Irish Americans). The ethnic background of a person often identifies his or her culture and way of life (foods, dating patterns, etc.)

A note on nationality and national origin:

Nationality refers to the country of which a person is currently a citizen. National origin, often used to identify a person's ethnic background, refers to where their ancestors came from. For example, a person who is identified as an Italian American is one who is an American citizen, but whose ancestors came from Italy.

RELIGION

There is no precise definition for "religion." However, most definitions of religion list several common elements: a set of beliefs about a god; a set of customs and practices; and an organization, such as a church, which oversees the conduct of religious practices. Many different religious groups emigrated to the United States to escape religious persecution. As a result, Americans belong to a wide variety of religious faiths. Our government follows a practice outlined in the U.S. Constitution, that Church and State must be separate from one another. Even so, members of some religious groups, such as Catholics and Jews, have faced acts of private discrimination in various periods of our history.

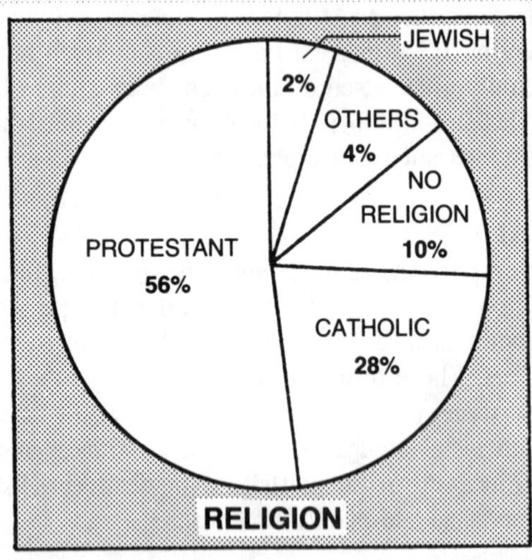
JEWISH
2%
OTHERS
4%
NO
RELIGION
10%
PROTESTANT
56%
CATHOLIC
28%
RELIGION

SOCIAL CLASS

Another way Americans have traditionally organized themselves is into social classes (working class, upper middle class, etc.). This refers to people of similar income and education, who work in similar kinds of jobs and live in similar communities. While a person is born into the social class of his or her parents, he or she can move into a different social class based on education, work and luck. The movement of individuals from one social class to another is called **social mobility**.

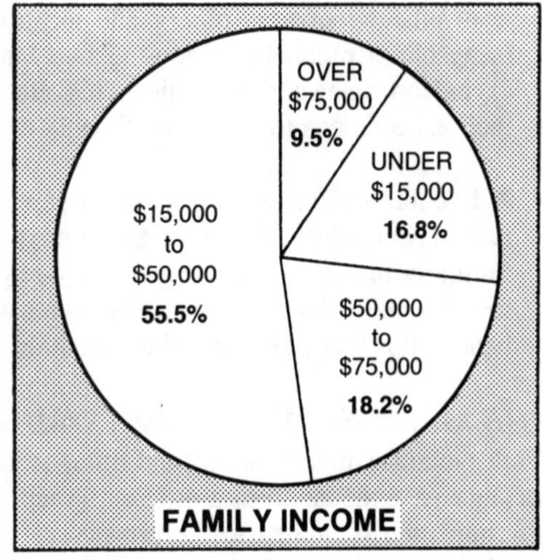
OVER
$75,000
9.5%
UNDER
$15,000
16.8%
$15,000
to
$50,000
55.5%
$50,000
to
$75,000
18.2%
FAMILY INCOME

Having had the opportunity to read about each of these classifications, how might you *now* define yourself? Return to the chart at the start of this section and make any adjustments you feel are appropriate.

STUDYING THE EXPERIENCES OF DISADVANTAGED GROUPS

Much of what you study in American history deals with the actions of our government and business leaders. For most of our history, these national leaders have been wealthy white Protestant males. However, studying this group does not really give us a full picture of American life. To truly understand our nation's history and character, we need to study the experiences of Americans outside this limited group. Even more importantly, our own progress towards full social equality will depend in part upon our understanding of the past deprivations and struggles of disadvantaged groups. Sometimes we refer to these groups as **minorities**, since their experiences differed from those of the majority or dominant group. We usually tend to include women as one of the deprived groups, although this group actually constitutes the majority, not a minority.

In other sections of this book, you will review the experiences of particular minorities and disadvantaged groups in detail. Here we will take a brief look at the general patterns of prejudice and discrimination that many of these groups have faced.

THE ROOTS OF PREJUDICE

The word prejudice comes from a joining together of *pre* and *judge*. It refers to a person's having attitudes and beliefs against people from other racial, ethnic, class or gender groups. What causes people to be prejudiced? Why are prejudices often so difficult to eradicate? Social scientists studying these problems have identified several mechanisms that explain how these prejudices develop and spread:

- **Psychological Factors.** People often feel more familiar and friendly with those in the same racial, ethnic, class or gender group. Lack of familiarity with members of other groups often leads to thinking in **stereotypes**, in which prejudiced individuals make negative generalizations about members of other groups based on a few hasty observations. They look on people from other groups as outsiders. For psychological reasons, they come to believe that their own group is the best. This **ethnocentrism** increases their own personal self-esteem. They believe they are superior because other groups are inferior.

- **Influence of Tradition.** We are not born with prejudices; we learn them from family members, friends and neighbors as we grow up. Members of the dominant group often looked upon people from other groups as inferior and incapable. For example, many men thought women were incapable of rational decision-making. Major institutions such as universities and government excluded women and minorities. This often led women and members of minority groups to limit their expectations to what they thought they could realistically achieve.

■ **Economic Competition**. In many cases, prejudice is increased by fears of economic competition. Poor whites feared competition with poor blacks who might work for lower wages. Similarly, union members feared that immigrants from Southern and Eastern Europe might accept lower wages. More recently, some men have feared the loss of jobs to women. Social scientists believe this fear of economic competition is often a major factor behind prejudice.

THE MANY FACES OF DISCRIMINATION

While prejudice refers to beliefs and attitudes about the members of a group, discrimination refers to actual acts against someone from a different group. Discrimination can take many forms. In some societies, discrimination is limited to the private acts of individuals. In other societies, discrimination against members of minority groups is supported by public law.

■ **Private Acts of Discrimination**. Even where people are treated equally under the law, private individuals may exercise their rights of private choice and refuse to associate with other individuals because of their race, ethnicity, social class or gender. Private discrimination makes it difficult for members of disadvantaged groups to get the best education or jobs, blocking their economic and social advancement. For example, many private clubs once excluded women, and at one time, the residents of many neighborhoods signed agreements promising not to sell their homes to members of certain racial or religious groups. Federal laws now prohibit these forms of discrimination.

■ **Legal Discrimination and Segregation**. In more extreme cases, minorities faced public discrimination supported by law. In some states, special laws once excluded some minority groups from political power or civil rights, making them second-class citizens. These legal disabilities in turn left members of the disadvantaged group open to economic exploitation and social oppression. For example, after the passage of Jim Crow laws in the South, African Americans were excluded from white public schools and separated from whites in the use of most public facilities.

■ **Enslavement, Expulsion and Genocide**. Sometimes actions against minority groups can be much more extreme. Earlier in our history, Africans were brought to America by slave traders and were bought and sold as though they were property. Native Americans were forcibly removed from their tribal lands and resettled on reservations. Many died from maltreatment and exposure to new diseases. The most extreme form of abuse is an attempt to eliminate a minority through extermination, known as **genocide** — murder of a whole group of people. The best-known example of genocide was the Nazi attempt to eliminate the Jews of Europe during World War II.

THE CHALLENGE OF A PLURALISTIC SOCIETY

For some disadvantaged groups, acts of resistance against exploitation and oppression have been almost continuous. In the 19th century, the leaders of many disadvantaged groups organized their own reform movements with the goal of improving their conditions. They attempted to establish a broader base of support by winning the sympathies of people outside their own group. The Holocaust during World War II and the Civil Rights Movement of the 1950s and 1960s were major turning points. The U.S. Supreme Court began reading new meaning into the "Equal Protection" clause of the 14th Amendment, and Congress passed new laws against discrimination. Leaders of other disadvantaged groups—women, Native Americans, and the disabled—followed the African-American activists in fighting to achieve benefits for their own group. As a result, the United States today is making greater efforts to accommodate the needs of all its citizens—fostering a society in which all groups participate in exercising political, economic and social power. However, this goal has presented challenges.

THE NEED FOR AGREEMENT

Americans need to agree on what efforts should be made to overcome the effects of past prejudice and to achieve equality among all groups. Should we establish a "color-blind" society (in which race is never a permissible factor in any decision), or should we take specific steps to compensate the members of disadvantaged groups for the effects of past discrimination (for example, admitting an additional number of candidates from disadvantaged groups into prestigious colleges)?

THE NEED TO PRESERVE IDENTITIES

Americans must find new ways to preserve their identities as members of distinct cultural and social groups while also cooperating with members from different groups in maintaining a common American identity. Can Americans strike a balance between loyalty to their particular group and loyalty to their society as a whole? Some scholars fear that the recent emphasis on ethnic or group identity threatens to weaken the American commitment to a common culture. They predict that instead of broadening American society to include all groups, the result will be hostile competition and a new fragmentation.

ANSWERING AN ESSAY QUESTION ON DIVERSITY

Essay questions about disadvantaged groups in America frequently appear on the RCT and Regents examinations. Let's take a look at an essay question that appeared on the January 1992 Regents:

At various periods in United States history, groups of people have been affected by specific actions or events.

Groups / Periods

Native American Indians / 1865 to the present
Factory workers / 1865 to 1920
Women / 1900 to 1925
Farmers / 1929 to the present
Japanese Americans / 1941 to 1945
African Americans / 1950 to the present

Choose *three* of the groups listed and for *each* one chosen:

- Identify a specific action or event that had an impact on the group during that time period
- Discuss a positive or a negative impact of the action or event on that group during that time period
- Discuss the extent to which the condition of the group has changed since the action or event

Most other of these types of essay questions follow a similar pattern:

THE GROUPS

The question will contain a list of social, ethnic and occupational groups — women, African Americans, Native Americans, Hispanics (Latinos), Asian Americans, Japanese Americans, Jewish Americans, factory workers, farmers, or the disabled. You will usually be asked to choose some groups from the list.

THEIR PROBLEMS

Often you will be asked to provide details on problems members of these groups faced — in what ways they were discriminated against or treated unequally. You should be ready to give specific examples of discrimination or unequal treatment. Let's look at a group that frequently appears on tests—African Americans.

> African Americans lived in the United States for many generations as slaves. Even after their emancipation from slavery, and up through the 1950s, they were discriminated against and segregated. They were excluded from the best schools and jobs; and in many states they could not vote or hold public office; they were even forced by law to use separate, inferior public facilities.

ATTEMPTS TO SOLVE THE PROBLEM

You will be asked ***either*** to give an example of a proposal by a reform movement to solve the problem ***or*** to give an example of a government action or program that attempted to solve the problem.

> In the 1950s, African-American leaders like Thurgood Marshall, a lawyer for the N.A.A.C.P., fought in the courts to end discrimination. In *Brown v. Board of Education* (1954), the Supreme Court prohibited racial discrimination in public schools. Other African-American leaders like Dr. Martin Luther King, Jr. used marches, boycotts, sit-ins, freedom rides and voter registration drives to end discrimination on buses, in restaurants and in public facilities.

EVALUATION OF THE SOLUTION

You will be asked to evaluate the solution; how well did it succeed in achieving equality for the selected group? Often you will be asked to consider whether that group still faces problems today.

> The Civil Rights Movement dramatically affected conditions for African Americans. As a result of the Civil Rights Acts of the 1960s, discrimination is now prohibited in housing, employment, education, and in the use of services open to the public. Far greater educational opportunities are available now than before the *Brown* decision almost forty years ago. There is a growing and prosperous black middle class in the professions and in positions of leadership. African Americans have become proud of their heritage. On the other hand, the Civil Rights Movement has not been totally successful. Legal barriers to progress have been removed but economic obstacles still remain. Unemployment is still higher among African Americans than among the general population.

CHAPTER 8

CHANGING AMERICA

In the period after the Civil War, life in America was changing drastically. Cities became more crowded as increased numbers of immigrants flooded into them. Life on the frontier was also undergoing change. Native Americans were moved out of lands that they had occupied for centuries. Wilderness areas vanished as settlers and farmers moved west.

— TIMELINE OF KEY EVENTS —

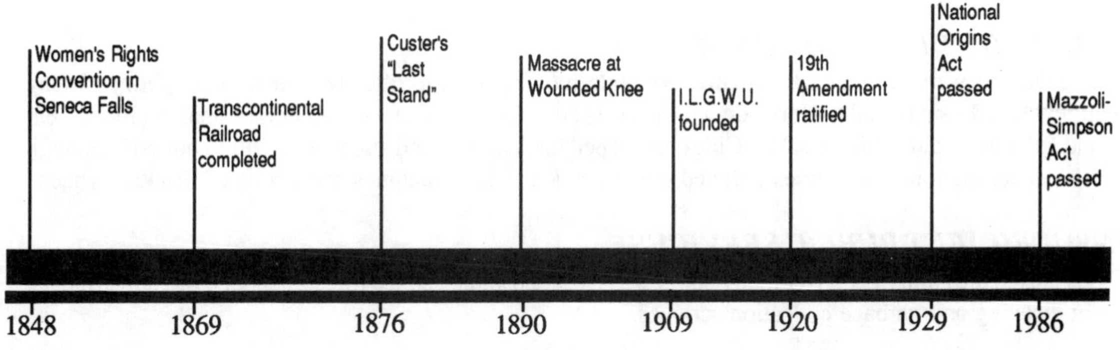

Women's Rights Convention in Seneca Falls
Transcontinental Railroad completed
Custer's "Last Stand"
Massacre at Wounded Knee
I.L.G.W.U. founded
19th Amendment ratified
National Origins Act passed
Mazzoli-Simpson Act passed
1848
1869
1876
1890
1909
1920
1929
1986

PART I: LIFE IN THE CITY

One of the most important results of industrialization was the rise of cities. Cities, and those who dwelled in them, especially immigrants and women, were greatly affected by the new problems of industrial life.

URBANIZATION

In 1865, most Americans lived in the countryside. By 1920, half of all Americans lived in cities. New York, Chicago and Philadelphia each had over a million people. This movement of people from the countryside to the cities is known as **urbanization.**

THE REASONS FOR URBANIZATION

Why did so many people move into the cities? There were many reasons:

THE ATTRACTION OF CITY LIFE

With the development of new factories, people moved to cities in search of jobs. Increased use of farm machinery reduced the number of farm jobs, forcing laborers and their families to seek work in the city. Some people were attracted by the cultural opportunities, amusements, entertainments and rich variety of city life. People sought the pleasures of museums, libraries, department stores and universities located in the cities.

THE FLOOD OF IMMIGRANTS

In the late 19th century, immigrants from Europe flooded American cities. In the largest cities, European immigrants often outnumbered native-born Americans. In the 20th century, African Americans and Hispanic Americans also moved into cities in large numbers in search of a better life.

CITIES FACE NEW PROBLEMS

American cities grew so quickly that municipal authorities could not deal adequately with all their problems.

OVERCROWDING AND CONGESTION

Whole families were crowded into **tenements** (single-room apartments often without heat or lighting). Many families shared a single toilet. Horse-drawn carriages crowded the streets of larger cities, making movement to and from work almost impossible. Cities developed haphazardly and streets were often not wide enough for the increased traffic. Factories polluted the air, and sewage sometimes contaminated drinking water.

INSUFFICIENT PUBLIC SERVICES

Cities lacked the ability to deliver many public services—hospitals, police forces, schools, fire departments, street cleaning and garbage collection services.

TENSIONS BETWEEN SOCIAL GROUPS

In the city, the very rich lived around the corner from the very poor. The closeness of the rich and poor increased the tensions of city-life, and made it more difficult for the poor to bear their horrible conditions.

POLITICAL CORRUPTION

Cities were run by corrupt "**political machines.**" Political bosses provided jobs and service for immigrants and the poor in exchange for their votes. The bosses then used their control of city hall to make illegal profits on city contracts. Nevertheless, the bosses at least provided some services to the poor at a time when government's role in dealing with social problems was strictly limited.

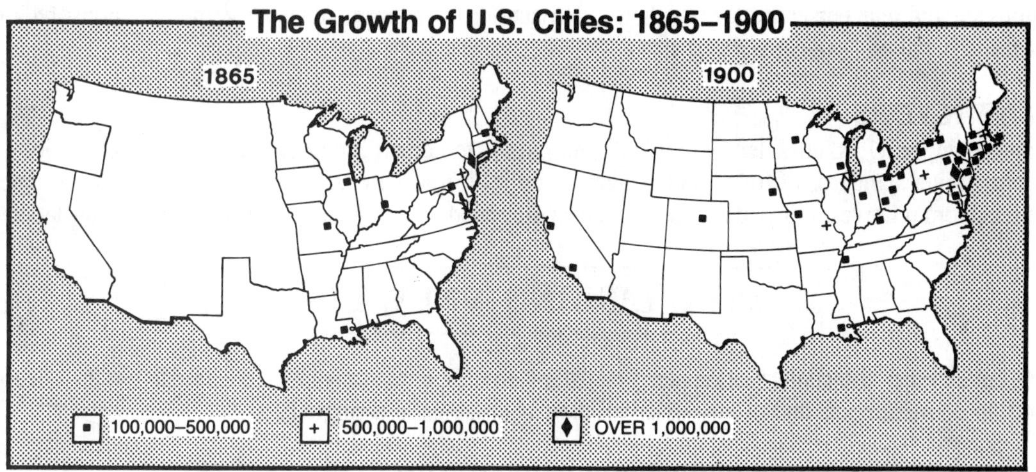
The Growth of U.S. Cities: 1865–1900
1865
1900
100,000–500,000
500,000–1,000,000
OVER 1,000,000

KEY ITEMS TO REMEMBER

Urbanization, tenements, "political machines"

IMMIGRATION: THE CHANGING FACE OF AMERICA

The United States has a unique population in that almost all of its people are immigrants or are descended from immigrants.

WHY THE IMMIGRANTS CAME

Immigrants have been attracted to America throughout its history. Their decision to come to America was influenced by the situation in their own countries, as well as by factors existing in the United States.

PUSH FACTORS

Conditions in the immigrants' native lands propelled or "pushed" them to leave. They came to escape horrible conditions of poverty. For example, the potato famine in Ireland in the 1840s caused the death of thousands and led a large number of Irish immigrants to come to America. Another major reason was to escape religious and political persecution. For example, Russian Jews fled from violent government-sponsored riots against them, called "**pogroms.**"

PULL FACTORS

Conditions in the U. S. attracted or "pulled" immigrants to come. They heard about the greater political freedom, higher standards of living and availability of jobs in America. News of these benefits was spread by letters from relatives, railroad advertisements selling land, and industrialists seeking to recruit laborers.

ESTABLISHING A NEW LIFE

Immigrants in the 19th century often faced hardships on the trip to America. They traveled in the cheapest steamship compartments and often carried all their belongings in a single bag.

THE PROCESS OF BECOMING AMERICANIZED

Becoming "Americanized" (learning to act, speak and be like others) was a gradual process. Often it was the children of immigrants, not the immigrants themselves, who became fully Americanized.

- **Initial Hardships.** Adjusting to life in their new land presented great difficulties. The new immigrants arriving after 1880 were extremely poor and usually settled in cities. Most did not speak English and were unfamiliar with American customs and culture. They lived in crowded, unsanitary apartments and worked at unskilled jobs for long hours at low pay. In addition, they faced hostility and discrimination from both native-born Americans and other ethnic groups.

- **Ethnic Ghettos.** To cope with their many problems, the immigrants usually settled down with other immigrants of the same nationality in urban neighborhoods known as **ghettos**. The immigrants felt more comfortable surrounded by those who spoke the same language, followed the same customs, and shared the same experiences. However, living in ethnic ghettos meant that they were cut off from mainstream American life, making it harder for them to become **acculturated** (learn the language and culture of their adopted land).

- **The Assimilation of the Immigrants' Children.** While some immigrants attended night school to learn English, most were too busy working or caring for families to spend much time learning a new language or culture. It was left to their children to attend public schools in order to learn English, and become familiar with American customs. In this way, the children were eventually **assimilated** (made similar to other Americans).

■ **Conflicts Develop.** Often the process of assimilation was accompanied by bitter conflict between generations. For example, the parents might insist on an arranged marriage for their children, while their children would insist on finding their own marriage partners according to the American custom. Most of the immigrants had no idea that in America they would find their most cherished beliefs and practices challenged by their children.

SHIFTING PATTERNS OF IMMIGRATION

THE OLD IMMIGRANTS (1607-1880)

Until the 1880s, most immigrants came from Northern Europe, especially Great Britain, Ireland, and Germany. In general, they were Protestant, except for the Irish, who were Catholic. Most of them spoke English. They came looking for the cheap farmland available in the west, and they often settled on the western frontier. There were no laws passed to limit these immigrants, since they were welcomed to America.

THE NEW IMMIGRANTS (1880-1920)

Existing patterns of immigration changed in the 1880s. Most of the "**New Immigrants**" came from southern and eastern Europe, especially Poland, Italy, Austria-Hungary, Greece and Russia. They were Catholic and Jewish, rather than Protestant. They were very poor, spoke no English, and dressed differently from northern Europeans. A trickle of Asian immigrants also came, until the first laws limiting immigration were passed.

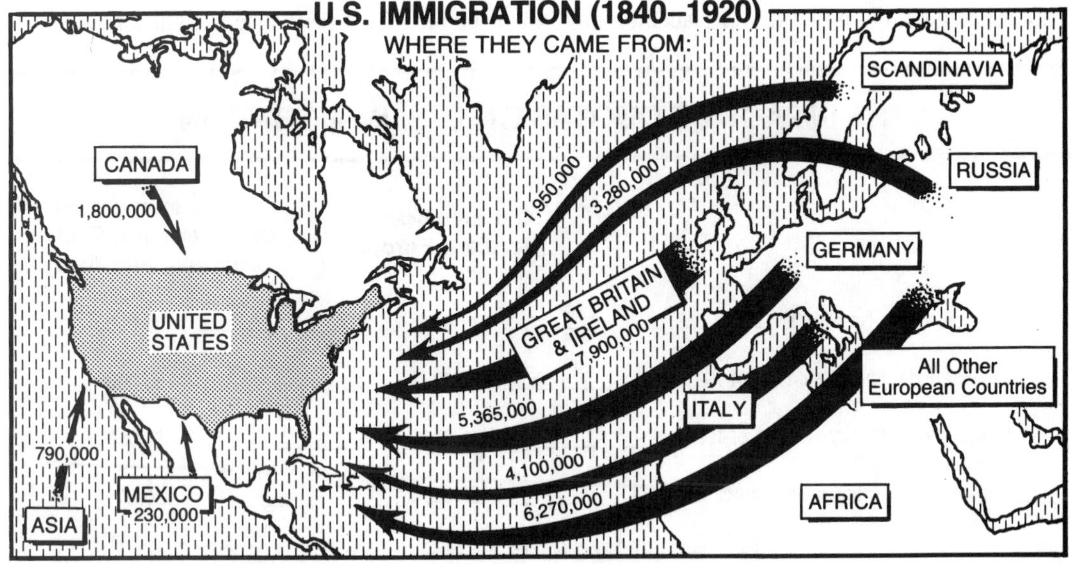
U.S. IMMIGRATION (1840–1920)
WHERE THEY CAME FROM:
SCANDINAVIA
1,950,000
RUSSIA
3,280,000
CANADA
1,800,000
GERMANY
GREAT BRITAIN & IRELAND 7,900,000
UNITED STATES
All Other European Countries
5,365,000
ITALY
4,100,000
6,270,000
790,000
MEXICO 230,000
ASIA
AFRICA

THE RISE OF NATIVISM

As the flood of immigrants grew at the end of the 19th century there developed a rising sentiment of nativist hostility. Nativists were **ethnocentric**, believing that native-born Americans were superior to foreigners and that immigration should be restricted. They argued that the "new" immigrants were inferior to "true" Americans, who were white, Anglo-Saxon, and Protestant (WASP). They were convinced that those of other races, religions, and nationalities were physically and culturally inferior. They feared that the New Immigrants would be impossible to absorb into American society, since they lived in ethnic ghettos and spoke their own languages. Finally, nativists believed that immigrants would lower living standards and take away jobs, since they were willing to work for such low wages.

EARLY RESTRICTIONS (1880-1920)

The first acts at limiting immigration were directed against Asians. The **Chinese Exclusion Act (1882)** was passed to satisfy anti-Chinese feeling in California against the flood of Chinese workers: all Chinese immigration was banned. In the **Gentlemen's Agreement (1907)** the Japanese government agreed to limit Japanese emigration to the United States to those who already had relatives living in America.

RESTRICTIVE IMMIGRATION (1920-1965)

After World War I, nativist feeling against immigrants led Congress to restrict immigration from Europe. These laws specifically discouraged the New Immigrants by establishing quotas for each nationality based on the existing ethnic makeup of the United States.

■ **Immigration Acts of 1921, 1924, and 1929** established a quota system aimed at preserving America's existing ethnic composition. Great Britain, Ireland and Germany were allowed the largest number of immigrants. This operated to limit the "New Immigrants." These acts were inspired by a desire for isolation in world affairs, fear of Communism and ethnic prejudice. Asians were banned, but no limit was placed on immigrants coming from the Western Hemisphere.

THE IMPACT OF QUOTAS ON U. S. IMMIGRATION

	Old Immigrants (Northern Europe)	New Immigrants (Southern and Eastern Europe, and Asia)
Average Yearly Total (1900-1914)	177,000	685,500
Allowed under Immigration Act of 1921	198,000	158,000
Allowed under Immigration Act of 1924	141,000	22,000
Allowed under National Origins Act of 1929	132,000	20,000

(All figures are approximate)

■ **McCarran-Walter Act (1952)** kept the quotas at the 1920 levels. Asian countries were allowed token immigration of 100 persons each. Total immigration outside the Western Hemisphere was set at 156,000.

■ **Immigration Act of 1965** was designed to be less biased than earlier immigration legislation, reflecting changes in our national values. Each country was given an identical quota of 20,000 immigrants. Preference was given to those with relatives in the U.S. or with valuable occupational skills. Although allowing greater immigration from southern Europe, Asia and Africa, the act limited immigration from Latin America — leading to a sharp increase in illegal immigration from Mexico and Central America.

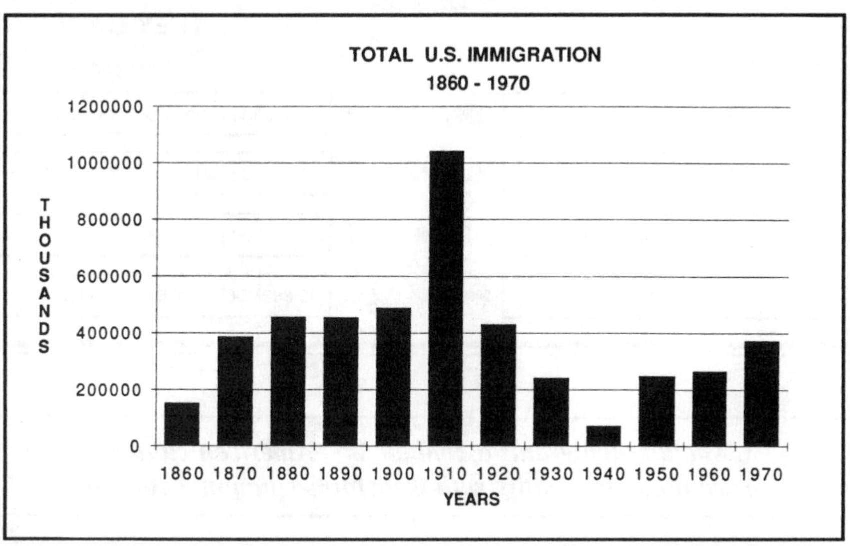
TOTAL U.S. IMMIGRATION
1860 - 1970
THOUSANDS
1200000
1000000
800000
600000
400000
200000
0
1860 1870 1880 1890 1900 1910 1920 1930 1940 1950 1960 1970
YEARS

Source: U.S. Historical Statistics

IMMIGRATION SINCE 1965

Since 1965, the largest number of immigrants have come from Latin America and Asia, with very few now coming from Europe. Today, the U. S. tries to limit total immigration to about 300,000. Because of these limits, there has been a sharp rise in illegal immigration. Perhaps a million "illegals" are entering each year.

■ **Refugee Act of 1980**. This act gave special status to **refugees**—people fleeing persecution in their native lands. It allowed an additional 50,000 refugees to enter the country each year. The president could also admit additional refugees in an emergency situation.

■ **Immigration and Control Act of 1986**. Often called the **Mazzoli-Simpson Act**, this act "legalized" all illegal aliens who had been in the United States continuously since 1981. Its purpose was to deal with the problems posed by massive illegal immigration. The act imposed stiff penalties on employers who hire illegal aliens.

■ **The Immigration Dilemma**. In the last two decades, America has opened its door to refugees from many nations, stirring a national debate over future immigration. In earlier times, the high cost of travel was a natural obstacle to immigration. In an age of cheap trans-portation, the U. S. could easily become flooded with people. We are a nation of immigrants, but we must restrict immigration. This poses a dilemma: How many people should we admit and who should they be? And how strictly should we enforce laws against " illegals?"

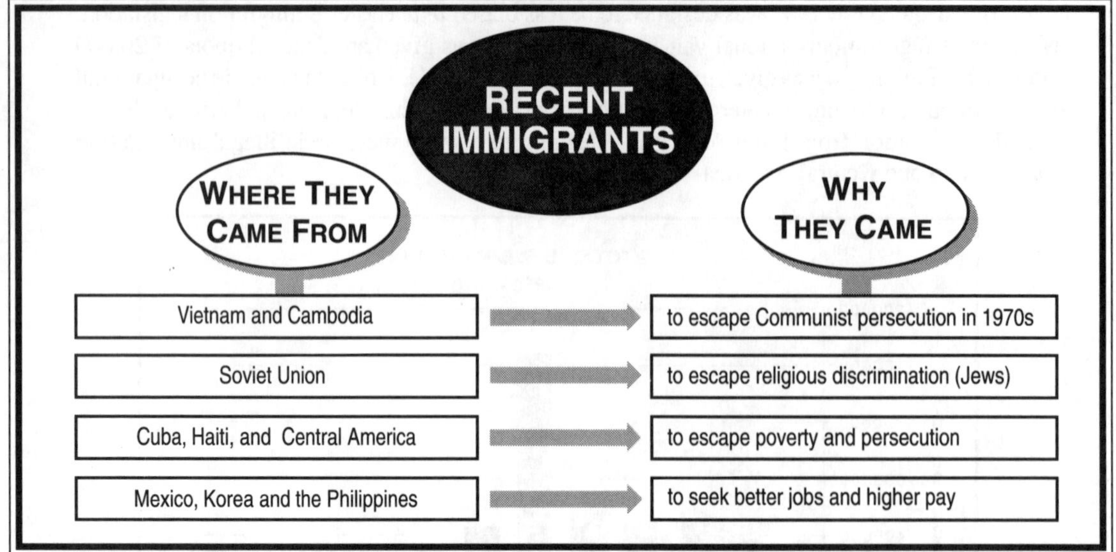
RECENT IMMIGRANTS
WHERE THEY CAME FROM
WHY THEY CAME
Vietnam and Cambodia
to escape Communist persecution in 1970s
Soviet Union
to escape religious discrimination (Jews)
Cuba, Haiti, and Central America
to escape poverty and persecution
Mexico, Korea and the Philippines
to seek better jobs and higher pay

Should immigrants assimilate into American culture or continue to identify with their former national culture?

POINT: ASSIMILATION	COUNTERPOINT: CULTURAL PLURALISM
Under the "melting pot" theory, by adopting American customs and culture, immigrants are "melted together" and made a part of America. Just as the immigrants and their children are blended into American life, many immigrant customs become a part of America's general culture, bringing about a more diverse and vibrant nation. This is most clearly seen in some of the foods we eat and some of the expressions in our language.	Under the "salad bowl" theory, America's heritage is not a uniform culture. Each ethnic group remains proud of its origins, culture, and special practices. Today, American society offers an example of cultural pluralism, with a great variety of customs and cultures living side by side. Each group, although possessing values in common with the other groups that make up America, retains its own unique identity.

KEY ITEMS TO REMEMBER

Nativism, ethnocentrism, Old Immigrants, New Immigrants, ghettos, acculturated, assimilation, "melting pot," cultural pluralism, "salad bowl"

THE WOMEN'S RIGHTS MOVEMENT: 1865-1920

THE TRADITIONAL ROLE OF WOMEN

In the mid-19th century, the United States was a **patriarchal** society; men held positions of authority and women were considered to be inferior.

INFERIOR LEGAL STATUS

Women were denied full equality of citizenship. They lacked the right to vote, to serve on juries or to hold public office. Women were excluded from public life and were left in charge of the home and children. In most states, once a woman was married her husband took control of her property and income.

INFERIOR ECONOMIC STATUS

Working-class women often had to work outside the home, usually in low-paying jobs as servants, laundresses, cooks and factory workers. Women were paid less than men for doing the same work. In addition, they were expected to work long hours and had little, if any, opportunity for advancement.

INFERIOR SOCIAL STATUS

Women were thought to be incapable of acting rationally or controlling their emotions. They received little schooling. No American colleges were willing to accept women.

THE STRUGGLE FOR SUFFRAGE: 1840-1870

Some women began to see their lack of equality and opportunity as a serious problem. These women began to organize themselves and to challenge the idea of male superiority.

EARLY LEADERS

Some women were already active in reform movements to help others. **Dorothea Dix** campaigned to improve conditions in prisons and for the mentally ill. **Harriet Tubman** and **Sojourner Truth** were leading abolitionists. **Harriet Beecher Stowe** had distinguished herself as the author of *Uncle Tom's Cabin*. The abolitionist movement helped trigger the movement for women's rights. Two abolitionists, **Elizabeth Cady Stanton** and **Lucretia Mott**, became the founders of the women's rights movement.

SENECA FALLS CONVENTION

In 1848, Stanton and Mott organized a Women's Rights Convention in Seneca Falls, New York. This event is considered the start of the women's rights movement in the United States. The convention passed several resolutions, proclaiming that women are equal to men and should be given the right to vote.

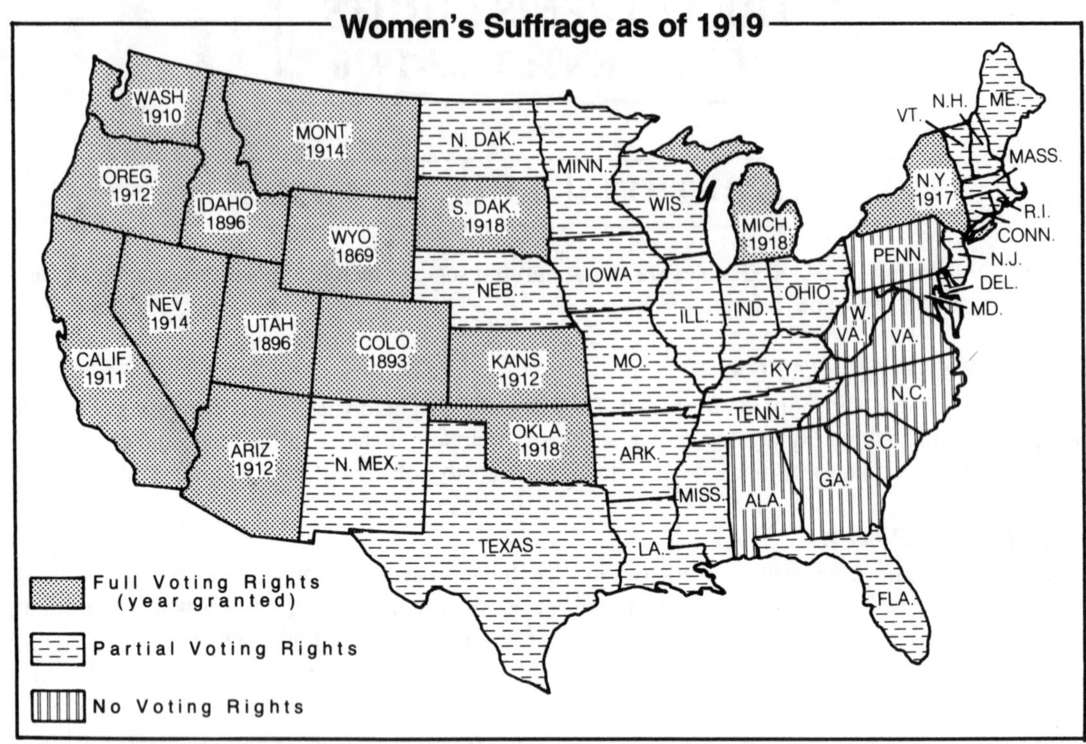
Women's Suffrage as of 1919
WASH. 1910
MONT. 1914
OREG. 1912
IDAHO 1896
WYO. 1869
N. DAK.
S. DAK. 1918
MINN.
WIS.
MICH. 1918
N.Y. 1917
VT.
N.H.
ME.
MASS.
R.I.
CONN.
N.J.
DEL.
MD.
PENN.
OHIO
IND.
ILL.
IOWA
NEB.
NEV. 1914
UTAH 1896
COLO. 1893
KANS. 1912
MO.
KY.
W. VA.
VA.
N.C.
TENN.
CALIF. 1911
ARIZ. 1912
N. MEX.
OKLA. 1918
ARK.
MISS.
ALA.
GA.
S.C.
TEXAS
LA.
FLA.
Full Voting Rights (year granted)
Partial Voting Rights
No Voting Rights

THE INFLUENCE OF THE CIVIL WAR

The North's victory in the Civil War and the emancipation of the slaves filled women reformers with the hope that freedmen and women would be given the vote at the same time. They were bitterly disappointed when the 14th and 15th Amendments gave citizenship and the vote to male freedmen, but not to women. In 1874, the Supreme Court ruled that although women were citizens, they had no constitutional right to vote.

ATTEMPTS TO ORGANIZE

The chief focus of the women's rights movement became securing the right to vote. The fact that women did not have **suffrage** (the right to vote) was a recognition of their inferior status in society and a violation of basic democratic principles. They were able to obtain suffrage in a number of western states, but could not succeed in passing a constitutional amendment that would require all states to give women the vote. By 1890, the failure to achieve women's suffrage led different women's groups to merge together into the **National American Woman Suffrage Association**, under the leadership of Stanton and **Susan B. Anthony**.

THE TRADITIONAL ROLE OF WOMEN CHANGES: 1870-1914

Industrialization brought about several important changes in the traditional role of women in society.

WOMEN ENTER COLLEGES

Since the mid-19th century, free public schools had been open to both boys and girls. The ability to read and write became increasingly important to women who were no longer confined to the home. Growing numbers of women obtained a college education. These women provided the backbone of the suffrage movement.

WOMEN WORK OUTSIDE THE HOME

The rise of industrial society created many new jobs. A large number of these were filled by women. For example, by 1919 one in five American workers was a woman. New inventions such as the sewing machine, typewriter and telephone led to increased employment opportunities for women. In addition, the spread of public education created a demand for teachers, most of whom were women.

THE IMPACT OF INDUSTRIALIZATION

As a result of industrialization, many families moved to cities in search of jobs. By 1920, half the women in America lived in cities. City life exposed women to new products and new ideas. These new products and labor saving devices—such as electric irons, washing machines, vacuum cleaners and refrigerators—helped to reduce housework. City living increased women's political and social awareness and contributed to women's working, marrying later in life and having smaller families.

THE 19TH AMENDMENT

During World War I, as men went off to Europe to fight for democracy, millions of women took their places, working in factories, mills and mines. It seemed odd to fight for democracy abroad while opposing it at home; it was hard for opponents of women's suffrage to deny that women were the equals of men. As a result, after America's entry into the war a proposed amendment was introduced into Congress, establishing that no state could deny a citizen the right to vote on the basis of sex; it became the 19th Amendment to the Constitution in 1920. It was a step forward in making the United States a true democracy of government by all the people. However, the passage of the amendment did not result in the drastic changes that its supporters had hoped for and that its opponents feared. Women did not sweep men out of public office; important inequalities between men and women persisted for several decades.

KEY ITEMS TO REMEMBER

Patriarchal, Seneca Falls Convention, suffrage, 19th Amendment

PART II: LIFE ON THE LAST AMERICAN FRONTIER

Just as life in American cities was affected by the rapid pace of industrial change, life on the last frontier was also transformed by America's industrial development.

THE WESTWARD MOVEMENT: 1860-1890

The so-called **frontier** generally defined the line separating areas of settlement from the "unsettled" wilder-ness territory. From another viewpoint, it could be said that the frontier marked the dividing line between areas where native peoples lived in traditional harmony with their natural environment, and areas where more technologically advanced peoples lived, who altered the natural landscape to meet their own needs.

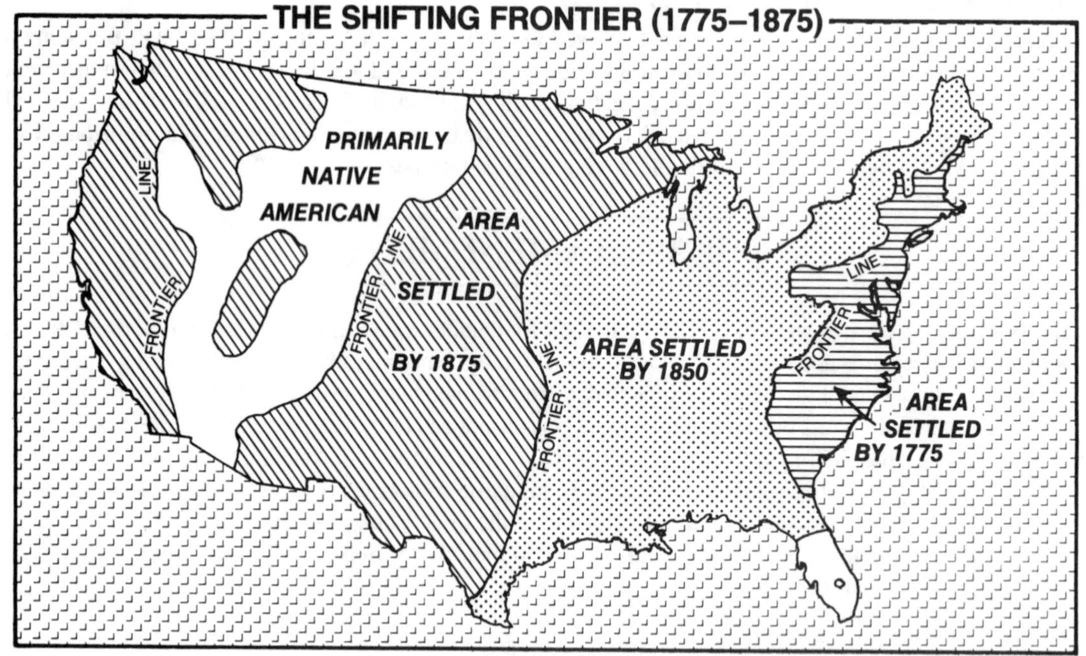
THE SHIFTING FRONTIER (1775–1875)
PRIMARILY NATIVE AMERICAN AREA
FRONTIER LINE
AREA SETTLED BY 1875
AREA SETTLED BY 1850
AREA SETTLED BY 1775

THE SETTLEMENT OF THE FRONTIER

Since the arrival of the first colonists, the frontier had moved slowly westwards. By the end of the Civil War, American settlers had occupied the mid-western prairies and established a foothold along the Pacific coast. Between these two lines was a vast expanse of territory, equal in size to all the rest of the

United States. This was the last frontier—the **Great Plains**. These lands provided a home to millions of buffalo and to the Native American Indians who lived off them. In the short space of thirty years, from roughly 1860 to 1890, the herds of buffalo were destroyed, the Indians were forced onto reservations, and the Great Plains were divided up into farms and ranches. By 1890, the U.S. government declared that the frontier wilderness was settled. There were several factors that led to this development:

THE DISCOVERY OF PRECIOUS METALS

Gold and silver were discovered in California, the Rocky Mountains, and the Black Hills of North Dakota during the second half of the 1800s. Thousands of prospectors and adventurers moved into the area in the hope of striking it rich. Rough-and-ready towns sprang up overnight. Often they collapsed just as fast.

THE ROLE OF THE RAILROADS

The railroads became one of the principal factors behind the settlement of the Great Plains. With the completion of the first transcontinental railroad in 1869, the journey from one coast to another was cut from several months to a few weeks. Railroads made it possible for ranchers and farmers to ship their cattle and grain to eastern markets.

THE AVAILABILITY OF CHEAP LAND FOR FARMING

Immigrants from Europe and farmers from the Eastern and Midwestern United States were attracted by the prospect of cheap land. The **Homestead Act** (1862) promised settlers 160 acres of free land if they farmed it for five years. Then, upon payment of a small fee, the settlers owned the land.

THE IMPORTANCE OF THE FRONTIER IN AMERICAN LIFE

By 1890, the Census Bureau announced that the American frontier no longer existed, since all parts of the country had been settled to some degree. Some historians, like **Frederick Jackson Turner**, claimed that the existence of the frontier had been a key factor in shaping and molding a unique American character:

- **Safety Valve.** The frontier allowed discontented people living in the East to escape to the freedom and openness of the West.
- **Individual Self-Reliance.** Isolated from the conveniences back East, each family on the frontier had to learn to survive on its own. This fostered a spirit of individualism and inventiveness in the American people. The frontier represented a golden opportunity for those willing to work to make their fortune.
- **Growth of Democracy.** Frontier people were distrustful and suspicious of government. As a result, people on the frontier promoted the growth of personal freedom, political equality among the sexes and greater involvement in political action. Western states were the first to adopt such measures as voting for women, the direct election of senators, and political primaries.

Critics of Turner's Theory. Turner's critics point out several weaknesses in his arguments. Although the frontier "officially" closed in 1890, more people settled in the west afterwards than before. Most people who settled the frontier did not come from the cities, so it is unlikely the frontier was a safety valve. Finally, plenty of cheap lands remained available just across the border in Canada.

The closing of the frontier greatly affected the foreign policy of the United States. Without a frontier, the nation had to look to foreign lands to supply raw materials and as a place to sell manufactured goods. This influenced the decision to establish overseas colonies in the late 1890s.

KEY ITEMS TO REMEMBER

Great Plains, frontier, Homestead Act, Turner's "frontier thesis"

THE FATE OF THE NATIVE AMERICANS: 1790-1990

EARLY RELATIONS WITH THE AMERICAN INDIAN

Native Americans, or American Indians, once occupied all of the continental United States. They were a people composed of many different groups, speaking hundreds of languages and dialects. Advancing white settlers, and European diseases like smallpox, severely reduced their numbers and pushed them westwards.

EARLY GOVERNMENT POLICY

From 1830 to 1890, the American government systematically followed a policy that pushed American Indians from their traditional lands onto government reservations in the West. Government policies usually followed a similar pattern. First, the government reserved lands for a tribe and signed a treaty with them. The tribe promised not to go beyond the borders of its lands. Individuals who did were captured and brought back. However, on each occasion when new settlers moved into the territory, the government broke its promise and the tribe was moved further westward again. This process was encouraged by several factors:

- In 1830, Congress ordered the removal of all American Indians to west of the Mississippi. Nearly one-quarter of the Cherokees perished on the journey westward, known as the "**Trail of Tears**."

- In 1869, the transcontinental railroad was completed. This, along with the passage of the **Homestead Act**, made western lands even more desirable.

- To protect settlers, federal troops were stationed in forts strung across the West. Clashes with the American Indians were inevitable. The **Indian Wars**, which pitted the settlers and federal troops against the American Indians, lasted about 30 years, from 1860 to 1890.

The Native Americans were doomed in their struggle against the settlers. In the end, the technological superiority of the United States government, the large number of settlers, and the destruction of the natural environment upon which the Indians depended for their livelihood overwhelmed the American Indians.

THE RESERVATION POLICY

Once the American Indians submitted to federal authority, they were settled on **reservations.** Reservation lands were usually small and often undesirable. The government promised food, blankets and seed for farming, but this policy clashed with tribal customs, since the Indians were traditionally hunters, not farmers.

Location of Major Native American Reservations: 1895

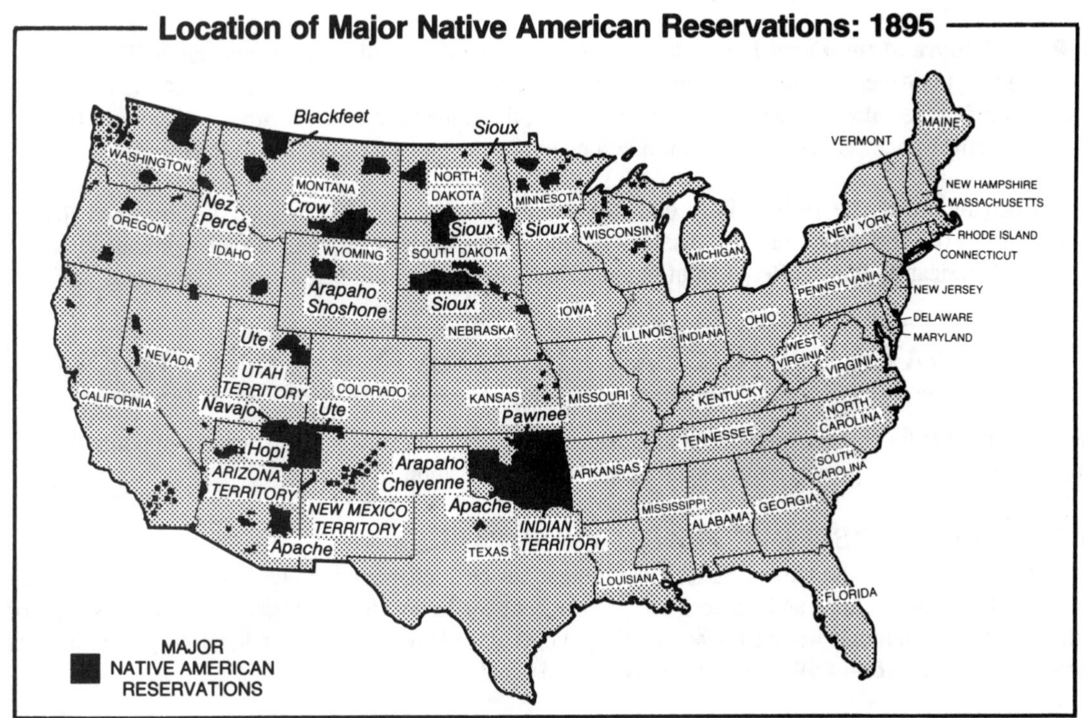
Blackfeet
Sioux
WASHINGTON
MONTANA
NORTH DAKOTA
MINNESOTA
MAINE
VERMONT
NEW HAMPSHIRE
MASSACHUSETTS
Nez Percé
Crow
OREGON
Sioux
Sioux
WISCONSIN
NEW YORK
RHODE ISLAND
CONNECTICUT
IDAHO
WYOMING
SOUTH DAKOTA
MICHIGAN
Arapaho Shoshone
Sioux
PENNSYLVANIA
NEW JERSEY
IOWA
NEBRASKA
OHIO
DELAWARE
MARYLAND
ILLINOIS
INDIANA
Ute
NEVADA
UTAH TERRITORY
WEST VIRGINIA
VIRGINIA
COLORADO
CALIFORNIA
Navajo
Ute
KANSAS
MISSOURI
KENTUCKY
Pawnee
NORTH CAROLINA
TENNESSEE
Hopi
ARIZONA TERRITORY
Arapaho
Cheyenne
ARKANSAS
SOUTH CAROLINA
NEW MEXICO TERRITORY
Apache
MISSISSIPPI
GEORGIA
ALABAMA
INDIAN TERRITORY
TEXAS
Apache
LOUISIANA
FLORIDA
MAJOR NATIVE AMERICAN RESERVATIONS

REFORMERS URGE AMERICANIZATION

Prejudice against American Indians was widespread. Nonetheless, some reformers began to protest the mistreatment of Native Americans. The most famous of these was **Helen Hunt Jackson**, who in her book *A Century of Dishonor* (1888) criticized the government for breaking its promises to the American Indians.

THE DAWES ACT (1887)

Many reformers felt that the American Indians, like the immigrants, should undergo **Americanization** by adopting American ways and institutions. The **Dawes Act** was passed to hasten the Americanization of the Indians. Under the provisions of the act:

- Native American tribes were officially abolished. Each male household was allotted 160 acres of reservation land as his own private property. Private property was expected to replace tribal land ownership, as each Native American became a farmer.

- Those who adopted this way of life were given United States citizenship and the right to vote. In 1924, all Native Americans were made citizens.

SHORTCOMINGS OF THE DAWES ACT

Although well-intentioned, the act was a terrible failure. It threatened the very survival of Native American culture.

- **The Failure of the Farm Program.** The act encouraged individual farm ownership. This was contrary to the American Indian tradition of sharing tribal lands. Many tribes had never engaged in farming; they had always been hunters. Furthermore, the lands they were given were often infertile, and the government never provided farm equipment or the assistance needed to learn farming.

- **Destruction of the Indian Way of Life.** Assimilation into American society threatened the destruction of tribal ways and customs. Reservation schools usually provided an inferior education. Many American Indians suffered from malnutrition, poverty and untreated health problems.

THE NATIVE AMERICAN DILEMMA IN RECENT TIMES

The main problem for Native Americans in the 20th century has been whether to assimilate into mainstream American society or to preserve traditional ways on the reservation.

ATTEMPTS TO PRESERVE TRADITIONAL VALUES

Generally, the policy of the United States Government has been characterized by a lack of understanding of Native American culture and values. The government made an attempt to show greater respect for traditional American Indian ways by reversing the policies of the Dawes Act. The Indian Reorganization Act (**Howard-Wheeler Act**) of 1934 sought to achieve this goal.

- The act stopped the breakup of reservations into individual plots of land. It restored elected tribal councils to govern the reservations.

- It attempted to improve the quality of Native American education while encouraging the practice of traditional crafts, customs and beliefs.

Many Native Americans welcomed these changes. Others, however, had already accepted Americanization. They were suspicious that the new approach was an attempt to keep them in an inferior status. Finally, promises to raise the living standards on the reservations were not fulfilled. Meanwhile, Indians who left the reservation for the cities faced widespread discrimination in finding jobs. All they found waiting for them was unemployment and poverty.

THE TERMINATION POLICY (1953-1963)

In 1953, the federal government again reversed itself in favor of Americanization. The government announced that it would provide job training and placement to help Indians blend into mainstream American life. At the same time, the Federal Government announced its intention of "terminating" (ending) its responsibility for Indians who remained on the reservations, transferring it to the state governments. The states, lacking the financial resources of the national government, were unable to provide the level of services previously given. As a result, the new policy, like all the previous ones, was largely a failure.

NATIVE AMERICANS BECOME MILITANT (1960s-PRESENT)

In 1963, the Federal Government abandoned its Termination Policy and swung back to encouraging tribal life on the reservations. In 1970, President Nixon announced that the Federal Government had solemn treaty obligations to the American Indian which it had no legal or moral right to terminate. Native Americans were given control of federal funds for housing, health care, education and economic renewal. Other programs were aimed at preventing discrimination against them. Nevertheless, many Native Americans felt these programs were not enough, and took a more militant approach to their problems. Under the slogan "**Red Power**," this new militancy took many forms.

- They formed a new organization, the **American Indian Movement** (A.I.M.) to mobilize public opinion behind Indian demands. Some protesters dramatized the plight of their group by temporarily occupying certain government installations and monuments, including Alcatraz Island and Wounded Knee, South Dakota.

- Some sought greater pride and respect for their heritage. They introduced the term "Native American," and protested against textbooks, television shows and movies with anti-Indian bias.

PROBLEMS OF NATIVE AMERICANS TODAY

Currently, there are about 1.4 million Native Americans, more than four times the number in 1890. The Native American population continues to grow, but it still faces very serious problems.

RESERVATION LIFE

Only about one-quarter of the Native American population lives on reservations. However, much of this land contains poor soil, is isolated and suffers from extremes in climate. American Indians living on reservations have some of the lowest incomes in the nation. They suffer from poverty, high unemployment, alcoholism, high suicide rates and high infant mortality.

CULTURAL CRISIS

Native Americans continue to suffer from a cultural crisis. Young American Indians must choose what to accept from traditional culture and what to accept from mainstream society. For example, traditional Indian culture was group-oriented while present-day American culture is more individualistic and profit-oriented. American Indian culture seeks to preserve the land and live in harmony with nature, while American businesses often seek aggressively to use environmental resources.

GOVERNMENT POLICIES

Unlike other minorities in America, Indians can cite government treaties guaranteeing their rights. Each year the federal government provides them with substantial aid. Nevertheless, Native American leaders maintain that government programs are under-funded. Tribes are often forced to compete for government funds, creating divisions among tribes.

KEY ITEMS TO REMEMBER

Native Americans, reservations, Dawes Act, American Indian Movement (A.I.M.)

PERSONALITIES OF THE PERIOD

SUSAN B. ANTHONY (SUFFRAGETTE)

Susan B. Anthony was a leader in the movement to abolish slavery and to achieve equal rights for women. She helped to found the National American Woman Suffrage Association in 1869. In 1890, she became the head of that organization. She traveled throughout the country lecturing at conventions to achieve the political right for women to vote. In her honor, the 19th Amendment is sometimes called the "Susan B. Anthony Amendment."

ELIZABETH BLACKWELL (PHYSICIAN)

In 1849 Elizabeth Blackwell became the first woman to receive a medical degree in the United States. She founded the first school in America devoted to training nurses. She was a leader in the movement to encourage women to become professionals — lawyers, doctors, ministers and teachers. Her sister-in-law became the first American woman to be ordained as a minister.

CYRUS McCORMICK (INVENTOR)

In 1831 McCormick invented the reaper, a horse-drawn machine used to harvest grain. Before this invention, farmers cut grain with a hand-held scythe. Since Western farmers were faced with a labor shortage, reapers allowed farmers to harvest more land with less labor. This invention helped spur western settlement.

GEORGE A. CUSTER (MILITARY LEADER)

In 1875, gold was discovered in North Dakota's Black Hills, and prospectors flooded the region. The Sioux, who occupied the region and considered it holy land, refused to move, and rose up in rebellion. In 1876 General Custer and his troops were sent in. At Little Big Horn his entire force was killed. Congress, prompted by this battle, voted additional money and troops to fight the Indians. Some army forces took revenge fourteen years later, when they gunned down Sioux men, women and children at **Wounded Knee**, South Dakota.

GERONIMO (TRIBAL CHIEF)

Geronimo, an Apache, typified the fighting spirit of some Native American leaders. He refused to accept being forced to live on a government reservation far from his original ancestral land. Geronimo was a fierce fighter who led his people to attack settlers along the southwest plains. He was finally captured in 1886.

For information about other personalities of this period, see Helen Hunt Jackson, Frederick Jackson Turner, Frederic Remington, George Catlin and Mark Twain, in the "Looking at the Arts" section.

THE CONSTITUTION AT WORK

A KEY AMENDMENT

NINETEENTH AMENDMENT (1920)
Women were given the right to vote.

KEY LEGISLATION

CHINESE EXCLUSION ACT (1882)
This act was passed in response to strong Nativist feeling against Chinese workers. The act excluded future Chinese immigration to the United States.

GENTLEMEN'S AGREEMENT (1907)
Japan protested a California school board's policy of segregating Asian school children. A compromise was worked out, ending the school board's policy of segregation in exchange for Japan's promise to limit Japanese immigration to the United States.

NATIONAL ORIGINS ACTS (1921, 1921, 1929)
These acts were passed after World War I, as part of the growing isolationist feeling in America. They limited immigration from eastern and southern Europe by establishing quotas based on the existing ethnic make-up of the United States. Immigrants from Asia were prohibited.

SUMMARIZING YOUR UNDERSTANDING

Directions: How well do you understand what you have just read? Test yourself by answering the following questions.

MAJOR ITEMS TO REMEMBER

On 3x5 index cards (as shown on pages 33-34), briefly define the following terms and concepts:

Urbanization	Assimilation	Seneca Falls Convention
Ethnocentrism	Nineteenth Amendment	Frontier
Native Americans	Dawes Act	National Origins Acts

AMERICA BECOMES URBANIZED

One of the most important developments of industrialization was the rise of cities. Summarize your understanding of this aspect of American life by answering the following questions:

- What factors contributed to urbanization in America?
- Describe some of the problems faced by people living in cities.

AMERICA'S IMMIGRANT POPULATION

The United States is unique, in that almost all of its people are immigrants or are descended from immigrants. Summarize your understanding of this aspect of American life by answering the following questions:

- What factors led immigrants to come to America? Describe some of the difficulties they faced in adjusting to life in the United States.
- Trace the changes in Congressional legislation dealing with immigrants coming to America.

THE CHANGING ROLE OF WOMEN IN AMERICA

Women sought to change their status from that of second-class citizens to equality with men. Summarize your understanding of this change by answering the following questions:

- Describe the status of women in the early to mid 19th century.
- Name some leaders of the Women's Movement, and state their contributions to the movement.
- What factors contributed to the changing role of women in American society?

THE FRONTIER IN AMERICAN HISTORY

The frontier had important effects on the course of American history. Summarize your understanding of these effects by answering the following questions:

- What factors contributed to the settlement of the frontier?
- What role did the frontier play in shaping America's historical and cultural development?

TREATMENT OF THE NATIVE AMERICANS

Federal government policy towards Native Americans has undergone many important changes. Summarize your understanding of these changes by answering the following questions:

- Trace the changing attitude of the Federal Government toward Native Americans.
- What are some of the current problems faced by Native Americans?

PERSONALITIES OF THE PERIOD

People often have an important influence on the political, economic or social life of their times. Summarize your understanding of this statement by completing a separate 3 x 5 index card (follow the procedures outlined on page 34) for each of the following individuals: ***Susan B. Anthony, Frederick Jackson Turner, Elizabeth Blackwell and Geronimo.***

TESTING YOUR UNDERSTANDING

Directions: Test your understanding of this unit by answering the following questions. Circle the number preceding the word or expression that correctly answers the statement or question. Following the short answer questions, answer either the RCT-type or Regents essay questions.

SKILL BUILDER: INTERPRETING A CARTOON

Base your answer to questions 1 through 3 on the following cartoon and on your knowledge of social studies.

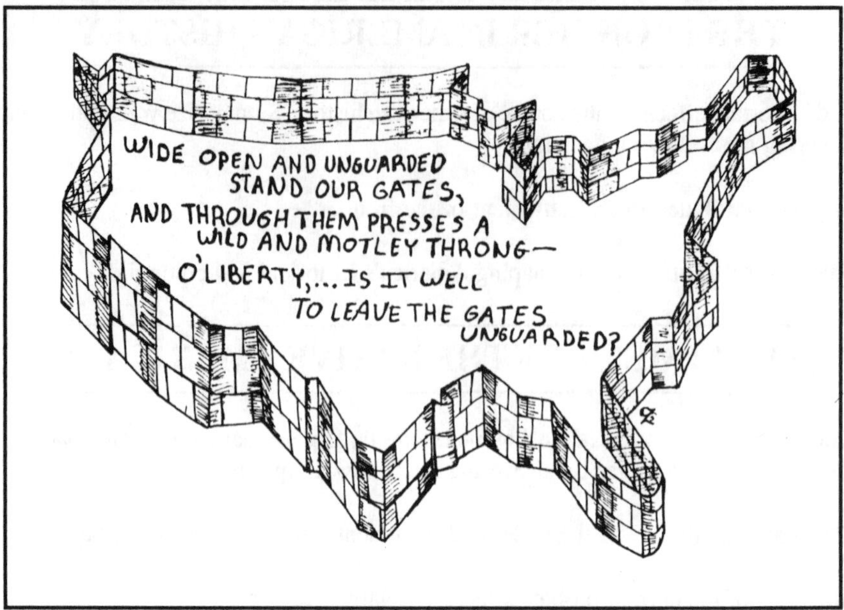
WIDE OPEN AND UNGUARDED
STAND OUR GATES,
AND THROUGH THEM PRESSES A
WILD AND MOTLEY THRONG—
O'LIBERTY,... IS IT WELL
TO LEAVE THE GATES
UNGUARDED?

1 The wall in the cartoon most likely represents
1 immigrants who wish to come to the United States
2 restrictive legislation preventing immigration
3 American poets writing about immigration
4 attempts to halt international terrorism

2 The main idea of the cartoon is that
1 immigrants need to be given positions of responsibility
2 equal opportunities are needed for all members of society
3 barriers are needed to prevent excessive immigration
4 immigrants in American society need to be more aggressive

3 A person supporting the views expressed in the poem could be labeled a(n)
1 nativist
2 abolitionist
3 feminist
4 imperialist

SKILL BUILDER: INTERPRETING SPEAKERS

Base your answers to questions 4 through 6 on the following speakers' statements concerning women's rights, and on your knowledge of social studies.

Speaker A: A woman's place is in the home.

Speaker B: The right to vote is an important right which belongs to every qualified citizen, male or female.

Speaker C: Women should be encouraged to work outside the home, but they should not expect to receive equal pay for equal work.

Speaker D: Equal educational opportunities should include equal athletic opportunities for all members of society.

4 Which speaker expresses the most prevalent attitude toward women held by American society during the 18th and early 19th centuries?
1 (A)
2 (B)
3 (C)
4 (D)

5 Which speaker expresses one of the main objectives of the Seneca Falls Convention of 1848?
1 (A)
2 (B)
3 (C)
4 (D)

6 Which is the most accurate conclusion that could be drawn from these speakers' statements?
 1 There is agreement on the need for an Equal Rights Amendment.
 2 Differences of opinion exist over the role of women in society.
 3 Most people favor giving women the right to vote.
 4 The role of women has remained unchanged over time.

SKILL BUILDER: ANALYZING A READING

Base your answers to questions 7 and 8 on the following quotation and on your knowledge of social studies.

"…. American social development has been continually beginning over again on the frontier. This rebirth of American life, this expansion westward with its new opportunities, its continuous touch with the simplicity of primitive society, furnish the forces dominating America's character. The true point of view in the history of this nation is...the West. The frontier is the line of most rapid and effective Americanization."

—Frederick Jackson Turner
The Significance of the Frontier in American History

7 According to Turner, American culture was primarily the result of the
 1 dependence of each generation upon its predecessors
 2 western settler's experience in adjusting to new surroundings
 3 pioneers maintaining contact with the settled areas
 4 influence of the frontier in making settlers more like Easterners

8 Which characteristic of the West as described by Turner most applies to contemporary society in the United States?
 1 simplicity of life
 2 new opportunities
 3 westward expansion
 4 frontier environment

---

9 The term "Native American" is used to refer to
 1 American Indians
 2 Hispanic Americans
 3 African Americans
 4 Asian immigrants

10 The term "suffrage" can be defined as
 1 the right to vote
 2 equal opportunity
 3 due process of law
 4 freedom of expression

11 Which statement is an example of ethnocentrism?
 1 "What we need is a return to the good old days."
 2 "My party's candidate can make our country strong."
 3 "Change is inevitable. We must attempt to adjust to new conditions."
 4 "Ours is a superior society, while all other societies are barbaric."

12 Which is a long-range effect of industrialization upon the status of women in Western societies?
 1 a decline of legal rights for women
 2 a decline in the importance of education for women
 3 an increase in employment opportunities for women
 4 an increase in the percentage of women in domestic occupations

13 The women's rights movement in the early 20th century focused its efforts primarily on securing
 1 cabinet positions for women
 2 reform of prisons
 3 civil rights for all minorities
 4 suffrage for women

14 The movement of people from the country to the cities in the late 19th century resulted in
 1 a decrease in the number of people able to read and write
 2 the development of crowded slums and unsanitary conditions
 3 a decline in economic growth
 4 the waste of farmlands

15 During the second half of the 19th century, the Federal Government encouraged the westward settlement of the United States by
 1 making low-interest loans to settlers
 2 paying western farmers to grow certain crops
 3 giving free land to homesteaders
 4 honoring Indian territorial claims

16 During the late 1800s, the policy of the U. S. government toward Native Americans was mainly one of
 1 transferring Native Americans from their homelands to government-designated areas
 2 encouraging Native Americans to retain their customs and traditions
 3 educating society about the cultural heritage of Native Americans
 4 shifting responsibility for Native American affairs to state governments

17 Native American Indians are unlike other minorities in the United States in that they can invoke rights guaranteed in
1 the Fourteenth Amendment
2 the Bill of Rights
3 treaties with the federal government
4 state constitutions

18 Which statement about immigration to the United States is most accurate?
1 Industrialization reduced the demand for cheap immigrant labor.
2 A diverse immigrant population helped create a pluralistic society.
3 Organized labor generally favored unrestricted immigration.
4 Most immigration legislation was passed to encourage immigration.

19 Which was a common complaint of nativist groups in the United States during the late 19th and early 20th centuries?
1 Congress failed to protect domestic industries.
2 The flow of incoming immigrants was too great.
3 Too many elected officials came from rural backgrounds.
4 Hiring people to work at government jobs was too selective.

20 An experience shared by most immigrants to the United States during the period from 1880 to 1920 was that they
1 frequently met with resentment
2 mainly settled in rural areas where cheap land was available
3 were rapidly assimilated into the predominant lifestyle
4 joined radical political parties to bring about economic reform

21 Which public school activity would probably be supported by an advocate of a pluralistic society?
1 compulsory reciting of prayers
2 creating ethnic studies courses
3 eliminating sports programs
4 censoring library materials

22 Which is the primary way that ethnic groups in the United States have helped shape the national identity?
1 Each group adopted the culture of earlier immigrants.
2 Each group contributed characteristics that became part of the general culture.
3 Each group attempted to become the dominant force in society.
4 Ethnic groups made large financial gifts in support of the fine arts.

23 Which helped prompt the passage of restrictive immigration legislation during the first quarter of the 20th century in the United States?
1 the demands of organized labor
2 lack of adequate food supplies
3 taxpayers' complaints about increased welfare costs
4 protests of city dwellers against overcrowded cities

24 The Gentlemen's Agreement and the Immigration Act of 1921 were reactions to earlier United States policies of
1 requiring proof of literacy in order for immigrants to be admitted
2 permitting unlimited immigration
3 limiting immigration to the upper classes
4 encouraging the immigration of scientists and intellectuals

25 Which is a major difference between immigration to the United States during the period 1860-1920 and immigration since 1970?
1 Immigrants today are not likely to experience discrimination.
2 There is a greater need for unskilled labor today.
3 The immigrants' countries of origin have changed dramatically.
4 Today's immigrants are easily assimilated into society.

26 Which development was a cause of the other three?
1 interest in overseas expansion
2 greater immigrant settlement in cities than in rural areas
3 limiting the flow of immigrants to the United States
4 the closing of the frontier

27 Which would be a primary source of information about immigrants coming to the U. S. in 1880?
1 a textbook chapter on 1880s immigration policy
2 a biography of a famous immigrant who lived during the 1880s
3 a news account about the re-opening of Ellis Island as a museum
4 a diary of an immigrant who came to the U.S. in 1880

28 The passage of the Immigration Acts of 1921 and 1924 indicated that the United States wished to
1 limit the flow of immigrants
2 encourage cultural diversity
3 welcome all immigrant groups
4 play a greater role in world affairs

29 The process of acculturation will occur more rapidly when a society
1 has a strong racist attitude
2 isolates specific ethnic groups
3 offers universal free education
4 has a high unemployment rate

30 A landless settler heading west in the 1870s would most likely have supported the passage of the
1 Dawes Act
2 Homestead Act
3 Sherman Anti-Trust Act
4 "Jim Crow" laws

RCT-TYPE ESSAYS

1 Before 1920, women in the United States faced many problems. They have tried to overcome these problems in many different ways.

Part A

List *two* problems that women in the United States faced before 1920.

1. ______________________ 2. ______________________

State *one* way in which women attempted to resolve one of these problems.

____

Part B

In your Part B answer, you should use information you gave in Part A. However, you may also include different or additional information in your Part B answer.

Write an essay discussing problems that women in the United States faced before 1920, and explain how they have attempted to resolve them.

2 Immigrants to the United States faced many problems. They have tried to resolve these problems in many different ways.

Part A

List *two* problems that immigrants faced when coming to the United States.

1. ______________________ 2. ______________________

State one way immigrants tried to resolve each of these problems. [State a different solution for each problem.]

1. ______________________ 2. ______________________

Part B

In your Part B answer, you should use information you gave in Part A. However, you may also include different or additional information in your Part B answer.

Write an essay discussing problems faced by immigrants to the United States and explain how the immigrants attempted to resolve these problems.

REGENTS-TYPE ESSAYS

1 At various times in its history, the United States has served as a land of opportunity for people of other nations.

Immigrant Groups / Time Period

Southern and Eastern Europeans / 1880-1920
West Indians / 1950-1980
Latin Americans / 1950-present
Asians / 1970-present

Select *two* immigrant groups from the list. For *each* one selected:

- Describe some of the conditions that the immigrants faced in their area or country of origin which led to their coming to the United States.
- Cite one problem encountered by that group as immigrants in the United States.
- Describe what actions or steps that group or its members took to cope with its problems.

2 Newcomers to urban areas have tended to live with people who are culturally similar to themselves in areas called ghettos. One sociologist has stated: "... the ghetto is both beautiful and ugly, kind and cruel, hope and despair, and a beginning and an end."

- Select one group of newcomers to urban areas of the United States in the ***19th century*** and describe to what extent the quotation reflects conditions experienced by that group.
- Select one group of newcomers to urban areas of the United States in the ***20th century*** and describe to what extent the quotation reflects conditions experienced by that group.
- Discuss to what extent the experiences of the two groups were different.

3 Throughout U. S. history, men and women have sought to improve society by participating in reform movements.

Reform Movements

Abolitionism	Organized labor
Women's rights	Native American rights

Select *two* of these reform movements, and for *each* one chosen:

- Identify one person or group associated with *each* of the movements selected and describe the influence of that person or group on the movement.
- Discuss the extent to which each movement has affected the quality of American life.

PERFORMANCE-BASED TASKS

Setting: Much has been written and portrayed in the movies about the lives and times of people settling the frontier. About one in every three settlers was either Mexican American or African American. Despite their large numbers, often very little can be found in American history textbooks about the role played by either of these groups in settling the frontier.

General Directions: In this exercise, you will have an opportunity to correct the problem by learning more about African Americans settling the frontier. First, read the four accounts below of African-Americans who lived on the frontier during the last half of the 19th century.

Nat Love: Although I was born Nat Love, most people called me by the name of Deadwood Dick. I was born into slavery in the year 1854. We were released from bondage after the Civil War. When I was 15, I left home to go west. I got a job as a cattle herder. However, I spent most of my time practicing to be a rodeo cowboy. In 1877, I proved to be a champion roper in the Deadwood Dakota rodeo. By out-roping and out-shooting the other cowboys, I became known as "the hero of Deadwood" or Deadwood Dick. During my life I spent time on cattle trails, gambled a lot, got into gun fights, both fought and made friends with Indians and spent some awful times on the wild frontier

Mary Fields: My name is Mary Fields, though most people called me Stagecoach Mary. I was born a slave in Tennessee. However, in 1884 at the age of 52, I moved to Montana. Despite being a woman, few men gave me trouble — I was six feet tall and weighed over 200 pounds, wore men's clothing, and smoked thick black cigars. Like many others on the frontier, I had my share of gunfights. I had a number of different jobs. For example, I carried the mail, ran a restaurant and drove a stagecoach, which explains my nickname. Despite getting older, I was still as tough as they come. At age 70, I owned a laundry. When a customer tried to cheat me by not paying his bill, I hit him on the jaw and knocked him down.

Bass Reeves: I was one of a number of black sheriffs who kept law and order in the west. In fact, I spent over 30 years as a lawman. Most of that time I spent as a deputy United States Marshal in Oklahoma's Indian Territory. I won a reputation as a great detective. Every outlaw in my territory came to fear the name Bass Reeves. Only one outlaw ever escaped after I caught him. Strange, though, most of those varmints never recognized that my special talent was the disguises I wore to fool those I went after. While it's not the thing I am proudest of, I won 14 shootouts (all against men who drew on me first) without ever suffering a wound.

B.K. Bruce: I escaped from slavery during the Civil War. Never in my wildest imagination could I believe that someday I would see the words "U.S. Senator B. K. Bruce." One of the causes I fought for was justice for the American Indian on the frontier. As a consequence of our selfishness, we had violated our treaties with the various Indian tribes. Little by little, it became apparent that our goal was to rid the continent of the Indians altogether. What we overlooked is the fact that the Indians are a vigorous, physical and intellectual people whom we should make every effort to save, not destroy.

Your Task: On the basis of these readings and further research you conduct in your school or public library, use the page provided to write a section of a textbook under the sub-heading, "African Americans on the Frontier."

AFRICAN AMERICANS ON THE FRONTIER

A KEY TO UNDERSTANDING CULTURE: LOOKING AT THE ARTS

People seem to have an inner drive to express their deepest beliefs, feelings and desires. The arts, such as literature, painting, architecture, photography, dance and music are some of the forms this drive for expression takes. Forms of artistic expression almost always reflect something about the society and time period in which they were produced. John Canaday summed it up best by stating:

> "A painting is ... a projection of the personality of the man who painted it, a statement of the philosophy of the age that produced it, and it can have a meaning beyond anything concerned with one {man} or only one period of time."

Although Canaday was discussing paintings, his statement applies to other artistic forms as well.

WHAT TO DO WHEN ANSWERING A QUESTION ON THE ARTS

In some essay questions on the RCT or Regents Examination, you will be asked to show how a form of art is a reflection of its times. The question may be presented in several different formats:

INTERPRETING AN ART WORK

You may be shown an individual work of art—a painting, a photograph of a building, or a literary selection. The question will then ask you (a) to interpret the picture, photograph or building; and then (b) to show how it reflects the times in which it was produced. To answer this type of question, you should ask yourself the following about the artwork:

- What is the theme or major point of the artwork?
- How does the artwork reflect the artist's views about the time period in which it was produced?
- In which time period was the artwork created?

This last question is an important one, for you must compare the theme shown in the artwork with the major themes that were dominant during that period of American history.

IDENTIFYING AN ARTIST'S WORK

This is the form that the majority of questions about the arts take. You are asked to describe how a particular artist reflects the time period in which the artist worked. This type of question differs from "interpreting an art work." In this type of question you are asked to discuss the major artistic achievements of the artist. Following is an example of a typical question of this kind:

> Certain books have had a significant impact on society. Some of these are:
>
> **Books**
>
> Thomas Paine — *Common Sense*
> Harriet Beecher Stowe — *Uncle Tom's Cabin*
> Helen Hunt Jackson — *A Century of Dishonor*
> Upton Sinclair — *The Jungle*
>
> Choose *two* works. For *each* one chosen:
>
> - Describe the main idea of the book
> - Discuss the impact of the work on society

To help you answer both the "interpreting an art work" and "identifying an artist's work" type of questions, it is important that you have some knowledge of the major themes running through each time period in American history. The following chart may be helpful to you.

TIME PERIOD	MAJOR THEMES
Constitutional Period	This period showed the heavy influence of European style and values on American life. It was also marked by a concern with patriotism and with themes showing independence.
Civil War Era	Here the major concern was with showing the injustices of slavery and the turmoil this was causing in the nation.
Growth of the American West	This period strongly reflected the influence and impact of the frontier on the American way of life.
The Gilded Age & The Progressive Period	This period reflected the excesses of business and the hardships faced by workers. Muckrakers and other writers, journalists and artists urged reform.
The Roaring Twenties	This period reflected the prosperity and good times enjoyed by many people in the nation. Some writers criticized American materialism.
The Depression and the 1930s	The major concern in this time period was with showing the economic problems faced by the nation.

World War II & the Cold War	This period was marked by feelings of instability and uneasiness over Nazi aggressions in Europe, followed by the growing threat of Communism.
The 1960s	This period was marked by the Civil Rights Movement and by discontent at home over the Vietnam War.
The 1970s	This period was generally one of experimentation, innovation, and the emergence of a distinct American style.
The Reagan-Bush Years: 1980s-1990s	The 1980s and 1990s have been marked by a search for traditional values, a celebration of the achievements of American free enterprise and a new patriotism.

Following is an overview of some of the most important authors, architects, painters and photographers in American history, and their impact on the nation.

AUTHORS

Author	Description of the Work	Its Impact on Society
Thomas Paine	In *Common Sense*, Paine urged the colonists to follow their destiny and break away from Great Britain. He ridiculed the idea of an island ruling a continent.	The pamphlet helped convince colonists to revolt against the English and fight for independence.
Alexander Hamilton	With the help of Madison and Jay, Hamilton wrote *The Federalist*, a collection of essays explaining the organization of the new Constitutional government and the advantages of adopting it.	These 85 essays were very influential in convincing Americans to ratify the new United States Constitution.
Harriet Beecher Stowe	In *Uncle Tom's Cabin*, Stowe described some of the horrors of slavery as they existed in the deep South.	The book helped stir Northern sentiment for the elimination of slavery. It gave renewed life to the abolitionist cause.
Helen Hunt Jackson	Jackson's book, *A Century of Dishonor*, criticized the federal government's policy of lies and broken promises to the American Indian.	Her book awakened the nation to the plight of Native Americans, and led to legislation that helped benefit the Native American cause.

Author	Description of the Work	Its Impact on Society
Mark Twain	His novel, *The Adventures of Huckleberry Finn,* was a social satire about a young boy and a runaway slave making their way down the Mississippi River.	Twain's novels helped to create a new style of American fiction. His works greatly influenced the language and style used by many future writers.
Frederick Jackson Turner	His essay, *The Significance of The Frontier in American History,* explained how the frontier shaped America's unique way of life.	Turner alerted the nation to the key role played by the frontier in the development of the United States.
Horatio Alger	In his late 19th century novels such as *Luck and Pluck,* Alger's heroes were always poor boys who through hard work and honesty were eventually rewarded with riches and honors.	His books helped popularize the American dream that almost anything could be achieved by working hard towards a goal.
Upton Sinclair	His novel *The Jungle* drew a vivid picture of unsanitary conditions in the meat-packing industry	The book shocked the nation, prompting legislation that regulated the food and drug industries.
F. Scott Fitzgerald	His novels related to the morality of the 1920s. He portrayed the wild life, the corruption and the striving for success and money that destroyed traditional values	He became the literary spokesman for the Jazz Age of the 1920s. His works reflected the fast-paced life style and enormous changes in values occurring in American society.
John Steinbeck	His most famous novel, *The Grapes of Wrath,* portrayed the plight of farmers during the Great Depression.	His novel alerted the nation to the terrible suffering and hopelessness facing migrant farm workers.
Betty Friedan	Her book *The Feminine Mystique* attacked the belief that women were happy staying at home as housewives.	Her book became the rallying point for the 1960s Women's Liberation Movement.
Ralph Nader	In *Unsafe At Any Speed,* Nader criticized automakers for being more concerned with profits than with building safe cars.	Nader's book pressured Congress into passing legislation forcing automakers to build safer cars.
Rachel Carson	Her book, *Silent Spring,* sounded an alarm to Americans about the harmful effects of insecticides and pesticides.	Her book led to a growth in the public's awareness for increased environmental protections and safeguards.

ARTISTS

Painters and sculptors often depict persons, scenes and lifestyles in their works, permiting later generations to "view" situations that they would otherwise be unable to see.

Gilbert Stuart: Stuart was a portrait painter who concentrated his talents on painting the heads and faces of famous people. His best known portrait of George Washington appears on the face of the dollar bill.

Frederic Remington: Remington achieved fame for his paintings, drawings and sculptures of life in the wild West. His works featured scenes of action and excitement associated with life in the west—cowboys roping a calf, or a cavalry charge against a group of American Indians.

George Catlin: Catlin was one of a unique group of artists. Often he would tag along on expeditions to the West. Catlin focused on frontier life, making it come alive for people in the East. His paintings featured Native Americans hunting, riding and performing ceremonial rituals.

Joshua Johnston: Born a slave, Johnston became the first African American to gain national recognition as a portrait painter. Although lacking formal training, he had great talent. His portraits of aristocratic families were noted for their attention to detail and use of light. His works hang in the National Gallery of Art, Howard University Gallery of Art, and the Fisk University Gallery of Art.

John Audubon: Audubon was an artist and naturalist who is best known for his illustrations of birds. In 1839, Audubon published *The Birds of America*, a four volume collection of his detailed and colorful bird drawings.

Thomas Eakins: One of America's most outstanding painters, Eakins depicted slices of everyday life in America. One of his best known works, *The Gross Clinic*, showed a surgeon during an operation. The painting created a sensation by showing surgical instruments and blood normally associated with surgery. This was seen by some as being too vulgar and realistic.

James A. Whistler: An artist of the late 1800s, Whistler was influenced by French impressionists. His most famous portrait, popularly called "Whistler's Mother," shows a profile view of a woman wearing a simple black dress, sitting in a straight back chair. His works hang in many major art galleries.

Mary Cassatt: A painter of the late 1800s and early 1900s, Cassatt is one of America's best-known women artists. Her favorite subjects were mothers and children. Cassatt's paintings are admired for their simplicity and pleasing use of pastel colors. Her works include "Mother and Child," "Lady At The Tea-Table" and "Modern Women."

"Grandma" Moses: Starting as an artist at age 70, Grandma Moses drew scenes of life on the farm and countryside. Her brightly colored paintings are often found adorning Christmas cards and calendars.

Jackson Pollock: Pollock became the symbol of abstract modern art by breaking with traditional-looking paintings. His paintings created a controversy because unlike traditional art works, they showed splashes and drips of bright paint crisscrossing a canvas.

ARCHITECTS

Buildings also reflect the times in which they are constructed. During the early period in American history, buildings reflected the European architectural style. As Americans moved from a rural to an industrial society, their architecture mirrored this development.

Louis Sullivan: Sullivan became the architectural mastermind behind the skyscraper. Believing that "form follows function," in 1890 he designed the first modern skyscraper in St. Louis —the Wainwright Building—which used a structural steel framework to permit the construction of a ten story building. Sullivan's skyscraper designs were to permanently change the skyline of America's cities.

Frank Lloyd Wright: In Wright's designs, the architecture of the buildings harmonized with the surrounding landscape. For example, if a building were constructed overlooking a waterfall, its exterior would reflect that feature. One of his most famous designs is the Guggenheim Museum in New York City.

I.M. (Ieoh Ming) Pei: Pei, best known for the many public buildings he has designed, carefully integrated his structures with their surrounding environment. Some of his works include the John Kennedy Memorial Library at Harvard University, the Payne Mellon Arts Center and the Mile High Center in Denver, Colorado.

PHOTOGRAPHERS

Photography was a mid-19th century development. Photographs are historical documents that allow us to travel back in time almost as if we were there when the photographs were taken. They are visual history lessons.

Matthew Brady: Brady set out to create a photographic history of the Civil War. His collection of photographs document the people, events and happenings that took place during the Civil War. His photographs have allowed future generations to view "with their own eyes" the suffering, destruction and devastation of the Civil War.

Dorothea Lange: Hired by a government agency during the New Deal, Lange traveled throughout the country taking pictures of life in rural America. Her photographs became famous because they depicted the suffering of the poor during the Great Depression.

Ansel Adams: Adams is best known for his regional landscape photographs, especially those of the American Southwest. His photos emphasize and promote conservation, nature, national parks and monuments.

CHAPTER 9

PROTEST AND REFORM

VOTES FOR WOMEN

As the United States transformed itself into an industrial nation, many Americans had trouble adjusting to this change. When the government failed to provide help, new political parties, such as the Populists and the Progressives, began to emerge. These new political parties gave a voice to those seeking reform.

— TIMELINE OF KEY EVENTS —

1887	1892	1900	1906	1910	1912	1913	1917	1920
Interstate Commerce Act passed	Populist Party founded	Theodore Roosevelt becomes president	Pure Food and Drug Act passed	N.A.A.C.P. formed	Woodrow Wilson elected	Income tax and Federal Reserve Act passed	United States enters World War I	Women gain vote; Progressive Movement ends

THE AGRARIAN MOVEMENT

AMERICA: A NATION OF FARMERS

Today, less than 2% of the population lives on farms. However, life in the United States was quite different in the 1870s, when the majority of Americans lived on farms.

THE PROBLEMS OF FARMERS: 1870-1900

In the late 19th century, farmers experienced great difficulties as food prices began to drop lower and lower, even though their expenses remained high. This situation resulted from a combination of factors:

- **Agricultural Overproduction.** The opening of the West had greatly increased the number of farms and the amount of land cultivated. At the same time, machinery and improved farming techniques increased the yield of each acre. Food prices fell as a result of high production and overseas competition.

- **High Costs.** Railroad companies knew that farmers, who had to ship their crops to market, had no choice but to pay whatever rates the railroads charged. Farmers also paid high prices for manufactured goods like fertilizer, farm machinery, clothing and furniture. A high protective tariff kept out cheaper European goods, keeping domestic prices artificially high.

- **Farmer Indebtedness.** Farmers often borrowed to buy land, make improvements, or purchase machinery. If the harvest was poor, farmers took out loans. Banks and lenders saw farmers as poor credit risks and charged them high rates of interest.

- **Periodic Natural Disasters.** Farmers are subject to the forces of nature: droughts, insect invasions and floods. A single bad year can wipe out the savings of many good years.

THE GRANGE MOVEMENT

With the rise of industrial society, farmers gradually began to see themselves as a special interest group. In 1867, the **Grange Movement** was organized. Their original purpose was to break the rural isolation of farmers and to spread information on new farming techniques. Within ten years, the Grangers had over 1.5 million members and moved into both the economic and political arenas.

- **Granger Cooperatives.** Grangers formed cooperatives which bought machinery, fertilizers, and manufactured goods in large numbers at discount. They sold their crops directly to city markets. But because of lack of experience and expertise, most of these cooperatives failed.

■ **The Granger Laws.** The farmers blamed the railroads for their difficulties. In several Midwest states, Grangers elected candidates to state legislatures who favored regulating the railroads. These states passed laws regulating railroad and grain storage rates.

Railroad companies protested that the new Granger laws took away the value of their property without "due process." In ***Munn v. Illinois*** the Supreme Court ruled that state governments could regulate railroads since they affected the public interest. In 1886, in ***Wabash v. Illinois*** the Court reversed itself, holding that states could not regulate the rates of railroads engaged in interstate commerce, since the Constitution gave this job to Congress. The Grangers then turned to Congress for help. In 1887, Congress passed the **Interstate Commerce Act** which created a regulatory agency to watch over the railroads and interstate commerce. (See The Constitution at Work section, later in this chapter, for more details on this act and court cases.)

KEY ITEMS TO REMEMBER

Grange Movement, *Munn v. Illinois*, *Wabash v. Illinois*, Interstate Commerce Act

THE POPULIST PARTY: 1891-1896

Because of the limited success of the Grange Movement, farmers continued to experience difficulties. In 1892, farmers joined forces with a new national political party, the **Populist Party**, which represented laborers, farmers, and industrial workers in the battle against railroad and banking interests. The Populists were convinced that rich industrialists and bankers had a stranglehold on government. They felt they could no longer rely on the Democrats or the Republicans. Like the Grangers before them, the Populists wanted the federal government to take on greater responsibility for the people's welfare. In 1892, the Populists held a national convention at Omaha, Nebraska, where a candidate was selected to run for president and a party platform was drawn up. Their platform contained many innovative proposals:

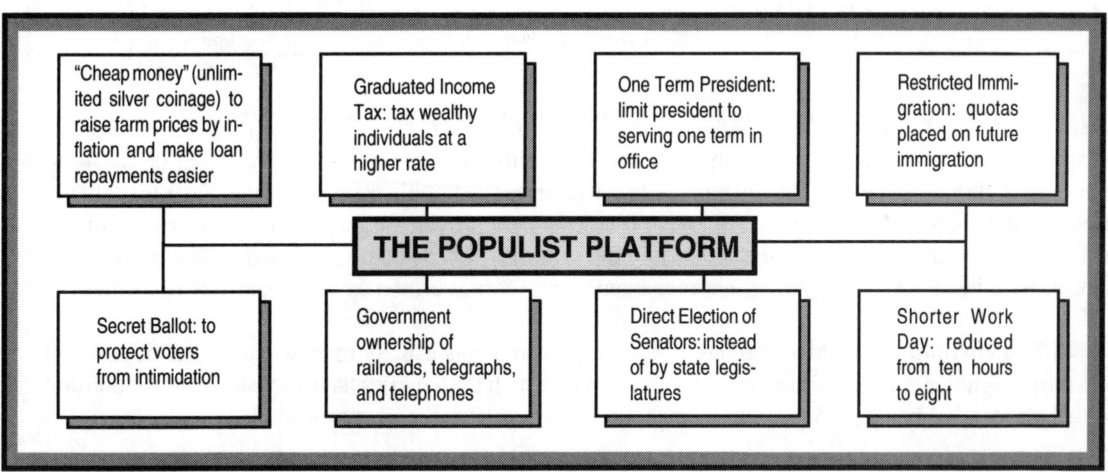
"Cheap money" (unlimited silver coinage) to raise farm prices by inflation and make loan repayments easier
Graduated Income Tax: tax wealthy individuals at a higher rate
One Term President: limit president to serving one term in office
Restricted Immigration: quotas placed on future immigration
THE POPULIST PLATFORM
Secret Ballot: to protect voters from intimidation
Government ownership of railroads, telegraphs, and telephones
Direct Election of Senators: instead of by state legislatures
Shorter Work Day: reduced from ten hours to eight

ELECTION CAMPAIGNS

With strongholds in the South, Northwest and Mountain states, the Populists turned their attention to getting candidates elected to office.

■ **Election of 1892.** The Populists elected 5 senators and received over 1 million votes for their presidential candidate. Soon afterward, the Depression of 1893 occurred. The Populists blamed the Depression on the scarcity of currency. Populist leaders decided to focus their attention on this issue.

■ **Election of 1896.** In 1896, the Democratic Party nominated **William Jennings Bryan** for president after he delivered a speech at the convention. His "**Cross of Gold**" speech praised farmers and denounced bankers for trying to "crucify mankind on a cross of gold." The Populists decided not to run their own candidate, and to support Bryan. Now that the Democrats had adopted so much of their program, a separate Populist Party seemed unnecessary. However, Bryan lost the election.

■ **Election of 1900.** This election pitted William Jennings Bryan against the Republican candidate **William McKinley**. McKinley's victory marked the end of the Populist Party. An improved economy, higher farm prices and greater use of scientific farming all helped to weaken interest in a separate farmer's party.

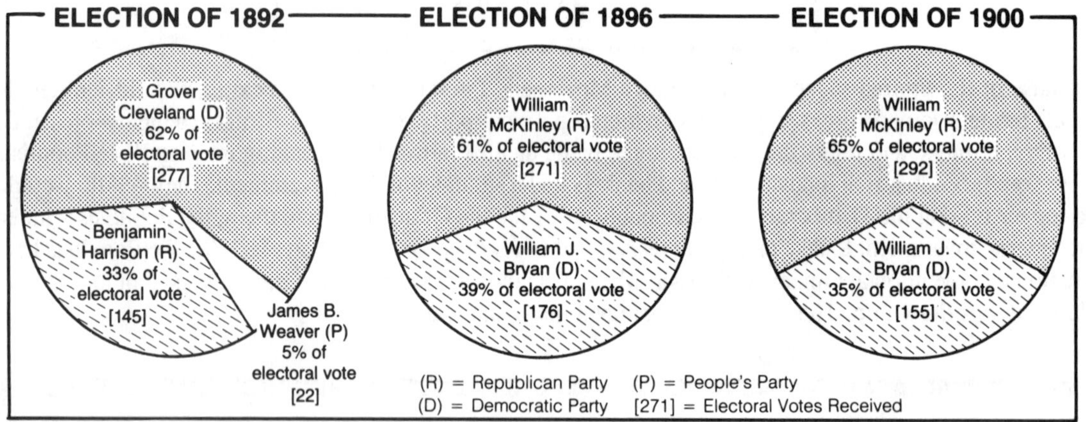
ELECTION OF 1892
ELECTION OF 1896
ELECTION OF 1900
Grover Cleveland (D) 62% of electoral vote [277]
Benjamin Harrison (R) 33% of electoral vote [145]
James B. Weaver (P) 5% of electoral vote [22]
William McKinley (R) 61% of electoral vote [271]
William J. Bryan (D) 39% of electoral vote [176]
William McKinley (R) 65% of electoral vote [292]
William J. Bryan (D) 35% of electoral vote [155]
(R) = Republican Party
(D) = Democratic Party
(P) = People's Party
[271] = Electoral Votes Received

THE LEGACY OF POPULISM: THE ROLE OF THIRD PARTIES

Many of the proposed Populist reforms, such as the graduated income tax, direct election of senators and the secret ballot, were later passed by other political parties. The Populists thus illustrate the role often played by third parties or independents in American politics—they provide an outlet for minorities to voice their grievances, generate new ideas and advocate new solutions. Occasionally, independents simply represent a protest against the existing parties, as when many voters demonstrated their support of Ross Perot in 1992.

■ **The Formation of Third Parties.** Third party movements usually form when the major political parties ignore a vital public issue. Some issues upon which third parties have focused include abolition of slavery, women's suffrage, temperance, farmer's grievances, and abortion.

■ **Influence of Third Parties.** If a third party is successful, one or both of the major parties will adopt its ideas—much as the Democrats adopted the program of the Populists. The best evidence of the influence of third parties is that many of their proposals have been passed into law.

KEY ITEMS TO REMEMBER

Populist Party, Populist Platform, "cheap money," "Cross of Gold" speech, third parties

THE PROGRESSIVE MOVEMENT: 1900-1920

DEVELOPMENT OF THE PROGRESSIVE MOVEMENT

The **Progressive Movement** first developed between 1900 and the start of World War I. Although the Progressives borrowed some ideas from the Populists, they were different. The Progressives were mainly middle-class and urban, while the Populists were working-class and rural people. In addition, the Progressives were more successful at acquiring political power than the Populists.

GOALS OF THE PROGRESSIVES

The primary aim of the Progressive Movement was to correct the political and economic injustices that resulted from America's rapid industrialization. The Progressives did not oppose industrialization, but they wanted to use the power of government to correct its evils so that all Americans, not just the wealthy, could enjoy better lives. To achieve this, they felt they also had to reform government itself, which had become corrupted by big business and political "bosses."

PRESSURES FOR REFORM

Reform has been a continuing process throughout American history. Reform movements are usually based on the belief that society can be made better. By 1900, a strong reform tradition already existed in America. This could be seen from the abolitionist movement, the temperance movement, the women's rights movement, and the Populists. The Progressives were one more example of Americans attempting to overcome difficulties by calling for reform. However, there were several specific reasons why the Progressive Movement emerged at this time.

■ **Problems Created by Industrialization.** The rise of industry brought many new social problems: brutal working conditions, child labor, political corruption, urban overcrowding, misuse of the environment, extreme inequalities of wealth, and the abuse of consumers.

■ **Middle Class Influence.** Progressive support came mainly from its middle-class members who felt threatened by the rise of big business and the creation of giant trusts, labor unions, and "political machines." Consumers had, in some sense, to organize to protect their interests .

■ **The "Social Gospel" Movement.** Progressives often acted out of a sense of moral responsibility derived from religion. Many Protestant ministers in the "Social Gospel" movement were especially concerned with the plight of the poor. Instead of accepting poverty as God's will, these clergymen called for social reforms, including the abolition of child labor and safer working conditions.

The abuses of industrial capitalism led some critics to demand an end to capitalism itself. Socialists believed that government should take over basic industries, while Communists believed that workers should seize control and abolish private property. Progressives rejected these schemes, but argued that some reform was necessary if social revolution was to be avoided.

THE IMPACT OF THE EARLY PROGRESSIVES

The Progressive Movement operated at many different levels of society and government.

THE MUCKRAKERS

The most influential of the early Progressives were the investigative reporters, writers and social scientists who exposed the abuses of industrial society and the corruption of government. These writers became known as "muckrakers" because they "raked" through the muck or dirt of American life in search of news. They examined the rise of industry and the abuses and corruption that led to the accumulation of large fortunes. They also examined business practices affecting the consumer, and the lives of the very poor and wretched. The muckrakers exposed many social evils and stimulated the cry for reform. In so doing, they set a model that is still at work today. Newspaper, magazine, and television journalists often stand as watchdogs over government, exposing problems, informing the public, and stimulating debate.

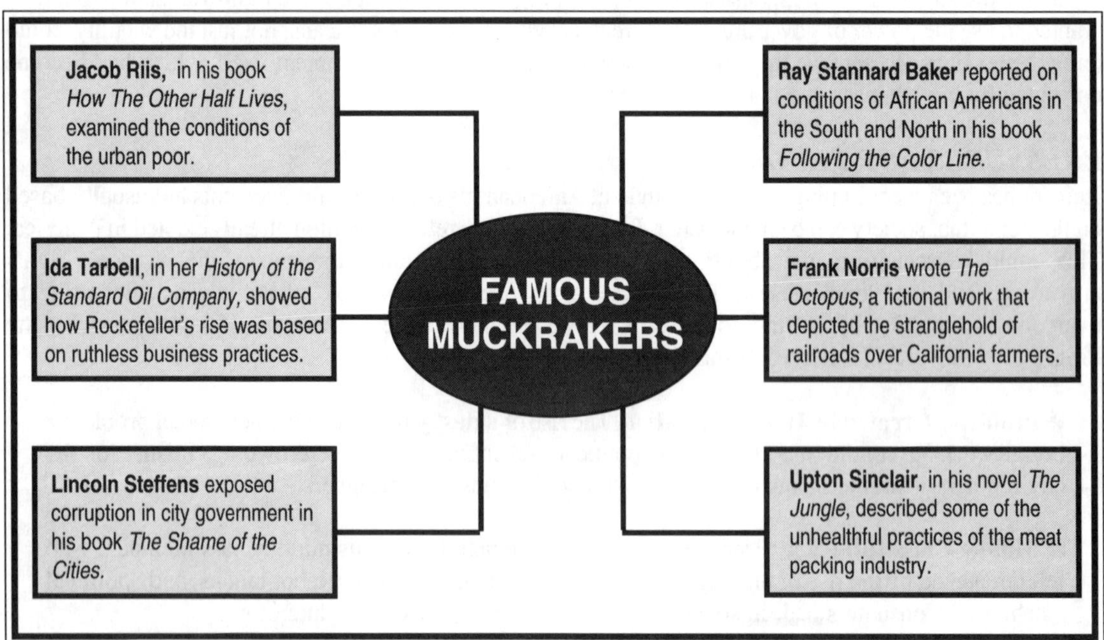
FAMOUS MUCKRAKERS
Jacob Riis, in his book How The Other Half Lives, examined the conditions of the urban poor.
Ida Tarbell, in her History of the Standard Oil Company, showed how Rockefeller's rise was based on ruthless business practices.
Lincoln Steffens exposed corruption in city government in his book The Shame of the Cities.
Ray Stannard Baker reported on conditions of African Americans in the South and North in his book Following the Color Line.
Frank Norris wrote The Octopus, a fictional work that depicted the stranglehold of railroads over California farmers.
Upton Sinclair, in his novel The Jungle, described some of the unhealthful practices of the meat packing industry.

THE SOCIAL REFORMERS

Some Progressives were so stirred by the abuses of industrial society that they made individual efforts at social reforms. **Settlement houses** were started in slum neighborhoods to provide services to the urban poor, such as child care, nursing of the sick, classes to teach English to immigrants, and help in obtaining naturalization. Other Progressives formed associations to promote social change and professional responsibility, such as the **N.A.A.C.P.** (National Association for the Advancement of Colored People) and the Anti-Defamation League (opposing religious prejudice).

MUNICIPAL REFORM

Many Progressives focused their attention on correcting abuses found at the town or city (municipal) level of government.

■ **Corruption in City Government.** Some cities grew so fast in the late 19th century that city services were inadequate. Adding to this problem, city government was often controlled by a "**political machine**" run by a political boss. Political machines provided the immigrants and the working poor with jobs, housing, emergency loans and help in obtaining citizenship. In exchange, these residents voted for candidates recommended by the boss. The machine then used its control to steal from the public treasury through bribes and padded contracts.

■ **Progressives Clean Up City Government.** Progressives replaced the rule of "bosses" with public-minded mayors. They expanded city services to take care of the problems of urban overcrowding, fire hazards, inadequate sanitation, and the lack of public services. In some cities, the Progressives introduced new forms of city government to discourage corruption.

THE REFORM OF STATE GOVERNMENT

As in municipal government, Progressives took special steps to free state government from corruption and the influence of big business, making government more responsive to the people. Many of the measures they took would later be adopted at the federal level:

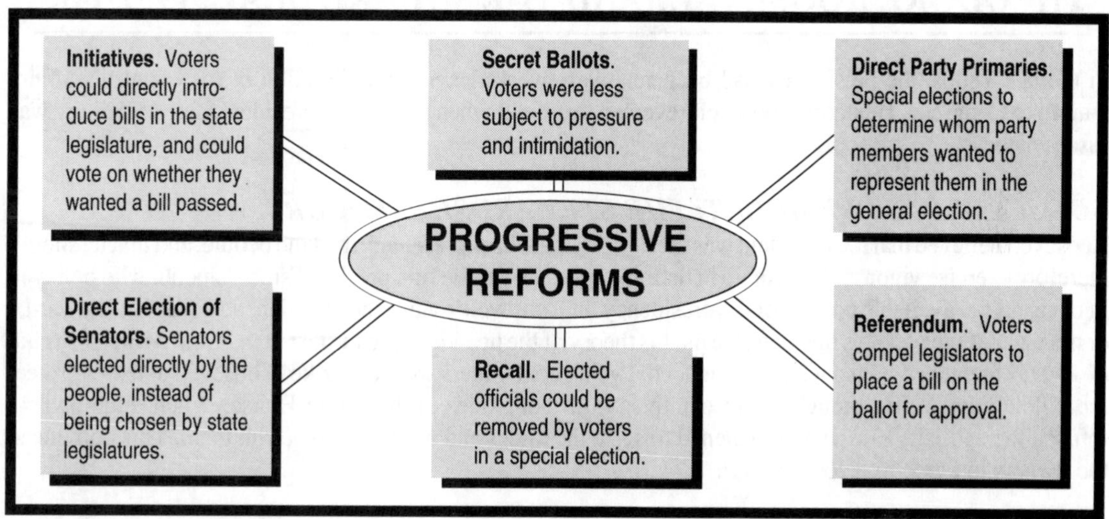
PROGRESSIVE REFORMS
Initiatives. Voters could directly introduce bills in the state legislature, and could vote on whether they wanted a bill passed.
Secret Ballots. Voters were less subject to pressure and intimidation.
Direct Party Primaries. Special elections to determine whom party members wanted to represent them in the general election.
Direct Election of Senators. Senators elected directly by the people, instead of being chosen by state legislatures.
Recall. Elected officials could be removed by voters in a special election.
Referendum. Voters compel legislators to place a bill on the ballot for approval.

States also enacted laws to deal with the worst effects of industrialization. These laws regulated conditions in urban housing and forebade the employment of young children. They also regulated safety and health conditions in factories, limiting the number of hours women could work and forcing employers to pay workers injured on the job (workers' compensation benefits). In addition, laws were passed aimed at conserving natural resources and establishing wildlife preserves.

REFORMS OF THE NATIONAL GOVERNMENT

In the late 19th century, corruption had been widespread in the federal government, much as in the state governments. Most of the corruption on the federal level came from the "**spoils system**," in which government jobs were used to reward people who made contributions to politicians or helped in their campaigns. However, in 1883, Congress passed the **Pendleton Act** which created a Civil Service Commission giving competitive exams and selecting appointees on the basis of merit (**merit system**).

KEY ITEMS TO REMEMBER

Progressives, muckrakers, political machines, initiative, referendum, recall, primaries, spoils system, merit system

THE PROGRESSIVE PRESIDENTS

THEODORE ROOSEVELT AND THE SQUARE DEAL: 1901-1909

In the late 1800s, the presidency had been relatively weak, leaving the direction of the country's affairs mainly to Congress. Theodore Roosevelt reversed this trend when he became president after McKinley was assassinated.

ROOSEVELT AS PRESIDENT: THE STEWARDSHIP THEORY

Roosevelt believed that the President was the one official who represented all of the people, and that he should therefore exercise vigorous leadership in their interest. He was the first president since Lincoln who believed in using all the available powers of the presidency. In Roosevelt's view, the president acted as the "steward," or manager of the people's interests. He put his theory of the presidency to the test in the **Coal Miners' Strike of 1902.** Threatened with a winter without coal when coal miners went on strike, Roosevelt acted to protect the public interest. He brought representatives from both sides to the White House. When mine-owners refused to negotiate, Roosevelt threatened to seize the mines and use the army to run them. This convinced the owners to agree to a compromise.

ROOSEVELT AS "TRUST-BUSTER"

Roosevelt revived the use of the **Sherman Anti-Trust Act** against large business consolidations called trusts. He did not attack all trusts. What he stood for was fair play. Therefore, he distinguished between "good trusts" and "bad trusts." Bad trusts were those that acted against the public interest. For example, Roosevelt challenged Rockefeller's Standard Oil Company. After Roosevelt left office, the Supreme Court affirmed breaking up Standard Oil. The Supreme Court borrowed Roosevelt's distinction between good and bad trusts by applying the Sherman Anti-Trust law to "unreasonable" trusts—those that harmed the public interest. Although Roosevelt did not break up a great many trusts, he established the principle that the government would act to break up harmful trusts. For this reason Roosevelt earned his reputation as "trust-buster."

SQUARE DEAL LEGISLATION

Roosevelt promised Americans a "Square Deal." He launched new laws to protect consumer health, regulate certain industries, and to conserve the nation's natural resources.

- **Protecting the Public Health.** Upton Sinclair's account of the meatpacking industry in his book *The Jungle* had shocked the nation. As a result, Congress passed the **Meat Inspection Act** (1906), providing for government inspection of meat. The **Pure Food and Drug Act** (1906), regulated the preparation of foods and the use of certain chemicals as preservatives.

- **Regulating Transportation and Communication.** Roosevelt increased the power of the Interstate Commerce Commission to regulate the railroads and the radio, telegraph, and telephone industries.

- **Conserving the Nation's Resources.** Roosevelt drew attention to the need to conserve forests, wildlife and natural resources. He stopped the practice of selling off public lands for development. He helped to form the National Conservation Commission. He also appointed conservationists, like **Gifford Pinchot**, to head agencies that dealt with natural resources.

WOODROW WILSON AND THE NEW FREEDOM: 1913-1921

In 1908, Roosevelt's friend **William Howard Taft** was elected President. In 1912, Taft was nominated again by the Republican Party. Roosevelt, who had become unhappy with Taft, decided to accept the nomination of a new third party, known as the Progressive or **"Bull Moose" Party**. This split in the Republican Party allowed the Democratic nominee, Woodrow Wilson, to win the election.

WILSON'S "NEW FREEDOM"

While Roosevelt was an emotional and enthusiastic president, Wilson was cool and logical. However, Wilson also believed in being a strong president who should use all the powers at his disposal. In the campaign of 1912, Wilson promised Americans a **New Freedom**, by taming big business, opening the way for greater competition and eliminating special privileges. He focused his attention on attacking the tariff, the banking system, and trusts. Wilson became a strong, reform-minded president, able to get several major legislative reforms passed by Congress.

■ **The Underwood Tariff** (1913). Wilson believed that high tariffs only benefited rich monopolists and hurt the average American. He enacted a law that lowered tariffs by about 25%.

■ **A Graduated Income Tax** (1913). In a graduated tax system, the rich are taxed at a higher rate on their income than less well off people. Wilson was able to introduce a federal income tax because the **Sixteenth Amendment**, ratified in 1913, gave Congress the power to tax personal incomes directly. Today the income tax serves as the main source of revenue for the federal government.

■ **The Federal Reserve Act** (1913). This act established 12 regional Federal Reserve Banks, which were to serve as "banker's banks." The act reformed the banking industry. Under the provisions of this act the federal government could regulate the amount of money in circulation by controlling the amount of money banks could lend.

■ **New Anti-Trust Legislation**. The federal government came to believe in the benefits of business competition, and sought to pass laws preventing any attempts to limit competition. In 1914, Wilson strengthened the Sherman Anti-Trust Act by passing the **Clayton Anti-Trust Act** (See the *Key Legislation* section at the end of this chapter). In addition, the **Federal Trade Commission Act** was enacted in an attempt to further protect consumers against unfair business practices by corporations.

THE PROGRESSIVE MOVEMENT COMES TO AN END

In 1914 World War I broke out in Europe. In 1917, Americans entered the war in a crusade "to make the world safe for democracy." Women's suffrage and Prohibition were both passed at the very end of the war—the final reforms of the Progressive Era. At the war's end, many Americans became disillusioned. The force of the Progressive Movement had spent itself on its major reforms; it lost its supporters and most of its appeal.

KEY ITEMS TO REMEMBER

Square Deal, Pure Food and Drug Act, Sherman Anti-Trust Act, Federal Reserve Act, Clayton Anti-Trust Act

PERSONALITIES OF THE PERIOD

IDA B. WELLS (REFORMER)

Ida B. Wells was a co-founder of the N.A.A.C.P. and a crusading journalist who worked tirelessly against the lynching of African Americans in the United States. As a result of her editorials and speeches against lynching, she faced personal threats, mob violence and a bomb attacks. None of these dangers were able to halt her crusade against lynchings.

JANE ADDAMS AND LILLIAN WALD (SOCIAL REFORMERS)

Jane Addams and Lillian Wald were both reformers in the settlement house movement. Settlement houses became places where poor people living in the inner cities could learn to read and write and obtain needed social services. In 1889, Jane Addams opened Hull House, a settlement house, in a slum area of Chicago. Four years later, Lillian Wald opened the Henry Street Settlement House in New York City.

ROBERT LA FOLLETTE (GOVERNOR)

La Follette, a leading Progressive, served as governor of Wisconsin from 1900 to 1906. He broke the influence of local political bosses and railroads over the Wisconsin legislature. Under his leadership, railroads were taxed at the same rate as other business properties. His reform measures also regulated public utilities and helped to conserve Wisconsin's forests and waters against industrial exploitation and pollution.

JOHN MUIR (CONSERVATIONIST)

John Muir was a conservationist and a crusader for protecting the beautiful landscape and natural wonders of America. A friend of President Theodore Roosevelt's, Muir helped convince him of the need to protect the environment. He is credited with bringing Yosemite in California into the national park system.

JOHN DEWEY (PROGRESSIVE EDUCATOR)

Dewey's approach to education was guided by the idea that a child learns best by doing. His methods placed less importance on book learning and more on teaching practical skills. In his experimental school, students ran all the services and carried out many other activities. He also believed that social usefulness was the best guide in deciding what subjects to teach. Dewey's beliefs became the basis of progressive education.

THE CONSTITUTION AT WORK

KEY AMENDMENTS

SIXTEENTH AMENDMENT (1913)

Congress was given the power to collect income taxes.

SEVENTEENTH AMENDMENT (1913)

The method for electing senators was changed from selection by state legislatures to direct election by the voters in each state.

EIGHTEENTH AMENDMENT (1919)

The manufacture, sale, importation or transportation of alcoholic beverages was prohibited. This amendment was later repealed by the 21st Amendment (1933).

NINETEENTH AMENDMENT (1920)

Women were given the right to vote.

KEY LEGISLATION

INTERSTATE COMMERCE ACT (1887)

This act prohibited railroads from charging different rates to different customers shipping goods the same distance. It also banned price-fixing agreements and the charging of more for short hauls than for long hauls over the same route. An Interstate Commerce Commission was created to investigate complaints and to enforce the act. The act marked the first step towards having the federal government curb unfair business practices. The I.C.C. became the first of many regulatory agencies created to watch over business.

FEDERAL RESERVE SYSTEM ACT (1913)

This act was an attempt by Congress to reform the banking industry. It created a central banking system composed of Federal Reserve Banks located in 12 different districts. The main purpose of the Federal Reserve Bank is to regulate the amount of money in circulation, by lending money to other banks.

CLAYTON ANTI-TRUST ACT (1914)

The Clayton Act toughened anti-trust regulations. In addition, the act limited the use of injunctions against unions, by exempting them from anti-trust suits. Prior to this act, businesses could claim that unions were "conspiracies in restraint of trade." This change in the status of unions was welcomed by organized labor.

KEY COURT CASES

MUNN v. ILLINOIS (1877)

Background: Midwestern farmers felt they were overcharged by railroads and grain warehouses. Illinois passed a law regulating the highest rate that could be charged by a railroad or grain warehouse. The railroads argued that Illinois was depriving them of their property without constitutional "due process" of law.

Decision/Significance: The Supreme Court upheld the right of a state to regulate railroads and grain warehouses because these businesses were closely related to the public interest. The ruling allowed states to regulate businesses which the state believed affected the public interest.

WABASH v. ILLINOIS (1886)

Background: Illinois passed a law penalizing railroads if they charged the same or more for shipping freight for shorter distances than for longer distances. The Wabash Railroad claimed that Illinois had no right to regulate prices on an interstate line even if the trip was within the state's borders.

Decision/Significance: The Supreme Court ruled against Illinois, stating that only Congress and not the states could regulate rates on interstate commerce. This ruling ended state regulation of most railroads, but opened the door to increased federal regulation in all cases affecting interstate commerce. It was followed by the Interstate Commerce Act.

SUMMARIZING YOUR UNDERSTANDING

Directions: How well do you understand what you have just read? Test yourself by answering the following questions.

MAJOR ITEMS TO REMEMBER

On 3 x 5 cards (as shown on pages 33-34), briefly define the following terms and concepts:

Populist Party	Federal Reserve Act	Grange Movement
Third Parties	Square Deal	*Wabash v. Illinois*
Muckrakers	Progressives	Interstate Commerce Commission Act

THE AGRARIAN MOVEMENT

The period of the 1870s through the early 1900s saw several fundamental changes in the lives of farmers. Summarize your understanding of these changes by answering the following questions:

- Describe some of the major problems facing farmers, and their attempts to overcome these problems.
- What was the legacy of the Populists?

THE PROGRESSIVE MOVEMENT

The Progressive Movement aimed at correcting certain abuses in American society. Summarize your understanding of this movement by answering the following questions:

- What were the goals of the Progressives?
- Who were some of the leading muckrakers of the Progressive Movement? Discuss some of the changes brought about by the muckrakers and other Progressives.

THE PROGRESSIVE PRESIDENTS

Theodore Roosevelt and Woodrow Wilson believed that the President should act to promote the public interest. Summarize your understanding of their ideas by answering the following questions:

- How did Roosevelt's Square Deal Program attempt to promote the public interest?
- How did Wilson's New Freedom Program attempt to promote the public interest?

PERSONALITIES OF THE PERIOD

People often have an important influence on the political, economic or social life of their times. Summarize your understanding of this statement by completing a separate 3 x 5 index card (follow the procedures outlined on page 34) for each of the following individuals: ***Upton Sinclair, Theodore Roosevelt, Woodrow Wilson, Jane Addams, Ida B. Wells, and John Muir.***

TESTING YOUR UNDERSTANDING

Directions: Test your understanding of this unit by answering the following questions. Circle the number preceding the word or expression that correctly answers the statement or question. Following the short answer questions, answer either the RCT-type or Regents essay questions.

SKILL BUILDER: INTERPRETING A CARTOON

Base your answer to questions 1 through 3 on the following cartoon and on your knowledge of social studies.

THE AMERICAN FARMER

1 The farmer in the cartoon would most likely have been a member of which political party in 1892?
1 The Democratic Party
3 The Populist Party
2 The Republican Party
4 The Federalist Party

2 What is the main idea of the cartoon?
1 Americans need more railroad safety laws.
2 The railroad industry is threatened by automobiles.
3 Farmers are at the mercy of the railroad industry.
4 Farmers must be protected from runaway inflation.

3 A direct result of the situation depicted in the cartoon was the
1 beginning of the Suffrage Movement
2 creation of the Interstate Commerce Commission
3 passage of the Dawes Act
4 establishment of the Freedmen's Bureau

SKILL BUILDER: INTERPRETING SPEAKERS

Base your answers to questions 4 through 6 on the speaker's statements and on your knowledge of social studies.

Speaker A: Our job is to report to the public about the crime, graft and corruption that exists throughout society. Unless these scandals are brought to light by crusading journalists like myself, the abuses in society will continue.

Speaker B: Government control must be shifted from the hands of the power brokers and political bosses to the people. Common people know what is best for them.

Speaker C: The national government must learn to keep its hands out of the affairs of business. If the government continues to regulate business, economic opportunities in the future will be threatened.

Speaker D: I am concerned about the increased number of children working in factories. We need laws to prevent our children from working in factories.

4 Speaker A could best be described as
1 a muckraker
3 a conservationist
2 a trust buster
4 a nationalist

5 Which speaker would most likely support the idea of laissez-faire capitalism?
1 A
3 C
2 B
4 D

6 Which speaker expresses beliefs held by such humanitarians as Jacob Riis and Ida B. Wells?
1 A
3 C
2 B
4 D

SKILL BUILDER: INTERPRETING A TABLE

Base your answers to questions 7 through 9 on the following table and on your knowledge of social studies.

TRENDS IN POLITICAL AFFILIATION IN THE U.S.

Year	Republican	Democratic	Independent
1979	22%	45%	33%
1978	23	49	28
1975	22	45	33
1972	28	43	29
1968	27	46	27
1964	25	53	22
1960	30	47	23
1952	34	41	25
1949	32	48	20
1944	39	41	20
1940	38	42	20
1937	34	50	16

7 According to the information provided in the table
1 there were more registered Republicans than registered Independents in 1979
2 the year 1937 marked an all-time high for registered Democratic voters
3 there were more registered Independents than registered Republicans in 1944
4 in 1964 there were more registered Democrats than Republicans and Independents combined

8 Which statement is best supported by the information in the table?
1 Since 1937, Americans have been gradually moving away from affiliations with traditional political parties.
2 During the 1940s, a greater percentage of Americans were independent than were affiliated with either major party.
3 Membership in the Democratic Party was at its lowest point during the 1960s.
4 The Republican Party made great gains in membership during the 1970s.

9 If the trend in the table continues, then it would be reasonable to expect that there will be
1 more registered Republicans than any other type of voter
2 more registered Democrats than any other type of voter
3 more Independent voters than registered Republicans
4 few people who will continue to vote in future elections

---

10 Which were factors that encouraged the growth of the Progressive Movement?
1 the influence of muckrakers, Populists and social reformers
2 the Stock Market Crash of 1929
3 racial conflict in the New South
4 the migration of population from cities to the countryside

11 Who is paired with the field in which he or she won national recognition?
1 Samuel Gompers — Women's Movement
2 Jane Addams — social reform
3 John Muir — prison reform
4 Dorothea Dix — conservation

12 The direct election of senators, the graduated income tax and the Pure Food and Drug Act were all measures introduced during the
1 Reconstruction Period
2 Progressive Era
3 Cold War
4 New Deal

13 Initiative, recall, and referendum are examples of
1 nineteenth-century foreign policies typical of imperialism
2 Progressive reforms aimed at making government more democratic
3 government regulations to control big business
4 conservationist measures adopted by Theodore Roosevelt

14 A supporter of the Grange Movement would probably favor
1 government regulation of railroads
2 abolishing private property
3 laissez-faire capitalism
4 women's suffrage

15 Which statement is most closely associated with William Jennings Bryan?
1 "Fifty-Four Forty or Fight"
2 "You shall not crucify mankind on a Cross of Gold"
3 "We have just begun to fight"
4 "I regret that I have but one life to give to my country"

16 Which event took place during the administration of Theodore Roosevelt?
1 emancipation of slaves
2 beginning of conservation of U.S. natural resources
3 founding of Standard Oil Company
4 start of the Grange movement

17 The United States Federal Reserve System was established to
1 serve as a source of loans for farmers
2 solve the problems of the Great Depression
3 balance the federal budget
4 regulate the amount of money in circulation

18 Which statement is supported by a study of the Progressive Movement in the United States?
1 The Progressives wished to ease immigration requirements.
2 The Progressives advocated responsible government to correct the evils of society.
3 The Progressives were opposed to the political views of the Populists.
4 The Progressives were supported by big business.

19 An economist studying the Progressive Era would most likely be interested in the
1 fate of Native Americans
2 election of William McKinley
3 policy of laissez-faire
4 work of social reformers

20 The muckrakers of the Progressive Era and the investigative reporters of our own day are similar in that both
1 seek to document corruption in United States life
2 advocate fewer government controls on the economy
3 try to increase the spirit of patriotism
4 call for expanded aid to economically less developed nations

21 Which statement about the Sherman Anti-Trust Act is the most accurate?
1 It gave powers to the states to regulate interstate railways.
2 It outlawed monopolies that restrict interstate commerce.
3 It established the Federal Trade Commission.
4 The Supreme Court ruled that it was unconstitutional.

22 A major aim of both the Grange and Populist movements in the United States was
1 the establishment of a gold standard for currency
2 mandatory government policies to curb inflation
3 passage of laws increasing federal regulation of monopolies
4 unlimited immigration of Asians

23 Which statement best describes many of the reforms proposed by the Populist Party?
1 They were just campaign promises.
2 They disappeared from public interest.
3 They were undesirable in a democratic country.
4 They were achieved by other political parties.

24 Political party primaries have helped increase public interest in the political process by allowing voters to
1 remove corrupt officials
2 select party candidates
3 attend nominating conventions
4 write party platforms

25 Both Theodore Roosevelt and Woodrow Wilson believed that the role of government in correcting economic inequalities should be to
1 own public utilities
2 find jobs for the jobless
3 replace company officials
4 regulate big business

RCT-TYPE ESSAYS

1 Leadership is important to the success of any political and social movement.

Leaders

Susan B. Anthony
Frederick Douglass
Samuel Gompers
John Muir
Jacob Riis
Jane Addams

Part A

Select *one* leader from the list: ______________________________

Identify a political or social reform with which that person was associated:

____

Select *another* leader from the list: ______________________

Identify a political or social reform with which that person was associated:

____

Part B

In your Part B answer, you should use information you gave in Part A. However, you may also include different or additional information in your Part B answer.

Write an essay discussing how certain leaders have been important to the success of a political or social movement.

2 The Progressive Movement sought to change society by introducing many reforms.

Part A

List *two* problems that existed in the United States before 1920. State *one* way the Progressive Movement tried to solve each problem through reform.

Problem	Attempted Reform
1. ______________	1. ______________
2. ______________	2. ______________

Part B

In your Part B answer, you should use information you gave in Part A. However, you may also include different or additional information in your Part B answer.

Write an essay discussing the problems faced by American society between 1890 and 1920, and explain how the Progressives attempted to resolve these problems.

REGENTS-TYPE ESSAYS

1 Leadership is an essential ingredient to the success of any political or social movement in history. Following is a list of leaders, paired with the movements they led.

Leaders / Movements

Elizabeth Cady Stanton / Women's rights
Frederick Douglass / Abolitionism
Samuel Gompers / Organized labor
John Muir / Conservationism
William Jennings Bryan / Populism
Theodore Roosevelt / Progressivism

Select *three* of the pairs listed above. For *each* pair selected, evaluate the success of the leader and his or her movement by discussing:

- The role of the leader in the movement
- Tactics used by the movement
- The effect of the leader and the movement on United States history

2 There have been many critical situations that presidents have had to face. In each situation the president has had to make a crucial decision.

Presidential Decisions

Abraham Lincoln / To issue the Emancipation Proclamation
Andrew Johnson / To follow Lincoln's Plan for Reconstruction
Theodore Roosevelt / To fight the influence of "bad" trusts
Woodrow Wilson / To fight for Progressive reforms

Choose *two* of the presidential decisions listed above. For *each* one chosen:

- Describe the situation faced by the president.
- Discuss reasons for the president's decision.
- Describe the opposing viewpoints.

3 Movements for reform have often developed in United States history.

Movements for Reform

Abolitionist Movement
Grange Movement
Labor Movement
Progressive Movement
Women's Rights Movement
Conservation Movement

Select *three* of the movements for reform from the list, and for *each* one chosen:

- Describe a specific problem that the movement attempted to solve
- Discuss a solution proposed by that movement.
- Discuss the extent to which the solution was successful in solving the problem.

4 At various periods in U. S. history, groups of people have been affected by specific actions or events.

Groups / Periods

Native American Indians / 1865-present
Factory workers / 1865-1920
Women / 1900-1925
Farmers / 1850-present
African Americans / 1850-1920

Choose *three* of the groups listed and for *each* one chosen:

- Identify a specific action or event that had an impact on the group during that time period
- Discuss a positive *or* a negative impact of the action or event on the group during that time period
- Discuss the extent to which the condition of the group has changed since the action or event

PERFORMANCE-BASED TASKS

Setting: The Progressive Era (1895-1920) was a period when many reform groups attempted to cure the evils caused by industrialization. During the Progressive Era a group of writers investigated and attacked social and economic injustice and political corruption. Theodore Roosevelt first used the term "muckrakers" to describe this group of investigative writers. Muckrakers used their writings to alert the American people to the need for reform. Some of the best-known muckrakers were:

- **Upton Sinclair**, a novelist, who wrote about the unsanitary conditions of the meat-packing industry. The account below is from Upton Sinclair's *The Jungle*:

  "There would be meat stored in great piles in rooms, and the water from leaky roofs would drip on the meat, and thousands of rats would race about on it. The packers would put poisoned bread to kill the rats. After the rats died, the rats, bread and meat would go into the hoppers together .... There was never the least attention paid to what was cut up for sausage: there would come all the way back from Europe old sausage that had been rejected, and that was moldy and white — it would be dosed with borax and glycerin, and dumped into the hoppers, and made over again for home use. There would be meat that had tumbled out on the floor in the dirt and sawdust, where the workers had tramped and spit uncounted billions of tuberculosis germs. It was too dark in the storage places to see well, but a man could run his hand over the piles of meat and sweep off handfuls of dried dung of rats."

- **Jacob Riis** photographed and wrote about the way immigrants lived in New York City tenement houses. Here is some of what he had to say in his book *How the Other Half Lives*:

  "It is said that nowhere in the world are so many people crowded together on a square mile as here. Here is a tenement that is seven stories high. It contains thirty-six families. In this house, where a case of smallpox was reported, there were 58 babies and 38 children that were over 5 years of age. In Essex Street two small rooms were made to hold a family of father and mother, 12 children and boarders. 330,000 per square mile are packed in here. The densest crowding in old London ... never went beyond 175,000.

  With the first hot nights in June, police dispatches record the killing of men and women by rolling off roofs and window sills while asleep. Life in the tenements in July and August spells death to an army of little ones whom the doctor's skill is powerless to save. Sleepless mothers walk the streets in the early dawn, trying to stir a cooling breeze to fan the brow of the sick baby. There is no sadder sight than this patient devotion striving against fearfully hopeless odds."

- **Lincoln Steffens**, in *The Shame of the Cities*, described some of the corrupt government practices that existed in the city of Philadelphia:

  "The honest citizens of Philadelphia have no voting rights. The machine controls the voting and practices fraud at every stage. 252 votes were cast in an area that had less than 100 legal voters in its boundaries. On the voting lists were the names of dead dogs, children and non-existent people. It was said that many whose names appeared on the Declaration of Independence were still voting in Philadelphia elections today."

General Directions: You will have an opportunity to correct some of the problems that you just read about in America in the early 20th century. Based on these readings and your own library research, you should:

- identify those conditions most in need of government action
- propose three laws to correct the conditions you identify.

This work may be completed individually or in groups. Use the form below to complete your assignment:

1. Condition: ______________________________

____

Law: ______________________________

____

2. Condition: ______________________________

____

Law: ______________________________

____

3. Condition: ______________________________

____

Law: ______________________________

____

A KEY TO UNDERSTANDING INTERNATIONAL RELATIONS: LOOKING AT FOREIGN POLICY

Many questions on the Regents Examinations and RCTs are about foreign policy. This section will help give you an overview of the nature of foreign policy.

WHAT IS FOREIGN POLICY?

Foreign policy is the conduct of one nation towards other nations. An example of foreign policy would be President Bush's decision to send soldiers to Saudi Arabia. On the other hand, domestic policy refers to a government's actions within its borders, such as Congress passing a new income tax law.

FOREIGN POLICY GOALS

The main objective of United States foreign policy is to act according to the nation's best interests. Many factors determine what the nation believes to be in its best interests.

NATIONAL SECURITY

The first and highest goal of American foreign policy is to protect our way of life. Each nation claims the right to protect itself against other nations. The U. S. does this through military readiness, by responding to acts of aggression, by economic development, by diplomacy, by alliances, and by participating in international organizations. For example, when Japan attacked Pearl Harbor, the U. S. Congress declared war.

PROTECTION OF AMERICAN CITIZENS AND INVESTMENTS

The United States also acts to protect American citizens overseas. For example, in 1990 in Kuwait and Iraq, concern for American hostages had a strong influence on foreign policy.

THE PROMOTION OF AMERICAN TRADE

The United States acts to promote the American economy. For example, when President Bush traveled to Tokyo, he was seeking to improve the U. S. balance of trade.

THE PROMOTION OF DEMOCRACY

The United States actively pursues spreading its political system—democracy. For example, President Wilson brought the United States into World War I to "make the world safe for democracy."

PROMOTION OF HUMAN RIGHTS AND INTERNATIONAL PEACE

The United States supports the causes of morality in international affairs. It realizes that the fate of each country ultimately depends upon the survival of the human species and the planet Earth. For example, the U. S. imposed sanctions on South Africa because of American moral opposition to apartheid.

WHO MAKES FOREIGN POLICY?

The U. S. Constitution gives control of foreign policy to the federal government. The states are prohibited from making foreign policy. To prevent one branch of the central government from becoming too strong, the Constitution divided control over foreign policy between the president and Congress.

PRESIDENTIAL FOREIGN POLICY POWERS

The president has the day-to-day control of foreign policy. The president is assisted in making foreign policy by the Secretary of State (a member of the Cabinet) and by officials in the State Department. Others assisting the president include the Central Intelligence Agency (C.I.A.), the National Security Council, and the Joint Chiefs of Staff. The foreign policy powers of the president include:

- serving as commander-in-chief of the armed forces.
- negotiating treaties with foreign countries.
- appointing and receiving foreign ambassadors and ministers. This gives the president the power to extend or deny diplomatic recognition to new foreign governments.

CONGRESSIONAL FOREIGN POLICY POWERS

Congress was given part of the power in formulating foreign policy. Primarily, this was done to act as a check or control on the president's powers over foreign policy. The foreign policy powers of the Congress include:

- declaring war.
- approving treaties and presidential appointments. A two-thirds vote of the Senate is required to ratify a treaty.
- regulating commerce with foreign nations.
- deciding how much money the president may spend on national defense.

In the 20th century, the ability to act rapidly and decisively has allowed the president to become the main focus in making American foreign policy, overshadowing the role of Congress. However, in times when the United States is not faced with a military crisis, the Congress has attempted to reassert some control over foreign policy.

OTHER INFLUENCES ON FOREIGN POLICY

Although the president and Congress have the constitutional power to make foreign policy, they are influenced in their decisions by others.

- **Special Interest Groups.** Businessmen, political action groups, environmental groups and others often lobby Congress or contact the president's staff to press their views.

■ **The News Media.** Newspapers, magazines, television and radio are extremely influential, since they decide what foreign news to report and how it is reported.

■ **Public Opinion**. Since the United States is a democracy, Congress and the president are very sensitive to the public's opinion. Both are mindful that it was the public that put them in office.

HOW TO EVALUATE FOREIGN POLICY

Evaluating or discussing a particular foreign policy is simply a process of deciding whether the best means were chosen to achieve a particular goal. To illustrate how this is done, let us examine the Cuban Missile Crisis.

STEP 1: WHAT IS THE GOAL?

The first step is to determine what was the immediate objective or goal of the policy. (Usually the objective will be related to one of the foreign policy goals previously discussed.)

Background: The Cuban Missile Crisis, October 1962

An American spy plane observed Soviet technicians building missile launch sites in Cuba. President Kennedy was told that the missiles being shipped to Cuba could be activated in a few days. Kennedy sought to have the missiles removed before they could be used to threaten the U.S.

Goal: National security by protecting the nation against a nuclear attack.

STEP 2: WHAT ARE THE ALTERNATIVES?

The second step is to examine the various choices that are open in order to achieve the goal or objective. In examining alternatives in foreign policy, there are always two extremes: go to war to obtain your objective, or simply do nothing. Between these two extremes there are many other options.

Alternatives: The Cuban Missile Crisis, October 1962

Kennedy and his advisors had a number of options:

- The United States could send nuclear weapons against Cuba.
- The United States Army and Navy could invade Cuba.
- United States jet bombers could destroy the missile sites.
- The United States could declare war and impose a naval blockade.
- The United States could appeal to the United Nations for help.
- The United States could do nothing.

- Any others? ______________________________

STEP 3: WAS THE BEST CHOICE ACTUALLY MADE?

In the final step, the choice selected is evaluated. Was this the best among the various alternatives? Did it succeed in reaching the goal? Did the policy assume any unnecessary risks or dangers?

Evaluation: The Cuban Missile Crisis, October 1962

Kennedy decided on a naval blockade of Cuba, preventing further Soviet shipments of missiles. Cuba was threatened with an invasion if the missiles were not removed. The United States offered to withdraw some U.S. missiles aimed at the Soviet Union and promised never to invade Cuba. Kennedy's naval blockade and threatened invasion, combined with the offer of United States concessions, convinced the Soviets to withdraw the missiles from Cuba. Although the objective was achieved, some critics claim the risk of nuclear war was too great.

MAJOR TYPES OF FOREIGN POLICY

Throughout U. S. history, our government has followed a variety of foreign policies in its relations with other nations. Many Regents Examinations and RCTs ask you to describe and give examples of these policies. For example, on the January 1991 Regents, the following foreign policy question appeared:

At various time periods, the United States has followed different policies in international affairs.

Policies / Time Periods

Isolationism - 1790 to 1825
Imperialism - 1890 to 1915
International Involvement - 1915 to 1945
Cold War - 1945 to 1985
Global Cooperation - 1985 to present

Select *three* of the policies and time periods listed. For *each* one chosen, explain why the United States followed the policy during the time period indicated. Discuss one example that illustrates how the United States followed the policy.

To help you to answer such questions, the following table summarizes the most important types of foreign policy.

POLICIES AIMED AT EXPANSION

Policy	*Description*	*Example*
Territorial Expansion	Buying or annexing territory to increase the size of a country	Louisiana Purchase and the Mexican Cession
Imperialism	The rule of one country over another, less powerful country	U.S. annexation of the Philippine Islands

POLICIES AIMED AT NATIONAL SECURITY

Policy	*Description*	*Example*
Neutrality	Avoiding taking sides in a dispute to prevent involvement in a foreign war	Advice given by Washington in his Farewell Address
Isolationism (Non-Involvement)	Refusing to become involved with other countries when that involvement could lead to war	U.S. policy in the 1920's and 1930's
Military Alliances	Two or more countries joining forces against a common enemy	U.S. participation in N.A.T.O.
Military Aid	Sending military supplies to help an allied or friendly power	Issuance of the Truman Doctrine
Collective Security	Relying on international organizations or military alliances to help strengthen national security	Participation in the United Nations and N.A.T.O.
Response To Aggression	Going to war when attacked, or when an ally is attacked	World Wars I & II
Containment	Preventing an enemy from gaining additional territory or spreading its way of life to new nations	Attempt by U. S. to halt Soviet influence in Europe and S.E. Asia
Detente	Reducing tensions between hostile nations	U.S.-Soviet relations under President Reagan

POLICIES AIMED AT STRENGTHENING U.S. DEFENSES

Policy	*Description*	*Example*
Military Preparedness	Protecting national security by being militarily prepared with a a strong army and navy	Reagan's increased defense spending in the 1980's
Nuclear Deterrence (Arms Race)	Having so many nuclear weapons that any nation will fear to launch an attack against us	Stockpiling of nuclear weapons in the 1950's

POLICIES AIMED AT FURTHERING U.S. VALUES OVERSEAS

Policy	*Description*	*Example*
Economic Aid	Giving dollars, supplies or expert advice to developing countries	Alliance For Progress and the Marshall Plan
Recognition of Foreign Governments	Presidents' power to send and receive ambassadors, giving them the power to recognize the legitimacy of a foreign government	U.S. presidents refused to recognize the Communist government of Russia, 1917-1933
Democracy	Attempts to make peace-loving nations friendly to the U.S.	Wilson's Fourteen Points sought "to make the world safe for democracy"
Promotion of Human Rights	Attempts to persuade foreign governments to respect their citizens' basic human rights	Signing of the Helsinki Accords
Disarmament	Attempts by the U. S. to bring about a reduction of military weapons in the world	S.A.L.T. Agreements with the Soviet Union

CHAPTER 10

AMERICA REACHING OUT

Early in American history, the nation's leaders followed George Washington's advice to avoid "entanglements" with Europe. However, at the end of the 19th century, the U.S. became more assertive in the Pacific and the Caribbean. After the Spanish-American War, the U.S. acquired its first overseas colonies. A second major turning point came in 1917, when America intervened in World War I. The results of the war disappointed many Americans, leading to a return to traditional isolationism.

— TIMELINE OF KEY EVENTS —

1796	1812	1823	1845	1846	1898	1915	1917	1919
Washington's Farewell Address	War of 1812 begins	Monroe Doctrine issued	Republic of Texas annexed	Mexican War begins	Spanish-American War	*Lusitania* sunk by German U-boats	U. S. enters World War I	Versailles Treaty

MILESTONES OF EARLY U.S. FOREIGN POLICY

U.S. FOREIGN POLICY TO 1812

As a new nation the United States was militarily weak and feared losing its recently achieved independence. As a result, it adopted a policy of **neutrality** by avoiding taking sides in European disputes and not becoming involved in foreign wars. During this period there were two notable foreign policy developments.

WASHINGTON'S FAREWELL ADDRESS (1796)

Washington, in his last address as president, cautioned Americans against entering into permanent alliances with foreign countries, especially with Europe. He wanted the nation to devote itself to developing its own trade and assuming leadership of the Western Hemisphere.

THE LOUISIANA PURCHASE (1803)

In 1803, France sold the Louisiana Territory to the United States for $15 million. The Louisiana Territory doubled the size of the United States. Although President Jefferson was uncertain if the Constitution allowed the federal government to buy territory, he went ahead with the purchase anyway.

A LARGER ROLE IN FOREIGN AFFAIRS: 1820-1898

THE WAR OF 1812

Departing from its previous policy of neutrality, the United States went to war with Great Britain in 1812. The war was begun to prevent British seizure of American sailors, to stop British support of American Indian raids in the northwest, and to protect freedom of the seas. Some Americans also wanted to seize Canada. The war ended in a stalemate, leaving things much as they were.

THE MONROE DOCTRINE (1823)

Napoleon's conquest of Spain led to the rise of independence movements in the Spanish colonies in Latin America. The United States recognized these nations' independence, but feared Spain might try to reconquer them. As a result, President Monroe issued the **Monroe Doctrine.** It announced that the United States would oppose any attempt by European powers to establish new colonies in the Western hemisphere or to reconquer former colonies that had declared independence. But Monroe also agreed not to interfere with any European colonies already in existence, such as Canada and Cuba.

The Monroe Doctrine was extremely important because it demonstrated to the rest of the world that the United States had special interests in the Western Hemisphere. The Doctrine was later used to justify frequent interference in the affairs of Latin American nations. During the late 19th and early 20th centuries, the enforcement of this policy dominated U. S. relations with Latin America.

MANIFEST DESTINY

Public opinion strongly supported continental expansion. In the 1840's, Americans came to believe that it was their "destiny," or future, to extend the United States from the east coast to the Pacific. Americans would benefit mankind by establishing their democratic institutions over this vast area.

■ **Annexation of Texas (1845)**. Americans began to settle in the Mexican province of Texas. In a dispute with Americans living in Texas, the Mexican leader **Santa Anna** was captured by Texan-Americans in 1836. To obtain his release, Santa Anna signed a treaty recognizing Texan independence. In 1845, Congress finally voted to annex Texas.

■ **Mexican-American War (1846-1848).** A dispute broke out between the United States and Mexico over the southern border of Texas. President Polk sent troops into the disputed area. He declared war, and Mexico was defeated. As a result, the United States acquired California, Nevada, Utah, Arizona, and parts of Colorado and New Mexico. In the final peace treaty, the United States paid $18 million for these areas.

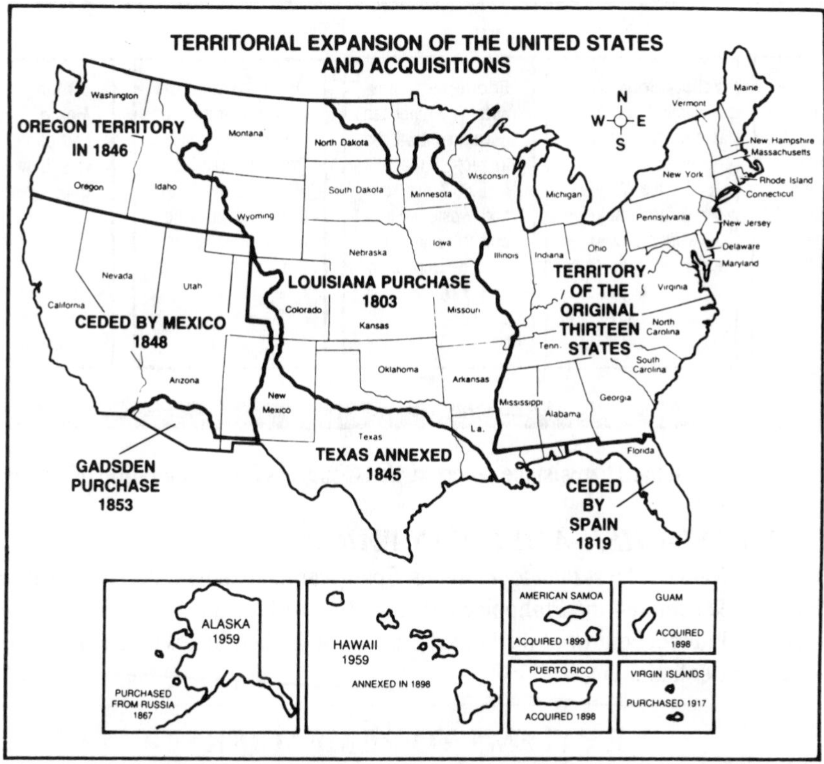
TERRITORIAL EXPANSION OF THE UNITED STATES AND ACQUISITIONS
OREGON TERRITORY IN 1846
LOUISIANA PURCHASE 1803
CEDED BY MEXICO 1848
TERRITORY OF THE ORIGINAL THIRTEEN STATES
TEXAS ANNEXED 1845
GADSDEN PURCHASE 1853
CEDED BY SPAIN 1819
N
W
E
S
Washington
Oregon
Idaho
Montana
Wyoming
North Dakota
South Dakota
Minnesota
Wisconsin
Michigan
Nebraska
Iowa
Illinois
Indiana
Ohio
Nevada
Utah
California
Colorado
Kansas
Missouri
Arizona
New Mexico
Oklahoma
Arkansas
Texas
La.
Mississippi
Alabama
Georgia
Florida
Tenn.
Maine
Vermont
New Hampshire
Massachusetts
New York
Rhode Island
Connecticut
Pennsylvania
New Jersey
Delaware
Maryland
Virginia
North Carolina
South Carolina
ALASKA 1959
PURCHASED FROM RUSSIA 1867
HAWAII 1959
ANNEXED IN 1898
AMERICAN SAMOA
ACQUIRED 1899
GUAM
ACQUIRED 1898
PUERTO RICO
ACQUIRED 1898
VIRGIN ISLANDS
PURCHASED 1917

■ **Additional Acquisitions**. The United States had three other major acquisitions. The **Gadsden Purchase**, bought from Mexico, completed American expansion in the southwest. In an agreement with Great Britain in 1846, the line dividing Canada and the United States was extended westwards to the Pacific. This gave the United States that part of the **Oregon Territory** that lay south of the line.

Lastly, in 1867, the United States purchased **Alaska** from Russia for $7.2 million. At first, Secretary of State William Seward's purchase met with ridicule, but it proved to be an important acquisition. In 1959, Alaska became the 49th state.

THE SPANISH-AMERICAN WAR OF 1898

The Spanish-American War marked a turning point in American foreign relations, because the United States went from a nation without colonies to one that controlled a vast overseas empire. In 1894, Cuba rebelled against Spain, seeking its independence. The Spanish army sent to Cuba used brutal force to crush the rebellion. Several factors led to American intervention in the dispute:

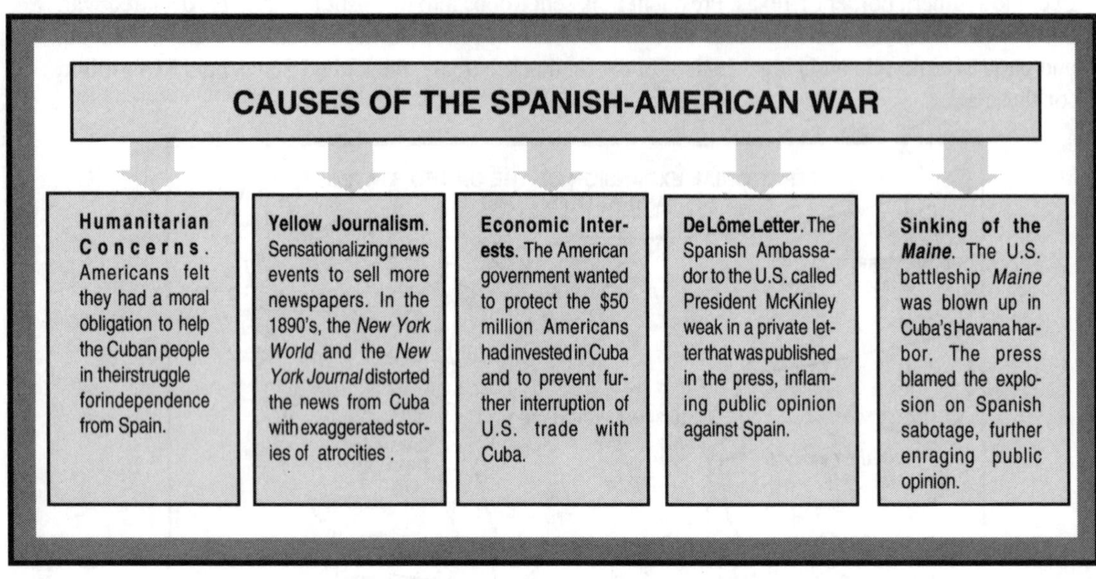
CAUSES OF THE SPANISH-AMERICAN WAR
Humanitarian Concerns. Americans felt they had a moral obligation to help the Cuban people in theirstruggle forindependence from Spain.
Yellow Journalism. Sensationalizing news events to sell more newspapers. In the 1890's, the *New York World* and the *New York Journal* distorted the news from Cuba with exaggerated stories of atrocities.
Economic Interests. The American government wanted to protect the $50 million Americans had invested in Cuba and to prevent further interruption of U.S. trade with Cuba.
DeLôme Letter. The Spanish Ambassador to the U.S. called President McKinley weak in a private letter that was published in the press, inflaming public opinion against Spain.
Sinking of the *Maine*. The U.S. battleship *Maine* was blown up in Cuba's Havana harbor. The press blamed the explosion on Spanish sabotage, further enraging public opinion.

President McKinley, finding it hard to resist the outcry, asked Congress for a declaration of war against Spain.

RESULTS OF THE SPANISH-AMERICAN WAR

The Spanish-American War lasted less than four months. Spain was no match for the superiority of American forces. The United States acquired the Philippines, Puerto Rico and Guam. Cuba became independent in name but fell under the indirect control of the United States. The United States thus emerged from the war with its own far-ranging colonial empire.

KEY ITEMS TO REMEMBER

Neutrality, Washington's Farewell Address, Louisiana Purchase, War of 1812, Monroe Doctrine, Manifest Destiny, Mexican-American War, Spanish-American War, yellow journalism, DeLôme Letter, *U.S.S. Maine*.

AMERICA BUILDS A COLONIAL EMPIRE

Since America was once a colony, many Americans felt uneasy about forcing colonial rule on others. Some Americans also thought that colonial rule violated the democratic principles of self-government. However, after the Spanish-American War the United States reversed its traditional policies by becoming an imperialist power. **Imperialism**, the control of one country by another, became a major foreign policy goal of the United States. There were several reasons for this transition.

REASONS FOR COLONIAL EXPANSION

NEED FOR RAW MATERIALS AND OVERSEAS MARKETS

The United States was now an industrial power. Colonies would provide needed raw materials for factories, a guaranteed market for manufacturers, and a place for farmers to sell their surplus crops.

STRATEGIC REASONS

Some Americans believed the acquisition of colonies would promote American naval strength. **Alfred Thayer Mahan**, in his book *The Influence of Seapower Upon History*, urged the United States to increase its wealth and power by developing a strong navy, building a canal through Panama, and establishing colonies in the Pacific and Caribbean. Most of his program was later adopted by President Theodore Roosevelt. Others saw colonial expansion as a means of showing that the United States was a great and powerful nation. They argued that European powers were carving up Africa, Asia, and the Pacific into colonies and that the United States should follow their example and grab something before there was nothing left.

ATTITUDE TOWARDS OTHER PEOPLES

Psychological attitudes and beliefs played a role in colonial expansion. Many Americans believed in "Anglo-Saxon superiority"—that Anglo-Saxons were a superior race and should rule over others. Others wanted to help other peoples around the world, believing that by spreading Christianity and American institutions, they would be helping other, less fortunate individuals.

AMERICAN INVOLVEMENT IN THE PACIFIC

After the Spanish-American War, the U.S. acquired a colonial empire in the Pacific Ocean with the acquisition of the Philippine Islands and Guam. American settlers helped bring about the annexation of Hawaii. Later, Samoa and Midway became American possessions.

THE PHILIPPINES

The Filipinos were bitterly disappointed when the United States annexed the Philippines at the end of the Spanish-American War instead of granting them independence. The Filipinos rejected American annexation and fought for their independence, until they were finally defeated in 1902. Afterwards, the United States built roads, hospitals and schools throughout the Philippine islands. Philippine independence was granted in 1946, just after World War II.

HAWAII

Hawaii consists of a group of islands in the Pacific Ocean. The islands provided a useful coaling station for United States ships traveling to the Far East. In the mid 19th century, American settlers built sugar and pineapple plantations on Hawaii. In the 1890's, **Queen Liliuokalani** tried to take political power away from the American landowners. In response, the American landowners organized a successful revolt in 1893. A provisional government, formed by Americans, asked to be annexed by the United States. At first Congress refused. After the outbreak of the Spanish-American War Congress reconsidered, and in 1898, it voted for annexation. Hawaii became the 50th state in 1959.

SMALLER PACIFIC ISLANDS: GUAM, SAMOA, & MIDWAY

Guam was taken from Spain in the Spanish-American War. Samoa had been under the joint control of Britain, Germany and the United States since 1889. In 1899, it was divided outright between Germany and the United States. Midway had been in American possession since 1867. These Pacific islands provided valuable naval bases and coaling stations for American ships traveling back and forth between Asia and the U.S.

U.S. POSSESSIONS IN THE PACIFIC

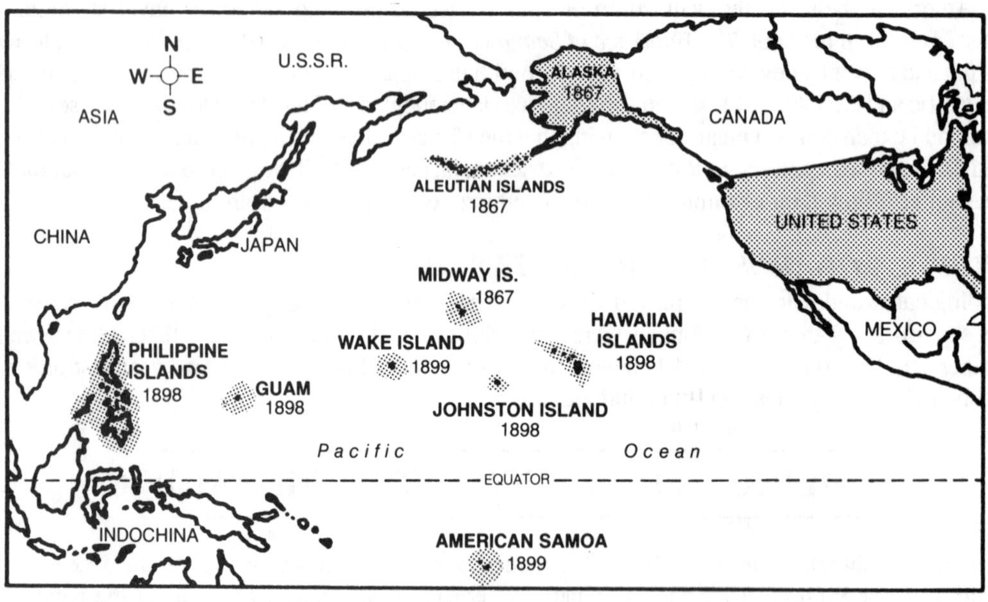
N
W
E
S
U.S.S.R.
ASIA
ALASKA
1867
CANADA
ALEUTIAN ISLANDS
1867
UNITED STATES
CHINA
JAPAN
MIDWAY IS.
1867
HAWAIIAN
ISLANDS
1898
MEXICO
PHILIPPINE
ISLANDS
1898
WAKE ISLAND
1899
GUAM
1898
JOHNSTON ISLAND
1898
Pacific
Ocean
EQUATOR
INDOCHINA
AMERICAN SAMOA
1899

AMERICAN INVOLVEMENT IN THE FAR EAST

The United States developed an active trade with China and Japan in the mid-19th century. After 1898, the control of the Philippines, Midway, Hawaii, Guam and Samoa made the United States an important Far Eastern power. This increased United States activity in the Pacific led to a more active role in the affairs of both China and Japan.

THE UNITED STATES AND CHINA

■ **The Open Door Policy in China (1899).** The United States was concerned that European powers would establish "spheres of influence" in China, cutting off areas from American trade. Secretary of State **John Hay** announced equal trading rights for all foreign nations in all parts of China. Even though the European powers never agreed to cooperate, Hay declared that the Open Door Policy was in effect.

■ **The Boxer Rebellion (1900).** A group of Chinese rebelled against the growing Western influence in China. These so-called "Boxers" threatened the lives of all foreigners in China. An international expedition was sent to crush the rebellion. The United States, fearing that Europeans and Japanese would use this as an excuse to dismember China, announced that the United States would oppose any attempts to carve it up. As a result, China's territorial integrity was saved.

THE UNITED STATES AND JAPAN

■ **The Opening of Japan (1853).** The United States opened an isolationist Japan to Western trade and influence when **Commodore Matthew Perry** landed there with American gunships in 1853. Soon afterwards, Japan became the first non-Western country to industrialize and adopt many Western ways. By the 1890's, Japan had turned itself around, and was also becoming an imperialist power, anxious to sell its goods on the Asian mainland. Japan defeated China in a war that lasted from 1894 to 1895, and gained control over Taiwan and Korea.

■ **President Roosevelt and the Russo-Japanese War (1905).** Japan surprised the West by defeating Russia. Americans did not wish to see either nation become too dominant in the Far East. When the Japanese invited President Theodore Roosevelt to mediate the conflict, he accepted. Roosevelt brought both sides to a peace settlement in the **Treaty of Portsmouth** (1905), and won the Nobel Peace Prize for his efforts.

■ **The Gentlemen's Agreement (1907).** Bad feelings between the United States and Japan increased when San Francisco excluded Japanese children from its public schools. Roosevelt halted the segregation of Japanese school children, and in exchange, the Japanese government promised to limit future Japanese emigration to America.

U.S. IMPERIALISM IN THE CARIBBEAN

As a result of the Spanish-American War, America acquired direct control of Puerto Rico and indirect control over Cuba, two islands in the Caribbean. The construction of the Panama Canal further contributed to American interest in this area. There were other reasons for U.S. interest in the Caribbean:

- **Hemispheric Security.** The United States sought to keep foreign powers out of the Caribbean because they could pose a possible threat to the United States

- **Economic Interests.** The Caribbean area was an important supplier of agricultural products, like sugar and tropical fruits, and provided a valuable market for United States goods and investments.

- **Importance of the Canal.** Once the canal was built, it became a strategic waterway permitting easy access between the Atlantic and the Pacific Oceans.

CARIBBEAN AREA

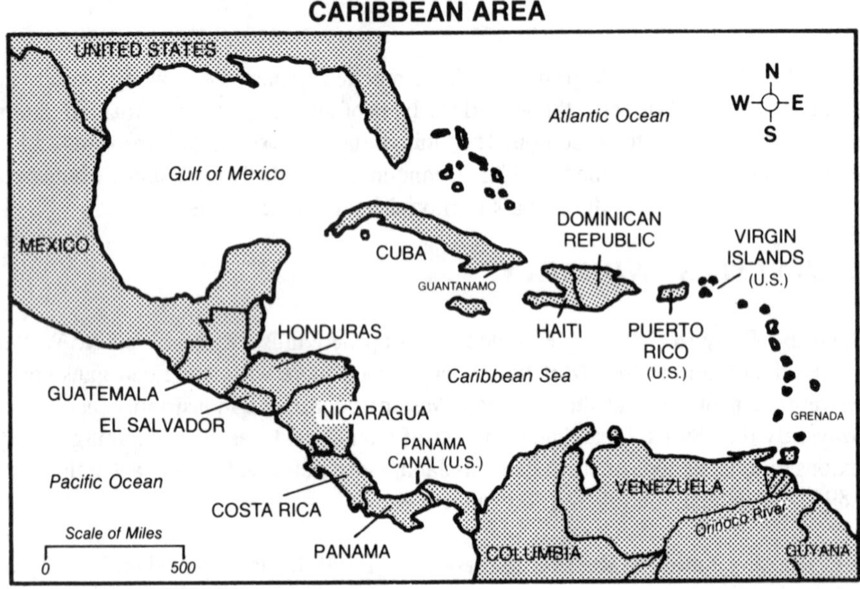
UNITED STATES
N
W
E
S
Atlantic Ocean
Gulf of Mexico
MEXICO
CUBA
GUANTANAMO
DOMINICAN
REPUBLIC
VIRGIN
ISLANDS
(U.S.)
HONDURAS
HAITI
PUERTO
RICO
(U.S.)
Caribbean Sea
GUATEMALA
EL SALVADOR
NICARAGUA
GRENADA
PANAMA
CANAL (U.S.)
Pacific Ocean
VENEZUELA
Orinoco River
COSTA RICA
Scale of Miles
0
500
PANAMA
COLUMBIA
GUYANA

CUBA: AN INFORMAL PROTECTORATE

Cuba is an island only 90 miles off the coast of Florida. This nearness has led Americans to take a keen interest in Cuban affairs. The **Teller Resolution** (1898), passed in the anti-imperialist climate before the Spanish-American War, stated that the United States would not annex Cuba. Consequently, Cubans were given their independence after the war, but despite the Teller Resolution, Cuba soon became a **protectorate** (an area under American control). American military forces remained on the island, and American businesses invested heavily in Cuba. Cubans were forced to agree to the **Platt Amendment**, which gave the United States the right to intervene in Cuban affairs at any time. The Platt Amendment was finally repealed when the United States reversed its policies towards Cuba in the 1930's.

PUERTO RICO

Puerto Rico became an American possession as a result of the Spanish-American War in 1898. By 1952 it became a self-governing U.S. Commonwealth. However, there has been controversy over its future status.

What should be the future status of Puerto Rico?		
POINT (Commonwealth): Puerto Rico has been a United States Commonwealth for almost 100 years, and should continue in that role. Puerto Ricans are American citizens, free to move anywhere in the United States they wish. In Puerto Rico, they pay no federal tax, and they can serve in the United States military.	**COUNTERPOINT (Statehood):** If Puerto Rico becomes a state, its people will be able to vote in U.S. elections, will be represented in Congress, and will receive more federal aid and other social services. However, Puerto Ricans will have to pay federal taxes; businesses may leave since they will have to pay federal tax on their profits.	**COUNTERPOINT (Independence):** Puerto Ricans identify strongly with Latin America and the culture of the Caribbean. If Puerto Rico becomes independent its citizens will have a true cultural identity, instead of feeling like "second-class" citizens in a larger country. Spanish would become the official language of the island, instead of English.

THE PANAMA CANAL

The Spanish-American War emphasized the importance of building a canal in Central America connecting the Atlantic and Pacific Oceans. By 1903, the U. S. decided to build the canal across the Isthmus of Panama. At that time Panama was a part of Colombia. The U. S. offered $10 million and an annual fee to Colombia for a strip of land on which to build the canal. The Colombians, seeking a better deal, delayed giving their approval.

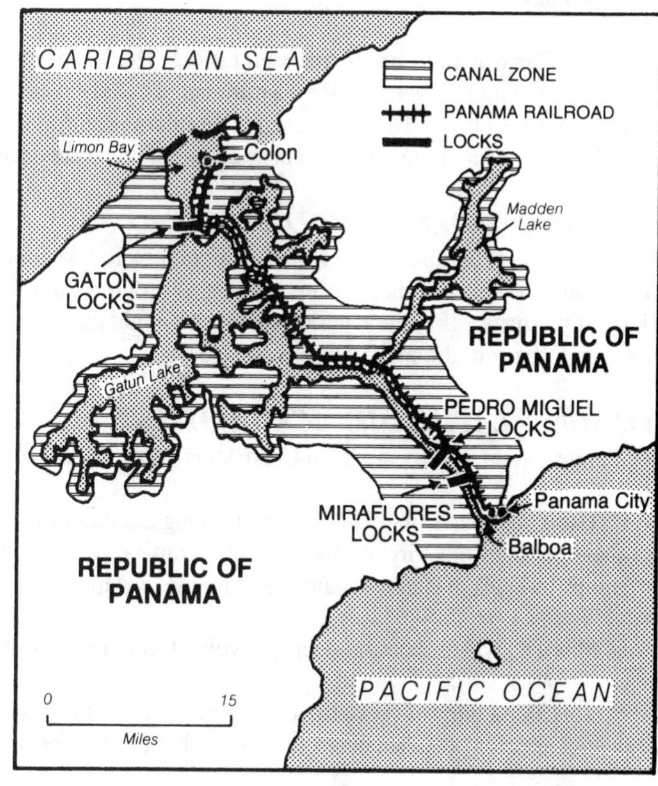
CARIBBEAN SEA
CANAL ZONE
PANAMA RAILROAD
LOCKS
Limon Bay
Colon
Madden Lake
GATON LOCKS
Gatun Lake
REPUBLIC OF PANAMA
PEDRO MIGUEL LOCKS
MIRAFLORES LOCKS
Panama City
Balboa
REPUBLIC OF PANAMA
PACIFIC OCEAN
0
15
Miles

■ **President Roosevelt Strikes A Deal.** President Theodore Roosevelt struck a deal with Panamanian rebels who wished to break away from Colombia and establish an independent Panama. U. S. warships prevented the Colombian government from putting down the rebellion. Roosevelt immediately gave Panama diplomatic recognition. In return, Panama allowed the U. S. to build the Panama Canal. The U. S. was given complete control of a 10-mile strip running through the center of Panama, called the **Panama Canal Zone**. Such policies greatly angered Colombia and many other Latin American countries. Construction of the canal was a monumental effort, taking over 10 years (1903-1914) to complete, costing thousands of lives and $400 million.

■ **More Recent Developments.** A discussion of the **Treaty of 1977** and the **Invasion of Panama (1989)** can be found in Chapter 14.

AMERICAN INTERVENTION IN THE CARIBBEAN

In the late 19th and early 20th centuries, American governments expanded the interpretation of the Monroe Doctrine. Often they intervened in the affairs of Latin America to protect growing U. S. economic investment.

■ **Venezuelan Boundary Dispute (1895).** When Great Britain threatened to use force to resolve a border dispute with Venezuela, the United States threatened to go to war. Fearing a war with the United States, Great Britain submitted the border dispute to American arbitration.

■ **The "Big Stick Policy" or "Roosevelt Corollary."** In 1904, Roosevelt barred European countries from using force to collect debts owed by the Dominican Republic. Roosevelt went one step further and declared that the United States would intervene and collect the debts for them, acting as an "international police power." This "corollary" to the Monroe Doctrine was also known as the "Big Stick Policy."

■ **The Caribbean as an "American Lake."** The Big Stick Policy was used so often by the U.S.to justify sending troops to the West Indies and Central America, that the Caribbean became known as an "American lake." Haiti, Nicaragua, Honduras and the Dominican Republic, like Cuba, became virtual American protectorates. These interventions were deeply resented by many Latin Americans.

TAFT AND "DOLLAR DIPLOMACY"

President Taft encouraged bankers and corporations to invest in profitable ventures in the countries of the Caribbean. The use of American investment to promote American foreign policy interests was known as "dollar diplomacy." If Latin American countries could not repay the American loans, the United States sent in troops to be sure the money was collected.

WILSON'S LATIN AMERICAN POLICY

Several important developments in Latin American affairs occurred during Woodrow Wilson's Presidency:

■ **The Caribbean.** In 1917 Wilson, seeking additional U.S. bases in the Caribbean to protect the Canal, bought the Virgin Islands from Denmark. To protect American interests, Wilson also sent troops to Haiti, Nicaragua, and the Dominican Republic.

■ **Mexico.** Wilson became deeply involved in the affairs of Mexico.

- **The Policy of "watchful waiting."** In 1913, the leader of the Mexican army murdered the elected president and seized control of the Mexican government. Wilson, refusing to give diplomatic recognition to this new government, said he would recognize only democratically-elected governments. This policy of non-recognition was known as "watchful waiting."

- **Pancho Villa.** Troops of the Mexican rebel leader "Pancho" Villa murdered several American workers in Mexico. Then they crossed the border and attacked a town in the U. S. Wilson reacted to these outrages by sending United States troops into Mexico. They remained almost a year, but never caught Pancho Villa. Wilson withdrew them in 1917, when the threat of U. S. involvement in World War I overshadowed Mexican events.

THE "GOOD NEIGHBOR POLICY" (1930-1945)

Under Presidents Hoover and Franklin D. Roosevelt, the United States abandoned the "Big Stick Policy" and attempted to improve relations with Latin American countries. Where Theodore Roosevelt had treated Latin American nations almost as U. S. protectorates, Hoover and Franklin Roosevelt sought to treat them as equals. Under the "Good Neighbor Policy" the United States agreed not to interfere in Latin America's internal problems, and relations between the United States and Latin American countries began to improve.

THE ORGANIZATION OF AMERICAN STATES (O.A.S.)

This organization was created in 1948 to provide a means for solving hemispheric disputes and problems peacefully through periodic meetings. It continues to serve as a legal channel for solving international disputes in Latin America.

KEY ITEMS TO REMEMBER

Imperialism, Open Door Policy, Boxer Rebellion, "Big Stick Policy," Platt Amendment, "dollar diplomacy," "Good Neighbor Policy," Organization of American States (O.A.S.)

THE UNITED STATES IN WORLD WAR I

EUROPEAN CAUSES OF WORLD WAR I

World War I was a global war fought with new destructive technologies. The outbreak of the war in Europe in 1914 had many causes:

NATIONALISM

Nationalism led to rivalries between France, Germany, Austria-Hungary and Russia. Austria-Hungary was still composed of many smaller nationalities, with each group wanting its own national state.

ECONOMIC RIVALRIES AND IMPERIALISM

The European powers had competing economic interests. German industrialization threatened the British economy. Russian interests in the Balkans threatened Austria-Hungary. Competing colonial claims created additional tension.

THE ALLIANCE SYSTEM

Starting in the 1890s, Europe divided into two large alliances: on one side stood Germany and Austria; on the other stood Russia, France and Great Britain. Every dispute involving any two of these countries threatened to involve all the others.

Allied & Central Powers WWI

The assassination of **Archduke Francis Ferdinand** by Slavic nationalists in 1914 was the immediate cause for the war. When Austria invaded Serbia to avenge the assassination, the various alliances brought Russia, Germany, Britain and France into the war. This escalated what might have been a minor regional crisis into a major European war. Moreover, World War I was a global war fought with new destructive technologies. New weapons—the machine gun, poison gas, airplanes and submarines—prevented either side from gaining a quick victory.

REASONS FOR U.S. INTERVENTION IN WORLD WAR I

The U. S. was not a member of either European alliance system. When war broke out, American leaders attempted to follow the traditional policy, stated in Washington's Farewell Address, of avoiding involvement in European conflicts. Yet despite their efforts at neutrality, the U. S. became involved in World War I. Why?

CLOSER TIES WITH THE ALLIES

Many Americans traced their ancestry to Britain. A common language and a common history tied Americans to the British. The United States, Great Britain, and France shared the same democratic political system. American trade to the Allies increased dramatically as the United States became the main source for Allied arms, supplies, food and loans.

GERMAN ACTIONS AND ALLIED PROPAGANDA

The actions of Germany as reported in Allied propaganda moved Americans closer to the Allies. Americans were shocked at Germany's violation of international law by its invasion of neutral Belgium, shooting of civilians and destruction of civilian buildings. A message (the **Zimmerman Telegram**) from the German Foreign Minister was intercepted and printed in American newspapers. It promised Mexico the return of New Mexico, Arizona and Texas if Mexico would help Germany in a war against the United States. This further inflamed American public opinion against Germany.

VIOLATION OF FREEDOM OF THE SEAS

The main reason for the American entry into World War I was the German use of **submarine warfare**, violating the United States right to freedom of the seas.

- **The British Blockade.** A British blockade prevented food and arms from being shipped to Germany. The German fleet was too weak to break the blockade. Using their fleet of submarines, the Germans retaliated by threatening to sink all ships delivering goods to Great Britain. Because the submarines were so small, Germany announced it would be unable to rescue survivors.

- **Sinking the Lusitania (1915).** A German submarine sank the British passenger ship Lusitania, killing over 1,000 passengers including 128 Americans. Anti-German feelings were stirred up when American newspapers reported this catastrophe. Wilson sent a strong protest to Germany, but refused to go to war over the incident.

- **The Sussex Pledge (1916).** After a German submarine attacked an unarmed French passenger ship, Wilson threatened to break off relations with Germany. Germany pledged not to sink any more ocean liners without prior warning or providing help to passengers.

- **Germany Uses Submarine Warfare (1917).** The Germans, suffering from near-starvation, took the risk of announcing they would they would sink ships in the blockaded areas. This was a clear violation of the American principle of "**freedom of the seas**" — the right of neutral nations to ship non-war goods to nations at war. When German submarines attacked three unarmed American merchant vessels, Wilson asked Congress for a declaration of war against Germany.

AMERICA GOES TO WAR: 1917-1918

AMERICAN IDEALISM

As an idealist and Progressive, President Wilson tried to broaden the American war effort from an attempt to defend "freedom of the seas" to a crusade for democracy. He told Americans that their aim in the war was to establish the ultimate peace of the world and to free its peoples. Wilson declared, "The world must be made safe for democracy." The American people found it inspiring to endure the war for such high-minded ideals. With a strong sense of moral superiority, they set out to save and remake the world.

THE WAR EFFORT AT HOME

Involvement in a major war led to important changes at home:

- **The Wartime Economy.** Wilson was given sweeping powers by Congress. He established a number of agencies—the War Industries Board, War Labor Board, and Food Administration—all directed at regulating the economy during the war. Railroads were placed under direct government control. Congress passed a Selective Service Act; millions of Americans were registered for the draft, while others were drafted or volunteered to enlist. Women often replaced men at the workplace.

- **War Costs.** The cost of the war, about $30 billion, was paid for by increasing taxes and selling war bonds to the public. About a third of the cost was spent in loans to Allies, turning the United States from a debtor to a creditor nation. (Instead of America's owing money to foreign countries, they owed money to America.)

- **Civil Liberties.** Civil liberties were curtailed to meet wartime demands. Espionage acts made it a crime to criticize the war effort. Some opponents of the war were sent to prison. The Supreme Court upheld some limits to free speech in *Schenck v. United States* . (See *The Constitution at Work* section for more details of this case.)

THE PEACE SETTLEMENT: THE TREATY OF VERSAILLES

Almost two million American troops eventually reached Europe, where they gave the Allies an overwhelming advantage in combat. Germany surrendered in November 1918. Even before the war ended, President Wilson announced America's war aims in his Fourteen Points. These reflected American idealism and Wilson's view that the war should be a crusade for democracy that would establish a lasting peace.

THE FOURTEEN POINTS (1918)

The Fourteen Points demanded that each nationality should have its own country and government. It called for freedom of the seas, equal trade, reduced armaments and an end to secret diplomacy. Wilson felt the most important point in his plan was the creation of a **League of Nations**. He hoped to create a world of peaceful, democratic nations in which future wars would be avoided.

THE VERSAILLES TREATY

Wilson traveled to Europe to negotiate the final peace treaty. He made a crucial mistake in not inviting influential Senators to accompany him, since the Senate would eventually have to ratify the treaty. Almost immediately, Wilson came into conflict with Allied leaders who wanted to impose a harsh treaty on Germany. Wilson had to make many concessions to their views in order to get their support for the formation of the League of Nations, which was to be included in the peace treaty. The final terms of the peace settlement and accompanying treaties were extremely harsh on Germany and the other Central powers:

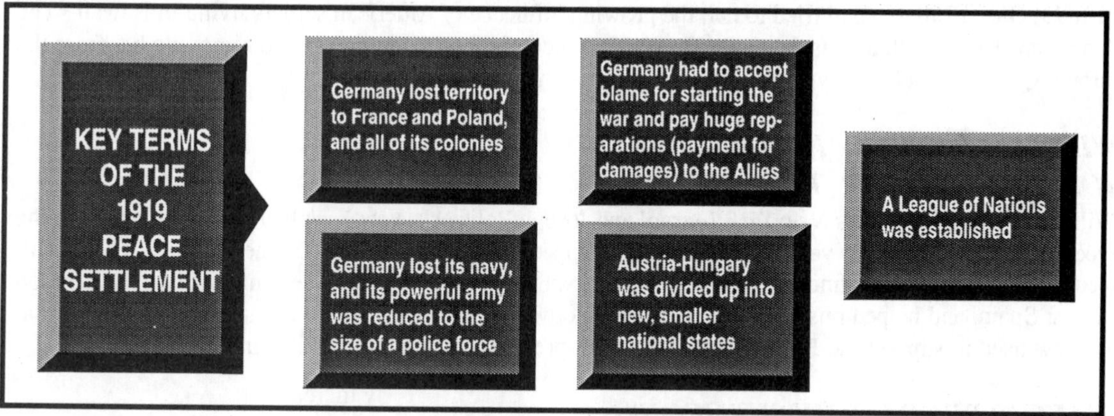
KEY TERMS OF THE 1919 PEACE SETTLEMENT
Germany lost territory to France and Poland, and all of its colonies
Germany had to accept blame for starting the war and pay huge reparations (payment for damages) to the Allies
Germany lost its navy, and its powerful army was reduced to the size of a police force
Austria-Hungary was divided up into new, smaller national states
A League of Nations was established

THE U.S. REJECTS PARTICIPATION IN THE LEAGUE OF NATIONS

Wilson hoped the League of Nations would discourage future aggression and wars. The League had no army of its own, but relied on the armies of its members to stop aggression. The League failed, in part because many major world powers, including the U. S, never became members. The American failure to join was due to the rejection of the Versailles Treaty by the Senate. Wilson needed a two-thirds vote in the Senate to ratify the Versailles Treaty. He rejected any compromises in the Treaty that were suggested by the Senate. Instead, he decided to appeal directly to the American voters for support, and went on a national speaking tour. However, Wilson had failed to gauge the feelings of most Americans, who had become disillusioned with U.S. participation in world affairs. During his speaking tour, Wilson suffered a stroke which left him partly paralyzed. Later, the Senate refused to ratify the Treaty, and the United States never joined the League.

THE UNITED STATES RETREATS INTO ISOLATION

Many Americans were disillusioned with the large costs and small gains the U. S. made as a result of its involvement in the war. They began to look once again to George Washington's earlier advice to avoid European entanglements, and turned their attention back to their own well-being at home. This marked a return to a policy of **isolationism**—refusing to become involved in other countries' affairs when that involvement might lead to war.

KEY ITEMS TO REMEMBER

Freedom of the seas, *Lusitania*, submarine warfare, Fourteen Points, Versailles Treaty, League of Nations. isolationism

PERSONALITIES OF THE PERIOD

QUEEN LILIUOKALANI (QUEEN OF HAWAII)

In 1893, Queen Liliuokalani tried to halt the growing influence of American settlers living in Hawaii. The Americans led a revolt against her rule. They were successful in seizing power and removing her from the throne. Queen Liliuokalani was the last ruling monarch of Hawaii.

WILLIAM RANDOLPH HEARST and JOSEPH PULITZER (PUBLISHERS)

William Randolph Hearst's *New York Journal* and Joseph Pulitzer's *New York World* were pioneers in the type of reporting known as **yellow journalism**. To appeal to general readers, both newspapers sensationalized stories about the treatment of Cubans under Spanish control. Their stories inflamed public opinion against Spain, and helped push the United States into war with Spain in 1898. Pulitzer donated funds that are now used to support the Pulitzer Prize, the most prestigious award in writing and journalism.

WALTER REED (ARMY SURGEON)

Americans living in Cuba and the Panama Canal were often stricken with yellow fever, a tropical disease. In 1900, Walter Reed, leading a medical team sent to find the cause of this illness, discovered that it came from the bite of certain mosquitoes. Within a year, after destroying the breeding areas of these mosquitoes, the disease was eliminated.

HENRY CABOT LODGE (SENATOR)

Lodge, a Massachusetts senator, was an isolationist who believed the U. S. should stay out of Europe's affairs. As chairman of the Senate Foreign Relations Committee, he led the fight against the U. S. joining the League of Nations. He succeeded in preventing the Senate from approving the Treaty of Versailles.

THE CONSTITUTION AT WORK

A KEY COURT CASE

SCHENCK v. U.S. (1919)

Background: During World War I, Schenck was arrested and convicted for publishing and distributing literature that encouraged men to resist the draft. Schenck claimed his First Amendment rights to freedom of speech and press had been violated.

Decision/Significance: The Supreme Court ruled that there are some limits to free speech. The Court said that free speech should not be used to protect someone from causing panic by shouting "Fire!" in a crowded theater when there is no fire. Total free speech could not be allowed in the face of a "clear and present danger." The decision became a guide by which to measure the limits of free speech.

SUMMARIZING YOUR UNDERSTANDING

Directions: How well do you understand what you have just read? Test yourself by answering the following questions.

MAJOR ITEMS TO REMEMBER

On separate 3 x 5 index cards (as shown on pages 33-34), briefly define the following terms and concepts:

Monroe Doctrine	Open Door Policy	Yellow Journalism
Spanish-American War	Good Neighbor Policy	Fourteen Points
Imperialism	League of Nations	Isolationism

AMERICA BUILDS A COLONIAL EMPIRE

In the aftermath of the Spanish-American War, the United States reversed its traditional policies by becoming an imperialist power. Summarize your understanding of this change by answering the following questions:

- What factors contributed to America's becoming a colonial power?
- Describe some of the dealings of the U. S. with the Philippines, Cuba, Hawaii, China and Japan.

U. S. POLICY TOWARD LATIN AMERICA

United States relations with Latin America in the 20th century have been primarily motivated by its economic interests in the region. Summarize your understanding of this statement by completing the following chart:

POLICY	DESCRIPTION OF THE POLICY
Monroe Doctrine	______________
Big Stick Policy	______________
Dollar Diplomacy	______________
Good Neighbor Policy	______________

MAJOR WARS: 1898-1918

The United States became involved in two major wars in the period between 1898 and 1918. Summarize your understanding of these wars by completing the following chart:

WAR	CAUSES	RESULTS
Spanish-American War	______________	______________
First World War	______________	______________

PERSONALITIES OF THE PERIOD

People often have an important influence on the political, economic or social life of their times. Summarize your understanding of this statement by completing a separate 3 x 5 index card (follow the procedures outlined on page 34) for each of the following: ***Alfred Thayer Mahan, William Randolph Hearst, Joseph Pulitzer,*** and ***Woodrow Wilson.***

TESTING YOUR UNDERSTANDING

Directions: Test your understanding of this unit by answering the following questions. Circle the number preceding the word or expression that correctly answers the statement or question. Following the short answer questions, answer either the RCT-type or Regents essay questions.

SKILL BUILDER: INTERPRETING A CARTOON

Base your answers to questions 1 through 3 on the following cartoon and on your knowledge of social studies.

THE NEW DIPLOMACY
ARBITRATION
EUROPE

1 The policeman in the cartoon most likely represents which American President?
1 James Polk
2 Theodore Roosevelt
3 William H. Taft
4 Woodrow Wilson

2 Which title best expresses the main idea of the cartoon?
1 The World For Sale
2 Miracle At Versailles
3 The World's Policeman
4 The Sinking Of The *Maine*

3 Which policy of the United States is depicted by the situation in the cartoon?
1 detente
2 isolationism
3 neutrality
4 imperialism

4 The most accurate statement concerning American foreign policy is that the United States has generally
1 acted according to its own national self-interest
2 reacted forcefully to imperialism around the world
3 formed alliances with countries in need
4 used military confrontation to solve disputes

SKILL BUILDER: INTERPRETING SPEAKERS

Base your answers to questions 4 through 6 on the speakers' statements and on your knowledge of social studies.

Speaker A: This nation should trade with any and all countries on a friendly basis, but should not take sides in other nations' disputes.

Speaker B: We should not become involved in alliances with other nations.

Speaker C: U.S. foreign policy should be devoted to expanding American power and influence.

Speaker D: We must be willing to bear any burden and pay any price to advance the cause of freedom.

5 Which two speakers agree most strongly about U.S. foreign policy?
1 (A) and (B)
2 (C) and (D)
3 (A) and (D)
4 (B) and (D)

6 The history of United States foreign relations with Latin America in the period 1880-1920 could best be used to support the views of speaker
1 (A)
2 (B)
3 (C)
4 (D)

7 Which speakers express views that are closest to the advice George Washington gave to the new nation in 1796?
1 (A) and (B)
2 (B) and (C)
3 (C) and (D)
4 (D) and (A)

SKILL BUILDER: INTERPRETING A MAP

Base your answers to questions 7 and 8 on the following map and on your knowledge of social studies.

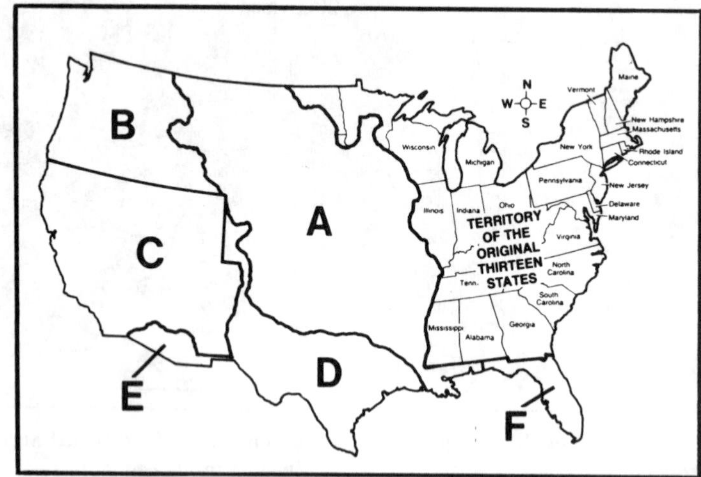
B
C
A
D
E
F
N
W
E
S
Maine
Vermont
New Hampshire
Massachusetts
New York
Rhode Island
Connecticut
Wisconsin
Michigan
Pennsylvania
New Jersey
Delaware
Maryland
Illinois
Indiana
Ohio
TERRITORY OF THE ORIGINAL THIRTEEN STATES
Virginia
North Carolina
Tenn.
South Carolina
Mississippi
Alabama
Georgia

8 The most appropriate title for this map would be
1 The Rise of American Imperialism
2 The Westward Expansion of the United States
3 The U.S. Acquires a Colonial Empire
4 U.S. Protectorates in the 19th Century

9 Which territory did the United States obtain from France?
1 A
2 B
3 C
4 D

10 A fundamental reason for the issuing of the Monroe Doctrine was to
1 halt the slave trade from Africa to the Caribbean
2 prevent European intervention in the Western Hemisphere
3 keep the United States out of World War I
4 protect the Panama Canal

11 Which concept refers to the American desire to expand westward in the 19th century?
1 collective security
2 balance of power
3 manifest destiny
4 mutual appeasement

12 A primary aim of the United States Open Door Policy was to
1 encourage the Chinese to emigrate to other countries
2 prevent European powers from dividing up China
3 develop China's industrial capacity
4 introduce democratic government into China

13 Which was a basic cause of World War I?
1 an American desire to seize overseas colonies
2 the European alliance system
3 tensions between the U. S. and the Soviet Union
4 the German invasion of Poland

14 Which foreign policy approach would advocates of the balance-of-power concept most likely support?
1 unilateral disarmament
2 establishment of military alliances
3 abolition of foreign trade
4 reliance on world organizations

15 Which headline best reflects the concept of imperialism?
1 "The Supreme Court Bans Segregation in Public Schools"
2 "United Nations is Founded in San Francisco"
3 "President McKinley Announces U.S. Annexation of the Philippines"
4 "President Bush Meets Gorbachev at Summit Conference"

16 The peace treaties ending the Mexican War of 1848 and the Spanish-American War of 1898 were similar in that both
1 gave land to the United States
2 addressed the issue of freedom of the seas
3 created a mutual defense pact
4 established a strong union of friendship

17 The most important reason for construction of the Panama Canal was the need to
1 increase the security of the United States
2 spread the U.S. way of life to less developed nations
3 encourage the economic development of Central America
4 stop the spread of communism in the Western Hemisphere

18 Which newspaper headline provides a modern example of the Monroe Doctrine?
1 "U.S. Declares War Against Germany"
2 "U.S. Troops Land in Korea"
3 "U.S. Ships Blockade Cuba"
4 "U.S. Sells Missiles to Saudi Arabia"

19 A principal reason why isolationists in the U. S. Senate objected to the United States joining the League of Nations was their opposition to
1 lower tariffs
2 freedom of the seas
3 potential military commitments
4 Soviet and German membership in the League Council

20 Evidence that the U. S. generally followed a policy of isolationism from 1919-1939 is that the United States
1 condemned Fascist aggression
2 rejected the policy of appeasement
3 refused to join the League of Nations
4 participated in disarmament

21 Which of the following provisions of the Treaty of Versailles reflects the influence of President Woodrow Wilson?
1 division of German colonies among the Allies
2 acceptance by Germany of full responsibility for World War I
3 establishment of a League of Nations
4 payment of reparations to the Allies by Germany

22 Which generalization about the origins of wars is best supported by the events that led to World War I?
1 Years of continuing international tension can lead to war.
2 A policy of appeasement can prevent the outbreak of war.
3 A revolution in one country can lead to war with other nations.
4 Religious hatreds often breed war.

23 "Why ... entangle our peace and prosperity in the toils of European ambition, rivalship, interest, humor or caprice?" Which action by the United States best reflects the philosophy expressed in this quotation?
1 passage of legislation restricting immigration
2 rejection of the Treaty of Versailles
3 enactment of the Lend-Lease Act
4 approval of the United Nations Charter

RCT-TYPE ESSAYS

1 The following timeline shows some major foreign policies in American history.

1796	1823	1899	1904	1933
Washington's Farewell Address	Monroe Doctrine	Open Door Policy	Big Stick Policy	Good Neighbor Policy

Part A

Select *one* foreign policy development: ______________________

State the main aim of the policy: ______________________

Select *another* foreign policy development: ______________________

State the main aim of the policy: ______________________

Part B

In your Part B answer, you should use information you gave in Part A. However, you may also include different or additional information in your Part B answer.

Write an essay beginning with this topic sentence:
Major foreign policies in American history often help to shape our relations with other nations in the world.

2 An important principle of foreign policy is that each nation attempts to protect its interests. Following is a list of foreign policies that the United States has pursued at various times in its history.

Foreign Policies

Imperialism	Neutrality
Isolationism	Intervention

Part A

Select *one* policy: ______________________

Define the policy: ______________________

Give *one* example in which the United States used that policy. ______________________

Select *another* policy: ______________________

Define the policy: ______________________

Give *one* example in which the United States used that policy. ______________________

Part B

In your Part B answer, you should use information you gave in Part A. However, you may also include different or additional information in your Part B answer.

Write an essay discussing how a country's foreign policy protects its interests.

REGENTS-TYPE ESSAYS

1 A major goal of a nation's foreign policy is to protect the national interest. The President of the United States is influential in developing and carrying out that policy.

Choose *two* of the presidents listed below. For *each* one chosen:

- Describe conditions that caused that president to develop a specific foreign policy to promote the national interest.
- Describe a specific action taken by that president to carry out that foreign policy.

Presidents

George Washington	James Monroe
William McKinley	Theodore Roosevelt
Woodrow Wilson	James Polk

2 Historically the foreign policy of the United States toward Latin America has changed over time. The following headlines illustrate some of these changes.

Headlines

Monroe Doctrine Announced
U.S. to Build a Canal in Panama
Taft Announces "Dollar Diplomacy" for Latin America
F.D.R. Introduces "Good Neighbor Policy"
U.S. Joins the Organization of American States

Choose *three* of the headlines. For *each* headline chosen:

- Describe the circumstances that led to the headline
- Discuss the major effects of the event

PERFORMANCE-BASED TASKS

Setting: Most Americans are uncomfortable with the idea of colonies. After all, this nation was once a colony of Great Britain, and we fought a war to end British colonial rule. Yet today, America controls five island colonies — Puerto Rico, the Virgin Islands, Samoa, the Northern Marianas, and Guam. Of the five, Puerto Rico is the largest and most populated island. Its people are American citizens, but a minority would prefer seeing Puerto Rico as an independent nation.

General Directions: Groups with strong opinions about certain issues often sponsor newspaper advertisements to convince the public to support their point of view. Study the arguments about the future status of Puerto Rico found on page 225. You should undertake additional research regarding the three possible options for Puerto Rico's future. Then, decide which of the three options for Puerto Rico's future status you most support.

Your Task: Use the form on the next page to create a newspaper advertisement. Your newspaper advertisement should consist of the following:

- an attention-grabbing headline
- a photograph or drawing to convey your ideas in the most dramatic way
- some text to accompany the picture and the headline

You should use as few words as you can to convey your message. An effective advertisement is concise, because an advertiser does not know how long people will spend reading it.

First, make some notes about the various ideas you want to get across in the ad. Decide which is the most important idea. Your headline should reflect the most important idea in some way. Many people only scan the headlines of advertisements. Therefore you need to catch the interest of your readers, to encourage them to read further.

Notes: ____

____

____

____

(Attention-Grabbing Headline)

(Photo/drawing/cartoon to let people know the idea you seek to communicate)

(Write your point of view: be brief, while making a convincing case)

LOOKING AT ECONOMIC POLICY

Questions on the RCT and Regents examinations often test your understanding of various aspects of economic policy. You learned something about our economy in "Looking At Economic Growth." This "Looking At" section focuses on the role of government in influencing the operation of our economy.

THE GOALS OF NATIONAL ECONOMIC POLICY

Since the late 19th century, the role of government in our economic life has changed. Earlier, most people believed in **"laissez-faire"** capitalism. This meant that the government should not interfere in the economy, except to act as a referee to ensure fair competition. Because of the Great Depression of the 1930s, the federal government began to take on a greater role in the economy. In 1946, this role became law when Congress passed the **Full Employment Act** which stated the goals of national economic policy. Today, the federal government has the responsibility to:

- **promote maximum employment**
- **promote maximum production**
- **fight inflation (rising prices)**

To help make Congress and the nation aware of what is happening in the nation, the president presents Congress each year with the *Economic Report of the President*, stating the economic concerns facing the United States.

MEASURING THE NATION'S ECONOMIC HEALTH

In measuring the health of our national economy, and in comparing it to the economies of other nations, economists look at several important statistical indicators:

GROSS NATIONAL PRODUCT (or GROSS DOMESTIC PRODUCT)
This is the value in dollars of all the goods and services produced in the United States in a single year.

PER CAPITA INCOME
This is the Gross National Product divided by the population. It gives us an indication of the average production of a single person.

UNEMPLOYMENT RATE
This measures the percentage of people who are actively looking for but cannot find work.

NATIONAL DEBT

This is the total of money owed by our national government to those who have lent it money.

INFLATION RATE

This measures how quickly money is losing its value because people are paying more for the same goods. When things seem to cost more than a few years ago, this is a sign of inflation.

ECONOMIC POWERS OF THE NATIONAL GOVERNMENT

In attempting to achieve its economic goals, the federal government has several instruments at its disposal.

THE POWER TO PROVIDE PUBLIC GOODS

Public goods are those goods paid for by tax money and used to serve the whole community. When you use public parks, schools or hospitals, you are receiving public goods. Public goods have always been a controversial issue in United States history. Some people think that government should just provide for our defense and nothing more. Others think that governments at all levels—local, state, federal—should provide additional services to improve the health and welfare of their people.

THE POWER TO REGULATE ECONOMIC ACTIVITIES

The government also acts as a referee to ensure a free market by:

■ **Encouraging Competition**: The government helps ensure that the marketplace remains competitive. Trusts and monopolies were outlawed by the **Sherman Anti-Trust Act** (1890). In addition, the government created commissions, such as the Interstate Commerce Commission (I.C.C.) and the Federal Communication Commission (F.C.C.) to act as watchdogs over certain industries. During the 1980s the federal government deregulated certain industries, such as airlines and telephones, to bring about increased competition.

■ **Protecting Workers and Consumers**: Both the federal and state governments have passed laws to protect workers and consumers. Some of the most important laws are the:

- **Pure Food and Drug Act** (1906), requiring manufacturers to list the ingredients of products on their labels.

- **Occupational Safety and Health Act** (1970), establishing health and safety standards in the workplace.

How the government regulates the economy remains a controversial issue. Some people think that government should allow the free play of the market to determine working conditions. Others feel that government must do more to ensure a healthy and safe working environment.

■ **Regulating International Trade**. The federal government also regulates trade through its power to impose **tariffs** (taxes on imports). Some people feel we need higher tariffs to protect our own industries. They argue these tariffs are needed to protect jobs against unfair foreign competition and to ensure that those industries that are vital to our security stay competitive. Others support freer trade, arguing that high tariffs interfere with world trade and raise prices of consumer goods.

■ **Ensuring Equal Opportunity.** Both the federal and state governments have enacted legislation to promote equality in the workplace. In 1972, the federal government passed the **Equal Employment Opportunity Act** requiring employers to pay equal wages to workers for equal work regardless of their race or sex. The government has also attempted to eliminate workplace discrimination that is based on sex, race, color, religion, or national origin.

■ **Protecting The Environment.** In 1972, the government combined 15 federal programs into a single federal agency, the **Environmental Protection Agency.** The E.P.A. sets strict standards for cleaning up the environment. Some critics want the E.P.A. to reduce its requirements, to allow the states to play a greater role in enforcing their own environmental standards. Supporters of the E.P.A. claim that national standards are needed, since local and state enforcement programs vary widely and often encourage abuses of the environment.

FISCAL POLICY

During the Great Depression, the economist **John Maynard Keynes** showed that a government can influence the rates of unemployment and inflation by its spending, taxing and borrowing policies. Keynesian theory states that:

■ if a country's economy is in a depression, the government should spend more than it receives in taxes. By hiring more workers and buying more products, the government ceates new jobs. Workers and businesses then spend more, creating further demand and stimulating production.

■ if there is a high rate of inflation, the government should collect more taxes than it spends. People and businesses will become more cautious about spending and borrowing money. With less spending, producers will have to lower their prices.

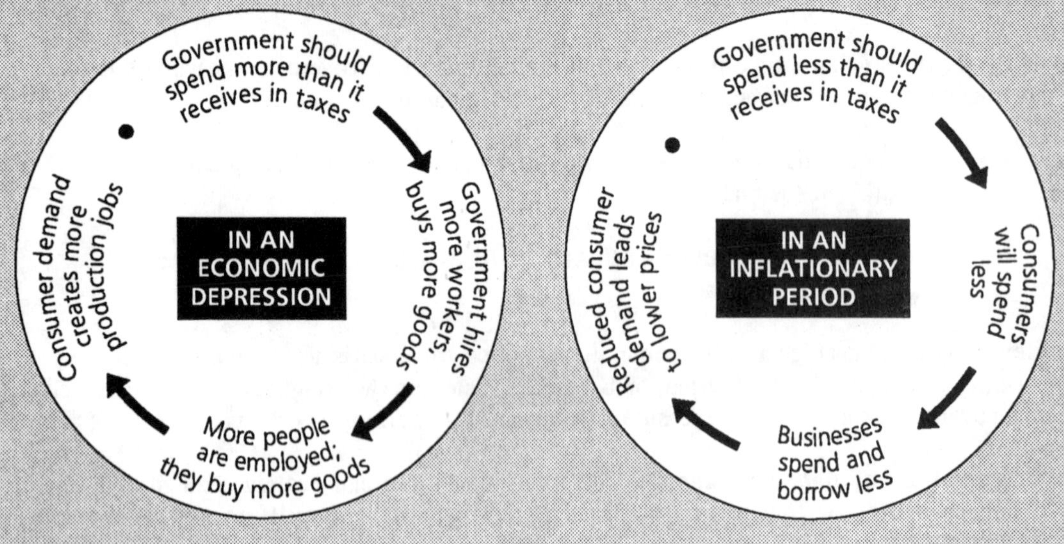
Government should spend more than it receives in taxes
Government hires more workers, buys more goods
More people are employed; they buy more goods
Consumer demand creates more production jobs
IN AN ECONOMIC DEPRESSION
Government should spend less than it receives in taxes
Consumers will spend less
Businesses spend and borrow less
Reduced consumer demand leads to lower prices
IN AN INFLATIONARY PERIOD

Keynes thus urged governments to take an active role in maintaining high levels of employment and stable growth. One trouble with Keynesian policy has been that spending and taxing programs are established by Congress. When asked to cut spending or to raise taxes to fight inflation, Congress has often refused to do so. This is because groups of voters usually fight proposed tax cuts that will hurt their interests. This is one of the main reasons why Congress has had a hard time reducing the federal deficit. Therefore, although fiscal policy is an excellent economic tool, political considerations can often affect its use.

MONETARY POLICY

Monetary policy is another tool used to stabilize the economy. Monetary policy relies on the government's ability to control the total money supply in the economy. This in turn affects the overall amount of business activity. The **Federal Reserve Act** (1913) established the Federal Reserve System. Today, the Federal Reserve's major role is to reduce wild swings in the business cycle. Its chief power lies in controlling the ability of banks to lend money.

- When there is a downswing in the economy, the Federal Reserve enlarges the money supply. As more money is pumped into the system, interest rates go down. Businesses usually borrow more because the cost of borrowing is less. Since businesses can borrow more, they can spend more, stimulating production and employment.
- When there is an upswing in the economy and inflation is rising, the Federal Reserve reduces the money supply. By limiting the amount of available money, fewer loans are made to businesses. Businesses borrow less and the pace of growth is slowed.

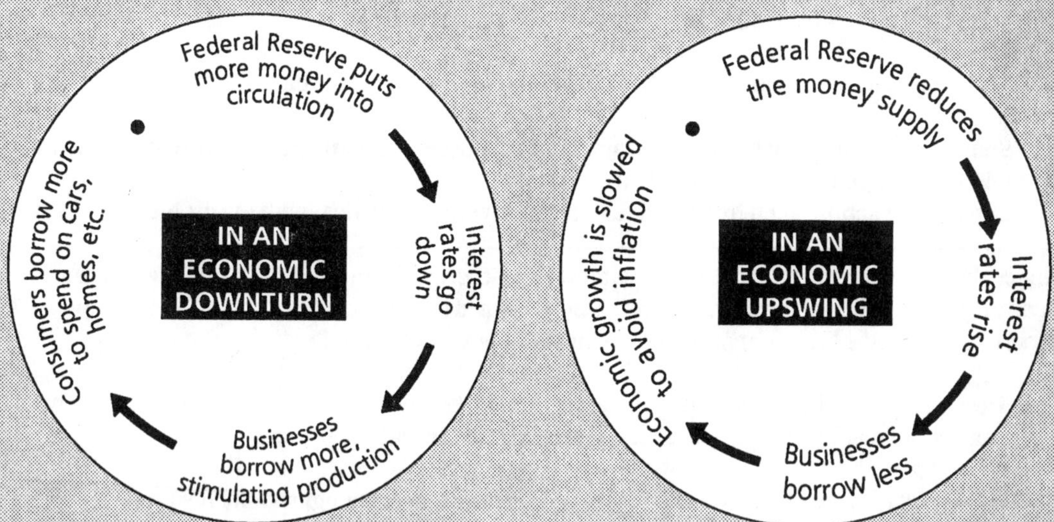

IN AN ECONOMIC DOWNTURN
Federal Reserve puts more money into circulation
Interest rates go down
Businesses borrow more, stimulating production
Consumers borrow more to spend on cars, homes, etc.
IN AN ECONOMIC UPSWING
Federal Reserve reduces the money supply
Interest rates rise
Businesses borrow less
Economic growth is slowed to avoid inflation

The chief limitations in the use of monetary policy are:

- Monetary policy is controlled by the Federal Reserve Board, an independent agency. Congress and the president have no direct control over its policies except through the appointment of its members.

■ The Federal Reserve assumes that businesses will respond to lower and higher interest rates. Sometimes they do not.

■ Monetary policy at home has effects overseas. Interest rates affect the strength of the dollar compared to foreign currencies. Federal Reserve policies influence the ability of American companies to compete overseas or to attract foreign investment. What may be good monetary policy for stabilizing the economy at home may weaken American industry abroad.

ANSWERING A QUESTION ON ECONOMIC POLICY

On occasion, the Regents or RCT will ask questions about specific economic problems faced by the nation at various moments in its history and the policies different administrations used to deal with those programs. For example,

> Economic problems have been a major concern in the United States in various periods since the Civil War. Some of these problems are listed below.
>
> **Economic Problems**
>
> | | |
> |---|---|
> | Rise of monopolies | Farm bankruptcies |
> | Bank failures | Inflation |
> | Trade gap | Budget deficit |
>
> Choose *three* of the economic problems listed and for *each* one chosen:
>
> • Show how the problem has been a major concern during a specific period since the Civil War
> • Discuss a major cause of the problem
> • Discuss one action taken by the United States Government to deal with the problem

Notice that in answering this question you must first describe the problem, then analyze its cause, and finally discuss a policy of the federal government designed to deal with the problem. For example, if you choose to answer the "rise of monopolies" you might write as follows:

■ **Describe the problem**. Monopolies were a problem because they gave a single producer control over an entire market. The producer could dictate prices because he faced no competition.

■ **Analyze its Cause**. Monopolies were formed when a producer bought up smaller producers. This was especially true in the late 1800s, when there were many new industries and very few government controls.

■ **Government Policies**. The U.S. government eventually responded by introducing new regulations aimed at preserving free competition. The Sherman Anti-Trust Act of 1890, the trust-busting activities of Presidents Roosevelt and Taft, and the Clayton Anti-Trust Act of 1914 all gave the federal government the power to break up monopolies.

CHAPTER 11

PROSPERITY AND DEPRESSION

The 1920s was a decade of political conservatism, economic prosperity and changing values. Unfortunately, the prosperity did not last. When the Great Depression started in 1929, the Hoover Administration proved incapable of restoring economic growth. Franklin D. Roosevelt, elected in 1932, promised a "New Deal" and introduced innovative programs to speed recovery. The New Deal greatly increased the size, power and responsibilities of the federal government.

— TIMELINE OF KEY EVENTS —

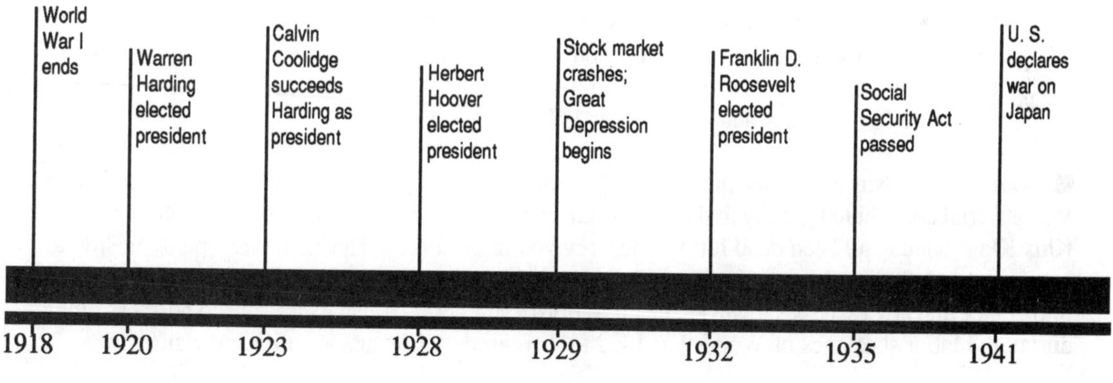
World War I ends
1918
Warren Harding elected president
1920
Calvin Coolidge succeeds Harding as president
1923
Herbert Hoover elected president
1928
Stock market crashes; Great Depression begins
1929
Franklin D. Roosevelt elected president
1932
Social Security Act passed
1935
U. S. declares war on Japan
1941

BOOM TIMES: THE 1920s

THE ROARING TWENTIES: 1919-1929

The 1920s, sometimes called the "Roaring Twenties," were good times for many Americans. However, beneath the appearance of calm and the desire for profit-making, America was experiencing fundamental economic and social changes. The real significance of the decade was less in its politics than in its development of twentieth-century values.

ADJUSTING TO PEACE, 1919-1920

The decade of the 1920s opened with the difficult task of adjusting to peace. Disillusioned by the outcome of World War I, the American public sought to follow a policy of **isolationism** in foreign affairs—refusing to become involved in other nations' disputes or problems. On the domestic front, the government stopped its massive wartime spending and soldiers returned home looking for jobs. This led to a temporary economic recession, lasting from the war's end until 1921.

THREATS TO CIVIL LIBERTIES

The 1920s also witnessed new attacks on civil liberties in American society.

■ **The Red Scare.** The Communists seized power in Russia in 1917 and attempted to spread their revolution to other countries. When a wave of strikes took place in the U. S. in 1919, people saw this as the beginning of a Communist revolution. This hysterical fear resulted in:

- **The Palmer Raids.** In 1919, Attorney General Palmer conducted raids against leading radicals and accused them of plotting to overthrow the government. Thousands of alleged agitators and radicals were arrested. Immigrant radicals were deported.

- **Sacco and Vanzetti Trial.** The hysteria affected immigrants as well. Two Italian immigrants, Sacco and Vanzetti, were convicted of committing murder during a robbery to obtain funds for an anarchist revolution. Although the evidence was insufficient, the two were found guilty and executed in 1927.

■ **Rise of Nativism and Racism.** The "Red scare" and the notoriety surrounding the Sacco and Vanzetti trial contributed greatly to the rise of **nativism** (a distrust and dislike of foreigners). The Ku Klux Klan, which had been dead for decades, revived in the 1920s. The Klan was openly hostile to immigrants, Catholics, Jews and African Americans. Most Americans rejected the Klan's excessive intolerance and lawlessness. However, the migration of southern African Americans to northern cities during the labor shortages of World War I led to increased racial tensions after the war.

THE REPUBLICAN PRESIDENCIES: HARDING, COOLIDGE AND HOOVER

In 1920, Republicans returned to the White House. They were to remain there for the next 12 years, through the prosperity of the twenties and the beginnings of the Depression that ended it.

POLICIES FAVORING BUSINESS

In general, Presidents Harding, Coolidge and Hoover followed policies favorable to American business. They supported **laissez-faire** policies, promoting minimum government interference in business activities.

■ **High Protective Tariffs.** Congress passed a series of tariffs that protected American manufacturers by keeping out foreign-made goods. For example, the **Hawley-Smoot Tariff Act** (1930) sought to restrict foreign imports by raising tariff rates to their highest levels in American history.

■ **Lower Taxes on the Wealthy and Corporations.** Congress slashed taxes on the rich and on corporate profits. As a result, a larger tax burden was shifted to the average wage earner.

■ **Lax Enforcement of Anti-Trust Laws and Regulations.** The president was deliberately lax in making use of existing laws regulating business. Business was given a free hand, and a large number of business mergers took place in the 1920s.

THE HARDING ADMINISTRATION (1921-1923)

Warren Harding, elected President in 1920, captured the national spirit when he called for a "return to normalcy:" a less ambitious foreign policy and prosperity at home. Under Harding, the U. S. did not join the League of Nations. The government imposed tariffs on foreign goods and restricted immigration. It also refused to cancel war debts owed by America's former allies. Harding's administration, like Grant's, also became famous for its scandals and corruption. In the **Teapot Dome Scandal**, it was revealed that one high-ranking official had leased out government land to businessmen in exchange for personal bribes.

THE COOLIDGE ADMINISTRATION (1923-1929)

Upon Harding's death, Vice-President Calvin Coolidge assumed the office of president in 1923. Coolidge came to symbolize old-fashioned values like honesty and thrift. Continuing Harding's pro-business policies, his motto was "the business of America is business." Because Coolidge's administration coincided with the business expansion of the 1920s, he received much of the credit for it. As a result, Coolidge was elected in 1924. He refused to run again in 1928.

THE HOOVER ADMINISTRATION (1929-1933)

In his 1928 campaign for the presidency, Hoover optimistically forecast that America was about to end poverty. Like other Republican leaders, he was greatly impressed by the achievements of business in raising American standards of living in the previous decades. He believed this was the result of the American system, in which individuals were given equal opportunities, a free education and a will to succeed. This "**rugged individualism**," as Hoover called it, spurred progress. He strongly felt that government interfering in business would only threaten the prosperity and progress of the nation.

FACTORS UNDERLYING THE ECONOMIC PROSPERITY OF THE 1920s

For many Americans, the decade of the 1920s was a prosperous period. Wages and employment opportunities increased, while business profits and production soared. We have seen that government policies were favoring business; however, there were several other factors underlying the prosperity of the 1920s.

THE RISE OF THE AUTOMOBILE

Probably the single most important factor in creating prosperity was the fact that the automobile came into widespread use during this period. In 1920, there were 8 million cars on the road. By 1930, there were three times that number. This enormous growth in automobile ownership profoundly affected American life.

■ **Effect on Business and Employment.** Automobile production required vast amounts of steel, glass and rubber, stimulating the growth of those industries. Motorists required paved roads, bridges, garages and gasoline stations. By 1929, one out of every nine workers was employed in an auto-related industry. Other industries declined; for example, shipping by railroad or horse-drawn wagon began to lose business to the growing truck industry.

■ **Changed Lifestyles.** Cars gave people greater mobility. Families were now able to drive away on vacation. The construction of larger suburbs around cities was made possible by the existence of the car. New school buses allowed larger, more centrally located schools. Students in remote and rural areas could now attend school regularly.

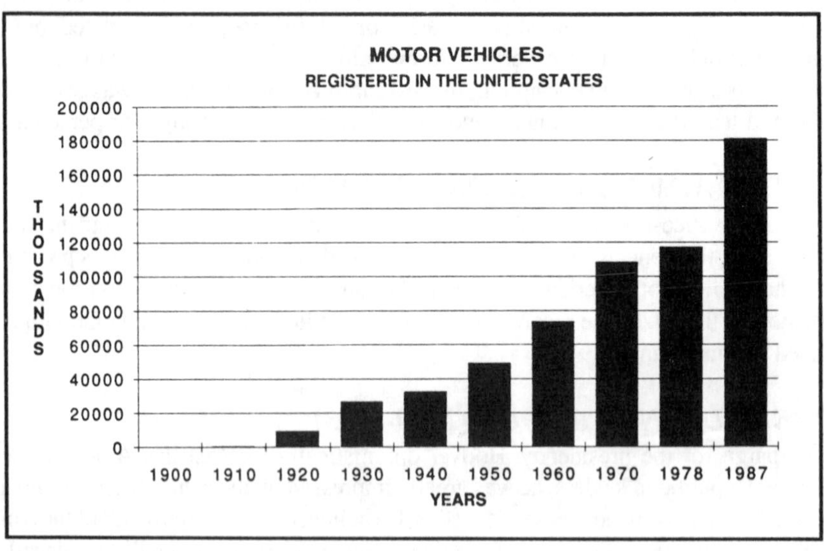
MOTOR VEHICLES
REGISTERED IN THE UNITED STATES
THOUSANDS
200000
180000
160000
140000
120000
100000
80000
60000
40000
20000
0
1900 1910 1920 1930 1940 1950 1960 1970 1978 1987
YEARS

Source: U.S. Historical Abstract

THE DEVELOPMENT OF OTHER NEW INDUSTRIES

Besides the automobile, there were several other new industries, mainly based on new uses of electricity. Electric household appliances like the vacuum cleaner, refrigerator and toaster were introduced. Radio and motion pictures became widespread. These industries created new jobs, produced generous profits, and changed the ways Americans lived.

MORE EFFICIENT PRODUCTION TECHNIQUES

During World War I, improvements in production techniques were developed for war production. These improvements were soon applied to industrial production. In the 1920s, the assembly line, the conveyor belt, the use of interchangeable standardized parts and other labor saving devices were applied to other fields, making American industry more efficient and productive. For example, by 1925 the Ford Motor Company had one car rolling off its assembly line every ten seconds.

THE AGE OF MASS CONSUMPTION

There were new patterns of consumption, creating mass markets for goods. Workers were earning higher wages and could afford to buy more products. The growth of advertising stimulated demand. Retailers developed plans for installment purchases and buying on credit: buyers paid only a small down payment to take an item home, and then paid off the balance in small monthly installments.

CULTURAL VALUES OF THE 1920s

The 1920s saw the emergence of new values. The greater mobility and material comfort afforded by the automobile and electricity were having an important impact on social patterns and cultural values. Some groups, notably women, the young and African Americans felt a new sense of power and freedom. Others felt threatened by the new currents of thought, and sought to preserve traditional values.

ATTEMPTS TO PRESERVE TRADITIONAL VALUES

At the start of the 1920s, rural America continued to regard the rise of urban society with suspicion. The revival of the Ku Klux Klan and laws restricting immigration were expressions of this impulse. The best examples of the effort to defend traditional values were Prohibition and the Scopes Trial.

■ **Prohibition.** Religious and women's rights reformers saw liquor as the cause of poverty, crime and the breakdown of families. In 1919, the states finally approved the passage of the **Eighteenth Amendment**, banning the sale of alcoholic drinks in the nation. In 1933, it was generally accepted that the "experiment" had failed because a large portion of the population refused to accept the ban on alcoholic drinks and the demand for illegal liquor stimulated the growth of organized crime. Prohibition was repealed by the **Twenty-first Amendment**, demonstrating that unpopular laws are often unenforceable.

■ **The Scopes "Monkey Trial."** Tennessee outlawed the teaching of the Darwin's theory of evolution because it contradicted the Bible's account of Creation. In 1925, John Scopes, a biology teacher, was arrested, tried and convicted for teaching evolution. The trial illustrated the clash between new scientific theories and older religious beliefs and values, a conflict which is still with us today.

NEW VALUES

In opposition to traditional rural values were the newer values of the period. These values included greater openness and self-expression, and an easing of restrictions on traditional morality. Certain groups were more affected than others.

■ **Women**. The decade opened with the 19th Amendment, giving women the right to vote. New household appliances reduced housework, and greater numbers of women went to college. Since more women started to work outside the home, their new political equality and economic independence led women to become more assertive. This brought about changes in manners and morals. Women began to smoke and drink in public. They stopped wearing restrictive clothing like long dresses, and began wearing short hair and skirts above the knees. Sexual behavior became more open as young women went out on dates without a chaperone.

■ **Youth and the Lost Generation**. Young adults were responsible for zany fads like flagpole sitting and marathon dancing. A group of writers, known as the **Lost Generation**, rejected the desire for material wealth. Young novelist **Sinclair Lewis**, in *Main Street* and *Babbitt*, ridiculed the narrowness and hypocrisy of American life. **F. Scott Fitzgerald**, in *This Side of Paradise* and *The Great Gatsby*, wrote about the confusion of his generation by showing that the search for purely materialistic success often led to tragedy.

■ **The Harlem Renaissance**. The 1920's is often referred to as the **Jazz Age**, reflecting the importance of African-American music. The center of the African-American community in the 1920s was in Harlem, in New York City. Here jazz music, with its syncopated rhythms and roots in Black spirituals, flourished. This re-awakening by African-Americans of pride in their culture is known as the Harlem Renaissance. Black poets like **Langston Hughes** and **Countee Cullen** expressed a new pride and sense of defiance. **Alain Locke**, in his book *The New Negro*, spoke out against racism. **Marcus Garvey**, stressing racial unity through education, self-help and racial pride, encouraged African Americans to take pride in being Black. He even planned a Back-to-Africa Movement.

■ **Popular New Heroes**. More leisure time gave people greater opportunity for entertainment. They turned to spectator sports, the radio, movies and magazines. This had a great impact on popular culture and values. The rise of new popular heroes resulted from a deep longing to preserve a sense of personal identity in an increasingly impersonal age of machines. **Charles Lindbergh** was the first person to fly solo across the Atlantic Ocean to Europe, and became a national hero and worldwide celebrity. Popular heroes from the sports world and movies, like Babe Ruth and Jack Dempsey, served as new role models.

KEY ITEMS TO REMEMBER

Red Scare, nativism, laissez-faire, Roaring Twenties, Teapot Dome scandal, "rugged individualism," Prohibition, Scopes "Monkey Trial," Jazz Age, Harlem Renaissance.

THE GREAT DEPRESSION: 1929-1940

Economies normally pass through good and bad periods that regularly repeat themselves. In economic theory, these up-and-down periods are referred to as the **business cycle**. The bad times are called **depressions**, characterized by business failures and high unemployment over an extended period. One of these low periods, the **Great Depression**, which lasted from 1929 to 1940, was the worst in our nation's history, not ending completely until the U. S. entered World War II. When the stock market crashed in 1929, it set off a chain reaction that first toppled the American economy and then spread to the rest of the world. What caused the economy to move from the prosperity of the 1920s to the severe depression of the 1930s?

CAUSES OF THE GREAT DEPRESSION

A variety of factors combined to bring about the economic collapse known as the Great Depression.

SPECULATION IN THE STOCK MARKET AND REAL ESTATE

In the 1920's, speculation—buying an item with the hope of reselling it at a higher price— reached new heights on the stock market and in real estate.

■ **Stock Market Investments.** Stocks are shares in corporations that can be bought and sold on the open market. As stocks rose in value, more people bought stocks hoping to "get rich quick." By 1929, stock prices had tripled from what they had been in 1920. Corporate and personal profits were soaring, while the federal government had reduced taxes on the rich.

■ **Buying On Margin.** To make matters worse, people were buying stocks on margin—paying only a small percentage of a stock's value, promising to pay the rest later. However, if the stock went down in value, individuals often did not have enough money of their own to make good on the losses. With margin buying, the stock market quickly became a national casino.

■ **Real Estate Buying.** People also invested in real estate, especially in Florida, with similar hopes of becoming rich quickly. The frenzy of stock market and real estate speculation created an atmosphere of easy money.

OVERPRODUCTION

The 1920s saw a rapid economic expansion as manufacturers made and sold new products like cars, radios and refrigerators. Many consumers lacked the purchasing power (money) to buy these goods. Manufacturers were producing more goods than they could sell. Advances in technology, especially the introduction of the tractor and the spread of electricity, brought about overproduction. As a result, farmers suffered as crop prices dropped sharply, and large numbers of them went bankrupt.

UNEVEN DISTRIBUTION OF INCOME

Not all groups had shared in the prosperity of the Roaring Twenties. In fact, almost half the population lived at or below the poverty level. Other groups faced special difficulties. Members of minority groups, especially African Americans, Hispanics and Native Americans continued to experience limited job opportunities, low paying jobs and high levels of unemployment. Workers in the declining railroad, coal and textile industries also faced hard times.

RESTRICTED INTERNATIONAL TRADE

American tariffs protected American markets but made it hard for producers to sell abroad, since other countries retaliated by setting up high protective tariffs of their own. Also, since foreign countries found it hard to sell their goods here, they had no way to earn dollars with which to buy American goods. The highest tariff of all, the **Hawley-Smoot Tariff**, went into effect in 1930 just after the stock market crash. The effect was to further restrict international trade.

SHAKY BANKING

During the 1920's the government failed to effectively regulate either the banking system or the stock market. Bankers invested their depositors' money in unsound investments. Many consumers, using easy credit, were buying more than they could afford. This vast over-extension of credit made the entire economy extremely vulnerable.

THE GREAT DEPRESSION BEGINS

THE STOCK MARKET CRASH

In 1929, the market turned sharply downward. On October 29th, the market crashed, driving prices to all-time lows. The stock market crash set off a chain reaction. Corporations could no longer raise funds, and business prospects became gloomy. People who lost their money in the stock market could not repay their loans, leading to bank failures in which thousands of people lost their life's savings. In this new economic climate, the demand for goods decreased. As prices fell, manufacturers closed their factories, leading to more unemployment. The country became caught in the grip of a vicious downward spiral. Soon, the Depression spread from the United States to Europe in a dramatic demonstration of world financial interdependence.

THE HUMAN IMPACT OF THE DEPRESSION

The Depression became a national nightmare. Businesses failed, half a million farmers lost their farms, one-quarter of the banks failed, and millions of people were out of work. There was no "safety net" as in today's economy—no unemployment insurance, retirement benefits or bank deposit insurance. Private charities were overwhelmed. People went hungry; children suffered from malnutrition. Millions depended on soup kitchens and bread lines for their food.

THE DUST BOWL

In addition to the financial disaster, the farmers of the Great Plains had to contend with natural disasters. A series of droughts in the early 1930s dried up crops and land, turning the soil into dust. Farmers were forced to abandon their farms, and many moved west to California.

PRESIDENT HOOVER FAILS TO HALT THE DEPRESSION

HOOVER'S PHILOSOPHY

Hoover followed his belief in **laissez-faire capitalism**. According to this theory, the market needed time to repair itself. When prices got low enough, people would start to buy goods again and employment would increase. Unfortunately, these predictions turned out to be false. Hoover rejected the demand that the federal government should provide direct payments to the unemployed and needy, believing that this would reduce the incentive to work and undermine the "rugged individualism" which he saw as the key to America's past success. Instead, Hoover felt that voluntary and private organizations, with government encouragement, should be the ones to give emergency relief to the needy.

HOOVER'S RESPONSE

Hoover held meetings with business leaders asking them not to lay off workers. He cut taxes and increased federal spending on public works projects. He directed a federal agency to buy surplus farm crops. In 1932, He finally established the **Reconstruction Finance Corporation** to give emergency loans to banks and businesses. Hoover believed that cheap loans would spur businesses, allowing them to expand. He thought the results of this expansion would soon "trickle down" to the average American. In general, Hoover's policies were too little, too late. Americans found his lack of leadership frustrating. Shanty towns, sarcastically called "**Hoovervilles**," sprang up on the outskirts of cities.

KEY ITEMS TO REMEMBER

Great Depression, business cycles, overproduction, stock market crash, "Hoovervilles"

FRANKLIN D. ROOSEVELT AND THE NEW DEAL

During the Great Depression, the main problem facing Americans was widespread unemployment. By promising to put Americans back to work with a **New Deal**, the Democratic candidate, Franklin D. Roosevelt, easily defeated Hoover in the election of 1932.

THE NEW DEAL WIDENS GOVERNMENT'S RESPONSIBILITIES

The **New Deal** was a major turning point in American history. It established the important principle that the federal government bears a major responsibility for the smooth running of the American economy.

FRANKLIN D. ROOSEVELT AS PRESIDENT

Roosevelt delivered not only a New Deal, but he did it in a style different from what people were used to.

■ **New Deal Philosophy**. Franklin D. Roosevelt saw the Depression as a national emergency as serious as any war, and he believed that the president's task was to find a way back to prosperity. The New Deal marked the final death blow to the older laissez-faire view that government and the economy should be completely separated. Under Roosevelt's leadership, the New Deal permanently increased the size and power of the federal government and made it primarily responsible for managing the nation's economy. As radical as it seemed at the time, the New Deal kept Americans from turning to more extreme solutions to the problems of the depression, as occurred in countries like Germany.

■ **F.D.R.'s Style**. F.D.R. brought a new way of doing things to the presidency. He assembled a group of extremely talented people to serve under him; many of his innovative ideas were drawn up by members of this "brain trust." In order to win public support, he explained his policies in informal radio addresses known as "**fireside chats.**" In public, F.D.R. was very optimistic, hopeful and confident. Part of Roosevelt's purpose was psychological: he wanted to restore public confidence so that people would begin buying and investing again.

NEW DEAL LEGISLATION: RELIEF, RECOVERY, REFORM

When President Roosevelt took office, he assembled Congress for a special session. The economic catastrophe permitted Roosevelt to push through major legislation that would have been difficult to pass in other less critical times. The New Deal was novel, both in its size and in its underlying assumption that the federal government had to take a more active role in running the economy. Roosevelt explained New Deal measures in terms of three "R's": relief, recovery, and reform.

RELIEF

Relief measures were short-term actions designed to tide people over until the economy recovered.

■ **The Banking Crisis**. Over ten thousand banks had failed since the Depression began. Roosevelt closed all the nation's banks just after his inauguration by declaring a **Bank Holiday**. Each bank was permitted to reopen only after the government inspected its records and found it was financially sound.

■ **Relief for the Unemployed**. One out of four of the nation's workers was unemployed, with no source of income. There was no unemployment insurance as there is today, and many were without any food or shelter. Roosevelt favored "work-relief"—giving people jobs.

- **The Federal Emergency Relief Act (1933)** gave money to state and local governments to provide emergency relief, and enabled millions of people to be hired for "make-work" projects.

- The **Civilian Conservation Corps (1933)** gave jobs to young people, such as planting trees, cleaning up forests and draining swamps. Members of the C.C.C. lived in camps supervised by army officers and received free uniforms and food.

- The **Public Works Administration (1933)** and **Works Progress Administration (1935)** both helped increase employment by building public works projects—schools, courthouses, roads, post offices and bridges. The W.P.A. also hired artists, writers and musicians to paint murals, write guidebooks, and produce plays and concerts.

■ **Relief to Homeowners and Farmowners.** Many people could no longer meet their mortgage payments. Banks and lenders were forced to foreclose (seize the property and throw people out of their homes and farms). The government passed legislation giving homeowners and farmers emergency loans.

RECOVERY

Roosevelt realized that the key to recovery was to stimulate production. Thus he designed his recovery measures to restore the economy by increasing incentives to produce and by rebuilding people's buying power.

■ **Priming The Pump.** Roosevelt believed in "pump priming:" putting a little "water" (money) into a dry pump (the American economy) to get it flowing again. The government hoped that by putting money into the hands of consumers, they would spend more, increasing the demand for products. This would lead to more workers being hired, increasing purchasing power. All the relief measures had this secondary purpose of priming the pump for recovery.

■ The **National Recovery Administration (1933)** was designed to help industry recover by increasing prices and reducing wasteful competition. Businesses were asked to cooperate voluntarily in following codes which set standard prices, limits on production, a reduced work week, and established a minimum wage. Anti-trust restrictions on price-fixing and collaboration were ignored. Although 95% of all industries joined the N.R.A., in 1935 the Supreme Court declared the N.R.A. unconstitutional on the grounds that the federal government had no power to interfere with businesses conducting activities within just one state.

■ **Agricultural Adjustment Acts (1933 and 1938)** sought to help farmers to increase farm prices by reducing farm output. Under the first A.A.A., the government simply paid farmers to plant less. The Supreme Court declared the act to be unconstitutional in 1936. In 1938, the second A.A.A. was passed. Under this act, farm surpluses were bought by the government and stored in government warehouses until prices went up. This act was successful in raising farm prices.

REFORM

Reform measures were aimed at correcting defects in the structure of the American economy, to make sure another depression would never strike again. Many of the reform measures were based on the idea that government should help protect individuals against risks they could not handle on their own.

■ The **Federal Deposit Insurance Corporation (F.D.I.C.),** created in 1933, insured deposits in banks so that people would no longer have to worry about losing their savings in the event of a bank failure.

■ The **Securities and Exchange Commission (S.E.C.),** formed in 1934, is a federal agency that watches over the operations of the stock market, preventing fraud and guarding against a stock market collapse. Companies selling stocks are required to provide accurate information to potential investors.

■ The **Social Security Act (1935)** was the single most important law passed by the New Deal; see The Constitution At Work on page 259.

■ The **National Labor Relations Act (1935)** transformed employer-employee relations; see The Constitution At Work on page 259.

■ The **Tennessee Valley Authority (1933)** was a New Deal experiment in public ownership. The T.V.A. built and maintained 21 large dams along the Tennessee River. This allowed the control of floods and the production of hydroelectricity. Construction of the dams brought greater prosperity to the area. The T.V.A. illustrates how the federal government was willing to step into a situation to meet local needs. It was controversial because the government kept ownership instead of turning facilities over to private utility companies.

THE NEW DEAL PROGRAMS AT A GLANCE

AGENCY/PROGRAM (Year Passed)	SOUGHT TO PROVIDE RELIEF BY:
C.C.C. (1933) Civilian Conservation Corps	giving young people jobs in parks & forests
W.P. A. (1935) Works Progress Administration	providing jobs to rebuild schools, roads, bridges
H.O.L.C. (1933) Home Owners Loan Corporation	helping people pay their mortgages with low cost loans
AGENCY/PROGRAM (Year Passed)	**SOUGHT TO PROVIDE RECOVERY BY:**
N.R.A. (1933) National Recovery Administration	regulating business production, hours of work & wages
A.A.A. (1933) Agricultural Adjustment Act	helping farmers by setting limits on crop production
AGENCY/PROGRAM (Year Passed)	**SOUGHT TO PROVIDE REFORM BY:**
F.D.I.C. (1933) Federal Deposit Insurance Corp.	insuring individual bank deposits against loss
T.V.A. (1933) Tennessee Valley Authority	developing the resources of the Tennesees Valley
S.S.A. (1935) Social Security Administration	providing protection against unemployment & illness

REACTIONS TO THE NEW DEAL

POPULARITY OF F.D.R. AND THE NEW DEAL

The public felt that Roosevelt was trying to do something to fight the Depression. This made him very popular, leading to a landslide victory in the 1936 Presidential election. In 1940, Europe was in the middle of World War II. Roosevelt broke with tradition by running for a third term, and was re-elected. In 1944, Roosevelt, believing the nation needed his leadership to get through the war, successfully ran for a fourth term. Only one year later, F.D.R. died. After his death, the **Twenty-Second Amendment** was passed, limiting future presidents to two elected terms.

ROOSEVELT'S COURT PACKING PLAN (1937)

Although the New Deal was generally popular, Roosevelt had some critics. He faced opposition from big business, especially in the early years of his administration. Some conservatives accused F.D.R. of attempting to establish a popular dictatorship. The greatest threat to the New Deal, however, came not from its critics but from the Supreme Court. In 1935-36, the Court held that both the N.R.A. and the A.A.A. were unconstitutional. Roosevelt feared the Court might soon declare all of the New Deal legislation unconstitutional. In 1937, he proposed that the president should be allowed to appoint a new Justice to the Court for each justice who did not retire after reaching age 70. This would have added six new appointments, giving Roosevelt control of the Court. F.D.R.'s attempt was viewed by many as an attempt to undermine the independence of the judiciary and upset the traditional balance of power. Despite his personal popularity, Roosevelt's court packing scheme was widely condemned by the public; Congress rejected the proposal.

EVALUATING THE NEW DEAL

Was the overall impact of the New Deal on American society good or bad?

POINT

- Reduced unemployment and gave immediate relief to those without food or shelter during the worst years of the Depression.
- Completed valuable public works projects like roads, buildings, bridges and dams.
- Established a "safety net" to protect Americans from financial ruin.
- Introduced new regulatory agencies, like the S.E.C., to prevent some of the causes of the Depression from recurring.
- Increased the power of organized labor by giving workers the right to form unions, a minimum wage and maximum working hours.
- Established the principle that the federal government should oversee the smooth running of the United States economy.
- Introduced government price supports for agricultural products to help the farmers.

COUNTERPOINT

- Increased the nation's indebtedness.
- Increased taxes to pay for all the new programs.
- Established the precedent that the national government could lower unemployment by spending more taxpayers' money.
- Increased federal regulation of business, interfering with the free market economy.
- Interfered in the operation of the free market by setting artificial price supports for farmers.
- Increased the degree of government interference in almost every aspect of American life.
- Increased the size of the federal bureaucracy
- Undermined the role of individuals by reducing the incentive to work.

KEY ITEMS TO REMEMBER

New Deal, "court packing" plan, Social Security Act, Federal Deposit Insurance Corporation.

PERSONALITIES OF THE PERIOD

WILLIAM C. HANDY (MUSICAL COMPOSER)

W.C. Handy is known as the "Father of the Blues." The blues is a type of sad music that gives expression to the inner soul and problems of the African-American experience in America. As a musical composer, Handy popularized the blues, making it part of the unique flavor of American music in the world.

HENRY FORD (AUTOMAKER)

Henry Ford developed the idea of building a gas-powered automobile. Ford's goal was to build cars that everyone could afford. He introduced the assembly line in 1914, increasing the efficiency and production by moving cars along an electric conveyor belt while workers completed their assigned task. By 1924, Ford was producing 1.6 million cars at a price of under $300 per car.

LANGSTON HUGHES (WRITER)

Langston Hughes is recognized as one of the nation's best poets. He often drew on his Harlem experiences in writing about what it was like to be an African American growing up in the United States. His poems, novels, plays and newspaper column made him one of the most versatile and talented writers of the Harlem Renaissance.

CARTER G. WOODSON (HISTORIAN)

Known as the "Father of Modern African-American History," Woodson developed the idea of having a Black History Month. Early in his career he realized that many important parts of African-American history were being overlooked, ignored and forgotten. He led the fight to have African-American history taught in the schools so that African-American students would gain a greater appreciation of their ancestors' contributions.

ELEANOR ROOSEVELT (HUMANITARIAN)

Eleanor Roosevelt, President Franklin Roosevelt's wife, served as her husband's eyes and ears by traveling throughout the country and later the world. A political activist, she strongly advocated women's rights and peace causes. She was also known as a champion of social programs to help the poor. Her greatest contribution was in helping to create the United Nations and in writing its Declaration of Human Rights.

For other personalities of this period, see F. Scott Fitzgerald and John Steinbeck in "Looking at the Arts."

THE CONSTITUTION AT WORK

KEY LEGISLATION

SOCIAL SECURITY ACT (1935)

This was the single most influential law passed by the New Deal. During the early Depression, Americans had no "safety net" to prevent them from being hurt by unemployment, illness or a death in the family. The Social Security Act set out to change this.

- **Unemployment Insurance.** Administered by the federal and state governments, workers were to receive unemployment insurance, paid for by a tax on employer payrolls.

- **Retirement Benefits.** Employees were to receive monthly payments after their retirement, paid for by a special tax on their wages combined with contributions from their employer. The same fund provided benefits to their spouses and children in the event of an untimely death.

Social Security coverage has grown to include helping the orphaned, disabled and chronically ill.

THE NATIONAL LABOR RELATIONS ACT (1935)

This act, often called the **Wagner Act**, gave workers the right to form unions, to bargain collectively, and to submit grievances to a new National Labor Relations Board. Unions grew rapidly with the support of this new law.

A KEY COURT CASE

SCHECHTER POULTRY CORPORATION v. U.S. (1935)

Background: President Roosevelt pushed the National Industrial Recovery Act through Congress to help the economy recover from the Depression. The act gave the president power to set up "codes of fair practices" for businesses involved in intrastate (within a state) commerce. The Schechter Poultry Corp. was convicted of failing to obey the act. They appealed their conviction on the basis that the act gave the president an unconstitutional increase in power. The Supreme Court ruled that the N.I.R.A. was unconstitutional.

Decision/Significance: The Court made it plain that Congress, even during a national crisis like the Depression, could not give the president any more powers than were specifically granted in the Constitution. The Schechter decision led to F.D.R.'s court packing plan. In 1937, the Court changed its direction, and began accepting most of the later New Deal legislation.

SUMMARIZING YOUR UNDERSTANDING

Directions: How well do you understand what you have just read? Test yourself by answering the following questions.

MAJOR ITEMS TO REMEMBER

On 3 x 5 cards (as shown on pages 33-34), briefly define the following terms and concepts:

Nativism	Red Scare	Great Depression
Prohibition	New Deal	Harlem Renaissance
Business cycles	Social Security Act	Court Packing Plan

ECONOMIC AND SOCIAL CHANGES

The period of the 1920's saw fundamental economic and social changes. Summarize your understanding of these changes by answering the following questions:

- What factors supported the economic prosperity of the 1920's?
- Describe some of the new values of the 1920's.
- Identify and state some of the contributions of the individuals associated with these changes.

THE GREAT DEPRESSION

The Great Depression of 1929-1940 had a profound effect on the nation. Summarize your understanding of this time period by answering the following questions:

- What were some of the causes of the Great Depression?
- Describe some of the programs used to restore the economy.
- What has been the overall impact of the New Deal on the nation?

PERSONALITIES OF THE PERIOD

People often have an important influence on the political, economic or social life of their times. Summarize your understanding of this statement by completing a separate 3 x 5 index card (follow the procedures outlined on page 34) for each of the following individuals: ***Herbert Hoover***, ***Franklin D. Roosevelt***, ***Marcus Garvey***, and ***Langston Hughes***.

TESTING YOUR UNDERSTANDING

Directions: Test your understanding of this unit by answering the following questions. Circle the number preceding the word or expression that correctly answers the statement or question. Following the short answer questions, answer either the RCT-type or Regents essay questions.

SKILL BUILDER: INTERPRETING A CARTOON

Base your answer to questions 1 through 3 on the following cartoon and your knowledge of social studies.

ALL I SAID WAS "GIMME SIX MORE JUSTICES!"

Source: Library of Congress

1 The donkey depicted in the cartoon symbolizes a
1 European nation
2 labor union
3 farm organization
4 political party

2 Which statement best expresses the main idea of the cartoon?
1 There are many legal problems facing the nation.
2 There is no justice in the United States.
3 Animals must be kept in cages to prevent damage.
4 There are limits to the powers of the president.

3 The cartoon indicates that the cartoonist would probably support the idea of
1 federalism
2 executive privilege
3 checks and balances
4 due process of law

SKILL BUILDER: INTERPRETING A LINE GRAPH

Base your answer to questions 4 and 5 on the following line graph and on your knowledge of social studies.

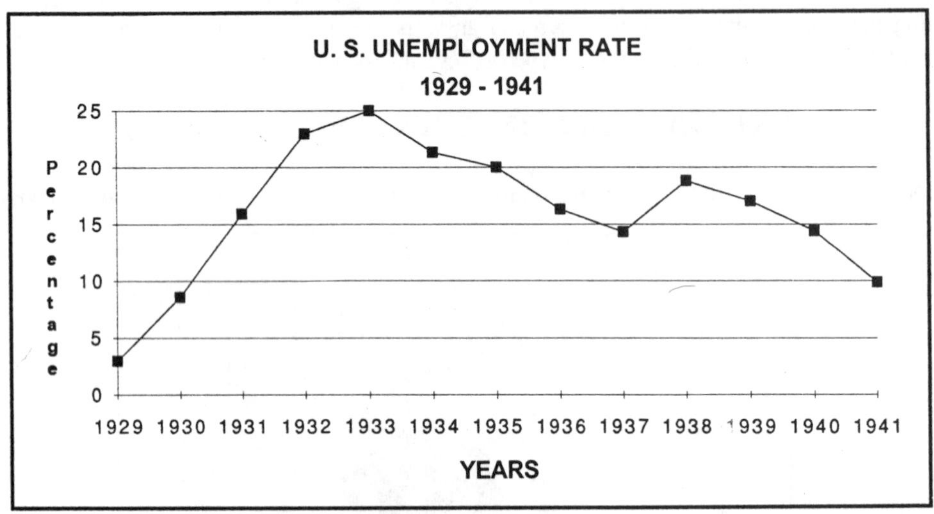
U. S. UNEMPLOYMENT RATE
1929 - 1941
Percentage
25
20
15
10
5
0
1929 1930 1931 1932 1933 1934 1935 1936 1937 1938 1939 1940 1941
YEARS

Source: U. S. Historical Abstract

4 In which year was the unemployment rate the highest?
1 1929
2 1935
3 1933
4 1941

5 Which governmental action would have been most beneficial to the U. S. economy during the period from 1931 to 1939?
1 a decrease in the money supply by the Federal Reserve
2 creation of additional state banks
3 increased federal spending on public works projects
4 an increase in foreign aid by Congress

SKILL BUILDER: INTERPRETING SPEAKERS

The following discussion refers to the New Deal era of the late 1930's. Base your answers to questions 6 through 8 on the speaker's comments and on your knowledge of social studies.

Speaker A: Our nation's economy has been ruined by costly government programs that destroy free enterprise and individual initiative.

Speaker B: I strongly disagree. Our economy will be helped by public works projects, unemployment insurance and old-age retirement insurance. This is a peaceful revolution.

Speaker C: We have had no revolution. We are witnessing the evolution of an idea that began in the days of Populism and Progressivism.

6 The evolutionary idea referred to by Speaker C is
1 a regulatory role for the government
2 the unlimited coinage of silver
3 civil rights for minorities
4 an income tax amendment

7 Speaker B's position is best illustrated by such measures as the
1 Securities and Exchange Commission and the Dawes Act
2 Reciprocal Trade Agreements Act and the Sherman Anti-Trust Act
3 Social Security Act and the Tennessee Valley Authority
4 National Recovery Act and the Pure Food and Drug Act

8 Which president based his economic policy on the idea expressed by Speaker A?
1 Franklin D. Roosevelt 3 Herbert Hoover
2 Lyndon Johnson 4 Abraham Lincoln

---

9 The "Harlem Renaissance" refers to the
1 artistic style of the first Dutch settlers to New York
2 regiment of African-American soldiers in World War I
3 flourishing of African-American literature and music during the 1920's
4 blossoming of Hispanic culture in New York during the 1980's

10 The major problem facing Franklin D. Roosevelt upon taking over the presidency was
1 inflated prices 3 factory overproduction
2 overseas trade imbalance 4 high unemployment

11 A major result of the New Deal was that it
1 eliminated poverty in the United States
2 extended the merit system in the civil service
3 destroyed the free enterprise system
4 expanded the power of the federal government

12 William C. Handy and Al Jolson are best noted for their accomplishments in the field of
1 literature 3 science
2 music 4 politics

13 Which was a basic cause of the Great Depression?
1 over-extension of credit and the stock market crash
2 shortages of consumer goods
3 collapse of the international gold standard
4 a rise in oil prices and higher farm prices

14 The primary purpose of the Social Security Act of 1935 was to
1 achieve integrated public schools
2 provide old age and unemployment insurance
3 regulate international trade
4 guarantee the collective bargaining process

15 The motto of the Harding, Coolidge, and Hoover administrations could best be expressed as
1 "We have not yet to begun to fight."
2 "Power to the people."
3 "The business of America is business."
4 "Speak softly, but carry a big stick."

16 The major significance of the Social Security Act of 1935 was that it
1 banned business trusts in the United States
2 raised tariff rates at the start the Great Depression
3 provided a "safety net" for people affected by a personal catastrophe
4 set business codes for industries engaged in intrastate commerce

17 Which generalization is best supported by a study of Prohibition in the United States?
1 Social attitudes can make certain laws difficult to enforce.
2 Increased taxes can affect consumer spending.
3 Morality can be legislated successfully.
4 People will sacrifice willingly for the common good.

18 Which statement best describes Franklin Roosevelt's New Deal programs?
1 They reduced the number of government employees.
2 They expanded the economic role of government.
3 They stressed the need for local government leadership.
4 They emphasized the importance of the gold standard.

19 What would someone be called who favored the decision in the Sacco and Vanzetti trial, the rebirth of the Ku Klux Klan, and the National Origins Act of 1924?
1 rugged individualist
2 imperialist
3 nativist
4 mercantilist

20 The terms N.R.A., W.P.A., C.C.C. would most likely be discussed in an essay dealing with the
1 causes of World War II
2 Progressive Movement
3 New Deal
4 Women's Movement

21 Which action is often viewed as the most serious attempt to undermine the independence of the judiciary?
1 Hoover's appointment of conservative Supreme Court Justices
2 Franklin D. Roosevelt's plan to reorganize the Supreme Court
3 appointing Supreme Court Justices to unlimited terms of office
4 periodic increases in the salaries of Supreme Court Justices

22 Which branch of the national government declared early New Deal legislation unconstitutional?
1 the Senate
2 the Supreme Court
3 the President
4 the House of Representatives

23 Which terms best describe the U. S. during the 1920s?
1 expansion and appeasement
2 depression and militarism
3 prosperity and isolationism
4 recession and imperialism

24 Which development led to the other three?
1 the introduction of new regulatory agencies
2 the Stock Market crash in 1929
3 the passage of the Social Security Act
4 increased government involvement in the economy

25 "... economic depression cannot be cured by legislative action or executive pronouncement... The contribution of government lies in [stimulating] voluntary programs in the community."

This quotation by Herbert Hoover suggests that in times of economic crisis
1 the national government should take full responsibility for solving economic problems
2 people should be patient and economic problems will solve themselves
3 private organizations, with government encouragement, should deal with economic problems
4 the government should not be expected to deal with economic problems since it did not cause them

RCT-TYPE ESSAYS

1 You have just been elected president of the U.S. One of the major problems you face as president is that the U.S. is in the middle of a severe economic depression.

Part A

List two problems that the United States would face as a result of this economic depression, and state two recommendations that might help to resolve these problems.

PROBLEM	**RECOMMENDATION**
1. ____________________	1. ____________________
2. ____________________	2. ____________________

Part B

In your Part B answer, you should use information you gave in Part A. However, you may also include different or additional information in your Part B answer.

Write an essay explaining how your recommendations would help to solve the economic problems faced by the United States.

2 **Postage stamps have long been means by which governments honor certain individuals.**

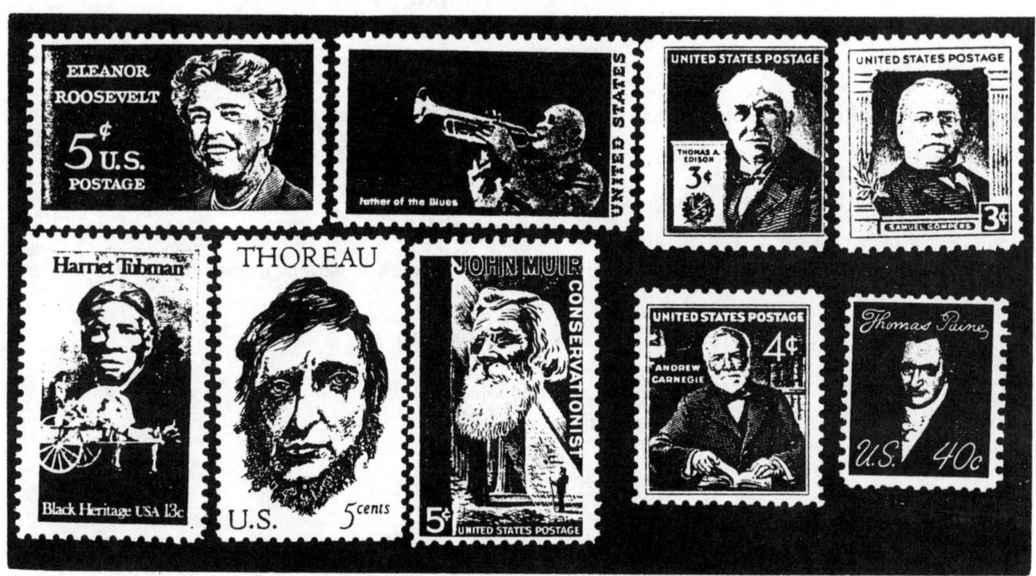
ELEANOR ROOSEVELT
5¢ U.S. POSTAGE
Father of the Blues
UNITED STATES
UNITED STATES POSTAGE
THOMAS A. EDISON
3¢
UNITED STATES POSTAGE
SAMUEL GOMPERS
3¢
Harriet Tubman
Black Heritage USA 13c
THOREAU
U.S. 5cents
JOHN MUIR
CONSERVATIONIST
5¢ UNITED STATES POSTAGE
UNITED STATES POSTAGE
4¢
ANDREW CARNEGIE
Thomas Paine
U.S. 40c

Top row: Eleanor Roosevelt, W.C. Handy, Thomas Edison, Samuel Gompers

Bottom row: Harriet Tubman, David Henry Thoreau, John Muir, Andrew Carnegie, Thomas Paine

Part A

Select *one* of the individuals shown: ______________________________

State that person's contribution to American society: ______________________________

____

Select *another* individual shown: ______________________________

State that person's contribution to American society: ______________________________

____

Part B

In your Part B answer, you should use information you gave in Part A. However, you may also include different or additional information in your Part B answer.

Write an essay discussing why certain people are honored by having their picture on a stamp.

REGENTS-TYPE ESSAYS

1 Historians have given different time periods names that sum up the major events of the period.

Historical Periods

Reconstruction Era
Progressive Period
The Roaring Twenties (1920's)
The Great Depression

Choose *three* of the historical periods listed above and for *each* one chosen:

- Identify the time period
- Explain why historians have given this time period its name

2 Economic problems have been a major concern in the United States at various times since the Civil War.

Economic Problems

Rise of monopolies and trusts
Farmers' difficulties
Depression
Stock market collapse

Choose *two* of the economic problems listed and for *each* one chosen:

- Show how the problem has been a major concern during a specific period since the Civil War
- Discuss a major cause of the problem
- Discuss one action taken by the United States Government to deal with the problem

3 Some congressional legislation has significantly changed the American way of life.

Congressional Legislation

Interstate Commerce Act (1887)
Sherman Anti-Trust Act (1890)
Pure Food and Drug Act (1906)
Federal Reserve System Act (1913)
Social Security Act (1935)
"Wagner Act" (1935)

Select *three* of the acts of legislation listed above and for *each* one chosen:

- Describe the specific features of the act
- Discuss its lasting significance on American life

PERFORMANCE-BASED TASKS

In this activity, you will act as an adviser to President-elect Franklin D. Roosevelt.

Setting: Roosevelt has recently defeated Herbert Hoover to become the next President of the United States. It is still some weeks before Roosevelt is scheduled to be inaugurated. You have been called to his office and asked to help him in drafting an inaugural address to be delivered to the nation.

General Directions: Before putting pen to paper you review newspaper stories with the following headlines:

- "MANY BUSINESSES GO BANKRUPT"
- "HALF A MILLION FARMERS LOSE FARMS"
- "ONE-QUARTER OF ALL U.S. BANKS FAIL"
- "THOUSANDS OF AMERICANS GO HUNGRY"
- "MILLIONS DEPEND ON SOUP LINES FOR FOOD"

You also study other information about economic conditions in the nation. In addition, you review suggestions for particular sections of the speech offered by members of your staff and other advisers to F.D.R.

Proposed Sections:

- "This great nation will endure as it has endured, will revive and will prosper. So first of all, let me assert my firm belief that the only thing we have to fear is fear itself."

- "Taxes have risen, our ability to pay has fallen, government is faced by a serious cut in income; the means of exchange are frozen. The withered leaves of enterprise lie on every side; farmers find no market for their produce; the savings of many families are gone."

- "We still have much to be thankful for. Plenty is at our doorstep. Our primary task is to put people to work. This can be accomplished by direct recruiting by government."

- "I shall ask Congress for broad executive power to wage a war against the Depression, as great as the power given to me if we were in fact invaded by a foreign foe."

- "The people of the United States have not failed. They have asked for direction under leadership."

Your Suggested Speech: After studying additional information about the Depression, you should write a suggested inaugural address of about 300 words. Use the memo outline suggested on the following page.

To: President-elect Franklin D. Roosevelt
From: You
Subject: Inaugural Address

- Begin with words that will build confidence and lift up the spirits of the American people.

____

____

- The body of the speech should address the conditions brought on by the Depression, and the measures you propose to introduce to fight the Depression.

____

____

____

____

____

____

____

- Your conclusion should leave people with the feeling that all Americans face these problems together, and that we must begin to fight the Depression now.

____

____

____

Your teacher might also ask you to deliver your speech to your classmates, to test its effectiveness for President-elect Roosevelt.

LOOKING AT THE IMPACT OF HISTORICAL DEVELOPMENTS

Have you ever seen the movie *Back to the Future*? In this film, the main character travels back in time and meets his mother while she is a teenager. His sudden appearance in his mother's teenage life triggers effects that threaten to change events so that he will never be born. Such time travel into the past may be wildly unrealistic, but part of the excitement of this film is that it reveals an important truth: if we could alter even a single past event, we might change the entire course of history.

Why is this? It is because every event has effects, and these effects in turn have still further consequences. Some events can affect the entire development and direction of a society. For example, decisions a society makes may affect its social organization, political structure, or economic activities. The nature of these structures then influences the later development of that society. Choices by leaders at critical turning points can be especially decisive. For example, a country's leaders may decide to go to war, which can lead to the complete altering of a country's political, social and economic systems.

CAUSE AND EFFECT

Historians are particularly interested in examining the relationships of cause and effect between events.

- The **causes** of something are the conditions or factors that led to it or brought it about. It would not have happened except for this cause. For example, turning the switch on a light is the cause of the light's going on.

- The **effects** of something are any of the things that have happened because of it — the results of a particular decision, development or event. For example, the light's going on was the effect of my turning the switch.

Cause ——————>	Effect
I turned the switch.	The light went on.

ANSWERING AN ESSAY QUESTION ABOUT HISTORICAL EVENTS

Very often the RCT or Regents Examination will ask a question about historical developments and their effects. The question will usually list historical events, movements or developments of various kinds, and ask you to discuss the event or development and its impact. An example of this type of essay question appeared on the June 1990 Regents:

Various factors in U. S. history have had an impact on the role of women in American society.

Factors

The Industrial Revolution	World War II
The Women's Movement	The media

a Choose *three* of the factors listed. Using specific examples, discuss the impact of each factor on the role of women in United States society.

b Show how present-day United States society has been affected by the changed role of women.

For this question, first think very carefully about each of the historical factors that you select. Begin answering the first part (**a**) of the question by listing on scrap paper all the ways in which each of these historical developments had effects on women. For example, you might include:

■ **The Industrial Revolution.** This event changed the way people lived and worked. Women worked in factories and lived in cities. Women enjoyed new opportunities but faced many hardships—working long hours for low pay in unsafe conditions.

■ **The Women's Movement.** In 1848 a Women's Rights Convention at Seneca Falls, New York passed resolutions proclaiming women's equality to men. This movement focused the cause of women on obtaining the right to vote. Eventually, success was achieved when the 19th Amendment was added to the Constitution. It was the first step for women in obtaining full equality. It opened the door for women to vote and achieve elective office.

■ **World War II.** This historical event had an important impact on women. Men were sent off to fight the war. Women filled their places in factories and offices, showing that women could work in these occupations as well as men. Many women were even recruited for non-combatant duty in the armed services. Nevertheless, when the war ended many women lost their jobs and most of them found themselves in traditional roles as housewives and mothers in the post-war baby boom.

For the second half of the question (**b**), think carefully about how changes in women's roles have affected American society today. Think about our political, social and economic structures.

■ **Politically.**

- How has the vote for women changed our politics?
- How many women run for political office?
- How many political campaigns concern women's issues such as child care and abortion?

■ **Socially.**

- How have the roles of women—especially in the work force—affected our social structure?
- Does it influence, for example, the way children are raised in the 1990s?

■ **Economically.**

- How have new roles for women affected our economic life?
- What kinds of positions do women now fill?
- What are the effects on American creativity and productivity?

NOTE: In discussing a historical event or development, consider answering the questions "who," "what," "when" and "where." Apply the same questions in discussing the results of an event or development.

LOOKING AT SPECIFIC TIME PERIODS

Sometimes the RCT or Regents will ask a question on a specific time period, like the 1890s, 1920s or 1960s. For example, the following question appeared on the June 1989 Regents:

Many of the developments of the 1920s have had a significant impact on American society.

Developments of the 1920s

Changing role of women
Widespread use of the automobile
Growth of nativism
Popularity of radio and motion pictures
Speculation in stocks and real estate
Clash between science and traditional values

Choose *three* of the developments listed. For *each* one chosen:

- describe the development that took place in the 1920s.
- show how that development has had a continuing effect on American society since the 1920s.

In this case, think about how the time period differed from what went on before it. What problems did people face in this time period? What unique approaches did the people of this period have for overcoming their problems? How could you characterize the spirit or flavor of that particular time? Was it a period of economic growth or decline? Was it a period of social and political experimentation? Was it a time of social conformity and repression? Most of all, think about how the economic events, politics and new ideas of the period were all related to one another. The literature and art of the period will also often tell you something of the spirit of the times.

CHAPTER 12

THE AGE OF GLOBAL CRISIS

In the 1930s dictatorships came to power in Germany, Italy, Spain and several other countries. When war clouds appeared in Europe and Asia, Americans were reluctant to become involved in another foreign war. However, Japan's attack on Pearl Harbor ended U. S. neutrality. American participation helped ensure an Allied victory in World War II. U. S. leaders regretted not trying to stamp out Nazi aggression in its infancy. In the post-war years, they resolved not to make the same mistake in the struggle against international communism.

— TIMELINE OF KEY EVENTS —

1935	1937	1939	1940	1941	1945	1947	1948
First Neutrality Act passed	F.D.R delivers his Quarantine Speech	Germany invades Poland	F.D.R. elected to a third term as president	Japan attacks Pearl Harbor; U. S. declares war	Atomic bomb dropped on Hiroshima	Truman Doctrine announced	Marshall Plan proposed

PEACE IN PERIL: 1920-1941

A RETURN TO AN ISOLATIONIST POLICY

Americans became disillusioned with their involvement in foreign affairs during World War I. In the 1920s, the U. S. returned to its traditional policy of isolation. Americans concerned themselves with events at home, and felt safely removed from events abroad because of the oceans that separated them from Europe and Asia.

The United States refused to join the League of Nations.
Many Americans became pacifists, renouncing participation in any war.
U. S. ISOLATIONISM AFTER WORLD WAR I
The U. S. insisted on collecting war debts from its former allies, Britain and France.
The U. S. passed high tariffs against European goods, and also restricted European immigration.

There were some exceptions to the trend towards isolationism: (a) In 1921, the United States hosted the **Washington Naval Conference**, in which European and Asian powers temporarily agreed to limit the expansion of naval armaments and the size of their navies; (b) in 1928, the U. S. promoted the **Kellogg-Briand Peace Pact**, which was signed by 62 countries and renounced the use of war; and (c) between 1923 and 1930, American bankers lent funds to the German government to help it cover its reparations (payments for war damages) to Britain and France. In 1930, this help was withdrawn because of the Depression.

THE ORIGINS OF WORLD WAR II IN EUROPE

The violence and spread of the Great Depression in the early 1930s led to the triumph of fascist leaders in Germany, Italy and elsewhere in Europe. New political beliefs like Italian Fascism and German National Socialism (Nazism) mixed together feelings of intense nationalism, racism and the worship of violence. **Adolf Hitler**, the leader of Nazi Germany, was determined to achieve the German domination of Europe. This aggression was the underlying cause of the start of World War II in Europe.

THE FAILURE OF THE LEAGUE OF NATIONS

The League of Nations, charged with the responsibility of preventing another war, proved powerless. The League failed for a number of reasons:

- The idea of **collective security**—that peaceful nations would band together to prevent war—was doomed when major countries like the United States and Russia failed to become members of the League. In addition, Germany and Japan left the League in the 1930s.

- Even those countries in the League (such as Britain and France) failed to take effective action. The League was unable to stop German rearmament, the Japanese invasion of China, the Italian invasion of Ethiopia in Africa, and German and Italian intervention in the Spanish Civil War.

APPEASEMENT FAILS: THE MUNICH CONFERENCE (1938)

In 1938, Hitler annexed Austria. Next, he demanded the Sudetenland, a part of Czechoslovakia with a large number of German-speaking people. At first, France and Britain promised to protect Czechoslovakia, but when Hitler threatened war, France and Britain backed down. At the Munich Conference, British and French leaders, seeking to avoid war, agreed to give Hitler the western part of Czechoslovakia. This policy of giving in to satisfy the demands of a potential enemy is known as **appeasement**. This policy failed, since it only encouraged Hitler to make further demands.

WORLD WAR II BEGINS: THE GERMAN INVASION OF POLAND

In 1939, Hitler made new demands in Poland. Fearing Hitler intended to dominate Europe, Britain and France refused to give in. Hitler responded by signing a peace treaty with the Soviet dictator, Stalin, in which the two agreed to divide Poland. When Germany invaded Poland in 1939, Britain and France declared war on Germany, beginning World War II.

THE U.S. PRESERVES A CAUTIOUS NEUTRALITY

In the early 1930s, the United States had been too absorbed in the problems of the Great Depression to become actively involved in world affairs. In addition, a Senate investigation (the **Nye Commission**), had revealed that some individuals profited greatly from America's participation in World War I. This helped to strengthen public opinion against new involvement in Europe.

NEUTRALITY ACTS (1935-1937)

Congress passed a series of acts designed to avoid bringing the United States into another war. The U.S. had become involved in World War I because German submarines had attacked American ships bringing supplies to Britain and France. To avoid a repetition of similar events, the neutrality acts prohibited Americans from traveling on the ships of nations at war. They also prohibited Americans from selling arms or munitions to countries at war. Americans were only permitted to sell non-military goods to such countries on a "**cash-and-carry**" basis (cash only). Congress later revised the neutrality acts, allowing Americans to sell arms to Britain and France, so long as the Allies paid in cash and transported the goods in their own ships.

CONTINUING NEUTRALITY

When Japanese forces invaded northern China, President Roosevelt told Americans in his **Quarantine Speech** (1937) that peaceful nations had to act together to quarantine (isolate) aggressive nations—otherwise aggression would spread further. Most Americans, however, were opposed to taking any form of military action. Even when Germany invaded Poland, most Americans still opposed entering the war, although they were willing to help the Allies with measures short of war.

AMERICA PREPARES FOR WAR

American leaders nevertheless began making preparations in case they were dragged into the conflict. Congress increased spending on the army and navy.

THE PEACETIME DRAFT

In 1940, just after Nazi Germany defeated and occupied France, Congress enacted the **Burke-Wadsworth Act**, the first peacetime draft. All men between the ages of 21 and 35 had to register and were subject to one year of military service.

THE LEND-LEASE ACT

Roosevelt proposed this act in 1941, to sell, lease, or lend war materials to "any country whose defense the president deems vital to the defense of the United States." Congress allowed funds for the production of ships, tanks, planes and other weapons. Soon afterwards, American battleships began protecting British ships carrying supplies to Britain. Critics of the program feared it might drag the U.S. into the war. Most Americans, however, supported helping the British.

THE FOUR FREEDOMS

In 1941, Roosevelt told Americans he hoped to establish a world based on "Four Freedoms": freedom of speech and expression, freedom of religion, freedom from want, and freedom from fear.

THE ATLANTIC CHARTER

Roosevelt met with British Prime Minister **Winston Churchill** aboard a ship in the Atlantic Ocean to discuss their objectives for a postwar world. The U.S. and Great Britain announced that they sought freedom of the seas, no territorial gains, and an end to war. The Atlantic Charter laid the foundation for the United Nations.

THE UNITED STATES ENTERS WORLD WAR II: 1941

President Roosevelt believed that U.S. entry into the war was inevitable. However, before he could bring the United States into the war, he had to win over public support. In 1941, armed American merchant ships were authorized to carry supplies directly to Britain. It seemed as though United States involvement in the war was just a matter of time. Surprisingly, it was not events in Europe but in East Asia that finally brought the United States into the war.

INCREASING UNITED STATES-JAPANESE TENSIONS

U.S. foreign policy toward Japan before the 1930s was characterized by only moderate interest. In 1937, Japan went to war with China. When Japan occupied Southern Indochina in 1941, the U.S. reacted by freezing Japanese assets in the United States and cutting off all trade with Japan. Roosevelt offered to resume trade only if Japan withdrew its forces from China and Indochina. Japan refused this demand.

JAPAN PREPARES A SURPRISE ATTACK

Japanese military leaders decided to attack Indonesia to obtain oil supplies they needed for their war effort. Realizing such a move would bring the United States into the war, they also decided to launch a surprise attack against the United States. Japan believed a surprise attack would catch the United States unprepared, eliminate American naval power in the Pacific, and allow Japan to fortify its position in the area. Japanese leaders did not want to conquer the United States, but they believed Americans would soon tire of the war and negotiate a compromise peace, leaving Japan in control of East Asia. On the morning of December 7, 1941, Japanese planes attacked the U.S. Pacific fleet in **Pearl Harbor**, Hawaii. The next day, Congress declared war on Japan. Four days later, Germany and Italy, who were allied to Japan, declared war on the United States.

KEY ITEMS TO REMEMBER

Isolationism, collective security, appeasement, neutrality acts, Quarantine speech, Lend-Lease Act, Four Freedoms, Atlantic Charter

THE UNITED STATES AT WAR: 1941—1945

The U.S. was now engaged in a war on two fronts—the Atlantic and Pacific. The government had to mobilize American manpower and production to meet its enormous war needs.

THE HOME FRONT

THE DRAFT

All able-bodied men between 18 and 45 were eventually liable for military service. One out of every ten Americans was in uniform at some point during the war. Before the war was over, more than fifteen million men had been drafted or had voluntarily enlisted. For the first time, women could enlist in the armed services. About one million African Americans also served, even though they suffered the indignity of being placed in segregated units.

WARTIME PRODUCTION

The final victory of the Allies was due in large part to the achievement of American wartime production. Two agencies, the Office of War Mobilization and the War Production Board, managed the war economy. They controlled the use of raw materials, the conversion of factories to wartime production, the production of consumer goods, and the rationing of essential items like gasoline.

THE LABOR FORCE

The draft and the expansion of production ended the unemployment of the Great Depression. A large number of workers went into the armed services and overseas. Many African Americans and women stepped in to fill the gaps in large numbers. The number of women in the work force also increased dramatically. Women took jobs in heavy industry. African Americans continued to migrate to northern cities.

PAYING FOR THE WAR

The cost of the war to the U. S. was about $350 billion, more than ten times the cost of World War I. Patriotic Americans bought "war bonds," to be repaid by the government with interest after the war was over. One economic impact of the huge war cost was that the United States changed from a creditor to a debtor nation.

THE FORCED RELOCATION OF JAPANESE-AMERICANS

The surprise attack on Pearl Harbor created fear among many Americans, especially on the West Coast, that Japanese-Americans might commit acts of sabotage. This fear of Japanese-Americans was racially-motivated in part, since there was no evidence that they were guilty of disloyalty. No similar relocation measures were taken against either Italian-Americans or German-Americans.

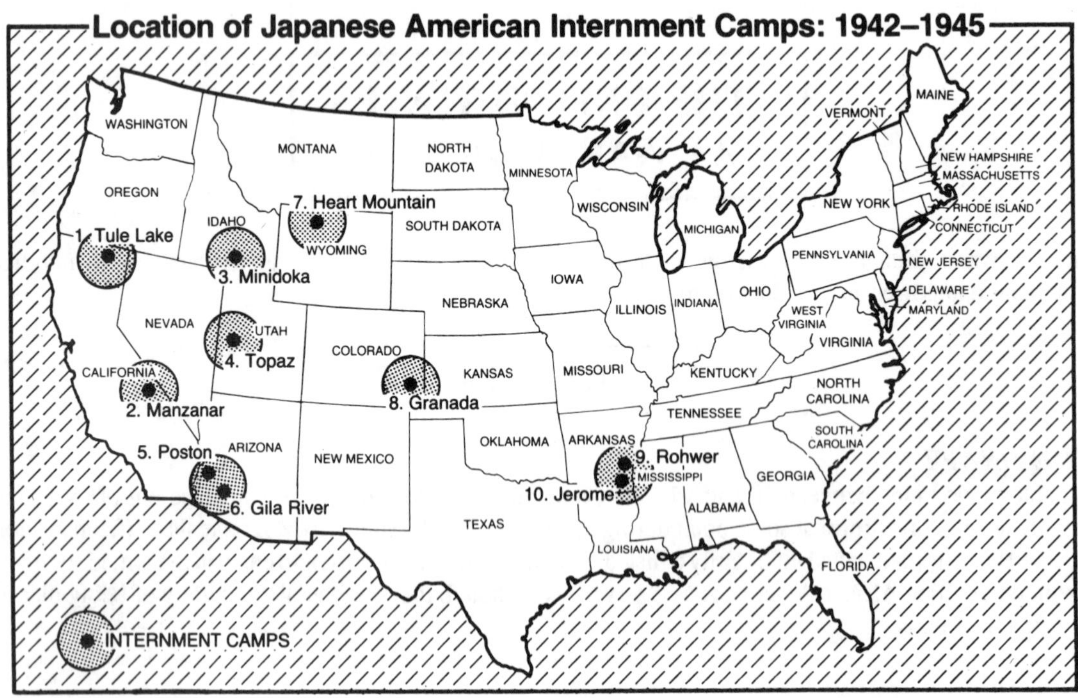
Location of Japanese American Internment Camps: 1942–1945
WASHINGTON
OREGON
IDAHO
MONTANA
NORTH DAKOTA
MINNESOTA
SOUTH DAKOTA
WYOMING
WISCONSIN
MICHIGAN
NEW YORK
VERMONT
MAINE
NEW HAMPSHIRE
MASSACHUSETTS
RHODE ISLAND
CONNECTICUT
NEW JERSEY
DELAWARE
MARYLAND
PENNSYLVANIA
OHIO
INDIANA
ILLINOIS
IOWA
NEBRASKA
NEVADA
UTAH
COLORADO
KANSAS
MISSOURI
KENTUCKY
WEST VIRGINIA
VIRGINIA
NORTH CAROLINA
TENNESSEE
SOUTH CAROLINA
GEORGIA
ALABAMA
MISSISSIPPI
ARKANSAS
OKLAHOMA
TEXAS
LOUISIANA
FLORIDA
CALIFORNIA
ARIZONA
NEW MEXICO
1. Tule Lake
2. Manzanar
3. Minidoka
4. Topaz
5. Poston
6. Gila River
7. Heart Mountain
8. Granada
9. Rohwer
10. Jerome
INTERNMENT CAMPS

■ **Relocation Centers.** Roosevelt ordered the forcible removal of Japanese-Americans to relocation centers, where they remained until after the war. Most were forced to sell their property and belongings at short notice. In the camps, they lived in primitive and crowded conditions.

■ **Increased Use of Presidential Power.** As during Abraham Lincoln's presidency, Roosevelt showed that presidential power often increases dramatically during wartime. Roosevelt justified his ordering of Japanese-Americans to relocation centers as a military necessity. The Supreme Court upheld the relocation camps in *Korematsu v. U.S.* (see Key Court Cases on page 288).

THE WAR AGAINST GERMANY

Roosevelt decided to focus American energies on defeating Nazi Germany first, since Germany was our most powerful and dangerous enemy. By the time the United States entered the war, Hitler was in control of most of Europe and North Africa.

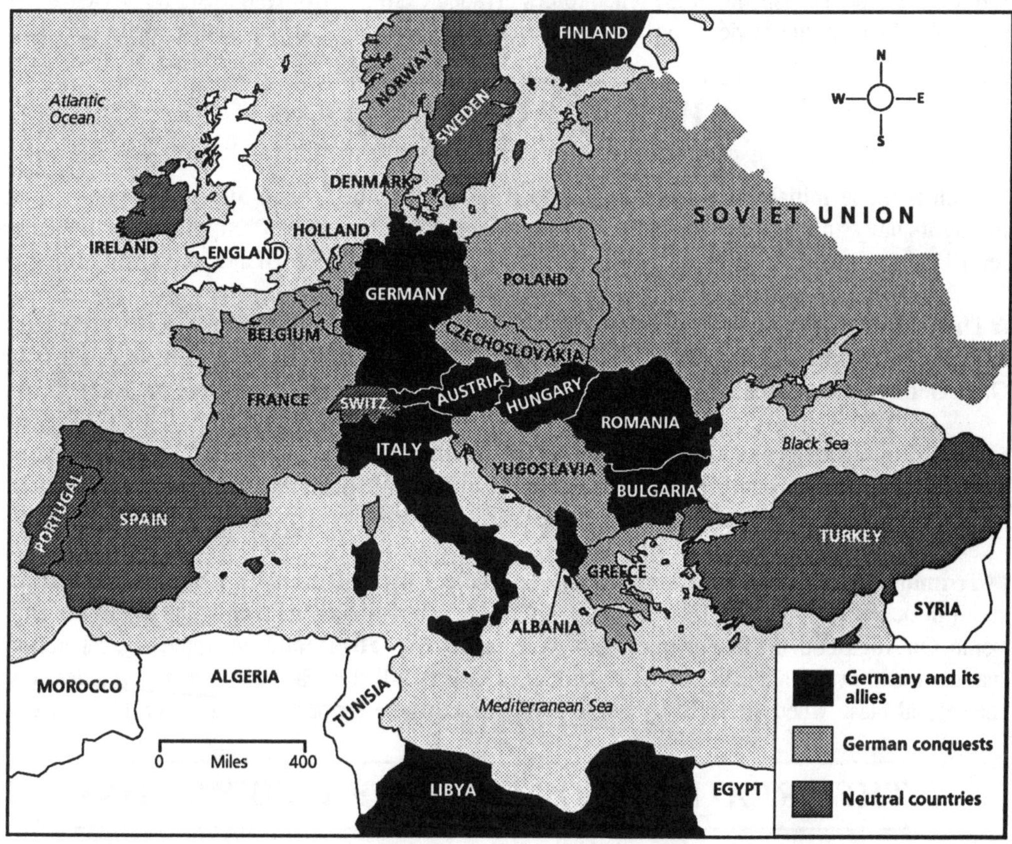
FINLAND
NORWAY
SWEDEN
Atlantic Ocean
N
W
E
S
DENMARK
SOVIET UNION
HOLLAND
IRELAND
ENGLAND
POLAND
GERMANY
BELGIUM
CZECHOSLOVAKIA
FRANCE
SWITZ.
AUSTRIA
HUNGARY
ROMANIA
Black Sea
ITALY
YUGOSLAVIA
BULGARIA
PORTUGAL
SPAIN
TURKEY
GREECE
SYRIA
ALBANIA
MOROCCO
ALGERIA
TUNISIA
Mediterranean Sea
Germany and its allies
German conquests
Neutral countries
0 Miles 400
LIBYA
EGYPT

■ **Hitler's Plan.** Hitler planned to reorganize Europe along racial lines. Germans were to compose a new ruling class, and other peoples would be turned into slaves. Jews, gypsies, Poles and certain others would be exterminated through mass murder. These plans led to the **Holocaust**—the slaughter of millions of Jews and other peoples in concentration camps, where they were gassed and their bodies were burned in large ovens.

■ **Early Fighting.** Hitler made his greatest mistakes when he invaded the Soviet Union in June 1941 and declared war on the United States in December 1941, before he had defeated Great Britain. In late 1941, the German advance into the Soviet Union was stopped just short of Moscow by the bitter cold of the Russian winter. Roosevelt and Churchill promised Soviet leader **Joseph Stalin** that they would open a second front against Germany in the west, to relieve the pressure on the Soviet army. Late in 1942 the Allies forces landed troops in North Africa. After defeating German forces there, the Allies advanced to Sicily and then Italy in 1943-1944. Meanwhile, the Soviet forces defeated the German army at Stalingrad and advanced toward Germany.

■ **The Collapse of Nazi Germany.** On **D-Day** (June 6, 1944), Allied troops landed in France on the beaches of Normandy. They moved quickly eastward, freeing Paris and reaching the German border. While American, British and Free French forces invaded Germany from the west, the Soviets entered in the east. In 1945, the Soviet army captured Berlin. Hitler committed suicide and Germany surrendered.

THE WAR AGAINST JAPAN

The Japanese made initial gains in Asia and the Pacific while the United States was preoccupied with rebuilding its navy and fighting Germany. Japan invaded and occupied the Philippines just after the attack on Pearl Harbor. Japan also occupied Hong Kong, Borneo, the Solomon Islands, Java and Singapore.

■ **The War Begins To Turn Against Japan.** In 1943, the U. S. regained naval superiority in the Pacific and American forces began "island-hopping," liberating islands from Japanese control, one at a time. Once Germany was defeated, the United States began preparations for a massive invasion of Japan.

■ **The Manhattan Project.** Before entering the war, the U.S. had begun the "Manhattan Project" to develop an atomic bomb in secret laboratories in New Mexico,. American leaders feared Nazi Germany might develop such a bomb first. The first atomic bomb was successfully tested in July 1945.

■ **Truman Decides to Use the Atomic Bomb.** President Truman feared an invasion of Japan might result in nearly one million U.S. casualties. To avoid such an invasion, Truman turned to the atomic bomb. On August 6th the first atomic bomb was exploded over **Hiroshima**, and three days later another was exploded over **Nagasaki**. About 100,000 people were killed in each city. Japan surrendered after the second blast, when the U. S. agreed to allow the Japanese Emperor to remain on his throne.

THE TREATMENT OF THE DEFEATED NATIONS

THE NUREMBERG TRIALS

The liberation of the concentration camps by Allied forces at the end of the war showed clear evidence of Nazi crimes. The discovery of millions of bodies, and the naked and half-starved survivors, indicated the full extent of Nazi brutality. The Allied leaders put many of the leading Nazis on trial for international aggression and "crimes against humanity" in Nuremberg, Germany, from 1945 to 1946. Those on trial attempted to defend themselves by stating they had only been following orders. Many were found guilty of committing atrocities and several were hanged or imprisoned for life, indicating that individuals are responsible for their actions, even in times of war.

"DENAZIFICATION" AND THE DIVISION OF GERMANY

Germany was occupied by the United States, Britain, France and the Soviet Union. The occupying powers introduced re-education programs, explaining to the German people the evils of Nazi beliefs. The division of Germany into different occupation zones led to the separation of Germany into two states, East and West Germany, which lasted for the next 45 years.

THE OCCUPATION OF JAPAN

The American General **Douglas MacArthur** was assigned the task of rebuilding and reforming post-war Japan. Under his leadership, the Japanese people were not punished for starting the war, but important changes were imposed to make Japan less aggressive and less imperialistic. Japan's overseas empire was taken away, and her military leaders were put on trial. Japan renounced the use of nuclear weapons and the waging of war, and was forbidden from having a large army or navy. A new constitution went into effect in May 1947, making Japan a democracy.

THE GLOBAL IMPACT OF WORLD WAR II

World War II was a disaster for much of the world. Over 50 million people lost their lives. Much of Europe, North Africa and East Asia lay in ruins.

U.S. MILITARY CASUALTIES IN MAJOR WARS

WAR (length)	NUMBER INVOLVED	WOUNDED	KILLED	TOTAL CASUALTIES
Civil War (4 years)	2,213,363	281,881	364,881	646,392
Spanish-American War (4 months)	306,760	1,662	2,446	4,108
World War I (1 year 7 months)	4,734,991	204,002	116,516	320,518
World War II (3 years 8 months)	16,112,566	670,846	405,399	1,076,245
Korean War (3 years 1 month)	5,720,000	103,284	54,246	157,530
Vietnam War (12 years)	8,744,000	153,303	57,702	211,005

U. S. Historical Abstract

The end of World War II brought about other important changes.

THE RISE OF THE SUPERPOWERS

The collapse of European power left the United States and Soviet Union as the two superpowers in command of the world. The United States had tremendous economic power and control of the atomic bomb. The Soviet Union had its large army, which occupied most of Eastern Europe. Their differences in viewpoint and in national interests rapidly led to the "Cold War."

THE FORMATION OF THE UNITED NATIONS

Despite the failure of the League of Nations, the victorious allies formed a new international peace-keeping organization: the United Nations.

■ **Aims.** Like the League of Nations, the **United Nations**' major aim was to maintain peace in the world, while trying to foster friendship and cooperation among nations. The U.N. also seeks to eliminate hunger, disease and ignorance.

■ **Collective Security.** Like the League of Nations, the United Nations relies on the concept of collective security. However, unlike the League of Nations, the United Nations has a **Security Council** that gives the larger powers a special role. The Security Council is responsible for ensuring peace and deterring aggression. It can investigate disputes, apply economic sanctions, or use military action to resolve disputes. Each permanent member nation on the Security Council has veto power over the Council's actions. For much of its history, friction between Communist and non-Communist countries on the Security Council prevented it from intervening in many international disputes.

KEY ITEMS TO REMEMBER

Pearl Harbor, Holocaust, "D-Day," atomic bomb, Hiroshima, Nagasaki, Nuremberg Trials, United Nations

THE COLD WAR: 1945-1965

The end of World War II left two great superpowers in control of world affairs—the United States and the Soviet Union. Although they were allies during World War II, they soon became rivals in a "Cold War." The war was "cold" only in the sense that because they had nuclear weapons the two superpowers never confronted one another directly in open warfare. However, their global competition led to frequent world crises and regional confrontations on every continent.

THE ROOTS OF THE COLD WAR

The roots of the Cold War lay in the competing ideological systems of the United States and the Soviet Union. The U. S. wanted to spread its democratic capitalist system, while the Soviet Union wanted to spread its system of Communism. It was inevitable that these two superpowers would clash in seeking their objectives. The Communist system was based on the ideas of **Karl Marx**. Some of its most important ideas were:

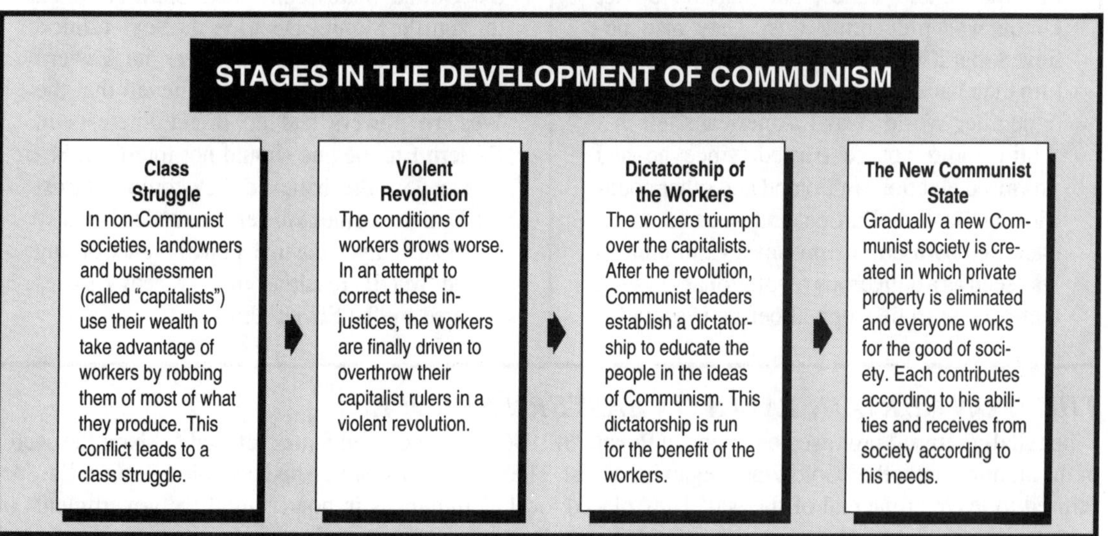
STAGES IN THE DEVELOPMENT OF COMMUNISM
Class Struggle
In non-Communist societies, landowners and businessmen (called "capitalists") use their wealth to take advantage of workers by robbing them of most of what they produce. This conflict leads to a class struggle.
Violent Revolution
The conditions of workers grows worse. In an attempt to correct these injustices, the workers are finally driven to overthrow their capitalist rulers in a violent revolution.
Dictatorship of the Workers
The workers triumph over the capitalists. After the revolution, Communist leaders establish a dictatorship to educate the people in the ideas of Communism. This dictatorship is run for the benefit of the workers.
The New Communist State
Gradually a new Communist society is created in which private property is eliminated and everyone works for the good of society. Each contributes according to his abilities and receives from society according to his needs.

THE U.S. AND SOVIET UNION: WARTIME ALLIES (1941-1945)

When Hitler's troops invaded the Soviet Union in 1941 and Japan attacked Pearl Harbor, the United States and the Soviet Union joined as allies in the struggle against Germany, demonstrating that alliances between rivals are often based on mutual self-interest. However, the Soviets resented the fact that the U. S. and Great Britain waited until 1944 to invade Europe. All this time the Soviet Army suffered the brunt of fighting the Nazis. American losses in World War II were 300,000 dead, compared to Soviet losses of 21 million.

POST-WAR PLANS: THE YALTA CONFERENCE (1945)

In 1945, Roosevelt, Churchill and Stalin met at Yalta in the Soviet Union to make plans for the future reorganization of Europe at the end of the war. They agreed on the formation of the United Nations. They also agreed that Germany would be divided into four separate occupation zones. Finally, the three leaders agreed to restore democratic government and allow free elections throughout the countries freed in Europe. Stalin gave his pledge to allow free elections in Eastern Europe after the war.

THE COLD WAR BEGINS

When Roosevelt died in 1945, Truman replaced him, and met with Stalin at Potsdam, Germany. At the **Potsdam Conference**, serious differences began to emerge, mainly over the future of Eastern Europe:

Who was to blame for starting the Cold War?	
THE AMERICAN VIEWPOINT American leaders felt that European countries wanted to become democratic societies like the United States, but that the Soviet Union was preventing this. They also believed that it would be a mistake for them to turn their back on European affairs as they had done after World War I. Americans felt that Stalin could not be trusted, since he had promised elections in Poland and other countries in Eastern Europe and seemed to be backing down on this promise. Communism was seen as a dangerous revolutionary system that needed to be stopped before it spread.	**THE SOVIET VIEWPOINT** Soviet leaders believed they had a right to control Eastern Europe. They felt that just as the United States controlled Latin America through the Monroe Doctrine, the Soviet Union should have the final say over its Eastern European neighbors. Stalin believed that the Western powers had no direct interests in Eastern Europe and should not interfere. Soviet leaders also believed they could not trust the U. S. and other Western countries because they had delayed the invasion of France during World War II, resulting in very heavy losses suffered by the Soviet Union.

THE IRON CURTAIN FALLS ON EASTERN EUROPE

When Stalin refused promised elections in Poland in 1946 and the United States refused to share the secret of the atomic bomb, the "Cold War" began in earnest. The Soviet army, which had occupied Eastern Europe, refused to leave at the end of the war. They placed local Communists in power in all the governments of Eastern Europe. Trade and communication between Eastern and Western Europe was cut off. It appeared that an **Iron Curtain** had fallen, closing off Eastern Europe from the West. Over the next forty years, travel and contact between East and West was limited and Eastern European governments became "satellites" of the Soviet Union. At periodic intervals, Soviet troops were sent to crush democratic uprisings by force in Hungary, Czechoslovakia and other nations in Eastern Europe. The Iron Curtain remained in place until 1989.

THE POLICY OF CONTAINMENT IN EUROPE

American leaders responded to the Soviet domination of Eastern Europe by developing a policy of **containment**. They attempted to avoid the mistakes of the appeasement of Hitler in the 1930s by reacting firmly against every attempt to spread Communist influence. American leaders did not attempt to overturn Communism where it already existed. Instead, they acted to contain it, by preventing it from spreading to any additional countries. This goal became the major concern of United States foreign policy.

THE TRUMAN DOCTRINE (1947)

Truman believed Communism was most attractive to people who were desperate and miserable. When Communist rebels threatened the governments of Greece and Turkey, President Truman gave these countries military aid. In his speech to Congress, he promised American support to any country fighting Communism. This declaration, known as the **Truman Doctrine**, marked the beginnings of America's policy of containment.

THE MARSHALL PLAN (1948)

The U. S. proposed that aid be given to the countries of wartorn Europe to help them rebuild their economies. General **George C. Marshall** proposed to help Europeans to avoid the turmoil and economic dislocations that had followed W.W. I. Supporters of the plan believed that economic aid would create strong European allies and trading partners for the United States. Americans thought that by fighting poverty in Europe, the peoples of Europe would become more resistant to the attractions and claims of Communism. The Marshall Plan was extremely successful: it speeded the economic recovery of Western Europe and created much good will towards the United States. Soviet leaders refused an offer of Marshall Plan assistance to the East.

THE DIVISION OF GERMANY AND THE BERLIN AIRLIFT (1948)

In 1948, the French, British and Americans decided to merge their zones of occupation in Germany into a single West German state. Berlin, the old capital of Germany, was located in the Russian zone but had also been divided up into four sectors, each occupied by a different power. The Soviets reacted to the merging of the western zones by announcing a blockade of West Berlin, closing all highway and railroad links to Berlin. The Western Allies began a massive airlift to feed and supply the city. Within a year, the Soviet blockade was lifted. At various times over the next 15 years, the Soviets placed renewed pressure on Berlin.

THE FORMATION OF NATO AND THE WARSAW PACT

In response to Cold War tensions, the U. S., Canada, and ten Western European countries formed the North Atlantic Treaty Organization (**NATO**) in 1949. Its purpose was to protect Western Europe from Communist aggression. It was based on the concept of **collective security**—each NATO member pledged to defend every other member if attacked. Through NATO, the U. S. extended its umbrella of nuclear protection to Western Europe. The Soviet Union responded to NATO by creating the **Warsaw Pact** with its Eastern allies in 1955.

MEMBERS OF NATO AND THE WARSAW PACT
MEMBERS OF NATO
MEMBERS OF WARSAW PACT
FINLAND
NORWAY
NORTHERN IRELAND
North Sea
SWEDEN
IRELAND
GREAT BRITAIN
DENMARK
NETH.
SOVIET UNION
EAST GER.
POLAND
English Channel
BEL.
WEST GERMANY
LUX.
CZECHOSLOVAKIA
Bay of Biscay
FRANCE
SWITZ.
AUSTRIA
HUNGARY
RUMANIA
ITALY
Black Sea
PORTUGAL
SPAIN
YUGOSLAVIA
BULGARIA
ALBANIA
TURKEY
GIBRALTAR
Mediterranean Sea
GREECE
AFRICA

FRICTION BEHIND THE IRON CURTAIN

During periods of friction behind the Iron Curtain, the United States never felt it should directly interfere where Soviet power was so firmly established. Although the United States loudly condemned Soviet acts of force, it did not intervene when Soviet troops suppressed an anti-Communist revolution in Hungary in 1956, erected the Berlin Wall in 1961 to prevent East Germans from escaping to the West, and invaded Czechoslovakia in 1968 to overthrow a reform government there.

CONTAINMENT IN ASIA

Just when American statesmen believed they had succeeded in checking the spread of Communism in Europe, the world's most populous nation in Asia turned Communist. This raised new questions for American leaders. Could they check the spread of Communism, not only in Europe, but everywhere on the globe?

THE FALL OF CHINA (1949)

Since the 1920s, Communist Chinese had been attempting to overthrow the Nationalist government. After World War II, fighting between the Nationalists and Communists intensified. In 1949, the Communists, led by **Mao Zedong,** finally defeated the Nationalist government of **Chiang Kai-Shek.** Chiang retreated to the island of Taiwan. On the mainland, Mao developed the world's largest Communist state. The United States responded by refusing to extend diplomatic recognition to the Communist government in China. Using its veto power in the United Nations, the U. S. prevented admission of Mao's China to the United Nations. The United States also pledged to protect the Nationalist government on Taiwan against Communist attacks.

THE KOREAN WAR (1950-1953)

Many Americans were shocked that the United States had not done more to prevent the fall of China into Communist hands. This affected the climate of opinion at the time of the outbreak of the Korean War.

■ **The Division of Korea.** Korea was ruled by Japan from 1910 to 1945. After World War II, it was taken from Japan and divided into two occupation zones. As had happened in Germany, a Communist government was set up in the Soviet zone (the northern part of Korea). Elections in the southern part of the country led to the creation of a non-Communist government there.

■ **The Korean War Begins.** In 1950, North Korea invaded South Korea in an attempt to unify the country under Communist rule. Truman, acting without an official declaration of war by Congress, ordered U.S. forces into South Korea to resist the invasion. Because of a boycott by the Soviet Union at the United Nations, the United States was able to pass a resolution sending United Nations troops to South Korea. This action marked the first time that an international peace organization used military force to oppose aggression.

■ **The Truman-MacArthur Controversy.** Truman sent World War II hero General Douglas MacArthur to command American forces. MacArthur surprised the North Koreans by landing at Inchon and then attacked North Korea, advancing up to the border between North Korea and China. This brought a large Chinese army into the war, forcing MacArthur's smaller force to retreat. MacArthur wanted to recapture control of China from the Communists, by using atomic weapons if necessary. When Truman refused such measures, MacArthur publicly criticized Truman. Truman dismissed him from his command, successfully asserting civilian control over the military.

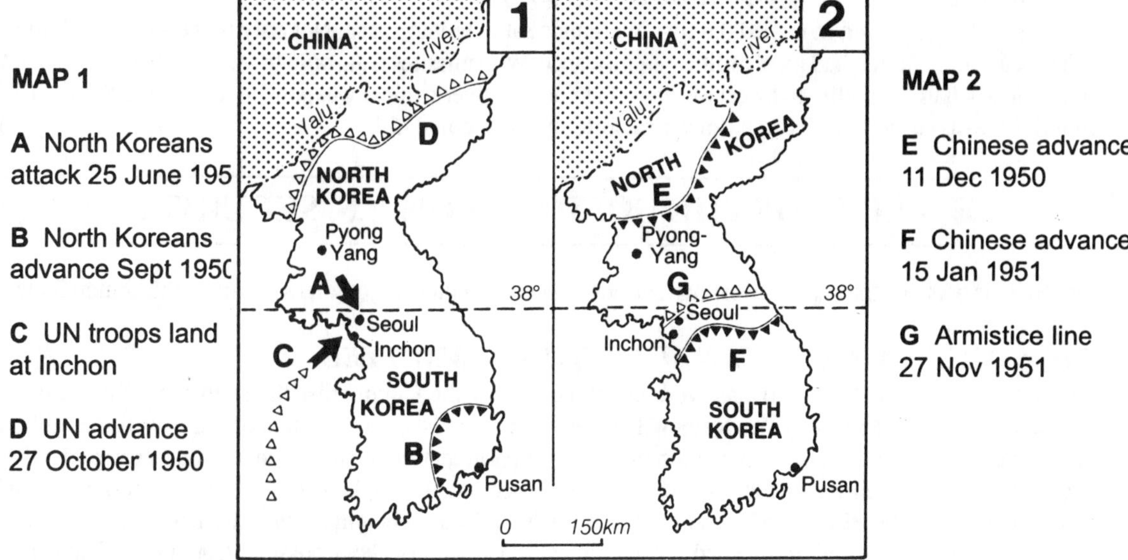
MAP 1
A North Koreans attack 25 June 195
B North Koreans advance Sept 195
C UN troops land at Inchon
D UN advance 27 October 1950
1
CHINA
Yalu river
NORTH KOREA
Pyong Yang
A
D
38°
Seoul
Inchon
C
SOUTH KOREA
B
Pusan
0 150km
2
CHINA
Yalu river
NORTH KOREA
E
Pyong-Yang
G
38°
Seoul
Inchon
F
SOUTH KOREA
Pusan
MAP 2
E Chinese advance 11 Dec 1950
F Chinese advance 15 Jan 1951
G Armistice line 27 Nov 1951

In 1952, **Dwight Eisenhower** was elected President on a pledge that he would find a way to end the war in Korea. An armistice was signed in 1953, ending the war. It left Korea divided exactly as it had been before the North Korean invasion three years earlier.

THE NUCLEAR ARMS RACE BEGINS

In 1945, the United States was the sole atomic power. It held this monopoly of power for only a short time. American leaders refused to share the secret of the atomic bomb with other countries. Congress gave the President control over these weapons. However, by 1949 the Soviet Union developed its own atomic bomb. The nuclear arms race began in earnest in 1952. The United States developed the hydrogen fusion bomb, vastly more powerful than the earlier atomic bomb. The Soviet Union exploded its first hydrogen bomb less than a year later, showing that the gap between American and Soviet nuclear technology was narrowing.

MASSIVE RETALIATION

American leaders in the 1950s decided to rely more on American nuclear weapons for defense than on large numbers of troops. These nuclear weapons acted as a **deterrent**—the Soviet Union would be deterred or prevented from attacking the United States because if it attacked, the United States would damage or destroy the Soviet Union with its large arsenal of nuclear weapons. This defense by threat of massive retaliation was cheaper than maintaining large numbers of conventional forces. However, it was less flexible. American leaders soon realized that in almost all situations nuclear weapons could not be used because they were so dangerous. They were a weapon of last resort, whose use could only be justified if the very survival of the nation were at stake.

THE SOVIET LAUNCH OF SPUTNIK (1957)

In 1957, the Soviet Union launched the first man-made satellite into space. Not only was this the beginning of the "space race," but it had great military significance. With missiles that could travel into space, the Soviet Union clearly had the ability to target missiles that could deliver nuclear weapons to the United States. The United States launched its first man-made satellite into space in 1958.

EFFECTS OF THE COLD WAR ON U.S. SECURITY

The tensions between the superpowers had serious effects on matters of internal security in the United States.

THE HOUSE UN-AMERICAN ACTIVITIES COMMITTEE

Following World War II, Americans were concerned about the Communist threat in the United States. President Truman ordered **Loyalty Review Boards** to be established. Under this order, over three million Americans were investigated. Participation or even past participation in an extremist group or organization was viewed as being un-American. On very little evidence, many people were accused of "un-American" acts. Congress conducted its own loyalty checks through the House Un-American Activities Committee. The Committee even questioned Hollywood actors, directors and writers about possible Communist leanings.

THE ROSENBERG TRIALS

As the Cold War grew more intense, Americans became ever more concerned with internal security. In 1950, **Julius and Ethel Rosenberg** were arrested for spying and charged with selling secret information about the atomic bomb to the Soviet Union. The Rosenbergs were found guilty and executed for espionage (spying). As in the Sacco and Vanzetti case of the 1920s, many Americans had serious doubts about the Rosenbergs' guilt.

THE McCARTHY HEARINGS

In 1950, a Senator from Wisconsin, **Joseph McCarthy**, rocked the nation by claiming that he knew the names of hundreds of Communists that had infiltrated the State Department. Although McCarthy was never able to prove any of his claims, his charges frightened Americans. **McCarthyism**, the method used by Senator McCarthy, has since become identified with the making of accusations without offering any evidence in support. Like the Red Scare in the 1920s, his allegations served to create fears of a possible Communist conspiracy in the United States.

KEY ITEMS TO REMEMBER

Cold War, Yalta Conference, Iron Curtain, policy of containment, Truman Doctrine, Marshall Plan, Berlin Airlift, NATO, Warsaw Pact, Korean War, massive retaliation, nuclear deterrent, Sputnik, Loyalty Review Boards, McCarthy hearings

PERSONALITIES OF THE PERIOD

ALBERT EINSTEIN (SCIENTIST)

Albert Einstein, a German physicist who immigrated to the United States, was responsible for helping to develop nuclear fission—splitting an atom to release enormous energy. Einstein's "theory of relativity" made him the most important physicist of modern times. In 1939 Einstein wrote to President Roosevelt warning that the Nazis were secretly working on an atomic bomb. As a result, Roosevelt began a "crash program" to develop an atomic bomb. The bomb that was developed was exploded over Hiroshima and Nagasaki, forcing the Japanese to surrender in World War II.

JACKIE ROBINSON (BASEBALL PLAYER)

Robinson broke the "color barrier" by becoming the first black person to play major league baseball. Before he was hired by the Brooklyn Dodgers in 1947, African Americans were limited to playing only in the Negro Leagues. Initially meeting with resistance and hostility, Robinson's talents and skills permitted him eventually to achieve acceptance. In 1962, he was voted into the Baseball Hall of Fame at Cooperstown.

DOUGLAS MacARTHUR (MILITARY LEADER)

Douglas MacArthur was the Allied Commander of U.S. forces in the Pacific region during World War II. When a Japanese invasion forced him from the Philippine islands, he vowed to return. Two years later he did return, driving the Japanese from the Philippine islands. MacArthur went on to supervise the occupation of Japan after the war and to serve as Commander of U.S. forces in the Korean Conflict. When he sought to broaden the war by dropping atomic bombs on China's industrial centers, President Truman dismissed him.

THE CONSTITUTION AT WORK

KEY LEGISLATION

NEUTRALITY ACT OF 1939

At the request of President Roosevelt, Congress passed the Neutrality Act of 1939, permitting the United States to sell war goods to any nation that paid cash and would carry it away on their own ships. The intent of the act was to assist Britain and France in their fight against German aggression, while permitting the United States to remain neutral.

LEND-LEASE ACTS (1941)

This act, requested by President Roosevelt, authorized the United States to lend or lease war materials to the British in their battle against Nazi Germany. Under the terms of this act, the United States gave over $50 million in aid to Allies fighting the Germans. This marked the first significant step towards U. S. involvement in World War II.

A KEY COURT CASE

KOREMATSU v. UNITED STATES (1944)

Background: Many Americans feared that Japanese-Americans would become involved in acts of espionage and sabotage on behalf of Japan. President Roosevelt issued an executive order requiring Japanese-Americans to move from their homes to inland relocation camps. Korematsu was convicted of continuing to remain in a restricted area. He believed his constitutional rights had been violated.

Decision/Significance: The Supreme Court, indicating that constitutional liberties may be limited in wartime, upheld the decision of the national government to deny Japanese-Americans their rights because of perceived military necessity. Almost 50 years later, Congress apologized and voted to pay compensation to the families involved.

SUMMARIZING YOUR UNDERSTANDING

Directions: How well did you understand what you have just read? Test yourself by answering the following questions.

MAJOR ITEMS TO REMEMBER

On 3 x 5 cards (as shown on pages 33-34), briefly define the following terms and concepts:

Neutrality	Nuremberg Trials	Containment
Pearl Harbor	Marshall Plan	Korean War
World War II	Truman Doctrine	McCarthyism
Holocaust	Cold War	*Korematsu v. U.S.*

PEACE IN PERIL: 1920-1941

Americans were quite disillusioned following their involvement in World War I. This fact was strongly reflected in their foreign policy attitudes. Summarize your understanding of this period in American history by answering the following questions:

- Trace the development of United States foreign policy in the period from 1920 to 1941.
- Why was the League of Nations unable to prevent World War II?
- What factors contributed to the start of World War II?

WORLD WAR II

United States involvement in World War II had a profound and lasting impact on the nation and its people. Summarize your understanding of the war by answering the following questions:

- Describe the plight of Japanese-Americans living on the West coast at the start of World War II.
- Why did President Truman decide to use the atomic bomb against Japan?
- Why were the leaders of Nazi Germany put on trial at the end of World War II?

THE COLD WAR PERIOD

The end of World War II saw a dramatic change in relations between the United States and its former ally, the Soviet Union. Summarize your understanding of this relationship by answering the following questions:

- Why were the Soviet Union and the United States distrustful of each other?
- How did American leaders hope to prevent Soviet expansion in Europe and Asia following World War II?
- In what ways was fear of the Soviet Union reflected in the internal affairs of the United States?

PERSONALITIES OF THE PERIOD

People often have an important influence on the political, economic or social life of their times. Summarize your understanding of this statement by completing a separate 3 x 5 index card (see page 34) for each of the following individuals: ***Douglas MacArthur***, ***Harry S. Truman***, ***Joseph McCarthy***, and ***Jackie Robinson***.

TESTING YOUR UNDERSTANDING

Directions: Test your understanding of this unit by answering the following questions. Circle the number preceding the word or expression that correctly answers the statement or question. Following the short answer questions, answer either the RCT-type or Regents essay questions.

SKILL BUILDER: INTERPRETING A CARTOON

Base your answers to questions 1 through 3 on the following cartoon and on your knowledge of social studies.

WESTERN EUROPE
EASTERN EUROPE

1 This cartoon is concerned with relations between the United States and
1 Africa
2 Cuba
3 the Soviet Union
4 South America

2 Which statement best expresses the main idea of the cartoon?
1 Peaceful coexistence will never work.
2 Europe is divided into two camps.
3 Barriers between Eastern and Western Europe are disappearing.
4 A nation's internal problems are best resolved by compromise.

3 The cartoonist would most likely support a U. S. foreign policy of
1 isolationism
2 containment
3 colonialism
4 imperialism

SKILL BUILDER: INTERPRETING SPEAKERS

Base your answers to questions 4 through 6 on the speakers' statements and on your knowledge of social studies. The speakers are discussing U.S. foreign policy.

Speaker A: The U.S. has always had difficulty maintaining a credible foreign policy in Latin America. We must do what is in the best interests of all nations in the Western Hemisphere. We must, however, avoid the mistakes and distrust created by our past dealings with Latin America.

Speaker B: We must contain the Communists in the eastern Mediterranean. They are threatening Greece and Turkey. If these nations fall to Communism, I fear our interests in the Middle East and other parts of the world will be endangered.

Speaker C: After World War II, Europe was in ruins. It is our responsibility to prevent the economic collapse of this vital area. We must work to achieve a healthy economy for Western Europe if we wish to prevent its fall to the Communists.

Speaker D: The U.S. must develop a foreign policy that will ease tensions with the Soviet Union. We must stop the foolish competition between us.

4 Which speaker would support Franklin D. Roosevelt's Good Neighbor Policy?
1 (A) 3 (C)
2 (B) 4 (D)

5 Which speaker was referring to the Truman Doctrine?
1 (A) 3 (C)
2 (B) 4 (D)

6 To which time period were the speakers probably referring?
1 1850-1890 3 1930-1970
2 1900-1930 4 1970-1990

SKILL BUILDER: INTERPRETING A MAP

Base your answers to questions 7 through 9 on the following map and on your knowledge of social studies.

ALLIED ADVANCES IN THE PACIFIC

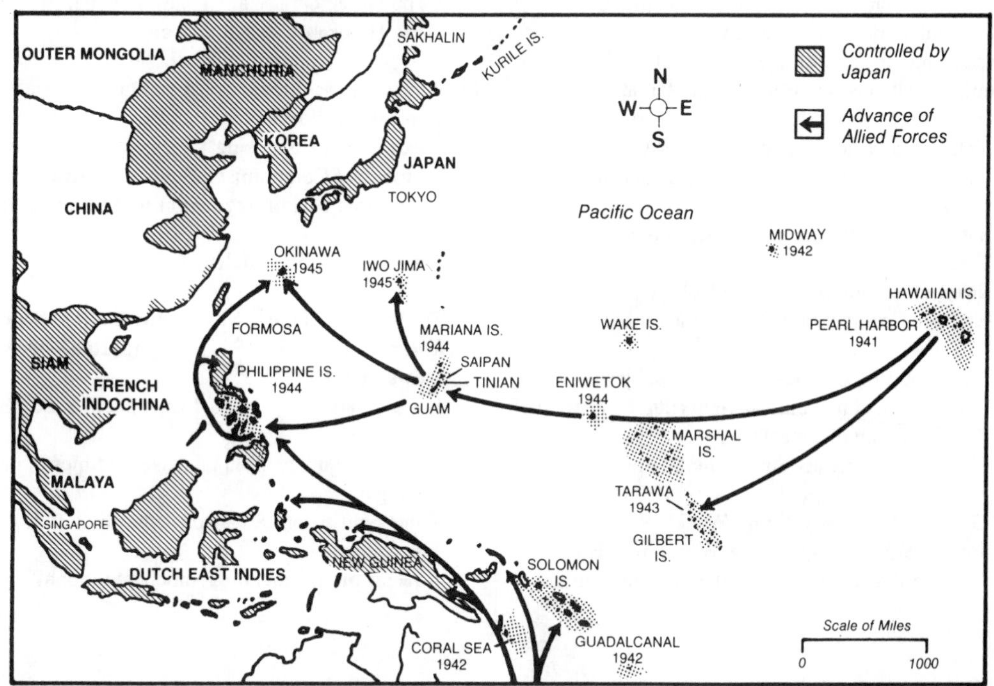
OUTER MONGOLIA
MANCHURIA
SAKHALIN
KURILE IS.
KOREA
JAPAN
TOKYO
CHINA
N
W
E
S
Controlled by Japan
Advance of Allied Forces
Pacific Ocean
MIDWAY 1942
OKINAWA 1945
IWO JIMA 1945
FORMOSA
MARIANA IS. 1944
SAIPAN
TINIAN
GUAM
WAKE IS.
HAWAIIAN IS.
PEARL HARBOR 1941
SIAM
FRENCH INDOCHINA
PHILIPPINE IS. 1944
ENIWETOK 1944
MARSHAL IS.
MALAYA
SINGAPORE
TARAWA 1943
GILBERT IS.
DUTCH EAST INDIES
NEW GUINEA
SOLOMON IS.
CORAL SEA 1942
GUADALCANAL 1942
Scale of Miles
0
1000

7 How far is the island of Iwo Jima from Japan?
1 approximately 1000 miles
2 approximately 3000 miles
3 approximately 750 miles
4 approximately 2500 miles

8 In which sequence were the islands taken by the allied forces?
1 Marshal Islands — Wake Island — Iwo Jima
2 Guam — Philippine Islands — Okinawa
3 Gilbert Island — Solomon Islands — Guadalcanal
4 Midway — Wake Island — Japan

9 Which pair of countries were members of the Allied Forces?
1 France and Germany
2 U.S. and Great Britain
3 Japan and Canada
4 Korea and China

---

10 Which was an example of appeasement?
1 The U.S. Neutrality Acts of 1935 and 1937
2 The German occupation of the Rhineland in 1936
3 The agreement to give the Sudetenland to Hitler in 1938
4 Germany's invasion of Poland in 1939

11 Which was a major goal of U.S. foreign policy in the years between W.W. I and W.W. II?
1 isolation from European military conflicts
2 the containment of Communism
3 active membership in the League of Nations
4 military alliance with France and Great Britain

12 Which was a basic cause of World War II?
1 tensions between the United States and the Soviet Union
2 nationalistic rivalries within the Austro-Hungarian Empire
3 the aggressiveness of Nazi ideology
4 European competition for colonies in Africa

13 Which group of U.S. residents was subjected to the greatest loss of constitutional rights during a period of U.S. military involvement?
1 Hispanic-Americans during the Spanish-American War
2 German-Americans during World War I
3 Japanese-Americans during World War II
4 Chinese-Americans during the Korean conflict

14 The bombing of Hiroshima and Nagasaki resulted in
1 the outbreak of World War II
2 United States entry into the war against Japan
3 the dawn of the atomic age
4 a decrease in the spread of Communism

15 Which was a major result of World War II?
1 Great Britain and France helped rebuild the Soviet Union
2 a power vacuum led to a Cold War between the U.S and Soviet Union
3 Germany gained control of Eastern Europe
4 Italy was divided into two countries

16 The term "Cold War" refers to
1 U.S. neutrality before World War II
2 Prime Minister Chamberlain's attempts to appease Hitler
3 the border dispute between the Soviet Union and Communist China
4 a period of hostility between the United States and Soviet Union

17 A term paper dealing with "McCarthyism," the Rosenberg trial, and loyalty oaths would probably be titled
1 The Cold War and U.S. Security
2 The Treatment of Japanese-Americans in the U.S.
3 The Nuremberg War Crimes Tribunal
4 The Holocaust and Its Effects

18 Which characterized world politics just before the outbreak of World Wars I and II?
1 existence of opposing alliances
2 growth of Communist influence in Western nations
3 increased acts of aggression by Western democracies
4 a decline in imperialism

19 The decision of the U.S. Supreme Court in the case of *Korematsu v. U.S.* (1944) is important because it shows that
1 the Court is always a firm upholder of personal liberty
2 racial prejudice often increases in times of national danger
3 the right to protest against the draft is limited in wartime
4 racial discrimination is unconstitutional

20 The principal defense used by most Nazis tried at Nuremberg after World War II was that they had been
1 following orders given by their superiors
2 serving the good of humanity
3 carrying out universal ethical principles
4 reflecting the popular will of their society

21 Which was a fundamental principle expressed by the WarCcrimes Tribunal at Nuremberg following World War II?
1 National leaders and their followers are responsible for their wartime actions.
2 National policies followed during wartime cannot be criticized after the war.
3 Individuals acting in the name of the state cannot be prosecuted for their actions.
4 No action is a crime if it happens during wartime.

22 Which is a valid conclusion based on a study of the Holocaust?
1 World opinion is effective in stopping genocide.
2 Savage acts can be committed by an advanced society.
3 People should not become involved in partisan politics.
4 Military commanders cannot be held responsible for acts committed during wartime.

23 U.S. aid to Western Europe after World War II was intended primarily to
1 create a tariff-free Common Market
2 provide the United States with badly needed raw materials
3 bring about political unity in Europe under U.S. leadership
4 rebuild the economies of European nations to strengthen them against Communism

24 Which U.S. military involvement was the result of a presidential order rather than a declaration of war by Congress?
1 War of 1812
2 Spanish-American War
3 World War I
4 Korean War

25 A study of the Red scare of the 1920s and the McCarthy Era of the 1950s would show that
1 large numbers of Soviets had infiltrated high levels of the Federal Government
2 fears of subversion can lead to the erosion of constitutional liberties
3 Communism gains influence in times of economic prosperity
4 loyalty oaths by government employees prevent espionage

RCT-TYPE ESSAYS

1 The relationship between the U.S. and the U.S.S. R. during the period of 1945 to 1965 has been called the "Cold War."

Part A

Define the term "Cold War:" ______________________________

Identify *two* examples of Cold War policies of *either* the United States or the Soviet Union.

1. ______________________________

2. ______________________________

Part B

In your Part B answer, you should use information you gave in Part A. However, you may also include different or additional information in your Part B answer.

Write an essay explaining why the relationship between the U.S. and the U.S.S.R. during the period of 1945 to 1965 has been called the "Cold War."

2 Wars are important events in history which can have different causes and lasting effects.

Wars

Spanish-American War	World War II
World War I	Korean War

Part A

Select *two* wars from the list. For *each* war selected, identify a cause of the war, and one of its results.

WARS	CAUSE	RESULT
______________	1. ______________	1. ______________
______________	2. ______________	2. ______________

Part B

In your Part B answer, you should use information you gave in Part A. However, you may also include different or additional information in your Part B answer.

Write an essay beginning with the following topic sentence:

Wars are important events in history which can have different causes and lasting effects.

3 Nations go to war for many different reasons.

Part A

List *two* factors or causes that played a role in the U. S. entry into W.W. II.

1.____

2.____

Part B

In your Part B answer, you should use information you gave in Part A. However, you may also include different or additional information in your Part B answer.

Write an essay discussing some of the reasons that led to the United States entry into World War II.

REGENTS-TYPE ESSAYS

1 The U. S. Department of State has developed goals to guide foreign policy decisions of the United States. Among these goals are:

- Deterring or resisting aggression.
- Bringing about a closer association of the nations in the world.
- Helping democratic nations recover from the devastation of war.
- Striving to end the arms race and reduce the risk of war.
- Assisting a genuine world community based on cooperation and law.
- Punishing war criminals guilty of crimes against humanity.

a Select *two* significant U.S. foreign policy decisions since 1898. Using specific information, explain how *each* decision supported one of the goals listed above.

b Discuss how *one* of the goals listed above has been a source of major controversy within the United States since 1898. (Provide specific information to support your answer.)

c Explain how *one* foreign policy goal listed above has interfered or conflicted with the foreign policy goal of another nation since 1898. Use specific information in your answer.

2 Americans were shocked by a series of events before and during World War II. The following headlines mention some of those events.

Headlines

Britain, France and Germany Reach Agreement at Munich, 1938
Congress Approves Lend Lease, 1941
Japan Attacks Pearl Harbor, 1941
Supreme Court Rules on Korematsu Case, 1944
Nazi Leaders Put on Trial at Nuremberg, 1945

Choose *three* of the headlines. For *each* one chosen:

- Describe the circumstances that led to the headline
- Discuss the major effects of the event

3 Important issues have often been created or intensified by U.S. participation in wars. Each war in the list below is paired with a specific issue created or intensified by U.S. participation in that war.

Wars / Issues

U.S. Civil War / Status of blacks in society
Spanish-American War / U.S. acquisition of an overseas empire
World War I / Growth of nativism
World War II / Changing roles of minorities and women

Choose *two* of the pairs from the list above. For *each* one chosen:

- Explain how the issue was an outgrowth of the war
- Discuss an impact of the issue on U.S. society

4 At various times, the United States has followed one or more of the foreign policies listed below.

Foreign Policies

Imperialism
Isolationism
Containment
Nonrecognition
Formation of military alliances
Reliance upon international organizations

Choose *three* of the policies listed above. For *each* one chosen, discuss a specific application of that policy by the United States. Include in your discussion one reason why the United States applied that policy and one result of the application of that policy.

PERFORMANCE-BASED TASKS

Setting: Important decisions that have long-lasting effects and international impact are often made by world leaders. One of the most far-ranging decisions was President Truman's decision to drop the atomic bomb on Japan. The war in the Pacific had been raging for nearly four years. Although Japanese leaders were working to arrange some kind of surrender, progress was moving at a slow pace. President Truman's military advisers informed him that an invasion of Japan could cost 1 million or more American casualties. This was the situation facing President Truman when he learned that American scientists had created a new weapon — the atomic bomb.

TRUMAN JUSTIFIES THE BOMBING (1945)

I set up a committee of top men and asked them to study with great care the implications the new weapon might have for us ... It was their recommendation that the bomb be used against the enemy as soon as it could be done. They recommended further that it should be used without specific warning, and against a target that would clearly show its devastating strength. I had realized, of course, that an atomic bomb explosion would inflict damage and casualties beyond imagination. The scientific advisers of the committee concluded that no technical demonstration they might propose, such as over a deserted island, would be likely to bring the war to an end. It had to be used against an enemy target. Also, Prime Minister Churchill of Great Britain told me, without hesitation, that he favored the use of the atomic bomb if it might aid to end the war.

I wanted to make sure the bomb would be used as a weapon of war, dropped on a military target. Hiroshima was selected because it was a key military target.

Below is a view opposing President Truman's decision to drop the bomb on Japan.

JAPAN'S REACTION TO THE BOMBING

How can a human being with any moral responsibility use a weapon of such destruction, which at a single stroke can annihilate so many people? This is not war, this is not even murder. This is a crime against humanity. This shows the Americans, who have always claimed to be the champions of fairness, are nothing but liars. It is ironic that in 1937, the United States protested against the Japanese bombing in China. But where its own actions were concerned, the U.S. government saw nothing inconsistent in committing the same crime on a vaster scale.

What greater atrocity can there be than the wiping out at one stroke of the population of a whole city — men, women and children. Hiroshima was a city populated by civilians, not a military target. The United States may claim that such an action was required because Japan refused to surrender unconditionally as the United States had demanded. But the question of unconditional surrender has not the slightest relevance to the question of whether it is justified to use a weapon of mass destruction.

General Directions: The decision to use the atomic bomb has been debated endlessly by historians, government leaders, and editorial writers. For example, some historians claim that the United States dropped the bomb to show its military power to the Soviet Union, rather than to defeat Japan. Using the two sources above and other sources you find through library research, write a 300-word editorial for the Daily Gazette, under the headline that appears below.

EDITORIAL PAGE OF THE DAILY GAZETTE

USING THE ATOM BOMB: THE RIGHT OR WRONG DECISION?

LOOKING AT OUR LEGAL SYSTEM

Americans are justly happy that they live under the rule of law— a system that protects the individual from random and impulsive acts by the government or from unfair treatment by neighbors. This section will briefly review how this system of laws works.

WHAT IS LAW?

A **law** is a rule that tells people to do something or not to do something. Usually there is a **penalty** or some other consequence for breaking the law. There are several law-making bodies in our legal system. The most familiar to you are legislatures—such as the U.S. Congress or your state legislature in Albany; your county or town may also have a legislative body with law-making authority. In addition to legislatures, agencies sometimes are allowed to make rules which have the binding powers of law. For example, the I.R.S. (an agency that collects federal income taxes) has the power to make rules with the force of law. The military can also set some legal standards for its members. Finally, executives can sometimes issue orders or regulations which have the force of law. A Presidential order, for example, has legal authority.

WHAT DO THE COURTS DO?

You have often heard that courts "apply" or "interpret" the law, but what does this mean? No general rule can ever be so precise that it can foresee all the particular situations that might arise. For this reason, we need courts to apply the laws to specific situations, to see whether or not particular circumstances fall within the rule.

> For example, a sign reads, "NO VEHICLES IN THE PARK." We are fairly certain this means no cars or trucks in the park, but what about bicycles? Suppose we decide bicycles are excluded because they are a danger to pedestrians. What about baby strollers? What about wheelchairs? Are they "vehicles" in the sense intended by the sign?

As you can see, courts must interpret the words of a law to decide exactly what the law means. Sometimes they might want to consider the purpose of the rule (or what was said about the rule when it was made) to determine whether it applies to a particular situation or not.

> A court might say that the purpose of the rule, "NO VEHICLES IN THE PARK," is to avoid danger to pedestrians. Since wheelchairs and baby strollers pose no danger to pedestrians, they are not "vehicles" in the sense intended by the rule.

Because we live under the "rule of law," we want each person in the same circumstance to be treated similarly. Courts look to the decision of other courts to see how to treat particular cases. In general, courts follow the example of other courts unless there is some strong reason not to do so. The opinions of judges therefore provide another source of law, known as **common law**. Rules made by judges still control many areas, unless a legislative body has chosen to replace these judge-made rules by passing its own specific laws.

TYPES OF CASES

Courts actually perform several functions. They enforce criminal laws by putting those accused of crimes on trial and sentencing them. They enforce other government regulations by penalizing offenders. They also decide **civil cases**—disputes between private parties which may involve family law (divorce or child custody), business law (contract disagreements) or personal injuries.

In enforcing laws, preventing crimes, and acting as a final arbiter, courts help to preserve social order. Parties may not agree with court decisions, but they generally agree with the procedures used by courts to arrive at these decisions, making unfavorable decisions more acceptable to the losing party.

In any court proceeding, each party has certain rights—to engage an attorney, to hear the opposing evidence, to present its case, and to appeal the decision. In criminal cases and some civil cases, the defendant also has the right to a trial by **jury**. Even in these cases, the trial judge plays an important role. He decides what evidence can be admitted into consideration, and instructs the jury on the applicable laws and what issues they are to decide. All these guarantees — known as "due process" rights — ensure that each side gets a fair opportunity to persuade the judge and jury that it is correct.

OUR FEDERAL SYSTEM OF JUSTICE

In our federal system we have two levels of government: the state governments and the federal government. We also have two levels of courts: the state courts and the federal courts.

ORGANIZATION OF THE UNITED STATES COURT SYSTEM

FEDERAL COURTS	NEW YORK STATE COURTS
U.S. Supreme Court	N.Y. State Court of Appeals
U.S. Courts of Appeal ("Circuit Courts")	N.Y. State Appellate Division of Supreme Court
U.S. District Courts (Trial Courts)	N.Y. State Trial Courts

Trial courts at the state level can hear most cases. The federal courts are more limited; they try cases which involve federal law or which are between citizens from different states. Trial courts generally hear each side present its case, including the examination of witnesses and the submission of evidence. These are the kinds of courts you frequently see on television. When the trial court gives its verdict, the parties have the right to appeal to an appellate court. The appellate court usually cannot overturn the decision on the basis of the facts, since it is generally limited to reviewing the issues of law presented by the case. Did the trial court apply the law correctly to the facts presented by the case? If the appellate court decides that the trial court misunderstood or misapplied the law, it can overturn the decision. Often the case is sent back to the trial court, to be retried on the basis of the instructions of the appellate court.

THE ROLE OF THE SUPREME COURT IN OUR LEGAL SYSTEM

The U.S. Supreme Court operates as the highest "Court of Appeals." It can hear appeals from both the federal courts and from the state courts (when these involve issues of federal law or the U.S. Constitution). Moreover, its power of review is totally left up to the Court's own judgment, since the nine Justices of the Supreme Court are free to pick which appeals they will decide. Being able to decide only a few hundred cases each year, they usually choose those cases of greatest political and legal significance.

The members of the Constitutional Convention debated whether the Supreme Court should be able to review the constitutionality of laws before they were passed. They decided that it was better if the Court heard cases after the laws were passed. They felt that people involved in an actual dispute would present their ideas more sharply, and that the facts surrounding a real dispute would allow the Justices to weigh the possible effects of their decision more soundly. Therefore, the Supreme Court only decides the constitutionality of a law *after* a dispute arises and is appealed to the Supreme Court.

The Supreme Court plays two roles. It determines how a law should be applied to a case. Many Supreme Court decisions do not concern the constitutionality of a law—only whether the law was applied as Congress intended. The Court's second role accounts for its importance in our political life; it can decide whether a law itself is unconstitutional. It can therefore reject a law it believes violates the Constitution, and the only way to override the Court's decision is then to pass an amendment to the Constitution.

AREAS OF GREATEST SUPREME COURT ACTIVITY

As you study American history, you may find the sheer number and complexity of Supreme Court decisions to be overwhelming. But in fact the Court has had its main impact in a limited number of areas. To help you review, the Supreme Court decisions you have studied are categorized below by subject area:

POWERS OF OUR FEDERAL GOVERNMENT

Case	*Importance of Decision*	*Page*
Judicial Review (Decisions establishing the power of the Court)		
Marbury v. Madison (1803)	Established the Supreme Court's power to declare laws unconstitutional.	89
Commerce Power (Decisions to regulate interstate commerce)		
Gibbons v. Ogden (1824)	Upheld Congress's right to regulate interstate commerce.	96
Wabash v. Illinois (1886)	Gave Congress power to regulate interstate railroad rates.	202
Schechter Poultry v. U.S. (1935)	Overruled earlier New Deal legislation.	259
The "necessary and proper" clause		
McCulloch v. Maryland (1819)	Expanded Congressional power on the basis of this clause.	95
Executive Privilege		
U.S. v. Nixon (1974)	Presidents cannot use executive privilege to obstruct criminal investigations.	338

INDIVIDUAL RIGHTS

Case	Importance of Decision	Page
Free Speech (First Amendment)		
Schenck v. U.S. (1919)	Upheld an individual's right to free speech unless it presented a "clear and present danger."	232
N.Y. Times v. U.S. (1971)	Upheld the right of *The New York Times* to print the "Pentagon Papers."	351
Hazelwood School District v. Kuhlmieier (1988)	School authorities can regulate school-sponsored student forms of expression, like newspapers.	380
Texas v. Johnson (1989)	Flag burning is a form of political protest that is a protected form of free speech expression.	381
Rights of Criminal Defendants (4th, 5th, 6th and 8th Amendments)		
Mapp v. Ohio (1961)	Evidence seized in an unreasonable search is not allowed to be used in a court of law.	317
Gideon v. Wainwright (1963)	A state must provide a free lawyer if a person is too poor to afford one.	317
Miranda v. Arizona (1966)	Persons in police custody must be informed of their constitutional rights.	317
Rights of Privacy (5th and 14th Amendments)		
Roe v. Wade (1973)	Upheld a woman's right to an abortion in the first three months of her pregnancy.	314
Planned Parenthood v. Casey (1992)	Reaffirmed Roe, but allowed states to make some special requirements to assure informed consent.	314
Cruzan v. Missouri (1990)	Upheld a person's "right to die" rather than to prolong life with new medical technology.	381
Equal Protection of the Laws (5th and 14th Amendments)		
Plessy v. Ferguson (1896)	As long as a state gives "separate but equal" facilities it is permitted to separate blacks from whites.	120
Korematsu v. U.S. (1944)	Upheld the relocation and detention of Japanese-Americans in W.W. II based on military necessity.	288
Brown v. Board of Education (1954)	Court overturned Plessy, saying segregated public schools were "inherently unequal."	303
Univ. of California v. Bakke (1978)	Upheld affirmative action programs, but ruled against setting specific racial quotas.	352
Richmond v. Croson (1989)	Limited affirmative action programs by ruling against certain state and local race-based plans.	381

CHAPTER 13

AMERICA IN UNCERTAIN TIMES

WE DEMAND
VOTING RIGHTS NOW!
UAW SAYS:
END SEGREGATED RULES IN PUBLIC SCHOOLS
WE MARCH FOR JOBS FOR ALL NOW!
WE DEMAND EQUAL RIGHTS NOW!

The 1950s and 1960s were an important time of social reform. The Civil Rights Movement sought equality for African Americans. The Women's Liberation Movement helped win greater civil and social rights for women. Presidents Kennedy and Johnson introduced programs to improve the conditions of the nation's poor. An activist Supreme Court enlarged the rights of citizens in the fields of civil rights, elected representation, and criminal procedure.

— TIMELINE OF KEY EVENTS —

1954	1961	1962	1963	1964	1966	1973
Brown v. Board of Education decision	Bay of Pigs invasion	First American in space Cuban Missile Crisis	March on Washington President Kennedy assassinated	Civil Rights Act passed Johnson announces "War on Poverty"	National Organization for Women formed	*Roe v. Wade* decision

THE EISENHOWER YEARS: 1953-1960

DOMESTIC POLICY UNDER EISENHOWER

The 1950s were essentially a period of recovery and economic growth. People whose lives had been disrupted by World War II settled down to work and have families. President Eisenhower continued to preserve the New Deal programs. The period was marked by several important developments.

THE "BABY BOOM:" A TIME OF DEMOGRAPHIC CHANGE

It was a time of extremely high birth rates, known as the "**baby boom**." The **G.I. Bill** for veterans made it easier to secure loans for houses. Developers built cheaper, mass-produced housing. As a result, home ownership increased by 50% between 1945 and 1960. The suburbs, areas outside of cities, grew much faster than the cities themselves. The movement of middle-income families from cities to suburbs led to a declining tax base and reduced services in the nation's inner cities.

ECONOMIC PROSPERITY

America came to dominate international trade and was the world's largest producer of goods. The demand for consumer goods reached all-time highs. Millions of automobiles and television sets were sold in the 1950s. The use of refrigerators and other appliances became widespread. The gross national product (GNP) doubled in the fifteen years from 1945 to 1960.

CONFORMITY

There was an emphasis on conformity in American society. Unusual ideas were regarded with suspicion and hostility. Fear of Communism strengthened the dislike of non-conformist attitudes. Television, popular music and magazines emphasized the values of family life, conformity and "togetherness."

FOREIGN POLICY UNDER EISENHOWER

Eisenhower gave control over foreign policy to his Secretary of State, **John Foster Dulles**. Dulles saw the struggle against Communism in moral terms—a fight of good against evil. Dulles believed in containing the spread of Communism by preventing the Soviets from gaining any additional territory. In 1957, Eisenhower announced he would send U.S. forces, if requested, to any Middle Eastern nation defending itself against Communism. This extension of the containment policy to include the Middle East came to be known as the **Eisenhower Doctrine**.

THE CIVIL RIGHTS MOVEMENT

The Civil Rights Movement of the 1950s and 1960s was a major turning point in American history, not only in achieving equal rights and better conditions for African Americans, but also in transforming American society. Women, other ethnic minorities, the disabled and the younger generation all followed the trail-blazing efforts of the leaders of the Civil Rights Movement in making America more open and pluralistic.

THE EMERGENCE OF THE CIVIL RIGHTS MOVEMENT

The United States had held out the promise of equality to African Americans at the end of the Civil War, but the aftermath of Reconstruction put an end to these hopes. Many Americans understood that the treatment of African Americans in some parts of the nation was highly inconsistent with the democratic ideals stated in the Declaration of Independence and the U.S. Constitution. The Civil Rights Movement did not suddenly spring up overnight in the mid-1960s. Some leaders had been fighting for equality since the 19th century. Events in the 1940s and 1950s, however, were especially important in the movement's later development.

THE TRUMAN YEARS (1945-1953)

World War II brought the United States into a struggle to defend democracy. More than one million African Americans joined the armed services during the war years, encouraging African Americans to raise their voices for greater rights and equality at home. In 1946, just after the conclusion of the war, President Truman appointed a special Committee on Civil Rights. Its report, issued in 1947, called for ending segregation in American life. In 1948, Truman ordered the desegregation of the armed forces and an end to discriminatory hiring practices in the federal government. In 1947, **Jackie Robinson** became the first African-American major league baseball player.

BROWN v. BOARD OF EDUCATION OF TOPEKA, KANSAS (1954)

The *Brown* decision was vital to the emergence of the Civil Rights Movement.

■ **Background**. Starting in the 1930s, black lawyers in the N.A.A.C.P. began challenging the doctrine of "separate-but-equal" facilities established in 1896 in ***Plessy v. Ferguson***. They began by challenging the exclusion of African Americans from white schools in the South. The climax of their efforts came in 1954. N.A.A.C.P. lawyers appealed a lower court ruling to the Supreme Court, arguing that Linda Brown, an African-American student, was denied admission to an all-white public school near her home. The N.A.A.C.P. alleged that segregated public schools denied African-American children the "equal protection" of the law that was due to them under the Fourteenth Amendment. In addition, the N.A.A.C.P. argued that the education received by African-American students was inherently (by its very nature) inferior—since it gave them a psychological message that they were not good enough to be educated with white students.

■ **The Decision.** Chief Justice **Earl Warren** wrote the unanimous decision in *Brown*, declaring that segregation in public schools was unconstitutional. "Separate-but-equal," Warren wrote, has no place in the field of public education: "Separate educational facilities are inherently unequal." Enforcement of this decision was left to the lower federal courts, which were to see that local school districts complied with the desegregation order. Although the court ruled that this should be done "with all due deliberate speed," it took many years before the decision was fully complied with.

■ **Significance.** The case marked the end of legal segregation in public schools and an important turning point in the Civil Rights Movement. The decision showed that the Supreme Court was now willing to become involved in controversial social issues. In addition, the decision illustrated how changing social, political and economic conditions can often affect the Court.

MILESTONES OF THE CIVIL RIGHTS MOVEMENT

A young minister, **Dr. Martin Luther King, Jr.**, emerged in the late 1950s as the main organizer and leader of the Civil Rights Movement. King, like Thoreau and Gandhi, believed in the philosophy of **non-violence**: passive resistance to unjust laws could eventually change the attitude of the oppressor without the use of force. King carried out this resistance through **civil disobedience**: if a government passed an unjust law, people would oppose it with non-violent techniques such as boycotts, picketing, sit-ins and demonstrations.

THE MONTGOMERY BUS BOYCOTT (1955-1956)

The system of segregation in Southern states prevented African Americans from sharing restaurants, water fountains or seats on buses with whites. King and other African-American leaders focused their attention on stopping segregation on buses in Montgomery, Alabama. When **Rosa Parks**, a seamstress, was arrested for refusing to give up her seat to a white passenger, local black leaders used the occasion to begin a 13-month boycott of Montgomery's public buses. King was made the leader of the boycott. African Americans organized car pools and cabs to take boycotters to work. The boycott showed that African Americans could unite successfully to oppose segregation.

LITTLE ROCK, ARKANSAS (1957)

Southern states deliberately delayed putting the *Brown* decision into effect. When the governor of Arkansas was unable to provide protection to nine black students seeking to attend an all-white high school in Little Rock, President Eisenhower sent in federal troops to provide that protection. The following year, the governor closed the school and asked for a postponement of the integration plan. The Supreme Court ruled against any delays and forced the reopening of the school.

SIT-INS (1960) and FREEDOM RIDES (1961)

Sit-ins began when African-American students sat at a "Whites Only" lunch counter in the South. The tactic was soon copied by students who supported the Civil Rights Movement throughout the South. According to federal law, segregated seating and facilities for interstate passengers were unconstitutional. **Freedom Rides**, consisting of interracial groups riding buses through the South, were used to help provoke confrontations so that the federal government would be forced to intervene. Freedom Riders often faced violence and death from those who opposed integration.

KING'S LETTER FROM A BIRMINGHAM JAIL (1963)

King and other leaders focused their activities on achieving desegregation in Birmingham, Alabama. When King led a march into the city, he was arrested. From jail he wrote a "Letter From a Birmingham Jail" explaining why he felt it was necessary to build up tension to achieve equal rights, and why African Americans could no longer wait to obtain their constitutional rights. Television showed the rest of the nation the brutal tactics used by the Birmingham police in breaking up marches and protests. As a result of the protests, downtown stores agreed to desegregate lunch counters and hire African-American employees.

THE MARCH ON WASHINGTON (1963)

Martin Luther King, Jr. and other civil rights leaders called for a March on Washington in support of a civil rights bill introduced into Congress by President Kennedy. More than a quarter of a million people took part in the march. King gave his most famous speech, "I Have a Dream," in which he said he looked forward to the day when Americans of all colors would live together peacefully. The following year, King was awarded the Nobel Peace Prize.

THE CIVIL RIGHTS ACT OF 1964

This important act, based on the power of the federal government to regulate interstate commerce, attempted to end discrimination based on race, color, religion or ethnic origin. The Supreme Court later upheld the constitutionality of the act, which:

- Prohibited discrimination in hotels, restaurants, trade unions, and places of employment doing business with the federal government or engaged in interstate commerce. It also prohibited discrimination in employment on the basis of sex, and threatened to cut off federal aid to school districts with segregated schools.

- Broadened the federal government's power to register voters, and established the **Equal Employment Opportunity Commission** to enforce its provisions regarding employers and trade unions.

THE STRUGGLE TO ACHIEVE VOTING RIGHTS

Earlier civil rights acts (1957 and 1960) had given federal courts the power to register black voters in the South. Despite these measures, most African Americans were still denied the right to vote by poll taxes, literacy tests, and fear. Civil rights organizations tried to register black voters in the South, without much success. In 1964, the civil rights leaders turned their full energies to registering black voters and encouraging them to vote. They saw the vote as an important vehicle of political, economic and social change.

- **Twenty-fourth Amendment (1964)**. This amendment eliminated poll taxes in federal elections.

- **Selma March**. In 1965, Martin Luther King went to Selma, Alabama, to organize a protest march demanding the vote for African Americans. When the demonstrators were attacked, President Johnson reacted by announcing that he would introduce a Voting Rights Bill.

- **The Voting Rights Act of 1965**. This act ended all poll taxes and suspended literacy tests where these were used to prevent African Americans from voting. The act led to a substantial increase in the number of black voters, and eventually to African Americans filling many political offices.

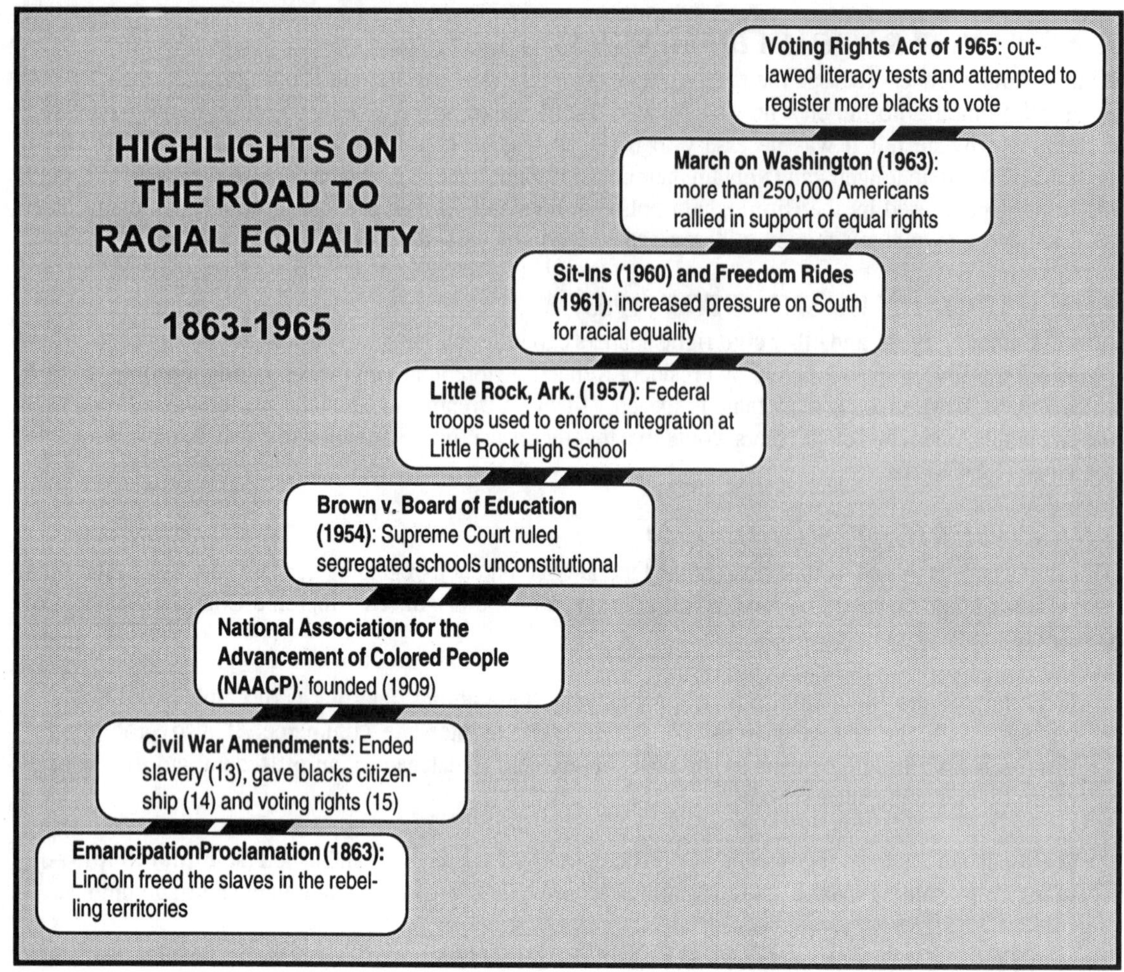
HIGHLIGHTS ON THE ROAD TO RACIAL EQUALITY
1863-1965
Voting Rights Act of 1965: outlawed literacy tests and attempted to register more blacks to vote
March on Washington (1963): more than 250,000 Americans rallied in support of equal rights
Sit-Ins (1960) and Freedom Rides (1961): increased pressure on South for racial equality
Little Rock, Ark. (1957): Federal troops used to enforce integration at Little Rock High School
Brown v. Board of Education (1954): Supreme Court ruled segregated schools unconstitutional
National Association for the Advancement of Colored People (NAACP): founded (1909)
Civil War Amendments: Ended slavery (13), gave blacks citizenship (14) and voting rights (15)
EmancipationProclamation (1863): Lincoln freed the slaves in the rebelling territories

AFFIRMATIVE ACTION (1965)

In 1965, President Johnson signed an executive order requiring employers and institutions with federal contracts to raise the number of minority and female employees to correct past imbalances. Affirmative action programs have increased minority representation in colleges and in the professions. However, critics question the continuation of some affirmative action programs, calling them "reverse discrimination."

INCREASING AFRICAN-AMERICAN MILITANCY

Despite the achievements of the Civil Rights Movement, many African Americans, especially the young, believed changes were not coming fast enough. They disagreed with Dr. King's policy of cooperation with sympathetic whites and his program of non-violence.

THE GHETTOS ERUPT (1965-1968)

In the North, African Americans faced segregation almost as much as in the South, except that Northern segregation was the product of residential living patterns rather than the outcome of state laws. Black frustration finally erupted in a series of riots that shook Northern cities three summers in a row. The climax to these urban riots occurred in the spring of 1968, when Martin Luther King was assassinated in Tennesee. In cities across the nation, rioters smashed windows, overturned cars and started fires. The **Kerner Commission**, appointed to investigate the causes of the urban unrest, reported that the lack of job opportunities for African Americans, urban poverty and white racism were the chief factors behind the riots.

THE BLACK POWER MOVEMENT

The new militants believed in **Black Power**—that blacks should use their votes to win concessions from government, control their own communities, patronize their own businesses, and free themselves from the economic, cultural and political domination of whites.

- **The Search For A New Identity**. Many of the militants were influenced by the achievements of the nations of Africa in obtaining independence from their former colonial rulers. These African-American intellectuals began to search for the roots of their own cultural identify. They did not simply want to imitate whites or be absorbed into mainstream American culture. They felt African Americans should be proud and that "Black is beautiful."

- **Malcolm X** questioned Dr. King's ideas of non-violent resistance. Malcolm X thought that African Americans should meet violence with violence and could not depend on the inner goodness of other people. A follower of Elijah Muhammad, he broke with the Black Muslims in the 1960's and formed his own organization. As an early leader in the **Black Power Movement**, he believed African Americans should control their own businesses, schools and communities. Malcolm X was assassinated in 1965.

- **New Groups Emerge.** Traditional groups, such as the Southern Christian Leadership Conference, the N.A.A.C.P., the Urban League and the Congress of Racial Equality favored non-violent methods and cooperation with sympathetic whites. However, new groups now emerged which challenged the leadership of these traditional African-American organizations. The **Student Non-Violent Coordinating Committee**, which once recruited both black and white members, began discouraging white participation. The **Black Muslims** believed African Americans should form their own state and adopt Islam as their religion. The **Black Panthers** demanded that the U.S. government pay "reparations" to blacks.

KEY ITEMS TO REMEMBER

N.A.A.C.P., desegregation, *Plessy v. Ferguson, Brown v. Board of Education,* Sit-ins, Freedom Rides, "Letter From a Birmingham Jail," March On Washington, Twenty-Fourth Amendment, Civil Rights Act of 1964, Voting Rights Act, affirmative action, Black Power.

THE KENNEDY PRESIDENCY: 1961-1963

In 1960, a young New England senator was elected president. John F. Kennedy set a new tone for the presidency in his inaugural address, when he told Americans that the "torch of government" was being passed to "a new generation." He pledged that Americans would "pay any price, bear any burden, meet any hardship, [and] support any friend" in defense of freedom. He challenged Americans to "ask not what your country can do for you" but "what you can do for your country." His speech ignited the spirit of American idealism.

DOMESTIC POLICY UNDER KENNEDY

In sharp contrast to the complacency of government in the Eisenhower years, President Kennedy's **New Frontier** symbolized the vigor of youth. His administration was marked by several important developments:

THE SPACE PROGRAM

To counter the Soviet space program, Kennedy announced that the United States would place a man on the moon by the end of the decade. During Kennedy's administration, the first American traveled in space: **John Glenn** became the first American to orbit the earth in 1962.

STALLED DOMESTIC PROGRAMS

Kennedy proposed a tax cut to stimulate the economy, the creation of a new Department of Urban Affairs, the creation of Medicare, and an increase in federal aid to education. None of these measures passed under Kennedy, but many were later passed by Congress as part of President Johnson's "Great Society" program.

A CULTURAL REAWAKENING

The President and Mrs. Kennedy brought an elegant style and an appreciation of culture to the White House. They invited as honored guests poets, painters, writers and musicians from all ethnic groups, to celebrate the nation's rich cultural heritage.

FOREIGN POLICY UNDER KENNEDY

Kennedy came into office at the height of the **Cold War** (the struggle between the U. S. and the Communist world). He believed that Eisenhower had relied too much on "massive retaliation." Kennedy wanted the United States to offer a "**flexible response**"—to reply firmly to Communist aggression at whatever level it appeared. Kennedy increased military spending and built up the armed services.

CONTAINMENT IN LATIN AMERICA

In 1959, Fidel Castro and his guerillas overthrew the dictator ruling Cuba. Castro promised Cuba a democracy, but established a Communist dictatorship. One of Kennedy's greatest problems was Communism in Cuba, only 90 miles from Florida. He feared the spread of Communism from Cuba to other Latin American countries.

- **The Bay of Pigs Invasion.** In 1961, Cuban exiles, armed and trained by the United States, invaded Cuba at the Bay of Pigs. However, President Kennedy refused to give the rebels air support during the invasion, and they were defeated by Castro's army. This was a major foreign policy failure for the Kennedy Administration.

- **The Alliance for Progress (1961).** To meet the Cuban challenge, Kennedy created the Alliance for Progress, a program offering grants and loans to Latin American nations to promote economic progress, increased trade and land reform.

- **The Cuban Missile Crisis.** In 1962, the United States discovered that Cuba was secretly building bases for Soviet missiles. Many feared that the U. S. might be subject to a nuclear attack. Kennedy imposed a naval blockade on Cuba and threatened to invade if the missiles were not withdrawn. The world was on the brink of nuclear war. Soviet Premier Krushchev agreed to withdraw the missiles in return for a pledge that the United States would not invade Cuba. The Cuban Missile Crisis was seen as Kennedy's greatest foreign policy success.

THE PEACE CORPS

Kennedy created the Peace Corps, a program in which American volunteers went abroad to developing countries in Africa, Asia and Latin America to apply and communicate their skills. The program continues to operate today.

THE JOHNSON YEARS: 1963-1968

The nation was stunned when President Kennedy was assassinated by Lee Harvey Oswald in November 1963 in Dallas, Texas. Vice-President Lyndon Johnson became president.

DOMESTIC POLICY UNDER JOHNSON

Soon after taking over the presidency in 1963, Johnson put forth a group of far-reaching proposals for social legislation.

THE GREAT SOCIETY

Johnson's aim was to turn the United States into a "Great Society" by opening up opportunities for all Americans and improving their quality of life. His "Great Society" was the most ambitious program of social reform sponsored by any president since Roosevelt's New Deal. When Johnson was elected president in his own right in 1964, he sponsored additional legislation extending his Great Society program:

■ **Civil Rights Act.** Johnson convinced Congress to pass the most comprehensive program of civil rights legislation since Reconstruction. This included the **Civil Rights Acts of 1964**, the **Twenty-Fourth Amendment** abolishing poll taxes, and the **Voting Rights Act of 1965**. The previous section on the Civil Rights Movement contains a fuller discussion of these acts.

■ **Tax Cut.** A reduction of $11 billion in personal and corporate income taxes, originally proposed by Kennedy, was pushed through Congress by Johnson. The purpose of the tax cut was to stimulate the economy by placing more money in the hands of investors and consumers.

■ **The "War on Poverty."** Johnson called for a "war on poverty." The **Economic Opportunity Act** (1964) created a new government office to administer the programs established by the act. These included the **Job Corps**, a program to train underprivileged youths, and **VISTA** (Volunteers in Service to America), a domestic "Peace Corps" of volunteers performing services in depressed areas.

■ **Federal Aid to Education.** The Elementary and Secondary Education Act of 1965 gave over $1 billion to local school districts. The Higher Education Act provided funds for scholarships and created a National Teacher Corps. "Head Start" provided money to prepare underprivileged youngsters for elementary school. All federal aid was made conditional on the desegregation of local school districts.

■ **Aid to Cities.** The Housing and Urban Development Act created a cabinet post in charge of programs aimed at helping the nation's cities. Billions in aid were spent on urban planning, slum clearance, housing assistance for the poor, and the reconstruction of buildings.

■ **Medicare Act of 1965.** The Social Security program was expanded to provide medical care, hospital insurance and post-hospital nursing for persons over the age of 65.

THE GREAT SOCIETY FALLS VICTIM TO THE VIETNAM WAR

Despite the massive federal money spent on the Great Society, many Americans remained in poverty. Meanwhile, Johnson's involvement in the Vietnam War became increasingly costly, forcing him to withdraw funding from Great Society programs. Because of his failure to achieve victory in Vietnam, Johnson finally announced he would not seek another term as president in 1968. Nevertheless, the passage of civil rights legislation and Medicare have been a lasting achievement of the Johnson era.

FOREIGN POLICY UNDER JOHNSON

The major foreign policy event of the Johnson administration was the escalation of American involvement in Vietnam. This topic is discussed fully in Chapter 14.

KEY ITEMS TO REMEMBER

New Frontier, Peace Corps, Cuban Missile Crisis, Great Society, War on Poverty, Medicare

THE YOUTH CULTURE OF THE SIXTIES

THE ROOTS OF THE SIXTIES CULTURE

Because of the post-war "baby boom," a large number of Americans reached their twenties in the 1960s and early 1970s. This generation was influenced by the prosperity of the 1950s, the new permissive methods of child care introduced by experts like **Dr. Benjamin Spock**, and the wide exposure to the world that came from watching television. In their adolescence, the baby boomers were also exposed to the idealism of the Kennedy and early Johnson years.

A NEW REBELLIOUSNESS

Unlike the college students of the 1950s, the baby boomers had high expectations and an open, questioning attitude. They objected to the social rules of their elders. This attitude eventually led to a spirit of rebelliousness. The baby boomers, as they came of age, objected to the bureaucracy and impersonal, machine-like lifestyle of corporate America. They challenged the materialism of those in charge of American society, whom they called the "Establishment." They were shocked at the Establishment's indifference to the poverty, pollution and other problems existing in America and throughout the world.

NEW FORMS OF RECREATION

The new "**Youth Culture**" was especially influenced by rock music. The Beatles from England introduced new fashions and long hair for males as early as 1963. Long hair became a symbol of the new culture. The Youth Culture was equally affected by greater sexual freedom, aided by the development of oral contraceptives ("the pill"), and by the availability of drugs like marijuana and LSD, a hallucinogen. They adopted new fashions, like bell-bottomed trousers, beads and colorful clothing to set themselves apart from their elders and more traditional lifestyles. Some of the so-called **hippies** dropped out of mainstream America altogether and went to live on self-sufficient communes.

THE ANTI-WAR MOVEMENT

Many youths were intensely political. In the late 1960s, their concerns focused on the increasing American involvement in Vietnam. In 1968, young people began to protest the nation's involvement in the war. In 1969, several students were killed by National Guardsmen during anti-war demonstrations at Kent State. In 1970, most university campuses were closed by students protesting the American invasion of Cambodia. Protests continued until the United States withdrew from the war in 1973.

KEY ITEMS TO REMEMBER

The Establishment, youth culture, hippies

THE WOMEN'S LIBERATION MOVEMENT

One of the most important events of the 1960s was the birth of the Women's Liberation movement.

WOMEN FROM THE 1940s TO THE 1960s

After achieving the right to vote with the passage of the 19th Amendment in 1920, women continued to make gradual progress. During World War II, millions of women filled jobs left by the departure of men, as they had in World War I. Women were recruited for the first time in the armed services for non-combatant duty. Nevertheless, women still earned less than men, and were expected to give up their jobs when the men returned. The post-war years seemed to indicate that women's progress had reached its peak. Movies, television and popular magazines all tended to reinforce the image of a woman as a mother and housewife.

THE WOMEN'S LIBERATION MOVEMENT IS BORN

Many women were dissatisfied with their roles as housewives. They wanted freedom to express themselves in careers and to earn money as men did. Unlike the earlier women's rights movement, which had focused its efforts primarily on securing suffrage (voting rights) for women, the Women's Liberation Movement of the 1960s was directed mainly at achieving economic and social equality. There were several reasons why the movement suddenly emerged at this time.

■ **Influence of the Civil Rights Movement**. Many of the leaders of the Women's Liberation Movement had been activists in the Civil Rights Movement. They adopted the same techniques to promote women's rights, such as organizations, lobbying, demonstrations, boycotts, and strikes.

■ **Dynamic Leadership**. Highly-educated and talented women provided dynamic leadership. In 1963, **Betty Friedan's** book *The Feminine Mystique* denied that all women were happy and content leading lives as mothers and housewives. She pointed out that women were as capable as men and should be permitted to compete for the same jobs and careers. In 1966, Friedan and others formed the **National Organization of Women (NOW)**, which became the chief voice of the Women's Movement. Later, **Gloria Steinem** founded a monthly magazine, *Ms.*, which was devoted to women's issues and concerns. Women social scientists like **Margaret Mead** and **Simone de Beauvoir** argued that women's low status was due to sociological factors rather than biological necessity.

■ **Contraception and the "Sexual Revolution."** Women like **Margaret Sanger**, the founder of the birth control movement in the U. S., had long sought to publicize the facts about contraception. In 1942 she had founded a group that eventually became the Planned Parenthood Foundation. Freudian psychology made people more open about their sexual feelings. Sex education courses began to be taught in the schools. Birth control pills protected women from pregnancy. In this new atmosphere, the Women's Movement objected to women being treated as "sex objects" instead of full human beings.

RESULTS OF THE WOMEN'S LIBERATION MOVEMENT

The goals of the Women's Liberation Movement were greater freedom and a fuller social and economic life.

■ **Education.** As a result of the Equal Access To Education Act (1972), universities receiving federal support cannot discriminate on the basis of sex in admissions. Affirmative action programs promoted the hiring of women. Finally, fairer treatment of women was achieved in admissions to military academies, law and medical schools and graduate business schools.

■ **Employment.** The Women's Movement sought to establish equal employment opportunities. Women wanted to have positions of responsibility. They wanted laws requiring companies to grant maternity leave and federal aid for child-care centers. They have been partially successful. The **"Equal Pay" Act (1963)** requires companies to pay the same wages to men and women for the same work. The **Civil Rights Act (1964)** bans discrimination in hiring on the basis of sex. However, critics charge that most women are still not receiving equal pay for equal work. Jobs with large numbers of women employees—such as nursing—offer lower pay than jobs filled by men with equivalent skills.

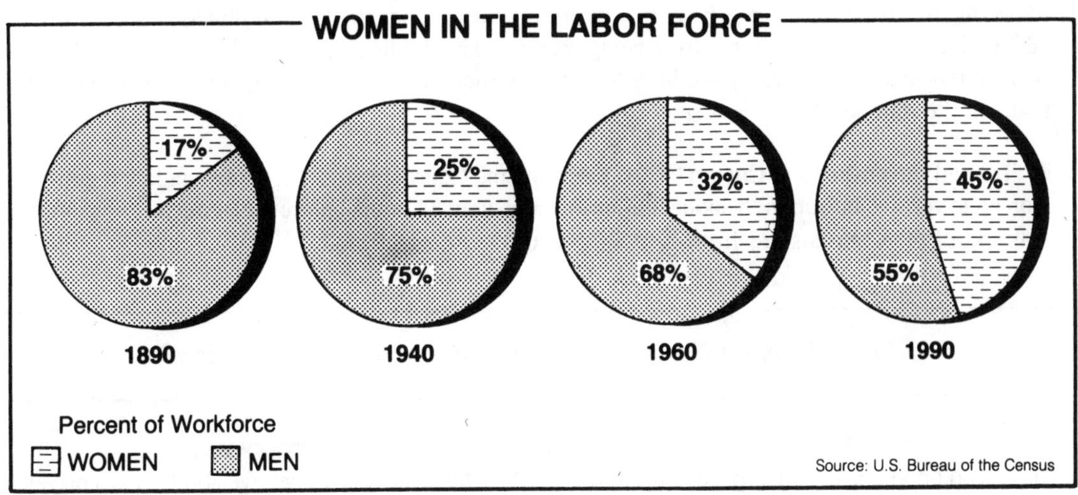
WOMEN IN THE LABOR FORCE
17%
83%
1890
25%
75%
1940
32%
68%
1960
45%
55%
1990
Percent of Workforce
WOMEN
MEN
Source: U.S. Bureau of the Census

■ **New Popular Attitudes.** Feminists argued that achieving liberation from traditional roles and inferior status could only be done by changing people's attitudes. They objected to beauty contests and introduced "Ms." to replace Miss and Mrs. (which reveal a woman's marital status). They urged that men and women share domestic chores. They fought against sexist language (police*man*, fire*man*), and the use of women as sex objects in advertising. Feminists opposed sex discrimination in textbooks that ignored women's contributions and experiences. They lobbied for more research on women's diseases like ovarian and breast cancer and on problems like rape and domestic violence.

THE EQUAL RIGHTS AMENDMENT FAILS

One failure of the Women's Liberation Movement was its inability to secure the passage of the Equal Rights Amendment (ERA), a constitutional amendment guaranteeing women equal rights with men. Opponents of the amendment argued that women already had equal rights. Others feared that passage of the ERA would require women to be eligible for the draft (compulsory military service). Although passed by Congress in 1972, the amendment fell short of the required number of states needed for ratification.

THE ABORTION ISSUE

Abortion is the deliberate termination of an unwanted pregnancy. In the 1960s and 1970s, many states still had laws banning abortions. Feminists believed that women should have the right to decide whether or not to have an abortion. Pro-choice rights became a rallying cry of the Women's Movement. The Supreme Court then became involved in this highly controversial issue:

- **Roe v. Wade (1973).** Jane Roe (an assumed name) tried to terminate her pregnancy. She was arrested for violating a state law making abortion a crime unless the pregnant woman's life was endangered. The Court weighed the interests of the mother and the fetus, and ruled that a woman's constitutional right to privacy guaranteed her the unrestricted right to an abortion in the first three months of pregnancy and restricted rights to abort in the second three months. In the last three months, the interests of the fetus prevailed over the rights of the mother. This ruling by the Supreme Court overturned state laws prohibiting all abortions in the first three months of pregnancy.

- **Webster v. Reproductive Health Services (1989).** The Supreme Court upheld a Missouri law restricting the use of state funds by clinics performing abortions. The law prohibited abortions from taking place at public facilities or from being performed by public employees. The Court upheld the right of the state to pass restrictive laws limiting abortion. The ruling reopened the entire abortion issue on the state level.

- **Planned Parenthood v. Casey (1992).** The Supreme Court upheld a Pennsylvania law requiring women to receive information about childbirth and to wait 24 hours before receiving an abortion. A majority of the Court also reaffirmed its support of the *Roe* decision.

Should Women Be Denied the Right To Have an Abortion?

POINT	COUNTERPOINT
Those who oppose abortion argue that each life is precious. They believe that life begins at conception, that abortion is murder, and that to abort a fetus is to put it through a painful death. Abortion opponents believe that only God should determine who lives and who dies, and that the state has an obligation to protect the fetus. If a woman is uninterested is protecting her fetus, then the state should take up the cause of the unborn.	Pro-choice advocates believe abortion is a private matter, best left to a woman and her doctor. They argue that it is unclear at what point human life begins, and object to the religious beliefs of one group being imposed on others. They believe that women should have the right to control what happens to their own bodies, and that this is a basic human right. If abortions are banned, they argue, this will only prevent safe, legal abortions and increase dangerous "back alley" abortions.

KEY ITEMS TO REMEMBER

NOW, ERA Amendment, abortion, *Roe v. Wade*, Right-to-Life, Pro-Choice

PERSONALITIES OF THE PERIOD

RACHEL CARSON (ENVIRONMENTALIST)

Rachel Carson was a leader in the movement to educate Americans about the dangers of pesticides. Her book, *Silent Spring*, written in 1962, sounded the alarm for Americans to wake up to the destruction of plant and animal life caused by using insecticides and pesticides. She warned that the time would come when wildlife would die out and the food supply would become too contaminated for human use.

RALPH NADER (CONSUMER ADVOCATE)

Ralph Nader's book *Unsafe At Any Speed* exposed the failure of the auto industry to provide safe cars. He attacked the automakers for being more concerned with profits than in creating a safe car. His book prompted Congress to pass legislation that made cars less dangerous. Nader continues his muckraking efforts on behalf of consumers in many other areas.

CESAR CHAVEZ (UNION ORGANIZER)

Cesar Chavez, a union organizer for Mexican-American farm workers in California, led a non-violent strike against the California grape growers. His 1965 strike and boycott of California grapes won national attention and support. His actions succeeded in obtaining better working conditions and higher pay for his migrant workers. He also helped to organize other groups, such as lettuce pickers.

JONAS SALK AND ALBERT SABIN (SCIENTISTS)

Salk and Sabin were scientists who developed the vaccines to prevent the spread of the crippling disease of polio. Salk injected dead polio viruses into his patients to help them develop an immunity. Sabin found it was more effective to use a live-virus in a vaccine that could be taken orally. Their efforts all but eliminated polio in the 1950s. Awarded a medal for Distinguished Civilian Achievement by Congress, Salk continues to work as a microbiologist, seeking a cure for AIDS.

THURGOOD MARSHALL (FORMER SUPREME COURT JUSTICE)

Thurgood Marshall, appointed by President Johnson in 1967, was the first African American to sit on the Supreme Court. As a lawyer for the N.A.A.C.P. Defense Fund, which he helped to found, Marshall had argued the *Brown v. Board of Education* case before the Supreme Court in 1954. His later appointment to the Court capped a glorious legal career that ended when he retired in 1991 due to ill health.

S.I. HAYAKAWA (SENATOR)

S.I. Hayakawa, a Japanese-American, was a noted scholar and expert on the English language, and served as a college president. He was also elected by the voters of California to the U. S. Senate. Hayakawa was active in the fight to have English adopted as the official language of the United States.

For other personalities of this period, see Louis Sullivan, Grandma Moses and Betty Friedan in "Looking at the Arts."

THE CONSTITUTION AT WORK

KEY AMENDMENTS

TWENTY-FIFTH AMENDMENT (1967)

The original Constitution did not provide for a procedure to be followed when a president became disabled and could not function. After President Kennedy's assassination, the 25th Amendment was ratified. It called for the vice-president to assume the presidency after the death or resignation of the president. Also, procedures were established for determining when a president was too disabled to continue discharging the duties of the presidency.

KEY LEGISLATION

CIVIL RIGHTS ACT OF 1964 and CIVIL RIGHTS ACT OF 1968

One of the most significant achievements of Johnson's Great Society program was the Civil Rights Act of 1964. The act forbade discrimination in voting, employment and public accommodations. In addition, it established an Equal Employment Opportunity Commission to ensure fair treatment for all minorities. The Civil Rights Act of 1968 extended the prohibition on racial discrimination to include the sale or rental of housing.

MEDICARE ACT OF 1965

The Social Security program was expanded to provide medical care, hospital insurance and post-hospital nursing for persons over the age of 65.

KEY COURT CASES

— THE WARREN COURT —

During the Kennedy and Johnson years, the Supreme Court under Chief Justice Earl Warren, became a strong supporter of civil rights. In its interpretations of the Constitution, the Warren Court defended what it saw as the rights of individuals. The Court became a major instrument of social change, protecting rights that other institutions seemed too weak to defend.

Some critics opposed this judicial activism, arguing that the Court should leave these questions to the elected branches of government. Other critics felt that the Warren Court went too far in creating rights—especially increasing the rights of the accused, which made it difficult for police to protect society. However, the Warren Court acted out of a sense of responsibility to protect individual rights which it believed arose out of the Constitution. When other branches failed to protect those rights, it believed it was the duty of the

Supreme Court to intervene as soon as an appropriate case came into its jurisdiction. The most important example of this was *Brown v. Board of Education*, discussed earlier in this chapter. Some of the other important cases of the Warren Court are summarized here:

MAPP v. OHIO (1961)

Background: Dollree Mapp was suspected of hiding gambling equipment in her home. When the police arrived to search her house, Ms. Mapp refused to admit them. When she tried to prevent the police from entering, Ms. Mapp was arrested. A search turned up obscene materials prohibited by an Ohio law. Ms. Mapp believed her Fourth Amendment rights had been violated.

Decision/Significance: The Supreme Court agreed with Ms. Mapp that her right to be protected against "unreasonable searches and seizures" had been violated by the police. This case prevented state and local officials from using in a court evidence that was obtained in an unlawful search.

BAKER v. CARR (1962)

Background: In the late 19th and early 20th centuries, America's population had grown rapidly. Large numbers of people had moved from rural areas to cities. Frequently, state legislatures failed to redraw their electoral districts. As a result, the population in some rural areas was over-represented, while some cities were under-represented in their state legislatures and in Congress.

Decision/Significance: In the past, the Supreme Court had refused to rule on this matter, claiming that the issue was political, not legal. The Court now asserted that federal courts can reapportion legislative districts. The decision led to new electoral districts being created that were approximately equal in size, on the "one person, one vote" principle.

GIDEON v. WAINWRIGHT (1963)

Background: Clarence Gideon was arrested for petty larceny. He was too poor to afford a lawyer, and was not provided with one. His request for an attorney was rejected because under Florida's laws a lawyer was only appointed for a defendant in a capital case.

Decision/Significance:The Court ruled that Gideon's Sixth Amendment right to a lawyer, even in a non-capital case, had been violated. The case required all states to provide free counsel for anyone who could not afford one.

MIRANDA v. ARIZONA (1966)

Background: Ernesto Miranda was arrested for raping and kidnapping a young woman. After appearing in a police line-up, Miranda confessed to the crime. The police never told him he had the right to remain silent and did not have to answer their questions. He was also never informed that he could have a lawyer present to advise him.

Decision/Significance: The Supreme Court overturned Miranda's conviction. The police are now required to inform all suspects of their constitutional right to remain silent, to have a lawyer present during questioning, and to warn them that their remarks could be used against them. These are known as "Miranda" rights.

SUMMARIZING YOUR UNDERSTANDING

Directions: How well did you understand what you have just read? Test yourself by answering the following questions.

MAJOR ITEMS TO REMEMBER

On 3 x 5 index cards (as shown on pages 33-34), briefly define the following terms and concepts:

Brown v. Board of Education	Equal Rights Amendment	Affirmative Action
Right-to-Life / Pro-Choice	Black Power	*Roe v. Wade*
Civil Rights Movement	Great Society	The Warren Court

THE CIVIL RIGHTS MOVEMENT

The Civil Rights Movement of the 1950s and 1960s was a major turning point in American history. Summarize your understanding of this movement by answering the following questions:

- What were some important milestones reached by the Civil Rights Movement on the road to equality?
- Why did the Civil Rights Movement become more militant in the 1960s?

THE KENNEDY AND JOHNSON ADMINISTRATIONS

During the Kennedy and Johnson presidencies, many changes took place in the United States. Summarize your understanding of these changes by answering the following questions:

- What changes occurred in U. S. foreign policy during the Kennedy presidency?
- How did the Great Society of President Johnson attempt to extend social reforms in the nation?

SIXTIES CULTURE

The 1960s were marked by a shift in tradition and a spirit of rebelliousness. In what way did the the sixties reflect this growing sense of restlessness?

THE WOMEN'S LIBERATION MOVEMENT

Unlike the earlier women's right's movement that focused its efforts primarily on securing voting rights for women, the Women's Liberation Movement was directed mainly at achieving economic and social equality. Summarize your understanding of this movement by answering the following questions:

- What factors brought about the Women's Liberation Movement?
- What were some of the accomplishments and shortcomings of the Women's Liberation Movement?
- How has the debate on abortion divided the nation?

THE WARREN COURT

The Warren Court became the defender of minorities and the rights of the accused. Summarize your understanding of the Warren Court by answering the following questions:

- Which cases, decided by the Warren Court, sought to achieve equal rights for minorities and to protect those accused of a crime?
- How did each case cited achieve equal rights for minorities and extend protections for those accused of a crime?

PERSONALITIES OF THE PERIOD

People often have an important influence on the political, economic or social life of their times. Summarize your understanding of this statement by completing a separate 3 x 5 index card (follow the procedures outlined on page 34) for each of the following individuals: ***Martin Luther King, Jr.***, ***Betty Friedan***, ***Rachel Carson***, and ***Ralph Nader***.

TESTING YOUR UNDERSTANDING

Directions: Test your understanding of this unit by answering the following questions. Circle the number preceding the word or expression that correctly answers the statement or question. Following the short answer questions, answer either the RCT-type or Regents essay questions.

SKILL BUILDER: ANALYZING A CARTOON

Base your answer to questions 1 through 3 on the following cartoon and on your knowledge of social studies.

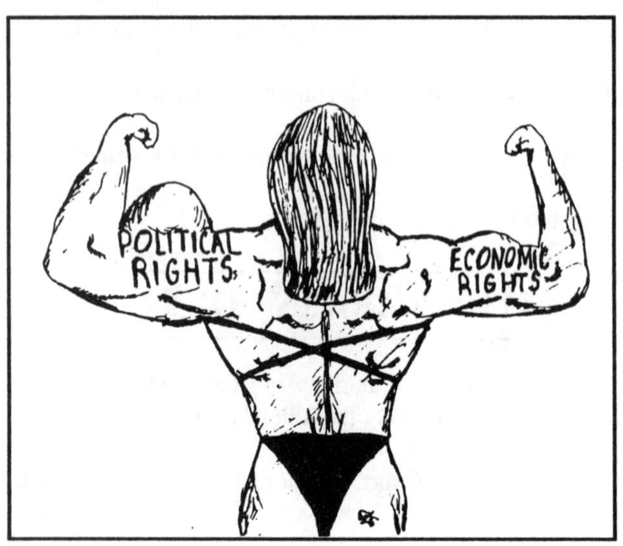
POLITICAL RIGHTS
ECONOMIC RIGHTS

1 Which person would most likely argue that the cartoonist has accurately represented the position of women in America today?
1 a feminist
2 a woman weight-lifter
3 an industrialist
4 a farmer

2 What is the main idea of the cartoon?
1 Women have equal political rights with men.
2 Women need to achieve full economic rights.
3 All people are created with equal rights.
4 Political rights are more important than economic rights.

3 Which situation would the cartoonist most favor?
1 an increased role for women in the workplace
2 women being excluded from military service
3 a reduced role for women in government
4 limitations placed on abortions

Following are quotations from the writings of three African American authors. Base your answers to questions 4 and 5 on their statements and on your knowledge of U.S. history.

Author A: "The Negro must have a country, and a nation of his own.... Don't encourage them to believe that they will become social equals of the whites in America, without first on their own account proving to the world that they are capable of evolving a civilization of their own."

Author B: "Our greatest danger is that in the great leap from slavery to freedom, we may overlook the fact that the masses of us are to live by the production of our hands and fail to keep in mind that we shall prosper in proportion as we learn to dignify and glorify common labor and put brains and skill into the common occupations of life."

Author C: "We went in for agitation. We pushed our way into the courts. We demanded the right to vote. We urged and pushed our children into college. We encouraged Negro art and literature. We studied African history in season and out of season. We declared that the colored races were destined at least to share in the heritage of the earth."

4 Twentieth-century black nationalist leaders would probably agree most strongly with the statements of authors
1 A and B
2 A and C
3 B and C
4 A, B, and C

5 Which person would be most likely to support the views of Author A?
1 Malcolm X
2 Martin Luther King, Jr.
3 Thurgood Marshall
4 Jesse Jackson

Base your answers to questions 6 through 8 on the following quotation from a U.S. Supreme Court decision and on your knowledge of social studies.

"We conclude that in the field of public education the doctrine of 'separate but equal' has no place. Separate educational facilities are inherently unequal. Therefore, ... the plaintiffs ... are, by reason of the segregation ..., deprived of the equal protection of the laws guaranteed by the Fourteenth Amendment."

6 In which time period was the decision from the Supreme Court probably rendered?
1 1860-1890
2 1900-1920
3 1920-1940
4 1940-1970

7 This quotation from a Supreme Court decision marked a reversal of the decision originally stated in
1 *Plessy v. Ferguson*
2 *Gideon v. Wainwright*
3 *Roe v. Wade*
4 *Miranda v. Arizona*

8 This Supreme Court decision is based on the idea that segregation in education is likely to
1 deny some individuals the chance to make social and economic progress
2 create unnecessary administrative problems in the nation's schools
3 place excessive burdens on school transportation systems
4 result in unfair tax increases to support dual school systems

---

9 Which person is correctly paired with the movement with which she is associated?
1 Jane Addams / Suffrage Movement
2 Betty Friedan / Feminist Movement
3 Rachel Carson / Right-to-Life Movement
4 Eleanor Roosevelt / Environmental Movement

10 A member of NOW would most likely favor
1 giving power to state governors
2 increasing military spending
3 greater opportunities for women
4 black separatism

11 In *Roe v. Wade*, the Supreme Court ruled that
1 racial segregation in public schools is unconstitutional
2 the Court has the power to declare federal laws unconstitutional
3 women deserve equal pay for equal work
4 the right to privacy allows women to have abortions

12 The terms "hippies," "youth culture" and "anti-establishment" would most likely be discussed in an essay dealing with which decade?
1 The 1940s
2 The 1950s
3 The 1960s
4 The 1980s

13 The study of the art, music and literature of a nation helps us to better understand its
1 economic progress
2 political development
3 cultural values
4 technological advancement

14 Roosevelt's New Deal and Johnson's Great Society shared the idea that
1 foreign trade should be cut to a minimum
2 the federal government should help with the economic needs of the less fortunate
3 taxes should be raised to stimulate consumer spending
4 key industries should be nationalized

15 Which description best characterizes the decisions of the U.S. Supreme Court of the 1950s and 1960s under Chief Justice Earl Warren?
1 activist, with a liberal approach to interpreting the Constitution
2 cautious, with a philosophy of strictly following the Constitution
3 traditional, with a stress on States rights
4 conservative, with an emphasis on "cracking down" on criminals

16 The basic difference between the beliefs of Malcolm X and Martin Luther King, Jr. concerned the
1 use of violence to achieve racial equality
2 desirability of racial equality
3 issue of American commitments in Africa
4 issue of pride in being black

17 Which statement best describes an important part of the African American experience during the period between W.W. I and W.W. II?
1 Many blacks moved back to the South to recapture their roots.
2 Racial tensions increased because of the black migration to Northern cities.
3 The influence of the Ku Klux Klan declined significantly.
4 Successes by black soldiers in W.W. I led to better treatment of blacks.

18 In the case of *Brown v. Board of Education* (1954), the Supreme Court decided that
1 racially segregated public educational facilities are unconstitutional
2 busing children to overcome segregation is constitutional
3 the use of civil disobedience to achieve legal rights is constitutional
4 closing public schools to avoid integration is permitted

19 Which statement is most clearly illustrated by the Supreme Court decision in *Brown v. Board of Education*?
1 The Constitution ensures federal control of education in the states.
2 Racial prejudice no longer exists in the United States.
3 Non-whites have gained economic and political equality with whites.
4 The Court's interpretation of the Constitution can change over time.

20 With which statement would a believer in the philosophy of Dr. Martin Luther King, Jr. be most likely to agree?
1 All laws in society should be obeyed.
2 Demonstrations against unjust laws are morally correct.
3 Civil disobedience is damaging to society.
4 Violence is acceptable if the cause is just.

21 The movements led by Mohandas Gandhi of India and Martin Luther King, Jr. were similar in that both
1 supported attempts to overthrow the established government
2 advocated civil disobedience to bring about social change
3 appealed solely to the upper classes for financial support
4 campaigned for national political office

22 The equal protection clause of the 14th Amendment to the U.S. Constitution has been used by the federal government to justify its intervention in state matters concerning
1 civil rights
2 appointment of judges
3 the granting of corporation charters
4 regulation of currency

23 Which development was a result of the other three?
1 The Civil Rights and Voting Rights Acts of the 1960s were passed.
2 African Americans were barred from voting in several states.
3 State laws supported racial segregation.
4 The Civil Rights Movement was formed.

24 Which activity best illustrates the idea of affirmative action?
1 An organization actively recruits qualified women and members of minority groups for an on-the-job training program.
2 A corporation hires people on a first-come, first-hired basis.
3 A university's sole criterion for admission is performance on an entrance examination.
4 A graduate school accepts all students who apply.

25 "Under a government which imprisons any unjustly, the true place for a just man is also a prison."
—Henry David Thoreau

Which idea would Thoreau most strongly support?

1 social control
2 conformity
3 suspension of civil liberties
4 civil disobedience

RCT-TYPE ESSAYS

1 Leadership is an essential ingredient to the success of any social or political movement.

Leaders

Malcolm X	Betty Friedan
Martin Luther King, Jr.	Rachel Carson
Ralph Nader	Cesar Chavez

Part A

Choose *one* of the leaders listed above. ______________________________

Identify the field with which that person is associated: ______________________________

Choose *another* leader listed. ______________________________

Identify the field with which that person is associated: ______________________________

Part B

In your Part B answer, you should use information you gave in Part A. However, you may also include different or additional information in your Part B answer.

Write an essay explaining why leadership is an important ingredient for the success of any political or social movement.

2 Throughout U. S. history, various groups have fought against discrimination.

Groups

African Americans	Hispanic-Americans
Asian-Americans	Native American Indians
Women	

Part A

Choose *two* of the groups listed above. For each group chosen, list one form of discrimination faced by the group, and state one way in which that group fought against the discrimination.

GROUP	FORM OF DISCRIMINATION	HOW GROUP OPPOSED IT
1. ____________	1. ____________	1. ____________
2. ____________	2. ____________	2. ____________

Part B

In your Part B answer, you should use information you gave in Part A. However, you may also include different or additional information in your Part B answer.

Write an essay explaining how various groups throughout U. S. history have fought against discrimination.

3 Since 1865, African Americans have faced many problems. They have tried to resolve these problems in different ways.

Part A

List *two* problems that African Americans have faced since 1865. State *one* way African Americans have tried to resolve each problem.

PROBLEM	ATTEMPTS TO RESOLVE THE PROBLEM
1. ____________	1. ____________
2. ____________	2. ____________

Part B

In your Part B answer, you should use information you gave in Part A. However, you may also include different or additional information in your Part B answer.

Write an essay discussing the problems African Americans have faced since the Civil War and explain how they have attempted to resolve these problems.

REGENTS-TYPE ESSAYS

1 Leadership is an essential ingredient for the success of any political or social movement. Listed below are various leaders paired with the movements they led.

Leaders/Movements

Eleanor Roosevelt / Human Rights
Martin Luther King, Jr. / Civil Rights Movement
Betty Friedan & Gloria Steinem / Women's Liberation Movement
Ralph Nader / Consumerism
Cesar Chavez / Rights of Migrant Farm Workers

Select *three* of the pairs listed above. For *each* pair selected, evaluate the success of the leader and movement by discussing:

- the role of the leader in the movement
- tactics used by the movement
- the effect of the leader and the movement on United States history

2 Developments in the United States often give rise to controversy. Controversies have arisen over each of the following statements:

Statements

- No group should use violence to achieve its goals.
- Women should be given the same pay as their male counterparts.
- Employers should have the right to hire anyone they want.
- President Kennedy should have bombed Cuba during the Cuban Missile Crisis.
- All the workers in a company should belong to a union.

Select *two* statements from the list above. For *each* statement selected:

- Identify the controversy that has arisen over the statement
- Briefly discuss the historical origins of the controversy
- State one argument in favor and one argument opposed to the position taken in each statement you have chosen.

3 Although the form it takes often changes with time, discrimination has existed and continues to exist in the United States among different peoples and groups.

Groups

Women
African Americans
Hispanic-Americans
Asian-Americans
Native American Indians

Select *two* groups from the preceding list. For *each* group selected:

- Describe one form of discrimination experienced by the group prior to 1900.
- Describe a different form of discrimination experienced by the group since 1900.

4 Throughout United States history, there have been many instances where political, economic, or social difficulties led to demands for reform. In response to these demands, movements or programs such as those listed below developed.

Movements / Programs

Agrarian Protests / 1870-1900
Progressivism / 1900-1920
New Deal / 1933-1945
Great Society / mid-1960s
Women's Liberation Movement / mid-1960s

Select *two* movements or programs from the list above and for *each* one chosen:

- Describe a specific problem that led to the movement or program
- Describe a specific reform advocated by the movement or program to deal with the problem
- Discuss the extent to which this reform was successful in solving the problem

PERFORMANCE-BASED TASKS

Setting: One of the most controversial decisions in the history of the U.S. Supreme Court was handed down by the Warren Court in *Miranda v. Arizona*. Hailed by most supporters of civil liberties as a victory for individual rights, it was attacked with equal emotion by conservatives throughout the nation as another attempt to undermine the efforts of law enforcement officials.

General Directions: It is May, 1966. You are an Associate Justice of the Supreme Court of the United States. You have just heard arguments in the case entitled *Miranda v. Arizona*. Here is what you were presented with:

Facts of the Case: Ernesto Miranda, a poor 23-year-old Mexican-American, was arrested by the police in Phoenix, Arizona. He was charged with kidnapping and rape. At the police station, Miranda was identified as the perpetrator by the victim. Police officers questioned Miranda for two hours in the interrogation room. At first, Miranda claimed he was innocent. However, by the end of the two hours, Miranda signed a written confession of his guilt. Later the police admitted that neither before nor during the questioning had Miranda been advised of his right to consult with an attorney before answering any questions. In addition, he had never been told of his right to have an attorney present during questioning by the police.

Relevant Part of the 5th Amendment
"(No person) ... shall be compelled in any criminal case to be a witness against himself ..."

Relevant Part of the 6th Amendment
"In all criminal prosecutions, the accused shall enjoy the right to ... have the assistance of counsel for his defense."

Arguments Favoring Miranda
"The Fifth Amendment privilege against self-incrimination is available to an individual swept from familiar surroundings into police custody and subjected to the techniques of persuasion described in the standard police interrogation manuals. Such an individual is not under compulsion to speak. No statement obtained from a person under these circumstances is admissible. In order for a statement of guilt to be admissible the following four warnings must be effectively given: (1) you have the right to remain silent; (2) anything you say can and will be used against you; (3) you have the right to talk to a lawyer before being questioned and to have him present when being questioned; and (4) if you cannot afford a lawyer, one will be provided for you before any questioning if you so desire."

Arguments Favoring the State of Arizona
"The thrust of the argument made in favor of Mr. Miranda will discourage any future confessions at all. Historically, the privilege against self-incrimination did not apply at all to the use of out-of-court confessions. The Fifth Amendment has never been thought to forbid all pressure to incriminate oneself. This is not to say

that any punishment is permissible. Furthermore, it is wrong to say that the Fifth Amendment requires tha one must have a precise knowledge of one's rights before they can be waived. In fact, it must be recognize at the outset that police questioning allowable under the Fifth Amendment may inherently entail some pressure on the suspect and may seek advantage in his ignorance or weaknesses."

Your Task: As you prepare to write your decision in the case, the two most important questions raised by its facts are the following:

- Were Miranda's rights against self-incrimination (5th Amendment) violated?
- Were Miranda's rights to an attorney (6th Amendment) violated?

After consulting the Fifth and Sixth Amendments to the U.S. Constitution and hearing the arguments presented by both sides, you are ready to write an opinion reflecting your point of view. Be sure that your decision answers the two most important questions raised by the case. In addition, be prepared to defend your point of view before the class.

DECISION IN THE CASE OF MIRANDA VS. ARIZONA

In the matter of *Miranda vs. Arizona,* I rule that ______________________

____

____

____

____

____

____

____

____

____

____

LOOKING AT LEADERSHIP

Throughout American history, our national leaders have made decisions that have had important effects on the lives of others. What is it that makes a person a great leader? What makes someone into a person that others are willing to follow? A leader needs to have a vision for the future, an ability to communicate this vision to others, and the power to motivate others to act.

TYPES OF NATIONAL LEADERS

Three types of leaders have had a significant impact on American history: our residents, the leaders of our social movements and economic enterprises, and our authors.

PRESIDENTS OF THE UNITED STATES

The President of the United States is the chief executive of our federal government. As head of state, the president symbolizes the United States. The president has charge over foreign policy, military preparedness and national economic policy. Today, the president is also the leader of a major political party and can communicate to millions of Americans through television. Both the political skills that help a person attain the presidency, as well as the powers of the presidency itself, make the president an important national leader. Recent presidents have been personally responsible for major economic, political and social changes in the United States. In preparing to answer essay questions, you should familiarize yourself with the most frequently mentioned presidents and their administrations:

George Washington*
James Monroe
Abraham Lincoln*
William McKinley
Theodore Roosevelt*
Woodrow Wilson*
Warren Harding*
Franklin D. Roosevelt*
Harry Truman
John F. Kennedy*
Lyndon Johnson*
Richard Nixon*
Jimmy Carter*
Ronald Reagan*

(* appeared two or more times)

SOCIAL REFORMERS AND BUSINESS LEADERS

Unlike the president, the leaders of our major social movements and economic enterprises do not hold high political office and do not have the powers of the United States government at their disposal. Instead, they share an ability to manage and mobilize people. Great reformers and social leaders — like Martin Luther King, Jr. — are able to organize people into powerful groups that push for major social changes and better conditions for their supporters. Great leaders of business — like Henry Ford — are similarly able to organize people and direct their activities towards a common purpose: the production of goods and services in the most efficient way possible. In their different ways, both the social reformer and the business leader have major impacts on society. The economic, social and political leaders that appeared most frequently on past examinations include:

Susan B. Anthony*	Dorothea Dix	Eleanor Roosevelt*
William Jennings Bryan	Frederick Douglass	Margaret Sanger
John C. Calhoun	Marcus Garvey	Elizabeth Cady Stanton
Andrew Carnegie	Samuel Gompers*	Harriet Tubman
Chief Joseph	Martin Luther King, Jr.*	

AUTHORS

Writers also act as leaders by introducing the rest of us to new ideas and ways of doing things. New ideas and powerfully-expressed communications can have a major impact on the course of history. Some of the most frequently tested authors appearing on past Regents and RCTs include:

Rachel Carson*	Sinclair Lewis	John Steinbeck
Betty Friedan	Arthur Miller	Harriet Beecher Stowe*
Helen Hunt Jackson	Ralph Nader*	Ida Tarbell
Harper Lee	Upton Sinclair*	

ANSWERING AN ESSAY QUESTION ON NATIONAL LEADERS

Often a Regents examination or an RCT will ask you to answer an essay question dealing with the impact of our presidents or other prominent leaders and writers.

WHAT TO DISCUSS IN ANSWERING QUESTIONS ON PRESIDENTS

Questions on the presidents expect you to be familiar with the main problems of the period and the chief policies of the presidents listed. Usually in questions about presidents you are asked to either evaluate decisions made by presidents, to rate their performance, or to identify statements made by presidents. To answer these questions you basically have to:

(1) identify the problems faced by a particular president during his administration
(2) describe the policies advocated by that president to deal with those problems
(3) evaluate the effectiveness of these policies by discussing their effects

WHAT TO DISCUSS IN ANSWERING QUESTIONS ON SOCIAL REFORMERS AND BUSINESS LEADERS

Although the information you provide in your answer will depend on whether you are asked about the leader of a social movement or an economic enterprise, your essay should focus on:

(1) What group or enterprise did this person lead?
(2) What problems did the group or enterprise face?
(3) What policies or programs did this leader favor?
(4) What were the effects of these policies?

WHAT TO DISCUSS IN ANSWERING QUESTIONS ON AUTHORS

Writers are people who use the written word to change the way people think. Often they call attention to a problem or issue, focusing the nation's attention on that problem. Just as often they suggest new solutions.

Your answer about a writer should focus on the following:

(1) What area did this person write about?
(2) What did people believe about this subject before reading this author's work?
(3) What contribution did this author make in writing an article, poem or book?
(4) What was the impact of this writing on others?

A MODEL ANSWER TO A REGENTS QUESTION

Let's take a look at a sample Regents essay dealing with individual leadership. The following essay appeared on the August 1991 Regents:

Many individuals in United States history have identified conditions in American society that needed change and have used a variety of means to bring about change. Some of these individuals are listed below.

Individuals
Harriet Beecher Stowe
Susan B. Anthony
Chief Joseph of the Nez Perce
Margaret Sanger
Marcus Garvey
Martin Luther King, Jr.
Ralph Nader

Choose *three* of the individuals listed and for *each* one chosen:

- Describe a condition in American society.
- Explain how the individual attempted to change the condition.
- Discuss the effect the individual's efforts had in bringing about the desired change.

One of the individuals found in this essay question is Martin Luther King, Jr. Using the questions listed earlier for discussing the leader of a social movement, your essay would consist of the following:

MARTIN LUTHER KING, JR.	
(1) What group did this person lead?	Dr. King emerged in the late 1950s as the main organizer and leader of the Civil Rights Movement.
(2) What problems did the group face?	The Civil Rights Movement began in response to the harsh treatment of African Americans. They had seen their rights eroded by state laws and practices and faced abusive treatment. For example, African Americans in the South were legally segregated in schools and made to use separate drinking fountains. In addition, they lived in fear of being terrorized by groups such as the K.K.K. whenever they asserted their constitutional rights.

(3) What policies or programs did this leader favor?	Dr. King believed in the philosophy of non-violence. If a government passed an unjust law, he believed people should oppose that law with non-violent techniques. He felt that by passively resisting unjust laws, the attitude of most people would eventually change. King was very effective in his use of civil disobedience. Through the use of peaceful boycotts, pickets and demonstrations, pressure was placed on Congress and the president to act.
(4) What were the effects of these policies?	King and his followers brought an end to public segregation. The Civil Rights Act of 1964 was passed, prohibiting discrimination in public transportation, hotels and restaurants. The Voting Rights Act (1965) suspended literacy tests as a requirement for voting. In addition, President Lyndon Johnson signed an executive order instituting a policy of affirmative action, leading to increased minority representation in colleges, businesses and the professions.

Of course, in the essay you write you would include material corresponding to each numbered question, but without writing the questions themselves.

HOW THIS BOOK CAN HELP YOU ANSWER QUESTIONS ABOUT OUR NATIONAL LEADERS

This book contains several unique and important features designed to help you answer any question on the RCT or Regents Examination that concerns these leaders. For example, the names of presidents, important leaders and writers are always highlighted in the text in **bold** print. In addition, each main chapter of this book contains the following sections:

PERSONALITIES OF THE PERIOD

Here you will find a short paragraph about some of the important people who lived during the period covered by the chapter. Each paragraph contains background information and discusses the person's impact on the nation and the world.

SUMMARIZING YOUR UNDERSTANDING

Here you will find essay questions asking you to summarize the essential information about several of the most important people discussed in the chapter. If you follow our suggestion of preparing 3 x 5 index cards for each of these individuals, you will compile an excellent study aid for the RCT or Regents Examination.

TESTING YOUR UNDERSTANDING

Here you will often find essays that test your knowledge about influential people. These essays are designed to mirror the type of essay you will actually be required to answer on the Regents or RCT.

CHAPTER 14

THE LIMITS OF POWER

The 1970s were marked by uncertainty at home and abroad. Under President Nixon, the U. S. withdrew from Vietnam and opened diplomatic relations with Communist China. Under Presidents Ford and Carter, the nation sank into an economic recession, and U. S. prestige suffered when American hostages were held captive in Iran. The 1980s saw President Reagan return the nation's economy to prosperity, but at the cost of a greatly increased national debt. Although President Bush had great success on the international scene, his biggest challenge domestically has been to get the American economy moving towards prosperity again.

— TIMELINE OF KEY EVENTS —

1969	1972	1973	1974	1980	1986	1989	1990
U. S. astronauts land on the moon	Nixon re-elected Watergate affair begins	War Powers Act passed U. S. withdraws from Vietnam	Nixon resigns; Gerald Ford becomes president	Reagan elected; Iran frees the American hostages	Iran-Contra investigations held	U. S. invades Panama, captures Noriega	U. S. forces sent to the Persian Gulf

THE VIETNAM WAR: 1954-1973

In the 19th century, Indochina (Vietnam, Laos and Cambodia) came under French rule. During World War II Japan seized control of Indochina. After Japan's defeat in 1945, Vietnamese nationalists, led by **Ho Chi Minh**, declared Vietnam independent. When France refused to recognize the new Vietnamese government a nine-year war followed. In 1954, the Vietnamese won a decisive victory, forcing the French out of Indochina. At the **Geneva Conference** that followed, Laos and Cambodia were made into independent states. Vietnam was divided into two: Ho Chi Minh and the Vietnamese Communists were left in control of the north and a non-Communist state was established in the south. The country was to be reunited after elections were held in 1956.

MILESTONES OF U.S INVOLVEMENT IN VIETNAM

After the Geneva Conference, the U.S. replaced France as South Vietnam's principal supporter. South Vietnam refused to hold the promised elections for the unification of Vietnam. Soon after, Vietnamese Communists (**Vietcong**) with North Vietnamese support began a guerrilla war against South Vietnam's government.

THE WAR EFFORT UNDER PRESIDENT KENNEDY (1961-1963)

President Kennedy, responding to requests for help, sent aid and military advisers to assist in fighting the Vietcong. American leaders, believing in the **Domino Theory**, feared that if South Vietnam fell to the Communists, other Asian countries would also fall, like a row of dominos. This would allow Communism to spread until it posed a direct threat to the United States. Many Americans felt that standing up to the Communists could halt this spread, reflecting a view popular after World War II, that Communism could be contained. They felt that a successful democracy could be built in South Vietnam that would serve as a model for other developing countries in Asia, Africa and Latin America.

CHINA
Hanoi
Gulf of Tonkin
HAINAN ISLAND
LAOS
Mekong River
Ho Chi Minh Trail
Former border between North and South Vietnam
THAILAND
Da Nang
CAMBODIA
VIETNAM
South China Sea
Saigon
Gulf of Thailand
Mekong Delta
Scale of Miles
0
200

THE WAR EFFORT UNDER PRESIDENT JOHNSON (1964-1968)

Under President Johnson, the United States became even more active in the defense of South Vietnam.

■ **The Gulf of Tonkin Resolution.** In 1964, Johnson announced that the North Vietnamese had attacked American ships in international waters in the Gulf of Tonkin. Congress quickly voted to give the president extraordinary military powers to act to stop North Vietnam's aggression. Many years later investigations revealed that the American ships had been in North Vietnamese waters in cooperation with South Vietnamese warships bombing North Vietnam.

■ **The U.S. Escalates The War Effort.** In 1965, the war in Vietnam escalated. Although Congress had not officially declared war, President Johnson used the Gulf of Tonkin Resolution as his basis for escalating the war. He ordered massive bombing raids of North Vietnam. Johnson hoped to wear down the North Vietnamese and to destroy their ability to supply Vietcong guerrillas fighting in South Vietnam. Johnson sent increased numbers of combat troops to Vietnam. By 1968, over 500,000 U.S. soldiers were stationed in Vietnam. Destructive new weapons like **napalm**, a type of fire bomb, inflicted terrible damage on the Vietnamese. Herbicides like **Agent Orange** destroyed the jungle cover used by the Vietcong to hide.

■ **The Tet Offensive.** In 1968, the Vietcong staged a massive attack throughout Vietnam, seizing many of South Vietnam's major cities. Once in control, they committed acts of terror, like the murder of South Vietnamese officials. Although American forces were finally able to drive the Vietcong from these strongholds, the offensive marked a turning point in the war. It showed the American public that victory by U.S. forces was far from being achieved.

THE WAR EFFORT UNDER PRESIDENT NIXON (1969-1973)

Nixon campaigned on a promise of an early "peace with honor." However, the war dragged on for five more years after he assumed the presidency. Under President Nixon, several important developments in the war occurred:

■ **Vietnamization.** Under Nixon's policy of "Vietnamization," the South Vietnamese army took over the brunt of the fighting. This allowed Nixon to gradually withdraw American forces from Vietnam. At the same time he increased the bombing of North Vietnam, and military aid to South Vietnam.

■ **Invasion of Cambodia.** The Nixon Administration believed the war would be shortened if supply routes (through Cambodia) from North to South Vietnam could be cut. In 1970 American troops invaded Cambodia.

■ **Diplomatic Overtures to China and the Soviet Union.** These overtures, described in the next section of this chapter, were aimed at putting pressure on North Vietnam from its Communist allies.

THE VIETNAM WAR FINALLY COMES TO AN END

In 1973, Nixon's representatives worked out a cease-fire agreement with the North Vietnamese, known as the **Paris Peace Accords**. The United States agreed to pull out its troops from Vietnam, and the North Vietnamese agreed to release American prisoners of war. Critics saw the treaty as nothing more than a dignified way for the United States to withdraw from Vietnam. In effect, the United States had lost the war. After the U.S. withdrawal, bitter fighting continued. Finally, both South Vietnam and Cambodia fell to Communist forces in 1975, and Vietnam was reunited under Communist leadership.

WHY THE U.S. WAS UNABLE TO WIN THE WAR

By the end of 1968, the United States had dropped more bombs in Vietnam than in all of World War II. The war was costing $25 billion a year. Yet the United States was unable to win the war for a number of reasons:

AN UNFAVORABLE GEOGRAPHY

The jungles and forests of Vietnam provided an ideal cover for guerrilla warfare and secret enemy movements. Vietnam's location next to Communist China made it easy for Communists to send a steady flow of supplies. American soldiers found the climate hot and uncomfortable.

COMMUNIST SUPPORT FOR NORTH VIETNAM

The North Vietnamese obtained large amounts of supplies and support from the Communist governments of China and the Soviet Union. American leaders did not invade North Vietnam or use nuclear weapons because they feared this might lead to possible Chinese and Soviet intervention.

POPULARITY OF THE NATIONALIST CAUSE

The North Vietnamese and some South Vietnamese looked upon Ho Chi Minh as the father of their country. They were fighting for independence and were willing to suffer large losses to obtain their goal: the removal of U.S. forces and the unification of the country. On the other hand, the disruption of the war weakened the government of South Vietnam. Corruption became widespread. Refugees choked the major cities. None of the governments that ruled South Vietnam was able to gain the support of most of the Vietnamese people.

THE USE OF GUERRILLA WARFARE

American soldiers were not well-trained for a guerrilla war. They did not know the Vietnamese language, the people or the terrain. The Vietcong hid among the other Vietnamese people and had the support of many of them, making it hard for the Americans to tell who was a friend and who was an enemy.

DISCONTENT AND DIVISION ON THE HOME FRONT

As the fighting in Vietnam dragged on and American involvement grew, the public became increasingly disillusioned with the conduct of the war. President Johnson told Americans that the war was being won, but newspaper reporters and television journalists told them otherwise. This led to a growing **credibility gap** as people began to lose faith in the reliability of their government.

■ **Doves v. Hawks.** The "doves" wanted the United States to withdraw from Vietnam. They saw the contest as a civil war between the North and South Vietnamese. They believed the United States was acting immorally by bombing civilians, burning villages and destroying the country. Meanwhile, the "hawks" supported the war and sought to halt the spread of Communism. They saw the war as defending an independent nation against a menacing Communist invasion.

■ **The Anti-war Movement.** Many young Americans began to distrust their government. Some rejected society, dropping out and joining in a growing anti-war movement. As public opinion turned against the war, marches, demonstrations and rallies increased dramatically. Young men burned their draft cards, college students shut down their campuses, and demonstrators protested at national political conventions and in Washington, D.C.

THE LEGACY OF THE VIETNAM WAR

Next to the Civil War, the Vietnam War was the most divisive war in American history — leaving deep wounds and lasting effects on the nation, many of which have not fully healed. Over 58,000 Americans died in the war and thousands of others suffered physical and psychological injuries. Over a million Vietnamese were killed, and over half the population of South Vietnam was left homeless. Cities and rice paddies were ruined, and the Vietnamese economy was left in shambles.

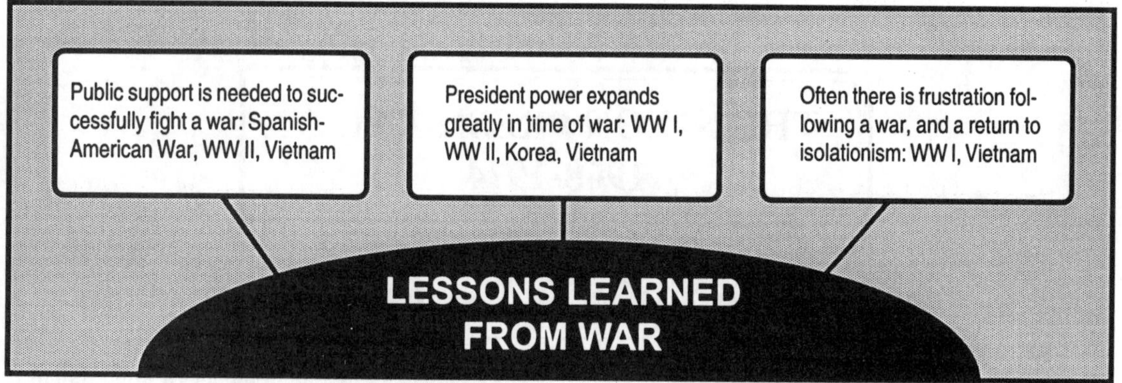
Public support is needed to successfully fight a war: Spanish-American War, WW II, Vietnam
President power expands greatly in time of war: WW I, WW II, Korea, Vietnam
Often there is frustration following a war, and a return to isolationism: WW I, Vietnam
LESSONS LEARNED FROM WAR

IMPACT OF PUBLIC OPINION

The Vietnam War, like the Spanish-American War, demonstrated to America's leaders that the success of government actions can be greatly affected by public opinion. In a democracy there must be popular support for government actions.

LIMITS ON PRESIDENTIAL WARTIME POWERS

In the Vietnam War, as in the Korean War, presidential wartime powers greatly expanded. As a result, in 1973 Congress attempted to claim a greater role in determining national policy by passing the **War Powers Act**, which limits the president's power to commit troops overseas. (See the Key Legislation section at the end of this chapter.)

LOSS OF U.S. PRESTIGE ABROAD

The war led to a crisis of confidence. Like the reaction after World War I, many Americans became concerned about our foreign commitments. As a result, the United States adopted a more isolationist approach in world affairs, ignoring many events in other parts of the world.

SOCIAL AND ECONOMIC IMPACT

Wartime expenses led to the abandonment of many Great Society programs begun under President Johnson. The war brought rising inflation to the American economy. Most importantly, there was a widespread distrust of their government by many Americans.

THE BOAT PEOPLE AND INCREASED U.S. IMMIGRATION

When the Communists seized control in South Vietnam, many Vietnamese, fearing perse-cution, fled on small boats to neighboring non-Communist countries. Thousands of these refugees immigrated to the United States

KEY ITEMS TO REMEMBER

Domino Theory, Vietcong, Gulf of Tonkin Resolution, Tet Offensive, doves, hawks, War Powers Act

THE NIXON PRESIDENCY: 1968-1974

NIXON AND THE IMPERIAL PRESIDENCY

The authors of the Constitution attempted to strike a balance between separate branches of government to protect Americans from the abuses of tyranny. However, the growth of presidential power in the last 50 years threatened to upset this Constitutional balance of power. Presidential authority was greatly expanded because the New Deal had given the President increased power over the economy; two world wars and the Cold War made foreign affairs far more important; and radio and television allowed the president to appeal directly to the public for support. This expansion of presidential power was taken to extremes during the Nixon Presidency. Some historians have referred to the use of presidential powers beyond those stated in the Constitution as the "**Imperial Presidency.**"

ACTING WITHOUT CONGRESS

Nixon made major decisions without Congress. He failed to consult or inform Congress about the bombing and invasion of Cambodia and Laos, mining of the harbors of North Vietnam, and his decision to open relations with Communist China. Nixon often refused to spend money voted by Congress for programs he disapproved of.

ABUSES OF POWER

Nixon used millions from public funds to remodel and refurbish his private homes in California and Florida. He used the C.I.A. and F.B.I. to collect information about his political enemies and to harass those who disagreed with his views. Nixon's staff placed illegal pressure on corporations to contribute to his re-election campaign fund.

DOMESTIC POLICY UNDER NIXON

In domestic affairs, Nixon replaced "Great Society" programs with revenue-sharing, attempted to curb inflation through wage and price controls, and made conservative appointments to the Supreme Court.

NIXON'S "NEW FEDERALISM"

Nixon believed that federal spending on social programs was often inefficient and wasteful, and he gradually scaled down President Johnson's Great Society programs. In place of federal welfare programs, Nixon proposed "revenue-sharing." He believed that local problems could best be dealt with at the local level. Nixon called this new division of responsibility between local and federal government the "**New Federalism**."

SUPREME COURT APPOINTMENTS

Nixon tried reducing the power of the federal government by appointing justices to the Supreme Court who favored "judicial restraint" over "judicial activism." He eventually appointed four of the nine justices of the Supreme Court.

NEW ECONOMIC TROUBLES

The 1970s saw rising prices, a new trade deficit and gradually rising unemployment. Government spending during the Vietnam War, troubles with the value of the dollar and rising oil prices all contributed to these problems. To combat inflation, Nixon cut government spending on social programs. He also imposed wage and price controls in 1971 and again in 1973. These attempts at controlling wages and prices were unsuccessful. The problem of inflation combined with unemployment—known as **stagflation**—continued to plague Presidents Nixon, Ford and Carter.

FOREIGN POLICY UNDER NIXON

Nixon believed the president's major role was to lead the country's foreign policy. His foreign policy successes included the United States withdrawal from Vietnam, opening diplomatic relations with Communist China, and beginning a detente with the Soviet Union.

THE VIETNAM WAR (1969-1973)

When Nixon became president in 1969, the main issue facing the country was the Vietnam War. As the fighting dragged on, Americans became disillusioned with the war. Nixon pursued a policy of "Vietnamization" of the war, shifting the fighting from American troops to the South Vietnamese army. He reduced America's troop strength in Vietnam, while increasing aid to South Vietnam, stepping up the bombing of North Vietnam, and invading Cambodia and Laos. In 1973, Nixon and the North Vietnamese agreed to sign the **Paris Peace Accords**. (See The Vietnam War, earlier in this chapter, for a fuller discussion.)

RE-OPENING RELATIONS WITH CHINA (1972)

Ever since the Communist take-over of China in 1949, the United States had refused to establish diplomatic relations with the Communists government there, and had instead treated the Nationalist Chinese government on the island of Taiwan as the official government of China. Nixon, however, visited Communist

China and restored normal diplomatic relations with the Communist Chinese. There were several reasons why Nixon took this step. He believed it was time for American leaders to come to terms with the rulers of China, who had been in power for 23 years. Nixon also felt that, as a strong anti-communist who would face little criticism at home, he would be the best American leader to restore relations with China. He hoped friendship with China would put pressure on North Vietnam to end the Vietnam War.

DETENTE WITH THE SOVIET UNION (1972)

Nixon also introduced a policy of **detente** (relaxing of strained relations) with the Soviet Union. In 1972, he became the first president to visit Moscow. During this visit Nixon signed the **S.A.L.T. I Accord** in which the United States and the Soviet Union agreed to limit the development of certain types of missile systems. Nixon also agreed to sell American grain to the Soviet Union, to help the Soviets cope with severe food shortages. When a war broke out in the Middle East in 1973, he used his friendship with Soviet leaders to persuade them not to intervene. The United States and Soviet Union then jointly pressured Israel and the Arab states to conclude a cease-fire.

CORRUPTION IN THE NIXON ADMINISTRATION

THE VICE PRESIDENT RESIGNS

Nixon had promised Americans a return to "law and order," but they soon learned that the government itself had become corrupt. In 1973 **Spiro Agnew** resigned as vice president when it was discovered he had taken bribes while serving as governor of Maryland. Under the terms of the 25th Amendment, passed after President Kennedy's assassination, Nixon appointed Gerald Ford to replace Agnew as vice president.

THE WATERGATE AFFAIR

In 1972 some C.I.A. agents, working for Nixon's re-election, were caught breaking into Democratic Party headquarters in Washington, D.C. This set in motion a series of events that led to Nixon's resignation:

- **The Cover-up**. Nixon might have admitted that the burglars were tied to some of his staff in the White House but had acted without his orders. Instead, he tried to cover up the investigation on the grounds of national security. The burglars were offered bribes to keep quiet. In the tradition of the Progressive Era, a group of investigative reporters were the first to report the possible links to the Nixon White House. A federal district court appointed a grand jury to investigate the break-in. The Senate also appointed an investigative committee. Lastly, the Attorney General appointed a special prosecutor to examine the Watergate Affair.

- **The Watergate Tapes**. In the Senate hearings, it was revealed that Nixon secretly recorded all of his White House conversations. Both the Senate Committee and the special prosecutor applied to hear the tapes. Nixon refused to hand them over, and gave only edited versions. Nixon also refused a court order to surrender the tapes, claiming **executive privilege**—that Congress was forbidden to question members of the executive branch without presidential approval. In ***United States v. Nixon*** (1974) Nixon contended that to obey the Court's demand would be to allow judicial control of the president, violating the separation of power provisions of the Constitution. The Supreme Court ruled that Nixon must turn over the tapes, reaffirming the principle that no one is above the law — not even a president.

The tapes revealed that Nixon had lied to the American people when he said he was not involved in the cover-up. They also disclosed other examples of executive wrongdoing.

■ **Nixon Resigns.** The House of Representatives moved to impeach Nixon. Fearing impeachment, Nixon resigned, and **Gerald Ford** then became president. As president, one of Ford's first acts was to pardon Nixon for any crimes he might have committed as president.

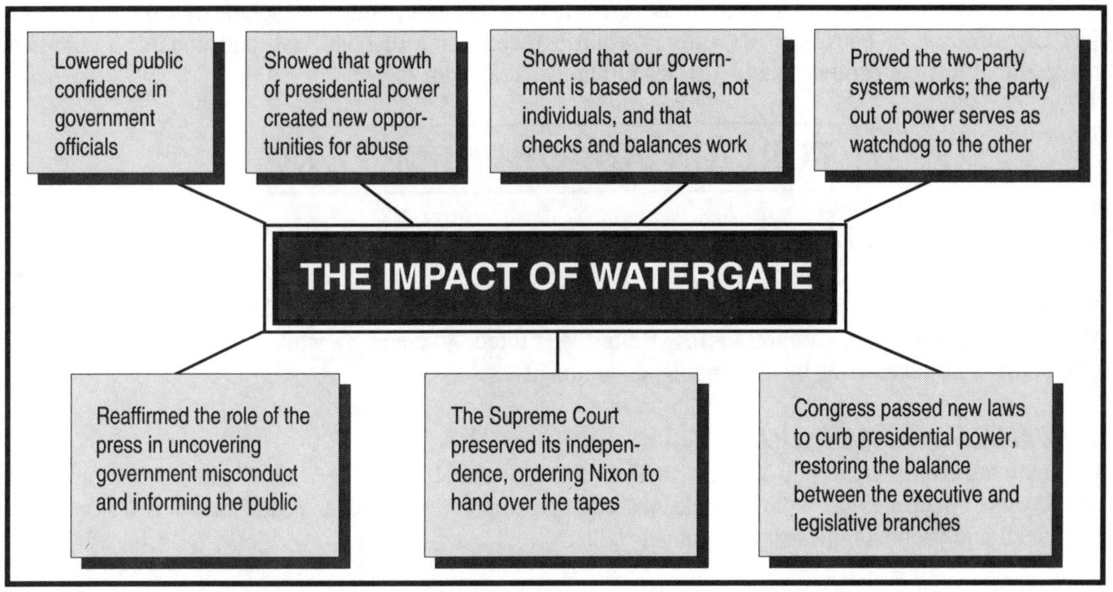
Lowered public confidence in government officials
Showed that growth of presidential power created new opportunities for abuse
Showed that our government is based on laws, not individuals, and that checks and balances work
Proved the two-party system works; the party out of power serves as watchdog to the other
THE IMPACT OF WATERGATE
Reaffirmed the role of the press in uncovering government misconduct and informing the public
The Supreme Court preserved its independence, ordering Nixon to hand over the tapes
Congress passed new laws to curb presidential power, restoring the balance between the executive and legislative branches

KEY ITEMS TO REMEMBER

Imperial Presidency, detente, SALT Accords, stagflation, Watergate Affair, executive privilege

THE FORD PRESIDENCY: 1974-1977

President Gerald Ford operated under an unusual handicap, since he was never elected as either vice president or president. Instead he had been appointed by Richard Nixon, a man who had resigned in disgrace. When Ford became president, one of his first acts was to pardon Nixon. This action came under heavy criticism, especially since Nixon had appointed Ford as his vice president.

DOMESTIC POLICY UNDER FORD

Ford's main worries were economic. The United States continued to suffer from "stagflation"—high unemployment combined with high inflation. Ford wanted to fight inflation by limiting government spending; the Democratic Congress wanted to increase government spending to fight unemployment. Much of the stagflation, however, was caused by the drastic rise in world oil prices. During the Arab-Israeli War of 1973, the Arab nations had learned to cooperate in using oil as a political weapon. After the war, **OPEC** (the Organization of Petroleum Exporting Countries), consisting of both Arab and non-Arab members, realized that this cooperation could also lead to higher prices for their oil.

FOREIGN POLICY UNDER FORD

INDOCHINA FALLS (1975)

Ford's inability to lead Congress became evident when the government of South Vietnam fell to North Vietnamese forces in 1975. When Ford asked Congress for new funds in a last-ditch attempt to save the South Vietnamese government, Congress refused. Ford was forced to stand by while both South Vietnam and Cambodia were taken over by Communist governments.

THE HELSINKI ACCORDS

Ford maintained Nixon's policy of detente with the Soviet Union. In 1975, the United States, the Soviet Union and 33 other countries signed the Helsinki Accords, agreeing to recognize the post-World War II boundaries as official and promising to respect "human rights."

THE CARTER PRESIDENCY: 1977-1981

Ford lost the 1976 Presidential election to Jimmy Carter in part because many Americans still blamed his party, the Republicans, for the misdeeds of Watergate. Carter, a retired naval officer and former governor of Georgia, was elected as an "outsider" to Washington politics.

DOMESTIC POLICY UNDER CARTER

Carter's chief problems at home were economic. Inflation went over 10%, interest rates rose to 20%, and unemployment remained high. The United States become heavily dependent on imported oil, as oil prices skyrocketed.

THE ENERGY CRISIS

To deal with the energy crisis, Carter created a cabinet-level Department of Energy. He asked for a special tax on large automobiles, but special interest groups blocked passage of the bill. Carter's request for a "windfall profits" tax on excess profits earned by oil companies,due to oil price increases was granted, but Congress denied him the power to fix prices or ration gasoline. Attempts to develop synthetic fuels were also rejected by Congress in favor of grants and loans to private companies developing solar and renewable energy or synthetic fuels. Oil prices and fuel shortages continued throughout the Carter years. Partly due to the oil crisis, inflation and interest rates soared in 1979. Carter cut federal spending, but inflation did not come down until two years into the Reagan presidency.

THE ENVIRONMENT

Carter had a strong record in environmental protection. The Waste Clean-Up Act of 1980 provided funds for the clean-up of toxic dumpsites through a special tax on chemicals. Finally, following an accident at the **Three Mile Island** nuclear reactor in 1979 in which radiation was released, the Nuclear Regulatory Commission established stricter standards for nuclear plants.

OTHER POLICIES

Carter appointed women and members of minorities to judicial and government posts. He supported the passage of the **Equal Rights Amendment** (guaranteeing equal rights for both sexes), but not enough states ratified it. He also sponsored the Bilingual Education Act, which requires that public schools provide special instruction to students who are still in the process of learning English.

FOREIGN POLICY UNDER CARTER

HUMAN RIGHTS

Carter wanted the United States to assert its world leadership by setting a moral example for other nations. He made human rights a high priority: He condemned apartheid in South Africa, and cut U. S. aid to dictatorships that violated human rights. He also pressured the Soviet Union to grant freedom of speech to Soviet dissenters and to allow Soviet Jews to emigrate.

THE PANAMA CANAL TREATY (1977)

Carter felt the United States should set an example for the world by doing the right thing and respecting local feelings. In 1977, he negotiated a new arrangement for control of the Panama Canal. The treaty returned control of the Canal Zone to Panama, except for the canal itself. The U. S. agreed to turn over the canal to Panama in 1999. In exchange, Panama gave the U. S. the right to defend the Canal from attack.

THE CAMP DAVID ACCORDS (1978)

Carter's greatest foreign policy achievement was the **Camp David Accords**. Egypt and Israel had been enemies since the creation of the state of Israel in 1948. Egypt and Israel had been at war in 1948, 1956, 1967 and 1973. Carter invited both Egypt's President Anwar Sadat and Israel's Prime Minister Menachem Begin to Camp David, where an agreement between the two leaders was reached in September 1978. In extending this invitation, Carter asserted America's leadership role and interest in achieving stability in the

Middle East. Under the Camp David Accords, Israel agreed to return the Sinai Peninsula to Egypt in exchange for a peace treaty and the establishment of normal diplomatic relations between the two countries. The peace treaty was signed in 1979. Sadat and Begin were awarded the Nobel Peace Prize, but other Arab leaders denounced the agreement because it failed to provide a homeland for the Palestinians.

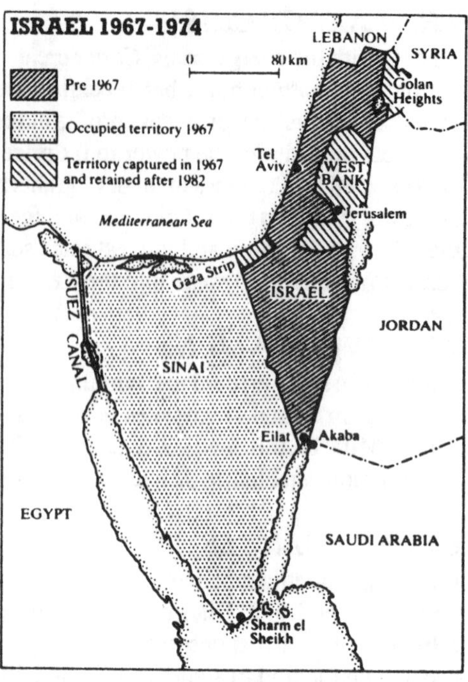
ISRAEL 1967-1974
0
80 km
Pre 1967
Occupied territory 1967
Territory captured in 1967 and retained after 1982
LEBANON
SYRIA
Golan Heights
Tel Aviv
WEST BANK
Jerusalem
Mediterranean Sea
Gaza Strip
ISRAEL
JORDAN
SUEZ CANAL
SINAI
Eilat
Akaba
EGYPT
SAUDI ARABIA
Sharm el Sheikh

THE IRANIAN REVOLUTION AND THE HOSTAGE CRISIS (1978-1979)

The Shah (ruler) of Iran was a strong ally of the United States and a fierce anti-Communist. However, he was also a dictator who used secret police and brutal measures against his opponents. In 1978, widespread popular demonstrations broke out against the Shah's rule and he fled the country. Meanwhile, religious leaders who were hostile to the United States took control of Iran. The United States faced resentment for having helped the Shah and for backing Israel. In retaliation, Iranian students seized the staff of the U. S. Embassy in the Iranian capital. Fifty staff members were kept hostage and held for 444 days. Carter froze Iranian assets in American banks. Although Carter tried to free the hostages, all of his attempts failed. The image of the United States at home and abroad suffered because of Carter's inability to obtain the prompt release of the hostages. Negotiations finally led to the return of the hostages, only moments after Carter left office and Reagan became president.

U.S.-SOVIET RELATIONS

Carter continued the Nixon-Ford policy of detente with the Soviet Union. He signed the S.A.L.T. II Treaty, an arms control agreement which limited the number of nuclear missiles for each superpower. However, the treaty was never ratified by the Senate because of the Soviet invasion of Afghanistan in 1979. The invasion of Afghanistan thus brought a temporary end to detente. Carter halted grain sales to the Soviet Union, called for a boycott of the 1980 Olympics in Moscow, and postponed ratification of the S.A.L.T. II agreement.

KEY ITEMS TO REMEMBER

Helsinki Accords, human rights violations, Camp David Accords, Panama Canal Treaty, Iranian Hostage Crisis

THE REAGAN PRESIDENCY: 1981-1989

President Reagan introduced far-reaching changes in both domestic and foreign policy. These changes brought a return to prosperity for many, but critics feared his policies would create major problems in the future.

DOMESTIC POLICIES UNDER REAGAN

Reagan felt that individuals and businesses in a free market were more efficient and better able to solve economic problems than government agencies. He believed businesses would become more successful if they could make decisions without government interference. Therefore, under his policy of **New Federalism**, Reagan began reversing the trend of increased federal responsibility and control that had started with President Franklin D. Roosevelt.

REAGANOMICS

When Reagan took office the key domestic problem was "stagflation"—high inflation and high unemployment. Reagan attempted to solve the problem with "**supply-side economics.**" He tried to make it easier for suppliers to produce goods. A large supply of goods would bring down prices, stopping inflation. Some called this strategy "**Reaganomics.**" In 1983, the economy finally began to recover. For the rest of the 1980s, Americans enjoyed a period of prosperity based on several factors:

■ **Cuts In Taxes and Domestic Spending.** Reagan cut taxes on businesses and the wealthy; he felt these groups were overtaxed and were the most likely to invest their income. Their investments would raise economic productivity, increase employment, and result in benefits that would "trickle down" to other groups. In order to finance a tax cut, Reagan reduced spending on federal welfare programs—food stamps, education, school lunch programs, aid for low-income housing and job training programs. At the same time he pledged a "safety net" of emergency aid for the "truly needy."

■ **Deregulation**. Reagan eliminated many federal regulations on industry, which he believed made businesses less competitive and hampered economic growth in some areas. He believed businesses would become more successful if they could make decisions without government interference.

■ **Increased Military Spending**. Sharply increased military spending stimulated the entire economy; it created a demand for many goods and services. This was paid for through "**deficit financing**," which meant that the government put more money into the economy than it received through taxes.

■ **Other Factors**. World oil prices stabilized, while the new Alaskan pipeline made the United States less dependent on foreign oil. New employment patterns created new jobs in some areas, such as computer processing and health care.

THE FEDERAL DEFICIT AND THE NATIONAL DEBT

Although Reagan brought an end to stagflation, new problems were created. The federal deficit is the amount that the federal government spends each year beyond what it collects in taxes. The deficit is paid for by borrowing. Reagan promised a **balanced budget**—one in which government spending was equal to taxes received. However, during Reagan's presidency the size of the federal deficit increased greatly, and the national debt more than doubled. This brought about sharp criticism of President Reagan because the long-term effects of the growing national debt may threaten future economic growth.

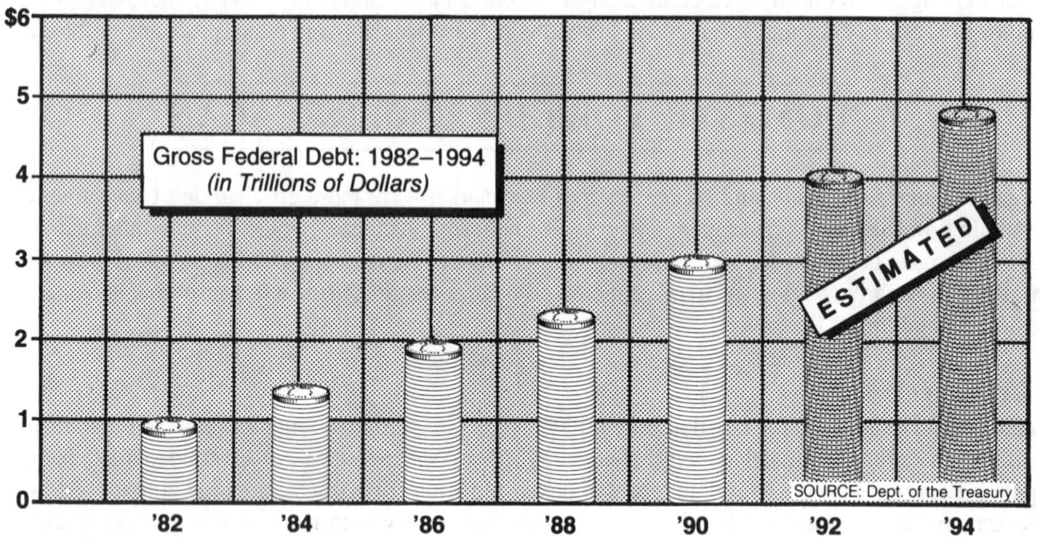
$6
5
4
3
2
1
0
Gross Federal Debt: 1982–1994
(in Trillions of Dollars)
ESTIMATED
SOURCE: Dept. of the Treasury
'82
'84
'86
'88
'90
'92
'94

THE TRADE IMBALANCE

Reagan's encouragement of free trade led to growing trade imbalances with Japan, South Korea, Taiwan, and West Germany. During the Reagan years the United States went from a creditor to a debtor nation (one that owes money). The United States bought more goods and services than it sold overseas. The imbalance led to the closing of steel mills and auto plants, the loss of millions of jobs, and a drop in the disposable income of Americans. Meanwhile, the same dollars used to purchase goods abroad flowed back to the United States as investments in U.S. properties or loans to the U.S. government to help finance the national deficit.

FOREIGN POLICY UNDER REAGAN

In his early years as president, Reagan set out to restore American confidence. He believed that the United States should continue to act as the world's defender of freedom and democracy.

THE REAGAN DOCTRINE

In 1986 President Reagan announced a new policy, known as the **Reagan Doctrine**. Under this doctrine the United States stated it would no longer confine itself merely to containing Communism, but would attempt to roll it back by aiding anti-Communist "freedom fighters" in their attempts to liberate their nations from Communist control.

■ **Increased Military Spending.** Reagan sharply increased military spending, which had diminished during the post-Vietnam period. He sent military aid to anti-Communist rebels in Afghanistan, Nicaragua, Angola and Cambodia. He also proposed a **Strategic Defense Initiative** (S.D.I.) or "**Star Wars**" defense against nuclear attack by use of lasers and other new technologies . The Star Wars plan disturbed Soviet leaders, who feared the expense of developing their own Star Wars technology.

■ **Military Intervention.** In 1983 President Reagan, acting under his powers as commander-in-chief, sent U. S. Marines to the island of **Grenada** in the Caribbean just after Communists had taken control. Reagan took this action to protect American medical students on the island and to prevent Cuba and the Soviet Union from using the island to export Communism to other island republics in the area. In Nicaragua, Reagan was aiding the anti-communist **Contra** rebels against the new **Sandinista** government, until Congress voted to cut off all aid to the Contras.

CRITICISM OF THE REAGAN DOCTRINE

Critics pointed out that Reagan's pro-democratic stand was inconsistent. He assisted anti-Communist freedom fighters but remained allied to non-Communist dictators in Chile, the Philippines and other parts of the world. Other critics pointed out that Reagan did nothing to fight Communism in areas where it was firmly established, like Eastern Europe. Finally, some critics feared that the Reagan Doctrine would lead the United States back into a Vietnam-like situation in Nicaragua.

THE WAR AGAINST TERRORISM

Terrorism is the use of bombing, assassination or kidnapping by groups to ensure that their voices will be heard. Terrorists strike without warning, instilling panic into civilians. Dealing with terrorists created a dilemma for Reagan as it had for previous presidents. American leaders wanted to show terrorists that they were not intimidated, but if they responded too harshly, terrorists might escalate their activities or retaliate by taking hostages. In addition to Americans being held in Lebanon throughout the Reagan-Bush years, there were other terrorist acts:

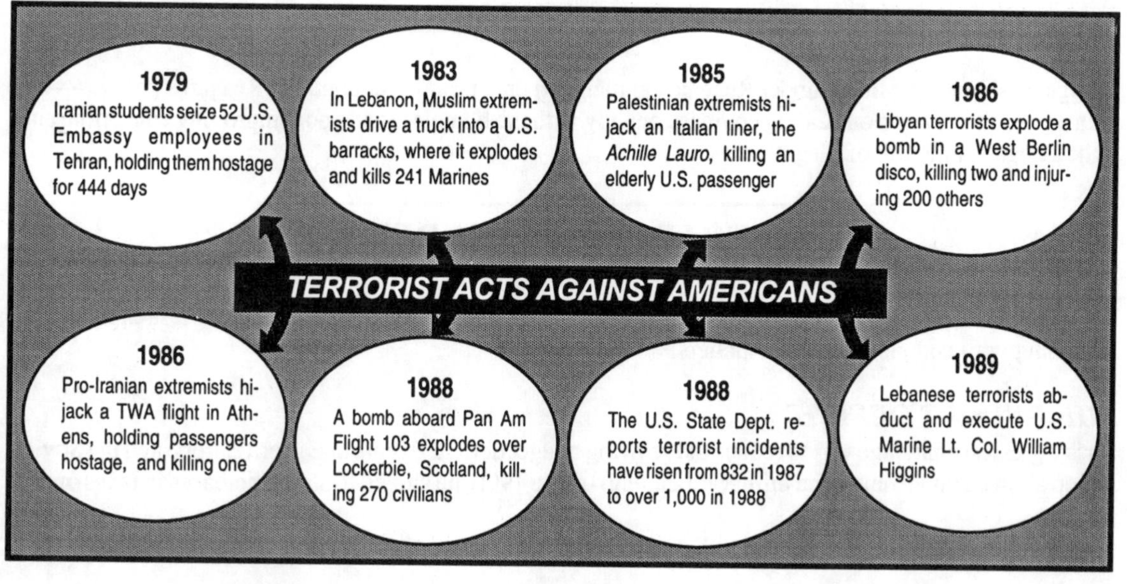
TERRORIST ACTS AGAINST AMERICANS
1979
Iranian students seize 52 U.S. Embassy employees in Tehran, holding them hostage for 444 days
1983
In Lebanon, Muslim extremists drive a truck into a U.S. barracks, where it explodes and kills 241 Marines
1985
Palestinian extremists hijack an Italian liner, the *Achille Lauro*, killing an elderly U.S. passenger
1986
Libyan terrorists explode a bomb in a West Berlin disco, killing two and injuring 200 others
1986
Pro-Iranian extremists hijack a TWA flight in Athens, holding passengers hostage, and killing one
1988
A bomb aboard Pan Am Flight 103 explodes over Lockerbie, Scotland, killing 270 civilians
1988
The U.S. State Dept. reports terrorist incidents have risen from 832 in 1987 to over 1,000 in 1988
1989
Lebanese terrorists abduct and execute U.S. Marine Lt. Col. William Higgins

THE IRAN-CONTRA AFFAIR

President Reagan tried to follow a policy of refusing to negotiate with terrorists. In 1986, the Reagan Administration went against its official policy by secretly selling arms to Iran in exchange for the release of American hostages in Lebanon. When this was revealed, there was widespread public criticism. Soon afterwards, it was discovered that the profits from the sales to Iran had been diverted to support the Contra rebels fighting the Communist government of Nicaragua. This violated an act of Congress forbidding further aid to the Contras. An investigation into the Iran-Contra Affair cleared the president of wrongdoing, but several Reagan officials were convicted of lying to Congress and were sent to prison.

THE TRIUMPH OF DEMOCRACY

During Reagan's second term democracy triumphed in many parts of the world. The U. S. provided a successful example of a prosperous, democratic society, in contrast to the economic difficulties faced by most Communist nations. In the Philippines and Latin America, many dictatorships and military governments were replaced by democratically-elected civilian governments. The Cold War ended when the failure of the Soviet economic and political system forced its leaders to introduce changes. Gorbachev agreed to withdraw Soviet troops from Afghanistan and to allow peaceful change in Eastern Europe. In 1987, Gorbachev and Reagan signed a major agreement dismantling thousands of intermediate range nuclear missiles.

KEY ITEMS TO REMEMBER

Reaganomics, supply side economics, deregulation, deficit financing, national debt, trade imbalance, Iran-Contra Affair, Reagan Doctrine, Star Wars, Grenada invasion, terrorism

THE BUSH PRESIDENCY: 1989 - 1993

George Bush, vice president under Reagan, campaigned on a promise to continue Reagan's policies—but with a greater emphasis on dealing compassionately with the homeless and poor, improving education, and fighting against the use of illegal drugs.

DOMESTIC POLICIES UNDER BUSH

Bush's previous experience had mainly been in foreign policy, and critics noted that he was less experienced in dealing with complex domestic matters.

THE BUDGET DEFICIT

Bush's greatest challenge was to reduce the growing budget deficit. Events in Eastern Europe and the Soviet Union allowed him to cut some military spending. In late 1990, he agreed to slight increases in taxes on the very wealthy in a compromise with Democrats in Congress. Despite these factors, Bush was never able to make a significant reduction in the budget deficit.

SUPREME COURT APPOINTMENTS

During 1990 and 1991, two liberal members of the Court resigned. Their resignations allowed Bush to appoint **David Souter** and **Clarence Thomas**, nearly giving conservatives control of the Court. The Rehnquist Supreme Court has toughened its treatment of criminal defendants and is making other important changes. (See Key Court Cases in Chapter 15).

THE RECESSION

The United States gradually moved into a recession in 1990. Economists identified several factors that caused this economic downturn.

- **Reduced Spending**. Large debt burdens carried by consumers, corporations, local and state governments and the national government led to reduced spending. In addition, reduced military spending led to a decline of defense-related industries.

- **Troubled Industries.** Problems surfaced in the construction industry, due to falling real estate prices and fewer house sales. Also, the banking industry was in trouble because of unsound investments and the drop in real estate values.

- **Rising Unemployment**. Lay-offs in the automobile industry increased, due to greater foreign competition. Joblessness reached over 8% in such large states as California, New York, Florida, Michigan and Illinois.

By early 1992, the recession had affected the political climate. President Bush's approval ratings, which had reached an all-time high after the Gulf War, began to drop as a consequence of the recession. The President was blamed for failing to recognize the early warning signs of the recession and for failing to do anything about it. The Federal Reserve, in an attempt to fight the recession, sharply lowered interest rates.

CIVIL RIGHTS AND CIVIL UNREST

As a result of the civil rights gains of the 1960s and 1970s and the growth of a sizeable African-American middle class, many Americans began to feel that special race-based programs were no longer needed to help minority Americans. In contrast, many minority leaders believed that their communities were still being denied equal opportunities. Minority frustrations boiled over in riots in Los Angeles in 1992, when an African-American motorist named Rodney King was stopped after a high-speed car chase, and a group of policemen beat him. The event was captured by a bystander with a video camera, and was shown on nationwide television. When the policemen were brought to trial for using excessive force, a jury found them not guilty. African-American and Hispanic neighborhoods erupted. Thousands of buildings in Los Angeles and other cities were looted and burned, and more than 70 people were killed. The riots called attention to the continuing plight of minorities, and to the problems of racial tension and hostility in America.

BUSH'S FOREIGN POLICY

Bush's major achievements were in the field of foreign affairs:

THE INVASION OF PANAMA (1989)

President Bush acted against Panamanian dictator and drug dealer **Manuel Noriega**. He ordered American forces to invade Panama, restore democratically elected leaders, and bring Noriega to the United States to face drug charges. Noriega was convicted, and sent to federal prison.

U.S.-SOVIET RELATIONS

Bush continued Reagan's policy of detente with the Soviets. Within two years of his inauguration, Eastern Europe moved from Communism to democracy, the Berlin Wall was torn down and Germany was reunited. In addition, democratic changes took place in the Soviet Union. Bush strongly supported Soviet leader **Mikhail Gorbachev** in August 1991 by failing to recognize Communist leaders who temporarily seized the government in a coup. After resuming power, Gorbachev had hoped to get the leaders of the Soviet Republics to agree to a new Treaty of Union. However, by the end of 1991 each republic decided to secede from the Union. The Soviet Union was dissolved and replaced by a looser arrangement known as the **Commonwealth of Independent States**. Gorbachev resigned from public life. Bush recognized the newly independent republics and offered them economic assistance.

THE GULF WAR (1990)

The Gulf War was George Bush's greatest foreign policy success.

- **Background.** Iraqi leader **Saddam Hussein** had developed a powerful military machine and stockpiled a large supply of chemical and biological weapons. In August 1990, Hussein invaded its tiny neighbor Kuwait, capturing its vast oil wealth and extending Iraq's borders. He seized foreigners as hostages, but fortunately released them. Many feared Hussein would try to extend his power throughout the Middle East. In response, the U.N. placed an economic blockade on Iraq and voted a deadline for Iraq to leave Kuwait.

- **The U.S. Response.** President Bush saw the incident as the occasion for forming a **New World Order** of peaceful countries united against aggression. He increased U.S. troop strength in the area to nearly 500,000 soldiers and began to carefully gather international support. When last-minute attempts at diplomacy failed, American and U.N. coalition forces launched an air attack against Iraq shortly after the deadline expired.

- **Operation Desert Storm.** President Bush promised the American people that Operation Desert Storm, as the war became known, would not turn into a long drawn out affair like Vietnam. Much of the arsenal of modern U.S. weaponry was unleashed against Iraq. For weeks, allied bombers and missiles pounded away at Iraq with deadly accuracy. In the final attack, coalition forces mounted an invasion of Kuwait, attacking the Iraqi troops there. The invasion of coalition forces ended the war in a matter of a few days. In February 1991 Hussein agreed to remove all Iraqi troops from Kuwait and pay damages to Kuwait. Some Americans believed the war should have continued until Hussein was removed from power, but President Bush kept to his original intention of freeing Kuwait, and declared a cease-fire.

■ **Effects of the Gulf War.** The crisis was significant because it was the first major challenge to world order since the end of the Cold War. The war had important effects. (1) **Advanced Technological Warfare** enhanced American prestige. The world was amazed at the latest U.S. technology, such as computer controlled, laser-guided "intelligent" missiles that evaded radar and entered buildings with pinpoint accuracy. (2) **Kurdish Massacres** in northern Iraq. The Kurds, a distinct cultural minority, revolted against Hussein and sought to establish a nation of their own. When Hussein began a massacre of the Kurds, Bush ordered American forces to stop the killing and to create safe refugee camps for them. (3) **Destruction of the Environment** was unleashed by Hussein. He ordered the dumping of crude oil into the Persian Gulf and set the oil wells of Kuwait aflame, killing plant and animal life and causing billions of dollars of damage.

SOMALIA

In August 1992, Bush began a humanitarian airlift of food and supplies to war-torn Somalia in northeastern Africa, where millions faced starvation. When local warlords and bandits continued to steal and threaten and rob food shipments, President Bush, acting under a U.N. mandate, sent U. S. troops to Somalia in the final month of his presidency. They were later withdrawn by President Bill Clinton.

KEY ITEMS TO REMEMBER

"Most Favored Nation" status, Kurds, Commonwealth of Independent States, Operation Desert Storm.

THE CLINTON PRESIDENCY 1993 - PRESENT

The Presidential election of 1992 was unusual in that it was a three-way contest. The Republicans attempted to focus the nation's attention on "family values" instead of economic issues, but Bush was hurt by the public's belief that he was not doing enough to fight the recession. The Democratic candidate, Bill Clinton, was helped by the emergence of **Ross Perot**, a Texas billionaire, as a third-party candidate. Perot's main focus was on the problems that had emerged in the Reagan and Bush years — such as the growth of the national debt and the flight of jobs overseas. In contrast, Clinton succeeded in unifying different groups within the Democratic Party — all of which were anxious to end 12 years of Republican control of the White House. He offered voters an agenda of change and a willingness to tackle problems like the national debt and health care. Bill Clinton was elected President with 43% of the popular vote.

DOMESTIC POLICIES UNDER CLINTON

Clinton promised America an ambitious agenda of reform He began his Presidency with a number of new programs. However, like many presidents, he had difficulty in obtaining Congressional support.

THE BUDGET DEFICIT

Democrats controlled Congress during the first two years of Clinton's term, but he still had some difficulty passing his early budgets. His first budget reduced some federal spending, increased income taxes for the wealthy and included a new tax on gasoline. These steps helped reduce the federal budget deficit.

HEALTH CARE REFORM

Clinton had promised to reform health care if elected. He appointed his wife, **Hillary Clinton**, to head a task force. The key feature in Clinton's proposal was to give every American guaranteed health insurance. Increased cigarette taxes were to help finance the new system. Employers would pay for most health insurance for their workers, and a national health board would control medical costs. Opponents feared greater government involvement in health care. Many alternative plans were soon proposed. No plan received enough support to pass Congress. The failure to reform health care was a major defeat for the President.

CRIME BILLS

President Clinton was successful in passing a major crime bill which increased funds for local police departments, introduced a five-day waiting period before an individual could purchase a handgun, increased money for prisons, and banned the sale of assault weapons.

SUPREME COURT APPOINTMENTS

Presidents Reagan and Bush had appointed conservatives to the Supreme Court; many feared the new conservative majority would overturn the Court's previous decisions on abortion, affirmative action and individual rights. Clinton appointed two moderates to the Court: Ruth Bader Ginsburg and Stephen Breyer.

ECONOMIC RECOVERY

Clinton's domestic measures and trade policies helped restore some confidence in the U.S. economy. By his second year in office, unemployment was down and consumer spending and business profits were up. However, the Federal Reserve Board, which controls the amount of money in circulation, increased interest rates to prevent rising prices. This step slowed the rate of economic growth.

CONGRESSIONAL ELECTIONS

In 1994, for the first time in 40 years, Republicans won control of both houses of Congress. This was seen as a sign of public dissatisfaction with the Clinton Presidency. Many voters were upset with tax increases, catering to special interest groups and the return of big goverment. During the campaign, many Republican candidates signed a document they called the "**Contract With America.**" This Contract promised lower taxes, less government regulation, and less federal spending on social programs. Led by the Speaker of the House, Newt Gingrich, Republicans introduced a number of new bills. However, their proposed balanced budget amendment, as well as term limits for Congress, failed to pass.

THE PRESIDENTIAL ELECTION OF 1996

By 1996, President Clinton had restored much of his popularity by opposing many cuts in spending proposed by the Republican Congress. Many Americans were particularly upset when they thought Republicans would cut Medicare and Medicaid. The economy was prosperous, and Clinton easily defeated Republican challenger Bob Dole, with almost 50% of the popular vote.

FOREIGN POLICY

Clinton had come to the White House with limited experience in foreign affairs. Some of his greatest successes, however, have been in foreigh policy. As President, Clinton made trade and economic issues his top priority. Congress passed NAFTA and revised GATT (an international agareement to lower world tariffs). Clinton has reduced U.S. export controls and reopened trade with Vietnam. He has also participated in trade summits with leaders from Asia, Latin America and Europe.

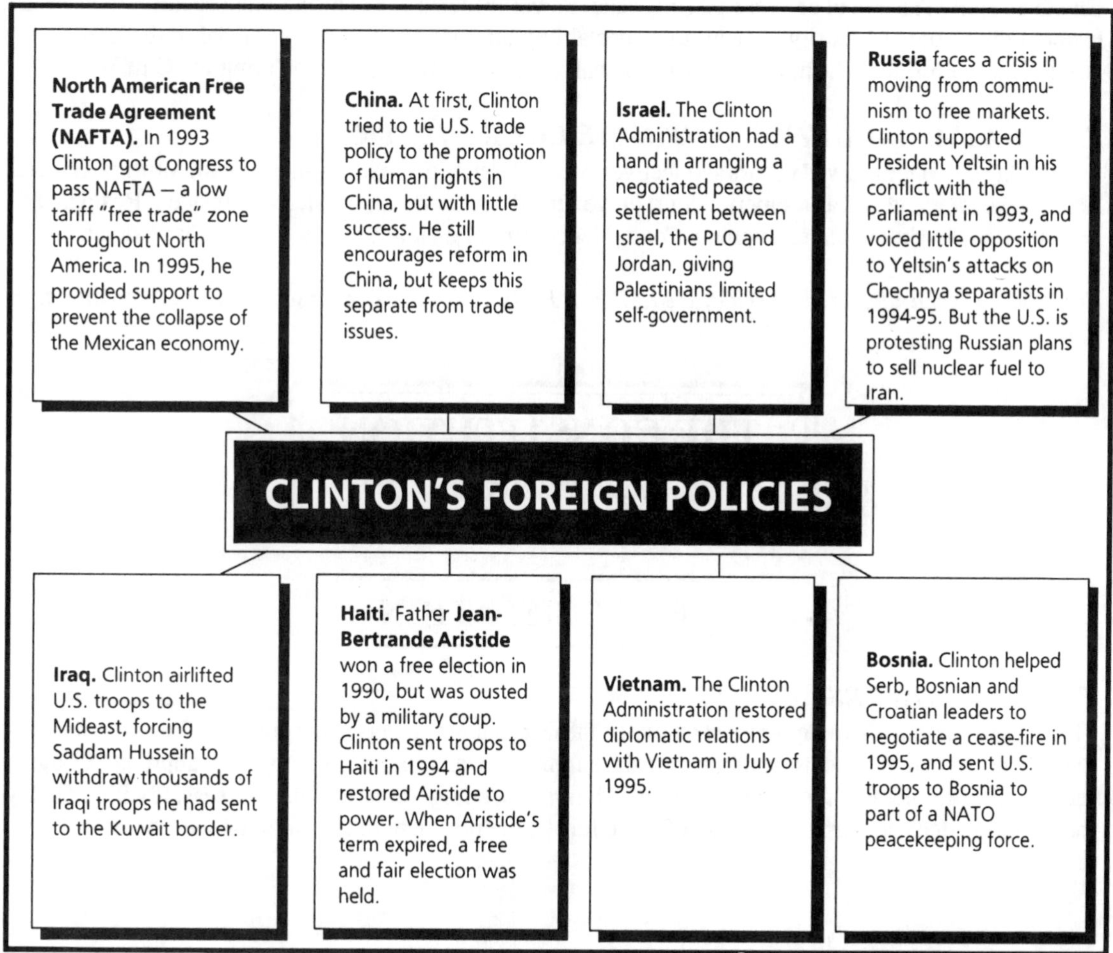
CLINTON'S FOREIGN POLICIES
North American Free Trade Agreement (NAFTA). In 1993 Clinton got Congress to pass NAFTA — a low tariff "free trade" zone throughout North America. In 1995, he provided support to prevent the collapse of the Mexican economy.
China. At first, Clinton tried to tie U.S. trade policy to the promotion of human rights in China, but with little success. He still encourages reform in China, but keeps this separate from trade issues.
Israel. The Clinton Administration had a hand in arranging a negotiated peace settlement between Israel, the PLO and Jordan, giving Palestinians limited self-government.
Russia faces a crisis in moving from communism to free markets. Clinton supported President Yeltsin in his conflict with the Parliament in 1993, and voiced little opposition to Yeltsin's attacks on Chechnya separatists in 1994-95. But the U.S. is protesting Russian plans to sell nuclear fuel to Iran.
Iraq. Clinton airlifted U.S. troops to the Mideast, forcing Saddam Hussein to withdraw thousands of Iraqi troops he had sent to the Kuwait border.
Haiti. Father **Jean-Bertrande Aristide** won a free election in 1990, but was ousted by a military coup. Clinton sent troops to Haiti in 1994 and restored Aristide to power. When Aristide's term expired, a free and fair election was held.
Vietnam. The Clinton Administration restored diplomatic relations with Vietnam in July of 1995.
Bosnia. Clinton helped Serb, Bosnian and Croatian leaders to negotiate a cease-fire in 1995, and sent U.S. troops to Bosnia to part of a NATO peacekeeping force.

PERSONALITIES OF THE PERIOD

NEIL ARMSTRONG & EDWIN ALDRIN (ASTRONAUTS)

In July 1969, 600 million television viewers watched Neil Armstrong and Edwin "Buzz" Aldrin step out of their lunar module and walk along the surface of the moon. This accomplishment ended a struggle, begun in 1957, to catch up to the Soviets in the "space race." It marked an enormous achievement for American technology and helped boost American prestige world-wide.

COLIN POWELL (CHAIRMAN, JOINT CHIEFS OF STAFF)

In 1989, President Bush nominated Colin Powell, a four-star general, to be the new Chairman of the Joint Chiefs of Staff. The son of Jamaican immigrants, Powell became Reagan's national security advisor and restored the National Security Council to respectability after it was rocked by scandal in the Iran-Contra Affair. Under President Bush, Powell provided calm and inspiring leadership during the Gulf War.

SANDRA DAY O'CONNOR (SUPREME COURT JUSTICE)

Sandra Day O'Connor served in various elective posts in the state of Arizona—as assistant Attorney General, as a state senator and and as a superior court judge. In 1981, she was nominated by President Reagan to fill a vacancy on the United States Supreme Court. Her confirmation made her the Court's first woman justice.

For other personalities of this period, see I.M. Pei, Jackson Pollock and Ansel Adams in "Looking at the Arts."

THE CONSTITUTION AT WORK

KEY LEGISLATION

THE WAR POWERS ACT (1973)

This act was passed to help Congress set limits on the war-making powers of the president. Passed in response to the concern that presidents could involve the nation in a war without Congressional approval, Congress required the president to inform them within 48 hours of sending troops to fight overseas. If within 60 days the Congress does not approve the use of these forces, the president must withdraw the troops.

KEY COURT CASES

— THE BURGER COURT —

The Warren Court put the Supreme Court into the national spotlight as an instrument of social change. The **Burger Court** (1969-1986), like the Warren Court before it, continued to believe in judicial activism—that the Supreme Court has a responsibility to safeguard the Constitution against violations by other branches of government. In general, it emphasized societal rights over individual rights.

NEW YORK TIMES v. U.S. (1971)

Background: The U.S. Government tried to block publication in *The New York Times* of a classified study on Vietnam policy, commonly referred to as the *Pentagon Papers*. The government argued that it should be allowed to limit freedom of the press when the nation's security was at stake.

Decision/Significance: The Supreme Court supported *The New York Times*' right to publish the documents, ruling that national security was not threatened by the release of the report, and that the government's attempted censorship was unconstitutional.

ROE V. WADE (1973)

See page 314 for details.

UNIVERSITY OF CALIFORNIA v. BAKKE (1978)

Background: Alan Bakke, a white male, was denied admission to a medical school which had accepted African Americans, Chicanos and Asians with less desirable academic credentials. The medical school contended that special admissions were being used to correct past racial discrimination. Bakke argued that this was reverse racial discrimination.

Decision/Significance: Although the Supreme Court ordered Bakke admitted to the school, it said schools could take race into account as a factor in admissions. However, they could not have specific quotas for different racial groups. The decision was significant because it upheld the principle of affirmative action.

— THE REHNQUIST COURT —

The **Rehnquist Court** (1986-present) has seen a shift in membership. Many have stated that the newer members appointed by Presidents Nixon, Reagan and Bush tend to be conservative rather than liberal. The Rehnquist Court has been reversing some of the decisions of the Warren and Burger Courts, especially in the matters of abortion rights, affirmative action programs, and the rights of defendants in criminal cases. See pages 380-381 for some of the key decisions of the Rehnquist court.

SUMMARIZING YOUR UNDERSTANDING

Directions: How well did you understand what you have just read? Test yourself by answering the following questions.

MAJOR ITEMS TO REMEMBER

On separate 3 x 5 index cards (as shown on pages 33-34), briefly define the following terms and concepts:

War Powers Act	Helsinki Accords	Commonwealth of Independent States
Imperial Presidency	Camp David Accords	Trade Imbalance
Watergate Affair	Reaganomics	Iran-Contra Affair

THE VIETNAM WAR

The Vietnam War left deep wounds in this nation, many of which have not fully healed. Summarize your understanding of the Vietnam War by answering the following questions:

- Trace the steps leading to United States involvement in Vietnam.
- Why was the United States unable to win the war in Vietnam?
- What has been the legacy of the war in Vietnam?

THE NIXON AND CARTER PRESIDENCIES

The Nixon and Carter presidencies were marked by successes in foreign policy coupled with difficulties in domestic affairs. Summarize your understanding of these presidencies by answering the following questions:

- What factors contributed to the growth of presidential power in the 20th century?
- Describe some of the domestic difficulties and foreign policy successes of the Nixon and Carter presidencies.
- How did the Watergate Affair show the strengths as well as the weaknesses of the American system of government?

THE REAGAN, BUSH AND CLINTON PRESIDENCIES

Presidents Reagan, Bush and Clinton were involved in important developments at home and overseas. For each president, describe some of the important events during his term and how he reacted to them.

PERSONALITIES OF THE PERIOD

People often have an important influence on the political, economic or social life of their times. Summarize your understanding of this statement by completing a 3 x 5 index card (see page 34) for each of the following: ***Richard Nixon***, ***Jimmy Carter***, ***Ronald Reagan***, ***George Bush***, ***Sandra Day O'Connor***, and ***Colin Powell.***

TESTING YOUR UNDERSTANDING

Directions: Test your understanding of this unit by answering the following questions. Circle the number preceding the word or expression that correctly answers the statement or question. Following the short answer questions, answer either the RCT-type or Regents essay questions.

SKILL BUILDER: INTERPRETING A CARTOON

Base your answer to questions 1 through 3 on the following cartoon and on your knowledge of social studies.

1 Which concept is most clearly reflected in the cartoon?
1 checks and balances
2 judicial review
3 federalism
4 national supremacy

2 Which president is depicted in the cartoon?
1 Jimmy Carter
2 Richard Nixon
3 Ronald Reagan
4 George Bush

3 The main idea of the cartoon is that the
1 Congress and the president often disagree.
2 The executive branch is the main one in the federal government.
3 Congress holds the nation's purse strings.
4 The president's programs are quite popular.

SKILL BUILDER: INTERPRETING SPEAKERS

Base your answers to questions 4 through 7 on the statements of the following presidential advisors and on your knowledge of social studies.

Advisor A: Mr. President, your continued spending on defense programs at the present rate has left the nation facing an enormous deficit. Even though you personally oppose a tax increase, we must have one.

Advisor B: You can no longer continue to defy the courts. Your administration is faced with a political scandal. This constitutional crisis has been brought on by your claims of executive privilege, putting you in direct opposition to the judicial branch of the federal government.

Advisor C: You must act to condemn acts of terrorism. We cannot permit the forcible seizure of our diplomats by foreign terrorists. Action is called for in this situation—you must do something!

Advisor D: Your responsibility as president is to determine our foreign policy. This constitutional grant of power will support your goal of removing an unfriendly foreign leader from power to protect our Caribbean interests.

4 Which president is receiving advice from advisor A?
1 Eisenhower
2 Nixon
3 Carter
4 Reagan

5 Advisor B is most likely speaking to which president?
1 Eisenhower
2 Reagan
3 Carter
4 Nixon

6 Advisor C is probably describing the United States involvement in the
1 Iranian Hostage Crisis
2 Gulf of Tonkin
3 Bay of Pigs invasion
4 invasion of Panama

7 Which situation would advisor D most likely have supported?
1 Iranian hostage crisis
2 Camp David summit meetings
3 passage of the New Deal
4 invasion of Panama

SKILL BUILDER: ANALYZING A TIMELINE

Base your answers to questions 8 through 10 on the following timeline and on your knowledge of social studies.

TWENTIETH CENTURY EVENTS IN VIETNAM'S HISTORY

1940	1954	1963	1967	1971	1973
Vietnam battles Japanese invaders in W.W II	France is forced out of Vietnam	17,000 U.S. military advisers sent to Vietnam	500,000 U.S. troops sent to fight in Vietnam	200,000 anti-war protesters march on Washington	U.S. forces withdraw from Vietnam

8 During which time period were U. S. military forces first sent to Vietnam?
1 1940 to 1954
2 1954 to 1967
3 1967 to 1973
4 after 1973

9 The timeline indicates that the United States and Vietnam were
1 involved in a military conflict
2 economic trading rivals in Asia
3 sharing advanced technology
4 military allies against the French forces

10 Which conclusion is best supported by information in the timeline?
1 Vietnam has often fought against foreign invaders.
2 Vietnam's government lacks a democratic tradition.
3 Years of warfare have left Vietnam in economic ruin.
4 In 1973, North Vietnam was taken over by South Vietnam.

---

11 Which was a basic cause of American involvement in the Vietnam War?
1 religious differences between North and South Vietnam
2 American fear of Communist expansion in Asia
3 the North Korean invasion of South Vietnam
4 placement of Soviet nuclear weapons in Vietnam

12 Which event took place during the administration of George Bush?
1 invasion of Panama
2 passage of the Civil Rights Act
3 passage of the New Deal
4 the Watergate scandal

13 During President Reagan's time in office, his federal budget proposals came under sharp criticism because they have
1 lowered interest rates and decreased inflation
2 increased social welfare spending
3 resulted in very large deficits
4 advocated raising the income tax

14 The Reagan Administration faced its greatest difficulties in Central America in
1 Nicaragua
2 Honduras
3 Guatemala
4 Costa Rica

15 United States actions in the Vietnam War demonstrated that
1 the domino theory is an effective military tactic
2 military policy in a democracy is influenced by popular opinion
3 advanced technology ensures victory
4 limited use of tactical nuclear weapons can be successful

16 Which statement best reflects President Reagan's "New Federalism"?
1 the federal government should be given greater power
2 taxes should be raised to reduce the federal deficit
3 the federal government should give power back to the states
4 military spending should be cut to provide funds for social programs

17 The final outcome of the Watergate Affair was significant because it reinforced the idea that
1 the government is based on the rule of laws, not on individuals
2 the chief executive has nearly unlimited powers
3 Congress is ineffective in dealing with a Constitutional crisis
4 the Supreme Court is afraid to make decisions involving the presidency

18 During the administration of President Nixon, U. S. policy toward China was characterized by
1 attempts to introduce democracy into China
2 increasing hostility and isolation
3 the signing of a mutual defense pact
4 a relaxation of strained relations

19 The main similarity between the Korean War and the Vietnam War was that both wars
1 involved the issue of freedom of the seas
2 sought to achieve religious freedom
3 tried to limit the spread of Communism in Asia
4 attempted to restore a king to power in Asia

20 Which source would be most helpful in locating information about Vietnam's topography?
1 an atlas of Southeast Asia
2 a history text describing U. S. involvement in Southeast Asia
3 a State Department bulletin describing diplomatic affairs in Asia
4 the memoirs of a Vietnam war veteran

21 The Gulf of Tonkin Resolution and the sinking of the *U.S.S. Maine* are similar in that both events
1 prevented the spread of Communism
2 brought the U. S. to war
3 brought democratic government to Asia
4 encouraged European immigration to the U. S.

22 Which statement best describes reaction in the United States after both W. W. I and the Vietnam conflict?
1 The United States increased its policy of global intervention.
2 America became more cautious about involvement in world events.
3 The United States paid large indemnities to its wartime enemies.
4 Congress quickly voted funds to expand the military.

23 Which factor had the greatest influence on the decisions of the U. S. government to enter the Spanish-American War and to withdraw from the Vietnam conflict?
1 campus demonstrations
2 pressure from large corporations
3 power of the press
4 advice of the military

24 Which is the best explanation of why presidential power increased during the Vietnam War?
1 Congress was afraid to exercise its Constitutional powers.
2 The Constitution was suspended during wartime.
3 The president was in a position to act quickly and decisively.
4 In wartime, the Constitution puts all power into the president's hands.

25 "I believe that it must be the policy of the United States to support free peoples who are resisting attempted subjugation by armed minorities or by outside pressures. I believe that our help should be primarily through economic and financial aid...."

—Harry Truman

The ideas in the quotation were used by President Reagan to justify U. S. intervention in the affairs of
1 Central America
2 Western Europe
3 Vietnam
4 Canada

RCT-TYPE ESSAYS

1 Presidents can be graded on the deeds that they accomplished while in office.

Presidents

John Kennedy	Jimmy Carter
Richard Nixon	Ronald Reagan
Gerald Ford	George Bush

Part A

Choose *one* of the presidents listed above. ______________________________

List *two* accomplishments or failures that occurred during that president's term of office.

1. ______________________________ 2. ______________________________

Using the list at right, what grade would you give this president? __________

Excellent	90-100
Good	70-90
Fair	60-70
Poor	10-60

Part B

In your Part B answer, you should use information you gave in Part A. However, you may also include different or additional information in your Part B answer.

Write an essay explaining why you gave that particular grade to the president.

2 Foreign policy decisions made by U. S. presidents often have an important and far-reaching impact.

Part A

The following chart lists six 20th-century U. S. presidents and one important foreign policy decision made by each.

President	The President's Decision
Truman	Ordering the dropping of an atom bomb on Hiroshima
Johnson	Sending U. S. troops to Vietnam
Nixon	Signing a peace treaty to end the war in Vietnam
Carter	Helping to bring about the Camp David Accords
Reagan	Greatly increasing the U.S. defense budget
Bush	Sending U. S. troops to fight Iraq

Choose *one* of these presidents: ______________________________

State why the president made that decision: ____

Choose *another* president: ______________________________

State why the president made that decision: ____

Part B

In your Part B answer, you should use information you gave in Part A. However, you may also include different or additional information in your Part B answer.

Write an essay explaining how foreign policy decisions made by U. S. presidents often have an important and far-reaching impact.

REGENTS-TYPE ESSAYS

1 Presidential decisions have had an important effect on the United States and the world. Following are headlines representing important presidential decisions:

Headlines

"McKinley Asks for a Declaration of War Against Spain"
"Wilson Wants Senate to Approve the Treaty of Versailles"
"Truman Orders a Bomb Dropped on Hiroshima"
"Kennedy Orders Blockade of Cuba"
"Johnson Increases Military Forces in Vietnam"
"Carter Signs Camp David Accords With Sadat and Begin"
"Bush Orders Operation Desert Storm Against Iraq"

Select *three* of the headlines listed, and for *each* one:

- Describe the circumstances which led to the decision
- Discuss *two* major results of that decision

2 In a past survey, historians graded U.S. presidents on characteristics such as leadership qualities, accomplishments, crisis management, political skills and integrity. Some presidents and their grade levels are listed below.

High Grades	Low Grades
Abraham Lincoln	Andrew Johnson
Theodore Roosevelt	Ulysses S. Grant
Woodrow Wilson	Warren Harding
Harry S Truman	Jimmy Carter
Franklin D. Roosevelt	Richard Nixon

a Select *one* president from each group. For *each* president selected, discuss to what extent you agree or disagree with the historians' rating of that president. [Use specific historical information to support your position.]

b Identify *any* president *not* listed above and state whether you would give that president a high or low grade. Support your position by using specific historical information.

3 In attempting to measure how successful a person has been as president of the United States, the following qualities have been identified as important:

- Communication skills
- Ability to interpret the mood of the country
- Ability to project a positive public image
- Willingness to initiate bold programs
- Firmness, yet willingness to compromise

Select *three* qualities from the list which you think are the most important qualities necessary for success as a president. For *each* one selected, show how this quality contributed to the success of a specific United States president during his presidency. [Use a different president for each quality.]

PERFORMANCE-BASED TASKS

Setting: The Vietnam War was this nation's longest war — costing the lives of over 58,000 American soldiers, and an estimated 3 million Vietnamese. Despite the high cost in lives and money, the United States was never able to achieve its goal of preserving a separate, independent South Vietnam free of Communism. Some critics of American involvement in Vietnam believe that U.S. Presidents knew the war could not be won. These critics argue that U.S. Presidents continued to wage the war either because they feared losing the next election or because they did not want to become the first President in U.S. history to lose a war.

General Directions: Your task is to pretend you are a member of Congress in 1968, a critical time during the Vietnam War. A fellow member of Congress has just introduced the following resolution:

> **Resolved**: That the President of the United States should immediately withdraw all U.S. forces from the Republic of Vietnam.

As a member of Congress, you must decide whether you favor or oppose this resolution. Before making your decision, you should conduct further research in your school or local library. Remember that you must make your decision based on information that was known in 1968 — not on the basis of what we know today. In reaching your decision, you should consider:

- the objectives of the United States government
- whether a withdrawal or continuation of the war would further those objectives.
- the effects of withdrawal on the future of South Vietnam and Southeast Asia.
- how a withdrawal would affect America's relations with its other allies
- how the war could have best been fought
- whether an independent South Vietnam had any prospects of survival

Your Task: Once you decide on your position, you should prepare a three to five minute speech to present to "Congress" — your class. To prepare for your presentation, you should make notes on notecards and practice delivering your speech to a friend. After the speeches are delivered, the "Congress" should continue to debate the resolution, and finally take a vote. You will be graded on how well you support your position and how well you know the material for your speech.

LOOKING AT CONTROVERSIAL ISSUES AND PROBLEMS

Many essay questions on the RCTs and Regents Examinations ask about current concerns, issues and trends facing the United States. An example of this kind of question appeared on the June 1992 Regents:

> In the United States today, people hold different viewpoints concerning controversial issues. Some of these areas of controversy are listed below:
>
> **Areas of Controversy**
>
> | | |
> |---|---|
> | Capital punishment | Censorship |
> | Right to die | Health care funding |
> | Affirmative Action | Homelessness |
>
> Choose *three* of the areas of controversy listed and for *each* one chosen:
> - State an issue involved in the controversy
> - Discuss two different points of view concerning the issue
> - Describe a specific action taken by government or a group to deal with the issue

This section will help give you an overview of what you need to know to answer this type of essay question.

CONCERNS

There are many concerns that affect the United States and touch upon the lives of its citizens. Part of the challenge of the future will be to deal with these concerns.

THE QUESTION

A question about these concerns will usually focus on several major problems introduced by a general statement. For example, a typical general statement beginning such a question could be:

> Many of the major problems facing the United States during the 1980s will continue to challenge the nation in the 1990s.

The types of problems listed will be those affecting the nation's well-being at home or those that involve the country with other nations. The concerns most often cited are:

Domestic Problems	Global Problems
AIDS Epidemic	International Terrorism
Increasing Health Costs	Drug Trafficking
Homelessness	Trade Gap
Budget Deficit	Human Rights Violations
Drug Epidemic	Debt Crisis
Rising Crime Rates	Political Instability in the World
Farm Crisis	U.S. relations with other countries
Environmental Pollution	Damage to the Ozone Layer

Let's examine how to answer this type of essay question.

A GENERAL APPROACH

Although there are different things that may be asked about these problems, generally most of the questions will focus on:

(a) **Defining the Problem.** Here you are expected to describe the nature of the problem. A helpful hint might be to go through a mental checklist — *who, what, where, when* — in describing or defining the problem.

(b) **Identifying the Causes.** Here you are expected to explain why or how something came about. "Causes" are the various reasons that led to the problem. For example, why is homelessness increasing? Or why is the United States experiencing a trade gap?

(c) **Explaining the Effects.** Here you are expected to explain the effects or impact that the problem is having on society. What, for example, has been the impact of the AIDS epidemic on hospitals and health care?

(d) **Providing Some Solutions.** Here you are expected to discuss some actions that

- have been taken by government agencies or private institutions to help solve the problem
- you might recommend to help solve the problem

For example, what steps could government take to control air pollution? The Clean Air Act limits automobile emissions and requires state governments to conduct tests before licensing factories. What other steps would you recommend?

To improve your study habits, when you read about a current concern, you should think about all four of these aspects: can you *define* the problem, *identify* the causes, *explain* the effects, and *provide* some solutions? Some important concerns facing us today are explained in the following chapter.

ISSUES

Throughout your U. S. History course, you have learned about enduring issues that touch upon aspects of the U.S. Constitution. Unlike a *concern*, where most people agree that there is a problem to be solved, an *issue* is one in which there are two opposing or contrary viewpoints.

THE QUESTION

Most often questions about issues are introduced by some general statement. For example, a typical general statement beginning such a question could be:

> In the United States, situations frequently occur in which the interests of individuals come into conflict with the perceived needs of society. Listed below are several issues that may lead to such conflict.

This type of question tests your understanding of opposing viewpoints on a particular issue. The issues most often cited are:

Gun control	Affirmative action
Prayer in schools	Death penalty
Right to die	Drug testing
Welfare programs	Abortion

Let's examine how to answer this type of essay question.

A GENERAL APPROACH

Although different things may be asked about these issues, most of the questions will focus on:

(a) **Defining the Issue**. Here you are expected to describe the issue. A helpful hint might be to go through a mental checklist — *who, what, where, when* — in defining the issue. For example, some people believe the death penalty should be used to punish murderers. Others believe this is "cruel and unusual punishment" in violation of the U.S. Constitution.

(b) **Explaining Opposing Viewpoints.** Here you are expected to tell about the two conflicting sides of the issue or controversy. You may be asked to bring in one or more arguments used by each side in support of its viewpoint. Opposing viewpoints on several important recent issues are presented in the next chapter.

(c) **Dealing with the Issue**. Here you are expected to discuss or explain some recent action taken by the government or private group on the issue.

To improve your study habits, when you read about a social issue, you should think about all three of these aspects: can you *define* the issue, *explain* the viewpoints, and *discuss* government or private actions taken on it?

TRENDS

A trend is a pattern of change that points in some direction. Several trends are visible today that will have an impact on our future.

THE QUESTION

Most often questions about trends are introduced by a general statement. For example, a typical general statement beginning such a question could be:

> Technology has greatly affected American society since the end of World War II. Listed are several areas in which technological developments have brought about change in American society.

These questions test your understanding of patterns of change. Most often you will be asked to discuss trends taking place in the following areas:

- Technology
- Health Care
- Role of Women
- Education
- Workplace
- Population Growth
- Cultural Diversity

Let's examine how to answer this type of essay question.

A GENERAL APPROACH

Although there are different things that may be asked about trends, most of the questions will center on:

(a) **Defining the Trend**. Here you are expected to describe the trend or development. A helpful hint might again be to go through a mental checklist — *who, what, where, when* — in defining the trend. For example, how has the role of women in the home, in the workplace and in politics changed over the past 100 years?

(b) **Predicting the Effects**. Here you are expected to discuss the effects or impact that the trend has had or will have on society. For example, what effects do you think continued world population growth will have on global resources?

To improve your study habits, when you read about a trend or development, you should think about both of these aspects: can you *define* the trend and *predict* its effects?

CHAPTER 15

PROSPECTS FOR THE FUTURE

During its first two hundred years the United States faced many problems and changes. The nation handled most of its troubles with great success. But what does the future hold for the United States as it enters its third century as a nation? In learning to deal with past challenges, the United States has emerged a richer and stronger nation. However, Americans cannot relax, since present and future generations will face new and unique challenges. This chapter explores some of these emerging challenges.

KEY CONCERNS

DOMESTIC CONCERNS

There are many problems that affect the nation and touch upon our lives. Let's take a look at some of the key concerns facing the nation today.

THE AIDS EPIDEMIC

Acquired Immune Deficiency Syndrome (AIDS) is a virus that prevents the body's internal defense system from fighting disease. People die from the disease when they are no longer able to fight off infection. It is transmitted from one individual to another through the exchange of body fluids, especially through sexual contact, infected hypodermic needles, and infected blood transfusions. Very little is known about exactly where or how the disease originated. Some communities were slow to respond to AIDS because only certain groups—particularly homosexuals and illegal drug users—were affected at first. Some community leaders did not want to encourage sexual activity among teenagers by teaching them about "safe sex."

■ **Impact.** The Centers for Disease Control report that since 1981 over 160,000 Americans have contracted AIDS. Since the start of the epidemic, over 82,000 Americans have died from the disease. In 1990 alone, over 31,000 AIDS patients died. Future death projections are even bleaker. The epidemic is leading to overcrowded hospitals and rising health care costs, threatening to strain the entire health care system.

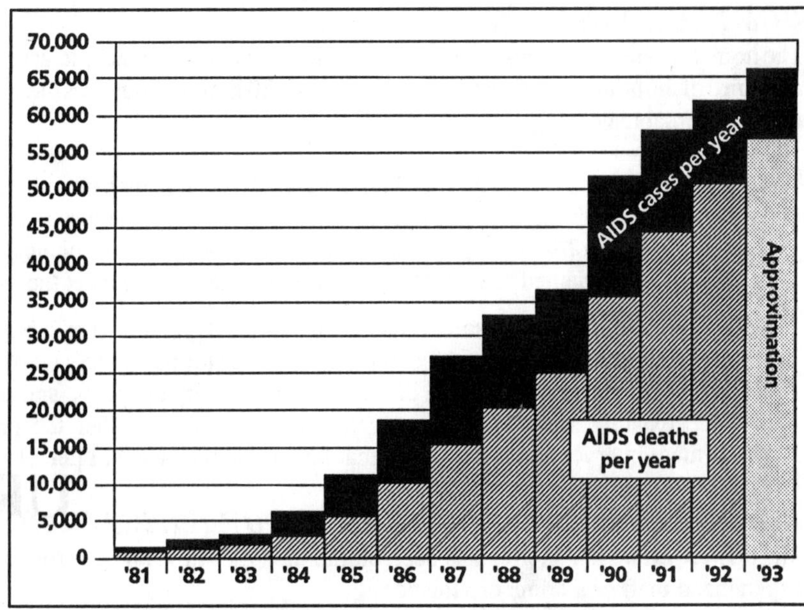
70,000
65,000
60,000
55,000
50,000
45,000
40,000
35,000
30,000
25,000
20,000
15,000
10,000
5,000
0
'81
'82
'83
'84
'85
'86
'87
'88
'89
'90
'91
'92
'93
AIDS cases per year
AIDS deaths per year
Approximation

Source: U.S. Department of Health and Human Services/Centers for Disease Control

■ **Actions.** Although the government has been spending billions of tax dollars on research, treatment,and education, there is still no cure. Currently, the only approved treatment for AIDS is the drug AZT.

INCREASING HEALTH COSTS

Health costs have become the fastest-rising item in the average household budget. Advances in medical technology have made it possible to save more lives, but have also led to drastic increases in the costs of treatment and research. Health insurance premiums have risen dramatically. One out of every three Americans is either uninsured (37 million) or underinsured (50 million). For these people, health insurance is either too expensive or insurance companies refuse to sell them a policy because of a pre-existing medical problem. Many Americans are now demanding national health insurance to provide free or inexpensive health care to all. Others fear national health insurance would reduce the existing quality of health care.

■ **Federal Action.** In 1965, Congress passed the **Medicare** bill, to provide citizens aged 65 and older with low-cost hospital insurance. Health costs for the U.S government are expected to triple between 1990 and 2000. As costs continue to rise, there is concern about future cuts in the Medicare program.

■ **State Action.** The states created **Medicaid** programs to help needy people below the age of 65 with their medical costs. But with medical costs continuing to climb, new and innovative ways need to be found by state governments to keep medical costs down.

■ **The Clinton Health Care Plan.** President Clinton has proposed a significant change in the system of American health care—See page 350.

HOMELESSNESS

The homeless are sometimes depicted as derelicts or mentally ill people who sleep in doorways. However, one-third of the homeless are families. Even though 20% of the homeless have full-time jobs, they are unable to find affordable housing.

■ **Causes.** The reasons for the problem are varied. As housing demand increases, housing shortages develop. Persons living on a minimal income often find themselves on the street as rents rise above their ability to pay. Many people do not have the educational and technical skills necessary in today's technologically oriented society to earn a sufficient income to meet the high cost of housing.

■ **Recommendations.** One solution would be for local governments to build subsidized, low-income housing. Others have suggested federal tax incentives for developers who build low-income housing; the sale of foreclosed homes at a discount to community agencies; and the use of tenant groups to renovate existing apartments. However, many question whether the problem can be solved by government intervention. They stress that the problem is deeper than a lack of money.

RISING CRIME RATES AND THE USE OF ILLEGAL DRUGS

Since 1975, crime in America has been on the increase. In 1988, one-fourth of all American households experienced theft or a crime of violence.

■ **Causes.** Some crimes are committed by poor and disadvantaged people who seem unable to break out of the cycle of poverty. The reasons most frequently offered for the rising crime rate involve the frustration of those who live in poverty, the availability of guns, and the violence spurred by television and movies. Much crime is also drug-related. The United States consumes sixty percent of the world's illegal drugs. One in four users becomes a dealer, selling to friends, neighbors and fellow workers to support the user's drug habit. Many of these drugs, like heroin and cocaine, are addictive and can cause death.

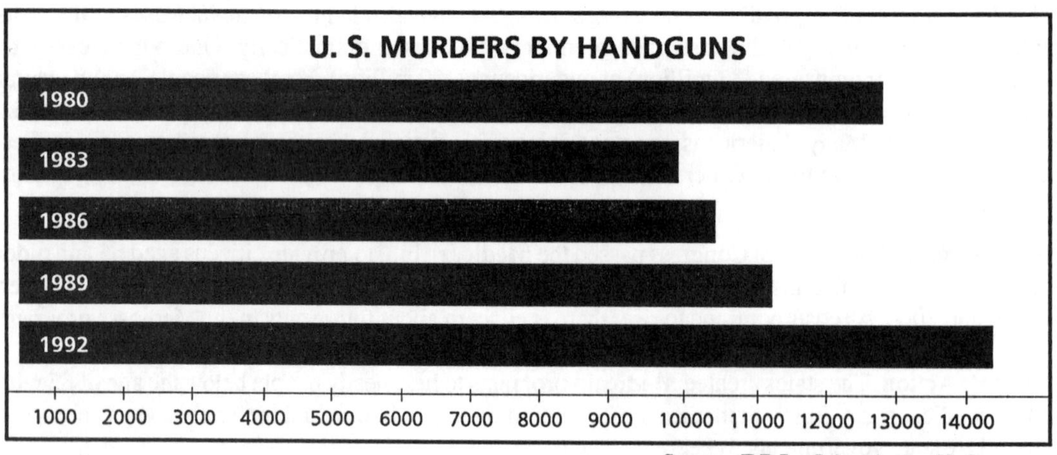
U. S. MURDERS BY HANDGUNS
1980
1983
1986
1989
1992
1000 2000 3000 4000 5000 6000 7000 8000 9000 10000 11000 12000 13000 14000

Source: F.B.I., *Crime in the U. S.*

■ **Suggested Solutions.** Some people believe more police, longer prison terms and tougher gun control laws are the answer. Others suggest more jobs, training programs and drug rehabilitation clinics might help eliminate the underlying causes of crime. They also emphasize the need for greater efforts to educate young people about the dangers of illegal drugs.

EDUCATION

Education is essential for a democracy to function effectively. Education is also viewed as the road to improved status in society. However, America's public schools are facing a crisis. Almost 23 million Americans are illiterate, and another 40 million can only read on an eighth grade level. Illiteracy is growing by 2.3 million people each year. High school dropout rates are approaching 30%, with inner city rates closer to 60%. In many states (Kentucky, Montana, New Jersey and Texas) courts have ruled that existing public school financing and educational systems are unconstitutional because of their failure to provide adequate schooling to needy children. American students consistently finish below students from most other industrialized nations in math and science achievement. Many employers wonder where the future workers will come from to fill the highly complex jobs needed in our technologically advanced society.

■ **Suggested Solutions.** Some educators have urged a system which would allow parents to receive a **voucher** for public funds, permitting them to select any school they wished for their children. Other suggestions include improved teacher salaries, innovative approaches to teaching and a greater emphasis on teaching basic skills. Still others urge more mandatory testing of all students for both skills and achievement.

THE ENVIRONMENT

Environmental protection is now a primary concern of Americans.

■ **Garbage Disposal.** America's industrial society creates billions of tons of garbage daily. Where to put this garbage creates serious problems. Burning garbage emits harmful toxins into the atmosphere. Ocean dumping contaminates the water and threatens marine life. Landfills are closing because they no longer have available space. New ways—such as **recycling**—need to be used to manage this growing problem. Americans must also reduce the amount of waste they generate.

■ **Water Pollution.** Factories sometimes dump toxins (poisons) and other wastes into our water supply. Accidents, especially those involving oil tankers, can result in oil spills covering hundreds of square miles of ocean and seashore, killing plants and wildlife.

■ **Air Pollution.** When fossil fuels such as coal and oil are burned to create energy, they dump pollutants into the air. This can have negative effects on the atmosphere.

- **Acid Rain.** Many of the pollutants released into the air by industrial fumes and automobile exhausts turn into acids. These acids get washed out of the air when it rains or snows. When these pollutants return to the ground, they are often toxic, killing fish, destroying forests and eroding soil. The U. S. government is enacting stricter standards to control these acid-forming agents; the Clean Air Act has already imposed limits on the levels of some chemicals allowed in the air.

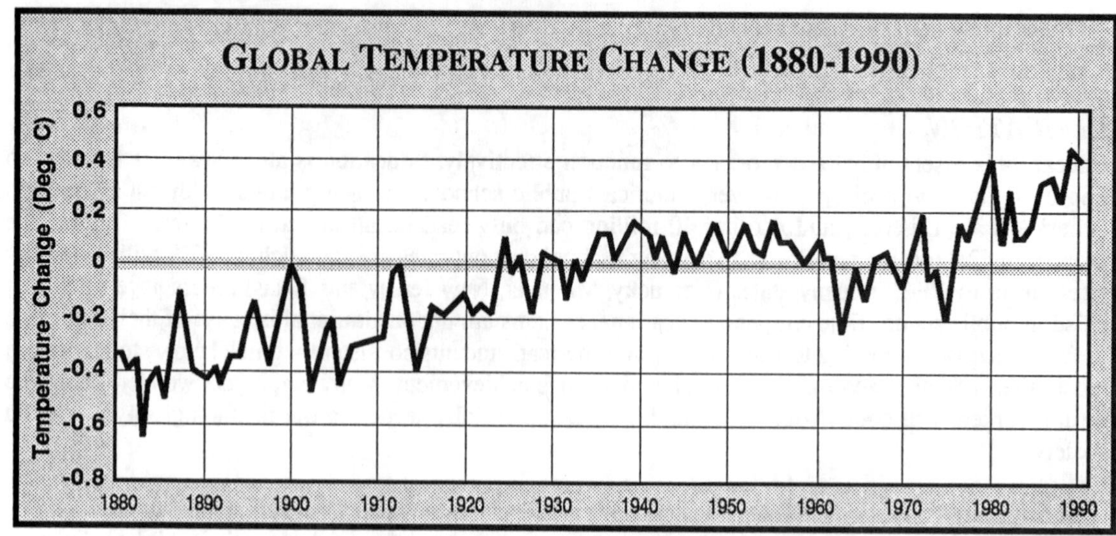
GLOBAL TEMPERATURE CHANGE (1880-1990)
Temperature Change (Deg. C)
0.6
0.4
0.2
0
-0.2
-0.4
-0.6
-0.8
1880
1890
1900
1910
1920
1930
1940
1950
1960
1970
1980
1990

Source: NASA Goddard Institute for Space Studies

- **Global Warming.** Pollutants in the air block heat from escaping harmlessly into space. The resulting **greenhouse effect** may permanently raise temperatures enough to cause farmlands to become deserts, rivers to dry up, and polar ice to melt, raising seas to dangerous levels. As more fuels are burned to supply electricity for air conditioners and cars, the problem will become worse.

- **Erosion of the Ozone Layer.** The ozone layer, which absorbs ultraviolet radiation that passes through the earth's atmosphere, is rapidly being thinned because of the use of certain types of fluorocarbons. Too much ultraviolet radiation can lead to skin cancer. Legislation has been proposed to limit the production and use of these harmful fluorocarbons.

■ **Resource Management.** The oil shortages of the 1970s made Americans aware that the earth's resources are limited. As a result, there has been a movement towards greater conservation, increased efforts at recycling, and additional federal and state legislation to protect the nation's resources.

■ **Deforestation.** The destruction of forests reduces the variety of plant and animal life and also decreases the world's production of oxygen.

■ **International Cooperation.** Environmental concerns cross national borders. The U. S. negotiates with foreign governments to reduce pollution and conserve world resources. In 1992, U. S. leaders participated in the **Rio Conference** ("Earth Summit") to discuss protection of the global environment.

THE BUDGET DEFICIT AND THE TRADE IMBALANCE

For a full discussion of these problems, see Chapter 14.

GLOBAL CONCERNS

The shrinking world has resulted in a growing sense of global interdependence, creating a situation in which events and relations between the U. S. and other nations are more important than ever to our own future.

HUMAN RIGHTS VIOLATIONS

Human rights refer to the rights we believe each person deserves as a human being, such as freedom of speech, thought, assembly, travel and participation in government. Human rights violations often take place in countries where there is only one political party in power. Usually this party does not tolerate political dissent or freedom of expression, and it severely limits each citizen's rights of movement and travel. Citizens are in constant fear of arbitrary arrest, imprisonment, torture, or death. Similar violations occur when a country is in the grip of civil war between rival groups.

POLITICAL INSTABILITY

Changing political situations in many areas of the world have heightened threats to world stability and peace.

- **Eastern Europe and former Soviet Union.** In 1989, the Soviet Union ended its indirect control of Eastern Europe. Democratic governments replaced Communist puppet governments. Today, the political situation changes almost daily. Eastern Europeans have high expectations from the recent changes, yet their economic systems are not as advanced as Western Europe. Perhaps most important, many of the different nationalities in this region cannot decide whether to cooperate or to break up into separate states. Yugoslavia is in a state of civil war, as are some of the former Soviet republics. U.S. foreign policy in the area is also undergoing change. Some U.S. business leaders would like to invest in the area, but others are afraid of future instability.

- **The Middle East.** The disagreement between Israel and its Arab neighbors over their boundaries and the fate of the Palestinians has been a constant source of warfare and tension. A recent compromise between Israeli and Palestinian leaders brings some hope of future peace. Americans continue to be concerned about the future of Arab-Israeli relations, realizing that any conflict in the region is capable of involving the United States. Americans are also concerned about Saddam Hussein, who remains in power in Iraq, and about the fundamentalist regime in Iran.

- **Somalia.** U.S. troops went to Somalia to stop widespread starvation caused by drought and local warfare. Now the U.S. hopes to withdraw without leaving Somalia in chaos.

ARMED CONFLICTS AROUND THE WORLD IN 1991

COUNTRY	KILLED (1991)	BASIS OF THE CONFLICT
Afghanistan	2,000	Islamic rebels continue to fight among themselves.
Burma (Myanmar)	5,000	Ethnic minorities fight the government.
India	6,500	Sikhs (Punjab) and Muslims (Kashmir) fight for independence.
Mozambique	2,000	Rightist rebels battle the government.
Somalia	20,000	Rival clans are fighting for government control.
Sri Lanka	11,000	Hindu Tamils are fighting the Buddhist Sinhalese majority.
Sudan	2,000	Islamic Fundamentalists government forces fight black rebels.
Yugoslavia	6,000	Croats and Serbs battled over Croatian independence.

KEY ITEMS TO REMEMBER

AIDS, homelessness, acid rain, global warming, global interdependence, human rights violations

KEY ISSUES

Throughout U. S. history, there have been critical issues that created contrary or opposing viewpoints. The following are some of the key issues facing Americans today.

GUN CONTROL

Should limits be placed on a citizen's right to own a gun?	
YES. Guns should be used by the police, whom we hire and train to enforce our laws, and not by average citizens. Guns give people a false sense of security. More often they kill through accidents the law-abiding citizen and not the criminal. Guns found in the homes of law-abiding citizens often wind up in criminal hands, leading to the deaths of innocent victims. Guns wrongly promote a "kill" mentality in society.	***NO.*** The 2nd Amendment of the Constitution gives citizens the right to own guns. Weapons used prudently can provide a means of self-defense for citizens. Those who support a citizen's right to own guns claim that in communities where citizens are permitted to own guns, crime has decreased greatly. A survey of criminals found that they are more fearful of armed civilians than of law enforcement officials.

SCHOOL PRAYER

Should prayers in public schools be permitted?	
YES. The Constitution allows freedom of religion, not freedom from religion. By banning prayers in school, we surrender an important part of teaching values and ethics to our children. The wall separating church and state is often crossed: public funds are used to buy books and provide bus transportation for parochial students; tax exemptions are given to religious properties; chaplains are a permanent part of the military; and prayers are used to open each session of Congress. Why, then, should we prohibit school prayers?	***NO.*** School prayers violate the constitutional separation of church and state. Praying in school infringes upon students who do not wish to take part in such activities by holding them up to embarrassment and ridicule by teachers and students. Besides, praying is a personal and private act, and should not be performed in a public school. Students are free to pray at home or in a place of worship at any time before or after school. Why, then, should we allow school prayers?

THE RIGHT TO DIE

Does a person have a right to choose a painless death?	
YES. The quality of life is the key, not life itself. When someone faces pain and suffering without hope of a cure, the government should not stand in the way of permitting a peaceful, painless death with dignity. Those who execute a **living will** have already made a choice. If they are hopelessly ill, such persons prefer that no heroic steps be taken to keep them alive, or that they receive **euthanasia** (mercy killing). This is more dignified than being forced onto life support systems when suffering and incurably ill.	***NO.*** Every life has value; it is ethically and legally wrong to help someone die. Life is a gift from God, and it is immoral to take that decision away from God. Doctors who help to carry out an "assisted suicide" are not healers, but executioners. Doctors should concern themselves with relieving pain, and not becoming killers. Finally, if the choice of painless death is made legal, many elderly will feel pressured to kill themselves for the good of their family, even though they don't really want to die.

AFFIRMATIVE ACTION

Should affirmative action programs be encouraged?	
YES. Affirmative action programs require employers to remedy past acts of discrimination by special efforts to hire women and minority members before hiring others who may be equally or better qualified. Such actions are necessary to help these groups overcome years of discrimination. Many women and minorities do not have the resources to overcome their economic conditions on their own. Also, the people in positions of power in hiring and recruiting are mainly white males. Special help is needed for minorities to achieve full equality.	***NO.*** Affirmative action programs that seek to end discrimination against women and minority groups result in reverse discrimination against white people and males. Artificial quotas to hire certain people based on race or sex serve only to undermine our national efforts to achieve a truly "color blind" society. Such programs actually lower a minority group's self-esteem by showing them that they are unable to get ahead on their own. Quotas that force businesses to hire unqualified members create increased hostility.

THE DEATH PENALTY

Should there be capital punishment?	
YES. Those who are critical of the death penalty must look beyond narrow individual interests and take into account the interests of society. Penalties must fit the crime; to do less makes a mockery of justice. Potential murderers may be deterred if they know they might be executed. Criminals have to respect and fear the law; the death penalty ensures that. High murder rates are found in societies with no capital punishment.	***NO.*** Capital punishment has never proven to be an effective deterrent to crime. The death penalty is revenge. It violates a person's right to life by subjecting that person to a cruel and inhuman punishment. Executing criminals is cruel; it causes them to suffer a prolonged period of anguish before the execution. It is also expensive because of the court appeals involved. Death is irreversible; juries are human and can make mistakes.

DRUG TESTING IN THE WORKPLACE

Should an individual be required to submit to drug testing?	
YES. Drug abuse is increasing daily. If drug testing is permitted in the workplace, a fear of testing positive may deter future drug use. Submitting to physical exams by employers is not new. Businesses and insurance companies often require exams before hiring someone or issuing an insurance policy. Testing employees for drugs allows companies to protect themselves by weeding out applicants who may be weak in character, use drugs at work, or engage in possible criminal activities against the company.	***NO.*** A person is believed to be innocent until proven guilty. Drug testing assumes people are guilty until they are proven innocent by testing negative. Drug testing is an invasion of a person's privacy. What an individual does in his or her off-hours is no concern of the employer. Allowing testing permits employers to use economic intimidation to force compliance with government laws. Companies should not be in the business of enforcing the law. Drug tests are notoriously unreliable, and a person has no protection against a possible mistake.

KEY ITEMS TO REMEMBER

Living will, euthanasia, death penalty, gun control, affirmative action, drug testing

KEY TRENDS

Throughout American history some trends have had an important impact on the development of the nation and its people. Let's take a look at some of the key trends today.

THE COMPUTER REVOLUTION

Developments in the computer field are leading the revolution in technology today. Although computers have been around since 1945, each year new and more imaginative ways are found to use them. The computer has made significant contributions to improvements in the quality of life in the United States by altering the way we live. The computer makes possible the use of countless labor-saving machines and equipment. Often faulted for eliminating jobs, the computer industry has more than compensated for that trend by adding millions of additional jobs in the service sector.

GENETIC ENGINEERING

In 1953, two scientists, Watson and Crick, identified DNA as the universal mechanism for heredity. Since then, scientists have been moving closer to tracking down each of the estimated 100,000 human genes on 23 chromosomes. This development is leading to a revolution in the field of genetic engineering.

■ **Elimination of Disease.** Medical researchers are on the verge of a medical revolution in genetic engineering. Thousands of diseases such as cancer, cystic fibrosis, sickle-cell anemia and Tay-Sachs disease may be caused by the malfunctioning of specific genes. If the genetic markers that cause such diseases can be found and corrected, the possibilities for eliminating diseases and human imperfections are endless.

■ **Impact.** Advances in genetic marking have some people concerned about the future potential of this new technology. If scientists are capable of selective breeding, will they try to create a superior race? Many new ethical questions are raised by this technology.

THE ROLE OF WOMEN

The Women's Movement has accomplished a great deal, but feminist leaders argue that much more still needs to be done. Some reformers believe that women still need to achieve equal pay for equal work, since women working full time currently earn only 70% of what men do, on average. The number of women executives has more than doubled, but women still face many closed doors in the workplace. Women's leaders also argue that more women are needed in political office. They believe this would focus more attention on such issues as child care, sexual harassment, maternity leave, more equitable divorce settlements and less government interference with the right to an abortion. But feminist leaders do not all agree on future goals, and are divided between those who favor special rules for women and those who support complete equality with men.

THE WORKFORCE

A well trained, abundant, highly-motivated work force was the foundation upon which American economic success was built. However, the number of young people entering the labor force is now declining. The labor shortage is expected to reach 23 million by the late 1990s.

■ **Increased Qualifications.** Qualifications for entry level jobs are rising faster than the number of workers able to fill them. As **automation** (the use of machines to replace human labor) in companies increases, different types of skills will be needed. For example, auto mechanics today must be able to operate complex pieces of machinery and need to understand complex service manuals to repair highly sophisticated automobiles.

■ **Challenges.** Traditional work values seem to be declining. Low educational achievement and high dropout rates indicate a dismal future for America's work force. Recent studies have shown that one in eight employees reads at a fourth grade level. The telephone company recently reported that only 2,000 out of 57,000 applicants were able to pass an entry-level test that measured basic skills.

To help meet the pressing need for workers in the future, some companies are becoming more involved in educational reform. They are training employees to read and write, adopting schools, donating expensive office equipment, helping train teachers and offering scholarships to needy students.

THE CHANGING FACE OF AMERICA'S POPULATION

■ **An Aging Population.** America's population is growing older. In 1900, only 4% of the population was 65 or older. By 2030, the number of elderly persons is expected to grow to 21%. This will present profound challenges to individual families as well as to the nation as a whole.

- Issues affecting the elderly will get greater political attention, since the elderly will carry more political influence because of their high rate of voter participation.

- Currently, 25% of the federal budget is spent on the elderly, but this amount will increase significantly as new demands are made on the government for additional housing, hospitals, nursing homes and other long-term care facilities.

■ **Shifts In Population.** Americans traditionally lived their entire lives in the place where they were born. Today, the average American moves once every 5 years, and cities are now losing population to the suburbs. Between 1950 and 1980, the percentage of people living in suburbs almost doubled.

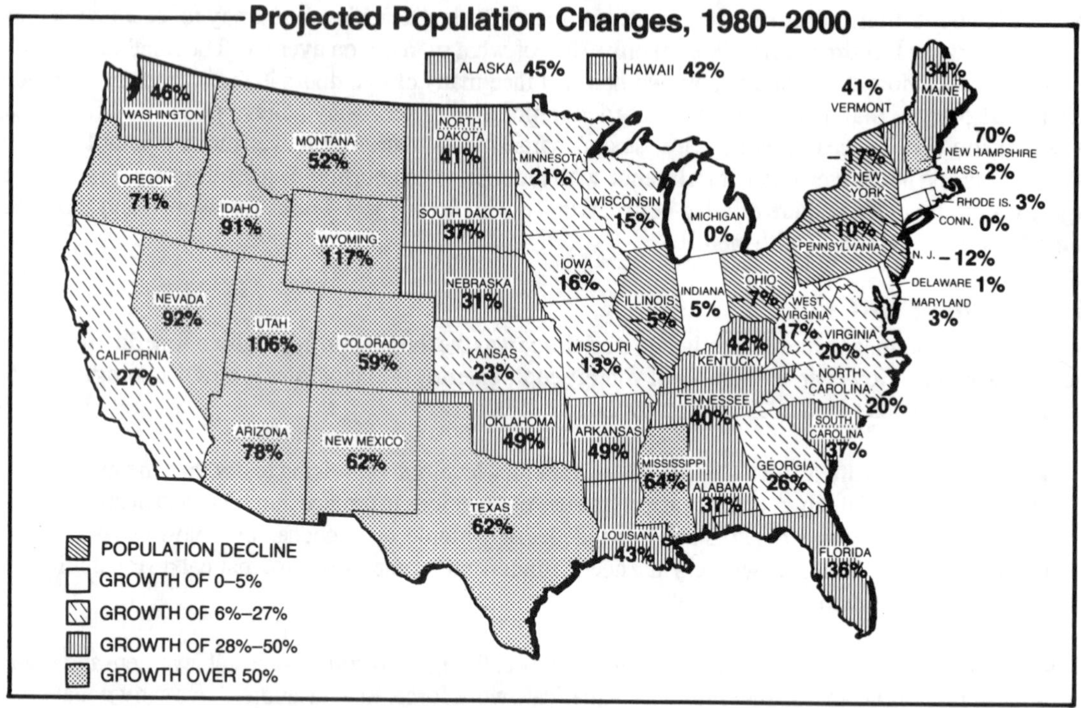
ALASKA 45%
HAWAII 42%
WASHINGTON 46%
OREGON 71%
CALIFORNIA 27%
NEVADA 92%
IDAHO 91%
MONTANA 52%
WYOMING 117%
UTAH 106%
ARIZONA 78%
COLORADO 59%
NEW MEXICO 62%
NORTH DAKOTA 41%
SOUTH DAKOTA 37%
NEBRASKA 31%
KANSAS 23%
OKLAHOMA 49%
TEXAS 62%
MINNESOTA 21%
IOWA 16%
MISSOURI 13%
ARKANSAS 49%
LOUISIANA 43%
WISCONSIN 15%
ILLINOIS -5%
MICHIGAN 0%
INDIANA 5%
OHIO -7%
KENTUCKY 42%
TENNESSEE 40%
MISSISSIPPI 64%
ALABAMA 37%
GEORGIA 26%
FLORIDA 36%
SOUTH CAROLINA 37%
NORTH CAROLINA 20%
VIRGINIA 20%
WEST VIRGINIA 17%
PENNSYLVANIA -10%
NEW YORK -17%
VERMONT 41%
MAINE 34%
NEW HAMPSHIRE 70%
MASS. 2%
RHODE IS. 3%
CONN. 0%
N. J. -12%
DELAWARE 1%
MARYLAND 3%
POPULATION DECLINE
GROWTH OF 0–5%
GROWTH OF 6%–27%
GROWTH OF 28%–50%
GROWTH OVER 50%
Projected Population Changes, 1980–2000

In addition, the traditional centers of population, the Northeast and Midwest, are declining. The fastest-growing areas in the nation are the sun-belt states of Nevada, Arizona, and New Mexico, the Northwest (Washington, Oregon, Idaho), and Florida. As a result, the fastest growing states will gain representatives at the expense of the northeast and midwestern states (see map on the following page).

How Congressional Representation Has Changed Following The 1990 Census

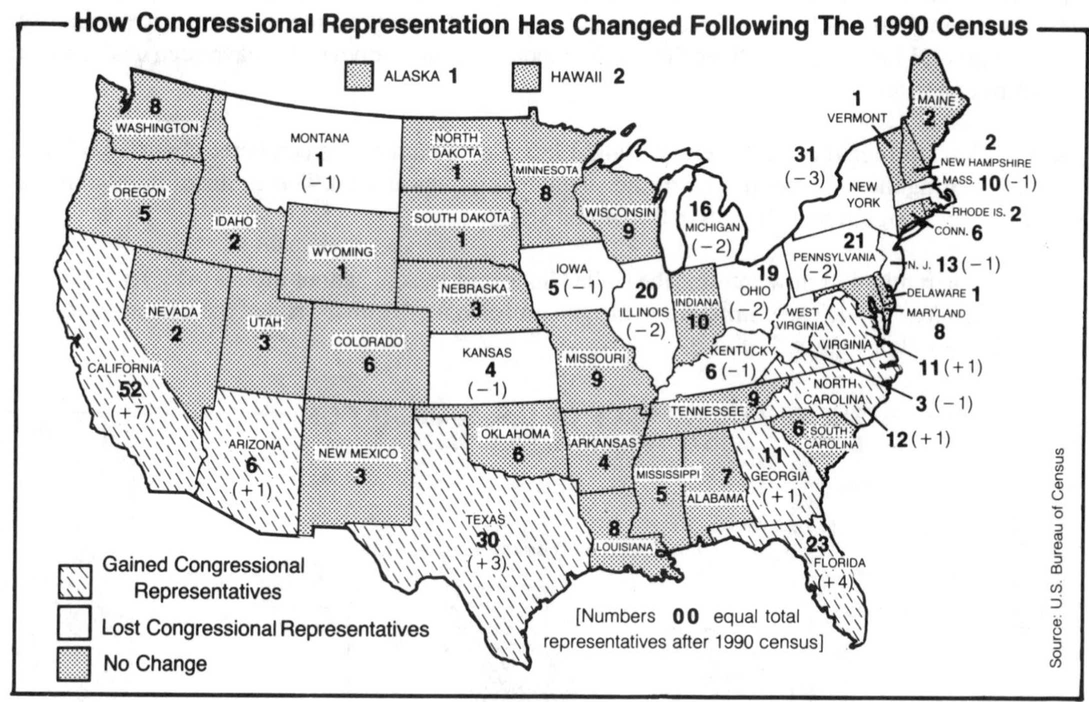
ALASKA 1
HAWAII 2
WASHINGTON 8
OREGON 5
CALIFORNIA 52 (+7)
IDAHO 2
NEVADA 2
MONTANA 1 (−1)
WYOMING 1
UTAH 3
ARIZONA 6 (+1)
COLORADO 6
NEW MEXICO 3
NORTH DAKOTA 1
SOUTH DAKOTA 1
NEBRASKA 3
KANSAS 4 (−1)
OKLAHOMA 6
TEXAS 30 (+3)
MINNESOTA 8
IOWA 5 (−1)
MISSOURI 9
ARKANSAS 4
LOUISIANA 8
WISCONSIN 9
ILLINOIS 20 (−2)
MICHIGAN 16 (−2)
INDIANA 10
OHIO 19 (−2)
KENTUCKY 6 (−1)
TENNESSEE 9
MISSISSIPPI 5
ALABAMA 7
GEORGIA 11 (+1)
FLORIDA 23 (+4)
SOUTH CAROLINA 6
NORTH CAROLINA 12 (+1)
VIRGINIA 11 (+1)
WEST VIRGINIA 3 (−1)
PENNSYLVANIA 21 (−2)
NEW YORK 31 (−3)
VERMONT 1
MAINE 2
NEW HAMPSHIRE 2
MASS. 10 (−1)
RHODE IS. 2
CONN. 6
N. J. 13 (−1)
DELAWARE 1
MARYLAND 8
Gained Congressional Representatives
Lost Congressional Representatives
No Change
[Numbers 00 equal total representatives after 1990 census]
Source: U.S. Bureau of Census

■ **Changes in the Ethnic and Racial Population.** In the 21st century racial and ethnic minority groups in the United States will outnumber whites. It is estimated that by 2056, white Americans will be a minority. Projections indicate that the Hispanic and non-white populations will increase dramatically, while the white population will show no increase. These changes carry important implications for the nation.

- The present trend toward **bilingualism** will continue, and white Americans will feel increased competition in the job market.
- Elected officials will place a higher priority on the needs of racial and ethnic minorities. Such a change might lead to increased racial and ethnic conflicts within society.
- The core curriculum now taught in most schools may change, with less emphasis on traditional European history. National values traditionally based on Western culture may undergo change.

■ **Challenges Posed by Ethnic and Racial Diversity.** Some see the movement to achieve full equality for African Americans and Hispanic citizens as this nation's greatest revolution. Although the Civil Rights movement achieved a great deal for minorities, racial discrimination still persists. Unemployment, crime, teenage-pregnancy, infant mortality, illegal drug use and other symptoms of poverty continue to remain higher among minority groups. Two major areas that the Civil Rights movement concentrated on were housing and education. Much was accomplished, but total equality in both of these areas has proven elusive. For example, inner-city schools are as segregated today as they were 40 years ago. The 1992 Los Angeles riots indicated the frustrations felt by some urban minority communities. Many people believe that while important gains in civil rights have been made, much remains to be done.

■ **The New Immigrants.** Between 1970 and 1986, illegal immigrants numbered about 5.5 million people. During the same period, 9.6 million legal immigrants arrived. This influx of immigrants is bringing about significant changes in the United States.

- Most immigrants now entering the United States come from nations in Asia (41%) or Latin America (37%). These immigrants are generally isolated from the rest of the United States by their language and culture.

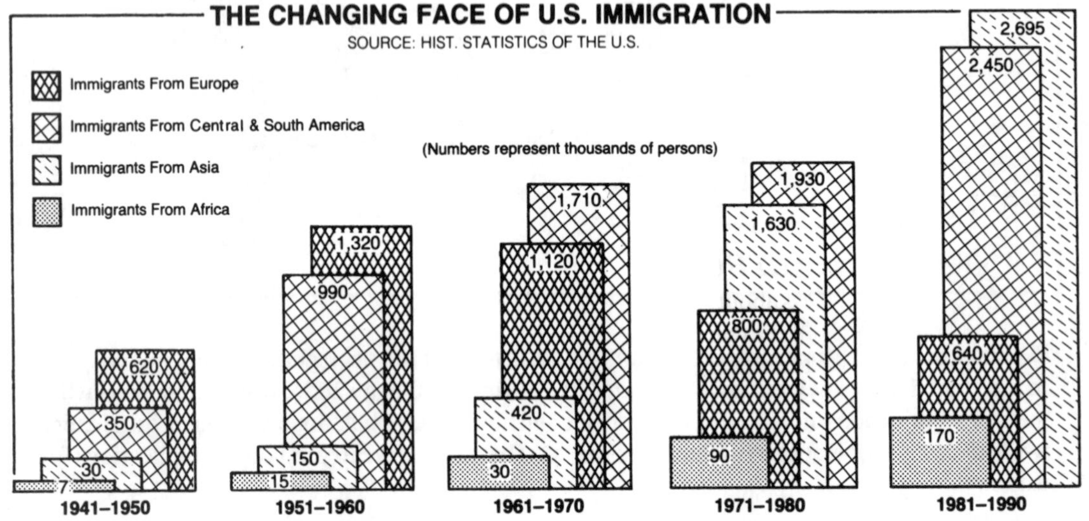
THE CHANGING FACE OF U.S. IMMIGRATION
SOURCE: HIST. STATISTICS OF THE U.S.
Immigrants From Europe
Immigrants From Central & South America
Immigrants From Asia
Immigrants From Africa
(Numbers represent thousands of persons)
620
350
30
7
1,320
990
150
15
1,710
1,120
420
30
1,930
1,630
800
90
2,695
2,450
640
170
1941–1950
1951–1960
1961–1970
1971–1980
1981–1990

- Most immigrants are quite young and of child-bearing age. This will have an important effect on the nation's public school system. Public schools will face severe challenges in assimilating the children of these immigrants into mainstream society. They tend to settle in a few states and cities, creating a greater impact in those areas beyond what their total numbers would suggest.

Recent historic levels of immigration have created a major national debate on whether immigration should be reduced, stopped or increased. If steps are taken to reduce legal immigration, it is not clear what measures would succeed in curbing the tide of illegal immigrants.

EXPANDED RIGHTS FOR THE DISABLED

Over 43 million Americans suffer from some form of disability. With such a large political power base, the handicapped led a successful movement attacking discrimination against the disabled. For example, a physically-challenged worker generally earns about 64% of what others would earn in the same job. In 1990, Congress passed the **Americans with Disabilities Act**, banning discrimination against the handicapped. The law extended to the disabled the same protections against discrimination given to African Americans, women, and ethnic minorities in the 1960s and 1970s. Some businesses have complained about the cost of building entrance ramps, additional elevators, and installing special equipment. These businesses contend that the costs will run into billions of dollars if they are forced to carry out provisions of the act requiring that stores and office buildings be made fully accessible to the disabled.

KEY ITEMS TO REMEMBER

Technology, genetic engineering, voucher system, Americans with Disabilities Act

PERSONALITIES OF THE PERIOD

TONI MORRISON (AUTHOR)

Toni Morrison writes novels about life in America from an African-American perspective. Her books *Song of Solomon*, *Beloved* and *Jazz* established her as one of America's leading writers. Her characters and their struggles illuminate the troubles of a society afflicted by racial prejudice. A creative writing teacher at Princeton University, she became the first black woman to receive the Nobel Prize in literature, in 1993.

JESSE JACKSON (CIVIL RIGHTS LEADER)

In 1984, Jesse Jackson challenged Reagan for the presidency, becoming the first major African-American candidate for president. In the 1960s, he assisted Martin Luther King, Jr. in the Civil Rights Movement. Since Dr. King's assassination, he has become the most prominent and important African-American leader in the nation. He has been in the forefront of a number of national organizations to help the poor and oppressed achieve political and economic equality.

SALLY RIDE & GUION BLUFORD, JR. (ASTRONAUTS)

Both Sally Ride and Guion Bluford, Jr. are part of NASA's space shuttle program. In 1983, Sally Ride became the first woman to fly on the space shuttle. Later that same year, Guion Bluford, Jr. had the distinction of being the nation's first African-American astronaut to venture into space.

AN WANG (BUSINESSMAN)

An Wang immigrated to America from China and became a giant in computer technology. In 1951, he invented an essential part of a computer's memory. Using this invention and his ability as a leader in computer technology, he founded his own company, Wang Laboratories. This company has been in the forefront in linking computers to word processors, as well as other types of office equipment.

THE CONSTITUTION AT WORK

KEY LEGISLATION

AMERICANS WITH DISABILITIES ACT OF 1990

This act, signed by President Bush, prohibits discrimination against the disabled in employment, public accommodations, transportation and telecommunications. Defining anyone who has a mental or physical impairment as disabled, the act guarantees that they will be treated equally in their jobs and be given easy access to office buildings, stores, restaurants, stadiums, trains and buses.

KEY COURT CASES

EPPERSON v. ARKANSAS (1968)

Background: A teacher was fired for violating an Arkansas law that prevented her from teaching human evolution (the theory that mankind is descended from a lower order of animals). The teacher claimed her right to teach evolution was protected by the First Amendment.

Decision/Significance: The Supreme Court ruled that the Arkansas law violated the **Establishment Clause** of the First Amendment. This clause states that a "wall of separation" exists between between Church and State. Neither a state nor the national government can establish a church or an official religion. Neither can pass laws which promote a particular religion or favor one religious point of view over another. The ruling indicated that the Court would accept nothing less than complete religious neutrality in public schools.

NEW JERSEY v. T.L.O. (1985)

Background: T.L.O., a student at a New Jersey high school, was caught smoking in the bathroom. After being taken to the vice-principal's office, her purse was searched. Cigarettes, drug items and other incriminating evidence were found in her purse. T.L.O. argued that searching her purse was a violation of her Fourth Amendment right against "unreasonable searches and seizures."

Decision/Significance: The Supreme Court supported the school officials. Unlike the police who need to show "probable cause," school officials need only show "reasonable suspicion" to conduct a search. This is because school authorities must be given the power to maintain a safe learning environment.

HAZELWOOD SCHOOL DISTRICT V. KUHLMEIER (1988)

Background: The principal of a public high school objected to several student articles in the school newspaper and forbade their publication. The students challenged this ruling as a denial of their right of free speech.

Decision/Significance: The Court held that while students have free speech rights, they are not the same as those of adults outside the school. In particular, school authorities have the right to regulate school publications and other forms of student expression to ensure that they are in keeping with the "educational mission" of the school.

TEXAS v. JOHNSON (1989)

Background: As a protest against the Reagan Administration, Mr. Johnson set the American flag afire. He was convicted under a Texas law that made such flag-burning illegal. Johnson challenged the state law as a violation of free speech rights.

Decision/Significance: The Court held that Johnson's flag-burning was expressive conduct protected by the First Amendment. This amendment protects political statements of this type—no matter how disagreeable it might be to most of society.

CITY OF RICHMOND v. J.A. CROSON (1989)

Background: Although 50% of the citizens of Richmond, Virginia were African American, less than 1% of its construction contracts were going to minority contractors. To remedy the situation, the city established an affirmative action program. Contracts would be awarded to builders who sub-contracted 30% of the job to minority-owned businesses. White contractors claimed this was reverse discrimination.

Decision/Significance: The Court held that the Richmond program was unconstitutional. A state or local government can only use racial classifications if it can show a need to remedy a specific local pattern of racial discrimination in the past. Only Congress and not local authorities could use race-based plans to remedy the general racial discrimination that had once occurred throughout society. This decision is important because it may limit the operation of many affirmative action programs.

CRUZAN v. DIRECTOR, MISSOURI DEPARTMENT OF HEALTH (1990)

Background: After an auto accident, Nancy Cruzan was left in a permanent coma, and was sustained by life support systems. After doctors determined there was no chance for recovery, her parents petitioned the courts to remove her artificial feeding system. Under Missouri law, Nancy's life had to be preserved unless there was proof that Nancy herself would have wished to end it.

Decision/Significance: The Supreme Court upheld the Missouri state law. The Court refused to give her parents permission to end Nancy's life. The Court left it to the states to define under what conditions relatives can make the decision to end the life of a person who is in a vegetative state, so long as the state's requirements are reasonable ones.

SUMMARIZING YOUR UNDERSTANDING

Directions: How well did you understand what you have just read? Test yourself by answering the following questions.

MAJOR ITEMS TO REMEMBER

On a separate sheet of paper, briefly define the following items:

AIDS
Americans with Disabilities Act
Greenhouse effect
Technology
Acid rain
Abortion
Global interdependence
Affirmative action
Human rights violations

KEY CONCERNS

The United States is faced with a number of key concerns. Summarize your understanding of these concerns by completing the following chart:

CONCERN	CAUSES	IMPACT	RECOMMENDATIONS
Environmental Threats			
AIDS epidemic			
Homelessness			
Crime rate			
Education			
Budget Deficits			
Human Rights Violations			

KEY ISSUES

There are a number of conflicts focusing on key issues in the United States today. Summarize your understanding of these issues by completing the following chart:

ISSUES	EXPLAIN THE OPPOSING VIEWPOINTS
Prayer in schools	
Right to die	
Affirmative action	
Drug testing	

KEY TRENDS

There are a number of key trends taking place in our nation that will have an impact on many people. Summarize your understanding of these trends by completing the following chart:

AREA	DESCRIBE ITS EFFECT/IMPACT
Computer revolution	
Genetic engineering	
Population changes	
Increasing ethnic and racial diversity	

TESTING YOUR UNDERSTANDING

Directions: Test your understanding of this unit by answering the following questions. Circle the number preceding the word or expression that correctly answers the statement or question. Following the short answer questions, answer either the RCT-type or Regents essay questions.

Base your answer to questions 1 through 3 on the following cartoon and on your knowledge of social studies.

DEFENSE SPENDING
SOCIAL PROGRAMS

1 The cartoonist is primarily concerned with the
 1 growing power of the presidency
 2 current state of military preparedness
 3 declining cost of social programs
 4 rising cost of government spending

2 Which statement best summarizes the main idea of the cartoon?
 1 Congress lacks the power to deal with problems facing the nation.
 2 Congress feels defense is more important than social programs.
 3 Social and defense programs need additional funding.
 4 Defense and social programs are too costly and must be reduced.

3 Which person would most likely agree with the cartoonist?
 1 a highway engineer
 2 a taxpayer
 3 an army General
 4 a person receiving food stamps

Base your answers to questions 4 through 6 on the speaker's statements and on your knowledge of social studies.

Speaker A: I own this land and have the right to do with it as I wish. If I sell it for apartments, I can make more money than if I sell it for use as single homes or for recreation areas.

Speaker B: Apartments would create too much demand on the water supply and sanitation facilities. The land should be used for parks.

Speaker C: The community is in an uproar. Crime has doubled. People are afraid to come out at night. Something has to be done.

Speaker D: Housing in our neighboring city is inadequate to meet the needs of the people. Our area has a responsibility to help solve this problem.

4 Speaker C would most likely favor a(n)
1 closing of nuclear plants
2 war on drugs
3 decrease in oil consumption
4 increase in the defense budget

5 Many environmentalists would probably be in agreement with the statement of speaker
1 A
2 B
3 C
4 D

6 The values of a free enterprise system are most evident in the statement of speaker
1 A
2 B
3 C
4 D

Base your answers to questions 7 through 9 on the following chart and on your knowledge of social studies.

CRIME IN AMERICA
(per 100,000 population)

Year	Violent Crimes	Property Crimes	Drug Arrests
1980	5,950	5,353	256.0
1985	5,207	4,651	346.0
1989	5,741	5,078	423.4

7 According to the chart, what is the rate of violent crimes (per 100,000) committed in 1989?
1 5,950
2 5,741
3 5,207
4 5,078

8 According to the chart, which statement is most accurate?
1 America has the highest crime rate in the world.
2 Most crime in America is on the decline.
3 Drug arrests are on the increase.
4 Property crime figures have remained the same throughout the 1980s.

9 The trend in the chart could be used to support the argument that
1 crime is a continuing problem in America
2 the government does not care about criminal rights
3 the population is declining
4 most crime can be prevented

---

10 Which has generally encouraged upward social mobility in the United States?
1 the existence of public education
2 the establishment of local zoning regulations
3 the adoption of state segregation laws
4 the system of federalism

11 Which contributed most to the development of the suburbs in the United States during the 20th century?
1 improvements in transportation systems
2 a decrease in the average per capita income
3 an increase in the number of women employed in industry
4 a desire by the middle class to develop original ideas and styles

12 "We live in a time when knowledge of world affairs is no longer simply nice to have or a luxury. It is essential to a nation's well-being."

This quotation is based on a recognition of the crucial role in today's world of global
1 jingoism
2 nativism
3 interdependence
4 assimilation

13 In the United States, the achievements of modern medical technology have resulted in a major controversy concerning the
1 distribution of medical services to various regions of the country
2 proper role of corporations in medical research
3 retraining of doctors in new techniques
4 definitions of life and death

14 Which will most likely be a major effect of the increasing life expectancy in the United States?
1 an increased effort by advertisers to capture the youth market
2 a surge in public school construction
3 an increase in the political power of retired people
4 a growth in the power of college students as a special-interest group

15 "If a nation expects to be ignorant and free, in a state of civilization, it expects what never was and never will be."

Which idea is most strongly supported by this statement?
1 compulsory education
2 a strong central government
3 universal suffrage
4 government's right to tax

16 Based on current trends, which statement about the future of the United States is most accurate?
1 The number of people living on farms will rise dramatically.
2 There will be an increase in the urban tax base.
3 The size of the elderly population will decrease.
4 There will be an increased need for skilled workers.

17 One major difference between the population of the U.S. today as compared to the population of the U. S. in the future is that
1 the U. S. population will decrease
2 a larger proportion of Americans will live in the Northeastern states
3 there will be a growth in the number of people employed in manufacturing
4 non-white Americans will eventually outnumber white Americans

18 Which statement best describes the present condition of American women?
1 More women are now entering the work force than ever before.
2 The role of women has not changed over the past 50 years.
3 Fewer women are interested in career occupations.
4 Fewer women are seeking a college education.

19 Which would be the best example of the policy of "affirmative action"?
1 giving food to minority members who are homeless
2 providing public housing to the elderly
3 helping minority members achieve equality in college admissions
4 lowering the voting age requirement for minority members

20 Which statement would be most difficult to prove?
1 Increased ultraviolet radiation is passing through the ozone layer.
2 Illegal drugs enter the United States from foreign lands.
3 Possession of nuclear weapons increases the danger of nuclear war.
4 The nation's values will undergo enormous changes in the future.

RCT-TYPE ESSAYS

1 Many of the problems that faced the U. S. during the 1980s continue to challenge the nation in the 1990s.

Problems

AIDS epidemic
Increasing health costs
Threats to the environment
Drug epidemic
Homelessness

Part A

Choose *one* of the problems listed above. ______________________

List *two* ways that this problem will present a challenge for the nation in the 1990s.

1. ______________________

2. ______________________

Choose *another* of the problems listed. ______________________

List *two* ways that this problem will present a challenge for the nation in the 1990s.

1. ______________________

2. ______________________

Part B

In your Part B answer, you should use information you gave in Part A. However, you may also include different or additional information in your Part B answer.

Write an essay explaining how some of the problems that faced the nation in the 1980s will continue to challenge the nation during the 1990s.

2 A number of major issues divide Americans today.

Major Issues

Death penalty	Right to die
Abortion	Gun control
Prayer in public schools	Drug testing in the workplace

Part A

Choose *two* of the issues listed. For *each* issue selected, list one argument in favor and one opposed.

ISSUE	ARGUMENTS IN FAVOR	ARGUMENTS AGAINST
1. ______	1. ______ ______	1. ______ ______
2. ______	2. ______ ______	2. ______ ______

Part B

In your Part B answer, you should use information you gave in Part A. However, you may also include different or additional information in your Part B answer.

Write an essay explaining why certain major issues divide Americans today.

3 Many recent developments will have a significant impact on the future economic and social life of Americans.

Developments

Population shifts
Impact of technology on the workforce
Global economic interdependence
Proportion of elderly in the population

Part A

Choose *one* of the developments listed. ______

Identify the development. ______

State *one* result that this development will have on society. ______

______

Choose *another* development listed. ______

Identify the development. ______

State *one* result that this development will have on society. ______

______

Part B

In your Part B answer, you should use information you gave in Part A. However, you may also include different or additional information in your Part B answer.

Write an essay explaining how many recent developments will have a significant impact on the future economic and social life of Americans.

REGENTS-TYPE ESSAYS

1 Many of the major problems facing the United States during the 1980s will continue to challenge the nation during the 1990s.

Problems

AIDS epidemic	The farm dilemma
Rising health care costs	Drug epidemic
Threats to the environment	Homelessness

Choose *three* of the problems from the list above. For *each* one chosen:

- Describe the nature of the problem.
- Explain why solutions to the problem are difficult to achieve.

2 Listed below are issues confronting Americans today.

Issues

Affirmative action programs	Prayer in public schools
Abortion	Right to die
The death penalty	Gun control

Select *three* of the issues listed, and for *each* one chosen:

- Discuss a controversy related to the issue.
- Identify one specific argument on each side of the controversy.
- Discuss one specific government action taken to resolve the problem.

3 Many recent developments will have a significant impact on the future economic and social life of Americans

Developments

Ethnic/racial population changes
Genetic engineering
Global economic interdependence
The computer revolution
Increasing environmental pollution
Increasing proportion of elderly people

Choose *three* of the developments listed. For *each* one chosen:

- Describe the development
- Show how this development will have a significant impact on the political, economic or social life of the United States

4 In the United States today, there is sometimes a demand for constitutional amendments.

Possible Amendments

A ban on abortion
Repeal of the right to bear arms
Requirement of a balanced federal budget
Allowing prayer in public schools
Equal rights for women
One six-year term for the office of the presidency

Select *three* of the possible amendments. For *each* one chosen, discuss specific arguments given by both the proponents and opponents of the possible amendment.

PERFORMANCE-BASED TASKS

Setting: As we move closer to the 21st century, Americans must grapple with the question: what do we want our country and world to be like in the future? One way to answer this question is to survey the ideas and opinions of Americans.

General Directions: Have your friends, classmates, relatives, and neighbors participate in the survey that follows. Add as many questions as you like.

SURVEY ABOUT AMERICA'S FUTURE

1. In the future, I would like people to be able to retire at an early age.
   ❒ Agree ❒ Disagree ❒ I'm not sure

2. I would like to see abortions totally banned in the United States.
   ❒ Agree ❒ Disagree ❒ I'm not sure

3. I hope the family continues to remain the basic social unit in our society.
   ❒ Agree ❒ Disagree ❒ I'm not sure

4. I believe education in the future should be more career oriented.
   ❒ Agree ❒ Disagree ❒ I'm not sure

5. I hope life will become more rural and slower paced.
   ❒ Agree ❒ Disagree ❒ I'm not sure

6. I want to see the power of the Federal government increase and grow stronger.
   ❒ Agree ❒ Disagree ❒ I'm not sure

7. I want to see the power of local governments increase and grow stronger.
   ❒ Agree ❒ Disagree ❒ I'm not sure

8. I would like to see less controls and regulations at every level of government.
   ❒ Agree ❒ Disagree ❒ I'm not sure

9. Government should limit the size and profits of all major U.S. corporations.
   ❒ Agree ❒ Disagree ❒ I'm not sure

10. The government should give more support to entertainment and the arts.
    ❒ Agree ❒ Disagree ❒ I'm not sure

11. I would like to see a more religious America.
    ❒ Agree ❒ Disagree ❒ I'm not sure

continued...

12. I believe there should be greater restrictions on the use of credit and credit cards.
❒ Agree ❒ Disagree ❒ I'm not sure

13. We should provide more public transportation and limit the use of private cars.
❒ Agree ❒ Disagree ❒ I'm not sure

14. I would like to see greater participation by people in governmental decisions.
❒ Agree ❒ Disagree ❒ I'm not sure

15. I want less government concern about world affairs and more with life in the U.S.
❒ Agree ❒ Disagree ❒ I'm not sure

16. I want all racial and gender groups in the nation to have equal power.
❒ Agree ❒ Disagree ❒ I'm not sure

17. I believe universal health care should become a right guaranteed by the goverment.
❒ Agree ❒ Disagree ❒ I'm not sure

18. I would like to see some of the powers of the press limited.
❒ Agree ❒ Disagree ❒ I'm not sure

19. I hope the pace of technological change slows down.
❒ Agree ❒ Disagree ❒ I'm not sure

20. I would like see the nation's growth rate limited by mandatory birth control.
❒ Agree ❒ Disagree ❒ I'm not sure

21. I want to see the power of labor unions more strictly controlled.
❒ Agree ❒ Disagree ❒ I'm not sure

22. Generally, I think the future will be better than today.
❒ Agree ❒ Disagree ❒ I'm not sure

23. *(You suggest one)* ____________________________
❒ Agree ❒ Disagree ❒ I'm not sure

Your Task: After you have completed your survey, select those questions that relate to either a political, economic or social aspect of American life. Then, prepare a one-page report summarizing your conclusions. In your report, you should compare your conclusions to the findings of other pollsters and writers who have tried to take the pulse of Americans as we approach the year 2000. Two such writers who have tried to assess the shape of the future are Alvin Toffler and Paul Kennedy.

LOOKING AT THE MOST IMPORTANT CONCEPTS AND TERMS

In your final preparation for the RCT or Regents Examination, it would be helpful to review important key concepts and terms. The following list comprises those items that appear most often on RCT and Regents examinations. They represent the concepts and terms we feel you must know in order to do well. However, we also recommend that you go back to each chapter and review the major terms and concepts found there.

Affirmative Action: Private and public programs designed to make up for injustices against groups that were discriminated against in the past. For example, a company might recruit and hire women and African Americans instead of others who are equally or better qualified.

Amendments: Additions to the U.S. Constitution. For example, the First Amendment, protecting free speech and religious freedom against government abuse, was an addition to the original Constitution. Amendments have to be approved by 2/3 of each House of Congress and by 3/4 of the states.

Articles of Confederation (1781-1787): The first constitution used to govern the United States. The Confederation kept the states together during the American Revolution. Its major weakness was that it put too much power in the hands of the state governments and gave too little power to the national government. It was replaced by the Constitution of 1787.

Bill of Rights: The first ten amendments to the U.S. Constitution. The major purpose of the Bill of Rights was to protect individual liberties from possible abuse by the national government.

***Brown v. Board of Education* (1954)**: An important Supreme Court decision declaring racial segregation in public schools to be unconstitutional because separate facilities in education are "inherently unequal." The case marked an important turning point in the Civil Rights Movement.

Capitalism: An economic system in which natural resources and the means of production are privately owned rather than state controlled. Prices, production and distribution are determined mainly by competition among sellers. Consumers are free to choose what they wish to buy from what producers make available. Supporters of capitalism say it leads to efficient use of resources. Critics claim it can sometimes create extreme inequalities among individuals.

Checks and Balances: The system created by the U.S. Constitution to ensure that the national government does not become too strong or oppress those it governs. Each branch of the federal government has been given ways to stop ("check") the other branches. For example, the President (executive branch) can veto bills passed by Congress (legislative branch). In this way, neither the President nor Congress can take on dictatorial powers.

Civil Rights Movement: A movement during the 1950s and 1960s that sought to achieve equal rights and better living conditions for African Americans. It was important because it moved the nation closer to the ideas stated in the Declaration of Independence and the U.S. Constitution that all people are created equal and entitled to equal protection of the laws. The Civil Rights Movement also had an important effect on expanding the rights of other groups, like women, Hispanic Americans, and the disabled.

Cold War (1945-1991):Refers to the rivalry between the two superpowers—the United States and the Soviet Union—after World War II. The Soviet Union tried to spread its system of Communism, while the United States attempted to contain it. The two superpowers never went to war against one another because of the threat of nuclear weapons, and the rivalry remained a "cold" war.

Collective Bargaining: Negotiations between the management of a company and a union representing its workers. Collective bargaining sessions often involve lengthy discussions about wages, hours, working conditions, benefits and other items of mutual concern.

Collective Security: A type of foreign policy in which a nation relies on either international organizations or on military alliances to strengthen its national security. For example, the United States obtained some collective security by its participation in NATO.

Concurrent Powers: Powers that can be used by both our federal and state governments. An example of a concurrent power is the power to tax, which can be exercised by both the federal government and New York State.

Constitution: A written set of rules that establish how a government operates. The U.S. Constitution describes the structures and powers of the United States government. All government actions must follow these rules.

Containment: The foreign policy that the United States used to halt the spread of Communist influence during the Cold War. Americans did not try to overturn Communism where it was established, but tried to "contain" it by preventing its spread to additional countries.

Corporation: A company chartered by a state and recognized in law as a separate "person." Corporations are permitted to issue stocks, or shares of ownership, to investors. Each shareholder is a partial owner of the corporation, but is not liable for the corporation's debts beyond the extent of his or her investment. An example of a corporation is IBM (International Business Machines Corporation).

Declaration of Independence (1776): A document issued to explain to the world the reasons for America's decision to declare independence from Britain. The Declaration stated that the purpose of government is to protect individual rights and property. If a government fails to do this, the Declaration said the people have a right to alter or abolish that government. The Declaration is important because it laid the foundation upon which the U.S. government now rests.

Deficit: The amount of money that a government spends beyond what it collects in taxes. For example, if the federal government spends more money in its budget that it receives in taxes, it will have a deficit. Deficits can be harmful since they must be paid for by borrowing and may threaten future economic growth.

Democracy: A system of government in which citizens of society participate in the decisions of government either by voting directly on issues brought before them or by electing people to represent them in the legislature. The United States is a representative democracy because Americans elect their own government leaders.

Due Process of Law: The right of an individual to a fair and impartial trial or proceeding before being punished or deprived of property or other rights. Every person is entitled to be told of the charges against him and to be able to explain or defend himself. No one can be punished or deprived of property according to established laws. In major criminal cases, each person has the right to be tried by a jury.

Elastic Clause: Found in the U.S. Constitution, this clause expands the power of our federal government by giving it whatever additional powers are "necessary and proper" for the carrying out of those powers that the Constitution specifically lists as belonging to it. For example, under the "elastic clause" Congress has the power to establish a national bank if it feels this is necessary for the collection of taxes, even though a national bank is not mentioned in the Constitution.

Electoral College: A special group of electors who are chosen to elect the president. It was made a part of the Constitution because the Framers did not fully trust leaving the election of the president up to the people. Today, the electors follow the selection of the voters of their state. Each presidential candidate wins either all or none of the electoral votes of each state. It is possible to win a majority of the popular vote, but still lose the vote in the Electoral College.

Ethnocentrism: A belief that one's race and culture are superior to others. For example, at one time many native-born Americans felt they were superior to all immigrants.

Federalism: A system for sharing power and authority between our national government and local governments. The U.S. Constitution, to avoid a concentration of political power, divided governmental power into two levels: the national level of government, which deals with national concerns; and the state level of government, which handles local affairs. The national level of government is usually known as the federal government.

Foreign Policy: The conduct of one nation towards other nations. Examples of foreign policy are President Bush's ordering troops into Panama or meeting with other world leaders at the international environment summit in Brazil.

Fourteenth Amendment (1868): A constitutional amendment passed after the Civil War. It prevented states governments from depriving citizens of property or liberty without "due process of law," and forced states governments to guarantee all their citizens "equal protection of the laws." The original purpose of the 14th Amendment was to safeguard the rights of the newly-freed former slaves in the South. The Supreme Court has interpreted the 14th Amendment as providing Americans with the same protections from acts by state governments that they have from acts of the federal government.

Freedom of Expression (also free speech): The right of an individual to speak freely without fear of imprisonment or punishment. In the United States, free expression is necessary for democratic government. However, even with free expression, one cannot make statements that directly threaten the safety of an individual or the community.

Frontier: An imaginary line separating areas of settlement from what was considered unsettled wilderness territory. In reality, the frontier marked the dividing line between where Native American peoples lived, and more densely populated areas where European-Americans and African-American peoples settled. By 1890 there was no longer any sharp dividing line.

Good Neighbor Policy (1930-1945): A policy in which the United States attempted to improve relations with Latin American countries by agreeing not to interfere in their internal problems and treating them more as equals. The policy sought to reverse earlier policies which had treated several Latin Americans nations as mere protectorates of the United States.

Grange Movement: An agrarian reform movement, begun in 1867, which sought to unite farmers into a single interest group to respond to their problems. For example, Grangers sought to elect candidates to state legislatures who favored lowering railroad rates.

Great Depression (1929-1940): The severe economic slowdown in the U.S. economy that resulted from the 1929 stock market crash. The Depression was marked by very high unemployment, increased business failures and a loss of business profits. The New Deal was later introduced to combat the Depression.

Harlem Renaissance (1920s): An awakening of African-Americans' pride in their culture. It was partly a result of the migration of Southern blacks to northern cities. Centered in Harlem, New York City, the Harlem Renaissance saw a flourishing of African-American music, poetry, and literature.

Hiroshima: A city in Japan selected as a target for the first atomic bomb used in warfare. The bomb, dropped on August 6, 1945, killed over 100,000 people and brought about the rapid surrender of Japan, ending World War II.

Immigration: The movement of peoples from other countries into the U. S. Immigrants were attracted to America to escape poverty and religious and political persecution in their native lands. Since World War I, immigration into the United States has been controlled by a series of national laws.

Impeachment: The act of removing a government official from office because of misconduct. For example, the president can be impeached and removed from office by Congress.

Imperialism: The political and economic rule by one country over another less powerful country. For example, the United States followed an imperialist policy when it annexed the Philippines after the Spanish-American War.

Industrial Revolution: A basic change in the way goods were produced. Instead of being made by hand at home, goods were made by machines in factories. The steam engine replaced human and animal power, making possible large-scale factory production, steamboats and trains.

Isolationism: The policy of any nation refusing to become involved with other countries when that involvement might lead to war. For example, the United States followed a policy of isolationism in the 1920s and 1930s.

Jim Crow Laws: Laws passed by Southern legislatures in the 1880s and 1890s that segregated blacks from whites. Jim Crow laws called for separate schools for blacks and whites, and required blacks and whites to ride in separate railroad cars and to use separate public facilities like bathrooms or park benches.

Judicial Review: The power of the Supreme Court to review acts of Congress and actions of the president to decide whether or not they are constitutional. The power of judicial review was first clearly established in the case of *Marbury v. Madison*.

Korean War (1950-1953): North Korea invaded South Korea in attempt to unify the country under Communist rule. President Truman ordered U. S. forces into South Korea to resist the invasion. The Korean War lasted three years and ended in a truce which left Korea divided as it was before the war.

Ku Klux Klan: A secret organization begun in the South in order to terrorize Southern blacks with threats and acts of violence, thus preventing them from asserting their full political and social rights. For example, some blacks were frightened into submission by having their homes burned.

Laissez-faire: A policy followed by the American government in the 19th century which left business free to operate with minimal government interference or regulation.

League of Nations: Organization originally proposed by Woodrow Wilson as part of his Fourteen Points; it later became part of the Treaty of Versailles ending World War I. The League was an international organization where nations could discuss their differences instead of resorting to war and aggression. The League failed to achieve world peace in part because many major world powers, including the United States and the Soviet Union, never became members. The League collapsed with the outbreak of World War II, and was replaced after the war by the United Nations.

Manifest Destiny: The belief of Americans during the 1840s that it was their destiny or future to extend the United States from the east coast westwards to the Pacific. As a result of this desire for continental expansion, the United States annexed Texas in 1845. The term developed a second meaning in the 1890s, when it was used to refer to America's "destiny" to acquire colonies in the Pacific.

***Marbury v. Madison* (1803)**: A case decided by the U.S. Supreme Court, which established judicial review. The Court claimed the power to determine which acts were constitutional, because it said the Constitution was the supreme law. The decision greatly strengthened the Supreme Court's own power by making it the final authority in interpreting the Constitution.

Marshall Plan (1948): A plan proposed by the United States to provide economic aid to the countries of Europe after World War II. The main purpose of the plan was to help these war torn nations rebuild their economies so that they would become more resistant to the attractions of Communism.

Melting Pot Theory: The view that immigrants should adopt mainstream American customs and culture so that they would be assimilated or made part of American society. As immigrants and their children blended into American society, they in turn helped create a more diverse and vibrant American culture.

***Miranda v. Arizona* (1966)**: A Supreme Court decision that required police to inform all suspects in their custody of their constitutional rights to remain silent and to have a lawyer present during questioning, and to warn them that their remarks could be used against them. These have become known as "Miranda" rights.

Monopoly: When a single seller achieves complete control of the production or distribution of a product or service. The aim of a monopoly is to eliminate competition so that the seller can control the price.

Monroe Doctrine (1823): Issued by President Monroe in an attempt to prevent future European colonization in the Western hemisphere. The doctrine was important because it established to the rest of the world that the United States had a special interest in the Western hemisphere. It was used by the United States in the 20th century to justify frequent interventions in Latin American countries.

Muckrakers: A group of journalists, writers and social scientists from the 1890s to the 1920s, who exposed the abuses of industrial society and the growing corruption of government. These writers "raked" through the dirt of American life in search of news. One of the most famous muckrakers was Upton Sinclair, who exposed the unhealthy practices that existed in the meat packing industry.

NATO: Organization formed in response to the rising tension of the Cold War following World War II. The United States, Canada and ten Western European nations pledged to defend each other if attacked. NATO (North Atlantic Treaty Organization) provides an example of collective security. During the Cold War, NATO helped prevent the further advance of Communism in Europe.

Nationalism: Has two separate meanings. For unified nations, it refers to loyalty or devotion to the nation, putting it above all other interests. For multi-ethnic countries, nationalism refers to the desire of each distinct group to have its own nation and government. This kind of separatism played an important role in the outbreak of World War I and in the recent breakup of the Soviet Union.

Neutrality: Policy under which a country does not take sides among warring nations. For example, the United States first followed a policy of neutrality when war broke out in Europe in the late 1930s.

New Deal: The program that Franklin D. Roosevelt introduced to overcome the Great Depression. It was important because it established the principle that the federal government bears major responsibility for the smooth running of the American economy. It marked an end to the laissez-faire view that government and the economy should be completely separate. The New Deal also introduced many important specific programs, such as Social Security and government insurance of bank deposits.

Nuremberg Trials (1945-1946): Following World War II, the leading Nazis were put on trial at Nuremberg by the Allies for "crimes against humanity." The trials resulted from the discovery of millions of half-starved and dead bodies found in German-run concentration camps. The trials were important because they showed that individuals could be held responsible for their actions, even in times of war or when they acted with government authority. Similar trials were conducted in Japan against Japanese war criminals.

Open Door Policy (1899): A policy in which the United States announced equal trading rights for all nations in all parts of China. Soon afterwards, the United States also announced its aim to preserve Chinese independence and unity. This was important because it helped prevent the dismemberment of China.

***Plessy v. Ferguson* (1896)**: A Supreme Court ruling that allowed states to separate blacks from whites so long as "equal" facilities were provided. In effect, this decision gave Southern states permission to con-tinue passing segregation laws. This decision was later overturned in *Brown v. Board of Education* (1954).

Political Party: A group of people working together to win elections and place candidates into public office. Usually party members share common goals. Although they did not exist in America when the Constitution was first written, political parties quickly emerged as an important feature of our democracy. The Democrats and Republicans are the two major political parties in the United States today.

Popular Sovereignty: In a democracy, such as the United States, the people hold the final power in government. The people exercise this power by selecting their representatives in elections. It is important because it is one of the key principles upon which our government is based.

Populist Party (1891-1896): Unable to rely on the established political parties, a group of farmers joined forces with workers to form the Populist Party to combat the power of banking and railroad interests on the national and state governments. The Populists never achieved national power but advocated a whole series of reforms that were eventually adopted, such as the progressive income tax.

Preamble: The introduction to the U.S. Constitution. It states the goals of our national government. For example, one of its goals is to ensure peace and harmony within the nation.

Progressive Income Tax: A system where wealthy individuals are taxed at a higher rate than others. For example, someone earning over $100,000 might be required to pay a 50% tax, while someone earning $10,000 would pay only a 5% tax. This was a major proposal of the Populists and Progressives.

Progressive Movement (1890-1920): A movement of reformers who sought to correct the political and economic injustices that had resulted from America's rapid industrialization. They wanted to use the power of government to correct the evils and abuses of big business. Two Progressives, Theodore Roosevelt and Woodrow Wilson, reached the presidency and introduced a series of Progressive reforms.

Protective Tariffs: Taxes placed on imported goods to protect domestic industries. Taxing Japanese cars to make them more expensive, so that American consumers will buy U. S. cars, is one example.

Reconstruction Era (1865-1877): The period right after the Civil War when Americans faced the task of unifying the nation, helping the freed slaves and rebuilding the South. How this was to be done created a bitter power struggle between the president and Congress. Congress briefly won control, continued military occupation in the South, gave African Americans full participation in Southern politics, and excluded former Confederate leaders. Reconstruction ended in 1877 when local Southerners gained control.

Reserved Powers: Refers to the exclusive powers given by the U.S. Constitution to the state governments. For example, the running of public schools is a reserved power of state governments.

***Roe v. Wade* (1973)**: A Supreme Court decision that overturned state laws prohibiting abortions. The Court ruled that a woman's right to privacy guarantees her the right to an unrestricted abortion in the first three months of pregnancy. This decision is important because it has created an enormous controversy in the United States concerning a woman's right to abortion.

Segregation: The separation of people by race. From the 1880s until the Civil Rights Movement in the 1950s and 1960s, many Southern states segregated blacks and whites in schools, on trains and in using public facilities. Such segregation is now illegal.

Seneca Falls Convention (1848): Organized by leading women reformers and considered the start of the women's rights movement. This meeting proclaimed that women were equal to men and should be given the right to vote.

Separation of Powers: The Constitutional system of separating the powers of the national government between the legislative, executive and judicial branches. It was created to prevent any individual or branch from becoming too powerful, and to prevent any individual or group from gaining control of the government.

Social Mobility: The movement of individuals from one social class to another. An example of social mobility would be the movement of a person from poverty to the middle class.

Social Security Act (1935): Act passed during the New Deal. It sought to provide a "safety net" for Americans affected by unemployment, illness or a wage-earner's death. Today millions of employees, after they retire, receive a monthly payment from a government fund of special taxes that were collected on their wages while they were working.

Spanish-American War (1898): A war between the United States and Spain over the treatment of Cuba. As a result of its victory in this war, the United States went from a nation without colonies to one with a far-reaching colonial empire.

Third Parties: Political parties other than the two mainstream parties. Unlike major parties which seek to join different groups into a majority, third parties usually concern themselves with a single issue rather than with obtaining power for its own sake. An example of a third party was the Populist Party in the 1890s.

Totalitarianism: A modern political system in which the government controls all aspects of life of the individual and the rights of speech and dissent are denied. Stalin's Soviet Union and Hitler's Nazi Germany are both examples of totalitarian states in which the leader's powers were unlimited and absolute.

Truman Doctrine (1947): Policy of limiting the spread of Communism in Greece and Turkey. President Truman offered these countries military aid and economic assistance, believing the best way to contain Communism was to provide support to any country fighting Communism.

United Nations: An international peace-keeping organization formed after World War II. The main aim of the U.N. is to promote international harmony, peace and economic development. Most nations of the world are members of the U.N. Unlike the earlier League of Nations, the United Nations gives special privileges to the world's most powerful nations, which act as permanent members of the Security Council.

Unwritten Constitution: Political practices that developed after the U.S. Constitution was written and put into effect. These practices became customary even though they are not formally a part of the Constitution. For example, both the cabinet system and our political parties are part of our unwritten constitution.

Urbanization: The movement of people from the rural countryside into the cities. The Industrial Revolution greatly increased the number of jobs available in the cities, while improvements in farm machinery made fewer workers needed on the land. Increasing urbanization occurred in the United States in the period following the Civil War and continued for most of the next century.

Vietnam War (1954-1973): The war fought between the United States and North Vietnam over the independence of South Vietnam. New and destructive weapons such as napalm and Agent Orange were used by the United States. The war was important because it was one of the most divisive in American history, leaving deep and lasting scars.

War Powers Act (1973): Act passed by Congress to set limits on the war-making powers of the president. It was passed in response to the events of the Vietnam War and Watergate, and anger at the fact that presidents had been able to involve the nation in a war without congressional approval. According to this act, the president must get congressional approval for sending troops to fight overseas or recall them within 90 days.

Watergate Affair (1972-1974): President Nixon, a Republican, was planning his re-election for a second term. A group of men working for Nixon's re-election were then caught breaking into Democratic Party headquarters in Washington, D.C. At first, Nixon denied involvement, but evidence later revealed he was deeply involved in the attempted cover-up. The scandal set in motion a series of events that led to President Nixon's resignation. This crisis lowered public confidence of Americans in their government.

Women's Rights Movement (1840-1870): Attempts by women to organize themselves in order to challenge male dominance. The chief focus of the movement was to secure the right to vote. The movement eventually led to the passage of the 19th Amendment which required all states to give women the right to vote. In the 1960s, the movement for equality for women revived under the name of the Women's Liberation Movement.

World War I (1914-1919): A major world war triggered by the assassination of Austrian Archduke Ferdinand. Conflicting nationalist aims in Europe led to the outbreak. The United States entered the war in 1917 on the side of the Allies (Britain and France) primarily over the issue of freedom of the seas. The United States emerged from the war as a major world power.

World War II (1939-1945): War caused by the aggression of Germany in Europe and of Japan in Asia. World War II was the most destructive war in history, killing 40 million people. The United States entered the war in 1941 when Japan launched a surprise attack against its Pacific Fleet stationed at Pearl Harbor. The United States emerged from the war, along with the Soviet Union, as a superpower.

Yellow Journalism: A technique in which news reports are intentionally sensationalized and distorted in order to sell more newspapers. Such a technique was used in the 1890s by some newspapers in reporting stories about alleged Spanish atrocities against the Cuban people. These reports caused the public outcry that led to the outbreak of the Spanish-American War.

CHAPTER 16

POST-TEST

Now that you have had an opportunity to review the various test-taking strategies and content chapters, you should take a post-test to measure your progress. To help you in this assessment, this chapter is composed of two examinations: an RCT-type examination and an actual Regents Examination from June 1990. You should take whichever test is appropriate for you. This post-test will help you identify any areas that you might still need to study. Good luck on this post-test!

AN IMPORTANT REMINDER: Before you begin answering the practice material found in this and the following chapter, you should review the important concepts and terms found in the "Looking at" section starting on page 391.

RCT-TYPE EXAMINATION

Directions: This practice test has two parts: Part I has 50 multiple-choice questions, and Part II has 4 essay questions (from which you must answer 2).

1 The main purpose of government is to
1 protect its citizens
2 provide jobs
3 encourage the arts
4 help the poor and disabled

2 The best evidence that a nation is a democracy is that
1 there is a system of civil and criminal courts
2 people have the right to vote
3 there is a strong presidency
4 the legislature is divided into two houses

3 Which document was written last?
1 the U.S. Constitution
2 the Articles of Confederation
3 the Declaration of Independence
4 the Bill of Rights

4 The term "checks and balances" refers to
1 the division of power between the national and state governments
2 the power of the Supreme Court to declare a law unconstitutional
3 the power each branch of government has over the other branches
4 the protection of individual liberties contained in the Bill of Rights

5 Which phrase best expresses the ideas contained in the Declaration of Independence?
1 "We have not yet begun to fight"
2 "All men are created equal"
3 "Give me liberty or give me death"
4 "A penny saved is a penny earned"

6 The Articles of Confederation were criticized for giving
1 too little power to the national government
2 too much power to Congress
3 the president the power to declare war
4 the Supreme Court the power to declare laws unconstitutional

7 A document that provides a framework for government is known as a
1 judgment
2 constitution
3 law
4 bill

8 The purpose of the U.S. Constitution separating the powers of government is to
1 make government more efficient
2 prevent one branch from becoming too powerful
3 give states power equal to that of the federal government
4 strengthen the military

9 Which situation most clearly illustrates the constitutional principle of federalism?
1 Congress hears the President's State of the Union Address.
2 A congressional committee kills a bill by majority vote.
3 The House of Representatives votes to impeach a federal judge.
4 State governors ask the federal government for more aid.

10 Which has been a major criticism of the Electoral College?
1 Each state has the same number of electoral votes.
2 Only members of the two major political parties can be elected.
3 The Senate must approve the outcome of the presidential election.
4 A candidate can win the popular vote but still lose the election.

11 The power of the Supreme Court to decide whether or not a law violates the Constitution is known as
1 a writ of habeas corpus
2 original jurisdiction
3 appellate jurisdiction
4 judicial review

12 The purpose of adding the Bill of Rights to the U.S. Constitution was to
1 guarantee the civil and political rights of individuals
2 insure the proper functioning of the checks and balances system
3 strengthen the authority of state governments
4 expand the power of the presidency

13 The topics "right to a lawyer," "double jeopardy," and "cruel and unusual punishment," would most likely be discussed in an essay dealing with
1 federalism
2 due process
3 separation of powers
4 denied powers

14 Which statement best reflects the views of Booker T. Washington?
1 African Americans should return to Africa.
2 Separate states should be set up for African Americans.
3 Vocational education is the key to success for African Americans.
4 African Americans must insist on political equality.

15 Which pair of people would most likely promote the idea of laissez-faire capitalism?
1 Ralph Nader and Gloria Steinem
2 Andrew Carnegie and John D. Rockefeller
3 Booker T. Washington and W.E.B. du Bois
4 Franklin D. Roosevelt and Upton Sinclair

16 Which statement about immigration since 1960 is most accurate?
1 Industrial growth in the Northeast has attracted most immigrants.
2 Most immigrants have come from Latin America and Asia.
3 Organized labor has pushed for easier immigration laws.
4 Most immigrants have been easily integrated into American society.

17 Which time period came first?
1 The Progressive Movement
2 The Reconstruction Era
3 The Roaring Twenties
4 The Great Depression

Base your answers to questions 18 and 19 on the following line graph and on your knowledge of social studies.

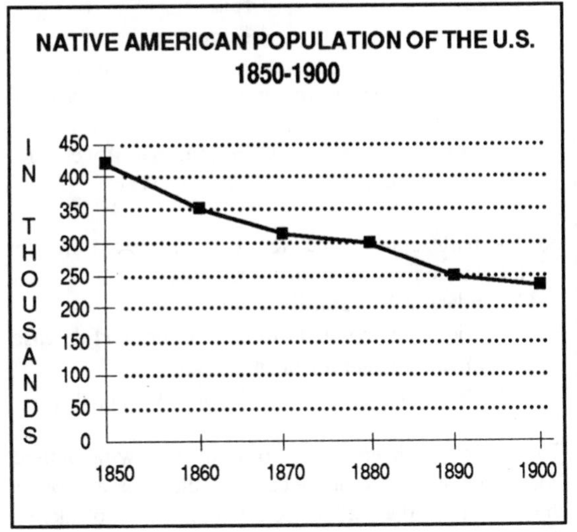
NATIVE AMERICAN POPULATION OF THE U.S.
1850-1900
IN THOUSANDS
450
400
350
300
250
200
150
100
50
0
1850
1860
1870
1880
1890
1900

18 In which year was the Native American population the greatest?
1 1850
2 1860
3 1870
4 1890

19 The most valid statement that can be drawn from the information in the graph is that
1 Native Americans have a higher birth rate than other Americans.
2 The Native American population grew sharply after 1900.
3 The Native American population declined sharply after 1850.
4 The general population of the country has doubled.

---

20 Which term refers to journalists who exposed social evils in the United States at the end of the 19th century?
1 carpetbaggers
2 abolitionists
3 muckrakers
4 scalawags

21 A major achievement of the Progressive Movement was that
1 racial discrimination was made illegal
2 political reforms were established
3 18-year-olds were given the right to vote
4 business leaders were freed from the worry of government regulation

22 Which event took place in the administration of Theodore Roosevelt?
1 the emancipation of slaves
2 the start of World War I
3 the building of the Panama Canal
4 the bombing of Pearl Harbor

Base your answers to questions 23 and 24 on the following speaker's statements and on your knowledge of social studies.

Speaker A: It is in our best interest to steer clear of involvement with other countries, since they are continually arguing over matters that do not concern us.

Speaker B: If we wish to survive, we must maintain friendly terms with other nations. We should encourage trade, not alliances.

Speaker C: I believe that it is our fate as a nation to expand our nation from the Atlantic to the Pacific coast.

Speaker D: To be successful our nation must develop its naval power, obtain colonies, and build a canal connecting the Atlantic and Pacific oceans.

23 Theodore Roosevelt would most likely have agreed with speaker
1 A
2 C
3 B
4 D

24 The policy referred to by Speaker C has been called
1 Monroe Doctrine
2 detente
3 policy of containment
4 Manifest Destiny

---

25 A basic purpose of the Monroe Doctrine was to
1 prevent European intervention in the Western Hemisphere
2 stop the spread of Communism in Latin America
3 halt the slave trade from Africa
4 keep the United States out of European conflicts

26 The term "manifest destiny" refers to the belief that Americans should devote their energies towards
1 industrial growth
2 equality and justice for all
3 westward expansion
4 freedom of religion

27 Which was a major aim of U.S. foreign policy during the administration of President George Washington?
1 maintaining neutrality in world affairs
2 supporting the British in their war against France
3 protecting the countries of the Western Hemisphere
4 creating an international peacekeeping organization

28 Isolationism was the primary foreign policy followed by the United States afterwhich war?
1 Spanish-American War
2 World War I
3 World War II
4 Korean War

Base your answer to questions 29 and 30 on the following cartoon and on your knowledge of social studies.

OF COURSE WE MAY HAVE TO CHANGE REMEDIES IF WE DONT GET RESULTS
FDR
REMEDIES
CONGRESS
NRA
CCC
AAA
CWA

29 The drug bottles on the table are meant to symbolize
1 New Deal programs
2 foreign policy programs
3 raw materials used in World War II
4 people opposed to Franklin D. Roosevelt.

30 Which statement best expresses the main idea of the cartoon?
1 The government should not interfere with the nation's economy.
2 Any branch of government can solve the nation's economic problems.
3 Government should aid in the solution of economic problems.
4 Economic crises lead to decreased government involvement.

31 Which musical art form originated in the United States?
1 jazz
2 opera
3 folk songs
4 symphony

32 Widespread unemployment was the major characteristic of the
1 Roaring Twenties
2 Great Depression
3 Progressive Movement
4 Vietnam War

33 The philosophy of the New Deal supported the idea that the federal government should
1 regulate and reform the economy
2 restrict its activities to foreign affairs and defense
3 own and operate major industries
4 reduce its role in helping the disadvantaged

Two items have been omitted from the following outline. For each blank space in the outline, select the number of the items from the list that best completes the blanks for 34 and 35.

ITEMS:
1. Equal Rights Amendment
2. Susan B. Anthony
3. Civil Rights Movement
4. Booker T. Washington
5. The March on Washington

THE TURBULENT 1960s

34 I. ____________________
  A. Early History
    1. Unfair treatment of African Americans
    2. Impact of African American organizations
  B. Milestones in African American History
    1. Montgomery Bus Boycott
35   2. ______________
II. Women's Movement
  A. The Movement is born
  B. Leaders of the movement

36 The development of the "Cold War" between the United States and the Soviet Union was a direct result of
1 World War I
2 World War II
3 Korean War
4 Vietnam War

37 Following World War II, the Truman Doctrine was enacted to
1 help Germany and Japan recover from damages caused by the war
2 rebuild the nations of Africa
3 prevent the spread of Communism in Greece and Turkey
4 eliminate poverty in Third World nations

38 Which situation is an illustration of the concept "detente"?
1 British declaration of war on Germany in 1939
2 U.S. grain sales to the Soviet Union in the 1970s
3 U.S. blockade of Cuba during the Missile Crisis of 1962
4 United Nations intervention in Lebanon in the 1980s

39 Racial prejudice often increases in times of national danger. The truth of this statement was illustrated in the Supreme Court case of
1 *Brown v. Board of Education* 3 *Korematsu v. U.S.*
2 *Roe v. Wade* 4 *Marbury v. Madison*

40 The bombing of Hiroshima and Nagasaki resulted in
1 the outbreak of World War II in Europe
2 United States entry into the war against Japan
3 the dawn of the Atomic Age
4 a decrease in the spread of Communism

41 Following World War II, the United States developed its policy of containment in response to the
1 spread of Soviet control over Eastern Europe
2 building of the Berlin Wall in Germany
3 partition of Palestine in the Middle East
4 spread of nuclear weapons in southeast Asia

42 During President Reagan's administration the federal deficit
1 was eliminated by a constitutional amendment
2 increased greatly
3 was reduced by new taxes
4 remained about the same

43 Which event took place during the administration of George Bush?
1 the Persian Gulf War
2 the bombing of Hiroshima
3 passage of the New Deal
4 the Watergate scandal

44 The growth of technology has resulted in
1 decreased in economic activity
2 reduced warfare among nations
3 increased international trade
4 growth in the national debt

45 The United States sells manufactured products to Third World nations and purchases raw materials from these nations. This fact illustrates
1 economic protectionism 3 global interdependence
2 pooling of resources 4 finance capitalism

46 Despite gains made by the women's movement, many women still do not have
1 the same earnings as men
2 legal protection against discrimination
3 the right to work
4 the right to hold elective office

47 What do Henry David Thoreau, Martin Luther King, Jr., and Dorothea Dix have in common?
1 They expressed a need for reform.
2 They were leaders of religious movements.
3 They were 20th-century labor union organizers.
4 They were important business leaders.

48 Which person is correctly paired with the field in which he or she achieved national fame?
1 Samuel Gompers — labor movement
2 John Muir — prison reform
3 Betty Friedan — medical discoveries
4 Rachel Carson — conservation

49 Which headline best reflects the concept of imperialism?
1 "The Supreme Court Permits Abortion"
2 "Germany Invades the Soviet Union"
3 "U.S. Annexes the Philippines"
4 "U.S. President Meets Soviet Minister at Summit Meeting"

50 Which event directly caused the United States to enter the Gulf War?
1 Soviet invasion of Afghanistan
2 Iraqi invasion of Kuwait
3 Egyptian seizure of the Suez Canal
4 Israeli takeover of the Sinai

PART II

ANSWER TWO QUESTIONS FORM THIS PART (20 CREDITS)

1 The U.S. Constitution gave each branch of the federal government several ways to "check" (stop) the other two branches.

Branches

The Presidency
The Congress
The Supreme Court

Part A

Select *two* branches from the list. For *each* branch selected, list the two other branches it checks, and identify one way that it can check each of the other branches.

BRANCH	BRANCHES IT CHECKS	HOW IT CHECKS EACH BRANCH
1. ________	A. ________	1. ________
	B. ________	2. ________
2. ________	A. ________	1. ________
	B. ________	2. ________

Part B

In your Part B answer, you should use information you gave in Part A. However, you may also include different or additional information in your Part B answer.

On a separate sheet of paper, write an essay describing how the U.S. Constitution gave each branch of the federal government several ways to "check" the other two branches.

2 Throughout U. S. history, various groups have tried different means of overcoming the problems facing them

Groups

Women
African-Americans
Laborers
Farmers
Physically Disabled

Part A

Select *two* groups from the list. For *each* group selected, identify *one* problem the group faced and *one* way they tried to overcome the problem.

GROUP	PROBLEM	OVERCAME PROBLEM BY:
1. ________	________________ ________ ________________________	________________________________ ________________________________
2. ________	________________ ________ ________________________	________________________________ ________________________________

Part B

In your Part B answer, you should use information you gave in Part A. However, you may also include different or additional information in your Part B answer.

On a separate sheet of paper, write an essay explaining how various groups throughout United States history have tried different means of overcoming the problems they faced.

3 Many social problems in the United States have had a widespread effects on American life.

Problems

AIDS epidemic	Homelessness
High crime rate	Pollution of the environment
Federal budget deficit	Education

Part A

Select *two* problems from the list. For *each* one selected, state the problem and state *one* effect of the problem on American life.

PROBLEM	IDENTIFY THE PROBLEM	EFFECT ON AMERICAN LIFE
1. ________	________________________	________________________________ ________________________________
2. ________	________________________	________________________________ ________________________________

Part B

In your Part B answer, you should use information you gave in Part A. However, you may also include different or additional information in your Part B answer.

On a separate sheet of paper, write an essay using this topic sentence: Many social problems in the United States have had widespread effects on American life.

4 Throughout U. S. history, American leaders have made decisions that have had important effects on the lives of Americans. Following is a list of some national leaders.

National Leaders

Theodore Roosevelt	Lyndon Johnson
Woodrow Wilson	Jimmy Carter
Franklin D. Roosevelt	Ronald Reagan
Harry Truman	George Bush

Part A

Choose *one* of the leaders listed. ______________________

Identify *one* of his decisions: ______________________

State how that decision had an effect on lives of Americans: ______________________

____

Choose *another* leader. ______________________

Identify *one* of his decisions: ______________________

State how that decision had an effect on lives of Americans: ______________________

____

Part B

In your Part B answer, you should use information you gave in Part A. However, you may also include different or additional information in your Part B answer.

On a separate sheet of paper, write an essay discussing how some American leaders have made decisions that have had important effects on the lives of Americans.

U.S. HISTORY AND GOVERNMENT REGENTS EXAMINATION: AUGUST 1996

PART I (55 credits)

ANSWER ALL 48 QUESTIONS IN THIS PART

Directions (1-47): For each statement or question, *circle* the number of the word or expression that, of those given, best completes the statement or answers the question.

1 The Declaration of Independence states that the fundamental purpose of government is to
1 guarantee the right to vote to all citizens
2 secure for the people their natural rights
3 provide for common defense
4 assure employment for people who are willing to work

2 Which statement is accurate about governmental power under the Articles of Confederation?
1 State governments had the power to collect taxes, coin money and control trade.
2 The executive branch of the central government was more powerful than the legislative and judicial branches.
3 The central government was made stronger than state governments.
4 The states with the largest populations had the most votes in Congress.

3 A compromise reached at the Constitutional Convention of 1787 was that
1 states were given the power to make treaties
2 congress became a two-house legislature
3 slavery was prohibited throughout the United States
4 an individual could could serve only two terms as President

4 To make all laws which shall be necessary and proper for carrying into execution the foregoing powers...

This clause in the United States Constitution has most often been used to
1 impeach members of the executive branch
2 increase the power of state governments
3 justify the principle of civil disobedience
4 broaden the authority of Congress

5 Before a bill becomes a federal law it must be
1 reviewed by the cabinet
2 passed by the Senate and the House of Representatives
3 approved by the Supreme Court
4 signed by the President

6 Which headline refers to a power granted only to the Federal Government by the United States Constitution?
1 "War Declared Against Germany"
2 "Reminder: File Income Tax Return Early"
3 "New Law Allows Right Turn at Red Light"
4 "Law Passed to Raise Drinking Age to 21"

7 According to the United States Constitution, the reason for conducting a census in the United States is to determine the number of
1 members of each ethnic group
2 people who are eligible to vote
3 people who are eligible for Social Security benefits
4 representatives to be elected by each state to the House of Representatives

8 The clause of the United States Constitution that provides the legal basis for public regulation of railroads is the
1 equal protection clause
2 commerce clause
3 due process clause
4 supremacy clause

9 It is the duty of the President to oppose and it is the privilege of the Congress to dispose. This statement refers to the concept of
1 federalism
2 popular sovereignty
3 judicial review
4 checks and balances

10 Presidents can most directly influence the future decisions of the United Sates Supreme Court by
1 impeaching justices with whom they disagree
2 encouraging the public to write letters to the justices
3 vetoing rulings of the justices
4 appointing new justices to the Court with the Senate's approval

11 Political parties and the President's Cabinet are considered to be part of the unwritten constitution because these groups
1 developed through custom and usage
2 represent the people's views more accurately than elected officials do
3 were created by amendments to the original Constitution
4 exist only at the state and local level of government

12 The decision of President George Washington to use the state militia to put down the Whiskey Rebellion in 1794 demonstrated that the
1 states were still the dominant power in the new nation
2 president was becoming a military dictator
3 federal government had no authority to impose an excise tax
4 new national government intended to enforce federal laws

13 The most significant effect of minor political parties in the United States is that they have
1 elected many of their party leaders to the Presidency
2 had little impact on the major parties
3 suggested reform ideas that later became laws
4 influenced only local levels of government

14 During the period from 1800 to 1865, the issues of States' rights, the tariff and slavery led most directly to the growth of
1 imperialism
2 sectionalism
3 national unity
4 industrialization

15 After the Civil War, a major goal of the Radical Republicans in Congress was to
1 gain voting rights for the newly freed slaves
2 rebuild the farms and factories of the northeast
3 restore the white plantation owners to power in the south
4 support the policies of President Andrew Johnson

16 The literacy test and the poll tax were devised mainly to
1 eliminate fraudulent voting practices
2 establish uniform national voting requirements
3 limit the number of African -Americans qualified to vote
4 raise money for political campaigns

17 Immigrants to the United States between 1890 and 1930 most frequently experienced discrimination because they
1 spoke different languages and had different customs
2 entered the competition for scarce farmland
3 were better educated than earlier immigrants
4 remained more loyal to their homelands than to the United States

18 During the late 1800's, the theories of social Darwinism were often used to justify the efforts of
1 federal officials to control state governments
2 Northern liberals to pass civil rights legislation
3 Southern farmers to increase cotton exports
4 big business to destroy its competitors

19 During the late 1800's, the growing of cash crops by an increasingly large number of farmers resulted in
1 greater isolation of farmers from American economic life
2 a shift from self-sufficiency to commercial farming
3 less food available for export
4 general economic prosperity for all farmers

Base your answer to question 20 on the following cartoon and on your knowledge of social studies.

BILL OF FARE
CUBA
PORTO RICO
PHILIPPINE ISLANDS
SANDWICH ISLANDS
McKINLEY

Boston Globe, May 28, 1898

20 This cartoon deals mainly with the concept of
1 imperialism
2 government overspending
3 isolationism
4 free trade

21 The primary goal of manifest destiny was the
1 abolition of slavery in territories held by the United States
2 removal of European influence from South America
3 expansion of the United States westward to the Pacific Ocean
4 secession of the Southern states from the Union

22 "You furnish the pictures and I'll furnish the war."

In 1898 when newspaper publisher William Randolph Hearst made this statement to artist Frederic Remington he was suggesting that
1 artists and writers resented being censored by the government
2 artwork made newspapers more interesting to read
3 journalism could be used to shape opinions and policies
4 journalists valued accuracy and objectivity

23 Ida Tarbell, Upton Sinclair, and Frank Norris all shared a belief that
1 monopolies were necessary for businesses to survive
2 reform was needed to control the abuses of business
3 the government should follow a laissez-faire policy
4 the public was unlikely to respond to calls for reform

24 The Granger Laws, the Interstate Commerce Act and the Agricultural Adjustment Acts are similar in that they all
1 protected the interests of big business
2 turned over significant Federal powers to the state governments
3 forced farmers to join cooperatives
4 attempted to address problems experienced by farmers

25 The main objective of President Woodrow Wilson's Fourteen Points was to
1 establish a military alliance with European nations
2 punish Germany for causing World War I
3 provide for a just and lasting peace
4 encourage open immigration in industrial nations

26 In the 1920's, one reason for placing restrictions on immigration to the United States was that
1 factory owners were hiring only native-born workers
2 Congress was concerned about radical ideas being brought into the United States
3 the United States was overcrowded and could not accept more immigrants
4 many foreign governments demanded the United States close its borders to immigrants

27 Which statement best explains a major cause of the Great Depression in the United States?
1 High income tax rates forced many workers into poverty.
2 Large quantities of foreign imports forced American companies out of business.
3 The government controlled almost every aspect of the American economy.
4 Factories and farms produced more products than Americans could afford to buy.

28 "They used to tell me I was building a dream,
With peace and glory ahead.
Why should I be standing on line just waiting for bread?
Once I built a railroad, made it run,
Made it race against time.
Once I built a railroad. Now it's done.
Brother, can you spare a dime?"

The words of this song suggest that the American dream of economic success
1 can be achieved only through hard work
2 holds its greatest opportunities during periods of war
3 is forfeited by people on welfare
4 can be shattered by forces beyond an individual's control

29 Republican opponents of President Franklin D. Roosevelt criticized the New Deal program on the grounds that it
1 spent more money than was taken in
2 weakened the power of the executive branch
3 failed to include labor legislation
4 promoted the ideas of laissez-faire economics

Base your answer to question 30 on the graph below and on your knowledge of social studies.

Bank Failures in the United States from 1926 to 1937

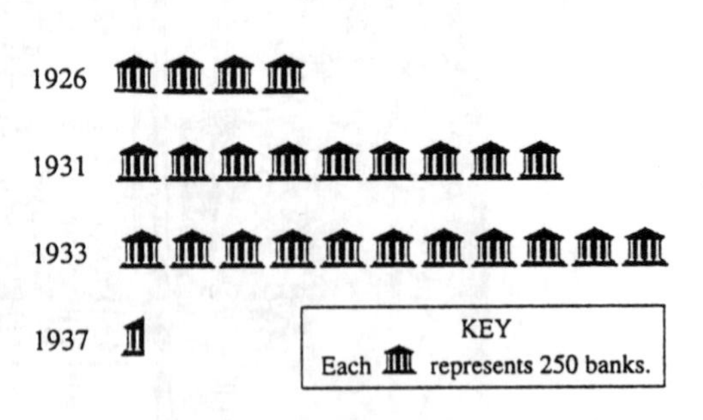
1926
1931
1933
1937
KEY
Each represents 250 banks.

Visualized American Government, 1957

30 The major reason for the change in the number of bank failures between the early 1930's and 1937 is that by 1937
1 new banking laws had restored public confidence in the nation's banks
2 most people were too poor to have any savings
3 the government had purchased and was now operating the nation's banks
4 most Americans had transferred their savings to European banks

31 President Franklin D. Roosevelt's court-packing proposal was criticized because it
1 attempted to give more power to the judicial branch
2 directly violated the Federal-state relationship
3 threatened the system of checks and balances in the Federal Government
4 violated the constitutional guarantee of the right to legal counsel

32 In the late1930's and early 1940's, the cash-and-carry policy and the lend-lease policy contributed to
1 ending tensions between the United States and Germany
2 involving the United States in European affairs
3 stabilizing the international money supply
4 expanding North American free-trade zones

33 The main reason for providing aid to Europe under the Marshall Plan was to
1 guarantee American factories a supply of cheap raw materials
2 create disagreements between western European nations
3 encourage the Soviet Union to withdraw from the United Nations
4 rebuild the economies of devastated European nations

34 Which concept is associated with the formation of the North Atlantic Treaty Organization (NATO)?
1 neutrality
2 isolation
3 collective security
4 appeasement

35 The term McCarthyism has come to symbolize
1 unfounded accusations of disloyalty and a climate of fear
2 the protection of constitutional rights of accused persons
3 integration in public education
4 attempts to encourage totalitarian dictatorships

36 Which trend occured in United States society in the 1950's?
1 The number of marriages and the birthrate declined.
2 Day care services for children became widely available.
3 Suburban areas developed rapidly.
4 The automobile became less important in people's lives.

37 During the 1950's United States foreign policy was characterized by
1 increased trade with Communist China
2 an alliance with the Warsaw Pact nations
3 economic aid to the Soviet Union
4 efforts to block communist expansion

38 In the 1960's, bus boycotts, lunch counter sit-ins and freedom rides were organized attempts to achieve
1 integration
2 black separatism
3 segregation
4 cultural diffusion

39 Which statement most closely reflects the views of Martin Luther King Jr.?
1 All Americans have a right to equality. Any means, including violence, can be used to attain it.
2 Unjust laws must be disobeyed and the consequences accepted peacefully.
3 African-Americans will never gain equality. We really have no choice but to have the two races separate.
4 African-Americans must be patient and aim first for economic advancement. Social and political equality will come later.

40 The Watergate investigation during President Richard Nixon's administration demonstrated that
1 Congress had lost much of its power and influence
2 impeachement is the only way for a President to leave office
3 the military has a great influence on government
4 separation of powers works effectively

41 The Federal Reserve System contributes to economic stability and growth by
1 controlling prices and wages
2 controlling the money supply and the availability of credit
3 regulating the purchase and sale of stocks and bonds
4 regulating the flow of exports and imports

42 Which is a common argument against raising tariffs on imported goods?
1 Domestic products are better made than foreign products are.
2 Foreign trading partners may retaliate and reduce their purchases of American made goods.
3 Foreign products are almost always more expensive than goods made in the United States.
4 Levying taxes on imports may be unconstitutional.

43 The domino theory was used by the United States as a justification for
1 participation in the Vietnam war (1960's-1970's)
2 extending diplomatic recognition to the People's Republic of China (1979).
3 negotiating with Iran to release American hostages (1979-1980).
4 sending armed forces to the Middle East. (1990-1991).

44 The reelections of Presidents Abraham Lincoln in 1864 and Franklin D. Roosevelt in 1944 were similar in that each
1 was later rejected by the electoral college
2 occurred during a major economic depression
3 resulted in a victory for a third party presidential candidate
4 showed that the American people were unwilling to change leaders during wartime

45 Sharecropping was a system of farming most common in
1 New England after the Revolutionary War
2 the Middle Atlantic States before the Civil War
3 the Southern States after the Civil Wa
4 the Pacific Northwest before World War I

46 During the 20th century, economic opportunities for women and minorities in the United States have increased most during periods of
1 war
2 recession
3 nativist agitation
4 overseas expansion

47 In recent years, a trend that many Americans consider a threat to the United States political process is the
1 declining number of political parties
2 increasing influence of political action commitees and lobbyists
3 rising number of senior citizens who vote
4 decreasing media attention on presidential election campaigns

48 One similarity between the Open Door Policy of the early 1900's and the North American Free Trade Agreement (NAFTA) of the 1990's is that both were intended to
1 lower tariffs on imports
2 improve relations in East Asia
3 expand economic links between nations
4 relax restrictions on immigration

ANSWER ONE QUESTION FROM THIS PART
[45]

1 Specific actions taken by United States Presidents on domestic issues have either increased or decreased the role of the Federal Government:

Presidents

Thomas Jefferson
Abraham Lincoln
Theodore Roosevelt
Woodrow Wilson
Herbert Hoover
Lyndon Johnson
Ronald Reagan

Choose *three* of the Presidents listed and for *each* one chosen:

- Discuss *one* specific domestic action taken by that President that had an impact on the role of the Federal Government in the United States.
- Explain how this action has either increased or decreased the role of the Federal Government. [5,5,5,]

2 Over the past 200 years the protections found in the United States Constitution have been both limitedand expanded by Supreme Court decisions.

Constitutional protections

Right to privacy	Right to legal counsel
Freedom of the press	Separation of church and state
Freedom of speech	Freedom of assembly

Choose *three* of the constitutional protections listed and for *each* one chosen:

- Discuss one specific United States Supreme Court case that deals with this constitutional protection. [The exact name of the case does not have to be given].
- State the court's decision in the case.
- Explain how the decision either limited or expanded the meaning of the constitutional protection. [5.5,5]

ANSWER TWO QUESTIONS FROM THIS PART

[30]

3 The United States has followed a variety of policies in its relations with Latin American nations. Some of these policies are listed below.

Policies

Containment	Territorial expansion
Immigration legislation	Economic assistance
Regulation of trade	Intervention

Choose *three* of the policies listed and for *each* one chosen:

- State a major goal of the policy as used toward Latin America.
- Discuss *one* specific action taken by the United States to achieve the goal. [Use a different action for each policy chosen.]
- Explain how the action affected the relationship between the United States and Latin America. [5,5,5]

4 Since 1900, actions taken by the United States government to solve economic problems have often led to the creation of other problems. Some of these actions are listed below.

Government actions

Regulating business activity	Setting interest rates
Setting a minimum wage	Using farm price supports
Reforming income tax regulations	Deficit spending

Establishing wage and price controls

Choose *three* of the actions listed,and for *each* one chosen:

- Discuss *one* specific economic problem that has occurred since 1900 that the action was designed to solve.
- Explain a different economic problem that resulted from that government action. [5,5,5]

5 Historians frequently use descriptive titles to characterize various periods in United States history.

Titles

Critical Period (1780's)
Reconstruction Era (1865 to 1877)
Last Frontier (1860 to 1890)
Gilded Age (1870 to 1900)
Roaring Twenties (1920's)
Cold War (1948 to 1990)

Choose *three* of these titles and for *each* one chosen:

- Explain why the title is used to describe the time period.
- Discuss how *one* specific event or trend during the period illustrates the meaning of the title. [5,5,5]

6 Technological developments often bring about significant changes in American culture. Some technological developments and the aspects of American culture they have changed are listed below.

Technological Developments — Aspects of American Culture

Cotton gin — slavery
Railroad — markets
Elevator — cities
Steel plow — farming on the Great Plains
Automobile — middle-class life style
Television — political campaigns
Computer — education

Choose *three* of the technological developments listed. For *each* one chosen, discuss *two* ways in which the technological development changed the aspect of American culture with which it is paired. [5,5,5]

7 Reform efforts have played an important role in United States history.

Reform efforts

Abolition
Labor movement
Temperance
Progressivism
Consumerism
Environmentalism
Women's movement

Choose *three* of the reform efforts listed and for *each* one chosen:

- Identify *one* goal of the reform effort.
- Describe *one* action taken to achieve that goal.
- Discuss the extent to which the action was successful in achieving that goal. [5,5,5]

CHAPTER 17

A TEST FOR FURTHER REVIEW

This chapter contains another U.S. History and Government Regents Examination, to provide you with an additional practice test and sharpen your test-taking skills.

U.S HISTORY AND GOVERNMENT REGENTS: JANUARY 1996

PART I (55 credits)
ANSWER ALL 48 QUESTIONS IN THIS PART.

Directions (1-48): For each statement or question, circle the number of the word or expression that, of those given, best completes the statement or answers the question.

1 "We hold these truths to be self-evident, that all men are created equal, that they are endowed by their Creator with certain unalienable rights, that among these are life, liberty, and the pursuit of happiness."

This quotation reflects beliefs mainly derived from
1 the Magna Carta
2 the divine right monarchs of Europe
3 John Locke's theory of natural rights
4 Marxist philosophy

2 The United States Government is considered a federal system because
1 the people elect national officials
2 both national and state governments exist within the nation
3 foreign policy is handled by state governments
4 each state has equal representation in the United States Senate

3 The flexibility of the original United States Constitution is due mainly to
1 its provision for the amending process and judicial interpretation
2 its guarantees of freedom and justice for all people
3 the extensive powers delegated to the executive branch
4 the willingness of the states to accept Federal control

4 Anti-federalists criticized the United States Constitution primarily because governing power was concentrated in the
1 State legislatures
2 President's Cabinet
3 delegates to the Constitutional Convention
4 National Government

5 "In framing a government which is to be administered by men over men, the great difficulty lies in this, you must first enable the government to control the governed; and in the next place, oblige it to control itself."

The passage from the Federalist Papers refers to the need for
1 a strong executive
2 a system of checks and balances
3 an independent military
4 a national education system

6 A member of the United States Congress must resign from Congress if elected or appointed to a position in the executive or judicial branch. This requirement is an example of
1 limited terms for Federal officials
2 judicial review
3 separation of powers
4 States rights

7 An example of the unwritten constitution in the United States is the
1 right of citizens to vote if they are 18 years old or older
2 rise of the two-party political system
3 right to freedom of speech
4 use of the electoral college system

8 The main purpose of lobbying is to
1 influence legislation on behalf of special interest groups
2 strengthen the power of political parties
3 increase the speed and efficiency of the law-making process
4 reduce the number of candidates in political elections

9 The two major political parties make their final selection of a Presidential candidate through
1 delegates' votes at a national party convention
2 decisions of the electoral college
3 actions of the State legislatures
4 citizens' choices in public opinion polls

10 Congress used the elastic clause provision of the United States Constitution when it
1 declared war against Germany in World War I
2 created the Federal Communications Commission (FCC)
3 passed the Hawley-Smoot Tariff of 1930
4 approved the President's nomination of Ruth Bader-Ginsberg to the Supreme Court

11 In 1823, the Monroe Doctrine was established mainly because the United States wanted to
1 keep control of Alaska and Hawaii
2 establish more colonies in Latin America
3 support England's attempt to keep its empire in Central America
4 warn Europe against any further colonization in Latin America

12 Which statement best explains President Abraham Lincoln's justification for the Civil War?
1 As an abolitionist, President Lincoln wanted to end slavery in the United States.
2 President Lincoln wanted to keep the South economically dependent on the industrial North.
3 President Lincoln's oath of office required him to defend and preserve the Union.
4 To keep the support of Great Britain and France, President Lincoln had to try to end slavery immediately.

13 A major result of the Civil War was that the
1 economic system of the South came to dominate the United States economy
2 Federal Government's power over the States was strengthened
3 members of Congress from Southern States gained control of the legislative branch
4 nation's industrial development came to a standstill

14 The Jim Crow laws of the post-Civil War Era were attempts by
1 the Federal Government to improve the status of African Americans and Native American Indians
2 state and local governments to restrict the freedoms of African Americans
3 states to ban organizations such as the Ku Klux Klan
4 the Radical Republicans in Congress to carry out Reconstruction plans

15 In the period from 1860 to 1900, the Federal Government encouraged the settlement of the West by
1 passing an increased number of liberal immigration laws
2 selling the most fertile public lands to Native American Indians
3 providing free transportation to settlers moving to the frontier
4 granting tracts of land to railroad companies to encourage construction

16 Which factor most limited the growth of labor unions during the late 1800s?
1 Most employers were very hostile toward workers' efforts to organize.
2 Most factory workers were satisfied with their wages and working conditions.
3 The Federal Government declared that unions were illegal.
4 Workers preferred to negotiate with factory owners as individuals rather than as members of a group.

17 In the 19th century, the major national labor unions wanted to improve the position of workers mainly by
1 obtaining the legal right to organize and bargain collectively
2 using government troops to settle labor disputes with management
3 supporting government ownership of major industries
4 endorsing a third political party for workers only

18 During the latter half of the 19th century, many business organizations in the United States combined into large corporations because
1 income levels for workers would be improved
2 government intervention in economic affairs would decline
3 efficiency in production methods could be increased
4 economic possibilities outside the United States could be explored

19 Many reformers who opposed the laissez-faire attitude of the late 19th century argued that
1 the National Government should not interfere in the activities of big business
2 national wealth could best be assured by the accumulation of gold
3 the idea of rugged individualism is vital to the nation's economic growth
4 government should protect society through the regulation of business

20 During the 1870s and 1880s, midwestern farmers found that earning a living was increasingly difficult because
1 prices of agricultural products were increasing
2 railroad companies charged high rates for transporting farm products
3 agricultural output was declining rapidly
4 farm labor was becoming more unionized

21 Why did the United States formulate the Open Door policy toward China?
1 to develop democratic institutions and practices in China
2 to prevent a European and Japanese monopoly of Chinese trade and markets
3 to establish a military presence on the Chinese mainland
4 to support Japanese efforts to industrialize China

22 The Populists believed that most of the United States economic problems would be solved by establishing
1 currency reform
2 postal savings banks
3 a national property tax
4 a renewed policy of open immigration

23 A major way in which the United States has practiced "economic nationalism" has been to
1 implement protective tariffs to help American industry
2 establish social welfare programs to aid the poor
3 pass legislation outlawing most monopolies
4 require industry to provide safe working conditions for employees

24 From 1900 to 1915, a basic aim of United States foreign policy was to
1 develop close economic ties with African nations
2 oppose revolutionary movements in western Europe
3 promote United States influence in Latin America
4 prevent the spread of communism in western Europe and Asia

25 In the period from 1890 to 1920, which development was the result of the other three?
1 labor union agitation in response to unemployment
2 Progressive Party pleas for compulsory education
3 public outcry following numerous industrial accidents
4 passage of child labor laws by individual states

26 A main purpose of President Theodore Roosevelt's trust-busting policies was to
1 reduce corruption in government
2 save the nation's banks
3 encourage competition in business
4 end strikes by labor unions

27 Since 1913, the United States banking system, interest rates, and the amount of money in circulation have largely been controlled by the
1 United States Supreme Court
2 Federal Reserve System
3 Federal Deposit Insurance Corporation
4 President's Council of Economic Advisors

28 The 1920s are sometimes called the "Roaring Twenties" because
1 foreign trade prospered after World War I
2 the United States assumed a leadership role in world affairs
3 political reforms made government more democratic
4 widespread social and economic change occurred

29 "You cannot extend the mastery of government over the daily working life of the people without, at the same time, making it the master of the people's souls and thought."

—*President Herbert Hoover*

The idea expressed in the quotation is a basis for President Hoover's belief that the problems of the Great Depression could best be solved by
1 nationalizing major industries
2 requiring business to pay a minimum wage to workers
3 relying mostly on private enterprise and individual initiative to improve economic conditions
4 creating government job programs for the unemployed

30 Which condition increased the negative effects of the Great Depression?
1 Factories had to decrease production because of low demand.
2 Low levels of unemployment created labor shortages.
3 The demand for imported products increased.
4 The Federal Government raised taxes repeatedly.

31 The main reason President Franklin D. Roosevelt attempted to increase the number of Justices on the United States Supreme Court was to
1 force the Court to hear cases involving the rights of minorities and women
2 speed up the Court's review of cases
3 increase the independence of the Court
4 make the Court more supportive of New Deal programs

32 A major result of President Franklin D. Roosevelt's New Deal was
1 a decline in the Federal deficit
2 an expansion of the power of the Federal Government
3 a change in the voting rights of women
4 a reinstitution of the gold standard for United States currency

33 In the early 1940s, the "destroyer-for-military-bases deal" with Great Britain and the Lend-Lease Act were evidence that the United States
1 recognized that its policy of neutrality conflicted with its self-interest
2 followed its policy of neutrality more strictly as World War II progressed in Europe
3 believed that the Allied policy of appeasement would succeed
4 wanted to honor the military commitments it had made just after World War I

34 A violation of civil rights that occurred in the United States during World War II was the
1 arrests made as a result of the Palmer raids
2 passage of an open immigration law
3 internment of Japanese Americans
4 forced removal of Native American Indians from their reservations

35 In the United States, the Red Scare of 1919 and the McCarthy Era of the early 1950s were periods of
1 severe economic depression
2 widespread support for groups promoting international anarchy
3 great growth in art, literature, and music
4 persecution of people suspected of holding anti-American political views

36 The "clear and present danger" ruling of the Supreme Court in *Schenck v. United States* illustrates the continuing conflict between
1 free speech and governmental authority
2 the use of search warrants and the rights of the accused
3 state powers and Federal powers
4 religious freedom and separation of church and state

37 Which generalization can most accurately be drawn from a study of Supreme Court cases *Plessy v. Ferguson* and *Brown v. Board of Education*?
   1 The Supreme Court has issued consistent decisions in cases involving rights of the accused.
   2 Supreme Court decisions are accepted without public controversy.
   3 The Justices believe that social issues are best left for state courts to decide.
   4 The Supreme Court has helped to determine public policy.

38 The Washington Naval Conference of 1921-1922 and the SALT talks of the 1970s between the United States and the Soviet Union both reflect the belief that
   1 civil wars within nations can create international hostilities
   2 escalating military buildups are one of the causes of war
   3 cultural exchange programs can reduce world tensions
   4 rivalry between nations over the control of natural resources is the major cause of conflict

39 A common purpose of the Truman Doctrine, the Marshall Plan, and the Eisenhower Doctrine was to
   1 carry out the United States policy of preventing the spread of communism
   2 insure the survival of the newly independent nations of African and Asia
   3 limit the proliferation of nuclear weapons
   4 provide medical aid to Latin American nations

40 The major goal of the civil rights movement of the 1960s was to
   1 establish a separate political state for African Americans
   2 gain passage of an equal rights amendment to the Constitution
   3 end segregation based on race
   4 permit unlimited immigration to the United States

41 In the United States, industrial unions of the 1880s and the 1980s had similar goals in that both campaigned for
   1 national health insurance
   2 better unemployment insurance
   3 greater job security and higher wages
   4 wage and price freezes

42 Which is a valid conclusion based on a study of the presidencies of Thomas Jefferson and Franklin D. Roosevelt?
   1 Strong third parties develop when the two major parties ignore popular demands.
   2 Presidential success depends mainly on a sympathetic Supreme Court.
   3 Economic crisis can force a President to suspend basic civil liberties.
   4 A President's political program may change in the face of current needs.

43 During which period in United States history were the amendments concerning the income tax, direction election of Senators, Prohibition, and women's suffrage enacted?
   1 Reconstruction
   2 The Gilded Age
   3 Progressive Era
   4 New Deal

Base your answer to question 44 on the cartoon below and on your knowledge of social studies.

CAPITAL GAINS TAX
U.S. Gov't
BUDGET DEFICIT
U.S.
COMPETITIVENESS
LIABILITY COSTS

"Here's yer problem—this here little Japanese doo-dad is blocking yer trade flow."

44 The point of view expressed in the cartoon is that the economy of the United States
1 suffers from many problems that cannot be blamed on other countries
2 needs another war to help the United States move from a debtor nation to a creditor nation
3 requires massive governmental action to restrict the amount of foreign goods imported to the United States
4 has been seriously weakened by the high cost of American labor

45 An original purpose of affirmative action programs was to
1 increase educational and employment opportunities for women and minorities
2 improve the American economy by guaranteeing that employees will be highly skilled
3 decrease social welfare costs by requiring recipients of public assistance to work
4 reduce the Federal deficit by increasing government efficiency

46 For the United States, the breakup of the Soviet Union has had the greatest effect on
1 import quotas
2 immigration policies
3 advances in technology
4 defense spending

47 A constitutional issue that was frequently raised about the United States involvement in the Korean conflict and the Vietnam conflict was the
1 right to regulate commerce with foreign nations
2 use of deficit spending to finance wars
3 lack of a formal declaration of war by Congress
4 Supreme Court's role in foreign policy decision-making

48 One result of the Persian Gulf War was that the United States
1 gained control of oil resources in the Middle East
2 liberated Kuwait from Iraqi control
3 brought about peaceful relations between Israel and its neighbors
4 obtained overseas colonies in the Middle East

PART II

ANSWER ONE QUESTION FROM THIS PART.

1 At the Constitutional Convention of 1787, the delegates frequently used compromise to resolve issues.

Controversial Issues

Commerce
Representation
Selection of a President
Slavery
Taxation

Choose *three* of the issues listed and for *each* one chosen:

- Identify a controversy involving that issue and discuss the opposing points of view held by delegates on that issue
- Describe the compromise reached by the delegates [5,5,5]

2 Issues in United States history have sometimes led to disagreements between branches of the Federal Government. Some issues involving disagreements between governmental branches are listed below.

Issues
Case of Marbury v. Madison (1803)
Impeachment of President Andrew Johnson (1868)
Ratification of the Treaty of Versailles (1919)
Taft-Hartley Act (1947)
War Powers Act (1973)
Watergate affair (1972-1974

Choose *three* issues listed and for *each* one chosen:

- Describe a disagreement between two branches of the Federal Government over the issue
- Explain how the disagreement was resolved [5,5,5]

PART III

ANSWER TWO QUESTIONS FROM THIS PART.

3 Since 1865, agents of change have acted to advance the cause of civil rights and civil liberties in the United States.

Agents of Change
Government
A non-governmental group
An individual

For *each* of the agents of change listed:

- Explain *one* action taken by that agent of change to help advance civil rights or civil liberties in the United States
- Describe the historical circumstances that led to the action [5,5,5]

4 During various periods in United States history, the Federal Government has followed different policies toward immigration.

- Chinese Exclusion Act 1882
- Chinese were not allowed into U.S.

Time Periods
Prior to 1880
1881 to 1920
1921 to 1964
1965 to 1996

a Choose *two* of the time periods listed and for *each* one chosen, describe an immigration policy by the United States during that time period and discuss a reason the United States followed that policy. [5,5]

b For *one* of the periods you chose in part a, describe a problem that arose in the United States as a result of the immigration policy of that period. [5]

5 Works of literature frequently reflect conditions in United States society.

Literary Works
The Red Badge of Courage by Stephen Crane
Huckleberry Finn by Mark Twain
Mark, the Match Boy by Horatio Alger
The Octopus by Frank Norris
The Great Gatsby by F. Scott Fitzgerald
The Grapes of Wrath by John Steinbeck
Bury My Heart at Wounded Knee by Dee Brown
Silent Spring by Rachel Carson

Select *three* of the works listed and for *each* one chosen:

- Discuss a main theme of the work
- Show how that theme reflected a condition in United States society [5,5,5]

6 The United States has followed different foreign policies at various times in its history.

United States Foreign Policies
Containment
Global involvement
Imperialism
Isolationism
Neutrality

a Choose *three* of the foreign policies listed and for *each* one chosen, define the policy, and using a specific historical example, show how the United States followed that policy. [Use a different example for each policy chosen.] [4,4,4]

b For one of the policies you chose in part a, discuss one problem the United States experienced as a result of following that policy. [4]

7 Some United States Presidents have instituted important economic programs.

Presidential Economic Programs
Theodore Roosevelt's Square Deal
Woodrow Wilson's New Freedom
Franklin D. Roosevelt's New Deal
Harry Truman's Fair Deal
Lyndon B. Johnson's Great Society
Ronald Reagan's New Federalism

Choose *three* of the programs listed and for each *one* chosen:

- Describe one specific goal of that economic program
- Show how a specific policy or law attempted to carry out that program [5,5,5]

INDEX